Eighty-Eight Years

PATRICK RAEL

Eighty-Eight Years

THE LONG DEATH
OF SLAVERY IN THE
UNITED STATES,
1777–1865

The University of Georgia Press
Athens & London

A Sarah Mills Hodge Fund Publication

This publication is made possible, in part, through a grant from the
Hodge Foundation in memory of its founder, Sarah Mills Hodge,
who devoted her life to the relief and education of
African Americans in Savannah, Georgia.

© 2015 by the University of Georgia Press
Athens, Georgia 30602
www.ugapress.org
Set in 10/13 Adobe Caslon Pro by Kaelin Chappell Broaddus

Most University of Georgia Press titles are
available from popular e-book vendors.

Printed digitally

Library of Congress Cataloging-in-Publication Data
Rael, Patrick.
Eighty-eight years : the long death of slavery in the United States, 1777–1865 /
Patrick Rael.
pages cm. — (Race in the Atlantic world, 1700–1900)
Includes bibliographical references.
ISBN 978-0-8203-3395-3 (hardcover : alk. paper) — ISBN 978-0-8203-4839-1 (pbk. :
alk. paper) — ISBN 978-0-8203-4829-2 (ebook) 1. Slavery—United States—History.
2. Slavery—Caribbean Area—History 3. Slavery—Political aspects—United States—
History. 4. Slavery—Political aspects—Caribbean Area—History I. Title.
II. Title: 88 years, the long death of slavery in the United States, 1777–1865.
III. Title: Long death of slavery in the United States, 1777–1865.
E441.R28 2015
306.3'620973—dc23
2014042982

British Library Cataloging-in-Publication Data available

FOR *Lola, Alison,* AND *Mom*

CONTENTS

FIGURES

ACKNOWLEDGMENTS

Americans are very used to hearing their own story. Most learn it a few times before graduating from high school, and many encounter it again a few times in college. They see it depicted in feature films and television documentaries, read many popular and scholarly books on it, and even live it themselves on weekends and vacations. For many of us, the past may be a foreign country where things are done differently, but it is not an unknown country, for we tour it often. This familiarity may obscure some unique qualities of our history. It is not easy to see anew our well-known tales, but the struggle to do so is worth it. This is a paradox of good history: sometimes, the familiar may be known only by rendering it a little bit strange.

As such an effort, I have sought to place one important American story, that of slavery's long demise in the United States, inside a larger story of the Atlantic world. Perhaps this way we may learn important lessons, or become excited anew about this aspect of our past. Things did not have to turn out the way they did. Our history owes to pieces of our past we would do well to become more conversant with.

I started this project wishing for a history that set the story of America's long abolition of slavery in the context of Atlantic slavery's demise. Hubris quickly gave way to humility. My first and most profound gratitude is thus reserved for the hundreds, if not thousands, of scholars whose tireless dedication to understanding the history of slavery and African-descended people in the Atlantic world has made possible a gesture as immodest as the one I have essayed. This book stands as a humble gesture of thanks for the herculean efforts of several generations of scholars. I hope that naïveté rather than arrogance has driven my work, and that my enormous respect for the vast scholarship required by this subject will be at least partially evident in the text and notes. There are places in these pages, though, where my debt to others is too great to leave to citations. Though I take full responsibility for any ways I may have misread them, I would like to acknowledge the inspiration of Ira Berlin, David Blight, Michael Craton, David Brion Davis, Seymour Drescher, Douglas Egerton, Stanley Engerman, Paul Finkelman, Eric Foner, Eugene Genovese, Leon F. Litwack,

James McPherson, James Oakes, Andrew O'Shaughnessy, Leonard Richards, Manisha Sinha, and Elizabeth Varon.

My goal has been to suggest some interpretive possibilities and help readers wrestle with the larger arc of antislavery and emancipation in the Atlantic world, all the while seeking to defamiliarize some aspects of our own history. My hope is for students of the American past to better understand that their story took place inside a much larger one. In working this way, I do not mean to suggest that American history is any more exceptional (and certainly not any better) than any other. As my colleague Daniel Levine is wont to argue about comparative history, "different things are different." Still, generalization is a necessary business of historians. I have used certain concepts, such as the tension between "periphery" and "metropole," as practical conceptual tools rather than methodological manifestos. The past stubbornly refuses to conform to the categories and patterns we construct for it, and its constant tendency to expose our arrogance in doing so keeps us humble and attentive. Inevitably, a work so broad, synthetic, and interpretive will inspire criticism, no doubt much of it warranted. Some feathers I have ruffled consciously and intentionally, confident in my own bent. Others I have done so inadvertently, out of the limitations of my own expertise. A work touching on so many subfields will doubtlessly draw fire from many directions. I bear full responsibility for any shortness in my grasp, but I do beg some sympathy for my reach.

I owe large debts to a number of colleagues, students, and friends. Derek Krisoff, once the senior acquisitions editor at the University of Georgia Press, enthusiastically endorsed my proposal for this book. Also at Georgia, Walter Biggins, Mick Gusinde-Duffy, and Beth Snead shepherded it to completion. They, along with my co-editors in the Race in the Atlantic World, 1700–1900 series—Richard Newman and Manisha Sinha—have been exceptionally helpful, as have many on its editorial advisory board. I am proud that our series bears the imprint of the Library Company of Philadelphia's Program in African American History, which has given so much to scholars in this field.

Bowdoin College helped fund the sabbatical that permitted me a year of uninterrupted writing. I am also grateful for Bowdoin's excellent library, and even more extraordinary library staff, including Ginny Hopcroft, Barbara Levergood, and Richard Lindemann. Also here in the piney woods, exceptional colleagues offered critical insights at crucial times. I particularly thank Dana Byrd, Tess Chakkalakal, David Gordon, Jessica Johnson, Steve Meardon, Jeff Selinger, Randy Stakeman, Femi Vaughan, and Allen Wells for their helpful thoughts. The blessings of teaching at a small liberal arts college are uncountable, but surely the greatest has been the chance to work with so many incredible students over the years. There is no way to list them all, but some whose investment in me helped me learn about matters in this book deserve special mention: Adam Baber, Caitlin Beach, Ethan Bullard, Tug Buse, Joy Cushman, Wes Fleuchaus, Josh Flowers, Jeremiah Goulka, Dave Holte, Diana Lee, Alexxa Leon, Alexis Little, Ben Lovell, Sean McElroy, Tina Nadeau, Anna Nutter, Scott Ogden, Kathryn Ostrofsky, Simon Parsons, Brian Powers, Kyle Ritter, Michael Shannon, Matt Spooner, Dave Thomson, Mark Veihman, and Kid Wongsrichanalai. As promised, I also give thanks to those in my spring 2013 intermediate seminar on Reconstruction, who proved as sharp a set of critics as one could wish for. Advising such students has been inspirational and transformative.

With this book I hope finally to earn the faith placed in me by the Gilder Lehrman Center for the Study of Slavery, Resistance, and Abolition, which generously supported an earlier sabbatical. I am grateful for the support and collegiality there of David Blight, Dana Schaffer, and Thomas Thurston. I also thank the Center for Africana Studies at Johns Hopkins University for inviting me to attend a five-week summer institute funded by the National Endowment for the Humanities, titled "Slaves, Soldiers, Rebels: Black Resistance in the Tropical Atlantic, 1760–1888." Organizers Stewart King, Ben Vinson, and Natalie Zacek, and the impressive array of scholars I had the pleasure to meet, generously shared their expertise through those sweltering weeks. I particularly appreciate Javier Aguayo, Pat McDevitt, and Srividhya Swaminathan.

I have benefitted from the intellects of many fine scholars, whose engagement with my ideas in professional settings has enriched my insights on matters discussed in these pages. In particular, I acknowledge Alan Guelzo, Leslie Harris, Paul Harvey, Graham Hodges, James O. Horton, Lois Horton, Leon F. Litwack, Waldo Martin, Joanne Pope Melish, John David Smith, John Stauffer, James Brewer Stewart, Clarence Walker, and Peter Wood. I am indebted to Ira Berlin, not only for his critical reading of the entire manuscript, but for his stellar example and generous mentorship. Special thanks go to Douglas Egerton and Donald Shaffer, whose close reading suggested many salutary additions, and saved me from many embarrassing errors. Fault for any that remain lies solely with me.

Many outside my field have sustained me through this effort. The opportunity to work with precollegiate teachers has deeply shaped my thinking about the way history might be written. For this, I am particularly thankful for the chance to work with those associated with the Maine Humanities Council, and especially Charles Calhoun, Martina Duncan, Anne Schlitt, and Sabrina Taliento, who have taught me so much about being a history educator.

Good friends reminded me of the many things to enjoy in life besides writing. In Brunswick, Dallas Denery and Lorry Fleming always offered a respite from the library or keyboard, usually in the form of excellent food and welcome amity. A large group of enormously congenial friends indulged me over many respites filled with board games. Roberto Confiño offered his long-standing friendship and unique connoisseurship of life, while Jack McKirgan lent his steady hand—often on my shoulder, sometimes on the pint glass. Leslie Darrell deserves my heartfelt appreciation for teaching this student of the past an awful lot about appreciating the present moment. And I am ever grateful for the many elegant transformations that have taken place in my long acquaintance with Marvin Breslow, a former teacher I am honored to call a good friend.

Finally, the diaspora of Washington Raels is blessedly small, but distance is distance. For helping me remember the importance of family, I owe thanks to Nancy Rael, Alison and Tim May, their wonderful children Megan and Peter, Chris Rael and Vlada Tomova, and their incredible little man, Sasha. Here in Brunswick, Mikaela and EmaLeigh Aschbrenner, along with their fabulous mom Ellen Meaney, who has survived so much with me, have taught me that with love, home can mean many things. May I share the amazing lessons Ellen has taught me with my most beloved Lola, who is always and forever first in my thoughts.

A House Divided

On June 16, 1858, Illinois Republicans anointed their new candidate for U.S. senator: Abraham Lincoln. At age forty-nine, Lincoln was a seasoned though hardly famous politician—a veteran of frontier political skirmishes between the Whig Party, to which he had long been loyal, and the Democratic Party of Andrew Jackson. Having gained only some slight military experience as a volunteer during the Black Hawk War of 1832, and having served for one term as an undistinguished member of the U.S. House of Representatives from 1847 to 1849, Lincoln had yet to demonstrate the political genius he would use to shepherd the nation through civil war. This June day in 1858 was a stepping stone on his path to that destiny.

On the occasion of accepting the nomination, Lincoln defined himself as a leader in the national movement to oppose the expansion of slavery into the unorganized western territories. His speech sought to galvanize the Republican Party in Illinois, which had inherited much of the defunct Whigs' constituency, while also adopting a new antislavery message, and warding off the specter that Stephen A. Douglas, the incumbent senator from Illinois and his chief political rival, might co-opt moderate Republicans and so retain his Senate seat in the upcoming election. It had been Douglas, after all, who had engineered the hated Kansas-Nebraska Act of 1854, which had focused national concerns on slavery by proposing that settlers in the western territory of Kansas could decide for themselves whether or not slavery would be permitted in their newly organized territory. To Lincoln, the act constituted a reminder—just one of all too many in the 1850s, as he saw it—that slaveholders were intent on enlarging their ability, over the national government if need be, to defend and even expand their "peculiar institution."

The speech was a masterpiece of rhetorical economy. In Lincoln's best fashion, it quickly made its point, delivering the key message in its first two minutes.

The lanky politician, yet to have grown his trademark whiskers, addressed the convention by speaking immediately to the Kansas-Nebraska Act. He declared that the ostensible purpose of passing the law, that of "putting an end to slavery agitation," had not been realized. In fact, the question of slavery had only become more fraught as a consequence of the act. Such was the vehemence and stridency of the national debate, in fact, that Lincoln now predicted that only a national crisis could resolve the issue. "A house divided against itself cannot stand," Lincoln intoned, echoing a passage from the Gospels. "I believe this government cannot endure permanently half slave and half free. I do not expect the Union to be dissolved—I do not expect the house to fall—but I do expect it will cease to be divided. It will become all one thing, or all the other."

Lincoln remained unclear as to the fate of slavery, as well as the means through which the issue would come to crisis. But he saw the nation as standing at a crossroads, with two possibilities before it. In one direction slavery would be limited: "The opponents of slavery, will arrest the further spread of it, and place it where the public mind shall rest in the belief that it is in the course of ultimate extinction." On the other course, though, "its advocates will push it forward, till it shall become alike lawful in all the States, old as well as new—North as well as South."[1]

This was a bold and harrowing prediction. Slavery lawful in the northern states as well as the southern? Such an utterance may have suggested gross hyperbole, if not downright paranoia. The nation was clearly divided between slave and free states, and for decades those north of the Mason-Dixon line had been at least nominally committed to the principle of universal liberty at the heart of America's founding. Yet Lincoln believed that of the two paths he had outlined, the one wherein liberty would fade seemed the more likely. Between the expansion of liberty or of slavery, Lincoln asked ominously, "Have we no tendency to the latter condition?"

Lincoln had good reason to fear the political power of the slaveholding states and their champions. Over the previous decade, this "slave power," as Lincoln's Republican colleagues often collectively labeled slavery's political defenders, had done much to strengthen the institution of slavery in response to decades of antislavery agitation. The Compromise of 1850 had guaranteed that much of the vast western land gained from Mexico in the war of 1846–48 would be open to the possibility of slavery. It also had strengthened existing fugitive slave laws, effectively extending southern power into the free states north of the Mason-Dixon line. The dissolution of the Whig Party had left the presidency open to a series of pro-South northern Democrats (known as "doughfaces" in the political slang of the day), while political opposition to the slave power had only slowly coalesced around marginal third parties. By the mid-1850s, important figures in the South had called to reopen the slave trade, as well as to wrest the Caribbean sugar island of Cuba from Spanish control for the purposes of expanding the slave regime.

Attacked though it had been, slavery was not shrinking, but growing. In 1854, Stephen Douglas had engineered the passage of the Kansas-Nebraska Act. This had permitted the possibility of slavery in the western territories on the principle of "squatter sovereignty," effectively repealing the Missouri Compromise of the 1820s, and threatening to upset the fragile sectional balance between free and slave states. The issue had come to blows, as antislavery Jayhawkers and proslavery Bushwackers engaged in ruthless guerrilla warfare in the Kansas Territory over the formation of a constitution and the outcome of elections. (One of the antislavery partisans, John Brown, was soon to launch his ill-fated, catalytic assault on the federal armory at Harpers Ferry, Virginia.) The issue of slavery in the territories had also drawn the attention of the U.S. Supreme Court, which in 1857 had declared that the slave Dred Scott had, like all other African Americans, "no rights the white man is bound to respect." The Dred Scott decision effectively nullified Congress's power to limit slavery in the territories, thus mooting the popular sovereignty provision of the Kansas-Nebraska Act, and opening all of the territories—from Minnesota to New Mexico—to slavery. And it seemed to be only a harbinger of things to come. Working its way to the Supreme Court was another important case, *Lemmon v. New York*, which had the potential to nullify the power even of the *states* to deny the enjoyment of slave "property" in them.[2]

But all was not lost. By the time Lincoln issued his House Divided speech in 1858, the forces opposing the slave power were organizing themselves into serious political challengers. In 1840, abolitionists had formed the Liberty Party to oppose the slave power, an effort taken up later by the Free Soil Party. The final incarnation of antebellum political antislavery, the Republican Party, had inherited their legacy, along with remnants of the Whig Party and dissident northern Democrats, to offer an umbrella for political antislavers and an array of single-issue reform interests. The avowed purpose of the party was to arrest the growth of the slave power, and particularly the spread of slavery into the western territories. Lincoln carried the political aspirations of his party with him, as his House Divided speech launched his campaign against Douglas for the Senate seat for Illinois. In a series of seven debates held across the state in 1858, Lincoln expanded upon his theme of the rising slave power, delicately threading the needles of public opinion with strands of argument drawn from traditions as diverse as antislavery, nationalism, and even white supremacy. Douglas went on to win the Senate seat, but "the Little Giant" would face Lincoln again, in the 1860 presidential battle. Heading the ticket for the northern wing of a now-divided Democratic Party, Douglas lost to Lincoln in a rancorous four-way election.

The Republican triumph in 1860 was the single most important factor in the nation's turn to civil war. Southern states threatened to break free of the federal compact, and thus destroy the Union, if the decision in the election was not undone. Lincoln, following through on the logic of his argument that the slave power sought to defend its beloved institution at the cost of the democratic process, insisted that he would have "none of it." As he wrote to a colleague in the midst of the secession crisis, "We have just carried an election on principles fairly stated to the people. Now we are told in advance the government shall be broken up unless we surrender to those we have beaten, before we take the offices." Lincoln accused secessionists of "extorting a compromise" with threats of disunion. "If we surrender," he wrote, "it is the end of us and of the government. They will repeat the experiment upon us ad libidium. A year will not pass till we shall have to take Cuba as a condition upon which they will stay in the Union."[3] Lincoln would opt for war with the secessionists over blackmailed conciliation. "Entertain no compromise in regard to the extension of slavery," he instructed a Republican negotiator during the secession crisis. If the conflict between slavery and freedom was indeed "irrepressible,"[4] as his prospective secretary of state William Seward had declared in a famous speech several years before, then accommodation made no sense. "The tug has to come," Lincoln wrote; "better now than later."[5]

"And," as Lincoln would recount in his second inaugural address in 1864, "the war came." The maelstrom that ensued decided which of the two paths that Lincoln had outlined in his House Divided speech the nation would take. By May 1865, the conflict was over. The Confederate nation lay in shambles. Over three million Americans, northern and southern, had risked their lives in combat, and three-quarters of a million had given all.[6] Untold suffering had been visited upon millions more. The president who had piloted the Union through the war lay dead, a martyr to the divided nation his election had created. As a result of innumerable battles and a calamitous loss of life, slavery's complete end was near and inevitable. In December 1865, the ratification of the Thirteenth Amendment to the Constitution abolished slavery in the United States.

None could have predicted all this in 1858. Certainly few foresaw that in a scant decade African Americans would be not only free, but full citizens of the nation, capable of voting and holding office. Even before the war, though, many Americans—both northern and southern—had agreed with Lincoln that some kind of crisis over slavery loomed. For decades, southern planters and their apologists had defended the slave regime against what they saw as the encroaching power of the free states. And for just as long, champions of "free labor" had excoriated the South for its slaveholding practices. The conflict was thus old—indeed, as old as the nation itself. For the United States had been established half slave and half free, and this had laid the foundation for a long struggle over the fate of slavery and the meaning of democracy in America.

Eighty-Eight Years

The Slave Power

For Lincoln and his Republicans, Union victory in the Civil War consummated the defeat of the slave power. What happened in the United States was a variation—singular, to be sure—on a theme that played out over the Atlantic Basin throughout the nineteenth century. The American Civil War was about many things, but above all it was about slavery and how slavery would end. The nineteenth century was the great age of slavery's abolition in the Atlantic world. Since the fifteenth century, the major European powers—England, France, the Netherlands, Spain, Portugal, Denmark, and Sweden—had embarked on expansive colonial adventures that required enslaved African labor to produce valuable cash crops for an expanding world economy. Now, several centuries later, the use of chattel bondage in these colonial empires was coming to an end. That movement began first in British America, as a direct consequence of the English colonies' effort to throw off the mother country and become an independent nation. But completing the process of abolition in the United States took a long time—far longer than anywhere else in the Atlantic world. Of all places in the New World, only the Spanish Caribbean and Brazil followed the United States in ending slavery, and did so with processes that occurred far more rapidly. For sure, everywhere in the Western Hemisphere the institution died as the result of an arduous process of contention and conflict. Only in St. Domingue (Haiti) and the United States, though, did slavery end in a violent spasm of national rebellion. And Haiti, for all the problems emancipation wrought, experienced the total destruction of slavery itself relatively quickly, while in the United States a nearly century-long gulf separated the nation's first moves toward abolition from the final consummation of that process. Nowhere else did a nation persist half slave and half free for anything like the nine decades the United States endured, from 1777, when the new state of Vermont wrote slavery out of its constitution, to 1865, when the Thirteenth Amendment to the U.S. Constitution was ratified.

This book explores those agonized eighty-eight years and their meaning. How is it that the nation became a "house divided against itself" when other nations that abolished slavery did not? Why did slavery take so much longer to die in the United States than elsewhere? And why did it take the Civil War—the fulcrum around which the American story turns—to end U.S. slavery? What was the relationship between the war and abolition? As Lincoln reflected in his second inauguration address, a slave "interest" located just in the South had "somehow" been the cause of the Civil War. But how, exactly? Why, in fact, had it even taken a war—and a war between two largely white societies, rather than the multiracial maelstrom that struck St. Domingue—to destroy slavery? What was it about the United States and its history that made its story of abolition unique? And what does this history reveal about other exceptional features of the American experience with race and slavery? Conversely—for every slave society possessed a unique story—what does the exceptional story of abolition in the United States suggest about the process of abolition throughout the Atlantic world?

This book diverges from previous studies of abolitionism by engaging this long, exceptional history in two ways. First, while many works have studied the history of the radical movement to immediately abolish slavery in the United States, which began in 1831 and lasted until the Civil War, fewer have explored as a whole the entire age of emancipation in U.S. history. Abolition here took place in two general waves. The first was the "neglected" period of antislavery agitation, which was triggered by the American Revolution and which we may say lasted until 1827, by which time eventual freedom had been provided for almost all African Americans in the North.[1] The second wave we might call the "radical" period, which lasted from the founding of immediate abolitionism by William Lloyd Garrison in 1831 through the end of the Civil War. Any complete view must understand the abolition of slavery in the United States through this longer temporal lens, exploring both periods and their connection to each other.

A long temporal lens incorporating the entire end of slavery in the United States also points us to a broader spatial frame of reference. The process of ending slavery was not, after all, a uniquely American one, it just took a unique form in America. African slavery ended not just here, but everywhere in the Atlantic world. Placing the experience of the United States in this comparative context reveals the unique qualities of the American experience with abolition, as well as highlighting fundamental aspects of slavery and abolition everywhere in the Atlantic world. By understanding what New World slave societies shared, we can better understand what made each one—particularly the United States—distinguishable. And we can also thus better understand the varied and mixed legacies of emancipation for the decades that followed.

The fundamental insight that such a comparison reveals is this: as Lincoln understood, the slave power of the American South possessed a remarkable degree of political potency, and this power helped it defend itself against a movement to abolish slavery that was itself the product of new social forces stirring in the economically developing world of the U.S. North. Lincoln's spare prose in his "House Divided" speech had captured the issue with stunning clarity. Republican fears of the plantation regime's overweening power were not political overstatement, but—at least in the context of the Atlantic world—a truism that lay at the heart of America's unique experience with race and slavery. The plantation regime of the U.S. South *was* powerful—more so, in fact, than any other analogous slave power in the Atlantic world. Abolition took so long in the United States, and entailed such a violent and arduous process, because the plantation regime in the South had an advantage unreplicated in most other slave societies in the New World. In much of the rest of the Atlantic, slavery was rooted in colonial appendages that lay within the borders of mercantile empires, but outside the European metropoles from which those colonial appendages were ruled. The exceptions were the Spanish Caribbean and Brazil, where the "slave power" was indeed dominant—so dominant, in fact, that no political power within their borders contested the right to own humans as property.

In the United States, however, the plantation complex lay within the boundaries of a nation developing its own urban centers, in which powerful antislavery ideas were slowly growing. These rising metropoles coexisted with the slave power in a nation organized by a federal compact wherein states were theoretically equal to each other, and quite powerful relative to the national government.[2] In fact, the slaveholding states of the South held an amount of political power in the nation utterly disproportionate with their relatively small populations. This preponderance of power in the U.S. plantation complex was what helped it maintain slavery for so long. And it also explains why a national bloodbath was required to end slavery once and for all.

To understand the unique experience of the United States with slavery and abolition requires an appreciation of the Atlantic dimensions of slavery and abolition. It is useful, then, to gloss the rise and fall of New World slavery—an impossible task in a few pages, but a useful one nonetheless, for providing a baseline for understanding how aspects of these massive global processes melded with or diverged from the American experience. In the process, some heuristic concepts will emerge that offer a shorthand of concepts and ideas useful throughout the investigation.

Historical mythology has long portrayed the expansion of Europe into the western Atlantic world in the heroic mold: as evidence of the Renaissance's expansion of the European intellect, as the individual achievement of remarkable explorers such as Christopher Columbus, or even as a historical inevitability attendant to Europe's rise to global dominance. Understanding the history of slavery, however, suggests just how deeply Europe's expansion into the Western Hemisphere was tied to two older, parallel, and related long-term trends that offer a far different picture: the emergence of centralized nation-states and the growth of merchant capital. Rather than marking a discrete moment in history, the colonization of what was to Europeans a new world was the result of processes already long under way, with national rivalry and commercial profit the key engines.

The steady expansion of the population in Western Europe after the fourteenth century fueled the growth of urban centers and the centralization of feudal principalities into nascent nation-states. From the fifteenth century through the seventeenth, strong monarchs emerged triumphant from perennial battles with aristocracies and the church in Spain, France, and England. Italian city-states lacked the expansive feudal hinterlands that fostered the emergence of strong central authority in these nations, but instead grew rich on trade in the prosperous Mediterranean. In cities such as Venice, Genoa, and Florence, merchants grew fat, acting as intermediaries between the Muslim traders of the eastern Mediterranean and the expanding populace of Southern and Western Europe. These political and commercial processes were linked and self-reinforcing: trade enriched the city-states, which expanded both urban populations and consumer tastes, thus creating an incentive for more trade and stronger administration. The rich trading cities of the Mediterranean (and, shortly after, Northern Europe) became prime targets of the developing dynastic nation-states, which also squabbled over contested fiefdoms, vague borders, and hereditary legacies. The eternal wars fought by European powers led to remarkably rapid innovations in military arts, but war was expensive, requiring further centralization of the monarchies and the development of still new mechanisms of finance and credit.

Colonial expansion served the economic and political needs of the emerging nation-states. No single commodity emblematized this fusion of commercial and political power more than sugar—a sweet, tall perennial grass that spread from Southern Asia to the Middle East in the centuries before the Crusades. Europeans prized sugar variously as a luxury item, a spice, a medicine, a preservative, and an alternative to bee honey as a source of sweetness. In the Middle Ages, as Mediterranean traders sought to break Muslim control of the sugar trade from the eastern Mediterranean, sugar production spread westward—first to islands such as Cyprus, Crete, and Sicily, and then onto mainland plantations in Iberia. Finally, it leapt out into the Atlantic. Frustrated with Italian control of

Mediterranean commerce, Spain and Portugal had moved first to explore the unknown ocean, using new ship designs to sail previously unnavigable waters and seek independent sources of profit. It was no coincidence that Christopher Columbus, who sailed under the sponsorship of the Spanish Crown, was a Genoese trader, well versed in the commerce and concerns of the western Mediterranean world. The Portuguese, perched on the western edge of the sea, first attempted sustained maritime exploration of the Atlantic, mapping the coast of Africa in the fifteenth century. Spain quickly followed, and the first instance of a continental European rivalry spilling out into the Atlantic Basin began.

Atlantic islands lying off the coast of Africa—the Azores, Madeira, the Canaries, the Cape Verdes, São Tomé, and Fernando Pó—offered the Portuguese and Spanish testing grounds for colonial expansion. "Discovered" by Iberian mariners in the fourteenth and fifteenth centuries, these islands offered semitropical or tropical climates that, when wet enough, proved excellent for the cultivation of sugar. Some of them, though, were inhabited—by Neolithic peoples who had migrated there from Northern Africa centuries before, only to lose the naval technology that could keep them linked to the African world. On the Canary Islands, the processes of European exploration, conquest, and exploitation all came together, as the Spanish pioneered the development of the plantation complex that would shortly after be transferred to the Caribbean. There, native peoples known as the Guanches were exterminated in a long campaign of conquest, with Spanish technology aided by Old World diseases that fell on the "virgin soil" of a population disconnected from Europe and Africa for millennia. The construction of sugar plantations quickly followed. Sugar, a labor-intensive crop that required a demanding harvest and refining process, benefitted from economies of scale, returning disproportionately greater returns for greater investment. Like tobacco, coffee, chocolate, and other New World products that would follow, sugar was also well suited as a trade commodity. High demand for sweeteners and stimulants from the New World made it profitable to grow. And because no one could live on sugar, there was no risk that it would be totally consumed where it was grown. Finally, in refined form sugar could easily be transported across great distances without undue risk of spoilage.

Slaves supplied most of the sugar plantations' insatiable demand for labor. Initially, unfree laborers were drawn from the Mediterranean's reservoir of bondsmen—captives taken in interminable religious wars with Islamic states, and labor from existing slave-trading networks that stretched from the Black Sea to trans-Saharan Africa. Increasingly, though, as enslaved natives and extant Mediterranean supplies proved insufficient for the huge labor demands of the Atlantic sugar mills, the Spanish slowly turned to a new source of workers—the sub-Saharan African slaves supplied to Portuguese traders by coastal chiefs.

For centuries, slaves had formed a crucial element in the workforces of medieval Europe and the Mediterranean. In Northern Europe, population decimations caused by plague and famine had steadily elevated the position of the most unfree workers to the states of serfs, landless laborers tied to their demesnes whose bodies nonetheless could not be bartered, sold, and moved. Steadily, enslavement became a status preserved for outsiders—most often, those defined as religious "infidels" by the Christian and Muslim states (such as Spain and the Ottoman Empire) locked in seemingly eternal combat for control of the fate of Europe and the Mediterranean.

The states and nonstate societies of sub-Saharan Africa had also long practiced "slavery" as an extreme form of social degradation. In many of these societies humans served as resources at least as valuable as land itself, and so constituted a critical measure of wealth. Yet while the lives of most of these slaves were unenviable in the extreme, slave status did not prevent a select few from becoming powerful. Indeed, in these forms of what we may term "Old World slavery," enslaved persons might over time, or even generations, acquire positions of prestige and power. Even in sub-Saharan Africa, those enslaved could over generations often assimilate, eventually erasing the original taint of slave status. Thus those who when initially enslaved could make no claims on the community—and hence become socially "dead," in Orlando Patterson's memorable formulation—might over time rise in status. Slave concubines might live to see their progeny make legitimate claims to inherited wealth. Enslaved court eunuchs in the Islamic world might command the ears of emperors. And slave warriors such as the Ottomans' dreaded corps of Janissaries or the Mamluk castes of Northern Africa could make or break their empires. While none of these forms of Old World slavery could in any way be described as benign or inherently humane, they nonetheless differed fundamentally from the rigid contours of the racial slavery that came to define the highly capitalistic worlds of the plantation Atlantic.

Such was the state of slavery in the Euro-Mediterranean world as the plantation complex moved to the western fringes of the Atlantic. The Spanish, employing the same naval innovations that had permitted Portuguese exploration of the African coastline, followed the trade winds to the Americas. Christopher Columbus attempted to establish sugar growing on Hispaniola on his second voyage to the New World, a telling sign both of his commercial motives and of the crop's significance in the process of exploration. In 1502, Spain imported its first African slaves to the Caribbean. While Columbus's Spanish overlords quickly became preoccupied with the wealth of native empires on the mainland Americas, other European powers divined the value of these tropical new lands as potential suppliers of sugar. The Portuguese, quickly mating ideal environmental conditions for sugar growing with the trade in bound labor they were already exploiting off the African coast, imported the sugar complex they had established on São Tomé to the northeastern coast of Brazil, which they had "discovered" and claimed in 1500. By the 1530s, *engenhos*, or sugar mills, dotted the Bahian countryside. As the Spanish had attempted in the Canaries, the Portuguese initially sought to augment their meager labor force by enslaving natives. As before, though, forces beyond the high mortality of plantation labor in the tropics worked against the colonizers: military conquest threw existing social systems into chaos, while virgin-soil epidemics such as smallpox decimated local populations. Native peoples fiercely resisted enslavement with all the advantages of those fighting on their home turf: knowledge of local conditions, and a vast frontier to meld into.

In their fifteenth-century African explorations, the Portuguese had begun to develop the alternative source of labor that fueled Brazilian sugar production. The Iberian nation was the first entrant into an Atlantic slave trade that ultimately carried over twelve million human beings across the Atlantic in the largest forced migration in human history.[3] Over time, every major European power would engage in the Atlantic slave trade—a commercial mechanism utterly devoted to the economic exploitation of New World agricultural production. At its nascence, however, the Atlantic slave trade appeared to differ little from systems of slave trading that had long existed in the Old World. In fact, the very notion of "slavery," like its modern opposite of "freedom," has changed over time. The familiar binary of slavery and freedom was itself a product of the very history of New World slavery we are examining. The dialectic emerged gradually in the Atlantic world as slavery grew alongside modern liberal democratic ideas. Ultimately, it wound up playing a vital role in the story of emancipation, but before that time, in the hierarchal orderings that have characterized most human societies throughout most of history, it makes sense to think not in terms of absolutes, but of degrees. On a range of degrees of liberty, "slaves" were merely the least free.

The Portuguese merchants who filled the Atlantic's burgeoning demand for labor thus drew upon, and in the process changed, social practices long extant. European traders bartered with coastal chiefs for a range of goods, humans constituting just one important category. The societies of sub-Saharan Africa, ethnically diverse and engaged in their own political conflicts, had long held humans in states that would today be defined as unfree: perhaps as captives taken in war, as pawns held for debt, or clients who produced for the kin group that held them. Life for those enslaved in this manner was hardly enviable. Yet neither was it likely to equal the horror experienced by those who endured the Middle Passage and enslavement in America. Whereas "slavery" in Africa was primarily a social system that served to expand the power of kin groups by adding to it valuable human resources, in the New World slavery was a labor system tied closely to the expansion of capitalism. And whereas the "slave" in Africa inhabited an unfortunate social status, it was not one tied to perpetual heredity (slaves could become incorporated into kin groups over time), definitions of "race" (enslavement was not reserved for one particular "race" since the notion of race in its modern sense did not yet exist), or permanent social degradation (some enslaved peoples could become very powerful proxies for their overlords). In short, diversity characterized the work, status, and destinies of "slaves" in much of Africa before the Atlantic slave trade.[4] In contrast, enslaved Africans in the New World occupied what became a clearly defined status: as human property to be bartered and sold like other trade goods, defined as slaves in perpetuity by the ascription of a particular "racial" identity, and deprived of all claims of rights as humans—all to serve a system of labor supply and labor subordination dedicated to the commercial exploitation of the natural world through the extraction or production of resources for sale in an international market.

Regardless of what it was to become, the new source of labor worked. By 1450, Portuguese slavers plying the coastal castles of sub-Saharan western Africa annually transported an average of more than five hundred slaves per year. By the turn of the 1500s, over eighty thousand Africans had found their way into the Atlantic slave trade.[5] Brazil's northeastern sugar colonies played host to a great number of these—perhaps fifty thousand by 1600. Eventually, Brazil would become the largest recipient of enslaved Africans, taking in over the course of slavery's long history there nearly four million slaves, or about 40 percent of the entire transatlantic trade.[6] But that was later. Here, in the sixteenth century, sugar took off, replacing the Atlantic islands as Europe's major source of sweetness. The boom lasted for a long time. In 1710, one scholar calculates, over five hundred mills operated in Brazil, producing over sixteen thousand tons of sugar that year.[7] Europe's taste for the sweetener knew only the bounds of cost, which in any case plummeted over time as sugar transitioned from luxury to staple. One historian estimates that from 1650 to 1800 England's consumption grew by 2,500 percent.[8]

In the early 1600s, Northern Europeans challenged the Portuguese, entering into both the Atlantic slave trade and colonization. The Dutch, having in the second half of the sixteenth century begun to establish what would become a worldwide trading empire, contested Portugal's claims in South America. In 1630, they wrested much of northeastern Brazil from Portuguese control. For the next twenty-four years, until the Portuguese reconquered their lost lands, Dutch merchants learned the methods and techniques of sugar agriculture, which they then transplanted to other colonies in the New World, particularly Surinam, on the northern coast of South America. So valuable was Surinam that in 1667 the Dutch were willing to trade New Amsterdam (which would later grow into New York) to England in order to retain control of it. The Dutch also elbowed their way into the Atlantic slave trade, capturing and temporarily holding Portuguese slave-trading forts on the west coast of Africa, just as they had overtaken Portuguese sugar colonies in Brazil. Between 1630 and 1674, Dutch ships were responsible for transporting seventy thousand Africans across the Atlantic.[9] Dutch merchants eventually supplanted the Portuguese slavers who controlled the *asiento*, the lucrative monopoly on the supply of slaves to the Spanish New World.

France and England also entered the game, vying as much for control of the international slave trade as for claims to prime croplands. Employing technologies initially carried by "refugees" from Dutch Brazil, planters on the English island of Barbados and the French islands of Martinique and Guadeloupe began raising sugar in the 1630s and 1640s.[10] By the end of the century, both nations had expanded their operations to larger islands taken from the overextended Spanish Empire: Jamaica for England and St. Domingue (the western portion of the island of Hispaniola) for France. So valuable were Caribbean sugar holdings that France, as had the Dutch with Surinam, chose to retain the tiny Caribbean sugar islands of Martinique, Guadeloupe, and St. Lucia over their expansive holdings on mainland North America; the 1763 Treaty of Paris thus ended the French Empire in North America, and Canada became British—all for the sake of sugar.

France and England entered the Atlantic slave trade briskly, with merchants from each trading off the asiento with Portuguese and Dutch concerns. French traders transported forty thousand Africans across the Atlantic in the seventeenth century, while British ones were responsible for nearly ten times that many. (After the Portuguese, who were in the trade for so long, England carried more slaves than any other single nation.[11]) Northern Europeans introduced not only new competitors into the scramble for New World colonies, but also financial and marketing innovations. For example, they pioneered the use of joint-stock companies in colonial ventures—such as the Virginia Company (England, 1606) and the Dutch West India Company (1621)—a novel method of pooling capital and sharing the huge risks that attended these costly enterprises. While state-sponsored private efforts eventually gave way to government's more efficient and consistent centralized administration, colonization always closely united commercial and national interests.

By Atlantic standards, England's efforts to establish cash-crop plantation agriculture on mainland North America initially constituted a marginal effort. In the scramble to claim the vast continent, Britain was only one, and a rather late, entrant. Spain had the earliest claims on the continent, and France arguably the strongest, when the first permanent English settlement began at Jamestown, Virginia, established in 1607, suffered through early deprivation and a futile search for mineral wealth until it finally alighted upon the formula that was reaping such profits in the Caribbean and Brazil. John Rolfe, a seventeenth-century English entrepreneur, first grew Virginia tobacco, a sweet hybrid of Caribbean and North American strains that could compete with the finer (but more expensive) Spanish product, in 1612. Tobacco, like sugar, proved an excellent colonial cash crop: once processed, it was an easily stored and transported luxury item that appealed to the European consumer market's growing appetite for stimulants, spices, and "dessert" products. Cash-crop production of tobacco for the European consumer market soon overtook the Chesapeake. By 1619, when Rolfe reported the arrival of "twenty negars" to the colony, Virginia was exporting more than twenty thousand pounds per year of the "noxious weede" back to England. The tobacco craze was on. In 1604, King James I of England had denounced smoking as "a custome lothsome to the eye, hatefull to the Nose, harmefull to the braine, dangerous to the Lungs, and in the blacke stinking fume thereof, neerest resembling the horrible Stigian smoke of the pit that is bottomelesse."[12] He dissuaded few. By the end of the 1600s, England could count on annual imports of up to thirty thousand pounds, much of it from Virginia and Maryland.[13]

Experience with sugar and tobacco in the New World established cash-crop agriculture for European consumer markets as one of the most viable motives for colonial settlement. But there were other crops, and other endeavors. These differences in settlement types and cash crops throughout the New World were vital to the history of slavery and abolition that unfolded. It is useful, then, to impose some sense of organization on these patterns and the factors that conditioned them. Following historian Philip Curtin, several useful models of European colonial settlement present themselves.[14] Of course, actual historical experience was messy, and did not scruple spilling out of ideal types constructed by later analysts, but such categories help highlight the major differences between colonial settlement patterns and point the way toward understanding their causes and consequences.

The first model, which Curtin labels *true empire*, is best exemplified by Spain's experience with the Aztec Empire in Central America and the Inca Empire in South America. In those places, Spanish conquistadores employed their advantages—superior military technology, cultural shock, and European diseases—to defeat centralized native states. With surprising ease, Spain thus quickly enjoyed the fruits of conquest, gaining the natural wealth—particularly gold and silver—the defeated states had compelled their subordinate populations to extract. One scholar estimates that in the 1500s the nation acquired 170 tons of gold and 8,200 tons of silver in this manner. By defeating native empires and appropriating their riches, Spain became the most powerful of all European states.[15]

No other European power was fortunate enough to encounter rich native empires that could quickly be conquered. Most native Americans were organized into less powerful states or nonstate societies. Not having extracted from the earth enormous caches of easily plundered gold and silver, and having the advantages of decentralization and knowledge of interior frontiers, they made unattractive and difficult targets for conquest and domination. But they did command land and labor power that Europeans sought to exploit in lieu of mineral riches. Here is where cash-crop agriculture fit in, as European entrepreneurs sought to enslave these native peoples and use their land to grow products for the European consumer trade. As in the case of Brazil, enslavement in the New World generally failed—native peoples died off, fled, or fought back—and African slavery took its place. Land expropriation, though, was another matter. Inexorably, Europeans took over the natives' land to grow crops.

Sugar was of course the most important of these. The white gold of the New World represented the quickest alternate source of wealth to conquest, albeit one that required intensive investment and effort to achieve its promised return. This investment actually proved to be a long-term advantage for the mercantile economies that sponsored sugar agriculture in the New World, for the investment required of sugar production helped foster the productive technologies, financial innovations, and credit mechanisms that further developed modern capitalism. While Spain quickly grew rich off of its New World empires, it just as quickly fell into a long, slow decline, fighting a centuries-long rearguard action against rival empires that pecked away at its hastily acquired riches. Those European powers that invested in the plantation complex (and Spain did finally turn to this, though too late, in Cuba) fared better in the long-term seas of international mercantile competition. Cash-crop agriculture represented the height of capitalist formation in the sixteenth and seventeenth centuries, and the lands dedicated to it we may label *exploitation colonies.*

While it is easy to think of European settlement as a process of transplanting Europe to the Americas, the success of exploitation colonies depended on climatic and geographic *difference* from Europe. The environmental conditions that favored the production of sugar and other New World products also made the Caribbean colonies unpalatable for European settler colonization. In the early modern period, the very features that now draw tourists to the tropics made them, without the benefits of modern hygiene and air conditioning, inhospitable and unwelcoming to potential migrants. Hot, humid climates nourished sugar, but also created a vicious disease environment to which Europeans were unaccustomed, and all too frequently succumbed. And the ferocity of the labor control necessary to compel enslaved peoples to work the arduous crop bred an ethos of hierarchy and domination in these societies that hardly made the colonial Caribbean an attractive destination for many Europeans. As a consequence, not many whites settled there. African slaves and their descendants dominated Caribbean populations. Historian Stanley Engerman figures that in the middle of the eighteenth century, 85 percent of the British Caribbean and 87 percent of the French and Dutch Caribbean were enslaved.[16]

In contrast to the exploitation colonies that grew topical products for the international market, other colonies established by Europeans occupied geographies and climates more akin to Europe than the Tropics. These "neo-Europes," as environmental historian Alfred Crosby has called them, favored the large-scale infusion of European settler populations, which undertook economic activities suited to New World conditions—such as fishing, trapping, timber production, and long-distance trade.[17] In neo-Europes throughout the Atlantic Basin, the Dutch and French concentrated on establishing outposts to *trading empires*, another of Curtin's categories of colonial settlement, rather than on transplanting their populations. For example, French settlements in the interior of North America served as entrepôts for a thriving fur trade, while Dutch settlements in places such as New Amsterdam and Cape Town offered key way stations for merchant ships that plied an ever-expanding worldwide network of trade.

Settler colonies formed where both environment and motives suited the large-scale migration of European populations and social institutions. While trade and commerce continued to figure prominently here (few moved to the New World without a desire for personal economic mobility), religious motives offered an additional impetus. The interminable religious struggles of early modern Europe had fostered a population of disaffected potential migrants who lent colonization a critical sense of religious purpose. The northern colonies of mainland North America most clearly embodied this model, as they were composed of large numbers of English settlers, who migrated in families and sought to re-create their own ideals of perfected English social and religious institutions. Puritan New England, for example, served to its founders as a "citty upon a hill" that might exemplify how a godly European community might form if permitted to establish itself largely free of Old World constraints.[18] Further south, Pennsylvania initially served as a haven for English Quakers, another dissenting Protestant sect. Surely, African slavery was an important institution in these northern colonies, just as it was throughout the Atlantic Basin, and indeed, in parts of Europe by that time. Yet, as historian Ira Berlin reminds us, we might more profitably think of such colonies as "societies with slaves" than as the "slave societies" of the Caribbean exploitation colonies.[19] New England—with its overwhelming white population and transplanted English mores, values, and culture—was a far cry from the British West Indies. While slavery played an important, and indeed long overlooked, role in the northern colonies, exploitation colonies were organized around the institution. Slavery, and what it was used for, was their very raison d'être.

Moving south through England's mainland North American colonies, the picture changed. As the climate and geography increasingly favored the production of cash crops using enslaved labor, so too the society itself manifested the characteristics of the exploitation colonies. These *hybrid colonies* combined elements of settler and exploitation colonies, generally in proportion to their suitability for each task. The tobacco-growing Chesapeake was an exploitation-oriented "slave society" with yet many characteristics of a settler society: a "neo-European" climate, a large white population, and social as well as commercial motives for large-scale transplantation of European populations and institutions. The significance of slavery was evident in large numbers of enslaved African-descended people, who accounted for 42 percent of Virginia's population on the eve of the American Revolution. It could not, however, compare with a Caribbean colony such as Barbados, where the enslaved amounted to 83 percent of the island's population, or Jamaica's, which stood at an incredible 93 percent. Further south on the mainland, the climate became more tropical, thus more well suited to the production of capital-intensive cash crops, and hence more Caribbean-like in its social composition and economic structure. On the Sea Islands off the coasts of South Carolina and Georgia, rice production rivaled sugar in the infrastructure and labor required for success. As a consequence, these hybrid colonies took on many of the characteristics of the Caribbean exploitation colonies they were originally meant to provision. Well over 70 percent of the population of some counties in colonial South Carolina was enslaved, at least before the Stono slave uprising of 1739 led the colony's leaders to squelch slave imports for the sake of white settlers' safety. On the eve of the Revolution, black people constituted 60 percent of South Carolina's total population.[20]

These variations on the theme of British mainland North America suggest that the colonies were no monolithic whole, but a group of discrete economies and societies, each of which reflected important differences in environment and settlement. Yet by other measures, the colonies *were* a united entity. For one, they were economically interdependent: colonies less suitable for cash-crop cultivation provisioned places given over almost wholly to cash crops. Imperial relationships united all in a network of trade and regulation intended to benefit the polities and commercial interests that had risked so much to establish them.

The colonies were thus politically subordinate to and economically dependent on the European states that had founded, supplied, peopled, and protected them.

Regardless of type, colonial relationships assumed a common form: governance of the empires happened back in the major cities of the European nations that had established them—which we may call the *metropole*. The metropole was the heart of the mercantile colonial empires—the place where administrative policy was formulated, where the sources of credit and finance were situated, and whence the military and diplomatic assets of empire were coordinated. Home to growing cities and large populations, and sites of intellectual and cultural innovation, the metropole was where consumer tastes were fashioned, and demand for products driven. In contrast, the colonies served as the *periphery* to this metropolitan *core*, producing the agricultural products that fueled profit and national power.[21]

Agricultural periphery and metropolitan core thus worked together. The colonies were commercial enterprises that represented the cutting edge of economic innovation and capital investment at the time, yet they were also state-run endeavors designed to aggrandize the powerful European nations that sponsored them. Commercial and national strength went hand in hand, as the great powers of Europe sought to use their colonial empires to enrich themselves in their continual contests for position and prestige—an idea that came to be known as *mercantilism*. Each nation's colonial empire, administered from thriving metropolitan centers such as London, Paris, or Amsterdam, existed to profit and strengthen the mother country. In this exchange, colonies were decidedly unequal partners. Empire was indeed expensive, but the cores grew fat on the wealth of colonies—fat enough, some historians have claimed, to help launch the industrial revolution of the late eighteenth and nineteenth centuries.[22] Meanwhile, colonies made some men in them rich, but these often lacked representation necessary to more successfully champion their interests back in the metropole, which after all they theoretically existed to serve. Laws stemming from Europe restricted trade from the colonial periphery so that profits would remain within the empire, and colonials lacked the representation necessary to more successfully champion their interests back home. England's Navigation Acts—a loose set of laws passed from 1651 to the American Revolution and beyond—best exemplified the idea, mandating that only English ships could carry goods from the colonies and "enumerating" certain colonial products, which could be carried only to Great Britain or other English colonies.

That was the theory. In practice effective administration of the laws designed to protect national monopolies was lax at best, beset by a small and inefficient bureaucracy (by today's standards anyway) and the difficulties of effectively governing a massive empire in an age of slow communication. Britain's mainland North American colonies benefitted from this "salutary neglect" in two ways: they developed traditions of local political autonomy rooted in English notions of "liberty" and grew their own economies while the mother country concerned itself with myriad other matters. By 1763, when Great Britain successfully ousted French competitors in North America and consolidated its claims, some colonies had enjoyed a century and a half of prosperous, fairly independent development. The British mainland colonies thus encompassed a wide range of economic endeavors—from exploitation-oriented cash-crop economies to settler-oriented trade economies that would soon embark on their own takeoff into the industrial future. By the time the borders of a new nation were drawn, these varied economies—and, more important, the differing social worlds they bred—would exist within the boundaries of a single country.

By the second half of the eighteenth century, the major European powers had fully developed thriving New World mercantile empires established on the production of cash crops using the enslaved labor of Africans and their descendants. These empires had well served to aggrandize their domestic economies and aid the European states in their endless national competitions with each other. Yet at the very height of this system, the empires came tumbling down. In the half century from 1775 to 1825—a mere blip on the world-historical scale—the leading New World powers of England, France, and Spain were all beset by calamitous revolutions that sundered many colonial holdings from their European sponsor states. After a little more than another half century—by 1888—Atlantic slavery, the labor system that had built the colonies, was dead. Thus ended a long chapter in the history of the emergence of the modern world: the rise of modern world capitalism with the expansion of Europe, based upon what strikes us as the decidedly uncapitalistic and unmodern institution of chattel bondage.

Several forces came together in the eighteenth century to create a series of revolutionary crises that ultimately destroyed slavery. The mercantile empires had been hugely profitable for the nations and private investors associated with them. We need not go so far as to accept Eric Williams's argument that the slave trade provided the resources that launched Britain's industrial takeoff to acknowledge that colonial endeavors played vital roles in the development of the European economies. That development drove the metropolitan cores toward forms of economic organization—nascent industrialization—that would ultimately displace the power of the plantation complex in the empires. In short, proponents of a new form of capitalism were beginning to wrest control of the state from proponents of an older form: plantation capitalism.

At the same time, the mercantile empires were dangerously overextended. Recall that these globe-spanning overseas empires served to aggrandize European nations that had been at more or less continual war since they had emerged from their feudal past. War, however, was expensive and risky, particularly for state apparatuses that were minuscule by modern bureaucratic standards. Moreover, war and its costs were no longer confined to Europe. In what may justly be termed the first true world wars, continental conflicts—the War of Spanish Succession (1701–14), the War of Austrian Succession (1740–48), and the Seven Years' War (1756–63)—began to spill over into the colonies. The North American analogues of these—Queen Anne's War (1701–13), King George's War (1744–48), and the French and Indian War (1754–63)—swept the mainland English colonies up into a defense of the empire. When the dust settled, Britain emerged triumphant in North America. But the expense had strained to the utmost the treasuries of all the powers involved, and ultimately broke the backs of the mercantile empires. In England, the need to recover the costs of defending the empire led Parliament to begin enforcing its long-ignored mercantile policy, which merely demanded that the colonies help finance their own defense; colonists' rejection of those measures led directly to the American Revolution. In France, impending financial ruin caused by a century of interminable war and absolutist rule led King Louis XVI to call for new taxes through the Estates General, a move that sparked the French Revolution in 1789. And in Spain, overextension and weak administration combined with the continental wars resulting from the French Revolution created opportunities for colonial autonomy throughout Spanish possessions in the New World. The forces unleashed by the fiscal crises of the great powers thus converged to create the dual phenomena of revolution in the metropole and independence movements in the colonies.

The first episode in this "Age of Democratic Revolution"[23] began with a colonial independence movement, the American Revolution, that illuminated vulnerabilities in all the mercantile empires. In part, these weaknesses actually owed to success. Mercantilism worked well when the economies of metropole and colony complemented each other, as with the case of slave-produced cash crops. Because they were grown in peripheries environmentally distinct from the European cores, New World products such as sugar and tobacco complemented rather than competed with English commercial enterprises. There could be friction, as metropolitan creditors and middlemen sought to maximize their profits at the expense of the New World planters beholden, and often deeply indebted, to them. And the maturation of colonies over time tended generally to foster a spirit of independence everywhere, especially among the "creole" generations of colonists actually born in the New World. But in general plantation and metropole worked together to enrich all.

Of greater concern were colonial economies with a paucity of cash-crop staples to complement the mercantile empires. Consider, for example, the British mainland colonial North. Lacking the lures of cash-crop agriculture, the northern colonies scrambled for ways to make profits, building their economies on the exploitation of resources from the frontier. The northern colonies grew, but on extractive industries, shipbuilding, and commerce—the latter endeavors coming to compete with rather than complement the economic enterprises of the metropole. In short, as the northern colonies successfully developed from their colonial foundations of dependence, they came to look more like cores and less like peripheries: mercantile, urban, and industrializing. Merchants and traders in these colonies chafed under the restrictions of the mother country's mercantile policy, which artificially inflated the cost of imported goods (which in theory could come only from the empire's manufacturers), and stifled the growth of colonial trade (by restricting it to the possessions of the mother country). Weak administrative systems combined with distance and inconsistent policy to make enforcement of the mercantile provisions ineffective and tension-fraught. Colonials invoked their rights as citizens of the metropole (for example, their status as "Englishmen") to argue for more favorable trade policy, only to be rebuffed by governments that saw no need to extend to subordinate overseas colonies the same political liberties and economic benefits that prevailed in the mother country.

Intellectual currents in the Atlantic world lent the colonists' grievances the authority of transcendent principle. Wherever revolutionaries sought to throw off the yoke of absolutist rule, they relied upon new ideas of human society and government that were emerging in the Atlantic world. The Enlightenment, an intellectual movement of eighteenth-century America, Britain, and continental Europe, rejected the divine right of kings to rule, and called instead for governments that served the governed rather than the governors, with popularly elected representatives who adhered to written constitutions. Relying upon these ideals of democratic liberalism, revolutionaries throwing off established authority could claim devotion to principles that transcended the manmade political order—the brotherhood of man, the fundamental equality of all, and the undeniable right of self-rule—and thus justified what otherwise would have been (and to many still was) simple treason. Under Enlightenment principles, to cast off the political shackles of an oppressive government constituted not rebellion against a king, but loyalty to principles now claimed to be universal. As Thomas Jefferson, the great American revolutionary put it, "Resistance to tyrants is obedience to God."

Other colonies followed England's mainland thirteen in the search for independence. The Spanish colonies of Central and South America resembled the colonial North in important respects. These "societies with slaves" featured small populations of unfree Africans, but sizable *mestizo* populations composed of those with a mixture of Spanish, Native American, and African heritage. These free people of mixed heritage often found common cause with more well-to-do creole populations, composed of American-born whites of "pure" Spanish heritage. Both felt slighted by mercantile policies that benefitted the mother country at the expense of those born and bred in the colonies, who favored free trade with other empires and other measures to promote the economic and political independence of the colonies. When Spain sought to reform its colonial policies in the late 1700s, these local elites sought even more control. At the turn of the nineteenth century, when Europe erupted in a generation of constant warfare, those opportunities only widened.

The Enlightenment ideology that stoked the fires of revolution in the colonies also had deep impacts back in the metropolitan cores. Notions of universal human liberty fueled dissent in the rigid political hierarchies of the centralized nation-states that had emerged just as Europe was beginning its expansion into the Atlantic. Whereas the American Revolution invoked Enlightenment ideas to argue that those in the periphery had a right to rule themselves, the French Revolution of 1789–99 used the new liberalism to topple an absolutist monarchy, and transform the very social system of the most highly developed metropole in the world. The ensuing conflagration reverberated throughout the Atlantic world. While European nations feared that France might export its radical social revolution, the colonies of all nations found themselves caught in the midst of political chaos back in the metropole. From 1791, when the First Coalition of European nations joined forces against revolutionary France, to 1815, when the seventh such coalition finally defeated the French Emperor Napoléon at Waterloo, Europe found itself embroiled in almost constant, total warfare. The colonies suffered from disrupted trade and sometimes rampaging armies, but also benefitted from the independence fostered when war weakened imperial control of the mercantile system.

As a consequence of the Napoleonic Wars, independence movements carved nine new countries out of Spain's crumbling New World empire. Napoléon's invasion of Spain in 1807 cut the colonies off from the imperial control that had stifled independence. Long-dissatisfied colonial dissidents capitalized on this power vacuum and, under the leadership of revolutionaries such as Simón Bolívar and José de San Martín, wrested independence from Spain in a series of long and bloody conflicts. By 1825, only Caribbean islands—Cuba, Puerto Rico, and Santo Domingo—remained under imperial control. Such was the disruption on the continent that the Portuguese Crown actually relocated itself to its premier colony, Brazil, which in a relatively bloodless revolution gained its independence from the mother country in 1822.

The ideology underlying these revolutionary movements played a critical role in the abolition of slavery. Ideas of self-rule and universal equality were deemed dangerous enough in the hierarchical societies of Europe, but in the Atlantic world of African bondage they were truly explosive. Colonial revolutionaries throughout the New World invoked Enlightenment principles of democracy, none more than the slave owners and plantation overlords of places such as Virginia. But slave-owning revolutionaries confronted an enormous problem: the ideology that justified their otherwise treasonous rebellions offered arguments that *anyone*, including the enslaved, might use to claim freedom from oppression. The Enlightenment-inspired ideology of the colonial independence movements, then, lent enormous momentum to antislavery ideas that had long been brewing on the margins of Atlantic society. Abolitionism transformed in the course of the 1700s, growing from a strange belief held by some dissenting Protestant Quakers into a secular idea that pervaded revolutionary societies.

It is hard to understate the significance of this shift. Because of the Atlantic revolutions, it suddenly became possible for masses of people to imagine that slavery, a practice of most human societies for virtually all of human history, could be eradicated. Whereas previous to this point all understood that the condition of the slave was debased and unfortunate, very few could have imagined slavery itself as something that could be, let alone should be, destroyed. Enlightenment ideology and the revolutions it fed rendered slavery abolishable by consigning it to the realm of outdated and oppressive governmental systems. Slavery's defenders went from having to justify why only Africans were enslaved to having to justify why *anyone* should be enslaved. It was indeed still possible to argue on behalf of slavery, but only by writing African-descended people out of the category of humanity—a strategy that slavery's defenders did in fact develop, relying on the very biological sciences the Enlightenment had birthed.

Slavery was totally destroyed first in St. Domingue, a place where these swirling revolutionary forces converged in a perfect storm of political and social upheaval. This complex story, which is detailed in the pages ahead, amounted to this: local colonial elites had taken advantage of the chaos created by a metropolitan revolution back in the European core to aggrandize themselves and launch a colonial independence movement justified by Enlightenment ideology, only to have it hijacked by a massive uprising of the enslaved—a move that ultimately succeeded because the racial demography of this rich exploitation colony so heavily favored blacks over whites. Haiti became the only place where a slave revolt successfully destroyed the slave regime and replaced it with a free republic. But it became a byword throughout the slaveholding Atlantic world, a specter of the "horrors" of revolution even more terrifying than the excesses of the French revolutionary government of 1793–94. To the enslaved and oppressed, it became a beacon of possibility.

Nowhere else in the Atlantic world did slavery die as it did in Haiti. Slave revolt played a necessary role in the process of emancipation everywhere, but only in Haiti was it even close to sufficient to liberate all. Elsewhere, three dominant patterns characterized the process of abolition. In the first, which we may term *revolutionary abolitions*, slavery ended as a consequence of colonial independence movements, which abolished the institution partly as an exigency of war, and partly as an expression of commitment to the revolutionary principles underlying revolt. This was the pattern throughout mainland Spanish Latin America, which by the nineteenth century was largely composed of societies with slaves rather than exploitation-oriented slave societies. Revolutionary forces could risk putting their principles into practice, particularly when the enslaved proved willing to trade their loyalty and military service for freedom in the wars of independence. In 1823, Chile and Mexico abolished slavery; the Central American states, which were then united into a single confederation, followed the next year. Other countries followed with a series of gradual measures, such that by the start of the American Civil War slavery was largely dead in mainland Spanish Latin America.

In the second pattern of abolition, European metropoles imposed abolition on their colonies. Two forces within these national colonial empires clashed. Those with an interest in thriving exploitation colonies, who had long held considerable political power back in the mother country, put up a fierce defense against the antislavery thinking brewing out of the industrializing, democratizing cores—a set of ideas we might term *metropolitan abolitionism*. These notions gained popular support where the capitalist economies were most highly developed, notably England and the U.S. North. New forms of economic organization were displacing old, and where manufacturing and urbanization gained ground, slavery increasingly came to be viewed as an unnecessary and archaic form of labor, as disconsonant with the economic imperatives of the new economy as with a bourgeois moral order dedicated to the virtues of "free labor."

The fight between the planter interest and metropolitan abolitionists took place in two stages: a first battle against the slave trade and a later struggle against slavery itself. Abolitionists in England—not coincidentally the most advanced economy in the world—led the way. Rooted in Quaker communities which had over the course of the eighteenth century increasingly advocated ameliorating the condition of the enslaved, the British abolition movement dates from the formation of antislavery societies in 1780s. Established in 1787, the Committee for the Abolition of the Slave Trade brought together the leading lights of the movement. It was led by William Wilberforce, a charismatic member of Parliament who had been inspired by John Newton, the former slave trader who renounced his past and converted to abolitionism (Newton penned the hymn "Amazing Grace" in honor of his redemption). Thomas Clarkson, another evangelical convert, became the movement's chief propagandist. Among his successes was the promotion of *The Interesting Narrative of the Life of Olaudah Equiano, or Gustavus Vassa, the African* (1789), the story of the Atlantic world's most famous former slave and black advocate of freedom. Another antislavery radical, Granville Sharp, propelled into the courts the plight of runaway slave James Somerset. In *Somerset's Case* (1772), Lord Mansfield, the chief justice of the King's Bench, ruled that slavery was "so odious, that nothing can be suffered to support it, but positive law"—a decision interpreted to mean that slaves setting foot on the free soil of Britain were thus made forever free.

Still, success came slowly. In 1789 Wilberforce first spoke out in Parliament against the international slave trade, and in 1791, he introduced the first bill to end Britain's international slave trade. But West Indian planters bitterly opposed the movement, while the French Revolution diverted popular attention and brought suspicion on antislavery's reforming zeal. It was not until 1807, in the midst of Britain's struggle against Napoléon's France, that an abolition bill succeeded. With England out of the slave trade, the nation's economic interests dictated the suppression of other nations' slave traders, lest other nations enjoy benefits England had forsaken. England began a feat of high-seas interdiction imaginable only with the earth's mightiest navy. Its famed West Africa Squadron freed about 160,000 African captives on Brazilian and Portuguese slavers between 1811 and 1867.[24] In 1815 at the Congress of Vienna, slave-trading powers such as the Netherlands and France responded to such pressure by agreeing to shut down their slave-trading operations. The Portuguese and Spanish trades were permitted to continue for some time, and of course illegal trading persisted, but the weight of international law and opinion now fell on the practice.

Upon the success of the Slave Trade Act, Wilberforce reportedly asked a friend, "What shall we abolish next?" The answer, of course, was slavery itself. It took another quarter century and other champions, though, for England to topple slavery in its own holdings. The end of the international slave trade did spell eventual doom for English slavery, for under rigorous work regimes and in unhealthful environments slave populations could never reproduce themselves naturally. Yet the slave regime remained politically powerful, just as slavery itself remained extremely profitable. Slowly, however, abolitionism gained traction— not only among metropolitan populations, but also among the enslaved themselves, who from the stirrings of metropolitan reform brewed up a new kind of slave revolution. Mass resistance had been a persistent feature of plantation slavery from the very start, but in the Atlantic world of the liberal nineteenth century, it took on new forms and new significance. In the prerevolutionary period, group violence directed at the slave regime could at most hope to remove some of the enslaved into precarious communities of runaway "maroons" in the interior. In the age of abolition, all this changed.

Three slave uprisings in the British West Indies—the Easter Rebellion that took place on Barbados in 1816, the Demerara Rebellion of 1823, and Jamaica's Christmas Rebellion of 1831–32—reflected the critical, often unappreciated significance of slave thought and behavior in the process of emancipation. Each calamity demonstrated that the enslaved had ears, and—as contemporary whites complained—listened to those abolitionist arguments "conveyed by mischievous persons" or overhead from "the indiscreet conversations of Individuals."[25] Whereas earlier instances of mass resistance had done little to link the cause of the slaves with broader metropolitan reform movements, these rebellions were predicated on them. In each, well-organized uprisings sought to leverage impending reforms of the slave regime into greater freedom, with slave leaders frequently claiming that "their good King had sent Orders that they should be free."[26] Disaster greeted each as well, as plantation rulers and the rebellion-wary government brought down with stunning ferocity the full force of English arms. While in the narrow sense the rebellions failed, claiming the lives of hundreds of rebel leaders and leaving metropolitan citizens aghast, they nonetheless belied for the British public any claims that the slaves did not wish for their own liberty.

As a consequence, public opinion moved in fits and starts toward complete emancipation. Finally, in 1833, Parliament passed the Slavery Abolition Act. This measure, which went into effect in 1834, abolished slavery throughout most of Britain's colonial possessions, and provided monetary compensation to slave owners for their losses. It also created a system of apprenticeship, through which slaves would remain unfree for a limited number of years, thus protecting the principle of property rights, guaranteeing labor for former owners, and providing a period of "adjustment" to liberty. When this system was dismantled in 1838, the last slaves in the British Caribbean were free, and the Atlantic world had witnessed its first instance of complete metropolitan abolition.

Other European powers followed suit, France first. The vicissitudes of the Revolution complicated France's path to abolition considerably. The revolutionary government had abolished slavery in French colonies in 1794, largely as an acknowledgment of the realities of slave rebellion in the Caribbean. Napoléon, however, restored slavery in 1802, as part of his plan to revivify the French mercantile economy against the might of Britain. France would not see an abolition movement emerge until the 1820s, with the Committee for the Abolition of the Slave Trade and the Society for Christian Morals. Even then, abolitionism in France remained confined to a small political elite, which shied away from the popular mobilization so reminiscent of both the late revolution and the abolitionism of recent English enemies. The establishment of a liberal constitutional monarchy under Louis Philippe succored abolitionist hopes, but antislavery in

France from 1830 to 1848 remained plagued by gradualism, effective planter resistance, and the intransigence of the king. Not until the political unrest of the
1840s did a popular abolitionist movement take hold. Led by Victor Schoelcher,
the French Society for the Abolition of Slavery expanded French antislavery
through the adoption of Anglo-American abolitionists' populist tactics, and
eventually embraced immediate abolition. When the Revolution of 1848 deposed Louis Philippe and installed the Second Republic, slaves in the French
Caribbean pressed for their freedom through riots and protests. Schoelcher,
newly empowered as undersecretary of state, drafted the decree that abolished
slavery immediately and without compensation. In 1848, France thus abolished
slavery for the second time.

Denmark, which had been the first European nation to abolish its slave trade
(1803), followed in France's wake, legislating in 1848 the end of slavery in its colonial dominions: the islands of St. Thomas, St. John, and St. Croix. The Netherlands was the last national power in Northern Europe to follow. In 1848 the fall
of slavery on the French half of St. Martin led Dutch St. Maarten to relinquish
the institution, and in 1863 the Netherlands abolished slavery in its remaining
Caribbean colonies. Even more than in France, abolitionism in Northern Europe never evolved into a popular movement that excited the sympathies of the
metropolitan public; rather, ending slavery merely ratified trends that seemed as
progressive as they were inevitable. Before the end of the American Civil War,
then, every major European power except for Spain had ended slavery in their
Atlantic colonies.

The final pattern of abolition in the New World characterizes what we may
term the *late abolitions*—those happening well after the fulcrum of the American Civil War. In this pattern, metropolitan cores largely imposed abolition on
the agricultural periphery across national borders—Puerto Rico in 1876, but particularly Cuba in 1880 and Brazil in 1888. Spain had controlled Cuba since the
days of discovery, but Cuba had entered the sugar game late, in the nineteenth
century. Nonetheless, it became one of the most important sugar-producing
centers of the nineteenth-century world, dependent utterly on unfree labor.
In 1860 Cuba produced over half a million metric tons of sugar, and as late as
1877 over 70 percent of those who worked that sugar were enslaved.[27] Brazil's
geographic expanse and economic diversity had propelled it past a decline in
its northeastern sugar industry. In the eighteenth century, gold mining in the
central regions had helped slavery thrive, and in the nineteenth century coffee
growing in the southern part of the nation exploded, increasing the demand for
slaves just as the slave trade was dying elsewhere. As classic slave societies, the
plantation regimes of nineteenth-century Cuba and Brazil found themselves increasingly distanced from the economically developing world as a whole. While

Western Europe and the U.S. North had been industrializing since the 1790s, Cuba and Brazil clung to a labor system increasingly considered reactionary, archaic, and inhumane. Both depended on declining European nation-states that had failed to industrialize as quickly or as completely as their more powerful neighbors. Brazil was a late and slow entrant into the industrial economy, and Cuba remained a sugar colony of Spain until 1902. In many ways, the industrializing world was bypassing Brazil and the Spanish Caribbean, committed as they—and their Euro-American creditors—remained to the still-profitable fruits of the plantation. Many in the metropole could thus view abolition in these societies as, as Seymour Drescher has put it, "a belated provincial rendezvous with progress."[28]

Abolitionism in the Spanish Caribbean stemmed not from internal mass movements that characterized the earlier wave of emancipations, but from impulses that came largely from without. Both societies comprised agricultural peripheries that generally lacked powerful metropolitan centers—even back in the old colonial cores—to champion abolition from within. True, internal movements to abolish slavery did develop in both places, especially Brazil, as planters seeking to make the most of declining fortunes found ways to salvage their self-interest by advocating gradual and compensated abolition, and as intellectual currents placed a premium on erasing the slight of national "backwardness" associated with slavery. Yet the foundational pressure was exogamous, coming from the European metropoles that had already abolished slavery, and that increasingly controlled systems of credit and finance in the periphery, even across national boundaries. It came particularly from Britain, which had taken up abolition as an ideological commitment, a national mission, and a strategic interest. Having effectively abolished most of the international trade in slaves shortly after the Napoleonic Wars, England employed formal and surreptitious diplomacy, its considerable economic might, and its even more impressive arms to pressure these late, weak holdouts into mass emancipation. England thus "colonized" abolition throughout the Atlantic Basin, much as it had colonized slavery in an earlier period.[29] Perhaps because of these external forces, patterns of emancipation in Cuba and Brazil exhibited intensified versions of a phenomenon apparent wherever gradual schemes of abolition were employed: in both places, as slavery's legal end loomed, many enslaved people became free through a range of practices and arrangements worked out on the ground. In addition, planters sought to reconstitute the plantation labor force through new forms of labor, from immigrant wage laborers to semifree "coolies" from East and South Asia.

In Cuba, a movement for independence from Spain melded with the general decline of Atlantic slavery to precipitate mass emancipation. A wave of revolutionary activity occurred in 1868—there, in Puerto Rico, and even in Spain itself, as reform elements throughout the Spanish Empire took advantage of popular unrest. The uprising in Cuba began in the less profitable eastern provinces, and soon embroiled the entire island. The success of liberal reformers in Spain fostered the rise of a modest metropolitan abolition movement, which bore fruit in the Moret Law of 1870. This measure liberated children born to slaves but kept them bound to their former owners; it also freed slaves at the age of sixty, as well as those *emancipados* who had been taken up in the suppression of the slave trade. Cuban planters resisted implementation, while Spanish reformers complained that the law fell short. In 1873, reform forces succeeded in achieving abolition in Puerto Rico, albeit through a system of apprenticeship and indemnification for planters. Emancipation came later to Cuba, where the plantation complex, especially on the western part of the island, remained immensely profitable. In 1878, the Pact of Zanjón concluded the Ten Years' War between Cuban revolutionaries and the restored Spanish Crown, in the process liberating those slaves who had fought in the conflict. With slavery now badly degraded by the effects of war and prior emancipations elsewhere, the Spanish Cortes Generales (parliament) signed an abolition law in 1880 that, like previous ones in the Atlantic, replaced slavery with a period of apprenticeship. These *patroncinados* were to remain under control of their former owners for eight years, but—also following previous Atlantic history—the system declined before its mandated conclusion. By 1886, only twenty-five thousand remained to be liberated by the early end of the system.

Slavery in Brazil fell in three general waves. The first phase, which demonstrated the power of exogamous metropolitan forces in compelling abolition, was marked by a showdown with Great Britain over the international slave trade. Building on a series of treaties signed with Brazil since its independence in 1822, England pressured Brazil diplomatically to adopt its own measures to stem the trade. In the 1840s, Britain used its powerful navy to enforce these treaties through aggressive interdiction, fomenting a military crisis that posed Brazil with a choice between national humiliation or slave trade abolition. In 1850, Brazil chose the latter, legally ending its own international trade. The next move came in 1871, with the passage of the Rio Branco (or "free womb") law, which freed all children of slaves born after the law's passage. Recent abolition in the United States and pending abolition in the Spanish Caribbean contributed to the internal push for this measure, which the sugar planters of the Brazilian northeast helped broker. With slave imports abolished, they reasoned, the transition to free labor was inevitable, especially in the declining sugar economy rather than in the dynamic coffee economy of the south. Easing Brazil into abolition through gradual measures like the Rio Branco law, which provided for the apprenticing of formerly enslaved children, ensured a temporary stream of labor, and staved off immediate disaster. Only in the last stage of abolition in Brazil did a full-blown, Anglo-American-style abolition movement emerge (under the figure of Joaquim Nabuco), and a southern-style proslavery movement never did. Enslaved people enjoyed the fruits of Brazilian abolition even before the "Golden Law" formally ended slavery throughout the nation in May 1888. With the institution tottering, the enslaved abandoned plantations en masse throughout the country, or negotiated with slave owners to trade early liberty for a guaranteed term of service. With the passage of the Golden Law—the last measure to abolish slavery in the New World—nearly three-quarters of a million enslaved peoples were liberated, a number much smaller than the 1.2 million registered as slaves just four years earlier.[30] Slavery died in the New World with not a bang, but a whimper.

Against this context, the abolition of slavery in the United States occupies a singular place. In many respects, the nation followed the example of England, pioneering a form of metropolitan abolitionism that well complemented its expanding economy. It is notable, for example, that England and the United States outlawed the international slave trade within one year of each other (1807–8). The northern states of the Union also emulated the Spanish-speaking mainland Latin American nations, which abolished slavery as a direct consequence of colonial independence movements built on revolutionary ideology. Vermont, which ended slavery in its 1777 constitution, and Massachusetts, which abolished slavery by judicial decision in the 1780s, were the very first polities in the New World to end slavery on their own. Yet abolition in the entire United States was not completed as a consequence of the revolutionary struggle for independence, for the South retained slavery as a vital element of its exploitation-oriented agricultural economy. As with Cuba and Brazil, slavery in the South was a profitable enterprise that had to be ended largely through the imposition of abolition from powerful metropolitan sources outside the agricultural periphery. But because in the United States the "slave power" of the agricultural periphery lay within the borders of the nation, and was thus quite powerful indeed, the forces of the metropole were not strong enough to do as those in England had done and abolish slavery within the boundaries of its own nation. Rather, it took compulsion, in the form of a devastating civil war, to accomplish this feat. The U.S. experience then constitutes a hybrid of all three forms of abolition, to which must be added a degree of violence reminiscent of the Haitian example. Why this was is the subject of the chapters that follow.

SECTION 1

The Age of Revolution

CHAPTER 1

Impious Prayers
Slavery and the Revolution

THE LOUDEST YELPS
Colonial Complaints and the Revolutionary Paradox

Samuel Johnson was not a man to bandy words. In the midst of Britain's imperial crisis with its mainland North American colonies, the renowned lexicographer and pamphleteer exercised his polemical skills to attack upstart colonials who complained of "taxation without representation." Those who held slaves, the Tory argued, had little business proclaiming the virtues of liberty. "How is it that we hear the loudest yelps for liberty among the drivers of negroes?" he famously wondered.[1]

This frequently cited illustration of American hypocrisy is seldom explored in detail. The pamphlet in which it appears—titled *Taxation No Tyranny: An Answer to the Resolution and Address of the American Congress* (1775)—reveals much about the slaveholding colonies' connection to their mother country on the brink of the American Revolution. Johnson's first concern was not slavery—in the pamphlet his "loudest yelps" jibe appears incidental—but the political character of empire. Colonials, he noted, argued that to be taxed without direct representation in Parliament denied their rights as Englishmen. Johnson replied that even in Britain few commanded the vote, and thus the colonists were "represented by the same virtual representation as the greater part of Englishmen."[2] Besides, the colonial relationship obviated Americans' right to direct representation, though not their obligation to obey their rulers. Colonies simply did not enjoy the same political privileges as did those at home. In Johnson's formulation, those departing for America had "voluntarily resigned" their right to direct representation "for something, in their opinion, of more estimation": the opportunity offered in America. "By his own choice," Johnson argued, the colonist "has left a country, where he had a vote and little property, for another, where he has great property, but no vote." Colonial subjects therefore possessed "the happiness of being protected by law, and the duty of obeying it."[3]

But what of liberty? Sympathetic ears in Britain, including influential members of Parliament, worried about undermining the liberties of Englishmen regardless of where they lived. Johnson had little patience for such concerns. "Chains need not be put upon those who will be restrained without them," he aphorized. Freedom existed in tenuous balance with subjugation, liberty with order. Some might claim that "liberty is the birthright of man, and where obedience is compelled, there is no liberty." Johnson replied simply, "government is necessary to man, and where obedience is not compelled, there is no government." It was at this point, in countering colonists' reliance on the doctrine of universal human liberty, that Johnson targeted the gulf between American principle and practice. "We are told, that the subjection of Americans may tend to the diminution of our own liberties," Johnson wrote. "If slavery be thus fatally contagious, how is it that we hear the loudest yelps for liberty among the drivers of negroes?" Johnson's point was thus not simply that the most ardent advocates of liberty in America seemed to have little problem enslaving fellow humans. It was that the practice of slavery did not seem to obviate the pursuit of liberty. In fact, he intimated, the two might have been linked. Somehow, the colonials had developed radical notions of liberty while practicing the most extreme form of oppression known to the Atlantic world.[4]

Perhaps this was no coincidence. Historian Edmund Morgan has suggested that radical notions of liberty emerged in the colonies alongside, and indeed because of, the development of slavery. Morgan argues that privileged colonial plantation barons could afford to preach equality and democracy, and thus enlist the political loyalties of less privileged whites, precisely because a caste of completely oppressed black slaves ensured that all whites could share a common freedom—a principle scholars have termed *herrenvolk democracy*.[5] As Morgan put it, "Aristocrats could more safely preach equality in a slave society than in a free one. Slaves did not become leveling mobs, because their owners would see to it that they had no chance to." What was more, the practice of enslavement may have lent a special poignancy to claims for liberty. The Virginia Founders Morgan studied "may have had a special appreciation of the freedom dear to republicans, because they saw every day what life without it could be like."[6] British Parliamentarian Edmund Burke, in a fitting riposte to Johnson, stated as much in 1775. Wherever slaves figured prominently in the population, he said, "those who are free, are by far the most proud and jealous of their freedom." For them, freedom was "not only an enjoyment, but a kind of rank and privilege." Because slaves occupied the lowest orders of society and lived in misery, free people equated liberty with privilege. "Liberty looks, amongst them, like something that is more noble and liberal."[7] Ideas of freedom and slavery thus developed out of a complex dialectical relationship with each other. In the plantation periphery of colonial America, notions of political equality grew out of their distinction from the practice of enslavement. As some became less free, others could become more so. The very notion of liberty, Morgan contends, evolved alongside its opposite.[8]

Samuel Johnson had put his finger neatly on the issues. For one, he had intuited some uniquely New World sources for the emergence of revolutionary notions of liberty, which depended absolutely on the further degradation of Africans who arrived on American shores already deprived of rights. For another, he succinctly described the political relationship between a mother country determined to subordinate its colonies to national interests and colonies equally dedicated to their own autonomy. And his criticisms reflected many Britons' justifiable confusion over colonial grievances. Had not the mother country only recently defended the colonials against rival native and European nations along the frontier? Indeed, the last of the great eighteenth-century wars for empire had begun in the mainland colonies, only later to spill over to the European continent. Unlike previous conflicts, the French and Indian War (known in Europe as the Seven Years' War) began in the periphery, when in 1754 a young colonial militia commander, George Washington, tussled with French forces in the backwoods of western Virginia and Pennsylvania. The colonies had called upon their mother country for aid, and aid had come, along with victory. At the cost of several thousand British casualties, England had gained control of much of the eastern portion of the Mississippi River Valley, expelled France from mainland North America, and markedly improved security along the western frontier.

It was understandable, then, for those in the mother country to expect some gratitude from colonies that had benefitted from England's protection, even to the point of soliciting payment for protection through taxes levied by Parliament. As Johnson put it, Britons might "think it reasonable, that they who thus flourish under the protection of our government, should contribute something toward its expense." (He grumbled that should England "restore to the French what we have taken from them . . . we shall see our colonists at our feet, when they have an enemy so near them.") But the colonies had enjoyed many decades of lax commercial regulation—years known as the "period of salutary neglect," in which American merchants had become accustomed to regulating their own commercial affairs largely unhindered by the mother country. What was in some English minds a long-standing and comprehensive system of mercantile regulation did not appear so to colonial eyes. Many in the colonies viewed with disdain the Navigation Acts, which Parliament had begun legislating in the 1650s as part of an ad hoc system of measures designed to extract maximal benefit from the colonies for the British Empire in its never-ending contests with other national empires, such as France, Spain, and the Netherlands. But the acts had never been comprehensively imposed, and now many colonists, associating freedom from regulation with their rights as "freeborn Englishmen," viewed demands for revenue as new impositions, not at all in keeping with the traditions of local governance they had grown accustomed to.

Eventually, of course, the colonies revolted. The story is too familiar, and too dense, to be anything more than sketched here. Tensions mounted in the early 1770s, as the Tory government in England squared off against colonial legislatures, particularly that of Massachusetts, over the question of revenue. In response to tax measures such as the Stamp Act of 1765 and the Townsend Duties of 1767, colonists—particularly in New England—resisted through increasingly direct action, such as the Boston Tea Party in 1773. Parliament sought to punish Massachusetts for its lead in instigating colonial defiance by imposing a series of measures known in America as the Intolerable Acts, which closed Boston's port, undermined Massachusetts's capacity for self-rule, and provided for the quartering of British troops throughout the colonies. The laws brought tensions to a head, and the showdown broke out into open conflict in April 1775, when British troops marched from Boston to Concord in search of munitions stored by the Massachusetts militia. On April 19, colonial militia squared off against British regulars; one among these—it has always been unclear who—fired the "shot heard 'round the world," and armed struggle began.

Seeing their interests threatened, other mainland colonies banded together. Having first organized in September 1774 to respond to the Intolerable Acts, delegates reconvened as the Second Continental Congress in May 1775, shortly after the Battles of Lexington and Concord. This Congress functioned as the effective national government for the remainder of the war, directing a military effort that ranged from Canada to the Carolinas and the Mississippi Valley to the Caribbean. Indeed, the Revolution resparked long-standing European rivalries, leading to a resurgence of the eighteenth century's worldwide wars for empire. Britain's European opponents sought to undermine the powerful island nation by supporting the colonies, often covertly through finance, trade, and arms, as did the Spanish and Dutch. Continental armies faced enormous disadvantages, as General George Washington's dreadful wintering at Valley Forge in 1777 made clear. But by winning a few clear victories, such as at Saratoga in 1777, and by simply remaining a viable fighting force, the colonials finally justified the formal intervention of France, Britain's great rival and the most powerful nation in continental Europe. This aid proved critical for Washington's successful siege of Yorktown in 1781, which ended military hostilities on the continent and brought a rebuffed Britain to the peace table. Great Britain, confronted by mounting losses, European support for the colonials, and the sheer costs of fighting a continental war across an ocean while simultaneously maintaining an enormous empire, let her thirteen mainland colonies go. After six years and the loss of perhaps fifty thousand killed and wounded Americans,[9] the war was over. The tally of war also imposed enormous financial burdens on all participants, particularly France, where financial disaster, and consequent revolution, loomed. The 1783 Treaty of Paris acknowledged the independence of the United States, also ceding them an enormous swath of western lands. Liberty had been won. But at the time when independence had been declared in 1776, every one of these new states sanctioned and practiced the holding of fellow humans as property.

NOTHING BUT CHATTEL
Liberty, Property, and Slaves

Johnson's "loudest yelps" quip posed the central questions for the revolutionaries: How could those arguing most ardently for liberty hold some in abject and complete servitude without becoming hypocrites? How committed were the patriots—not just to their own liberty, but to liberty as a universal principle? The point was not lost on the revolutionaries themselves, nor on those they held as slaves. With justice, succeeding generations have castigated the Founders for the disjuncture between their principles and their practice. Yet to dismiss the founding generation as merely hypocritical fundamentally mischaracterizes its thought world. The very disjuncture between slavery and freedom that permits modern observers to judge those such as Thomas Jefferson was itself in the process of historical formation at the time of the Revolution. This is, in fact, our subject.

The era of democratic revolutions that struck the Atlantic world in the half century from 1775 to 1825 birthed the widespread understanding of these two concepts, slavery and freedom, as we know them today. Recall that the Atlantic system of slavery had developed as a fundamental element of the expansion of European economies, and thus constituted an important stage in the growth of world capitalism. As this "merchant capitalism" developed in the early modern Atlantic world, it fostered a relatively narrow and absolute brand of bondage. "Slavery," which once described a broad range of particularly degraded social statuses in rigorously hierarchical social systems, transformed into the notion that humans (and their progeny in perpetuity) could be nothing but property. The transformation was neither seamless nor complete, for in certain times and places in the Atlantic world the enslaved could make critical claims rooted in their humanity. Yet, compared with the wide range of previous practices that have been termed "slavery"—from captive assimilation and debt peonage in sub-

Saharan Africa, to the powerful but unfree court eunuchs and warrior castes of the Ottoman Empire—it is safe to say that the expansion of the plantation complex into the New World brought with it the most highly capitalistic forms of servitude yet known. Of all slaves in world history, Atlantic ones were most likely to be defined in law as nothing but chattel.

This posed a problem, though. By the eighteenth century, the world of merchant capitalism was steadily enshrining bourgeois property relations, or the idea of human society as a world primarily composed of individuals who owned things, like land, livestock, or goods produced through labor. (Of course all of these, including one's own labor, could be bartered or sold, but this presumed a world of absolute ownership of things.) In fact, the rhetoric of rights surrounding the democratic revolutions of the late eighteenth and early nineteenth centuries often posed "liberty" as little more than the uncontested right to own and use property free of arbitrary molestation. The great theorists of liberalism, such as John Locke, had listed security in "the possession of outward things" among the very purposes that government should serve. As Locke had written in 1690, "the great and *chief end* . . . of Mens uniting into Commonwealths, and putting themselves under Government, *is the Preservation of their Property.*" Seventy-five years later, William Blackstone, whose influential *Commentaries on the Laws of England* (1765–69) the American revolutionaries widely referenced, listed "the right of private property," along with "personal security" and "personal liberty," among the "natural liberties" all men had a right to enjoy. So sacrosanct was property to Blackstone that the government could not expropriate it through taxes, "even for the defence of the realm or the support of government," except through citizens' own consent or the consent of their representatives.[10]

Grievances to the mother country during the revolutionary crisis clearly relied upon this understanding of property's relation to liberty. Colonists deprecated the Sugar Act of 1764, which for the first time imposed direct taxes on them for the purposes of alleviating the national debt. New York's state legislature declared to the House of Commons that where taxation occurs without consent, "there can be no Liberty, no Happiness, no Security." Freedom from such imposition was "inseparable from the very Idea of Property, for who can call that his own, which may be taken away at the Pleasure of another?"[11] Likewise, the Stamp Act Congress of 1765 charged that Parliament's appropriation of colonial property to supply British troops was "unreasonable and inconsistent with the principles and spirit of the British constitution,"[12] while the First Continental Congress declared property provisions of the Intolerable Acts "subversive of American rights."[13] Colonial patriot James Otis first penned the phrase "life, liberty, and property" in a 1764 pamphlet (Locke had used "life, liberty, or estate" in the *Second Treatise on Government*), a formulation appropriated and modified by later documents, like the Declaration and Resolves of the First Continental Congress (1774) and Virginia Declaration of Rights (1776). The Declaration of Independence's more famous phrasing—"life, liberty, and the pursuit of happiness"—merely sought an expansive view of property's importance to liberty.

The idea that humans might be included among the forms of property deemed justly inviolable raised thorny problems for the revolutionary generation. In precapitalistic worlds lacking absolute property rights, enslavement constituted merely an extremely unbalanced form of the exercise of "rights in persons," in which some in a social group claimed obligations from others. Marriage, for example, in which parties exchanged mutual obligations (one party obtained the wealth represented by the incorporation of a new person, while that person obtained a guarantee of protection), constituted a far more symmetrical relation. In contrast, one deemed an absolute slave could make no claims on others.[14] In most human societies and for most of human history, it makes more sense to think of "the slave" not as a category of property so much as a particularly degraded position among a range of statuses in hierarchical social orders.

The age of revolutions, with its commitment to equality under law, rejected the principle of freedom as a special preserve of social elites, and began posing the ideal social order in terms of the simpler binary of slave or free. In large measure, to be free was to exercise the right to own property; to be enslaved was to be that property. But in a world predicated on the ownership of things rather than on rights in persons, could humans hold other humans strictly as property? In an age slowly and arduously defining property as the centerpiece of the social compact, no consensus existed. Critical aspects of liberal theory suggested that humans themselves could not be property. Locke himself had written that "every man has a property in his own person: this no body has any right to but himself. The labour of his body, and the work of his hands, we may say, are properly his." Blackstone affirmed Locke, asserting that no man could sell away his right to personhood, for the capacity to own (and hence barter) resided in the very personhood that self-sale would barter away: "Of what validity then can a sale be, which destroys the very principles upon which all sales are founded?"[15] A man could thus trade his labor for a time, as in the case of indentured servants, who may have been regulated very much like slaves, but evolving liberal theory did not easily countenance that one's own body might become the property of another.

And yet slavery could indeed exist in such a world, as of course it did. Several moves made this possible. Consider first that the degradation associated with complete slavery had for several centuries in the European and Mediterranean worlds been reserved for extreme outsiders. Mediterranean Christian states, inheritors to a clear Roman tradition of slave law, and beset by unending religious conflicts with Muslim states to the east, had never ceased to enslave during times of war. Even in these instances, though, only captives taken in "just wars," such as those against the Muslim infidel, generally were considered enslaveable. Thus Locke, the great philosopher of bourgeois property, could consistently theorize that while man possessed an unalienable "natural liberty," conditions such as war could forfeit this fundamental right. The right of conquest gave victors absolute power over captive enemies otherwise subject to imminent destruction. Slavery—a kind of "social death" in Orlando Patterson's famous phrase[16]—constituted a temporary reprieve from a real death that might be executed at any moment. "This is the perfect condition of slavery," Locke wrote, "which is nothing else, but the state of war continued, between a lawful conqueror and a captive."[17] Slavery was thus a hugely unequal bargain: the captor temporarily spared the life of the captive to extract the benefit of his or her labor; all the captive got was to live an uncertain moment longer.

Preserved from earlier days, Locke's "just war" loophole faced challenges as one moved out of the Mediterranean. Throughout much of Northern and Western Europe, slavery had declined sharply around the turn of the first millennium, transforming into forms of serfdom such as villeinage, in which servants could not be freely bartered, but were nonetheless tied to the land and possessed very limited rights and a great many obligations. The Black Death of the fourteenth century further enhanced peasants' status by creating conditions of labor scarcity, which in most of Europe led to increased physical mobility and often higher wages for the laboring masses. In England in particular, the decline of medieval slavery fostered a widespread presumption of freedom by default. While infrequent cases on the issue in English common law left a schizophrenic record of precedents, slavery uniformly appeared as an exception applied to those lying far outside the customary boundaries of civic inclusion—and perhaps outside the confines of Britain itself. As the court was said to have stated in Cartwright's Case in 1569, "England was too pure an air for a slave to breathe in."[18]

Not until the seventeenth-century formation of an overseas plantation empire did Great Britain's legal system confront the need to wrestle again with the limits of unfreedom. At that time it found itself confounded by critical questions: To what degree were the laws of England also the laws of the colonies? Could slavery exist in one but not the other? Everywhere slavery took hold in the New World, local systems of governance formulated laws to legalize, define, and protect the practice; they closed loopholes to freedom such as the promise of emancipation upon Christian baptism, adumbrated clear definitions for once interchangeable words such as "servant" and "slave," and legitimated a range of mechanisms masters might employ to control their slaves. Yet the boundaries between metropole and periphery proved distressingly porous. While Atlantic slavery developed in the New World context, not even the Old was insulated from it, and nearly ten thousand enslaved Africans arrived in Western Europe over the course of the Atlantic slave trade.[19] Was slavery thus being introduced into "free" Europe? At the very time liberty was emerging as the default status of freeborn Englishmen, the colonial periphery was coming to assert the legal legitimacy of slave status elsewhere, and perhaps even back in the metropole. The question pressed, could humans be property? If so, where, and why?

No single moment better exemplified, and indeed reified, the geographical division between lands that could and could not permit slavery than the English Lord Mansfield's 1772 legal decision in what is known as Somerset's Case. Brought from Boston to Britain by his owner in 1769, the slave James Somerset promptly ran away. When he was recaptured and held on a Jamaica-bound vessel, friends appealed to the Court of the King's Bench for a writ of habeas corpus, demanding that Somerset's imprisoners demonstrate the legality of confining him. Relying on a thin trail of precedent, Lord Mansfield, the judge, concluded that in England the natural presumption of freedom was so strong, and slavery was so "odious" to it, that only "positive law"—a direct assertion of legality—could sustain slavery. In England, none existed. While colonial codes may have supported slavery abroad, Parliament had never sanctioned it at home. As soon, then, as Somerset had set foot on English soil, he had become free.[20] In the process, so too did the over ten thousand African slaves held in Britain.

To be sure, the decision was not without limits. Mansfield had never intended to abolish slavery and fretted over "the inconveniences and consequences" his decision entailed. Practically speaking, though, the case was interpreted as a sweeping abolition, helped by the efforts of early abolitionists like Granville Sharp, who widely publicized the decision. Yet there remained thorny questions over the relation between the law in England and the law of the colonies. Mansfield's dictum effectively asserted that while humans could not become property in a land of freedom (England), they might become so elsewhere, particularly in English dominions that depended absolutely on the sanctity of slave property. Benjamin Franklin condemned the ruling for its half-hearted approach to the question of liberty: "Pharisaical Britain! to pride thyself in setting free a single Slave that happens to land on thy coasts, while thy Merchants in all thy ports are encouraged by thy laws to continue a commerce whereby so many hundreds of thousands are dragged into a slavery that can scarce be said to end with their lives, since it is entailed on their posterity!"[21] A few years later, the fledgling British antislavery movement noted the same inconsistency. Asked the English poet William Cowper in verse, "We have no slaves at home:—Then why abroad?"[22]

Mansfield had thus affirmed the emerging value of British liberty at home in the metropole while simultaneously preserving the labor wealth in the periphery that had made that metropole a prosperous advocate of property's sanctity. But the vague and tenuous nature of the decision—this was no sweeping, bright-line ruling, just a single, albeit powerful, precedent—demonstrated the contingent quality of the question of slave property. England seems to have decided that, at home at least, people could not be chattels—movable pieces of personal property. The colonies, though, went by different rules, a disjuncture that eroded the authority of slaveholders everywhere. In a telling reminder of how impossible it was to insulate the plantation from the public sphere, even the enslaved learned of the ruling. In 1773, a Virginia master seeking the recapture of two runaways believed that his fugitive property "will endeavour to get out of the Colony, particularly to *Britain*, where they imagine they will be free (a Notion now too prevalent among the Negroes, greatly to the Vexation and Prejudice of their Masters)."[23] Of course, the problem for those such as Franklin, leaders of the mainland colonies that would revolt two years later by calling upon their natural rights as freeborn Englishmen, was this: Would they unite to form a nation so free that no one within its borders could be held as property? Or would they define their precious property rights in such a way that they could continue to hold humans as they did land or goods?

While Lord Mansfield tentatively resolved the question of whether humans could be property in England but not the colonies, there were yet other ways to square the practice of slavery with the presumption of liberty. Hypocrisy was, of course, always a possibility. Locke, for one, fell prey to his own sophistry. His *Fundamental Constitutions of Carolina* (1669) imposed a largely feudal system of governance on the colony for which he was a proprietor. As an investor in the Royal Africa Company he staked his financial future on slave trading, and as secretary to the Council of Trade and Plantations he aided the government in setting policy on slavery in English dominions, despite knowing full well that not all the millions of Africans transported across the Atlantic could have been captives in just wars.

What, though, if those Africans were of such a nature that they somehow fell outside the category of beings who innately possessed natural rights to property, if only in themselves? Perhaps slavery could be compatible with liberty, but only if those enslaved did not constitute a portion of the "all men" the Declaration of Independence would shortly declare to be free and equal. The critical question thus became, were people of African descent part of the community of mankind? On the one hand, eighteenth-century theorists clearly posited some fundamental rights as belonging to all, without qualification. Blackstone, for example, viewed natural rights as "the absolute *rights* of individuals . . . such as would belong to their persons merely in a state of nature, and which every man is entitled to enjoy, whether out of society or in it."[24] By this measure, it seemed impossible to deprive any human of basic liberty.

Many contemporaries, though, clearly viewed Africans as radically distinct from Europeans, and deeply deficient in revered qualities of "civilization." No less a philosopher than David Hume admitted that he was "apt to suspect the Negroes and in general all other species of men (for there are four or five different kinds) to be naturally inferior to the whites. There never was a civilized nation of any other complexion than white, nor even any individual eminent either in action or speculation. No ingenious manufacturers amongst them, no arts, no sciences."[25] This statement appears as a footnote in a famous essay from 1748, "Of National Characters," which argues against the idea that environmental conditions determined the qualities of peoples and "nations," instead ascribing them to innate principles transmitted from generation to generation over time. Hume, like fellow thinkers of the Anglo-American Enlightenment, wrestled deeply with the consequences of blacks' alleged innate inferiority on the prospects for liberty. Thomas Jefferson himself, writing during the American Revolution, believed that the "real distinctions which nature has made" among the "races" unfitted blacks for the delicate, precious privilege of taking part in common systems of democratic governance. Based on his extensive personal experience, Jefferson declared that "varieties of the same species, may possess different qualifications," or markers of refined civilization, and he found blacks deficient in all respects. "This unfortunate difference of colour, and perhaps of faculty, is a powerful obstacle to the emancipation of these people," he wrote. "Deep rooted prejudices entertained by the whites; ten thousand recollections, by the blacks, of the injuries they have sustained; new provocations; the real distinctions which nature has made; and many other circumstances, will divide us into parties, and produce convulsions which will probably never end but in the extermination of the one or the other race."[26]

At the same time, Enlightenment thinkers worried deeply about freedom's prospects in a slaveholding land. The French philosophe Montesquieu stated, "Slavery not only violates the Laws of Nature, and of civil Society; it also wounds the best Forms of Government; in a Democracy, where all Men are equal, Slavery is contrary to the Spirit of the Constitution."[27] Jefferson in particular argued that slaveholding degraded habits of virtuous liberty in both master and slave. "The whole commerce between master and slave," he wrote, "is a perpetual exercise of the most boisterous passions, the most unremitting despotism on the one part, and degrading submissions on the other." An entire society thus "daily exercised in tyranny" could not bode well for liberty. "With what execration should the statesman be loaded," he asked, "who permitting one half the citizens thus to trample on the rights of the other, transforms those into despots, and these into enemies." Yet while Jefferson considered slavery an undoubted blight, his belief in blacks' innate inferiority led him to declare mass emancipation impractical. Not only were blacks incapable of self-governance, if permitted by liberty to mix with whites they would degrade the quality of white racial stock. "Among the Romans emancipation required but one effort. The slave, when made free, might mix with, without staining the blood of his master. But with us a second is necessary, unknown to history. When freed, he is to be removed beyond the reach of mixture."[28] In Jefferson's formulation, there was no easy way out. As he would put it decades later, "We have the wolf by the ear, and we can neither hold him, nor safely let him go. Justice is in one scale, and self-preservation in the other."[29]

The biological qualities of black people, then—the nature and causes of their many alleged deficiencies—became vital subjects. For many, this was a question for a burgeoning science of nature and race, and remained very much open through the nineteenth century. At the time of the American Revolution, several theories abounded. Some, such as the German scientist Johann Friedrich Blumenbach, argued that there was but one family of man, with Africans a part of it. Physical differences among mankind owed to distinct histories and developments from a common origin. This position (known as "monogenesis") allowed others, such as Philadelphia doctor and Founder Benjamin Rush, to argue that because only mutable factors of environment had created distinctions among men, Africans should be entitled to the same rights as others. The opponents of monogenesis, such as French naturalist Georges Cuvier, believed in "polygenesis," or the idea that the different "races" of mankind descended from separate instances of creation. In the hands of nineteenth-century racial scientists, polygenesis became a potent argument for denying black people, slave or free, fundamental rights. At the time of the American Revolution, such theories offered tantalizing possibilities for considering the natural rights of Africans.

None of these men resolved the critical issues for all and sundry. The point is that the question of slavery's relation to liberty was legitimately contested, and would be for some time. Did liberty include the freedom to own humans as property? In the intellectual world of the Founding Fathers, the distinction between chattel slavery and a freedom based on individual property holding was in the process of formation. The last century of slavery's existence would, in fact, consist largely of the story of how different parts of the Atlantic world dealt with the question. The very process of resolving it bequeathed to us modern definitions of "liberty" and "slavery" that we hold as normative today, a distinct set of self-evident truths. Ultimately, of course, the polities of the Atlantic decided that humans could not be held as property, and rendered the practice illegal, and they found new ways to compel labor without degrading it to the legal status of property. But in Jefferson's day, the questions of Africans' qualities as a "race," and of the boundaries of the "all men" supposedly created equal, remained very much alive. It could be, in fact, entirely consistent with revolutionary principles to argue that the same natural right to own property guaranteed men's rights to hold property in the form of outsiders who had come to American shores, or were born there already enslaved.

INEXCUSABLE INCONSISTENCIES
Slavery and the Call for Abolition in Revolutionary America

The birth of ideas of American freedom, then, owed much to the presence of slavery. As Samuel Johnson suggested, ideas percolating in the revolutionary Atlantic—radical ones like the natural equality of men and the rejection of hereditary social preference, and even more conservative ones such as the sanctity of private property—contributed directly to ideas of freedom, just as they made the question of slavery's consistency with liberty more pressing. The words and ideas of colonial rebels conspicuously relied on understandings of slavery to frame their cause, moving the question from the theoretical to the very real.

Colonists understood their interests in ideological terms that elevated liberty over obedience. This was a critical move, for only novel ideas of governance could make legitimate a defiance of authority that otherwise constituted nothing more than simple treason. Parliament, the colonists' legitimate (if "virtual") representative in England, had levied reasonable taxes; now the colonists refused to pay. For conservatives like Samuel Johnson, as well as those such as Thomas Hobbes before him, disobedience to lawful civil authority led inexorably to anarchy and disorder, the correlates of tyranny. The challenge for the colonists was to demonstrate how England's lawmakers had passed illegitimate laws. The concept of liberty as a natural right supplied revolutionaries with a principle that transcended older notions of unconditional obligation to the state, such as the notion of kings' "divine right" to rule, supplanting them with the idea of men's innate right to liberty, which superseded all. Society was not a "leviathan," in which individuals submitted to arbitrary authority because it was preferable to a brutal state of nature. Instead, it was a social compact, in which the rulers owed the ruled good governance in exchange for obedience. When lawful governors ruled unlawfully and threatened liberty, they forsook the protections of sovereignty, and justified revolt. As Thomas Jefferson's adored motto asserted, "rebellion to tyrants is obedience to God."[30]

Such ideas had long been forming.[31] Revolutionaries' arguments drew upon the political principles of the eighteenth-century Enlightenment, England's own liberal tradition, and the "country party" republicanism of English political dissidents. Distance had incubated a long-standing tradition in English political thought that was deeply suspicious of the concentration of centralized authority. The experiences of the English Civil War and Glorious Revolution in the seventeenth century had broken the Crown, replacing its sovereignty with that of Parliament, which acted with a restored monarchy as the supreme representatives of the people and nation. Enlightenment thinking gave colonists notions of limited government, social contract, elected government, the separation of powers, and written constitutions with clearly enumerated rights. Meanwhile, commercial success demonstrated that imperial demands were unnecessary for, and even detrimental to, many of the colonies' economic well-being. Closely associating liberty with the protection of property rights, colonials closed the loop: to tax the colonies was to attack their property, and hence their liberty.

It was at this point, then, that the American revolutionaries called upon the idea of servitude to perform powerful rhetorical work.[32] Relying on their intimate knowledge of the subject, they came to associate their subordinate political status in the imperial relationship with "slavery." For example, in 1774, New York statesman John Jay penned a list of grievances for the Continental Congress that invoked the specter of servitude in the colonials' defense. Jay believed that Britain had become an agent of "slavery and oppression." The mother country was "forging chains for her friends and children" with a policy that amounted to a "ministerial plan for enslaving us." He concluded by vowing that the colonials would "never submit to be hewers of wood or drawers of water for any ministry or nation in the world."[33] For Silas Downer, a Son of Liberty from Rhode Island, nonconsensual taxation placed colonists "in the lowest bottom of slavery"; if their rulers could "take away one penny from us against our wills," he wrote, "they can take all."[34] Bostonians took the lead in invoking the slavery metaphor. In the Suffolk Resolves of 1774, they closed their courts in defiance of Parliament's Intolerable Acts, warning colonists that should they "basely yield to voluntary slavery" then "future generations shall load their memories with incessant execrations." The same year, John Hancock envisioned the spirits of the martyred patriots of the Boston Massacre of 1770, "delivering the oppressed from the iron grasp of tyranny" and transforming "the hoarse complaints and bitter moans of wretched slaves" into "cheerful songs."[35]

More familiar with slavery, southerners invoked the metaphor as well. In his famous "Give Me Liberty or Give Me Death" speech of 1775, Virginia's Patrick Henry stirred his auditors with the cry, "There is no retreat but in submission and slavery! Our chains are forged! Their clanking may be heard on the plains of Boston!" William Tennant, a Charleston minister, sermonized in 1774, "The Question is of no less of Magnitude than whether we shall continue to enjoy the Privileges of Men and Britons, or whether we shall be reduced to a State of the most abject Slavery."[36] No less a light than George Washington wrote that in the present crisis "we must assert our Rights, or Submit to every Imposition that can be heap'd upon us; till custom and use, will make us as tame, & abject Slaves, as the Blacks we Rule over with such arbitrary Sway."[37]

Slavery, then, consisted of depriving naturally free men of their fundamental liberties, and particularly their right to hold property. In answer to the charge that those in the colonies had forfeited some of their rights, patriots responded that this was impossible. In a fitting reply to Samuel Johnson's claim that the colonists' forbears had forsaken English liberty for the promise of social mobility in America, a Boston town meeting resolved that by choosing to migrate, early colonists had in no way renounced their rights as Englishmen. "The right to freedom being the gift of God Almighty, it is not in the power of man to alienate this gift and voluntarily become a slave."[38] Boston attorney James Otis had made the same case as far back as 1764. "In a state of nature no man can take my property from me without my consent," he reasoned. "If he does, he deprives me of my liberty and makes me a slave." Unlawful taxation constituted an unjust deprivation of property, and hence a violation of fundamental civil liberties. "The very act of taxing exercised over those who are not represented appears to me to be depriving them of one of their most essential rights as freemen," Otis argued.[39]

For the American revolutionaries, slavery was not simply a poignant simile, it was an actual political condition, characterized by a complete lack of political liberty, or the capacity to protect property. "Under the term liberty," sermonized Boston minister Simeon Howard, "may naturally be comprehended . . . every thing that is opposed to temporal slavery." Colonists' political subordination to Britain was not simply *like* slavery; it *was* slavery. Lacking direct representation in Parliament, the right to peaceably assemble, the ability to pursue wealth free of the arbitrary molestation of direct taxation, and other rights the Founders considered fundamental constitutional liberties, rebelling colonists considered themselves literally enslaved. Howard preached, "Where the subjects have no constitutional right to do any thing to prevent or remove such an evil, they are already slaves."[40]

These were not uniquely American ideas, but part of an evolving tradition of thinking about property and liberty shared across the Atlantic. Back in England, supporters in Parliament such as Edmund Burke assented to the understanding of slavery as the deprivation of man's natural right to enjoy property. Arguing to repeal the tea duty, Burke lashed out against imposing on colonists the dual burdens of mercantile trade constraint and direct taxation. "Tell me," he asked his opponents, "what one character of liberty the Americans have, and what one brand of slavery they are free from, if they are bound in their property and industry by all the restraints you can imagine on commerce, and at the same time are made pack-horses of every tax you choose to impose, without the least share in granting them."[41] Shortly after, he argued that colonists sought only the liberty due all Englishmen: "Slavery they can have anywhere," he admonished the ruling Tory government, but "freedom they can have from none but you."[42] The destruction of liberty was slavery; those who sought to deny the liberty of others enslaved them. The key justifications of the colonies' rebellion all cited this similar cause: a deprivation of property amounting to enslavement. In 1774, the First Continental Congress accused Britain of pursuing a set of policies "which demonstrate a system formed to enslave America,"[43] while the Second justified taking up arms against the mother country by asserting that it had evinced a "cruel and impolitic purpose of enslaving these colonies by violence."[44] The Declaration of Independence itself can be understood as little more than a catalog of the "long train of abuses and usurpations" (twenty-seven of them) against the colonies, which demonstrated "a design to reduce them under absolute Despotism," namely slavery.[45]

It was inevitable that an ideology so fiercely dedicated to individual liberties, and so assertive of the fundamental natural rights of man, would clash with the practice of slaveholding. With liberty so bound up with the concept of property, the apparent paradox of a liberty-loving people holding slaves could not be lost on the American revolutionaries. Throughout the rebelling colonies, Americans wrestled, deeply and genuinely, with the significance of their revolution on the practice of slavery. Radicals like James Otis felt compelled to denounce chattel bondage as a practice antithetical to liberty, worrying, as Jefferson would, of the effects of slavery on free society. "Those who every day barter away other men's liberty will soon care little for their own," he prophesied.[46] Others found it impossible to "remain insensible and inattentive to the Treatment" of fellow men who were "kept in the most deplorable State of Slavery," particularly "at a time when the general Rights and Liberties of Mankind" had "become so much the Subjects of universal Consideration."[47]

It proved difficult indeed to apply the metaphor of enslavement without extending it to those who were actually enslaved. Many of the founding generation noted, and warned, of the dangers of hypocrisy. "If domestic Slavery is agreeable to the Will and Laws of God, political Slavery is much more so," warned Philadelphia's Benjamin Rush.[48] In 1773, a Boston printer dared append to John Allen's *Oration upon the Beauties of Liberty* a plea for liberty from four enslaved men, declaring that he could not ignore that "near one sixth part of the inhabitants of *America* are held in REAL *Slavery.*"[49] Abigail Adams wrote candidly to her husband John in 1774, "I wish most sincerely there was not a slave in this province. It always appeared a most iniquitous scheme to me—to fight ourselves for what we are daily robbing and plundering from those who have as good a right to freedom as we have."[50]

The revolutionaries clearly understood their weakness on the point. At the very least, the self-interest of those who needed the sanction and succor of foreign nations compelled them to avoid charges of invoking transcendent principle opportunely. Already risking treason and rebellion, the Founders could ill afford adding hypocrisy to the tally by appearing to be selective in their employment of justifying principles. In this way, the ideology of the Revolution created powerful and very real rhetorical exigencies that could not be ignored; adherence to the doctrine of natural rights logically compelled the Founders to consider the plight of their own enslaved. Some made this link early on. "Oh! Ye sons of liberty," asked minister Nathaniel Appleton in the wake of the Stamp Act Crisis, "Is your conduct consistent? can you review our late struggles for liberty, and think of the slave-trade at the same time, and not blush?" Appleton feared that "had Great Britain thrown this inconsistency in our faces, . . . all mankind [would] have laughed at our pretensions to any just sentiments of Liberty, or even humanity."[51] With the next crisis, such moments came. English conservatives like Samuel Johnson were not alone in condemning colonial hypocrisy. English reformers, such as Thomas Day, called upon Americans to put principle in practice, and free the slaves. "If men would be consistent, they must admit all the consequences of their own principles," he wrote to an American friend. "You and your countrymen are reduced to the dilemma of either acknowledging the rights of your Negroes or of surrendering your own."[52] Loyalist critics in America made similar arguments. Take the point-by-point rebuttal of the Declaration of Independence issued by Thomas Hutchinson, who until 1774 was the much-reviled governor of Massachusetts. In considering the document's assertion of "life, liberty, and the pursuit of happiness" as natural rights, Hutchinson questioned whether the rebels were justified in "depriving more than an hundred thousand Africans of their rights to liberty."[53]

Such logic led inexorably to calls among American patriots for general emancipation. "If liberty is one of the natural and unalienable rights of all men," asked New Jersey minister Jacob Green in the midst of the Revolution, "how unjust, how inhuman . . . to violate this right? Britain is attempting to violate it; we in America have a long time been in the actual violation of it."[54] New York's John Jay also equated the cause of the liberty-yearning slave with that of the rebellious colonist, even as he continued to hold slaves himself. In 1777, he urged that New York's new state constitution provide for eventual abolition,[55] and endorsed a resolution by the state constitutional convention calling for the end of slavery. "Till America comes into this measure," Jay wrote in private correspondence in 1780, "her prayers to Heaven for liberty will be impious."[56] Such phrases echoed the thoughts of Thomas Jefferson, whose ruminations on the injustice of bondage caused him to "tremble" when he reflected that "God was just." Unlike Jefferson, however, Jay suspected that blacks' natural capacities were "probably" equal to whites', which to him made American hypocrisy all the more damning. "To contend for our own liberty and to deny that blessing to others," he would later write, "involves an inconsistency not to be excused."[57] Jay was not alone. In 1784, Richard Price declared that until the new states abolished the slave trade, "it will not appear that they deserve the liberty for which they have been contending. For it is self-evident that if there are any men whom they have a right to hold in slavery, there may be *others* who have a right to hold *them* in slavery."[58] In 1780, John Cooper, a member of the Continental Congress from New Jersey, summed it up effectively. Consistency with republican principles dictated the emancipation of the slaves, lest the entire Revolution amount to nothing more than the statement "that we are resolved not to be slaves, because we ourselves mean to be tyrants."[59]

The notion of slavery's abolition had been bandied before white and black abolitionists began spreading the word at the time of the Revolution. While critics of Atlantic slavery can be traced back to Bartolomé de Las Casas, a Spanish Dominican who spoke out against enslaving Native Americans in the Spanish colonies in the sixteenth century, most historians locate the origins of antislavery in North America to a 1688 petition that protested the practice of slaveholding. The signers, members of the Quaker sect living in Germantown, Pennsylvania, argued that both the golden rule and liberty of conscience dictated that Quakers "must, likewise, avoid to purchase such things as are stolen."[60] Twelve years later, the 1700 publication of a pamphlet titled *The Selling of Joseph*, written by Samuel Sewall, a justice on Massachusetts's Superior Court, labeled the slave trade "man-stealing," and declared, "It is most certain that all men, as they are the sons of Adam, are co-heirs, and have equal right unto liberty, and all other outward comforts of life." In the later decades of the eighteenth century, individuals such as John Woolman and Anthony Benezet, who converted to Quakerism, championed the abolition of slavery. Benezet in particular sought to create an antislavery movement rooted in appeals to the common humanity of all mankind, including the enslaved. Writing of the slaves to early British abolitionist Granville Sharp, Benezet asked, "Did not he that made them make us, and did not One fashion us before we were born?"[61]

To these early calls for abolition based purely on the grounds of Christian humanity, the Revolution lent the enormous weight of the national founding narrative, in the process spreading the antislavery gospel through a largely secular and civic evangelism. Arguments for abolition based on Christian principle faced considerable hurdles, not least of which was the Bible's apparent sanction of servitude in many instances—an argument raised by innumerable critics of these early advocates of abolitionism. Antislavery men could respond that the servitude practiced by God's chosen people constituted a distinct case or special exception, but the point had to be debated—and was, endlessly, right up to the eve of slavery's complete obliteration in the United States. The proper practice of

Christianity might require the humane treatment of slaves, or perhaps even their emancipation. But more compelling in the last quarter of the eighteenth century was the notion that slavery violated the transcendent principles upon which the new nation had been established. So long as so many Americans staked and sacrificed so much for their commitment to all men's natural right to liberty, it became very difficult to argue that the actual enslavement of Africans should be more easily countenanced than the virtual one of colonists.

The ideology of the Revolution thus created the antislavery cause. Of course, ethical qualms with slavery had long been the featured player in arguments to end the institution. And the emergence in Atlantic public discourse of "moral sentiment," or the value of imagining oneself in the position of unfortunate others, proved a necessary component of antislavery thought. (In fact, scholars have suggested that theories of moral sentiment did themselves draw from the same intellectual currents of the late Enlightenment that were implicated in the spread of notions of liberty.[62]) But it is difficult to imagine how a successful mass movement to end slavery could have evolved out of a world unfamiliar with the precepts of democratic revolution.[63] As we have seen, the categories of the very world that had created revolution—the tension between liberty and tyranny, and the notion of the individual's absolute right to own and enjoy property—had given shape and meaning to the practice of slavery. As citizens of the eighteenth-century Atlantic world knew it, slavery would not have been intelligible without those categories. Similarly, though, neither would abolition, or the idea of slavery as a social practice that could, and should, be eliminated.

Thus a grand irony of Atlantic history: the same Atlantic world that had created the brutal and highly capitalistic forms of slavery that existed throughout most of the New World also created the ideological preconditions for the complete obliteration of slavery. European nations and entrepreneurs had appropriated Old World forms of bondage, converting them into a massive system of labor expropriation that defined slaves as nothing but property—the very category of thing their economic revolution was coming to sanctify. But the very forces they unleashed—a modern world of merchant capital, with its privileging of bourgeois property rights, and its consequent tendency to view the world in terms of a simple binary between free (those who could own property) and slave (those who were property)—began to erode the ideological underpinnings of their central institution by raising knotty questions about the limits of freedom and the boundaries of property.

In sum, the forces that created New World slavery eventually created the possibility of New World slavery's demise. To say this is to give no special credit to the Western European societies that had settled across the Atlantic. Certainly it would be folly to suggest that the eventual emergence of abolitionism could ever atone for, let alone excuse, such an exceptionally abusive system of slavery, responsible for enslaving over twelve million in Africa, and consigning American-born generations to further captivity. But it is the case that if we are to seek the origins of the idea stream that would impel the actual destruction of the slave systems of the New World, we would look in vain outside the Old and New World metropoles of the most successful colonial empires.

African Americans were nonetheless integral players in this process. Those who were enslaved did not miss the bitter irony of slaveholding patriots' cause, nor the ideological currency of their paeans to liberty. If colonists could invoke the natural right of revolution because they viewed direct rather than indirect taxation as an appropriation of their property that was tantamount to enslavement, then how much more justified were the slaves of such men in shaking off their fetters? Virtually simultaneous with white revolutionaries' questioning of the link between liberty and slavery, similar statements by African Americans appeared. In 1773, four enslaved African American men petitioned the Massachusetts legislature for their freedom, boldly starting with an ironic swipe at the colonials' freedom struggle: "The efforts made by the legislative of this province in their last sessions to free themselves from slavery gave us, who are in that deplorable state, a high degree of satisfaction. We expect great things from men who have made such a noble stand against the designs of their *fellow-men* to enslave them. We cannot but wish and hope, Sir, that you will have the same grand object—we mean civil and religious liberty—in view in your next session."[64]

Unheeded, black Bostonians repeated their request three years later. Their petition, which the legislature also ignored, expressed the signers' "Astonishment that It has Never Bin Considred that Every Principle form which Amarica has Acted in the Cours of their unhappy Dificultes with Great Briton Pleads Stronger than A thousand arguments in favowrs of your petioners."[65] The objective was clear: leverage freedom through charges of hypocrisy and colonial commitments to liberty. Whites could live up to their ideals by freeing the slaves, or they could keep them but at the cost of appearing to be false to their own principles. Similar appeals appeared in the legislatures of the northern colonies throughout the period, particularly in the new northern states. In 1779, Connecticut blacks, writing to those who were "nobly contending, in the Cause of Liberty," declared slavery a "detestable Practice," and themselves "Convinced, of our Right (by the Law's of Nature and by the whole Tenor, of the Christian Religion, so far as we have been taught) to be free."[66] Twenty African Americans in New Hampshire asserted that "private or public tyranny and slavery, are alike detestable to minds conscious of the equal dignity of human nature," thus exhibiting their remarkable understandings of the ways their white contemporaries were discussing liberty.[67]

It is hard to underestimate the significance of blacks' efforts to parlay the rights rhetoric of the American Revolution on behalf of their own liberty. Obviously, the enslaved found it useful to employ the principles of their masters for their own ends. Yet their petitions bespeak much more than simplistic mimicry and a selfish interest in their own cause. How, for one, did the slaves come to know that it might be profitable to call patriotic slaveholders out on their commitment to liberty, or to point out their own use of the slave metaphor? Clearly, they learned of new possibilities for liberty by attending closely to the world around them. In a pamphlet titled *A Dialogue Concerning the Slavery of the Africans* (1776), Samuel Hopkins, a Congregational minister and early opponent of slavery from Massachusetts, described how he thought the process worked in the context of revolutionary America. "The poor negroes look on and hear what an aversion we have to slavery and how much liberty is prized," he described. "Often hearing it declared publicly and in private as the voice of all that slavery is more to be dreaded than death, and we are resolved to live free or die, &c. &c.," the slaves "attend their own wretched situation more than otherwise they could," quickly concluding that "the slavery the Americans dread as worse than death is lighter than a feather compared to their heavy doom."[68] Though he overestimated the role of new ideas and underplayed the enslaved's preexisting desire for liberty, Hopkins hit close to the mark. By attending to the tumultuous, shifting ideas around them, enslaved African Americans quickly gleaned the revolutionaries' struggle.

It was but a short leap to fathom that if British subjects in the colonies had an ironclad claim to liberty, the slaves' must be made of steel. In the process of debating their status and rights, these enslaved African Americans laid claim to the discourse of the public sphere,[69] or the arguments and ideas swirling about in the cosmopolitan worlds of the Atlantic seaboard cities. Ports such as Boston, New York, and Philadelphia were not isolated hinterlands but thriving commercial centers, connected by links of transportation, media, and finance to other centers of ideological production in the Atlantic world. Mobilizing in such cities through the printing press and the pulpit, in the courts, and on the street, African Americans took part in a hemisphere-wide public discussion over the meaning and limits of liberty. They thrust themselves into these debates, appropriating the revolutionary tradition for themselves, refashioning it and in the process becoming co-fabricators of the multiple meanings of freedom, alongside a wide range of other actors, from radical plebeian masses to the intellectual and economic elites who commanded the colonial legislatures.

We must be careful not to easily assume that African Americans' notions of freedom thus came from whites. Concepts traditionally used to describe the processes of cultural transformation experienced by African-descended people

in America, such as "integration" or "assimilation," do no justice to their experience with revolutionary ideology. These concepts latently suppose a "dominant"
culture, or normative set of largely static ideas, which a "minority" group somehow imbibes, thus replacing what had come before. This almost algebraic approach to cultural interaction, whereby the slaves became less "African" as they
became more "American," is as inaccurate as it is reductive. For of course there
was no single dominant or normative set of values in the fiercely dynamic world
of revolutionary era America, just as there was no monolithic "African" cultural
heritage to retain or lose. Furthermore, ideas are not quantities of mass that occupy the finite containers of human bodies, but are instead immensely complex
formations that can easily accommodate layers of meaning, which can be retained for generations across time and space. And as blacks' rapid embrace of
revolutionary principles suggests, concepts of liberty no more belonged to Europeans than to anyone else. Culture is not property, after all. To imagine ideas
in this light—as somehow inherently "white" or "black"—is to uncritically assent
to the very Lockean concepts that the revolutionary age was defining and refining. So when African Americans drew upon revolutionary ideology to argue in
behalf of their own freedom, they did far, far more than simply adopt a convenient argument. In the process of debating existing concepts of liberty, African
Americans fashioned new concepts of liberty. Their very presence as completely
unfree "slaves" had made it impossible for colonials to argue for their own independence without questioning the foundations of their society. In the decades
to come, blacks' continual manipulation of powerful public sphere concepts like
freedom would play a critical role in shaping the struggle that would eventually
yield the complete destruction of slavery in the United States.

WHAT THE ENTHUSIASM OF LIBERTY COULD DO
The Revolution, Military Service, and Emancipation

African Americans did more than simply write about their thirst for liberty. In the course of the Revolution itself, they acted on their commitment, risking their lives as soldiers on both sides. To the enslaved, the Revolution posed
agonizing questions of loyalty. Should they side with masters who spouted an
airy rhetoric of equality that they hesitated to apply to all? Or did blacks' best
chances lie with the opponents of those who held them in bondage? If most of
the enslaved chose the safest route of waiting and watching until matters resolved themselves, significant numbers acted on choices as complex and diverse
as were the slaves themselves. Yet the tally was not equal, for if raw numbers
stood for anything, England received the bulk of the benefit of black service, a
telling reminder of the enslaved's rejection of American hypocrisy. It is estimated

that a total of thirty thousand people of African descent served during the war in all its theaters. Roughly five thousand served in the Continental Army, and another thousand fought for America at sea. On the mainland, about twelve thousand fought for Britain, while another, oft-forgotten, twelve thousand offered their service to England in the Caribbean.[70]

Shifting official policy on both sides of the war defined the choices available to African Americans. Neither combatant began the conflict with abolition as a goal. British governors of the colonies, not sharing the rebels' high-flown rhetoric, began the war concerned with maintaining a social order, including slavery, that seemed swiftly to be careening out of control. The American revolutionaries, in contrast, started the war with ideological commitments far more inclined to universal freedom, but with severe practical constraints. Needing to maintain and control their human property, many slaveholding rebels considered their principles, even if sincerely felt, a luxury they could ill afford. When in 1778 William Livingston, the revolutionary governor of New Jersey, discreetly asked the state's assembly to consider mass emancipation, members rebuffed him, declaring the state in "rather in too critical a Situation to enter on the consideration of it at that time."[71] Opponents of abolition in Pennsylvania thought that the midst of war was not "the proper time" to consider freeing slaves in the state; rumors of liberty would lead "desperate" and "ignorant" southern slaves "to a demand of an immediate and entire freedom," resulting in "disorders" and "cruelties" that would further ravage the war-ridden country.[72] Any discussions of emancipation would have to wait until the successful conclusion of the war.

In time, though, both sides came to understand the practical value of using their bondsmen to fight. The need for security and defense against enemies gave each cause to consider reinitiating a practice as old as the colonies themselves—of arming the enslaved, eventually trading their military service for freedom. The incentives were mutually reinforcing for both combatants: for one side to consider arming slaves made it imperative for the other to consider doing so as well, lest it concede the entire advantage of armed slaves to its enemy. In the American Revolution, both sides, in varying ways and to varying degrees, steadily relinquished an initial commitment to maintaining slavery in favor of the military expedience of arming slaves. While both sides approached the matter in a highly provisional way, American solutions in particular had a strongly sectional geographic character, which portended ill for the future.

The British, hard-pressed and with less to lose by such a prospect, arrived there first. Several in Britain had foreseen the prospect of arming slaves should rebellion arise in the colonies. In 1772, John Murray, Earl of Dunmore and the royally appointed governor of Virginia, had concluded that the slaves constituted a liability in the defense of the colony. Many American slave owners "trembled at the facility that our enemy would find in Such a body of men, attached by no tye to their Master nor to the Country," reasoning that in the event of war the mass of bondsmen would be "ready to join the first that would encourage them to revenge themselves" on their oppressors.[73] When the crisis unfolded in 1775, a pamphlet written by a British traveler to the colonies urged the authorities to attack the colonists through their slaves. "Proclame *Freedom* to their Negroes," he suggested. "Then how long would they be a people? They would soon cry out for pardon, and render unto CÆSAR the Things which are CÆSAR's."[74] The point was not lost on the revolutionaries. Jefferson worried that slavery destroyed "amor patriae," or love of country, in African Americans, "for if a slave can have a country in this world, it must be any other in preference to that in which he is born to live and labour for another."[75]

The slaves' questionable loyalty loomed heavily over the entire revolutionary project. The trouble pertained particularly in those areas in the colonies most deeply beholden to slavery: the lower South plantations of South Carolina and Georgia, and the Chesapeake regions of Virginia, Maryland, and Delaware. Even before the war, planters in the lower South had viewed their powder-keg societies as a source of vulnerability on the world stage. Many planters considered southern slaves "necessary, but very dangerous Domestics, their Number so much exceeding the Whites."[76] They constituted a potentially rebellious class, exploitable by an enemy willing to offer a likely inducement such as liberty.

As war loomed, the problem grew. In 1774, James Madison conveyed reports of a recent slave conspiracy, in which "a few of those unhappy wretches met together and chose a leader who was to conduct them when the English troops should arrive." These slave rebels thought—"foolishly," Madison wrongly believed—that the British would be coming "very soon and that by revolting to them they should be rewarded with their freedom." Urging that such conspiracies "should be concealed as well as suppressed," Madison worried that "if America should come to a hostile rupture, I am afraid an Insurrection among the slaves may well be promoted."[77] In South Carolina, where slaves constituted nearly half of the state's entire population on the eve of the American Revolution, concern ran particularly high.[78] Back in 1766 Christopher Gadsen had called his native South Carolina "a very weak province," for "having such a number of slaves amongst us." In June 1775, South Carolina's legislature organized a militia (all white, of course) expressly to resist a feared British invasion of Charleston, which it was believed would accompany an instigated slave uprising. The assembly cited "the dread of insurrection," which "a wicked and despotic ministry" might inspire, as one of the "causes sufficient to drive an oppressed people to the use of arms."[79]

The lower South's dense population of enslaved Africans clearly alarmed revolutionary authorities. In 1775, John Adams reported a "melancholy" discussion with "gentlemen" from Georgia and South Carolina who feared that a small British army proclaiming freedom to the slaves could quickly raise twenty thousand troops. Notably, he remarked that the enslaved had a "wonderful art of communicating intelligence among themselves," noting that news "will run several hundreds of miles in a week or fortnight."[80] In fact, concerns over Britain's arming of the slaves sparked the outbreak of the Revolution in Virginia. As tensions led to military showdown in the spring of 1775, Royal Governor Lord Dunmore used British troops to remove gunpowder from the magazine in the capital at Williamsburg. Colonists massed at the governor's palace, demanding the return of the gunpowder on the pretext that they feared servile rebellion. In their words, "some wicked and designing persons have instilled the most diabolical notions into the minds of our slaves, and . . . therefore, the utmost attention to our internal security is become the more necessary."[81] Dunmore responded by threatening them with just this prospect. "If any insult is offered me, or those who have obeyed my orders," he stated, "I will declare freedom to the slaves, and lay the town in ashes."[82] The assertion did nothing to calm the situation. Shortly after, Dunmore fled with his family to a royal warship offshore, reporting to his superior in England his intention to "arm all my own Negroes and receive all others that will come to me who I shall declare free."[83]

That November, Dunmore carried out his threat, declaring martial law in Virginia and promising freedom for slaves and servants "appertaining to Rebels" who might take up arms for the king. In the following months, some eight hundred slaves or more accepted Dunmore's bargain, fleeing plantations to join British forces. Colonials howled. "Hell itself could not have vomited anything more black than this design of emancipating our slaves," a Philadelphian croaked.[84] In Virginia, the *Gazette* somewhat disingenuously warned the enslaved, "Be not then, ye Negroes, tempted by this proclamation to ruin yourselves"; Dunmore stood not with bondmen's "present masters, who pity their condition," but with the "English merchants" who sought "to repeal our kind and merciful acts."[85] George Washington worried that the proclamation might have a "snow ball" effect on the already apparent problem of slave flight, and declared Dunmore an "arch-traitor to the rights of humanity" who "should be instantly crushed, if it takes the force of the whole Colony to do it."[86] For Virginia's legislature, the proclamation further confirmed British designs on American liberties. That Dunmore could "by his single fiat, . . . strip us of our property, can give freedom to our servants and slaves, and arm them for our destruction," clearly evidenced the confiscatory "system of tyranny adopted by the ministry and parliament of *Great Britain*."[87]

So vehemently did the Founders oppose British-fomented slave insurrection that they ranked it among the grievances they listed in the Declaration of Independence. Thomas Jefferson's initial draft of the declaration had included a vociferous attack on the slave trade: "He has waged cruel war against human nature itself, violating its most sacred rights of life and liberty in the persons of a distant people who never offended him, captivating & carrying them into slavery in another hemisphere or to incur miserable death in their transportation thither."[88] In this, Jefferson may justly have been criticized for perversely displacing blame for the colonies' practice of slavery and slave trading onto a monarch whose courts (in the Somerset case) had only recently ruled slavery illegal in England.[89] Instead, the South Carolina and Georgia delegates to the Continental Congress lambasted him for writing against a slave trade they themselves wished to continue. Even some of Jefferson's colleagues from the North "felt a little tender under those censures," Jefferson recalled, "for tho' their people have very few slaves themselves yet they had been pretty considerable carriers of them to others."[90] While Congress struck Jefferson's slave trade clause, though, some scholars believe that the declaration retained an oblique reference to slavery in the phrase, "He has excited domestic insurrections amongst us." It seems likely that in this compromise language Jefferson conflated British support of Tory Loyalists with British incitement of slave rebellion. In the preamble of the Virginia state constitution, which he had recently penned, Jefferson had offered a similar list of grievances, placing "inciting insurrections of our fellow subjects" just before "prompting our negroes to rise in arms among us."[91]

Regardless, Dunmore's proclamation represented an ad hoc response to an immediate crisis, not a comprehensive policy pursued by the Crown. For most of the war, British commanders remained ambivalent about the employment of slave soldiers. As critics like Edmund Burke commented, the slaves had no more reason to trust Britain than the revolutionaries: "Must they not a little suspect an offer of freedom from that very nation which has sold them to their present masters?" he asked. "An offer of freedom from England would come rather oddly, shipped to them in an African vessel . . . with a cargo of three hundred Angola negroes."[92] Yet as the mother country found its empire increasingly threatened by enemies seeking to make the most of its conflict with the colonies, its war became increasingly global and its need for allies more imperative. The Revolution quickly spread. Skirmishes with Spain and France occurred in Florida and the Caribbean, and even as far away as India. In the West Indies, the British-held islands of Dominica, St. Vincent, Grenada, Tobago, St. Kitts, Nevis, and Montserrat were all taken by the French, whose aid made the revolutionaries' decisive victory at Yorktown in 1781 possible. As the toll of opponents and losses mounted, the prospect of attracting slave support with the promise of liberty proved irresistible. Freeing and arming rebels' slaves did triple duty: not only would each slave thus freed add one body to England's forces, it would deprive the rebels of one; more broadly, it would render all rebel slave property insecure.

Despite that Britain's pretenses to liberty seemed as questionable as rebels', more southern slaves chose service to the Crown over fealty to colony. They fled plantations in droves. Thomas Jefferson believed that Virginia lost an incredible thirty thousand slaves to flight in 1781, of whom a distressing twenty-seven thousand perished of disease.[93] Historian Gary Nash estimates that in the later years of the war in Virginia and South Carolina up to half of the healthy male slaves likely to escape fled their masters.[94] When permitted—for at times commanders forbade the recruitment of "Negroes, Mollatoes, and other Improper Persons"[95]—they enlisted in the British ranks, serving as attendants, guides, "pioneers," and soldiers. Few were treated well, for military rather than humanitarian logic had dictated the policy. Dunmore's Ethiopian Regiment saw action before being decimated by disease, while British-supported black guerrillas under a fugitive slave named Colonel Tye terrorized New Jersey from 1778 to 1780. Some, like Boston King, recorded their memories of the war, bequeathing to future generations invaluable insight into the complex motives of revolutionary era slaves.[96] Perhaps the greatest contribution African Americans made to the British war effort took place outside the United States. Recalling the hemispheric nature of the war, Philip D. Morgan and Andrew Jackson O'Shaughnessy estimate that twelve thousand blacks served Britain in the West Indies. All told, "the roughly twenty-four thousand slaves serving on the British side represented about 4 percent of the whole British war effort"—a remarkable figure.[97] In the end, black Loyalists' gamble paid limited dividends. It created freedom, sometimes only temporarily, for the tens of thousands who had fled plantations in Virginia, the Carolinas, and Georgia, and it had badly weakened slavery everywhere in the new states. While distressing numbers of slaves had perished in war, or had been denied the liberty they were promised, several thousand eventually found a qualified freedom—in the Canadian Maritime Provinces, Britain, or the newly established west African colony of freed slaves, Sierra Leone.

The rebelling colonies were hard-pressed to echo England's hesitant moves toward slave recruitment. Some revolutionary leaders believed that if slaves could be employed against the rebels, perhaps the best strategy would be to reverse the trick. Incorporate slaves into revolutionary armies, they argued, and gain the benefit of blacks' service while denying it to the British. In a pamphlet published in March 1775, the radical Thomas Paine had prophesied the coming crisis, suggesting the benefits of emancipation in gaining the slaves' loyalty. Should the slaves be freed, given property, "encouraged to industry," and offered "civil protection," he suggested, "they may become interested in the public welfare, and assist in promoting it; instead of being dangerous, as now they are, should any enemy promise them a better condition."[98] In 1779, Alexander Hamilton endorsed such a plan, supporting the recruitment of South Carolina slaves. "If we do not make use of them in this way," he wrote, "the enemy probably will." Emancipation, for Hamilton, was integral to the plan, precisely because it mobilized African Americans' loyalty in a manner consistent with "the dictates of humanity." He argued, "This will secure their fidelity, animate their courage, and, I believe, will have a good influence upon those who remain, by opening a door to their emancipation."[99]

Portentously, the northern and southern states divided on the matter. Emancipation offered a radical answer to the pressing problem of slave loyalty, but one anathema where slavery dominated the economy and social order. Southern fears of slave insurrection stifled the emergence of a policy of slave recruitment and manumission. For many planters, voluntarily relinquishing slave property amounted to little less than having it confiscated by British tyrants. The whole point of the Revolution, after all, had been the protection of property. Thus, Virginia declined to employ slave soldiers because its legislators "considered unjust, sacrificing the property of a part of the community to the exoneration of the rest."[100] Despite some calls for recruitment in the lower South, slaveholder intransigence impeded the formation of any policy. South Carolina's John Laurens reported to General Washington that his plan to enlist slaves had been "downed by the howlings of a triple-headed monster, in which prejudice, avaric, and pusillanimity were united."[101] Indeed, not only did these states never arm slaves, the interests of the lower South impinged on recruitment along the entire seaboard. John Adams rejected a New Jersey statesman's plan to recruit freed slaves in 1776, declaring, "Your Negro Battalion will never do. S. Carolina would run out of their Wits at the least hint of such a Measure."[102] In deference to such attitudes, the Continental Army began the conflict an officially white institution, despite the contributions of African Americans at early battles at Lexington, Concord, and Bunker Hill. In September 1775, General Horatio Gates explicitly forbade the enlistment of "any stroller, negro or vagabond." The next month, army commanders agreed to prohibit all people of African descent from serving in the Continental Army.[103]

Nonetheless, the dire need for manpower slackened resistance to black recruitment. General Washington's opposition slowly receded, and Congress followed. If enslaved blacks posed difficult questions, free ones did not. Upper South states such as Virginia found free African Americans more readily spared than the enslaved. No doubt, from the start of the conflict recruiting officers hungry for men turned a blind eye on some among these who claimed freedom but were still bound. While the Continentals represented the regular army of the entire United States, the states that supplied it with soldiers, and which also maintained their own militias, also played a vital role in the story of black recruitment. Inferior on the battlefield to regular troops, militias nonetheless served a critical purpose, acting as vital sources of information and constantly politicizing the countryside on behalf of American interests.[104] Militias proved widely variable in their recruitment patterns; particularly where slave populations were minimal, and examples of emancipation deemed less threatening to the overall social order, African Americans were more likely to be welcomed in them.

In the North, states less dependent on slavery found the trade of service for liberty easiest to make, and slowly began permitting the recruitment of free blacks and slaves into their militias. New England began the trend. Massachusetts formed the all-black Bucks of America company and permitted African Americans to serve in integrated units alongside whites. The First Rhode Island Regiment featured segregated companies of black soldiers; the enslaved among these were guaranteed freedom for service, while their owners were compensated by the state. In the South, only Maryland actively recruited slaves into its units, though Virginia permitted the enlistment of free blacks. And in the Carolinas and Georgia, where the militia functioned as much for slave control as for repelling foreign enemies, state legislatures fiercely resisted the possibility of slave enlistment. Still, by 1777, a Hessian officer could report the prevalence of African Americans slave and free among Continental forces: "You never see a regiment in which there are not negroes, and there are well-built, strong, husky fellows among them."[105] All told, an estimated six thousand African Americans fought for colonial independence.[106] Blacks served a range of roles, from building earthworks and fortifications to personally serving officers and fighting in frontline regiments. The names of these soldiers—Prince Easterbrooks, Peter Salem, Lemuel Haynes, Salem Poor, James Forten, Agrippa Hull, Prince Hall, and others—would be enshrined in a pantheon of black American heroes celebrated by later generations as "colored patriots" of the American Revolution.[107]

Whether they served America or England, though, slaves in arms fought first and foremost for liberty. In a sense, their assistance to both sides—whether in the cause of colonial independence or in defense of Britain—served a similar purpose. As dual expressions of the slaves' desire for freedom, both demonstrated, in no uncertain terms, that antislavery sentiment was not merely a logical consequence of revolutionary ideology, but the earnest wish of the slaves themselves. No clearer evidence in support of budding antislavery arguments could have been offered. The American Revolution thus constituted a new take on an old pattern. It was not the first time in Atlantic history when freedom had been traded for service. Since the founding of the colonies, plantation regimes in the periphery, often deficient in free white defenders and constantly threatened by national rivals, had frequently turned to their enslaved to help them in times of need. The decision had never been easy. Since plantations and slaves existed primarily to earn a profit through agricultural labor, any slave whose labor was diverted toward the security of the regime was necessarily removed from his primary purpose. Furthermore, arming slaves entailed transferring the means of violence from a military partly designed to subjugate slaves into the hands of the subjugated slaves themselves. With militias throughout plantation societies being as much directed at "domestic" enemies as at foreign, moving some from the category of the overseen to the category of the overseers undermined the fundamental divisions of the society as a whole.

Finally, military labor differed fundamentally from the work most slaves performed. While most plantation labor could be extracted by violence or its threat, good soldiers required degrees of cohesion and initiative that could not entirely be compelled. Though service in the modernizing armies of the early modern world subjected soldiers to intense discipline and rigid systems of authority, it did so in the service of the state and its interests. From the days of Machiavelli, the ideal had been soldiers willing to relinquish, voluntarily and temporarily, personal liberty to the state in exchange for the promise of civic inclusion and good governance.[108] The best soldiers, in fact, often enjoyed remarkable degrees of political inclusion. For example, in the middle of the seventeenth century, the democratically organized New Model Army of the Puritan Revolution did not lose a single important engagement, twice defeating the forces of the royalists, and successfully invading both Ireland and Scotland. Expense and the political risks of a politically empowered soldiery almost always precluded early nation-states from achieving this standard; this was for most the "age of absolutism," and the New Model was, after all, a revolutionary army. But the principle was clear: soldiers were not slaves. Though the daily lives of both may have been unenviable, soldiers were free, had rights, and could make claims on the state. Whereas soldiers could uphold or betray their country, slaves had no country. In the plantation zone, masters transferred these acknowledgments of soldiers' personhood to slaves very grudgingly indeed.

Nonetheless, it did happen. In the "cockpit of imperial rivalry"[109] that was the West Indies, sufficiently dire could be the need for arms that every slave society toyed with the practice. Particularly in the early days of the colonies, when claims on islands were most tenuous, white defenders scarce, and the racial caste system inchoate, Africans were not infrequently armed to fend off invasion. On Providence Island in the 1640s, Barbados in the 1660s, Bermuda around the turn of the eighteenth century, and Antigua at midcentury, English colonists armed slaves in significant numbers. The French were equally likely to put their slaves in arms.[110] In most of these instances, promises of freedom had accompanied the enlistment of slave soldiers.

In the Caribbean, where the practice of trading service for freedom had become familiar, emancipation through military service had consequences quite distinct from what would happen in mainland North America, where it was comparatively rare. Colonial authorities dealt with the danger represented by the precedent for emancipation by, ingeniously, establishing freed soldiers as custodians of the plantation regime. This pattern prevailed particularly in the exploitation colonies of the Caribbean. Where whites could constitute less than 10 percent of an island's population, local allies served critical roles in times of crisis. Emancipated slave soldiers, granted freedom and status, could serve in colonial militias designed not just to repel foreign invaders, but to maintain plantation control or combat runaway slave "maroons." The Caribbean's pattern of social stratification, wherein "free people of color" occupied the middle of a three-tiered caste system that featured enslaved Africans on the bottom and whites on top, owed in no small measure to this strategy of maintaining control of black populations through division. In the heavily black plantation societies of the West Indies, emancipated slave soldiers often formed the core of free communities of color with a distinct sense of identity as a privileged group, far elevated above the ranks of the enslaved. This pattern of social stratification recapitulated and intensified long-standing differences among African-descended people in these societies. White authorities, ruling exploitation colonies featuring overwhelming numbers of slaves and few whites, relied upon free people of color to act as a buffer caste, actively pursuing policies to divide their subordinate populations by creating a privileged group that protected the slave regime by serving as slave catchers, maroon fighters, and even slave owners themselves.

In the mainland colonies, the three-tiered system had never prevailed, though echoes of it could be found in regions with Caribbean-like demographic patterns, such as the areas around Charleston and Savannah. In the settler and hybrid societies of the mainland thirteen, a preponderance of whites in most areas obviated the delicate balancing act that took place in the Caribbean. As a consequence, slaves were rarely armed with anything like the readiness of the West Indies. In times of threats such as Indian wars, such moves were considered but most often rejected; even in the French and Indian War (1754–63), only a few slaves had served alongside white colonial troops.[111] And in the mainland thirteen no one ever discussed using slaves in the militia, since its primary function in the South was slave control, and since the white population was sufficient to fill its ranks.

When the prospect of emancipation through service in the Revolution did emerge on the mainland, it thus carried with it implications for a postemancipation world quite different from what prevailed in the West Indies. The mainland colonies, generally lacking a sizable and privileged middling caste of people of color who might serve as a buffer group between whites and the enslaved, so too lacked a strong tradition of having a clearly distinguishable rank of rights-limited people that the newly emancipated might join. Whereas in Jamaica or Antigua slave soldiers might be emancipated into long-established and clearly defined communities of free people of color, the mainland colonies could not offer whites similar assurance that freed slaves would remain inferior in law and social custom. There, most free people of color lived lives barely distinguishable from the enslaved; only a select few echoed the elite status of, say, the slaveholding *gens de couleur* of St. Domingue. Yet with large communities of free people of color being relatively uncommon on the mainland before the Revolution, there existed few laws to actively define them as subordinate. Emancipation in the revolting colonies thus entailed the possibility of civic and social equality—a powerful dissuasion for a large, white, and race-conscious population.

One final factor made the experience of emancipation through military service during the Revolution unique. A long history had established a close connection between military service and guarantees of freedom. The powerful new ideology of natural rights surrounding the American Revolution infused these older traditions of military service with new imperatives. In short, a military conflict posed as liberal revolution rapidly catalyzed moves toward emancipation. Military service lent calls for equality a weight that could not easily be ignored. When in 1780 seven free African Americans from Dartmouth, Massachusetts, complained that they were taxed despite "having no vote or Influence in the Election of those that Tax us," they pointedly noted that they had "cheerfully Entered the field of Battle of the defence of the Common Cause."[112] Though their immediate petition was denied, by 1783 propertied free blacks in Massachusetts were granted the vote. Thus while the rhetoric of liberty had created logical exigencies that pushed revolutionaries to extend liberty to the enslaved, the imperatives of war gave a practical impetus to this push, which was novel relative to previous attempts to arm slaves, and influential as a precedent for the future.

With the American Revolution, bargains of service for freedom began to carry a promise of national inclusion. Military service became inextricably linked with the full privileges of national citizenship. The democratic revolutions of the late eighteenth- and early nineteenth-century Atlantic proffered a new conception of the connection between the people and the state. In the burgeoning nationalism of the age, nations founded on principles of social contract found novel means of harnessing the energy of the people. Now promising responsive government in return for loyalty, governments founded on democratic principles could hope for hitherto unimagined levels of national commitment. One of the Hessian mercenaries who fought for Britain reflected admiringly on the commitment of Continental forces: "With what soldiers in the world could one do what was done by these men, who go about nearly naked and in the greatest privation? Deny the best-disciplined soldiers of Europe what is due them and they will run away in droves.... But from this one can perceive what an enthusiasm—which these poor fellows call 'Liberty'—can do!"[113] With the promise of personal freedom an even greater incentive than political liberty, it is easy to imagine why service might have attracted the enslaved. (It is also easy to see how highly gendered this sense of nationalism was. Only men, after all, were thought capable of rendering military service, and so the full privileges of citizenship were exclusively theirs.) All this meant that emancipation received an enormous, but highly qualified, boon from the Revolution. For when and where emancipation did happen, it would for many whites entail a critical problem: how did society preserve the privileges of racial caste in a world where slavery could no longer do that, and in a land where all men were alleged to have been created equal?

CHAPTER 2

Half Slave and Half Free
The Founding of the United States

WITH A WHIMPER
The First Emancipation

For all the revolutionary generation's concern that practice match principle, enacting liberty for people of African descent proved remarkably challenging. During the Revolution itself, with enthusiasm for liberty fueling a fierce struggle for national independence, a great many Americans asserted that dedication to liberty demanded the eradication of slavery. The devil, though, lay in the details of emancipation. When it came time to continue the work slave recruitment had begun and consider the actual mechanisms that would dismantle slavery and demonstrate the sincerity of the Founders' commitment to liberty, the internal paradoxes of revolutionary ideology became evident. Slavery did end in the northern states as a direct result of the Revolution, constituting some of the first instances in the Atlantic world whereby sovereign governments legally abolished the institution. Yet, as would happen often in later cases of general emancipation, the process was highly compromised, often taking place gradually, and compensating slave owners for their lost property. In one respect, though, the case of the United States was singular: unlike other places in the Atlantic world, in the United States slavery ended incompletely. The regionally divergent nature of the process as well as the unique form of government crafted by the Founders created the "house divided" that took a civil war to reunite.

The process of general emancipation began in the midst of the Revolutionary War itself, as political leaders in select northern states began seriously to doubt the ethics and utility of seeking to liberate themselves while holding slaves. With chattel bondage an important but secondary feature of their economies—recall the distinction between these "societies with slaves" versus the "slave societies" of the South—northern statesmen could more easily afford to put their principles into practice. As a signal of the tentative nature of these efforts, there was no central program, and even the earliest pronouncements of slavery's demise were muted, inchoate, and opaque. There was never a question as to whether the effort would be national or not. Certainly, antislavery reformers such as Anthony Benezet sought for the broadest emancipation possible; through tireless efforts such men built networks that spanned the states, and indeed the Atlantic. But so diffuse was national authority during the war, and so difficult were local efforts, that the thought of a coherent national policy of emancipation was beyond imagining. Not even after the war, at the constitutional convention that framed a stronger national state to replace the weak Articles of Confederation, was the national abolition of slavery even considered. The question was thus resolved state by state, on a case-by-case, geographically divided basis that provided for the eventual liberation of many slaves, but only in the North.

Fired by their own struggle for independence, statesmen, clergymen, and others began pressing for legal abolition during the war, citing once again the concern that Americans would appear hypocrites should they not act on their principles. In a typical example, toward the end of the war, David Cooper, a Quaker opponent of slavery from New Jersey, restated the cant—familiar by such time—that the practice of slaveholding imperiled the new nation's integrity: "Let not the world have an opportunity to charge her conduct with a contradiction to her solemn and often repeated declarations; or to say that her sons are not real friends to freedom; that they have been actuated in this awful contest by no higher motive than selfishness and interest."[1] Discrete movements emerged in every northern state to urge legislatures to enact concrete measures to end slavery, with New England leading the way. In Massachusetts the Assembly considered a bill to abolish the "wicked & unnatural Practice of holding Persons in slavery," while in Rhode Island antislavery Quakers such as Moses Brown took the lead in pressing for emancipation bills. Connecticut, too, considered a series of wartime abolition bills.[2]

These early proposals were highly qualified efforts. Most provided state compensation for slave owners, much as precursor bills permitting slave enlistment and emancipation had done. All provided freedom only for those born after a certain date (a principle called *post-nati* emancipation). Many sought to compensate slave owners for lost property directly through state coffers, or through graduating measures that fully freed the enslaved only after reaching a certain age, thereby indemnifying slave owners with guaranteed years of free labor. At no point was it suggested that the emancipated would be compensated for their lost years of labor, and most measures left the citizenship status of freed slaves unclear. These were thus not single, heroic events, but tentative half-steps toward freedom, which fared best in places where slaves were least populous and least central to the economy. The impulse to conserve the social order established under slavery was strong. State legislators saw themselves as confronting momentous issues, and grappling with consequences difficult to calculate; their caution was palpable at every step. The Massachusetts Assembly, for example, refused to move on a statewide abolition measure "from an apprehension that our brethren in the Other Colonies should conceive there was an impropriety" in its plan for abolition.[3] All such initial initiatives failed, victims of concerted but quiet legislative inertia rather than vocal public opposition. Legislatures tabled measures and let them die rather than risk speaking or voting against them, or they amended them beyond the point of acceptability.

When legislatures balked, though, events—compelled by the logic of the Revolution—might overtake them. In Vermont, for instance, the drafting of a new state constitution had signal results. In 1777, when the territory declared its independence, its state constitution, like many others, included a statement of rights reminiscent of the Virginia Declaration of Rights and the Declaration of Independence: "All men are born equally free and independent, and have certain natural, inherent and unalienable rights, amongst which are the enjoying and defending life and liberty; acquiring, possessing and protecting property, and pursuing and obtaining happiness and safety." Such declarations were, of course, notoriously vague; did they include people of African descent as well? Vermont clarified this by adding a statement that minimized doubt: "Therefore, no male person, born in this country, or brought from over sea, ought to be holden by law, to serve any person, as a servant, slave or apprentice, after he arrives to the age of twenty-one Years, nor female, in like manner, after she arrives to the age of eighteen years, unless they are bound by their own consent, after they arrive to such age, or bound by law, for the payment of debts, damages, fines, costs, or the like." In other words, because all were born free and equal, none could be sold. This was a stunning enactment of revolutionary precepts, written expressly into the fundamental law of the state. Still, the language was sufficiently vague to permit the possibility of holding black children as slaves until the time of their maturity, a feature of many states' later emancipation acts. (This was more likely a provision intended to permit the common practice of "binding" indigent children to families to prevent them from becoming a "charge" on public coffers.) Nonetheless, Vermont may justly lay claim to being the first sovereign polity in the New World to have legally ended slavery.[4]

No fireworks or public celebrations attended the moment. No shackles sprang loose, and there is no trace in the record that any Vermont slaves immediately fled their former masters to seek new lives in freedom. In fact, in such instances it could be impossible even to identify the discrete point at which slavery died. Given wartime distractions, the novelty of abolition, and weak political will, individual African Americans could and did remain enslaved for some time, even when it seemed slavery had ended. Vermont's legislature found it necessary to reinforce the point made in the Constitution, declaring that "the idea of slavery is expressly and totally exploded from our free government."[5] New Hampshire encountered even greater difficulties. Slavery ended there also through constitutional interpretation, a process that left considerable opportunity for the persistence of bondage. Many state leaders believed the institution dead by virtue of their 1783 constitution's assertion that "all men are born equally free and independent," yet at the time of the first federal census in 1790 New Hampshire recorded the presence of 157 slaves. Not until 1857 did the state finally pass a law clearly abolishing slavery and granting full citizenship rights to people of African descent.

Matters were even more unclear in Massachusetts, where slavery ended not through legislative efforts, which had failed, but as a consequence of a series of judicial cases regarding the interpretation of state constitutions' declaration of universal human equality. Since the 1760s antislavery activists had been bringing suits before the courts in an attempt to declare slavery illegal. When Lord Mansfield ruled in 1772 that the Boston slave Somerset was free by virtue of setting foot on British soil, some in the state interpreted the decision as applying to Massachusetts, too. In the early 1780s, several cases of slaves suing for their freedom helped clarify the matter. In one, an enslaved woman named Elizabeth Freeman, known at the time as Mum Bett, learned of the 1780 state constitution's declaration of natural equality and sought her liberty; "I'm not a dumb *critter*," she reportedly pleaded; "won't the law give me my freedom?"[6] In 1781 Thomas Sedgwick, a prominent attorney and delegate to the Continental Congress, brought suit on behalf of Bett and another slave, named Brom, successfully arguing that the new state constitution rendered them free.

Mum Bett's case provided the crucial precedent in Quok Walker's freedom suit, which is commonly held to have heralded the end of slavery in Massachusetts. As a boy, Walker had secured from his owner, James Caldwell, a promise to be freed when he reached the age of twenty-five. Caldwell died, leaving Walker to his widow, who married Nathaniel Jennison, a man undisposed to honor the bargain. Walker fled Jennison's household in 1781, at the age of twenty-eight, and worked nearby at another man's home. Jennison sued this man, also named Caldwell, for enticing away his slave. In a series of three cases, Walker's attorney, a prominent lawyer named Levi Lincoln, argued that servitude in Massachusetts violated the very principles for which the state had declared its independence. "Can we expect to triumph over G. Britain, to get free ourselves until we let those go free under us," he asked.[7] The court acceded. William Cushing, the chief justice of Massachusetts's Supreme Judicial Court, instructed the jury that because of the state constitution's declaration that "All men are born free and equal," slavery was "as effectively abolished as it can be by the granting of rights and privileges wholly incompatible and repugnant to its existence."[8] In 1783, the court thus ruled that "the idea of slavery is inconsistent with our own conduct and Constitution," and that therefore Walker was free.[9] Many in the state viewed the case as a universal precedent. Following it, few slaveholders had the confidence to enforce their claims to human property. By 1790, Massachusetts listed no slaves in its census. Yet no general abolition law followed, and slavery died in Massachusetts through general acquiescence rather than judicial fiat. Indeed, one could argue that, technically speaking, the possibility of slavery remained in Massachusetts until the ratification of the Thirteenth Amendment in December 1865.

Other New England states followed similarly circuitous routes to freedom. Toward the end of the Revolutionary War Rhode Island and Connecticut provided for an end to slavery through clear legislative processes. In 1779, Rhode Island banned the sale of slaves out of the state without their permission, but made little headway on general emancipation after the war. Pressed by the campaign of Quaker convert Moses Brown, the scion of a slave-trading family, Rhode Island's legislature passed a bill in 1784 providing that henceforth all children born of slaves would become free—girls at age eighteen, boys at twenty-one. In Connecticut, antislavery legislatures finally succeeded in passing through a quite gradual emancipation act in 1784—ironically, appended to the state's revised slave code. Similar to Rhode Island's, Connecticut's measure provided for post-nati emancipation, freeing newborn slaves once they had reached the age of twenty-five.

Emancipation faced an even rockier road in the mid-Atlantic, where slavery played a more important role in the economy. On the one hand, Pennsylvania's state legislature moved decisively to end slavery. Quaker abolitionists and the state's famously radical legislature of 1780 conspired to pass the nation's first legislated manumission act. For all the bill's novelty—it boldly declared slavery "repugnant" to natural liberties—it still freed no slaves immediately. Rather, it established a process of gradual, post-nati emancipation, freeing those newly born into servitude only after an excruciating twenty-eight years of bondage. The act went into force on March 1, 1784, the same date stipulated by the Connecticut and Rhode Island measures.

In New Jersey and New York, the struggle to abolish slavery long outlasted the Revolution. At the time of the first federal census in 1790, slaves in New York and New Jersey constituted over 6 percent of each state's total population, well over the 2 percent average for the northern states.[10] As the debates attending abolition measures in New York and New Jersey belong to the period of the Early Republic, they are considered in the next chapter; for now, a simple survey will suffice. The road was particularly tortuous in the Empire State, where the legislature began considering gradual emancipation measures in 1784 but did not pass the decisive bill until 1799. For sixteen years the fate of enslaved New Yorkers hung in the balance as politicians debated everything from former masters' responsibility for the moral instruction of the free to the emancipated's right to hold political office. Finally, on the eve of a new millennium, New York passed a bill freeing slave children born after July 4, 1799, indenturing women to their former owners until the age of twenty-five and men until twenty-eight.[11]

New Jersey's path to abolition was longest of all. Starting in 1778, when Governor William Livingston had sought, and lost, a bid for an emancipation measure, the state wrangled for over a quarter of a century with various emancipation proposals. Not until 1804 did the legislature pass a bill, which granted freedom to females born of slave parents at the age of twenty-one, and males at the age of twenty-five. As in other states' measures, the intervening years were to be occupied with service to former owners. In both New York and New Jersey, the state indemnified masters by permitting them to free their slaves early, only to receive from the government a monthly subsidy for the freedpeople's maintenance and care. Of all the northern states, New Jersey retained slavery the longest. African Americans born into slavery before 1804 remained bound; on the eve of the Civil War, the federal census continued to list eighteen "apprentices for life" as slaves.

The gradual emancipation measures initiated during the American Revolution constituted the leading edge of an Atlantic-wide movement that first challenged slavery and instituted its demise. Legislating even a distant end to slavery sent powerful shockwaves through all of American society. Wherever the end loomed, masters and slaves frequently engaged in fervent negotiations, striking deals for early liberty that secured the compliance of the enslaved but further undermined the institution. Despite the North's pioneering step, ambivalence and hesitation in revolutionary abolitionism were rife. Gradual emancipation temporized the issue of freedom, bargaining away the sanctity of the slaves' property in their own bodies in exchange for slaveholders' investments in human chattel. Whereas every emancipation measure compensated slaveholders for their loss, none even considered remunerating the slaves for the time they, not to mention their progenitors, had been denied their right to self-ownership. Clearly, the compact was grossly unfair; former slaves began lives of freedom without even a starting stake in a competitive market society. Had any possessed the temerity to question the arrangement, no doubt they would have been told that the mouths of gift horses should not be examined too closely. But because of this, gradual emancipation cannot be viewed as an unqualified endorsement of the principle of self-ownership.

The issue remained unresolved, not just between North and South, but even where abolition happened. Freedom came partly because it was owed to blacks as an essential feature of their humanity, but also as an act of white benevolence. Critically, this left open the crucial question of blacks' innate characters. Instead of compensating emancipated slaves for their travails, emancipation acts fretted that impoverished freedpeople might become a "burden" or "public charge" on society. Rhode Island's, for instance, required emancipating masters to demonstrate that those they freed were capable of supporting themselves in freedom. The long periods of "apprenticeship" required by all the laws were intended not just to compensate slaveholders for lost labor, but to provide a period of transition, during which blacks—whose morals allegedly had degenerated under the malign influence of slavery—might be sufficiently educated to not pose a threat to the public welfare. As one petition urging abolition argued, "if the Emancipation be gradual," the government could take action to suppress the freedpeople's "gross, flagrant, Idleness," and thus ease "fear of the Enormities which the Negroes may commit."[12] In each state where gradual abolition occurred, concerns about the consequences of emancipation shaped emancipation bills, directed slaveholder resistance to them, and intensified racial hostility after emancipation.

Further south, slaveholders' economic interests combined with general fears of a postemancipation world to entirely inhibit the success of mass emancipation movements. In the Carolinas and Georgia, abolition proposals never had a chance of success. But in the upper South states around the Chesapeake, a handful of plans emerged among those Founders who associated abolition with a fulfillment of the Revolution's promises of universal liberty. Thomas Jefferson considered several proposals for a general emancipation, but always balked—ever fearful, he claimed, that "the public mind would not yet bear the proposition."[13] Such measures never gained much traction in the legislatures. In 1785, Virginia, which was most disposed to consider ending slavery, rejected a Methodist petition declaring abolition the fulfillment of "the Glorious and ever Memorable Revolution."[14]

Despite the failure of general emancipation in the upper South, individual slaveholders could be moved by their faith in the Revolution's cause to manumit their slaves. While unlike their northern cousins they could not countenance complete abolition, Virginia, Delaware, and Maryland did pass measures permitting or easing private manumission. As the records of legal slave manumissions attest, many owners acted on their dedication to revolutionary principles, freeing individual slaves out of a commitment to the idea of natural equality.[15] The Founding Fathers themselves proved to be more hesitant. Despite their qualms, most, like Jefferson, retained their slaves. The great Virginia patriot Patrick Henry found his own slave owning similarly troublesome. "Would any one believe that I am Master of Slaves of my own purchase!" he wondered. "I am drawn along by ye general Inconvenience of living without them; I will not, I cannot justify it."[16] Henry held slaves for his entire adult life, though he permitted a few to be freed upon his death. George Washington, who built his fortune on plantation slavery, declared that "there is not a man living who wishes more sincerely than I do, to see a plan adopted for the abolition of it." Nonetheless, like Henry, he provided for the freedom of his slaves only when death freed him of his dependence.[17] Wealthy planters such as Washington sometimes enacted long-term plans for the manumission of their slaves, thus easing the transition to freedom by providing their freedpeople with limited educations, skills, or a stake in free life. When Virginia planter Robert Carter III manumitted five hundred of his bondspersons in the years after the war, he successfully established them as virtual sharecroppers on lands owned by his family and neighbors. Others, perhaps less wealthy and certainly more cynical, used revolutionary rhetoric merely to relieve themselves of the cost and care of burdensome older or unhealthy slaves.

The impulse to manumit in the upper South had enormous consequences. Historian Ira Berlin calculates that Maryland's free black population increased from 1,817 in 1755 to 8,043 in 1790. A scant ten years later, it numbered nearly 20,000, an increase of 144 percent. Virginia's free black population numbered around 1,800 in 1782, only to jump to 12,766 by 1790. By the turn of the century, it had risen 58 percent, to 20,124.[18] These Revolution-inspired manumissions altered the geographical character of enslaved and free black life. Whereas in the lower South free people of color had always been, and remained, the relatively well-to-do descendants of mixed racial unions and favored manumittees, in the upper South a large free black population emerged of quite different character. Manumitted indiscriminately out of ideology, the emancipated people of color in the Chesapeake region often began freedom with very little, and fared poorly. In contrast, the paternalistic mode of manumission in the lower South produced a historically privileged class of black people, often blessed with incomparable occupational skills and wealth. Some even became slaveholders themselves. These social distinctions created important differences in the collective identity of African-descended people in the U.S. South. Whereas elite people of color in cities such as Charleston and Savannah might easily see themselves as radically distinct from the enslaved, those of the upper South could view themselves as far more closely related to them—in time, blood, and the meager resources they commanded.[19]

A COMPACT FOR THE GOOD OF AMERICA
Slavery in the Framing of the U.S. Constitution

If the Revolution unleashed ideological forces that inadvertently divided the new country on the issue of slavery, the new Constitution drafted in 1787 enshrined that geographic division. While the paradoxes of liberal property theory made emancipation gradual, the nature of the new federal compact made it sectional. When in 1776 the Second Continental Congress took up the mission of drafting a national government to bind the states together during the Revolution, it understood its task as constructing a union of states that could stand united on the world stage, while strictly limiting the power of any central authority. According to the Founders, the abuse of such power had led to the "tyranny" that had warranted the Revolution, after all. Under the resulting Articles of Confederation, the United States of America was not a nation, but "a firm league of friendship," in which "each state retains its sovereignty, freedom, and independence." Unsurprisingly, the Articles made no mention of slavery whatsoever, leaving the matter entirely to the states. The presence of bondage could only be inferred from several passages in the Articles; references to "free inhabitants" and "free citizens," for example, clearly acknowledged the presence of their opposites. A provision requiring states to return those who cross borders when they "flee from justice" may also have counted, as it formed the basis of the fugitive slave clause of the 1787 constitution.

As the country's constitution from 1777 to 1789, the Articles were too weak, and the government built on them foundered. With no national currency, interstate trade proved difficult. Lacking a federal judiciary, competing claims among the states were impossible to adjudicate. And deprived of the power to tax the states, the national government starved for want of revenue. An inability to compel the states to contribute to a collective military undermined the very purpose of the compact, while the impossibly high threshold for amending the document—unanimous consent of all states—made these problems impervious to rectification.

When in 1787 delegates from the states met in Philadelphia to resolve the problems with the Articles, they embarked on the ambitious aim of utterly recrafting the national compact. Over the course of the convention, which met from mid-May to mid-September, fifty-five delegates participated, hailing from all states but one. (Rhode Island boycotted, fearing the convention would do exactly as it did, and overturn the weak Articles, under which small states possessed the same power as larger ones. Rhode Island remained contrary, refusing to ratify the resulting Constitution until 1790, when other states began speaking of expropriating its territory should it fail to join the Union.) Historian David Brion Davis finds that twenty-five of the fifty-five, or nearly half, were documented owners of human property, though some held "unproductive" slaves.[20] All understood the need for a stronger central authority, just as all appreciated the desire for a great deal of state autonomy within any reformulated republic. Delegates approached the proceedings with trepidation, for distinct interests of widely variable state populations would surely clash: the large versus the small, the eastern versus the western, the commercial versus the agrarian. Over time, though, the contest between slaveholding and nonslaveholding states became paramount. As James Madison, the architect of the convention, reflected midway through, "It seemed now to be pretty well understood that the real difference of interests lay, not between the large & small but between the N. & Southn States. The institution of slavery & its consequences formed the line of discrimination."

These forces clashed repeatedly at the convention, with the final document incorporating three primary compromises over slavery, and many small ones. The most pressing issue concerned the counting of slaves for representation in the lower house of the legislature, the House of Representatives. Whereas each state would command an equal number of votes in the upper house, representation in the lower house would be apportioned relative to the population of each state. More populous states would receive more representatives. The same principle would apply in the Electoral College, which selected the president; here, each state would receive electors equal to its number of representatives in the lower house, plus two. Small states howled at the proposal, fearing that their interests would be overridden by the majority. So too did delegates from southern states, who represented nearly half of the entire population of the nation. They well understood that one-third of that number was composed of slaves. Were these slaves not counted for purposes of representation, the population of southern states would drop from 49 percent of the national population to 39 percent.[21] Much was at stake in ensuring the representation that would protect the institution that was at the heart of their society, though one deemed repugnant to republicanism by many.

The solution was the three-fifths compromise, written into article I, section 2 of the Constitution. For purposes of computing the population of the states for determining representation, three-fifths of each state's slave population would be added to its free population. Known at the time as the "federal ratio," this method of determining population for purposes of apportionment overvalued the slaveholding states. As critics of the provision feared,[22] the compromise artificially inflated the South's influence in the House and Electoral College from the founding of the nation to the Civil War. In the first Congress, southern states were apportioned thirty of sixty-five seats in the House (46 percent); without the three-fifths clause, the South would have been apportioned only eighteen seats in a smaller House of forty-four seats (41 percent). In the first Congress, then, the three-fifths clause accounted for an 11 percent bonus for southern power. These figures did not change appreciably after the first federal census, of 1790, more accurately calculated the states' populations. The apportionment rules already favored smaller states to larger; with only 40 percent of the nation's free population at the time of the 1790 census, the South benefitted from this as well.

In the Electoral College, the small-state bonus and the federal ratio combined to once again give the southern states disproportionate power. Under 1788 apportionment, southern states commanded forty-two of ninety-one electoral votes (46 percent), despite being home to only 40 percent of the national free population. In the South, then, each individual commanded a larger share of each electoral vote than in the North. In the southern states, each free person's share of an electoral vote amounted to 107 percent of the national average, while in the northern states each free person's share of an electoral vote stood at 96 percent of the national average. The situation only got worse after the first federal census. Then, each electoral vote in the South represented only 20,525 people, while each in the North represented 25,590, a difference of 25 percent. Under the apportionment for 1792, each free southerner's share of an electoral vote was 113 percent of the national average, while the comparable figure for northerners was only 91 percent.[23] For the next seventy-eight years, the three-fifths clause would exercise extraordinary and far-reaching effects on American politics. In no other slaveholding society of the Atlantic was any slave power ever given such an enormous gift.

A second major compromise over slavery in the Constitution regarded provisions for coping with the problem of fugitive slaves. All conceded the role of a new federal government in returning to their home states those who "flee from justice" across state lines, just as the Articles of Confederation had done. Slave fugitives, though, constituted a knotty problem. For one, slaves were a kind of property apt, as was particularly evident during the Revolution, to "steal itself" by running away. What obligation did states relinquishing slavery have to return these fugitives? Did slaves fleeing to free states become free, as the Somerset principle suggested? Under the Articles, the problem was sufficiently well understood to have inspired efforts to legislate the return of fugitives. For example, the Northwest Ordinance, which Congress passed in 1787 to organize new western territories in the upper Mississippi Valley and Great Lakes region, prohibited slavery, but also guaranteed that "any person" escaping into the new territory "may be lawfully reclaimed" by those from whom they had fled.[24] Virtually the same language found its way into the new constitution. Article IV, section 2 included a clause providing that those "held to Service or Labour" in a state who, "escaping into another," would be "delivered up" to the owning party. The federal government had put itself in the business of returning runaway slaves.

A third major appearance of slavery in the Constitution concerned the international trade in slaves to the American states. This trade was a particular target of antislavery activists. Whereas domestic masters could (however disingenuously) claim that they merely purchased those who were already enslaved, treated them well, and offered them the privileges of Christian civilization, the trade itself had become notorious for its inescapable reduction of humans to mere property. The Continental Congress had prohibited importations of slaves from Britain in 1774, but the measure was designed more as a trade embargo against the enemy than as a humanitarian gesture for the slaves.[25] The Revolution halted the trade, and following the war many states maintained the prohibition as a matter of principle. As a facet of international trade, the commerce in slaves clearly fell under the purview of the new constitution. If the national government was to play a role in regulating trade between the states and foreign entities, it could surely speak to the "odious commerce" in slaves. Ultimately, delegates agreed on a provision that protected the slave trade for twenty years, during which Congress could levy a duty on each African imported into the country. After that point, Congress had the freedom, if it wished, to regulate the trade in some other way. James Madison excoriated the measure, predicting that "twenty years will produce all the mischief that can be apprehended from the liberty to import slaves." But Gouverneur Morris of Pennsylvania hoped it would "form a bargain among the Northern and Southern States."[26]

Such compacts conceded much to the slaveholding states: latent sanction for the practice of slaveholding, disproportionate representation in the House of Representatives and Electoral College based on their slave populations, federal protection of slave property through the fugitive slave and militia clauses (which guaranteed federal assistance in the event of slave insurrections), and federal protection of the supply of slaves from Africa for at least twenty years. Other components of the Constitution protected slavery indirectly by, for example, prohibiting the taxation of export goods produced largely through slave labor, or declaring that only "citizens" (hence, not slaves, and indeed not many free blacks) could access federal courts. In exchange, it had conceded virtually nothing but the Commerce Clause—the portion of article I, section 8 granting Congress the power to regulate trade between the nation and foreign entities, Native American tribes, and the states themselves. (Whereas the southern states wanted the Constitution to require a two-thirds majority for passing commerce measures in Congress, mercantile interests in the northeastern states wished for, and won, a simple majority.)

Southern delegates delighted in their success. Edmund Randolph argued to his Virginia constituents that in the recent convention "there was not a member of the Virginia delegation who had *the smallest suspicion of the abolition of slavery.*" Charles Cotesworth Pinckney of South Carolina crowed that "we have made the best terms for the security of this species of property it was in our power to make."[27] How had the South won so much, and at so little cost? The question looms particularly large when we acknowledge that it was precisely here, at the moment of the nation's founding, that the "house divided" began. Why did the Framers of the Constitution not take the opportunity to destroy slavery once and for all?

It was not that many Framers were unwilling to disavow slavery, or constrain the institution in any way. At the convention, Gouverneur Morris declared slavery "a nefarious institution" and "the curse of heaven." Likewise, Maryland's Luther Martin declared the importation of slaves "inconsistent with the principles of the revolution and dishonorable to the American character." (Martin held slaves at the time, as did others, like George Mason and James Madison, who also disavowed aspects of slavery at the convention.) At no point was contention more evident than on the vexed question of slaves as property. The issue came up foremost in the discussions that yielded the three-fifths compromise. How would apportionment in the House and Electoral College be determined: on the basis of people, or property? Which were slaves? Perversely, northern delegates tended to argue that for purposes of representation slaves should be considered strictly property and not people, while southerners contended that slaves should be counted among the general population, and thus as people. The logic was unmistakably mercenary: because counting slaves as people increased the South's representation in the House and Electoral College, southern delegates argued that slaves should be included "*equally* with the Whites" for purposes of representation.[28]

Unsurprisingly, northern delegates disagreed, for equally utilitarian reasons. Elbridge Gerry of Massachusetts resented that slaves should be included in the free population only for purposes of apportionment. Why should "blacks, who were property in the South," he declared, count toward representation "any more than the Cattle & horses of the North"? Asked Gouverneur Morris, "Upon what principle is it that the slaves shall be computed in the representation? Are they men? Then make them Citizens and let them vote. Are they property? Why then is no other property included?" William Patterson of New Jersey "could regard negro slaves in no light but as property. They are no free agents, have no personal liberty, no faculty of acquiring property, but on the contrary are themselves property, & like other property entirely at the will of the Master."[29]

Southerners turned the argument around. Pierce Butler of South Carolina responded that the matter at issue was the relative wealth of the states. Because "the labour of a slave in S. Carola. was as productive & valuable as that of a freeman in Massts.," he believed that "an equal representation ought to be allowed for them in a Government which was instituted principally for the protection of property." There it was again: if slaves were property, then the government had an interest in protecting masters' right to own them. As Pinckney of South Carolina affirmed, "property in slaves should not be exposed to danger under a Government instituted for the protection of property."[30] It worked; northern delegates accommodated. The three-fifths clause offered a compromise to southern delegates who, for purposes of representation only, wished slaves to be counted fully as people, and to northern delegates who wished them not to count at all. It was utterly inconsistent and entirely pragmatic, acknowledging the humanity of the enslaved, but only partially, and for reasons of sheer power.[31]

Many contend that in enacting such measures the Framers sacrificed abolition to secure national unity. The loss of abolition, it is suggested, was the price of keeping the lower South states in the fragile national compact. Pointed statements by representatives of the South support this contention. Scant weeks after signing the Declaration of Independence, South Carolina's Thomas Lynch had raised the threat of disunion in Congress, declaring "an end to the confederation" should questions persist regarding the legitimacy of slave property.[32] During the constitutional convention itself, lower South delegates repeatedly threatened disunion as the cost of ignoring their vital interests. "The true question at present," announced South Carolina's John Rutledge at a contentious moment, "is whether the Southern states shall or shall not be parties to the Union." When talk ran high of prohibiting the further importation of bound Africans, Charles Pinckney threatened that "South Carolina can never receive the plan if it prohibits the slave trade"; any measure prejudicial against slave states would be tantamount to "an exclusion of South Carolina from the Union."[33]

Time and again, opposing delegates acquiesced. In this instance, Roger Sherman of Connecticut yielded, suggesting that "it was expedient to have as few objections as possible to the proposed scheme of government." When dissatisfied with the question of counting slaves in the representation of southern states, William R. Davie of North Carolina declared that his state "would never confederate" on such terms, and that "the business was at an end." In response, Gouverneur Morris conceded that "it is in vain for the Eastern States to insist on what the Southn. States will never agree to"; he had come "to form a compact for the good of America." Hugh Williamson of North Carolina effectively captured the mood around these concessions to slavery. He declared "that both in opinion and practice, he was against slavery; but thought it more in favor of humanity . . . to let in South Carolina, and Georgia, on those terms than to exclude them from the Union."[34] In an important sense, then, slavery's defenders at the convention thought they were ransoming the Union in exchange for constitutional protections of slavery.

While this ransom thesis correctly assesses southern delegates' interests, it tends to exonerate the Framers as a whole. To argue that the Framers sought to destroy slavery but were stymied by others who sought first to protect it is to draw a false distinction and misplace responsibility. After all, the southern delegates were Framers, too—a fact often forgotten when the convention's antislavery efforts are praised. That some Framers gave way to others on so momentous an issue is hardly flattering to either party. Neither is it clear that the southern delegates possessed the power to scuttle the constitutional bargain. During the convention, the Carolinas and Georgia led the way in seeking to protect slavery and the slave trade. Had the other states not acquiesced, it is unlikely the Union would have been rent asunder. Historian Gary Nash sagely notes that it is unthinkable that the southern states, having risked all on independence, and suffered through the worst of the Revolution, would then have aligned themselves once again with Britain. Left alone, those states faced imminent crisis. Spain bordered them to the south, while Creek Indians threatened from the west. With less than 16 percent of the free population of the United States, and almost 35 percent of the slave, the lower South states could ill afford to go it alone.[35] George Washington offered the prevailing reasoning: "If a weak State, with powerful tribes of Indians in its rear and the Spanish on its flank, do not incline to embrace a strong general Government there must, I should think, be either wickedness, or insanity in their conduct."[36]

Other factors, then, must explain northern delegates' acquiescence to southern petulance. While many at the convention publicly disfavored slavery, very few seemed much inclined to do anything about it. Most Framers viewed dismantling chattel bondage as an issue wholly secondary to the primary task of forming a new nation. Regardless of their personal relation to the slavery question, all were willing to forego immediate action, expecting later generations to tackle the problem. Roger Sherman believed that "the abolition of slavery seemed to be going on in the United States and that the good sense of the several states would probably by degrees compleat it." Abraham Baldwin offered some vague hope that his state of Georgia might move in such a direction, but only if unprovoked: "If left to herself, she may probably put a stop to the evil," he offered weakly.[37]

For two primary reasons, delegates looked to the future rather than undertake hard work in the present. First, slavery and slave trading were practices so pervasive, and so deeply entrenched, that even the most ardent advocates of abolitionism viewed slavery's extirpation as the work of decades rather than weeks. For all the talk of slavery's incongruence with republican principles, and even despite the baby steps being taken in some northern states to gradually end the practice, slavery was a national institution, woven into the warp and woof of American life. Slavery and slave trading were being practiced almost everywhere in the United States. Despite the emergence of gradual abolition in the North, the region was still invested heavily in the slave economy. Northern seaport cities built ships that traded in slaves, just as northern financiers offered the credit and insurance necessary to conduct the trade. New England delegates at the federal convention voted for the twenty-year protection of the slave trade partly because of the enormous role their ports played in the commerce in slaves and slave-produced goods. What was more, slavery was quickly overrunning national borders, trailing pioneers into the trans-Appalachian West. The first federal census found that nearly seventy-five thousand white settlers had already flooded into the Kentucky Territory, bringing with them over twelve thousand slaves. Regardless of the desires of elites sitting in Philadelphia in the summer of 1787, slaves were in fact being rapidly moved into the West—a land of contested boundaries, native animosities, and intense international rivalries. Secretary of War Henry Knox described the frontier as a place wherein only "the sword of the Republic" was sufficient to compel "a due administration of justice, and the preservation of peace."[38]

Understanding the remarkable expansion of slavery into the West thus points to a second factor that helps explain why the Framers foundered so badly on the slavery issue. Slavery was not merely a national concern, but an international one. George Washington's insight on the foreign enemies threatening Georgia and South Carolina reminds us that the framing of the Constitution occurred not on a national stage, but the world stage. According to political scientist David C. Hendrickson, the Constitution can be viewed as a "peace pact" designed to resolve differences between thirteen distinct and rival nations existing among a host of other nations and empires.[39] Think, then, of the Constitution as a unique form of union—"unexampled in its origin," according to Madison[40]—that bound together fully independent polities as a means of mutual security *from each other* as much as from foreign enemies. John Adams perceived the "manifest danger" posed to the states from both foreign powers and "from one another."[41] Pierce Butler of South Carolina believed the interests of the slaveholding and nonslaveholding states "to be as different as the interests of Russia and Turkey."[42] Given such a view, it is easier to understand why the Framers envisioned a national government that was designed to deal only with matters between the states, or between the states and foreign powers. Local concerns and "domestic institutions" were to be left wholly and exclusively to state governments. Abraham Baldwin of Georgia "had conceived national objects alone to be before the Convention"; questions relating to slavery "were of a local nature" and thus off the table. Furthermore, as residents of a state on the periphery of the nation, Georgians feared they would lose "equal advantage" and thus stood against "yielding national powers" to a central government.[43] Local rule, particularly on slavery, offered the best security for the southern states, and entirely plausible given the intellectual framework that reigned.

None of this is to excuse the Framers in the least. Rather, it is to appreciate the key role that federalism played in bequeathing the nation its thorniest, and ultimately bloodiest, problem. The Framers were so committed to this form of union that the thought of a new central government imposing its power to abolish so sweeping and deeply rooted a practice as slavery was literally inconceivable. *The Federalist Papers*, the collection of essays written in defense of the Constitution during the ratification debates by James Madison, Alexander Hamilton, and John Jay, incessantly stressed that the new Constitution envisioned a collection of states, with national power sufficient only to keep the Union together. In the parlance of the day, it was a "federal" instrument rather than a "national" one. As Madison put it in *Federalist 39*, "the proposed government cannot be deemed a *national* one; since its jurisdiction extends to certain enumerated objects only, and leaves to the several States a residuary and inviolable sovereignty over all other objects." The only purpose of the overarching government was "to prevent an appeal to the sword and a dissolution of the compact."[44] This view of the overarching government's relation to the states permitted no room to impose so great a change in the "domestic relations" of a given state as that which the abolition of slavery would have entailed.

While the entire extirpation of slavery in America seemed beyond the bounds of plausibility at the convention, some Framers still sought to circumscribe slavery as much as possible. Abundantly aware of their limitations, they worked to ensure that the Constitution would do as little as possible to endorse the institution. The Framers sought to create a Constitution that would serve merely as the scaffolding of a union, and thus stand ostensibly moot on the morality of local practices. While to destroy slavery stood outside the purview of the convention, to excise as many references to it as possible stood within it. This effort succeeded to a large degree. Of course the word "slavery" itself does not appear in the Constitution, and would not until the Thirteenth Amendment used it to prohibit the practice explicitly in 1865; instead, the Constitution contains references only to "other persons," "persons held to service or labor," or "importation of Persons."

This was by design. Privately, John Dickinson, the Delaware statesman who had freed his slaves in 1777, fretted that "omitting the *Word* will be regarded as an Endeavour to conceal a principle of which we are ashamed."[45] Others saw it as a deliberate effort to avoid condoning slavery outright. Elbridge Gerry of Massachusetts argued that while the convention "had nothing to do with the conduct of the states as to slaves," it "ought to be careful not to give any sanction to it." Madison boldly declared that he "thought it wrong to admit in the Constitution the idea that there could be property in men."[46] This, then, became the Constitution's slavery, as well as its antislavery: chattel bondage as an acknowledged and legal practice, but not a social good, and one that might at some point in the future be eradicated. If some in later generations could label the Constitution "a Covenant with Death, an Agreement with Hell,"[47] others could claim something else. As Abraham Lincoln would put it in his Cooper Union Address of February 1860, the Framers viewed slavery "as an evil not to be extended, but to be tolerated and protected only because of and so far as its actual presence among us makes that toleration and protection a necessity."[48]

THIRTEEN OTHER COLONIES
Slavery Elsewhere in the Revolutionary Atlantic

It is easy to forget that the mainland colonies' departure from their mother country dented but did not destroy Britain's New World ambitions. As historian Andrew Jackson O'Shaunnessy reminds us, England's Atlantic empire included thirteen other colonies that did not rebel.[49] Even after the Treaty of Paris consummated the independence of the United States in 1783, England retained many of its possessions in the hemisphere: in mainland North America, Newfoundland, Nova Scotia, newly acquired Quebec, and holdings around Hudson Bay; in Central and South America, Belize, the Mosquito Coast, British Guiana, and the Falkland Islands. In the Caribbean, Britain controlled Barbados, St. Kitts and Nevis, Antigua, the Bahamas, Montserrat, Jamaica, Tortola and the British Virgin Islands, Dominica, Saint Vincent and the Grenadines, Grenada, and Saint Lucia. These Caribbean colonies, especially the great sugar producers of Barbados and Jamaica, constituted the most valuable of Britain's holdings in the Western Hemisphere. The same was true for other nations, of course. In the Treaty of Paris of 1763, the peace that ended the French and Indian War, France considered its sugar island of Guadeloupe—occupying but 620 square miles—a fair trade for all 200,000 square miles of its claims to Canada.[50] The calculation was not unreasonable, given the enormous wealth represented by Caribbean holdings. Between 1768 and 1772, North American goods constituted only 11.4 percent of all British imports by value; in contrast, goods from the British West Indies accounted for 27 percent, or nearly two-and-a-half times as much.[51] As grievous as was Britain's loss of the mainland thirteen, it would have paled in comparison to the deprivation of the British West Indies.

The economic and strategic significance of these islands reveals much about the American Revolution and the way it played out. Why, for instance, did only thirteen colonies revolt? Why not others on the mainland, such as Nova Scotia and Newfoundland? Why not any in the Caribbean? The answers suggest the significance of the mainland thirteen's unique position in the British Empire, poised between the exploitation model represented by many Caribbean colonies and the alternative templates of settler or trade colony. Recall that the colonists' main grievance against their mother country was commercial restraint amounting to a violation of liberty. These complaints came loudest from colonies like Massachusetts, where large settler populations were building cities with economies that increasingly competed with rather than complemented Britain's. Merchants and manufacturers chafed under imperial trade restraints that benefitted the mother country at the expense of the colony, such as trade duties on foreign goods that artificially increased their costs in American markets and requirements that only English ships could carry goods to and from the colonies. The marginal economies of British Canada shared few of these concerns. Lightly populated and even more lightly ruled, Newfoundland enjoyed freedom from the Navigation Acts, and thus had little to gain through independence. Nova Scotia was more populous, yet sparse enough to rely heavily on British protection and support. While many in that colony spoke up on behalf of American liberty during the crisis, a large British naval presence and its isolation from other colonies to the south kept it neutral. During the war, two small military expeditions failed to claim it for America, and the colony remained British.

Different interests compelled the British West Indies to maintain their ties to England. Whereas mercantile trade regulation stifled the growth of the mainland economies, the British West Indies actually gained from it. Parliament had passed the Molasses Act in 1733 at the behest of Caribbean planters, whom they hoped would benefit from the artificially high prices their sugar products would bring from residents of the empire. The Crown would enjoy much-needed revenue from protective duties imposed on sugar imported from the Caribbean to the mainland colonies. Mainlanders easily evaded the act through a widespread system of smuggling, which brought in cheaper sugar, molasses, and rum from the French Caribbean. When the Molasses Act was revised as the Sugar Act of 1764, Parliament's earnest enforcement of protective trade regulation in fact began the pattern of resistance among the mainland colonies that led to the Revolution. Rather than uniting the colonies, then, the slave economy divided them. While the northern colonies grew to chafe under a protection that rarely aided them, the monocultural West Indies lived and died by such policies. And the great wealth they accrued had afforded them the political capital required to ensure that their interests took precedence over those of the mainland north.

External security also compelled the West Indies to remain loyal to Britain. As isolated islands whose security lay largely independent of each other, Caribbean colonies faced the constant threat of invasion. From the founding of their New World settlements, European powers had traded West Indian islands with bewildering frequency. For example, English and French settlers fought over the tiny island of St. Kitts since its inception in 1624, uniting only to massacre the natives who stood in their way, or to defend themselves against Spanish raids.

Three times between 1624 and 1713, the French took complete control over the island, only to cede back a portion to England at the treaty table. The islands, then, lacked some of the military luxuries that space conferred on the mainland colonies. There, wide frontiers and vast distances served the Revolution well, making complete conquest almost impossible given a large and unyielding population. The situation was far more precarious in the islands, and the Revolution offered excellent opportunities for England's many rivals to exploit its imperial dismemberment. In the course of the conflict, France, then Spain and the Netherlands, declared war on England, and the islands changed hands once more.

The multinational fracas that emerged in the Caribbean dramatically impacted the war's outcome. As soon as France's entry threatened the West Indies, Britain found itself both spread thin and diverted. Troops were withdrawn from the mainland to defend the islands. In 1778, Britain conceded control of Philadelphia, the U.S. capital, to take the French island of St. Lucia. And the decisive victory at Yorktown in 1781 proved possible only because British ships had occupied themselves raiding the Dutch island of St. Eustatius while the French navy moved north to blockade British armies under General Charles Cornwallis on the banks of the Chesapeake. Even after Yorktown, the war continued for nearly two years, as Britain—having resolved to forego the conflict on the mainland—fought to gain back its losses in the Caribbean.[52]

In addition to the military vulnerabilities inherent in island colonies, white society there differed markedly from mainland analogues. As exploitation colonies dedicated to staple production, Caribbean islands offered little room for white people in roles other than on plantations or in the small bureaucracy. On the mainland, climate and geography made for "neo-Europes"[53] that drew long-term settlers of a middling sort; in the Caribbean, these factors dissuaded long-term habitation. The same climate that suited the region for tropical production imposed an atrocious disease environment on the islands, with staggering mortality even for those not compelled to toil under barbarous work regimes.

By the second half of the eighteenth century, absentee plantation ownership prevailed throughout much of the West Indies, in sharp contrast to the settler-creole ethos of the mainland.[54] To the extent possible, planter-entrepreneurs went to the islands (or, better yet, sent someone in their stead), extracted what they could from their subordinates and slaves, and returned home, having left few social institutions in their wake. For sure, those on the islands jealously guarded their precious property rights alongside their neighbors to the north. West Indian statesmen insisted on the right to be represented directly in the governments that taxed them, for example. "We think of the Doctrine of internal Taxations," one declared, "like our Brethren on the Continent." Conservative observers feared the spread of "principles of Republicanism," declaring their alarm that some West Indians had "caught the infection from America."[55] Some even went so far as Samuel Martin of Antigua, who adopted mainland metaphors when he asserted that the Stamp Act had reduced the colonies to the status of "slaves, to arbitrary power."[56] Overall, though, enormous wealth combined with an absentee mentality to create severely hierarchical social orders, which did little to nurture revolutionary egalitarianism—not even the tainted variety of herrenvolk democracy found in Virginia.

For all their talk of liberty, though, Caribbean planters depended mightily on the empire, for exploitation colonies were hotbeds of domestic insurrection. The fear of slave revolt provided the final, and crucial, reason why West Indian planters maintained their ties with Britain. All slave societies confronted the possibility of insurrection, but the colonies of the Caribbean were exceptional. Oppressive work regimes, constant infusions of young African men not born into slavery, and—most of all—massively skewed racial ratios, which rendered whites a small minority of the population, made them fertile breeding grounds for collective, violent resistance. In the middle of the eighteenth century, 85 percent of the population of the British Caribbean was enslaved. In Jamaica, the figure rose to over 90 percent.[57] West Indian planters sat on powder kegs. Between 1735 and the establishment of the United States in 1783, over a dozen revolts or advanced conspiracies occurred in the British Caribbean alone. Local authorities crushed planned rebellions in Antigua and Montserrat, while in the 1770s uprisings broke out on Tobago four times in five years. Jamaica was also prone, confronting major conspiracies in 1742, 1745, and 1766, and the largest open revolt to that time in the history of the British Caribbean: Tacky's Rebellion of 1760.

Contemporaries unanimously acknowledged the need for regular soldiers in the sugar islands. Jamaican administrator Edward Long recounted that planters were willing to pay for the presence of British arms to protect them "not so much from the French or Spaniards, as against the machinations of the many thousand slaves" who "grow the more formidable from their multitude."[58] Only well-disciplined regular troops—not unreliable local militias, and certainly not the runaway black "maroons" who lived outside the plantation regime but often made uneasy peace with it—could be counted on to prevent the "massacre and desolation" envisioned by the slaves' "diabolical plots" and "open Insurrection."[59] The difference in attitude toward British soldiers on the mainland and on the islands could not have been more clear. In 1770, the quartering of British regulars in colonial homes provoked the Boston Massacre; in 1771, the assemblies of Dominica, Grenada, and Tobago all demanded more of just such troops to protect their colonies from insurrection.[60] A few years later, during the Revolution itself, authorities discovered a major conspiracy on St. Kitts. Contemporaries suspected that another on Jamaica had been inspired by slaves' awareness of the "present unhappy disputes" with the mainland colonies, which drained forces from the island, and spread ideas of liberty through the *"House-bred Slave"* who overheard talk of the Revolution in his master's house.[61]

Compared to the Caribbean colonies, then, the mainland thirteen confronted fewer internal and external security threats, benefitted less (or not at all) from British trade policies, and nurtured strains of republican political ideology that combined to make them much likelier candidates for revolution. Yet the mainland thirteen differed markedly among themselves, with southern colonies inclining much more closely to the Caribbean exploitation model which benefitted from empire, and the northern toward a growing settler model that did not. This was evident in the lower South's reticence to enter the war, and in its protracted conservatism in prosecuting it. Both owed to the security needs of large slave societies. Southern planters' revolutionary enthusiasms were deeply tempered by the insecurity introduced by their slave populations.

Even after the war, with the immediate danger of insurrection past, the massive disruption of the system left a deep impression on the political sensibilities of southern patriots. In Virginia, the magnate Robert Carter Nicholas objected to a proposed state bill of rights because it included the phrase "all men are by nature equally free and independent." As slaves might use such language to seek their freedom, he feared that such a statement would be "the forerunner or pretext of civil convulsion."[62] South Carolina legislator Henry William De Saussure similarly dreaded broad assertion of the principle that "equality is the natural condition of man," for doing so would "instantly free the unfortunate slaves. . . . Inevitable ruin would follow both to the whites and to the blacks, and this fine country would be deluged with blood, and desolated by fire and sword."[63] So well understood were these sentiments that during the war itself, Britain bet all on a southern strategy, premised on the hope that Loyalists in the slave colonies would flock to the British cause, if only because they feared the threat of slave insurrection.

The southern states then, and particularly South Carolina and Georgia, were in many ways more naturally aligned to the interests of the Caribbean planters they often closely resembled. Both sets of colonies existed largely for their plantations. The slave populations of the mainland South did not match the 90 percent concentration of a Jamaica, but they could approach it. At the time of the first federal census in 1790, Beaufort and Charlestown Counties in South Carolina were over three-quarters enslaved. In Virginia nearly half the counties had a preponderance of slaves, and five were more than 60 percent enslaved.[64] Only geographic ties to other mainland colonies, and a richer tradition of white settlement, kept Georgia and South Carolina in the fold. As a consequence, the slave states of the South made strange national bedfellows with their northern counterparts. True, slavery was a shared institution. It had helped all of the colonies prosper, and slave labor contributed to the wealth of every British Atlantic holding. Yet varied dependence on slavery deeply divided the colonies, and shaped the Union they forged once independent. While the northern states steered themselves ever tentatively toward a world where people could not be property, the southern ones committed themselves ever more heartily to the principle. These divergent societies were held together in a federal compact that had been constructed loosely, in large measure to succor slaveholders who feared that strong national power would doom their bedrock institution.

The American Revolution had a final, largely unforeseen, consequence for the state of Atlantic slavery that proved significant indeed for the American "house divided." The loss of the mainland thirteen vastly weakened the "slave power" of the British Caribbean, and set England on the path of complete abolition. For the West Indies, the trouble with independence was that it disrupted vital trade connections. The mainland colonies served as crucial markets for Caribbean coffee, molasses, and rum. More important, the mainland supplied the islands with most of the basic goods necessary to run the plantation system. With all possible arable land on the Caribbean islands given over to the production of staples such as sugar, coffee, tobacco, indigo, and cotton, the West Indies depended on the continent for everything from basic foodstuffs to the materials required to package and ship their produce. Historian Selwyn H. H. Carrington puts it aptly, "In the 1770s the British West Indies received from the mainland colonies approximately one third of their dried fish; almost all of their pickled fish; seven eights of their oats; almost three quarter of their corn; nearly all of their peas, beans, butter, cheese and onions; half of their flour, quarter of their rice; five sixths of their pine, oak, and cedar boards; over half of their slaves; nearly all of their hoops; most of their horses, sheep, hogs, and poultry; and almost all of their soap and candles."[65]

The Revolution deprived the West Indies of this supply. In 1775, Parliament passed the Prohibitory Act, which imposed a naval blockade on the rebelling colonies, forbidding virtually all trade with them. On the islands, supplies dwindled, prices rose, and production fell. Nevis planter John Pinney complained that "the unhappy contest with American united with our internal distressed situation is truly alarming and will, I am afraid, cause the ruin of every individual."[66] When the war expanded into the Caribbean itself, matters only worsened. From 1775 to 1783, exports of sugar from the British West Indies to Great Britain fell from over 2 million hundredweight to not even 1.6 million. Rum exports fell from 2.3 million gallons to 1.9, and coffee from 55,000 hundredweight to 20,000.[67] These figures do not even address the loss of the American market for these goods. After the war, things remained bad. Britain maintained many restrictions on American trade to the British West Indies, but strenuous efforts to supply the islands from Canadian and British sources could not compensate for the loss. A vigorous smuggling regime and the slow reestablishment of trade with America proved insufficient to maintain the arc of growth the West Indies had exhibited before the war.

While historians debate whether or not the American Revolution initiated an uninterrupted decline in the plantation economy of the British West Indies, it is clear that the conflict damaged it badly, at least in the short term, and left a legacy of long-term weakness. As one measure, the supply of slaves to the British Caribbean fell from just over 150,000 in the period from 1771 to 1775 to not even 67,000 in the next five years. While this was undoubtedly a blessing for the Africans spared the horrors of Caribbean bondage, these numbers further reflect the damage done to the plantation economy. Caribbean slave populations could never reproduce themselves, as natural growth gave way to skewed gender ratios, oppressive work regimes, malnourishment, and devastating diseases. While slave imports to the British Caribbean rebounded to prewar levels in the 1790s, the lost years represented a devastating opportunity cost that could never be recouped.[68] The planter interest of the British West Indies never fully recovered.

Worse than the economic price of the Revolution were the political costs. The departure of the mainland thirteen left the West Indian planters bereft of powerful allies. While distance separated mainland from Caribbean planters, strong commercial ties had always linked them closely. Barbadian planters had begun South Carolina's plantation society, and South Carolina proprietors were granted control of the Bahamas. Movers and shakers in the Atlantic world crossed the Caribbean-mainland divide with regularity. For example, Eliza Lucas was born in Antigua in 1723, moved to South Carolina in her teens, took control over her family's plantation, and used Caribbean seedlings to develop the indigo that fueled much of the colony's staple economy. Her son, Charles Cotesworth Pinckney, become a prominent statesman and fierce defender of planter interests in the constitutional convention. The Revolution thus rent asunder a British plantation complex that once stretched from Barbados to the Potomac. The West Indian planter lobby in London could never again count on mainland friends. Likewise, southern planters in the United States found themselves steadily isolated in their new country, as slavery became a feature "peculiar" to their region of the nation.

In addition, the forces unleashed by the Revolution badly undermined the ideological foundations of slavery in the British West Indies. Some Britons, like Edmund Burke, had been sympathetic to the colony's pleas for liberty, and many, like Samuel Johnson, had connected that concern with the plight of the enslaved. It was virtually inevitable that revolutionary calls for abolition would emerge in England as well as in the United States. The antislavery spirit of the revolutionary era was a transatlantic affair. It drew sustenance from communication networks that stretched across the ocean, connecting Anthony Benezet and John Woolman in America with Granville Sharp and Thomas Clarkson in Britain, and these to Abbé Raynal and Abbé Grégoire in France. Antislavery societies sprang up in all three nations. In Philadelphia in 1775, Quakers founded the first antislavery organization in the Atlantic, the Society for the Relief of the Free Negroes Unlawfully Held in Bondage, later to become known as the Pennsylvania Abolition Society. Others, like the New York Manumission Society, quickly followed, and by 1793 similar institutions had appeared in Rhode Island, Delaware, Maryland, Virginia, and New Jersey; in 1794, delegates from all came together in the first American Convention for Promoting the Abolition of Slavery and Improving the Condition of the African Race. In Britain, reformers began the Society for Effecting the Abolition of the Slave Trade (also known as the Society for the Abolition of the Slave Trade) in 1787, while the Society of the Friends of the Blacks (Société des Amis des Noirs) began in France in 1788. Often composed of religious dissenters or political radicals, these institutions organized the first public campaigns to attack slavery, mobilizing public opinion through petition drives and aggressive media campaigns. They fought legal battles on behalf of slaves and free blacks, established benevolent institutions designed to "uplift" the free, and publicized the first accounts of slavery by African-descended people themselves.[69]

British abolitionists were notable in this latter regard, publishing the very first slave narrative in the English language, *A Narrative of the Most Remarkable Particulars in the Life of James Albert Ukawsaw Gronniosaw, an African Prince*, published in 1772. Others of note appeared shortly after—works such as *Letters of the Late Ignatius Sancho, an African* (1782), Ottobah Cugoano's *Thoughts and Sentiments on the Evil of Slavery and Commerce of the Human Species* (1787), and the most famous, *The Interesting Narrative of the Life of Olaudah Equiano, or Gustavus Vassa the African* (1789). Through these publications, British antislavers built important links to the Atlantic's first black activists. Cugoano had ties to abolitionist Granville Sharp, artist Richard Cosway, and the poet-artist William Blake; Equiano enjoyed the patronage of Selina Hastings, Countess of Huntingdon, and also worked closely with Sharp. For English abolitionists, the narratives functioned as important propaganda tools, lending critical moral authority to the movement. How could one oppose slavery, after all, without evidence that slaves did not like bondage?

The new British antislavery campaigns weakened slavery in the Caribbean by undertaking practical efforts, from founding educational institutions for African-descended people to sponsoring projects to colonize freed slaves in West

Africa. In the islands, thousands of blacks had risked their lives defending the empire, and deals struck during the war remained to be honored. Many of those slaves who had traded their service for liberty found themselves transported elsewhere in the empire: to Nova Scotia, where they were given substandard land and subjected to considerable prejudice; to London, which similarly marginalized them; or to the Bahamas, where they encountered lives not far different from those they had left. (The slaves of the white Loyalists who had evacuated America retained their status, and found themselves scattered, with their owners, throughout the British Atlantic.) British abolitionists lamented the plight of these blacks, and established a settlement for them on the western coast of Africa, in a land they named Sierra Leone. Designed as a showplace for the possibilities of emancipation, early efforts to establish such colonies foundered—underfunded and ill prepared, decimated by disease, and imperiled by hostile local people. A 1787 attempt failed utterly, but the next one, in 1792, took root, providing an important model for later abolitionists in other countries.

The emergence of a transatlantic abolition movement not only undercut the slave power of the British West Indies, but also dealt the entire institution of New World slavery an ideological blow from which it would never fully recover. The planter interest everywhere had been challenged. New bases of antislavery feeling and support had been seeded in the Revolution's new ideological challenge to the principle of property in man. Public opinion in the most highly developed and economically progressive metropoles of the Atlantic world had become divided. No matter how profitable slavery would be at particular places and moments, it would henceforth always be opposed by vocal and concerted detractors, sometimes backed by the power of the state. In the United States, the matter would take extraordinary time and effort to resolve, for the nation had been founded so peculiarly. In a draft of his first inaugural address, George Washington looked forward to the day when "mankind will reverse the absurd position that *the many* were made for *the few*; and that they will not continue slaves in one part of the globe, when they can become freemen in another."[70] He chose not to utter those words; nor did he ever acknowledge that the country he had helped found was not truly united, but was, in fact, part slave and part free.

The Early Republic

CHAPTER 3

A House Dividing

*Atlantic Slavery and Abolition in
the Era of the Early Republic*

TO DIE FOR THIS LIBERTY
Revolution and Abolition in the Caribbean

The United States encountered its earliest and most pressing foreign
policy crisis just as the states were arguing over ratification of the new Constitution. The Atlantic-wide revolutions that mainland colonists inaugurated in 1775
soon struck other European empires, challenging the young nation to grapple
with the logical limits of its dedication to universal principles of human equality. Huge implications for slavery in the United States attended these events. In
vastly expanding the realm of freedom in the Western Hemisphere, the Atlantic revolutions contributed to the isolation of the remaining slave societies. In
the United States, these events inadvertently contributed to the expansion and
growth of slavery in the American South, just as the North was gradually ex-
tinguishing slavery and experiencing a revolution in manufacturing and market
relations.

In important ways, the French Revolution of 1789 began in America. At
least, roots of it lay there, in the demands imposed by French participation in
the American war for independence. The latter conflict, like the other wars for
empire fought by the great European powers in the eighteenth century, drained
coffers faster even than it cost lives. Louis XVI, faced with a financial crisis even
his resourceful finance minister Jacques Necker could not forestall, was compelled to call the national legislature for the first time since 1614, in the hope
it would permit him to raise taxes. As is well known, this gathering of the Estates General unleashed pent-up social and political antagonisms, and ultimately
transformed a call for reform into one of the great revolutions of the Western
world.

In a more proximate sense, too, the Revolution had New World causes. In an illustration of how deeply connected were cosmopolitan metropole and colonial periphery, it took only rumors that important forces in Paris were arguing for the abolition of slavery to trigger a slave revolt on the French sugar island of Martinique in the late summer of 1789. This was mere months after the Estates General had begun meeting, and still before word had reached the island that a mob had stormed Paris's most imposing symbol of Crown authority, the Bastille, on July 14. The Martinique revolt began in August, when enslaved workers on two large plantations struck. "Armed with the tools that they use to cut sugar-cane," the island's governor related, they "refused to work, saying loudly that they were free."[1] The slaves claimed they had been liberated by "orders of the king," but that "rebellious people" on the island had resisted the decree. Local officials believed that a priest, apparently moved by antislavery sentiment, had stirred the slaves to insurrection. But the words of the enslaved themselves suggested considerable awareness of the emancipatory currents of Atlantic thought. "We are free," they declared, "and we want to die for this liberty." Others, revealing important and long-standing cleavages among people of color in the West Indies, complained that the "mulattos," or free people of color on the island, were "creating a plan for liberty for only themselves, when we are all of the same family." Clearly, the enslaved knew something of how free islanders were reacting to developments in France, and they knew that some back in the metropole had been pushing to ameliorate their condition. In short, they had been exposed to the intellectual currents of the Atlantic Enlightenment and had swept them up. They declared slavery to be "attacked by the laws, by humanity, and by all of nature, by the Divinity and by our good King Louis XVI."[2]

Martinique slaves were not the only ones. On St. Domingue, the most important and profitable sugar colony in the world, revolt was also brewing. With nearly five hundred thousand slaves, constituting 90 percent of the entire population, St. Domingue featured the largest and one of the most densely concentrated conglomerations of bound laborers in the Caribbean. Annually producing more sugar than the entire British West Indies combined, St. Domingue also featured one the most repressive slave regimes in the New World. In its day, it was the epitome of the modern experiment in labor exploitation and racial control. Still, among the islands it was not particularly well known as a site of conspiracy or revolt. From 1751 to 1757 Vodún priest François Makandal had led an unsuccessful uprising that had cost six thousand lives, but otherwise colonial St. Domingue had known surprising peace—at least compared to a competitor such as Jamaica, which confronted at least six major slave conspiracies or revolts from 1742 to 1776.

That changed in 1789. The meeting of the French Estates General, called for the first time in 175 years, raised crucial questions about the fate of the colonies. Enlightenment principles and the example of the American Revolution informed the gathering, inspiring a range of reform-minded parties to seek fundamental changes in the way the nation, and empire, were to be governed. The Third Estate of nonclerical, nonaristocratic "commoners" became ascendant, declaring itself a National Assembly representing all of France, and working toward the formation of a constitutional monarchy, which was implemented in 1791.

The colonies' connection to these events was complex. As politically subordinate to the French state, perhaps planter elites stood in relation to France as oppressed commoners did to the monarch. Yet how could masters who exercised complete domination over so many others ever pose themselves as dispossessed? Who best represented the revolutionary spirit in the French West Indies? The colony's complex social structure did not clarify matters. Geographically divided into three distinct regions, French St. Domingue was also home to the complex mix of social groups characteristic of exploitation colonies. At the top were about forty thousand whites, divided into *grands blancs*, composed of wealthy planters and major political functionaries, and *petits blancs*. These, made up of traders, artisans, and government officials, harbored long-standing resentments against their better-off white compatriots, who dominated island politics. About twenty-eight thousand *gens de couleur* (free people of color) helped fill the middling roles occupied by the petits blancs, and nurtured their own grievances at being systematically discriminated against on account of their color. Some, particularly in the south, were themselves large and powerful plantation owners, who owned considerable numbers of the nearly half a million slaves in the colony. Even slave society could be divided—into a minority of "creoles" born in the New World, and the bulk of African-born slaves brought to replace those who perished under intolerable work conditions and malicious disease environments. Critical differences in cultural assimilation and ethnic heritage could sunder these two groups, and fracture even subgroupings of Africans. Finally, large bands of runaway slaves, known as maroons, lived in precarious freedom on the margins of slave society. Throughout the Caribbean, such maroon societies had frequently extracted an unsteady peace from slave regimes. The Revolution exacerbated all of these divides. By concentrating energies on events in the metropole, it created an enormous power vacuum on St. Domingue. Just as significantly, the Revolution's ideas of natural rights offered ample justification for a wide range of groups seeking redress for long-standing complaints.

Everyone on the island took advantage of the revolutionary moment. The grands blancs moved first, sending unsolicited representatives to the Estates General in Paris while simultaneously seeking to shut the petits blancs out of power back in St. Domingue. The petits blancs resisted, and civil war between the two groups of white colonists erupted on the island in 1790. In the same year, the gens de couleur entered the fray. Vincent Ogé, a well-to-do free man of color who witnessed the outbreak of the revolution in France and resented racially prejudicial laws in St. Domingue, sparked in the northern part of the colony a revolt that whites there quickly and brutally crushed. The next year, though, the slaves themselves exploited the deep fissures that had divided free society on the island. Inspired by the Vodún priest Boukman Dutty, enslaved people in the northern part of the island launched a remarkably large and well-coordinated rebellion. Starting on August 20, several thousand slaves armed themselves, set alight plantations, and marched across the countryside, slaughtering whites. One contemporary remarked on the devastation by its sixth day: "The whites of six parishes were either refugees, prisoners, or corpses. Flames had consumed one hundred sugar works; and twenty thousand slaves, once peaceful and submissive, were now so many cannibals, threatening Cap Français with the same fate."[3]

Ideas from the French Revolution had filtered down to blacks in bondage, fusing with long-standing African cultural sensibilities to lend new energy to slave rebellion. For two years, the enslaved of St. Domingue had witnessed island whites use the rhetoric of the Revolution to demand relief from imperial trade constraints, and even independence; they then watched gens de couleur rely on revolutionary principles to argue against racially proscriptive measures on the free. Reflecting a pattern that would recur in later decades and in other slave societies, one plantation manager blamed the transmission of revolutionary principles to the enslaved on "the very indiscretion of the planters who show no restraint in their actions or their statements," as well as "writings that have long circulated in the colony and that the negroes knew about."[4] At the same time, all groups used revolutionary rhetoric pragmatically; interest, rather than a commitment to principle, predominated. Some slave rebels initially declared that they acted in defense of the French king, who was hastily wending his way toward execution, in so doing recalling a long tradition of African-Atlantic resistance relying on paternalistic discourse. "If the Negroes wore the colors of the counterrevolution, if they invoked a power that no longer exists," recalled one French officer who served in the conflict, "it is because the civil and military authorities who were fighting them wore the patriotic colors."[5]

Despite that the principles of democratic revolution were often invoked selectively and self-servingly, the revolutionary context marked a turning point in world history. The complex of events known as the Haitian Revolution helps us locate the birth of the United States in a broader Atlantic narrative—one foregrounding an omnipresent tension between slavery and freedom. Like the American Revolution, Haiti's struggle for independence demonstrated the unpredictable power of Enlightenment ideals unleashed in worlds of slavery. Like the American Revolution, the Haitian Revolution was a colonial independence movement originating in the periphery. And, like the American Revolution, it established an independent republic at least rhetorically committed to the principle of universal human liberty. But the Haitian example was singular, too, in that its promises of democratic liberty extended to the complete destruction of slavery on the island. The struggle for independence in the United States constituted a political revolution, for it drastically rearranged the contours of the British Empire, and created a new sovereign nation. Yet while its tumult approached the prospect of social revolution, it fell short; the basic patterns of class and racial ordering on mainland North America were shaken, but held. The Haitian Revolution, on the other hand, became a complete social revolution, which overturned the hierarchies of class and race that had been the very raisons d'être for the society in the first place. This was so precisely because society in St. Domingue had been so repressive. The American Revolution occurred across colonies disparately dedicated to slavery—from the "societies with slaves" of New England, to lowcountry counties in South Carolina and Georgia that mirrored the demographics of profitable Caribbean sugar islands. Haiti demonstrated the consequences of explosive revolutionary patterns in the most exploitative of all exploitation colonies. The result was the establishment of the first black republic of the modern world, and a stunning blow to slavery and racism throughout the Atlantic.

The founding story of that nation is immensely complicated, but worth surveying. Just as slave revolt was offing in the northern province around Cap Français, the west province became home to a battle between whites and gens de couleur over France's decree of civil equality for the latter, with both groups recruiting slaves into their forces. In 1792, the slave revolt in Cap Français spread to the two provinces to the south, which inspired the revolutionary government in France to extend full citizenship to the gens de couleur in hopes of salvaging the colony from complete overthrow by slave insurrectionaries. Then, in 1793, the further radicalization of the French government led to international war, as European monarchies fearful of the revolution's spread banded together to crush France and its revolution. Opening a front in that broader war, English and Spanish forces invaded St. Domingue, introducing two new players into a four-handed civil war involving grands blancs, petits blancs, gens de couleur, and slaves. In the ensuing struggle, alliances and allegiances shifted with bewildering rapidity. For example, early on, beleaguered grands blancs sought alliance with England, offering even to accept British sovereignty rather than lose to the gens de couleur. In contrast, French revolutionary governor Léger-Félicité Sonthonax actively enlisted the loyalty of the enslaved. Reprising a policy as old as the Caribbean colonies themselves, he promised them freedom in exchange for assistance against foreign rivals. Still, large numbers of slaves flocked to the army of Spain, which was seeking to invade French St. Domingue from the eastern side of the island, which it had long controlled. Finally, France itself devolved into the Reign of Terror, during which some forty thousand "enemies of the revolution" were summarily executed. The radical government affirmed trends already under way on the island, decreeing the complete abolition of slavery in all territories in February 1794. Slaves who had been fighting against the revolutionary government's representatives switched sides, securing victory for Sonthonax and France.

For the next ten years, armies composed of freed slaves and gens de couleur fought off British and Spanish invaders under the flag of revolutionary France, conquered the Spanish-controlled portion of the island, and then defeated the forces of St. Domingue native André Rigaud, who had established an independent state led by gens de couleur in the south province. With Sonthonax in nominal political control, military power lay with François-Dominique Toussaint Louverture, a remarkable black military leader who had been born a slave but had become free. Toussaint fought initially for the Spanish against the whites, and then changed sides with the declaration of mass emancipation. Steadily, Toussaint and his subordinates took control of the island and steered it toward independence, increasingly ruling for France only in name.

Throughout the period, these leaders confronted critical dilemmas over the fate of plantation labor on the island. All had partaken of revolutionary ideology, but what did the social revolution of France mean in the context of an exploitation colony? Believing the persistence of the plantation economy crucial for the island's future, Toussaint compelled emancipated slave workers back to the fields as wage laborers, a move that over time undermined his popular support. This tightrope walk between slavery and freedom presaged conundrums confronting all postemancipation societies, but developments in the metropole obviated their resolution in the French Caribbean. In 1799, Napoléon Bonaparte staged a coup d'état, took over the French state, and embarked on a historic campaign of imperial expansion. Imagining St. Domingue as the gem of a New World empire that would reach beyond the Mississippi River, Napoléon planned to disarm the island's sizable native armies and reinstitute plantation slavery—a policy also intended to appease the large planters and sugar magnates who had supported his takeover. Though Toussaint pledged his forces to Napoléon's commander, Charles-Victor-Emmanuel Leclerc, opponents succeeded in having Toussaint imprisoned and sent to France, where he died, a martyr to black freedom. Back on the island, dissent grew as field workers fled plantations to join guerrilla bands. Resistance to slavery's reimposition spread, and by the fall of 1802 military leaders who had once supported Leclerc's assertion of French sovereignty began siding with the guerrillas. Flocking steadily to the banners of Toussaint's lieutenant, Jean-Jacques Dessalines, blacks and free people of color rejected French rule, fought off Napoléon's army, and declared independence on January 1, 1804. The first black republic had been born.

The Haitian Revolution had enormous ramifications for slavery in the United States. A few American radicals sanctioned the insurrection on the basis of revolutionary principle. "Let us be consistent, Americans," wrote one Bostonian. "If we justify our own conduct in the late glorious revolution; let us justify those who, in a cause like ours, fight with equal bravery."[6] But the prospect of universal slave rebellion scared nearly everyone white, becoming the ultimate example—even more potent than the French Revolution's Reign of Terror—of the violent extreme to which revolution could tend. The fear and reaction created by events in the Caribbean paused Americans' own encounter with radical notions of liberty, which were already losing momentum in the wake of the new nation's founding.

Along with the "excesses" of the revolution in France, the "horrors of St. Domingue" led to a marked retrenchment in revolutionary enthusiasm in a country weary from war and struggling with the practicalities of establishing a new system of national governance. As early as 1782, George Washington had lamented the waning of revolutionary fervor. "That Spirit of Freedom which at the commencement of this contest would have gladly sacrificed every thing to the attainment of its object has long since subsided," he wrote, "and every selfish Passion has take[n] its place."[7] This retreat from radicalism had owed, in part, to slaveholding. Maintaining the security of slave property helped contain the revolution, ensuring that its impulses toward social leveling did not supersede the property-sanctioning component of revolutionary ideology. The need to secure slave property in the face of the Revolution's chaos helped restrain the "certain enthusiasm in liberty" Alexander Hamilton had celebrated, and this helped prevent a colonial independence movement from becoming a true social revolution. The Haitian example only further diminished the radical spirit of the Revolution by weakening even more the security of slave property. It epitomized American slaveholders' worst nightmares, and placed a premium on maintaining order, even at the expense of liberty.

Events in St. Domingue worked their way into American politics and statecraft. Washington himself rushed to lend arms and financial aid to the besieged whites of the colony. Shortly after news of the August 1791 slave uprising in Cap Français, he reassured the French ambassador that the United States would "render every aid in their power to our good friends and Allies the French to quell 'the alarming insurrection of the negros in Hispanola.'"[8] In ensuing years, the foundations of the American party system, in fact, took shape partly around the long crisis on the island. Paradoxically, conservative but Anglophilic Federalists struck more conciliatory tones on Haiti than did their opponents, the more radical but Francophilic Democratic-Republicans. While Washington pledged his support for France against slave rebels, his successor and fellow Federalist, John Adams, argued for a far more limited embargo of the insurrectionaries, on the theory that an independent but weak St. Domingue would best serve U.S. interests in the hemisphere. By its end, the Adams administration was trading with and supplying arms to Toussaint's regime as part of its "quasi-war" with revolutionary France. Hailing from an overwhelmingly white state with no slaves, the president had little to lose.

In contrast stood Thomas Jefferson, whose Democratic-Republicans won the presidency in 1800 in the first orderly transfer of power from one party to another in American history. The new, slaveholding president feared that the rebellion might inspire American slaves to revolt, and pursued a much more vigorous antirebel approach, despite that he had posed his party as the true custodian of the revolutionary tradition. Jefferson worried that "black crews, & supercargoes & missionaries" would carry the "combustion" of St. Domingue into the U.S. South, where it would "leven" the resentments of southern slaves into insurrection. One of his party confidants, Virginia Governor James Monroe, likewise feared the effects of the slave uprising on "all the people of colour in this and the States south of us, more especially our slaves."[9]

The insurrection warped the apparent commitments of the parties, exposing in particular the insecurity and hypocrisy at the heart of Jefferson's Democratic-Republicans. Federalist gadfly Timothy Pickering made hay of such contradictions, demanding to know how President Jefferson could oppose the slaves of St. Domingue in their struggle for liberty while supporting the equally bloodthirsty radicals of France. Given the atrocities committed on the continent, were not the oppressed revolutionaries of the island guilty only of having "skin not colored like our own"? He asked Jefferson, "If there could ever be an apology for Frenchmen, will it not apply with tenfold priority and force to the rude blacks of Santo Domingo?"[10] Nonetheless, Pickering himself, like other early Federalists, was no friend of rebellion. As staunch supporters of social order, such men had feared the spread of the *French* revolutionary energies to the United States. The prospect of blacks from the islands fomenting slave rebellion at home cowed everyone.

Throughout the young Republic, the Haitian Revolution heightened longstanding fears of slave violence and tempered excitement for radical political change. As modern history's first instance of overthrowing a slave society, it offered a model no one in power wished to emulate, and thus dampened enthusiasms, already waning, for broad schemes of abolition. Thousands of white and free colored refugees flooded American ports such as Philadelphia and Charleston, carrying savage stories of slave wrath. Many of these tales—such as the vision of black rebels brandishing a standard composed of "the body of a white child impaled upon a stake," or assertions that "pregnant women have been eviscerated"—do not find confirmation in the original eyewitness accounts, and were fabricated to attract the sympathy of metropolitan publics.[11] Refugees incited fears that agents of the rebellion sought to spread it to the southern United States; Jefferson himself found such claims sufficiently credible to warn John Drayton, South Carolina's governor, of "two Frenchmen, from St. Domingo" heading to Charleston "with design to excite an insurrection among the negroes."[12] The bondspersons who came with these slaveholding refugees, who may have numbered up to twelve thousand, energized African American communities with fresh doses of Afro-Caribbean culture and recent news of the struggle for liberty. As the largest American port closest to St. Domingue, Charleston served as refuge for many white islanders, and their slaves were thought to be particularly troublesome. In 1793 and 1796, widespread rumors of insurrection broke out in the city, with newspapers reporting that "the St. Domingo negroes have sown these seeds of revolt."[13] Word of Haiti seeped into Virginia as well, where white authorities overheard slave plotters discussing "how the blacks has [*sic*] killed the whites in the French island and took it a little while ago."[14] The great insurrection of 1791 established a precedent, horrifying for the advocates of slavery and racial order, of the possibilities of slave agency in the United States.

By arming slaves everywhere with the rhetoric of revolution, the Haitian example marked a critical turning point in the history of New World slavery. By yoking the cultural prestige of revolutionary ideology to long-standing traditions of collective and violent mass resistance, the Revolution offered slaves new possibilities for exploiting events in the metropolitan world on behalf of their own freedom. Invoking ideas of revolution helped ensure that thereafter slavery could be championed only as an exception to a presumed default state of nature: liberty. Slavery could be preserved for racial inferiors, or maintained as an economic expedient, but increasingly in metropolitan circles, doing either of these seemed to counter the natural order and God's will. The harnessing of revolutionary ideology to slave rebellion thus created extraordinary new potentials, altering the trajectory of collective slave violence for ever after. Any mass revolt would henceforth become subsumed under questions of liberty and freedom, emancipation and abolition. Finally, the Haitian Revolution made Atlantic what in the American Revolution had been merely continental. Whereas slave behavior had played an important role in the American Revolution, in St. Domingue it had determined outcomes. In the wake of the American struggle for independence, it was possible to imagine other colonial crises resolving without the enslaved playing the critical role. In the wake of the Haitian Revolution, every colonial crisis involving enslaved populations took on frightening possibilities for Atlantic slave powers.

REVOLUTIONS FOR LIBERTY
Revolution and Abolition in Latin America

This proved to be exactly the case when Spain's New World empire began dissolving in the first quarter of the nineteenth century. The process began as a consequence of the French Revolution, when Napoléon's invasion of the Iberian Peninsula disrupted the monarchies of Spain and Portugal, countries already struggling to manage large New World empires. The French emperor's Grande Armée crossed the Pyrenees in 1807, intending to capture Portuguese ports and seal French-dominated Europe from trade with Britain. Now juggling a weak king, court intrigues, and Napoléon's dominant army, Spain ceased to effectively rule its colonies, lending enormous impetus to simmering independence movements there. Creole elites in the colonies, reliant on Spanish power to maintain local hegemony and trade preferences, were not generally as predisposed to independence as their English counterparts in the northern colonies of mainland North America. But with a vacuum of leadership in the metropole, and power distributed across a variety of makeshift local juntas, autonomists in the colonies began to move.

Revolt began in Quito in 1809, quickly spreading to the rest of Spain's mainland possessions. By 1833, only the Caribbean islands of Cuba and Puerto Rico remained in Spanish hands. The conflicts that raged through the 1810s and 1820s were marked by shifting alliances involving creole elites, royalist sympathizers, local *caudillos* (charismatic militia leaders), and a range of nonwhite *castas*, including people of native American, African, and mixed racial descent. Motives were rarely clear-cut, and revolutionary principles often gave way to the particular interests of the groups invoking them. Most important, though, the exigencies of fighting extended wars across two continents made the issue of manpower vital. Much more than in the case of the American Revolution, the Latin American wars of independence relied upon the recruitment of African-descended populations, a process that vastly hastened the progress of emancipation.

While colonial Latin America was no mere Spanish replica of Britain's colonies on mainland North America, both nonetheless shared commonalities endemic to the mercantile empires of the eighteenth century. After several centuries of colonization, settlement, and trade, the economies of Spain's mainland colonies had matured markedly. Mining areas offered the greatest sources of wealth, but had done little to promote a foundation for long-term development. Coastal plains had proven favorable to the production of agricultural staples, such as the cacao produced in Venezuela. In both realms, exploited native labor and imported African slaves provided the bulk of the necessary workforce. Cities such as Caracas were, like those in Britain's northern colonies, becoming centers of trade and shipping. A thriving class of *criollo* (creole, or American-born) colonists benefitted in many ways from imperial security and trade protection, but also chafed under the constraints of mercantile restrictions. These groups often conflicted with *peninsulares* from Spain, who enjoyed greater wealth, privilege, and imperial preference. As were other imperial powers, Spain had been trying to reform its administration of the empire, but weak central government could not inhibit the emergence of calls for autonomy among creole elites in the New World, a phenomenon that broke free as a consequence of Napoléon's invasion of the mother country. Just as in British North America, the maturation of creole elites led to challenges to imperial rule. Likewise, in both sets of societies revolutionary ideology played a key role in sanctioning these challenges.

The Spanish American wars of independence, though, occurred in a much more explosive international context. While the American Revolution initiated a transatlantic crisis of empire, the Latin American independence movements evolved from the context of total war that developed from that crisis. France had deposed a king and placed the state in the hands of the people, only to watch a military authoritarian emerge who almost subdued the Western world. The West Indies had seen a civil war between rival groups of white elites overtaken by free people of color and then the slaves themselves, who converted it into the first instance of mass abolition achieved through collective violence. In this context, the crisis of Spain's imperial sovereignty transformed into a series of revolutions that swept up all in their maw. Events in St. Domingue fostered a wave of rebelliousness throughout the Atlantic. In 1795, for example, José Leonardo Chirino, the child of an enslaved father and native mother, led a revolt of free blacks and slaves in the Venezuelan coastal town of Coro. Apparently inspired by a visit to St. Domingue, Chirino called for application of the "French law" establishing abolition and racial equality. Chirino's band, putting plantation owners to the sword and fields to the torch, eventually succumbed to local forces, which hung and quartered him and brutally butchered his followers. Buenos Aires, Caracas, and Bahia also confronted revolutionary conspiracies, while Cuba witnessed a spate of rebelliousness in the second half of the 1790s.[15] Unlike earlier instances, such as Túpac Amaru's massive uprising of native peoples in Peru in 1780, these conspiracies and revolts tended to engage a wide range of social groups, from enslaved Africans to free people of color, and sometimes even radical white creoles. While challenges to imperial rule might express self-interest only through the rhetoric of rights and revolution, ideas were nonetheless important; they helped transform means and ends of the independence movements, which could now envision expanded privilege in the context of their own nation building, and nation building as an exercise in protecting free and independent citizens.

Independence movements in Spanish Latin America produced abolition because of the ways revolutionary ideology intersected with the circumstance of widespread war in mature, socially diverse colonial societies. As had happened in the English colonies that became the United States, the algebra of abolition balanced economic need against revolutionary ideology. Here, circumstances favored freedom in mainland Spanish South America over freedom in the American South. While slavery supplied critical labor in some places, most mainland Spanish colonies were better characterized as "societies with slaves" than as "slave societies." With African slavery in mainland colonial Spanish Latin America largely reserved for urban environments and select agricultural and mining areas, it became possible to imagine the end of the institution. In societies with large native populations long subjected to paternalistic systems of tribute labor such as the *encomienda*, *repartimiento*, and *hacienda*, African slavery supplemented labor needs, with enslaved Africans serving primarily along agricultural coastal plains and in cities. Over time, many had become free, and mixed with local native or white populations. Compared to the African-descended populations of Brazil, the Caribbean, and the U.S. South, the numbers were never that great. Around the turn of the nineteenth century, historian João Pedro Marques estimates, the Spanish mainland's nearly quarter million slaves were distributed widely, with the most important concentrations found in the seventy thousand of New Grenada (roughly contiguous with modern-day Colombia), sixty-five thousand among the Venezuelan cocoa plantations, forty thousand in Peru, and some thirty thousand in the Río de la Plata region of present-day Uruguay and northern Argentina.[16]

When the wars of independence gave ideological and practical impetus to mass emancipation, it became possible to imagine relinquishing formal slavery. When combined with revolutionary ideology, the imperatives of recruitment could outweigh the benefits that slavery had offered to a confined and relatively weak master class. Besides, just as peonage and semiservile labor would persist for native workers even after independence, so too might local elites continue to exploit African-descended laborers without formal slavery. When the wars of independence began making demands on military manpower, first colonial rebels and then loyalist forces began incorporating native and African-descended peoples into their armies. Trading freedom for service blurred the line between the slave and free, promised national inclusion for those freed, and began an almost inexorable process of dismantling chattel bondage. In some instances in revolutionary South America, such as during Simón Bolívar's Venezuela campaign of 1813, armies fighting for independence were composed almost wholly of free blacks and emancipated slaves. Culled from creole elites, revolutionary leaders such as José Francisco de San Martín and Simón Bolívar had initially not factored slavery into their movements. Over time, they came to connect revolution and abolition in ways similar to their North American counterparts. Bolívar, whose broad Atlantic travels had taken him to revolutionary Paris and the United States, called it "madness that a revolution for liberty should try to maintain slavery,"[17] and went on to trade the new Haitian republic a promise of general emancipation in Spanish South America for the military support of Haitian President Alexander Pétion.

In the course of achieving independence, the new states carved out of the Spanish Empire provided for freedom. As had occurred in the U.S. North, mass emancipation often happened gradually. "Free womb" laws, which slowly ended slavery by granting freedom to the offspring of slaves after a given term of service, appeared throughout the independent states. Complete and final abolition often followed, with the passage of further laws and constitutional mandates. Most often, these measures reified a decline already evident in practice, though resisted fiercely by slaveholders where they were powerful. Between slave recruitment, the decline of plantation control wrought by the havoc of war, and the impetus of abolitionist ideas among revolutionaries and the new states they formed, African-descended people were already becoming free. Chile took the fastest route to complete abolition, passing a free womb law in 1811 and abolishing slavery outright in 1823. Others followed. In 1822, the revolutionary government in Mexico freed slaves born on Mexican soil, and in 1829 abolished the institution entirely. Just to the south, the United Provinces of Central America—comprising the modern nations of Guatemala, Nicaragua, Honduras, El Salvador, and Costa Rica—abolished slavery in 1824 through a gradual free womb law. Gran Colombia, a confederation of newly independent states constituted by modern-day Venezuela, Colombia, and Ecuador, adopted a gradual free womb law in 1821. By 1831, all Spanish-speaking countries in mainland South America had begun the process of gradual abolition, and by the start of the U.S. Civil War, all but Paraguay (which followed in 1869) had formally completed it.[18]

Notably, the situation differed on the strategically critical islands of Cuba and Puerto Rico. Spain retained these possessions until 1898, during which time Cuba in particular grew into a large and profitable sugar colony. In a similar way, slavery had died only partially in British mainland North America. In the United States, revolutionary calculations had made the end of slavery possible, but only in the northern states that, like much of mainland Latin America, could be considered societies with slaves rather than slave societies. Both areas had undergone a process of revolutionary emancipation that, with the infamous exception of Haiti, provided the only model then known for ending modern slavery. Yet critical differences remained between the experiences of slavery in British and Spanish mainland colonies. Whereas Spanish Latin America remained divided between the Spanish-owned slave societies of the Caribbean and independent non–slave societies on the mainland, in the United States these two realms of slavery and freedom remained within the borders of a single nation. And while Cuba and Puerto Rico remained linked to a crumbling Old World empire, the slave power in the United States formed a powerful component of one of the most dynamic economies on the planet.

Along with the northern United States, Spanish mainland Latin America occupied one pole in a range of Atlantic experience, defined by its early provision of abolition resulting from colonial independence movements. On the other extreme was Brazil, where the quite different path to independence taken by Portugal's New World empire left slavery intact. With a wide expanse of mainland territory, Portuguese Brazil shared some of the economic diversity of mainland Spanish Latin America. From its start, though, Brazil had relied heavily on imported African slaves over native labor. For several reasons, the colony bound its fate early and firmly to the practice of chattel bondage. With no large native states to conquer, and with a climate and topography amenable to the profitable production of agricultural staples, Brazilian colonists demanded labor. With Portuguese traders ascendant in the early Atlantic slave trade, and the route to Brazil the shortest passage from African slave-trading centers, settlers had found a ready supply in enslaved Africans. From the sugar *engenhos* of the northeast in the sixteenth and seventeenth centuries to the gold and gem mines of eighteenth-century Minas Gerais and the coffee plantations outside of nineteenth-century Rio de Janeiro and São Paulo, slavery had largely supplied the labor needs of much of Brazil throughout its long colonial history. When the Atlantic world erupted in revolution, Brazil's elites were far too dependent on slavery to imagine abolishing it.

Nonetheless, this colony, too, broke free of its mother country. In the second half of the eighteenth century, Portugal had instituted reforms to streamline its imperial administration, just as the Spanish Crown had done through the Bourbon reforms. Under the Marquis de Pombal, Portugal had imposed a functioning mercantilist system on its colonies, which enhanced Crown control over trade, undermined the capacity of the church and nobility to siphon off royal revenues, and encouraged shipbuilding and manufacturing. As had Spain's similar campaign of late-colonial Bourbon reforms, the Pombaline reforms represented a step toward more rational imperial administration. But, also like the Bourbon reforms, they frustrated colonial elites who had prospered under the old system, leading to calls for greater autonomy. Then, in 1808, Napoléon's invasion of Iberia effectively sent the Crown into exile. The royal court relocated to Brazil, and Rio de Janeiro became the capital of the United Kingdom of Portugal, Brazil, and the Algarves—the only instance in which a European country came to be ruled from one of its colonies. The move inhibited nascent calls for autonomy, and tempered their militance when they nonetheless came to fruition. In 1822, Prince Regent Pedro of Brazil proclaimed nominal independence from Portuguese King João VI. The two-year war that followed was tame by the standards of the Spanish colonies, but—as elsewhere—still required the widespread recruitment of people of African descent, with the enslaved often offered liberty in exchange for service.

While mainland Spanish Latin America abolished slavery, and the United States ended slavery partially, Brazil remained wholly dedicated to the institution. With the royal court located in Brazil until 1821, it was difficult to frame the plight of creole elites in the master-slave terms common to the rhetoric of independence movements elsewhere. In addition, Brazil's war of independence may have been insufficiently desperate to convert "freedom for service" bargains into widespread emancipation. Mostly, though, the Brazilian economy simply depended too heavily on enslaved labor to imagine that the country could survive without it. Slave production remained a lynchpin of the Brazilian economy until 1888. As the century wore on, though, and as other Atlantic societies began dismantling the slave trade and then slavery itself, Brazil would fall increasingly out of step with hemispheric trends, leaving legacies of weak development and national backwardness problematic components of Brazilian national identity.

Brazil's story completes this broad survey of slavery's transformation from an Atlantic-wide phenomenon to one concentrated in particular regions. The northern states carved out of the English colonies on mainland North America had been the first in the New World to abolish slavery, albeit most did so gradually and with compensation to slaveholders. The toppling of slavery on Spanish mainland South America also came as a result of independence movements, and likewise often occurred gradually (though compensation often proved impossible for war-stretched new governments). In mainland Spanish Latin America, the planter interest had been insufficiently powerful to overcome the tumult and demands of the wars. But in the United States, the slave power had been particularly fortunate. It, too, had known a long war that had undermined the institution practically and ideologically. But it was geographically contiguous with states where slavery was being abolished. And those states, in the name of national unity, had conceded power in the national government to help protect it.

The chronology mattered much. The bloody experience of St. Domingue, which became the first and only New World society in which the enslaved themselves served as the prime movers in the establishment of a non–slave society, spurred these moves toward Latin American abolition, just as it elevated slaveholders' fears of slave rebellion where slavery remained. In turn, the widespread emancipations accompanying the wars of independence in Spanish Latin America impelled the decline of slavery in much of the Atlantic, and fostered the idea that liberty was the proper norm for Atlantic society. The spate of abolitions that had struck the Atlantic in the half century from 1775 to 1825 had transformed New World slavery mightily. From once being an accepted and practiced institution in every European colony on two continents, it was now confined to three primary realms: independent Brazil, the U.S. South, and Caribbean exploitation islands controlled by several European powers. Before the revolutionary emancipations in the Atlantic, slavery had been understood as a typical and expected feature of New World colonization. Afterward it could be seen only as an outlier of civilized society, a perhaps necessary but clearly brutal evil, or a violation of the natural order.

HOW SWEET THE SOUND
Atlantic Abolitionism and the Slave Trade

The age of democratic revolutions, and the Napoleonic Wars that followed, led the great powers of Europe to a critical reevaluation of the role of slavery in their empires. The wars wrought enormous dislocations throughout the European and Atlantic worlds. To those who lived through these decades of conflict, the world seemed transformed, as in many places it truly had been. Old notions of social order, built on hereditary aristocracy in Europe or on rigid racial ordering in the Caribbean, had been challenged to the core. Long-standing nations had fallen to Napoléon's armies, and the maps of Europe and the New World had been redrawn. Britain had lost half an empire, and the United States had been born. France had deposed a king and ended slavery, only to embrace an emperor and reimpose slavery. The slaves of St. Domingue had rejected this with unprecedented ferocity, defeating in succession the armies of three of the greatest nations in the world, and then founding an independent black republic. The figure of slavery had performed powerful ideological work, serving as a foil to principles of democratic Enlightenment, and embodying the worst of an older order that was dying away. It was thus no surprise that in the midst of this international maelstrom what had once seemed radical—the idea that slavery could and should be demolished—could increasingly become normative.

In the decades around the turn of the nineteenth century, the antislavery sentiment unleashed by revolutionary ideology was consummated in widespread calls to end the international traffic in slaves from Africa to the New World. The international trade, as opposed to the practice of slavery itself, had long drawn the ire of antislavery activists, stretching back to the earliest abolitionist statements. A Germantown, Pennsylvania, Quaker petition of 1688 had spoken out "against the traffik of men-body,"[19] while the mere title of Samuel Sewall's 1700 pamphlet, *The Selling of Joseph: A Memorial*, spoke volumes on the root problem of slavery. Whereas those who held slaves could contend that they treated their bondspersons well, those who engaged in the actual trade in humans had no such recourse. Reality differed, of course; even when slave owners did not live up to stereotypes of power-crazed sadists, their customary treatment of those in bonds seldom matched their paternalistic rhetoric. But the figure of commerce—the bartering of actual human bodies as things—encapsulated key ideological tensions confronting the revolutionary world. If the fundamental and "self-evident" rights of man included an inviolable right to private property, could humans fall into the category of property? The trend in the Atlantic world was to answer in the negative. To be charged with the care of dependents was a commonplace social relation unconfined to slavery; masters cared for apprentices, husbands for wives, and parents for children. But to sell humans as objects or beasts was quite another. No other image of slavery held as much power in the public mind as that of the inhumane treatment of Africans bound in chains, amassed in slave ships, and traded in the New World as goods. The face of early metropolitan antislavery, then, was the opposition to the slave trade.

British reformers were the first to put before the public lurid images of the international trade. These activists—including Quaker pioneers and early luminaries such as Thomas Clarkson and Granville Sharp—desired the complete end to slavery, but viewed the abolition of the trade in slaves as an easier, and necessary, first target. In London in 1787, they formed the Society for Effecting the Abolition of the Slave Trade, an organization dedicated to illustrating the horrors of the trade and convincing the public that it should be abolished. Using their command of the press, and relying on information gathered through observation and the firsthand accounts of African subjects of the trade, they launched an impressive public campaign. Pioneering virtually all the tactics employed by later mass humanitarian political reforms, they organized local committees throughout Britain, and issued a stream of anti-slave-trade propaganda. The powerful iconography of the early abolitionist movement—from Josiah Wedgwood's ceramic cameo of a kneeling slave asking "Am I Not a Man and a Brother?" to cutaway diagrams of slave ships like the *H.M.S. Brookes* showing Africans packed as tightly as sardines in a can—owed to these campaigns of public persuasion. In the hands of the early abolitionists, the English folk hymn "Amazing Grace," which celebrated the conversion of English sailor John Newton from slave trader to a life in the church, became one of the most recognizable songs in the English language. The campaigns resulted in a slough of petitions sent to Parliament requesting that Britain end its participation in the trade. In 1792, 519 petitions flooded the legislature, the most ever presented during a single session. As many as four hundred thousand different signatures appeared on these petitions, amounting to a staggering 5 percent of Britain's estimated 1790 population of eight million and perhaps 13 percent of the adult male population.[20] Several dozen abolitionist "saints" were even elected to Parliament itself, where the idealistic William Wilberforce led them in ceaseless agitation to end the trade.

The campaign was long and hard. Wilberforce began bringing bills before Parliament in 1791, repeating the effort almost every year thereafter through 1799. The measures all failed, sunk by a powerful planter lobby. This had been active and strong in England since at least the 1740s, uniting nonresident planters and merchants who traded in sugar and other New World commodities into a powerful political bloc, united by shared economic interests and social worlds. Organized into groups such as the Society of West India Planters and Merchants, these interests launched their own media campaign, issuing pamphlet after pamphlet attacking slave-trade abolitionists as incendiaries and fomenters of slave revolt. The point struck home. Once war with revolutionary France began in 1793, antislavery opinion confronted the added dilemma of being associated with radical ideas more generally. Slave trade defenders posed the slave uprising on St. Domingue as the logical consequence of revolutionary France's abolition of slavery, and warned of its repetition among English holdings should the slave trade be abolished. Abolitionists retreated. And yet, finally, Parliament did what it had been unable to do for so long. After a renewed campaign in 1804, abolitionists succeeded in introducing bills in Parliament that inched ever closer to success. At last, in 1807, slave trade abolitionists won. The Slave Trade Act made it illegal for British ships to engage in the trade, thus instituting an early and most significant such abolition in the Atlantic world. How had this come to pass?

The roots of the planters' ultimate failure may have rested in the historical trajectory established by American independence. Critically, the American Revolution had helped undo the West Indian planter interest in several ways. It had divided the interests of Britain's two major slaveholding centers by dividing the empire. The loss of the southern American colonies had left the planters without important allies in Britain who shared their general interests. Just as important, it had deprived the West Indians of critical markets within the empire—both to sell their goods and as sources of supply. In the wake of the Revolution, West Indies planters found themselves in the curious position of arguing for the continuation of mercantile-style trade protections for their produce, while also arguing for the opening up of free trade to provide access to critical American markets to sell it. It was a hard case to make, particularly among a public increasingly concerned with the inhumanity of slavery, and witnessing all too clearly slaves' manifest desires for liberty. Steadily, the planters had found themselves on the defensive.

With the turn of the nineteenth century, the course of Atlantic events gave new impetus to the British movement to abolish the international trade. The reenergizing of imperial rivalries in the Caribbean once again brought up the expense of maintaining empire, while the Haitian Revolution exposed the vulnerabilities of colonies built on the compulsion of huge slave majorities. The 1799 collapse of the sugar market from overproduction merely exposed the fragility of a system so dependent on distant production, forced labor, and unsteady markets. It may not have been that slavery had ceased to be profitable, as some historians have argued; just as sugar prices recovered, so too slave imports rose after their wartime interruptions. But, if only in the realm of public perception, something fundamental had shifted. Britons were slowly coming to see slavery as a system of production less than critical to the national interest, and perhaps not worth the moral cost of condoning what increasingly was seen as a "national sin."[21]

Britain's commitment to ending its trade put the world's most powerful naval empire behind efforts to cease other nations' practice. Its national interest now at stake, England began pressuring other nations to give up the trade, lest they enjoy the advantage of a profitable source of overseas commerce Britain itself had renounced. With Napoléon contending for domination of Central Europe, the promise of military support pressured England's wartime allies into denouncing the trade. The continental powers of Russia, Prussia, and Austria had little to lose by complying, and Portugal and Spain were in straits too desperate to argue much—though Spain's final suppression awaited 1820 and compliance remained a problem. From 1807 on, Britain sought, and gained, nominal commitments on the part of many European nations to end the trade: the Portuguese in 1810, Sweden in 1813, and France and the Netherlands in 1814. In 1815, England secured the condemnation of the trade at the Congress of Vienna, the body of international diplomats charged with refabricating the European order in the wake of the Napoleonic Wars. In this way, Britain pursued what some scholars term "diplomatic abolitionism," suggesting that the leading antislavery nation "colonized" abolition elsewhere. Apt though this formulation may be, the effort was difficult. As proper suppression of the trade could be achieved only through the interdiction of foreign ships on the high seas by British forces, compliance required small sacrifices of national sovereignty from foreign nations, an uneasy sell in a world of intense imperial rivalry. Slow compliance, weak enforcement, and constant smuggling still consigned nearly three million Africans to New World bondage between 1807 and 1866.[22]

Still, the effort was not without success. The British, Dutch, and Baltic traffic virtually ceased. Ships trading under the French flag restored the commerce in the years after Napoléon reimposed slavery, but in the 1830s stronger agreements with Britain severely inhibited their traffic. Many of these successes owed to the British navy's West African Squadron, which had been established specifically for the purpose of ceasing the trade. It assumed the overwhelming role, with the navies of France, the United States, and other nations playing bit parts. At its height in 1819, the squadron consisted of two dozen vessels with two thousand sailors, with bases at Fernando Po and Cape Town. Sierra Leone, the troubled West African colony of freed slaves pioneered by British abolitionists, became a refuge for many freed on the high seas. Historians estimate capture rates of twenty-five slave ships per year, with a total of some one thousand ships taken all together; five thousand Africans per year, perhaps one hundred sixty thousand in all, owed their liberation to these efforts.[23]

Everywhere, the slave trade looked headed for decline. In Spanish mainland Latin America, the wars of independence had done the work of abolishing it. When measures making the trade illegal there did not precede laws completely ending slavery, total abolition obviated the need for them. Spain itself, though, maintained the trade to Puerto Rico and especially Cuba, which in the wake of St. Domingue's demise quickly rose to become the world's premier producer of cane sugar. Between the nominal end of the Spanish slave trade in 1820 and the final end of slavery, traders shipped over 630,000 Africans to the New World on ships flying Spanish flags.[24] Brazil, now independent, held out the longest. Having inherited Portugal's agreement to limit the trade, Brazilian planters, now sovereign, sought to evade the legacy. Steady British diplomatic pressure finally resulted in a treaty declaring the slave trade to Brazil "piracy" in 1830. Even then, the persistence of the trade remained a critical source of tension with Britain, and over half a million slaves entered the country after that date. Fierce interdiction efforts in the 1840s led to a showdown between the two nations, in which British navies seized suspected slave-trading ships lying in the very ports of Brazil itself. Despite the affront to its national honor, Brazil demurred. In 1850, the Brazilian parliament passed a law forbidding the trade outright, choosing voluntary compliance over the further humiliation of imposition.

Against this narrative, the United States appears at first glance to have flown bold abolitionist colors. Congress actually preceded Parliament by three weeks in passing a measure abolishing the trade. In 1805, the national legislature took up the issue, anticipating the expiration of the twenty-year reprieve granted the trade in article I, section 9 of the Constitution. For many, the move to abolishing the commerce seemed a logical fulfillment of the promises implied at the constitutional settlement. Congress had already acted to limit the trade by, for example, prohibiting slave ships from being provisioned in American ports. New Jersey and Rhode Island had ended their trades in 1787, and Massachusetts, Connecticut, and New York soon followed. By the time Congress considered abolishing the trade, it remained legal only in South Carolina. State enforcement was lax, though; without the federal navy, such laws were too often observed only in the breach. President Thomas Jefferson himself had pressed Congress to outlaw the trade, thus removing Americans from their complicity in "those violations of human rights which have been so long continued on the unoffending inhabitants of Africa."[25] In both the Senate and House, politicians began drafting laws to abolish the trade as soon as constitutionally permissible.

The devil, as always, lay in the details. Examination of the debates in Congress over slave trade prohibition reveals the extent to which the interests of planters in the South drove the conversation and outcome. The slave trade debates constituted a signal instance in which early national politics was directed by the might of a slave interest empowered by full participation in the system of national governance. Southern members of Congress spoke vigorously for the interests of their section. What, for instance, was to be done with those Africans found on ships interdicted at sea? Southerners succeeded in ensuring that the courts closest to the sites of interdiction, which in all likelihood would be southern, would oversee the fate of these people. This principle of "forfeiture" meant that Africans rescued from slave ships in the international trade could quickly find their way back into bondage, and even bartered through the domestic trade within the United States. Forfeiture exposed the ambivalence of slave trade abolition in the United States: no Somerset principle would dictate unconditional freedom for interdicted slaves in the United States; Africans rescued from the international trade were very likely to find themselves caught up in the American domestic one.

Some northern members of Congress protested, insisting that the forfeiture provision placed the government in an untenable position. "By the same law we condemn the man-stealer and become the receiver of his stolen goods," opponents railed. "We punish the criminal, and then step into his place, and complete the crime which he had only begun. We ourselves do that which we prevent him from doing."[26] Others went further, arguing that forfeiture endorsed a "false principle" unauthorized by the Constitution, that "a property may be had in human beings."[27] Southern firebrands were chagrined. Invoking the Constitution's ambivalence just as effectively as did their opponents, they argued that state law prevailed where federal law was silent. The attack on forfeiture was an attack on the entire institution; "its effects strike at all property in slaves," they complained.[28] Finally, they played the trump card that had proven so valuable during the constitutional convention: the threat of disunion. Representative Peter Early from Georgia reacted to northerners' rejection of forfeiture with alarm, declaring that "the inhabitants of the Southern States would resist this provision with their lives." He urged his colleagues to pass the measure, for "we want no civil wars, no rebellions, no insurrections, no resistance to the authority of the Government."[29]

Such threats pervaded the southern response. Representative John Randolph of Virginia feared that future opponents of slavery might use abolition of the trade as "the pretext of universal emancipation," presciently declaring that "if ever the time of disunion between the States should arrive, the line of severance would be between the slaveholding and the non-slaveholding States."[30] Indeed, Randolph excoriated any interference with the domestic slave trade, announcing that "if the Constitution is thus to be violated, let us secede, and go home."[31] Ultimately, such tactics won the day. By a margin of just one vote, cast as a tie-breaker by Speaker of the House Nathaniel Macon of North Carolina, the effort to scuttle forfeiture lost, and the bill passed with the provision intact.[32] On March 3, 1807, President Thomas Jefferson signed it into law, and it went into effect on January 1 of the following year.

While both the United States and Great Britain legally abolished the slave trade nearly simultaneously, important differences distinguished the two efforts. Whereas Britain could claim that its abolition illustrated the nation's commitment to the principle of universal human liberty, slave trade abolition in the United States occurred in a way that actually upheld the principle of property in man. Furthermore, unlike the situation in the United States, England's abolition of the slave trade doomed chattel bondage in its slave periphery. Because harsh conditions ensured that the slave populations of the Caribbean exploitation colonies could not reproduce themselves, shutting down the future supply of Africans in bondage meant that the slave population of the islands would eventually die off, victim of the onerous conditions of West Indian servitude. In the United States, though, slavery had become a self-sustaining institution. Though ships openly smuggled slaves into southern ports well into the 1830s, foreign supply was no longer necessary to maintain the institution. With a self-reproducing slave population, the South became uniquely insulated, virtually impervious to diplomatic pressure from outside. If anything, the isolated nature of the southern slave regime worked to unite sections in the South that heretofore had been diverging. With an oversupply of slaves in its declining tobacco economy, the upper South states of Virginia, Maryland, and Delaware found a ready market in the lower South states of South Carolina and Georgia, which unceasingly demanded slaves to work rice and the new short-staple cotton that was being made so profitable by the invention of the mechanical cotton gin. Indeed, as the nation expanded into the Southwest, the demand for slaves would become unquenchable. As historians have shown, the upper South's ability to cater to this supply united the sections politically as well as economically.[33] A national "house" that might have splintered into subregions was becoming simply bifurcated, into a recognizable North and South.

AN EMPIRE OF SLAVERY
Expansion and the Slave Power in the Early Republic

At the same time that slavery in the United States was becoming a peculiarly southern institution, it was expanding westward as well. At the time of the nation's founding, some of slavery's critics had temporized on the Constitution's tacit endorsement of the principle of property in man, asserting that slavery would die a natural, or at least quiet, death. Washington himself had hoped that slavery would fall by "slow, sure, and imperceptible degrees."[34] The decline of the Chesapeake tobacco economy offered some support for such predictions, but the booming agricultural economy of the lower South belied them. Indeed, as the new century turned, sanguine assessments of slavery's imminent demise waned; slave production exploded into new territories carved out of western lands, or acquired from foreign powers. In 1803, the Louisiana Purchase added 828,000 square miles to the nation's existing 890,000, nearly doubling the size of the country at a stroke. The acquisition of Spanish Florida in 1819 added a further 72,000 square miles of territory, all of it southern. Slave owners and slave-grown crops spread into the new lands, raising difficult questions about the constitutional settlement and the fate of slavery. Increasingly, northern critics of the "slave interest" viewed Jefferson's expanding "empire of liberty" as something far less benign.[35]

The engine for the slave economy's expansion was, literally, an engine: the mechanical cotton gin, a machine that quickly performed the arduous task of separating cotton seed from the valuable silky fibers to which it was attached. First effectively developed by Eli Whitney in 1793, the gin revolutionized cotton agriculture, permitting efficient cultivation of short-staple cotton—a low-grade product that could be grown in a wide range of soils—throughout the South. Even the earliest hand-cranked mechanical gins could in one hour perform work requiring ten man-hours by hand. By the 1820s, factories were producing water-powered gins that multiplied this productivity many times. Annual cotton production in the United States soared—from 3,000 bales in 1790 to 73,000 just ten years later. By 1820 the nation produced 335,000 bales. By 1858 that figure had increased tenfold, and on the eve of the Civil War reached a remarkable 4.5

million bales.[36] By the mid-1830s, cotton exports to Great Britain and Europe constituted over half of the value of all American exports, a figure that remained fairly constant until the beginning of the Civil War.[37] Cotton cultivation expanded to every southern state, taking strong root first in the rich bottomlands of the lower Mississippi River Valley, which New Orleans served as the critical entrepôt. Riverside towns such as Natchez grew quickly from frontier outposts to critical trading centers. Soon, at the expense of native peoples forcibly relocated or simply decimated, cultivation spread throughout the middle portions of lower South states that had been carved out of Indian land. The national expansion of the United States was thus an affair deeply entwined with the health of slavery and the cotton economy. As the nation grew, slavery grew with it. In the first two decades of the new century, the slave states of Louisiana (1812), Mississippi (1817), and Alabama (1819) were added to the Union. By 1821, the tally of all states stood at twenty-four, evenly split into those where slavery had been (or was being) abolished, and those where slavery was positively protected by law and state constitution.

Rising slave populations kept pace with this expansion. At the time of the first federal census in 1790, the country enslaved almost 700,000 African-descended people. Two decades later the slave population had grown to 1.13 million, and by 1830 it had climbed to almost two million, or three times its 1790 level. The last years of the legal U.S. slave trade enhanced these numbers, and Africans continued to be smuggled into the country illegally afterward. Yet the vast majority of the growth owed to natural reproduction. In the process, slavery became an entirely southern institution. In 1790, the 40,000 slaves in the North constituted 6 percent—a small but notable proportion—of the nation's total population of enslaved people. By 1810, just after the closing of the slave trade, that figure was down to 27,000, a mere 2 percent of the national slave population. By 1830, only a few thousand black northerners remained enslaved, a telling but statistically negligible reminder of the national breadth the institution had once enjoyed.[38]

At the same time cotton cultivation boomed in the South, the northern economy was experiencing a distinct but related rise. The cotton that fueled southern economic expansion owed its value to new innovations in manufacturing, which made it a staple crop in the cloth production that helped drive the industrial revolution. In the United States, the process began with the emergence of technological changes that had originated in Great Britain and Western Europe, as new materials and new refining processes led to a revolution in manufacturing. Innovation blossomed, and the number of patents granted by the government rose—from 41 in 1800 to 155 in 1820 to 459 in 1840. Twenty years later, in 1860, 4,778 were issued. New materials and technologies, in turn, led to a revolution in the transportation of goods, people, and ideas across the nation. Roadways had been improving since the turn of the nineteenth century, when the nation boasted 1,200 miles of surfaced roads. New construction and paving technologies had helped these expand to 14,600 by 1825 and to 71,000 by 1850. New waterways, inaugurated by the opening of the Erie Canal in 1825, also heralded the new transportation age. By 1840 over 800,000 tons of freight moved over the Erie's network alone, a figure that tripled by the first year of the Civil War. New steamships plied the ever-expanding web of river roads, turning the Mississippi and Ohio River basins into two-way highways. At the same time, the "iron horse" revolutionized land transportation. In 1830, 23 miles of railroad track existed in the entire country. In five years there were over 1,000, and five years later still, in 1840, there were 2,800. On the eve of the Civil War, there were 30,000. These changes dramatically reduced the cost and time required to carry goods to market, thus increasing profits and creating incentives for further production and innovation.[39]

The transportation revolution brought to market new goods that were manufactured by new methods. As production moved from individual homes to centralized establishments, new systems of labor emerged to maximize productive efficiency. These new methods—mechanized production, interchangeable parts, and the specialization of labor in new manufactories—had vast social consequences. For one, cities grew in size and number. From 1790 to 1820 the urban population of the nation rose from just over 200,000 (5.1 percent of the total population) to nearly 700,000 (7.2 percent); in the next twenty years it grew to 1.8 million (19.8 percent).[40] The population of most American seacoast cities boomed in the early nineteenth century: Philadelphia's expanded by 150 percent from 1800 to 1830, while Baltimore's doubled. New York City's growth outdistanced them all. Already an important hub of commerce, shipping, and manufacturing, the city grew enormously around the turn of the century. By 1799, the value of the city's exports had grown to almost seven and a half times its 1791 level.[41] Growing by 1830 to two and a half times its size at the turn of the century, it outpaced in growth even expanding British industrial centers like Glasgow and Manchester.[42]

In and around such cities, the prevailing system of artisanal manufacture gave way to a new workforce composed of largely unskilled laborers, increasingly supplied from the ranks of displaced craftsmen, rural folk attracted to the urban economy, or European immigrants. Apprentices once destined to learn their entire craft and open their own shops now stayed in their un- or semiskilled occupations for life. Entrepreneurial artisans, who once took part in every part of the manufacturing process, became nascent capitalists who managed the labor of others or hired others to do so. Pioneered at sites such as Lowell, Massachusetts, the factory system of production employed laborers paid by hourly wages. Industrialization thus led to the emergence of modern social classes. Workers began to identify themselves through a cultural style that jealously guarded their declining workplace privileges and set them apart from the growing middle class, while a rising middle class just as assiduously sought to distance itself from "rough" laborers through "respectable" comportment and conspicuous display of their bourgeois status. The enormous social transformations in American life in the northern states amounted to much more than an industrial revolution; indeed, historians now speak of a "market revolution," which encompassed changes not just in technology and manufacturing, but also in social and mental worlds transformed by an expanding world of market connections, labor relations, and media communications.[43]

Documenting processes as large and complex as these is challenging, but it is instructive to relate the relative might of the industrializing U.S. economy, with its large population and highly diversified economy, to those of comparable New World societies. Contrast U.S. gross domestic product (GDP) in 1820 with its New World competitors. Economic historians calculate this figure at $12,548 million for the United States, rising to $18,219 in 1830. In contrast, Brazil's 1820 GDP stood at the equivalent to $2,912 million, rising to $4,959 in 1830; Jamaica's was $281 million in 1820, and fell to $217 in 1830, as slavery declined with the end of the slave trade. To put these figures in perspective, the U.S. numbers compared favorably with those of Great Britain and France, two of the largest economies in the world at the time, whose 1820 GDPs both hovered around the $36,000 million mark.[44]

Cotton fueled the industrial revolution that was responsible for this kind of success. In 1765, Britain had imported 3.36 million pounds of raw cotton, and exported 200,000 pounds of finished cotton goods; by 1825, it was importing 147 million pounds of raw cotton, which it converted into 30 million pounds worth of exported cotton goods.[45] The United States stood in complex relation to Britain's expanding textile industry. Its South supplied British looms with raw cotton, while its North constituted a rising competitor in the business of textile manufacturing; everywhere, its growing populations constituted a lucrative consumer market for the finished product. In 1825, the United States exported 131 million pounds of raw cotton to Great Britain, valued at over $30 million; it received back $11 million in finished cotton goods—the single largest category of British imports.[46] In essence, the U.S. North was coming to resemble the metropoles of Europe, with an expanding industrial base, rapid urbanization, and the formation of a large population of wage workers and consumers. The great difference, though, lay in the fact that in the United States, the agricultural periphery responsible for supplying raw materials critical for the manufacturing base lay within the boundaries of the nation itself and was fully empowered in the political process.

The expansion of the nation's borders in the first decades of the nineteenth century posed critical problems for a political system already tense over the fragile sectional compromise struck in 1787. Though slavery itself rarely dominated national anxieties—the threat of foreign rivals, or tensions between those in the urbanizing East and those in the frontier West, often claimed primacy—it could not be extricated from political debates, despite the most vigorous efforts to do so. As early as 1790, Congress pioneered a policy of studied silence on the potentially divisive issue. The Pennsylvania Society for Promoting the Abolition of Slavery condemned slavery and petitioned Congress to "devise means for removing the Inconsistency from the Character of the American People" and "promote mercy and justice toward this distressed Race."[47] Responding, both the House and the Senate composed committee reports endorsing the humanitarian principles of such petitions, but southern reticence proved fatal to them. Lower South representatives railed against the petition, complaining that the Constitution forbade any effort to end the slave trade before 1807 and avowing that any proposed federal efforts to free slaves "would never be submitted to by the southern states without a civil war."[48] Despite a close vote on the matter, Congress ultimately affirmed the Constitution's twenty-year protection of the slave trade as well as the right of southern states to hold slaves. Even more significantly, it had established a precedent with lasting implications: by responding to the antislavery petition with public silence, it had rendered the federal government neutral on the issue of slavery.

George Washington hoped that Congress had "at last put to rest" the sectionally divisive issue, but it would not die.[49] Whenever the boundaries of the nation expanded, it rose anew. The nation was born with an enormous swath of unsettled territory—British lands east of the Mississippi conceded to the United States at the end of the American Revolution. The Northwest Ordinance, passed in 1787 by Congress under the Articles of Confederation, organized the portion of this land north of the Ohio River, in the process excluding slavery from it. Southern interests were balanced when Congress similarly organized the territory south of the Ohio in 1790—but this time explicitly permitting slavery. Expansion did not, of course, stop there. It may fairly be said that America's greatest single instance of territorial aggrandizement owed to the paradoxical and unintended consequences of the slave revolution on St. Domingue. In defeating French attempts to reinstill slavery, the armies of revolutionary Haiti disrupted Napoléon's plans for a New World empire; instead, the emperor sold the Louisiana Territory to the United States in 1803. The Haitian Revolution thus bequeathed to the United States almost 900,000 square miles of territory, providing a vast new arena for slavery. Western lands fueled national expansion for decades, supplying the country with the territory, resources, and river-borne transportation networks necessary for it to become the most dynamic economy in the world. The Louisiana case demonstrated that, by introducing practical realities into what were usually abstract considerations, westward movement bedeviled efforts to enact commitments to universal freedom. The Louisiana Territory was already a slave land, occupied by people who owned, employed, and traded human beings. Its profitable exploitation depended, contemporaries believed, on the continued use of bound labor. As a southern congressman declared in debates over governance in Louisiana, "slaves must be admitted into that territory, it cannot be cultivated without them." Another argued that because only black people were capable of working effectively in its climate, "slavery must be . . . established in that country, or it can never be inhabited." The few upper South congressmen who opposed slavery in Louisiana did so only out of self-interested fears that it might "produce another St. Domingo."[50]

The sectional divide became particularly embittered as it became apparent that newly acquired lands threatened to vastly enhance the political power of the slaveholding states. Northerners, particularly New England Federalists, smelled in the Louisiana Purchase a plot to expand the power of the slave states and dominate the national government. Boston Federalist George Cabot argued that with the "federal ratio" operating in new states carved out of Louisiana, "it is so obvious that the influence of our part of the Union must be diminished."[51] With the promise of new slave states entering the Union, many northern politicians began doubting the wisdom of the compromises struck at the constitutional convention in 1787—in particular, the three-fifths clause. Some considered it "an original and radical defect in the form of government," while others feared that their forbears had unwittingly "made a *covenant with death*" in agreeing to the measure.[52] For the most ardent opponents of the slave power, the answer was to deny the application of the federal ratio in newly admitted states. William Ely, a western Massachusetts Federalist, engineered a resolution calling for a constitutional amendment abolishing the three-fifths clause, on the grounds that the Union could not persist "unless it be founded in principles which shall secure to all Free Citizens, equal political rights and privileges in the government."[53] The measure found no traction in Congress, but the point had been made: the fate of the Union depended on sectional harmony. Ardent Federalists pushed this principle to self-destructive extremes in 1814 during the Hartford Convention, when they openly discussed seceding from the Union and forming a "northern confederation." The call for northern secession amounted to political self-immolation for the party, yet Federalist opponents of southern power did succeed in establishing a critique of the three-fifths clause that would persist to the Civil War. Federalists such as Sereno Edwards Dwight, son of Yale President Timothy Dwight, issued screeds denouncing the "slave representation" permitted by the clause as a "rotten part of the Constitution," which "must be amputated."[54]

In these protests lay the roots of an argument that would reemerge time and again on the national stage: the "slave power" of the South represented a distinct interest, rooted in greed and domination, that sought to protect and aggrandize itself by undermining democracy and wielding uncontested political power. Clearly, there was much self-interest at work in northern politicians' efforts to undermine the slave power. Those who fiercely advocated limiting southern political might were mostly concerned with enhancing their own. At best, they reluctantly conceded the extension of revolutionary promises of equality to black people; at worst, they championed the forced removal of people they considered unassimilable racial inferiors. Yet if opposition to the slave power may not have drawn on the highest ideals of universal equality, there was more at work than simple self-interest. Federalist antislavery drew from values deeply rooted in the social worlds of the free states. It referred, obliquely but powerfully, to norms of American life developing out of conditions of dramatic social and economic change: those attending the political and economic revolutions the nation was so recently experiencing.

As political debates clarified the differences between the sections, there slowly emerged a vision of northern society that came to define slave society as its antithesis.[55] The depth of these commitments was apparent in many facets of the resulting ideology, but—by way of example—not least in the gender values evident in criticisms of the slave power. One Connecticut newspaper charged the slaveholding South with being full of "ignorant, effeminate and corrupt" men who "despise labor" for themselves and produced nothing but through their slaves. Others feared that "effeminate masters" would be unable to contain the "irreconcilable hatred" of rising numbers of slaves who threatened imminent uprisings.[56] When northern opponents attacked slaveholding as unmasculine because it fostered the luxury of idleness, they simultaneously defined their own masculine ideals as related to the ethic of the independent and individual producer, positing them as norms for acceptable society. This bundle of concerns evolved into what scholars have termed the ideology of free labor. By recalling free labor concepts in their rhetoric, northern politicians harnessed latent and deep-seated social values that proved far more vital than did ideas of race in combating slavery. If the Federalists and their elite vision of American society ultimately failed, they nonetheless bequeathed the twin pillars of all future political antislavery in the United States: the notion of the slave power and the virtues of free labor.

The tropes of slave power and free labor exhibited no simple paranoia, for despite the North's considerably larger population, the three-fifths clause cut severely into its advantage. In the First Congress, the apportionment for which was established by estimates of population in the Constitution, southern states controlled thirty seats, or 46 percent of the House of Representatives. By virtue of the federal ratio, this figure exceeded by twelve what without the clause would have been a mere eighteen seats. In the Second Congress, which was apportioned according to the 1790 census, the three-fifths clause secured the southern states fourteen seats they otherwise would not have enjoyed. Under a regime of apportioning seats strictly by free population, the North would have enjoyed a 19.0 percent advantage in the House; with the three-fifths clause, this lead was reduced to 8.6 percent.[57]

These differences mattered. Important pieces of federal legislation were passed by margins provided by the three-fifths clause. Scholars have established that it changed the results of over 55 percent of the legislative roll-call votes in the Sixth Congress (1799–1801). Southern overrepresentation was responsible for critical measures that aided the South, such as the Indian Removal Act of 1830, which cleared native-occupied lands for settlement and plantation agriculture.[58] The clause skewed the balance in the Electoral College with similar consequence. In the critical election of 1800, Jefferson's margin of victory owed to the five additional electoral votes Virginia commanded by virtue of the clause.[59]

The hyper-representation of the slave states also conferred a range of unpredictable and unforeseen benefits, which rippled through the halls of power at every level. To secure the alliances necessary to achieve southern support in the House, party leaders disproportionately favored southerners in the distribution of federal patronage and judicial appointments. The early party caucus system also gave unintended weight to southern concerns. With Jefferson's ascendant Republican Party rooted in the South and a much weaker Federalist Party siphoning off northern votes, northern Republicans found themselves dominated in caucus after caucus, despite representing far more constituents than did their southern party brethren.[60] Southern politicians understood, and reveled in, these realities, which the westward march of slavery promised only to enhance. George Mason of Virginia predicted that only a "few years" would pass before "the southern and western population should predominate," thus placing national power "in the hands of the minority." Even before the constitutional convention, Madison had predicted that southern states would accept the pact due to the "*expected* superiority" in population that they would enjoy in the near future.[61]

If Louisiana initiated northern fears of this power, debates over Missouri's admission into the Union placed them at the center of American politics. In the Missouri Crisis of 1819–21, questions of slavery and sectionalism organized national politics in unprecedented ways. The question arose as Missouri became the second state from the Louisiana Purchase to seek entry into the Union, in 1819. Under the Southwest Ordinance, Mississippi and Alabama had recently joined as slave states. Illinois had been admitted as a free state, but with several provisions that severely qualified its claim to the title, such as one permitting individual slaveholders to retain slaves (and their progeny) brought to the state before 1787 and another permitting the "indenture," or limited bound service, of black people into early adulthood. The prospect of yet another slave state entering the Union riled northern politicians. James Tallmadge, a Republican representative from New York, introduced an amendment to Missouri's statehood bill that prohibited the further introduction of slaves into the state, providing for post-nati emancipation for all newborn slaves after a period of apprenticeship. Effectively, the amendment amounted to a gradual emancipation act for the state. A two-year congressional battle ensued, with Tallmadge and his fellow New Yorker John W. Taylor leading the antiexpansion charge.

Speakers on both sides pontificated. Proslavery men argued that Congress had no right to restrict the terms on which new states might enter the Union, particularly on issues of property. Southern moderates argued that extension of slavery to Missouri actually served the cause of northern colleagues, for "diffusing" slavery across a wide expanse would spread it thinly, paving the way for gradual emancipation, and reducing the danger of slave revolt. Opponents invoked revolutionary principle, calling upon the inconsistency represented by the further spread of slavery in a land of freedom. Arthur Livermore, a representative from New Hampshire, supported the Tallmadge amendment because he hoped to "retrieve the national character" by enacting founding principles for all. Should the statehood bill pass unamended, he continued, "let us at least be consistent, and declare that our constitution was made to impose slavery, and not to establish liberty."[62]

Other restrictionists, though, used the Missouri debates to highlight the imbalance in political power conferred on the slaveholding states through the three-fifths compromise. John Quincy Adams reflected in his diary that the Missouri debates demonstrated to him "that the bargain between freedom and slavery contained in the constitution of the United States is morally and politically vicious." In addition to being "cruel and repressive," and "inconsistent with the principles on which alone our Revolution can be justified," the constitutional compromise struck with slavery in 1787 was "grossly unequal and impolitic." By viewing slaves as "persons not to be represented themselves, but for whom their masters are privileged with nearly a double share of representation," the Constitution had ensured "that this slave representation has governed the Union."[63]

Indeed, only southern overrepresentation had secured an outcome so favorable to the slave states. The critical vote on Missouri statehood in the House was a narrow ninety to eighty-seven—a victory that required all of Speaker Henry Clay's considerable skill at procedural manipulation to engineer, as well as the defection of fourteen northern representatives from their section. As historian Leonard Richards demonstrates, these northern defections were critical only because the South's overrepresentation brought its tally of support close enough to make them so. It is hard to imagine that northern congressmen, enjoying a clear majority, would have risked disloyalty to their section.[64]

In the end, Missouri entered the Union as a slave state, balanced by the simultaneous admission of Maine as a free state. In addition, no further slave states could be fashioned from the Louisiana Territory north of Missouri's southern border, the parallel of thirty-six degrees, thirty minutes. But the country had been badly shaken. Threats of disunion had flowed freely from all sides.[65] Thomas Jefferson's recollection of these events is well known: he considered the Missouri Crisis "a fire bell in the night," which portended "the knell of the Union." The compromise was a "reprieve only" from sectional discord—one that had established "a geographical line, coinciding with a marked principle" that "will never be obliterated," for "every new irritation will mark it deeper and deeper."[66] Jefferson himself, though, had championed the extension of slavery, as well as application of the three-fifths clause, to the entire Louisiana Territory. His Virginia colleague, Senator James Barbour, also viewed Missouri as a portentous divide, dramatically prophesying the apocalyptic civil war that was to come: "I behold the father armed against the son, and the son against the father. I perceive a brother's sword crimsoned with a brother's blood. I perceive our houses wrapped in flames, and our wives and infant children driven from their homes, forced to submit to the pelting of the pitiless storm."[67] On the other side, John Quincy Adams's disillusionment was equally palpable, to the point of wondering if the "wiser and bolder course" would not have been to let the Missouri Crisis rend the confederation. "This would have produced a new Union of thirteen or fourteen states unpolluted with slavery," which might have been able to rally other states around the glorious standard of "universal emancipation of their slaves."[68]

Such statements served partly as chits in a game of political brinkmanship being played out on the floors of the Senate and House. Yet they also revealed the degrees to which the Constitution had clearly not resolved fundamental issues over slavery, and how unlikely it was that the natural solution the Founders had hoped for would emerge on its own. The Missouri Crisis constituted a signal instance in which sectional concerns over slavery's expansion came to organize, and indeed temporarily dominate, national politics. A party political system built on broad national coalitions confronted enormous incentives to avoid sectionally divisive issues such as slavery, lest one party, in appearing to be sectionally extreme, concede the moderate center of political opinion to the other. Sectional issues threatened to split the parties and give the advantage to opponents, and were therefore studiously avoided. While by the time of the Missouri Crisis the withering Federalists could not even count on their old New England stronghold, the Republicans were a true national party and risked serious division over Missouri. Their own New York members had led the charge— a vast change from 1804, when New England Federalists had taken the lead in criticizing slavery's expansion.

The problem was that the issue was impossible to avoid. Because the three-fifths clause had woven slavery into the fabric of national political life, it affected the balance of power on all sectional issues. Whenever northern politicians felt the overweening power of southern statesmen, slavery was implicated, for only slavery had conferred on the South the overrepresentation that had so effectively served it. As the Missouri debate revealed, the problem for northern politicians was not so much that slavery itself was an institution that violated the fundamental principles of the nation and benighted its victims, but that slavery's defenders sought to manipulate the system of national governance in their own minority interest. By exercising unfair and disproportionate federal power, it was charged, they infringed upon the interests and liberties of free white people who lived in the states that did not permit slavery. The interests of the two sections being inimical, the slave power, it was thought, sought to protect itself by encroaching on the rights of the free. This violation of sectional comity undercut the entire experiment in democratic self-rule and imperiled the nation. The Constitution's hyper-empowerment of the slave states vastly protected the southern slave power, but at considerable cost: it generated sectional antagonism and provided slavery's critics with potent arguments. The political deck had been rigged at the nation's founding; the constitutional compromise had enshrined sectional inequity in the fundamental law of the land. Slavery was wrong not simply (or even) because it hurt slaves; slavery was wrong because it imperiled the government, and unity, of free whites.

In no rival slave country did slavery's expansion ever generate the political conflict it did in the divided United States. For example, Britain's expansion of its overseas colonial plantation complex in the second half of the eighteenth century had not seemed to pose a threat back in the British metropole. The acquisition of the Caribbean islands of Grenada, St. Vincent, the Grenadines, Tobago, and Dominica at the conclusion of the Seven Years' War in 1763 produced no national convulsions. The reticence of planters on the older islands to invite new competitors from within the empire signaled a lack of confidence driven by their growing weakness in the empire, while the perennial insecurity of Caribbean islands in an age of global warfare also inhibited the expansion of plantation slavery in newly acquired islands. Neither did the additions of Trinidad, St. Lucia, and Guyana around the turn of the century aggrandize the slave power of the British West Indies. With the abolition of the slave trade in 1807, and the emerging alternative of European beet sugar, which rose as a result of the Napoleonic Wars' interruption of the Caribbean cane sugar trade, prospects for the existing sugar complex, let alone opportunities for expansion, seemed bleak. It was not that sugar plantations did not grow, nor that abolitionists did not complain. But between questions over sugar's future in the periphery and an emerging consensus on the inhumanity of slavery in the metropole, political conflicts in Britain over the expansion of the plantation complex never came close to generating the animus they did in the United States. Even in the fiercest debates over the British slave trade, the *spread* of slavery never emerged as the central motif it did in the United States.

Brazil represents another pole on the range of political responses to the expansion of slavery in the postrevolutionary era. Unlike Great Britain, where a core of committed antislavers was emerging in the metropole, Brazil faced no internal political opposition to slavery's expansion. Slavery was broadly deemed a legitimate and necessary component of the national economy, and practiced virtually everywhere. The sugar region of the northeast had seen better years, and the mining regions of the center were declining in productivity. But the countryside in the south, outside of São Paulo and the national capital of Rio de Janeiro, became lucrative ground for the expansion of coffee production. In the middle of the eighteenth century, the southern portions of French St. Domingue had supplied half of the world's coffee, but the Haitian Revolution had disrupted production, opening up new possibilities in the prime growing lands of the Brazilian south. As cotton expanded across the southwestern frontier in the United States, coffee spread into the Paraíba Valley and Oeste Paulista of southern Brazil, placing huge new demands on existing sources of slave labor supply. As did cotton growing, coffee production occurred in lands cleared from the interior, and favored holdings that could be worked with smaller workforces and without the intense capitalization required of sugar. Yet as Brazil lacked a strong modernizing, industrializing core, wherein free labor was becoming the rule and antislavery metropolitan values prevailed, the spread of the coffee complex in Brazil never produced anything like the criticisms that cotton expansion encountered in the United States.

Between the British West Indies, where the slave power was most certainly on the defensive, and Brazil, where the slave power was so hegemonic that it bred even very little self-conscious identity as a slave power, stood the slave power of the U.S. South. It, too, produced agricultural staples that met ever-increasing demands from ever-growing publics. But in the race to keep up with a rapidly changing world economy, the South enjoyed important advantages over many other New World slave societies. The South's hyper-empowerment in its national government helped offset the proximity of antislavery critics within national borders, putting it on a par with the unassailed slave powers of Brazil and Cuba. Furthermore, the product the South grew, cotton, put the region in better relation to broader economic developments than did sugar or coffee. This was important because, as scholars such as Dale Tomich have noted, rapid industrialization, the expansion of finance and credit, and the growth of industrial wage labor as an efficient and normative mode of production threatened to relegate slave production to secondary status within the Atlantic economy.[69] Paradoxically, the industrial revolution and wage-labor capitalism had also helped create consumer tastes and a demand for products from the periphery. In no way did industrial society seek to destroy or negate the economy of the periphery; rather, it sought to subordinate it to the needs of the industrializing cores.

In the race to remain competitive with rising industrial sectors of the Atlantic economy, the southern slave power of the United States held relative advantages over its rivals. As historian Richard Graham has pointed out, its staple crop occupied a key position in a productive sequence at the forefront of the industrial economy.[70] Unlike sugar, coffee, cacao, or tobacco, cotton was no mere dessert product; it was not the end point in a chain of production creating consumer goods that the public increasingly expected to find cheap and plentiful. Rather, it was a raw good that lay at the beginning of an industrial process of textile production, the very one that fueled the industrial revolution. It hence attracted enormous capital investment, which resulted in the South markedly outpacing its agricultural competitors elsewhere in key measures of transportation infrastructure, industrialization, and agricultural innovation. The primacy of cotton in the most dynamic sector of the Atlantic economy impacted not just the South, but the United States as a whole. Shippers profited from moving cotton while textile manufacturers grew to compete with European producers, and creditors made fortunes from financing planters' purchases of new lands and enslaved workers. Northern producers of cloth and foodstuffs benefitted from supplying southern demand. In economic terms, everyone won.[71] Despite the searing critiques northerners would end up leveling at the alleged backwardness of the slave South, by all world-historical standards the region boasted the most highly developed economy of any slave society, anywhere. In contrast to its competitors in the Caribbean or even Brazil, the slave interest of the United States was well positioned indeed.

CHAPTER 4

To Become a Great Nation

Caste and Resistance in the
Age of Emancipations

LIBERTY MAY BECOME AN EVIL
The Problem of Freedom in the Postemancipation North

In the first three decades of the nineteenth century, the slaveholding states' strong position in the Union failed to be countered by a North as committed to free society as the South was to slavery. It did not hurt the South that the northern metropole to which it was connected was itself so ambivalent over the presence of slavery and nonwhite people in its midst. With slavery expanding westward in the South, and market relations expanding in the North, gradual emancipation was still under way. Political concern in the North about the "slave power" of the South portended ongoing national crises, but before 1831 moral qualms failed to arouse widespread public opposition to the practice of slavery, and certainly not to racial prejudice. Abolitionists in the Early Republic objected to slavery on religious grounds, but they constituted a small minority of elite reformers. The persistence of slavery in New York and New Jersey well into the early national period illustrated the North's reticence on issues of race. In 1790, enslaved African Americans constituted 6.2 percent of these states' total populations—the highest in all the North.[1] Every northern state found it difficult to end slavery unequivocally, but the process was especially troubled where bondsmen constituted important segments of the workforce. While slavery did gradually die in both of these holdout states, the process revealed a climate of postrevolutionary racial retrenchment that badly degraded the quality of freedom that the emancipated would enjoy.

In both New York and New Jersey, those inspired by revolutionary principles had argued for ending the institution. In New York, Governor John Jay had pressed for an abolition bill in 1785, arguing that "to contend for our own liberty and to deny that blessing to others, involves an inconsistency not to be excused."[2] New Jersey's William Livingston also pressed for a measure during the Revolution itself. In both states, though, slaveholders successfully repelled gradual abolition measures for a considerable time. Opponents of gradual abolition invoked arguments used in other states, made more powerful by stronger slaveholder interests. They relied on the familiar assertion that abolition constituted an illegitimate expropriation of legally held property in humans, calling emancipation measures "a solemn act of public ROBBERY." Arguing for "the respect due to property," they claimed that it would be "unjust and unconstitutional" to deprive citizens of their chattels "without making them a reasonable compensation."

Unsurprisingly, emancipation's supporters argued that it was unjust, if not unconstitutional, to hold other humans as property. Declared New York newspaperman Noah Webster, "*Property* in the persons and labors of other men, is a thing in itself absurd," and "a direct violation of the law of nature and society."[3] In truth, though, the issue was contested, and the impasse stalled the progress of emancipation measures in these states for years. Even antislavery politicians viewed moderation the best policy. In the midst of the Revolution, Gouverneur Morris, a New York member of the Continental Congress, tempered his call for the state "to dispense the blessings of freedom to all mankind" with the warning that "it would at present be productive of great dangers to liberate the slaves within this State." Delay, he believed, would be "consistent with the public safety."[4] Conceded Webster, "A *gradual* restoration of the blacks to their rights is all that is desired or can with safety be hazarded."[5]

Gradual was, indeed, the watchword of emancipation in New York and New Jersey, where legislatures consistently beat back efforts to pass emancipation measures until the turn of the nineteenth century. Chastened by rejection in the 1780s, emancipation's advocates in New York resteeled themselves in the 1790s, proposing new measures every year, just as William Wilberforce was doing with anti-slave-trade legislation in Britain. In 1799, they scored a major success with New York's first emancipation measure, which freed all children of slaves born after July 4, 1799, indenturing them to their former owners well into adulthood. By these provisions, the law would not legally free anyone before 1824, when women born of slave mothers would reach their maturity. Still, the diminution of slavery had begun. Enslaved people reacted to prospects for impending mass emancipation with a rash of flight, sinking into urban centers like New York City, where they might enjoy anonymous, tenuous lives in freedom. Owners seeking to extract remaining years of reliable service from their bondspersons often negotiated early releases from servitude in exchange for steady labor and financial compensation. Many enslaved African Americans purchased their own freedom with funds earned from extra work, in effect paying masters twice—

once for their usual unpaid labor, and again for their very liberty. When in 1817 New York's legislature passed a law providing for the freedom of all slaves ten years hence, the informal dismantling of slavery intensified.

A similar, though slower, process prevailed in New Jersey, where a post-nati emancipation measure did not pass until 1804. That law provided freedom for children of slaves born after July 4, 1804, upon reaching the age of twenty-one (women) or twenty-five (men). New Jersey never freed those born before this date, though the new state constitution of 1846 declared them "lifelong apprentices" with minimal legal protections.[6] In 1860, the federal census still listed eighteen bondspersons in the state, and slavery was not completely abolished in New Jersey until the Thirteenth Amendment ended the institution nationwide in 1865.

Debates over emancipation bills revealed the racial commitments of the society that had so hesitantly enacted the promises of the Revolution. Gradual emancipation posed what whites in all postemancipation societies regarded as a dilemma: what to do with African-descended people who were no longer enslaved. Many in the northern states of the Early Republic believed that, whether because of the habits inculcated by slavery or because of inherent racial deficiencies, black people constituted a dangerous element in free society. Against the Revolution's ideal of independent and civically invested men as ideal republican citizens, blacks were thought to fare poorly. Throughout the North, detractors— and even many defenders—of mass emancipation worried that the characters and proclivities of black people naturally unfitted them to participate equally in free society. New Jersey opponents of gradual abolition cited "the general misconduct of free negroes" and "the danger to which the state would be exposed from the manumission of so great a number."[7] Black people's "deep wrought disposition to indolence and laziness" supposedly went hand in hand with their "general looseness of passions and uncontrovertible propensity to gratify and satiate every thirst . . . without attending to the consequences."[8] Such statements attended discussions over emancipation in every northern state with a sizable black population, warning of the dangers freed slaves allegedly posed to community order and the fragile democracy.

These anxieties exposed the foundations of the racial caste society that emerged in the wake of the northern emancipations. As the North became free, it became ever more dedicated to assigning black people to the lowest rungs of the social and economic ladder, simply on the basis of race. The prime mover in the northern emancipations had been the ideology of the Revolution, rather than whites' enlarged estimation of blacks' capacity for freedom; the overwhelming concern that blacks may have been inherently different remained. Much room stood between complete enslavement and full citizenship, let alone social equality. The most frequent arguments made for mass emancipation were that slavery violated the principles of the Revolution and perhaps of Christianity, made hypocrites of liberty-loving Americans, and insidiously threatened the freedom of all. "Those who make slaves of the blacks," intoned one New York editor in 1785, "will likewise of the whites."[9]

Conspicuously absent from these worries that slavery warped the democratic fabric was much estimation of the enslaved, whom antislavery rhetoric portrayed as unfailingly debased, if only by an unjust institution. If slavery was bad because, as Jefferson had worried, it trained masters to antidemocratic tendencies, then it could hardly have been good for the slaves. Even those who spoke out against bondage did so on the grounds that, as Montesquieu had written, "slavery clogs the mind, perverts the moral faculty, and reduces the conduct of man to the standard of brutes."[10] The ambiguity over subject and object in such sentiments told much. The very degradation that made slavery abolishable also made its victims incapable of equality. Revolutionary discourse, with its concern for republican virtue and collective responsibility, excoriated the dependence inherent in servitude as dangerously antirepublican. But the same logic also suggested that the casualties of the institution were utterly unprepared for wielding the precious right of self-rule. Democracy was no trifle; it required incessant practice in the habits of civic virtue in order not to devolve into anarchy or tyranny. The enslaved had never had such practice, it was argued, and perhaps could not benefit from it anyway. As the American Convention for Promoting the Abolition of Slavery put it, "Liberty, may become an evil, without a previous qualification for its enjoyment."[11]

The antislavery minority thus harped incessantly on the need to "prepare" black people for freedom. White antislavery workers argued for careful supervision of free blacks, who "should be led from those habits of idleness, profligacy, and improvidence, consequent on slavery, into paths of sobriety and industry."[12] Lectures to free blacks constituted a staple of abolitionist literature. "It is by your good conduct alone," intoned the American Convention in 1796, "that you can refute the objections which have been made against you as rational and moral creatures, and remove many of the difficulties, which have occurred in the general emancipation of such of your bretheren as are yet in bondage."[13] To help ensure this uplifting of former slaves, antislavery societies constructed plans, such as the one Benjamin Franklin composed for the Pennsylvania Abolition Society, that free blacks be subject to visits from a "Committee of Inspection," which would oversee "the morals, general conduct, and ordinary situation of the free negroes."[14] Freedom, then, came with grave concerns over whether it was possible or not to remedy the moral and civic failings slavery had inculcated in slaves.[15]

In addition, slavery's elimination had removed from northern society a central principle of social division, and one that had conferred on the white majority an unfailing source of status. Despite its egalitarian rhetoric, revolutionary America was without question a class society, which the economic and social reorganizations of the Early Republic only furthered.[16] The presence of slavery had always provided whites on the lower end of the social spectrum some assurance that, no matter how lowly they might be perceived, there were always others beneath them. Now, though, with the category of "slave" no longer present to mark a distinction between working-class whites and blacks, northern society in the Early Republic seemed all the more committed to maintaining hierarchies of race. If slavery no longer distinguished a clear class of social subordinates, factors somehow embodied in black people themselves might do that work. Freedom thus paradoxically placed new premiums on arguments that blacks were, by their very natures, inherently inferior to whites. The northern emancipations in fact led to a marked redefinition of race, in which caste society's reliance on the institution of slavery gave way to rejuvenated faith in the concept of inherent and irrevocable biological difference. Revolutionary era paeans to the commonality of man and the unity of the human family faded. Claims that only degraded conditions produced degraded people succumbed to a resurgent faith that blacks' inferiority was likely innate and immutable.

These trends appeared in several realms. Not least were subtle changes in scientific arguments over race that emerged across the Atlantic, but particularly in the U.S. North. Revolutionary ideology, with its stress on universal human rights, tended to support a theory of race now termed "environmentalism," in which physical differences between humans were explained on the basis of environmental factors such as climate and geography. In environmental theory, Africans' long habitation in sunny equatorial zones explained their darker skin. Leading intellectual figures of the revolutionary era, such as Princeton University President Samuel Stanhope Smith, had advocated such views. Not everyone had acceded. Roots of an alternative view—"polygenesis," or the idea that multiple creations had spawned distinct species of man—were growing in the work of French naturalist Georges Cuvier and others. Jefferson himself, the embodiment of the American Enlightenment, expressed considerable ambiguity over the matter. Unwilling to decide whether Africans constituted "a distinct race" or were a people "made distinct by time and circumstance," he hazarded the "suspicion" that the races might nonetheless "possess different qualifications." Blacks' "unfortunate difference of colour, and perhaps of faculty," he wrote, rendered them inferior. Emancipation, he feared, would mean racial mixing, which in turn meant a degradation of white "blood" tantamount to racial suicide. In slave systems in which race was not a factor, Jefferson claimed, "the slave, when made free, might mix with, without staining the blood of his master"; but in America, the emancipated slave must be "removed beyond the reach of mixture."[17]

As these views suggested, environmentalism itself could slip easily into racial essentialism, or the view that each distinct "race" possessed inherent features that distinguished them from each other, morally and intellectually as well as physically. Benjamin Rush, Philadelphia's revolutionary era doctor and abolitionist, exemplified the process in his treatises on the causes of blackness. Arguing that Africans' skin color resulted from a disease akin to leprosy—originally contracted through Africa's "greater heat, more savage manners, and bilious fevers"—Rush contended that environmentally derived characteristics could become hereditary. While he used his conclusions to argue that Africans thus deserved "a double portion of our humanity," he also argued that their malady could be cured through massive bloodletting and the extensive inducement of "artificial diarrhoea."[18]

With distance from the Revolution, the fragile edifice of Enlightenment era environmentalism crumbled. In the Early Republic, ambivalence over environmentalism shifted into a growing faith in racial essentialism, and particularly the theory of polygenesis. Thinkers such as Charles Caldwell, who had studied with Benjamin Rush in Pennsylvania, began arguing forcefully that the Bible constituted the history not of all peoples, but only of the white race. According to this understanding of the biblical creation story in Genesis, which was called "pre-Adamism," God had made blacks along with the animal kingdom, before the sixth day.[19] In future years, an entire branch of biological science, which became known as the "American school" of ethnology, developed around the proposition that black and white people were not simply different varieties of the same family, but entirely different species. The very term Atlantic culture used to describe mixed-race people—*mulatto*—stemmed from the root word for mule, the sterile hybrid of differing animal species. Polygenesism, though often hostile to the biblically based defenses of slavery most frequently authored in the South, nonetheless held people of African descent in special contempt, thus fitting it well to serve as the ideological foundations of the racial caste society the North was pioneering. The birth of American racial science lay not in a slaveholding South seeking to justify its existence, but in an emancipating North seeking new ways to subordinate black people in the absence of slavery.

These trends in professional science followed rather than spawned popular culture's embrace of the notion of free black people's inherent inferiority. While in future decades the new science would become critical to denying black humanity, the work of denigrating people of African descent to the lowest rungs of northern society occurred first and most profoundly at the level of popular culture. Here, too, a transition from a more tolerant, revolutionary era environmentalism to the racial essentialism of the postemancipation age was apparent, nowhere more than in popular characterizations of black people made possible by inexpensive new technologies of print. In cheap broadsides and etchings designed to be humorous, a particular stereotype of black people emerged to articulate the white North's racial anxieties: the black dandy figure.

Consider one of the earliest of such images—an 1819 etching that appeared in Philadelphia, titled *A New Mode of Perfuming & Preserveing Clothes from Moths* (figure 4.1). In a streetscape, two white gentlemen outside a fashionable tailor's shop observe two young black men, dressed exactly like the whites, who are complimenting each other on how such fine clothing will help them woo ladies. It turns out, though, that the black men are imposters. They do not actually own their fancy clothes, but are only airing them out for the tailor, so the fine couture will not become moth-ridden in storage. Thus one of the white "swells" gripes, "Who knows but the suit I have on has been air'd in the same manner & perfumed too?" The implication, which is supposed to be horrifying, is that the white men are wearing clothing previously worn by the black men, and "perfumed" by the bad body odor frequently alleged of blacks. While

FIGURE 4.1. James Thackera, *A New Mode of Perfuming & Preserveing Clothes from Moths* (Philadelphia, 1819).
Historical Society of Pennsylvania, Philadelphia.

the image also lampoons the white men's obsession with fashion, its palpable racism trades on white fears that freedom has erased clear social distinctions between races, for emancipated blacks sought at every turn to appropriate the trappings of respectable whiteness. Text accompanying the image describes the scene thus: "The Black gentry aping their masters, dress quite as extravagantly, and frequently wear their clothes, long before they are cast off. They not only ape the dress of their masters, but also their cant terms, being well versed in the fashionable vocabulary."[20]

The black dandy figure in this image represented an addition to a long-standing cast of racial stereotypes. Earlier appearances of black figures in theatrical and literary humor had tended to partake of a long tradition of using social outsiders (such as blacks, servants, or the poor) to comment on the follies of social insiders by ridiculing pretenders to high social station. While black figures continued to serve this function, the black dandy constituted a new role for blacks—as those very pretenders. Whereas marginal blacks had once been used to poke fun at white dandies, they now became dandies themselves—as artificial as they were superficial. An 1829 etching from Philadelphia noted this theme with particular economy (figure 4.2). In one of the images in artist Edward Clay's satirical *Life in Philadelphia* series, two absurdly overdressed black

FIGURE 4.2.
Edward Clay, *Life in Philadelphia*, plate 4 (Philadelphia: S. Hart, 1829).
Library Company of Philadelphia, Philadelphia.

FIGURE 4.3. *Zip Coon, a Favorite Comic Song, Sung by Mr. G. W. Dixon* (New York: J. L. Hewitt, 1834).
Robert Cushman Butler Collection of Theatrical Illustrations, Manuscripts, Archives, and Special Collections, Washington State University Libraries, Pullman.

people meet on the street. Mr. Cesar asks Miss Chloe, "How you find yourself dis hot weader," to which she replies, "Pretty well I tank you Mr. Cesar[,] only I aspire too much!"[21] Miss Chloe's malapropism efficiently evokes the central fear of black social aspiration. The point of such images was clear: with freedom, black people sought to assume the appearance of bourgeois whiteness in dress, manners, and speech. The humor, though, was that this was a clear absurdity, given blacks' innate incapacities. Miss Chloe, after all, did not even understand the difference between aspiration and perspiration. The images thus worked by frightening, and then reassuring: newly freed blacks might try to "ape" the dress or speech of their betters, but their efforts would always fail. Incapable of assimilation, blacks would never be able to successfully assume the mantle of respectability. They would remain in their proper "place," and the color line could be preserved, even in freedom.

The new comic figure played a role in the birth of distinctly American entertainment forms, such as the blackface minstrel shows that became a national rage in the 1830s and 1840s. These traveling variety extravaganzas featured something for everyone, but working-class audiences particularly welcomed their denigrating racist humor. Now traversing the stage as the stock character Zip Coon (figure 4.3),[22] the black dandy consoled a broad range of white audiences that freedom would not erode the barriers between the races—that no matter how earnestly African-descended people sought to emulate the norms of middle-class whiteness, their inherent degradation would always out.

COLONIZATION, AMALGAMATION, OR ANNIHILATION
Enforcing Caste Society in the Free States

While racial science and popular culture pointed to the dilemmas posed by expanding black freedom in the North, two quite different phenomena offered solutions. One was for states to "reform" the rules determining eligibility to vote so as to exclude blacks from the elective franchise. Throughout the free states, the first decades of the nineteenth century witnessed a fundamental transformation in American politics. While the rhetoric of the Revolution had stressed the political empowerment of the common man and undermined colonial habits of social deference, the nation's early politics remained bound up in republican anxieties over civic virtue and constraints on democratic excess. Early crises over issues of class and revenue on the frontier—Shays' Rebellion in western Massachusetts in 1786 and 1787, the Whiskey Rebellion in western Pennsylvania in 1794, and Jan Fries's tax revolt among Pennsylvania Dutch farmers in 1799—convinced many national leaders of the dangers of widespread democratic participation, and helped consolidate national power in the hands of the privileged.[23] But with a new century, older patterns of deferential politics, in which elected officials were culled from the ranks of "best men" and local elites, steadily surrendered to broader participation in the electoral process. Westward migration and new frontier states shifted the balance of power away from the East. The consolidation of national politics in the wake of the War of 1812 and Panic of 1819 permitted the slow emergence of a true mass party political system, in which those out of power could be counted on to function as loyal opposition, dedicated to maintaining basic constitutional arrangements while also checking the mandate of the ruling party. Party rhetoric remained fractious, but all who sought political power came to understand the need to marshal a broad constituency. A wave of state action broadened the elective franchise. Northern states redrafted their constitutions, dropping property requirements to vote and ushering in what American historians once celebrated as the "age of the common man."

Such men did not include those of African descent. As free states dropped property requirements to vote, many added the word "white" to their constitutions for the first time, thus removing blacks from the electorate where some had once held the franchise. In 1818, Connecticut extended the vote to all white men who paid taxes or served in the militia, but denied the vote to free blacks. New York followed in 1821, when its new state constitution dropped property requirements for voting but added racial exclusions. In 1838, Pennsylvania did the same. New Jersey excluded blacks from voting in 1807, but did not drop its property requirement on white voters until 1844. Apart from those in Connecticut, New England blacks fared a bit better. In Vermont, New Hampshire, and Maine, no property qualification restricted voting, and race was no barrier. But, numbering a mere three-tenths of 1 percent of the total population of these states in 1820, blacks enjoyed little electoral power anyway. Rhode Island and Massachusetts never implemented racial exclusions to voting, but property qualifications prevailed in Massachusetts until 1821 and in Rhode Island until 1842. The situation was far worse in the new states of the West, which presented clean legal slates free of the racially egalitarian legacies of the Revolution. All new free states entering the Union before the Civil War did so without property qualifications for voting, but with explicit constitutional denials of black suffrage: Ohio (1803), Indiana (1816), Illinois (1818), Michigan (1837), Iowa (1846), Wisconsin (1848), California (1850), and Oregon (1859).

Debates over the suffrage exclusion that New York implemented at its state constitutional convention of 1821 illustrated the general pattern. Charges of political corruption provided the ostensible justification for disfranchisement. Some delegates complained that black New Yorkers were "too ignorant to know whether their vote is given to elevate another to office, or to hang themselves upon the gallows."[24] The real culprit, though, was black freedom itself. Whites could not halt the course of gradual emancipation, but they could still draw distinctions among the freed. At some point in the proceedings, nearly all advocates of franchise exclusion feared the specter of what was commonly termed "social equality." Delegate Erastus Root could not imagine poor blacks standing at the polls, equal to "those who ride in their coaches, and whose shoes and boots they had so often blacked." Whites would not countenance blacks on the militia training ground, in the jury box, or in their churches, so why let them vote? Conjectured one delegate, "If the time should ever arrive, when . . . the colours shall intermarry—when negroes shall be invited to your tables—to sit in your pew, or ride in your coach, it may then be proper to institute a new Convention, and remodel the constitution so as to conform to that state of society."[25]

No reasoned response was likely to alter such thinking. "Do our prejudices against their colour destroy their rights as citizens?" asked one delegate.[26] Others countered that restricting the vote only removed potential inducements to black social mobility. Rather than fostering a "sober and industrious" African American population, franchise exclusion would establish "a large, a perpetual, a degraded, and a discontented *caste*, in the midst of our population."[27] But such appeals fell deafly on the ears of a white majority so deeply invested in maintaining a stratified racial order. The convention removed all property restrictions on white men, only to impose a $250 property requirement on black voters. By 1826, further limits on white voting were removed, by which time only sixteen blacks in New York County possessed the property necessary to vote.[28] The Constitution of 1821 was long heralded as a victory of democracy over the forces of deference. But white New Yorkers had not erased social hierarchy; they had merely substituted old divisions of class and ethnicity among whites with the new primacy of race. In the age of the common man, African Americans paid the price for this *herrenvolk democracy* with their very rights.[29]

A host of legal limitations on black life buttressed the white supremacy implicit in suffrage restriction. Ohio laws required free blacks to register their presence and prove their liberty at county courts, fined whites for hiring free blacks lacking a state-issued certificate of freedom, and presumed in favor of slave owners when free blacks were accused of being fugitives from slavery.[30] A later law required blacks to post a bond of five hundred dollars when entering the state, which would be forfeited upon criminal behavior. Western states entering the Union thereafter all adopted similar provisions, which often remained on the books until abolitionists' legal efforts struck them down in the late 1840s. Some remained until the adoption of the Fourteenth Amendment in 1868. Oregon represented, like Ohio, another extreme case. Its territorial legislature required freed blacks to leave the state, and authorized county authorities to whip recalcitrant offenders every forty days until they complied.[31] In 1849, it simply forbade black settlement in the territory at all.[32] Virtually everywhere, free blacks were permitted to testify in court only against other blacks, and racial intermarriage was strictly forbidden. Throughout the free states, and particularly along the border with the South, free blacks were susceptible to capture and enslavement without full protection of law.

The goal was clear: exclude the immigration of blacks when possible, and define black citizenship as second-class when not. In the minds of many whites in the free states, blacks had themselves become synonymous with whatever problems slavery was thought to represent. Ridding themselves of the "curse of slavery" meant ridding themselves not simply of the institution, but of blacks themselves.[33] Collectively, such measures made a profound statement about the place of race in the Early Republic. In effect, the free states of the young country traded universal white manhood suffrage for racial exclusion. It was as if American society could not imagine the broadening of democracy to whites of all social classes without an equivalent restriction on blacks. White men of all social stations gained the suffrage only by denying it to free blacks, no matter how propertied. Here was a solution to the problem of potentially unruly lower orders: invest all whites in the political system by offering to the working class privileges now denied to blacks.

The exclusionary impulse evident in these racial restrictions found even stronger vent in a new national movement to "colonize" freed American blacks in settlements on the West African coast. Perhaps blacks, like slavery, could be removed entirely from the free states. Ideas for settling African Americans overseas had been floated for decades. British abolitionists had taken the lead in establishing the colony of Sierra Leone on the western coast of Africa in 1786, with the first fragile settlement of several hundred poor black (and some white) Londoners failing. A second settlement, in 1792, fared better. This group of twelve hundred was composed mainly of African American refugees from the Revolutionary War, who had accepted offers of British freedom only to find life difficult when relocated to the Canadian province of Nova Scotia. Over time, the colony became a haven for a wide range of African-descended people, including Jamaican maroons and Africans freed in interdicting the Atlantic slave trade. As in the United States, strong doses of practical consideration balanced whatever humanitarian idealism may have been at work in British plans for the colony. Black people were reluctant to resettle anywhere where their liberty and lives could be put at risk, but colony organizers such as Henry Smeathman were as interested in removing the black poor from the streets of London as they were in helping blacks establish a homeland.[34]

While challenged by practical problems and qualified by the limits of its organizers' racial egalitarianism, Sierra Leone became a potent symbol for American blacks seeking to escape the tightening noose of caste society in the North. It caught the attention of Paul Cuffee, a free black ship captain from New Bedford, Massachusetts, who dreamt of a land where African Americans could live free of the deepening prejudices around them. Encouraged by British abolitionists, Cuffee explored the possibilities of emigration on a visit to Sierra Leone in 1811. Returning inspired, he promoted emigration plans to American blacks, and even sent nine families to Sierra Leone—thirty-eight people in all—at his own expense.[35]

His interests dovetailed with those of white reformers formulating plans for an American version of British colonizationists' Sierra Leone Company: Robert Finley, a Presbyterian minister who rose to the presidency of Princeton University; Samuel John Mills, one of the founders of the American Bible Society; and Charles Fenton Mercer, a slaveholding Virginia congressman who became enamored of the possibilities of African colonization. In 1817 these men helped found the American Colonization Society (ACS), a benevolent organization dedicated to developing a colony of free black Americans on the shores of West Africa, in a land to the south of Sierra Leone. The plan attracted prominent backers, its leading lights numbering among the most prominent national figures in the land: James Monroe, Francis Scott Key, John Jay, Daniel Webster, Henry Clay, and Bushrod Washington. With this kind of backing, and the aid of state auxiliaries in border states such as Kentucky and Maryland, the effort yielded results. The ACS purchased lands in Africa that became Liberia, and from 1820 to 1843 transported 4,571 emigrants, mostly free blacks living in the slave states. Life was hard, with settlers beset by a paucity of supplies, poor administration by white benefactors, hostile African neighbors, and—most of all—a disease environment that claimed the lives of an enormous number of migrants, whom racial science and popular belief had erroneously supposed would be resistant. By 1843, historian Tom Shick demonstrates, only 1,819 of these original emigrants remained.[36]

In Liberia, the ACS sought to offer something for everyone, a potential solution to the problem of slavery that might appeal to both black and white people. As its newspaper offered, sending blacks "back" to Africa would provide a threefold benefit. First and most important, "we should be cleared of them," it stated, referring to free blacks. Second, the "partly civilized" settlers it sent to Africa would act as missionaries to help Christianize the benighted people of the continent. Last, "blacks themselves, would be put in a better situation" by escaping the prejudice that beset them in the United States.[37] This telling ordering of priorities suggested the deep ambivalence fundamental to the enterprise. At its start, though, the ACS attracted the energies of a broad array of Americans, including many important ones of African descent. To those such as Cuffee, colonization promised the aid of white benefactors in escaping the deepening oppression of the free North, establishing yet another black nation that could defend the interests of people of color everywhere and undermining slavery in the South. Finley discussed his plans with Cuffee, who supported his meeting in 1817 with Philadelphia black leaders James Forten and Richard Allen. Finley recorded that Forten, who was one of the wealthiest African Americans in Pennsylvania, became "animated on the subject." Emigration would let black Americans escape their "peculiarly oppressive situation," and, as the blacks of St. Domingue, "become a great nation." Allen, the cofounder of the first independent black church in the country, "spoke with warmth on some oppression which they suffer from the whites, and spoke warmly in favor of colonization in Africa."[38]

When presented to a public meeting of black Philadelphians, however, the proposal met with flat rejection. As Forten wrote to Cuffee, "Three Thousand at least attended, and there was not one sole that was in favor of going to Africa." Black Philadelphians simply did not trust their purported benefactors. Reported Forten, "they think that the slave holders want to get rid of them so as to make their property more secure." The masses' rejection of colonization chastened the leaders, but the dream of an independent black homeland did not die. Forten decided to "remain silent" on the issue in public, but privately grumbled that African Americans would "never become a people until they come out from amongst the white people."[39] Black leaders and elites nursed the idea, though, and over the course of the arduous decades to come they frequently resurrected hopes of contributing to a black nation elsewhere, like Haiti, or establishing a black state of their own—in central America, Canada, the American West, or elsewhere in Africa. While most African Americans rejected ACS-sponsored emigration, some prominent figures in African American life at the time—particularly those hailing from slavery-bound southern states—signed on, including Lott Cary, Daniel Coker, and John Brown Russwurm.

But in rejecting the scheme, three thousand of Philadelphia's African Americans had clearly, and rightly, sensed something amiss. The Colonization Society reflected the hardening logic of race in the age of emancipation. The ACS drew back from the revolutionary era's more idealistic antislavery to offer a practical solution to the "problem" of emancipation that was as congenial to white supremacy as it was to benevolent reform. In the same way that white supremacy qualified the abolition of the slave trade in the United States compared to that in Britain, so too colonization in the United States can be considered a degraded replica of its already-suspect English original. In the instance of England, the only other country to enact a comprehensive colonization plan for freed slaves, colonization efforts were clearly beset with racially paternalistic, if not downright exclusionary, tendencies.[40] But in the United States the Colonization Society had doubtful claims to any variety of antislavery at all, with Mercer himself vigorously denying that the ACS held any position on slavery. The ACS constituted a step backward from a more radical brand of antislavery, offering huge concessions to both southern slaveholders, for whom it remained mute on the morality of slavery, and northern free whites, for whom it promised a kind of ethnic cleansing. Its key premise reflected Jeffersonian reasoning: slavery was bad, but black people themselves were a blight on free society, and could not be permitted to remain in the country once freed. It viewed its strength as precisely the ability to appeal to a range of disparate constituencies. To black people it offered relief and the hope of a national homeland. But to slave owners it promoted not the end of slavery, but merely a solution to the problem of free blacks. And to northern whites it offered a vision of a racially pure republic.

The Colonization Society's public statements on the problems posed by emancipated slaves illustrates the point clearly. Free blacks were, "as a body, more vicious and degraded than any other which our population embraces," it contended. They constituted "a ragged set, . . . notoriously ignorant, degraded and miserable, [and] mentally diseased." For blacks, the ACS argued, their "freedom is *licentiousness*, and to many RESTRAINT would prove a blessing." The unique position in American society the free blacks occupied seemed particularly threatening. "Placed mid way between freedom and slavery," the Colonization Society asserted, "they feel neither the moral stimulants of the one, nor the restraint of the other." Claimed other colonizationists, "Contaminated themselves, they extend their vices to all around them, to the slaves and to the whites." Their inherent viciousness rendered them "repugnant to our republican feelings, and dangerous to our republican institutions." An editorial in the official organ of the society put it succinctly: "The African in this country belongs by birth to the very lowest station in society; and from that station *he can never rise*, be his talents, his enterprise, his virtues what they may." Free people of color constituted "a class by themselves—a class out of which *no individual can be elevated*, and below which, none can be depressed."[41] When challenged that such prejudice should not be catered to, colonizationists declared the problem intractable. They spoke of "the unconquerable prejudice of feeling against the African race that prevails so universally in the United States," lamenting the forces that mandated a separation of the races: "prejudices of colour, prejudices of habit, differences of physical conformation, inequalities arising from unequal intellectual cultivation, a dissimilarity of moral sense—the inevitable result of a state of freedom and a state of bondage." Expatriation presented the only option. One prominent colonizationist put America's choice baldly: "Slavery in this country must terminate in COLONIZATION, AMALGAMATION, OR ANNIHILIATION."[42]

The drives for African colonization and black disfranchisement in the 1810s and 1820s signaled a worsening climate of race relations in the wake of slavery's ending in the North. Revolutionary enthusiasm for liberty had only minimally influenced benign views of blacks' inherent equality, and the end of slavery had placed new premiums on considering their worthiness for civic inclusion in terms of innate biology. This was not a shift inclined to favor African Americans, as in the wake of slavery northerners began to understand the symbolic and material "wages" their whiteness could pay.[43] Public opinion in the North had retreated from the battle over slavery, only to re-form its lines against black equality. On both the right and left, the old wings of popular sentiment coalesced around a new center, best represented by the Colonization Society's Janus-faced concern, with black redemption on the one hand and black removal on the other. For those African Americans already blessed with nominal freedom, the encounter with colonization offered a critical lesson, which would have to be relearned generation after generation: slavery might die, but racial prejudice was something else. Freedom might mean an end to slavery, but it hardly meant an end to race.

COLORED CITIZENS OF THE WORLD
Black Institution Building and Black Agency in the Early Republic

Still, African Americans did become free in the northern United States. And despite that law and custom severely curtailed that freedom, they exercised their tenuous liberties to the full. The communities they created provided the social support otherwise denied African Americans, and responded to denigrating depictions of blacks in popular culture and racial science. In the process, they accomplished something remarkable. In building community in the decades after the Revolution, free African Americans in the North set forth some of the earliest and most powerful conceptions of black people *as a people*. More than in other places in the African diaspora at the time, the black North became the site where there emerged the notion that all people of African descent shared a common history and identity—in essence, an early form of black nationalism.

The first community institutions that free African Americans established functioned largely as extensions of the benevolent efforts of white reformers. Groups such as the New York Manumission Society and Pennsylvania Abolition Society organized the first schools for black children in the North, instilling in them the mission of uplifting African Americans from the "degradations" of slavery. Anthony Benezet, the Quaker abolitionist of Philadelphia, began educating black children in the 1750s, while New York abolitionists founded the African Free School in 1787. Over time, African Americans asserted control over their own schools, and the educational mission moved steadily out of white reformers' orbits. African Americans themselves established the African School in Boston in 1798, while black New Yorkers steadily wrested control of the African Free School from white benefactors. In Philadelphia, notable black citizens opened private educational institutions for black children. Even when independent, these free schools tended to endorse a view of education heavily dependent on the models established by white reformers, stressing moral education and racial uplift as much as classical training. But their elite orientation bore fruit in a remarkable generation of black leaders: in Philadelphia, Absalom Jones and Richard Allen; in Boston, William Cooper Nell; and in New York, Henry Highland Garnet and Alexander Crummell, among many others. These men would form the backbone of the national black leadership class that shepherded African Americans through the arduous decades to come.

The churches provided yet another avenue to independence and leadership. In 1787, Richard Allen and Absalom Jones refused to accept segregation in their church and were forcibly removed in the midst of prayer. Their protest led to the establishment of two of the first independent black churches in the country: Mother Bethel African Methodist Episcopal Church, which Allen founded in 1791, and the African Episcopal Church of St. Thomas, which Jones organized in 1792. Black New Yorkers established their first independent black church in 1800, the African Methodist Episcopal Zion Church, when James Varick led his coreligionists in a protest very similar to that in Philadelphia. Though beset with financial difficulties and the cloying interference of white churchmen, independent black churches became a staple of black community life in freedom. They provided not only spiritual nourishment in difficult times, but raised generations of leaders, assisted with efforts to educate African Americans, provided forms of public charity, and even functioned as small civil courts for their members. Independent black churches also became tenuous shelters for itinerant preachers—men such as John Jea and George White and women such as Jarena Lee, Zilpha Elaw, and Rebecca Jackson.[44] Rooted in the camp meetings and religious revivalism of the day, these figures could clash with the class elites who commanded the churches, and who insisted on "respectable" worship styles that often conflicted with the folk spirituality of the itinerants. But the roving preachers spread a message of spiritual egalitarianism and racial republicanism that they shared with the elite ministers.

In addition to schools and churches, free black communities created a host of Masonic, mutual aid, and literary societies. These offered not simply the immediate benefits of financial assistance or literacy, but the many indirect advantages of community organization. Social networks that were useful in all walks of life provided fora for elaborating understandings of the meaning of blacks' plight, and offered useful ways to expend energy on behalf of the individual and collective good. The burden was heavy. As Richard Allen and Absalom Jones reassured Philadelphia whites, "We are more earnestly endeavoring all in our power, to warn, rebuke, and exhort our African friends, to keep a conscience void of offence towards God and man."[45] And they did. Black leaders littered their encomia to liberty with calls for their "African brethren" to comport themselves respectably. Praising the efforts of the white reformers who had pressed for abolition of the slave trade, New York's Henry Sipkins lectured his black audience in 1809, "Let us by an upright and steady deportment merit a continuance of former favours, and evince to the world our high sense of gratitude."[46]

Proper comportment and moral and mental development would not just express appreciation for white benefactors, it would also disarm white critics, who posed black people as irredeemably inferior. As Jupiter Hammon had lectured free blacks, "If you are idle, and take to bad courses, you will hurt those of your brethren who are slaves, and do all in your power to prevent their being free."[47] Minister Peter Williams told his "beloved Africans" that "a steady and upright deportment" and "a strict obedience and respect to the laws of the land" would help blacks "form an invulnerable bulwark against the shafts of malice" cast by white society.[48] This gospel of racial uplift, which black leaders touted constantly to the nonelite, might surely have been met with some resentment by those who found it difficult to live up to the nearly impossible standards of virtue set forth. Others, though, would have found in community institutions opportunities to enact their commitment to personal and group growth. At the very least, the call for black "elevation" offered solace that in a hostile, largely uncontrollable world, everyone—regardless of how poor or powerless—might take part in a plan with historical and religious significance. God, wrote one black clergyman, "holds man responsible only for his moral conduct in the formation of his moral character, and on nothing more in his own existence has he control."[49] Even the most humble of northern blacks might take succor in thus appreciating both the potential and limits of their own agency.

Independent black institutions offered practical aid in the struggles to end slavery and make freedom meaningful. Schools and churches, literary and mutual aid societies—these had been born of need and racial strife, making them pioneers in activism and incubators of black leadership. As black institutions matured, and particularly as the dreaded Liberian colonization effort diverted the energies of potential white allies, black institutions became increasingly independent. The African Methodist Episcopal (AME) church broke free of all white ties in 1816, while at the African Free School in New York City black parents protested the condescension of white administrators. Later institutions built on this autonomy, presenting themselves as representatives of African Americans in the twin struggles against slavery in the South and racial prejudice in the North.

Black newspapers above all offered themselves as such a voice. In 1827 African Americans in New York City established the first black newspaper in the country, *Freedom's Journal*, which added a regularly published serial to the thriving collection of pamphlets, public sermons, and broadsides free African Americans had been penning since the days of the Revolution. Under the editorship of John Brown Russwurm, a free black native of Jamaica, and Samuel Cornish, a Presbyterian minister, the paper presented itself as an independent advocate of African Americans everywhere. "We wish to plead our own cause," the editors asserted in their inaugural edition; "too long others have spoken for us." The novelty of this famous assertion becomes apparent when contrasted with benevolent whites' long-standing history of sponsorship and interference with black institutions. *Freedom's Journal* represented a remarkable new effort to assert the interests of African Americans amid the cacophony of public discussion in northern cities. Its themes were not particularly new. The editors stressed the importance of moral and civic education, recalled the triumphs and tribulations of black heroes, rejected African colonization, and spoke out against the innumerable indignities blacks suffered in the nominally free North. But the mere notion that African Americans could regularly participate in public sphere discussions on a par with other Americans constituted a remarkable leap forward. Between 1827 and the start of the Civil War, at least a dozen and a half independent black periodicals appeared in the free states, edited by antebellum black luminaries such as Frederick Douglass, Martin Delany, and Samuel Ringgold Ward.[50] They remain remarkable illustrations of northern blacks' awareness that they stood virtually alone against the double evil of southern slavery and northern prejudice. In presenting themselves as alternatives to the vitriol spewed by the racially hostile "penny press" of northern cities, black newspapers like *Freedom's Journal* thrust African Americans boldly into American public life, as an equal people who sought to contest their public image.

The final institution black leaders created in this period, the national convention movement, was like earlier efforts triggered by the tightening grip of white supremacy. In August 1829, whites in Cincinnati, Ohio, rioted, attacking the part of town known as "Little Africa" in a torrent of violence designed to remind blacks of their inferior caste status. According to contemporary witnesses, for a week white thugs could be found nightly, "throwing stones, demolishing houses, [and] doing every other act of violence" imaginable. In the end, one African American was murdered and several more injured; numerous houses in "Bucktown" had been burned to the ground, their contents pillaged.[51] Many Cincinnati blacks decided to flee the city; some even left the country and emigrated to Canada. Back east, black leaders in New York, Philadelphia, and Baltimore used the occasion to coalesce the local efforts of black organizations into a national meeting. In February 1830, prominent African Americans from across the states met in Philadelphia. There they expressed solidarity with their brethren in Cincinnati, asserted their commitment to stating their grievances in print, endorsed migration to the "asylum of oppression" that was Canada, and organized a system for calling future conventions. National meetings convened from 1831 to 1835, and sporadically throughout the 1840s and 1850s.[52] In the course of their history, these gatherings foregrounded the most talented African American figures, providing a platform for some of their most eloquent appeals. They debated critical issues of strategy and tactics, and even contested the definitions of black leadership.[53] More than any other concern, the national convention movement sought to assert the legitimacy of African Americans on the public stage. It did so by, paradoxically, posing itself as a separate, quasi-governmental entity. Denied access to formal systems of politics, African Americans created their own. In the process, they laid claim to their rights and capacity to organize, as well as to the black elite's legitimacy as a national leadership.

Independent black schools and churches, mutual aid societies, the black press, and the black convention movement formed a matrix of institutions that set forth a three-pronged agenda for free black northerners. The first and most basic work, as we have seen, concerned inserting free African Americans into the public life of a hostile society. In worlds dominated by white supremacy, this was no mean feat, and it entailed very real risk to life and limb. The streets of the urban North could became literal battlegrounds, on which were fought struggles over ethnicity, class, and race. Black commentators never ceased criticizing the violence African Americans faced in merely appearing in public. Especially on "public days of recreation," Boston's Prince Hall charged, blacks were "shamefully abused," to the point where "helpless old women have their clothes torn off their backs, even to the exposing of their nakedness." In comparison, he wrote, "a slave in the West-Indies, on Sunday or holidays enjoys himself and friends without any molestation." Philadelphia's James Forten took it as "a well known fact" that on "days of public jubilee" such as the Fourth of July, blacks daring to step foot in the streets would be "assailed" by drunken whites. Thus, he asserted, "The day set apart for the festival of Liberty, should be abused by the advocates of Freedom," who would "sully what they profess to adore."[54] African Americans did not accept their public exclusion, but used their institutions to claim a full measure of civic equality. Neither did they forsake the streets. Instead, black leaders of these institutions organized their own parades and public celebrations, occasions that challenged white supremacy, and built solidarity with their own proletariat.[55]

Through their organizing and theorizing, independent black institutions in the North accomplished another important feat. They came to conceive of all people of African descent as a unified people. Recall the fractured state of black identity throughout the Atlantic world, where multitiered racial caste systems might divide the free from the slave, the light from the dark, or the creole from the African. Whereas other New World societies developed three-tiered racial hierarchies, in mainland British North America the "one-drop" rule assigned to one "race" all people with discernible African descent.[56] In the United States, white supremacy's ascription of a common, debased status for all people of African heritage unintentionally promoted a collective identity among the oppressed. Black people appropriated this ascribed unity, only to repose it as a potent source of collective power. The earliest writings of revolutionary era blacks had asserted their identity as "Africans," but in the postrevolutionary years the term came to connote the qualities of a prototypical nation, with its own distinct history and destiny. Jupiter Hammon, the elderly, educated slave of the Lloyd family of Long Island, New York, was among the very first to refer to his people in the language of nation, though he did so to promote a message of obedience. Addressing his "dear African brethren" in 1787, he hoped his auditors would find credible words coming from "one [of] your own nation and colour," and compared his message to that of the "apostle Paul, when speaking of his own nation the Jews."[57] John Marrant, the itinerant black Methodist, similarly posed African Americans as a "chosen generation" and "holy nation," who could achieve deliverance with the proper spiritual orientation.[58]

While these men wrote of spiritual redemption over time, the theme of Christian salvation took on decidedly civic implications. In 1808, Absalom Jones identified African Americans with the enslaved Israelites of the Old Testament, insisting that the abolition of the slave trade demonstrated that God had once again interposed in human affairs to deliver "the oppressed and distressed" from bondage.[59] Paul Cuffee sought to enact this deliverance, viewing African settlement as the foundation of a homeland for all people of African descent. Visiting Sierra Leone, he reflected that commerce would let the settlers "become a nation to be numbered among the historians' nations of the world."[60] And Richard Allen and James Forten's early excitement about the possibilities of Liberia stemmed entirely from their hopes that African-descended people might thus "become a people" and a "great nation." Throughout the young United States, a network of African-descended seamen and itinerant preachers spread spiritual messages of black national redemption: Boston King, David George, Prince Hall, John Jea, George Liele, Briton Hammon, and John Marrant. They joined other Atlantic figures—such as Ignatius Sancho, Olaudah Equiano, Quobna Ottobah Cugoano, and James Albert Ukawsaw Gronniosaw—to assert a black racial identity that overstepped the national borders that contained them. Of course, Haiti figured large in these early invocations of black nationalism, serving as a beacon of possibility. As Boston's Prince Hall lamented of African Americans' troubles in 1797, "Let us remember what a dark day it was with our African brethren six years ago, in the French West-Indies," when "all manner of torture" had been "inflicted on those unhappy people." But God, Hall suggested, had a way of bringing light out of darkness. "Thus doth Ethiopia begin to stretch forth her hand, from a sink of slavery to freedom and equality."[61] New England's Prince Saunders became so enamored with developing Haiti as a black nation that he moved there, and undertook strenuous efforts to recruit migrants from the United States and Britain.[62]

Nothing better emblematized this emerging collective consciousness than changes in the names African-descended people used to refer to themselves as a collective body. In the period between the Revolution and the emergence of the black convention movement in 1830, transformations in naming practices heralded a notion of black identity that embraced all people of African descent as a group united by a common history of oppression, and with a collective destiny of redemption. Colonial law in British America had referred to African-descended people under the terms "negroes, musteez, and mulattoes"—a tradition that persisted into the early national period. But following the Revolution, the institutions free blacks founded in the North most frequently labeled themselves "African," as in the African Methodist Episcopal Church, Free African Society, or African Marine Fund. In the 1810s, though, with the rise of the American Colonization Society, black leaders began to worry that "African" made a dangerous statement: perhaps even native-born blacks did not belong in America, and ought to be removed from the land of their birth. The African Baptist Church of Boston changed its name to the First Independent Church of the People of Color because, its congregants said, "the name African is ill applied to a church composed of American citizens."[63] The common term "negro" offered one alternative, but it sounded perilously close to an emerging racial epithet, "nigger," and was hence unacceptable.[64] Instead, black leaders began adopting a phrase commonly used in the West Indies to describe some people of African descent: *free people of color*. Its use in the United States reinforced by black refugees from St. Domingue, the phrase originally referred not to all blacks, but only those legally free, and likely boasting creole or mixed birth for several generations back. As we have seen, the French *gens de couleur* represented the elite among people of African descent; they were usually light-complected, and always much better off than the enslaved masses. But for black leaders in the U.S. North, the English-language version conjured useful associations with the most "respectable" classes of African-descended society. Black spokespersons appropriated it, and then, in a universalizing gesture, dropped the "free," and began applying "people of color" to all of African descent.

The phrase found steady usage among African Americans, white sympathizers, and eventually even the law. Blacks meeting in Richmond in 1817 to protest the American Colonization Society chose "free people of color" as a label for themselves, reflecting increasingly common usage while eschewing troubling references to Africa. In 1817, black Philadelphians called themselves "people of color" in the constitution of an educational society, while well-meaning whites in the New York Manumission Society termed newly freed blacks "Persons of Colour" in its annual reports.[65] Statutes began to reflect the new usage. Prior to 1830, most states above the Mason-Dixon line referred to African Americans in general under the clumsy rubric of "negro, mulatto, or mustee" (the latter describing one of mixed black and Native American descent). "Person of colour" occasionally appeared after 1800, but always alongside "negro" and "mulatto," as if to denote a distinct racial category.[66] Slowly, though, even legal terminology began to follow popular parlance. With social distinctions between differing people of African descent diminishing, laws began using "person of color" as an economical substitute for the weighty "negroes and mulattoes," as when an 1830 New York statute referred simply to "any person of colour."[67]

The transformation of "people of color" as it spread from the Caribbean to the U.S. North represented the democratization of a term originally intended for a small class of social and economic elites. In the hands of black northerners, *colored people* came to represent all people of African descent: the slave and the free, the dark-skinned and the light, the poor and the well-off. In 1827, the inaugural issue of *Freedom's Journal* dedicated itself exclusively to the interests of "free persons of colour," while an 1831 meeting of black people in Trenton, New Jersey, casually referenced "the free and slave man of color."[68] The use of a single name for the race promised to undermine forces that elsewhere had pulled apart a single identity for African-descended people. A correspondent to the *Colored American*, a black newspaper that appeared in 1836, put it well. The writer approved of the newspaper's name because it "fully embraces all colored persons of this country." To class people of color "as blacks and mulattoes, is to make the most unhappy divisions, to sow among them the seeds of discord and strife." The writer thought it "one of the greatest proofs of their improvement, that they consider themselves now more than formerly, as one people."[69] This vision was truly diasporic. As New York's William Hamilton put it, all black people were united under a common banner: "It makes no kind of difference whether the man is born in Africa, Asia, Europe or America, so long as he is proginized from African parents."[70] In 1829, the black radical David Walker—a man born in North Carolina who had then encountered a wide range of African-descended people in his moves to Charleston and Boston—addressed himself to "the Coloured Citizens of the World" in his militant *Appeal*.[71] By subsuming under one term distinctions which had divided black identity in other places in the New World, black leaders would unite a people often unified only by their shared experiences of racial proscription. "Colored" grouped under one banner everyone from the most "debased" slave field hands to the black "aristocracies" of the northern seaboard cities.

Finally, the body of thought emerging from independent institutions performed important ideological work by steadily asserting the primacy of blacks themselves in their own development as a collective body. Much of black protest was rooted in a tradition of prophetic thought that structured the experience of African-descended people into a historical narrative of (past) fall and (future) redemption. Over time, as northern black communities matured, black spokespersons shifted their thinking on the agents of their deliverance, moving from white abolitionist patrons to African Americans themselves. This movement followed the trajectory of black activism itself, which over time became ever more assertive, and ever more independent of whites. The earliest generation of free black leaders in the North had worked carefully to reign in freedpeople's aspirations for liberty, tempering their hopes for universal liberation with calls for subservience. For example, Jupiter Hammon cautioned his fellow bondspersons to think "very little" of their status in this world. "If God designs to set us free," Hammon intoned in 1787, "he will do it, in his own time, and way."[72] Deference and gratitude marked black public figures' early paeans to freedom. In Philadelphia, Richard Allen and Absalom Jones had termed the white antislavery workers who secured gradual emancipation "instruments in the hand of God for our good."[73] And in celebrating the abolition of the slave trade, African American spokespersons had lauded the efforts of the white abolitionists who had worked tirelessly for black freedom. Men such as John Woolman, Anthony Benezet, William Wilberforce, and Granville Sharp had been "instruments of divine goodness," their efforts "as the paternal hand rearing its tender offspring to mature years."[74]

Over time, though, free black spokespersons increasingly emphasized their own agency in the redemption of the race, and even of America. African colonization served as the fulcrum for this transition. While most free blacks rejected expatriation out of hand, they embraced its rhetoric of redemption, only to turn it back on itself. Colonizationists argued that American blacks would help redeem benighted Africans, whom they portrayed as "plunged in all the degradation of idolatry, superstition, and ignorance."[75] While some African Americans embraced this vision, most denounced the argument that intractable racism precluded blacks' progress in America. For Samuel Cornish, the logic of colonization amounted to "deifying prejudice and paying homage at the shrine of one of the grossest sins that every disgraced the human family."[76] A convention of black New Yorkers thus told the colonizationists in 1831, "We are content to abide where we are.... We do not believe that things will always continue the same."[77]

Indeed, through their own actions, black leaders came to see their people as agents of their own redemption. If whites proved unwilling or unable to liberate blacks, blacks themselves would become instruments in the hand of God— "Divine instrumentalities for Divine ends," as minister Jermain W. Loguen put it.[78] And if blacks were good enough to liberate Africa, they were good enough to redeem America. Rather than leave for Africa, the *Colored American* declared in 1837, "we will stay and seek the purification of the whole lump."[79] In 1809, Joseph Sidney could deliver an address celebrating the anniversary of the abolition of the slave trade the year before, in which he prayed God for white abolitionists' further intercession on behalf of blacks—that "some Wilberforce, some champion of African freedom" would arise to plead blacks' cause in the slave states.[80] By 1827, the black minister Nathaniel Paul could subsume the entire thrust of racial uplift into millennial visions of blacks' redemptive role on the world-historical stage. Lecturing black New Yorkers, he said, "Our conduct has an important bearing, not only on those who are yet in bondage in this country, but its influence is extended to the isles of India, and to every part of the world where the abomination of slavery is known."[81]

The self-redemption African Americans theorized in the first three decades of the nineteenth century grew out of a tradition of institution building that free black people pioneered after emancipation. When northern free blacks built community institutions, they established a foundation for a wide range of protest efforts in ensuing decades. This protest was, in turn, predicated on a notion of black identity that embraced people of African descent throughout the world, imagining them as a collective whole with a common history and destiny. Free black leaders' central theme of racial elevation, which began the century as deference to white benefactors and a defense against white slanders, became the centerpiece of a millennial project of national and even world redemption. As it matured, the matrix of institutions and ideas African Americans in the free North constructed amplified their power as potent advocates for the enslaved, and even inspired white allies to join the cause. For the meantime, though, the enslaved would have to rely primarily on themselves.

A RIGHT TO FIGHT FOR LIBERTY
Revolutionary Rebellion and Retrenchment in the Slave South

On the night of August 30, 1800, an enslaved Virginian sat huddled in a violent rainstorm, surrounded by fellows armed with clubs, field tools, hand-fashioned blades, a few muskets, and even some horses. The man, Gabriel, a tall twenty-four-year-old reputed to possess "courage and intellect above his rank in life," must have been experiencing unfathomable frustration. For months he and his fellows had been carefully planning rebellion, secretly developing a conspiracy that stretched from the state capital of Richmond to the countryside. According to testimony taken later, he and his lieutenants had recruited hundreds of insurrectionaries in Henrico and surrounding counties, including "400 Horsemen," and "all the Negroes in town," who numbered perhaps 1,000. He had had "12 dozen swords made," and had instructed followers to "commence the fight with scythe blades, until they could procure arms from the white people." He had even gathered guns, having amassed "six or seven pounds of powder" and "worn out 2 pair of bullet moulds in running bullets."[82] Now nature's violence had preempted his. The deluge—"the most terrible thunder Storm . . . that I ever witnessed in this State," according to a white contemporary—washed out the bridges linking nearby plantations, including Gabriel's home of Brookfield, to the target of Richmond. The plan had been to overtake the city's armory, capture Governor James Monroe, and ransom him for the slaves' freedom.

Now, though, the plot's leader could not even cross a river. Some of the insurgents made it to the appointed meeting place, but they were too few to launch a successful uprising. Gabriel sent frantic word, postponing the march until the next day. But the dawn brought even worse. Pharoah, a slave from a nearby farm who had only recently been recruited into the plot, informed on the conspiracy to his master, Mosby Sheppard, who sent word to Governor Monroe at his home in Albemarle. Armed whites descended on Brookfield, capturing a half dozen conspirators but missing Gabriel, who remained at large until turned in by yet another slave informant as the rebel leader sought passage on an outbound ship. As was ever the case in instances of slave insurrection, whites prosecuted conspirators swiftly and brutally. After two months of "trials," in which slaves had little recourse to legal procedure or representation, the authorities executed twenty-six slaves and deported others to nearby states.[83]

In Gabriel's rebellion the new nation confronted its first major slave insurrection. As such, the plot demonstrated the remarkable degree to which traditions of revolutionary radicalism had penetrated communities of the enslaved, lending old patterns of collective resistance remarkable new potentials. Over and over again, evidence collected in the trails of the conspirators revealed the suffusion of modern conceptions of liberty drawn from contemporary events across the Atlantic. According to one slave informant, Gabriel's band had "concluded to purchase a piece of silk for a flag, on which they would have written 'death or liberty'"—a clever riff on both Patrick Henry's famous 1775 oration, as well as the motto "Liberty to Slaves" which had been emblazoned on the banner carried by Lord Dunmore's Ethiopian Regiment during the Revolutionary

War. The principal coconspirators seem to have been well versed in revolutionary precept. One declared that he would offer the court no more information than what "General Washington would have . . . had he been taken by the British and put to trial"; he had staked his life "in endeavoring to obtain the liberty of my countrymen, and am a willing sacrifice in their cause."[84] Jack Bowler, another conspirator, declared that "we had as much right to fight for our liberty as any men."[85] Events on St. Domingue had also inspired Gabriel and his fellows. More than just news of the slave revolution there made it to Virginia. Since the state had, unlike its neighbors, failed to pass laws forbidding entry to the slaves of planter refugees from the island, it became host to a large number of African-descended people who had witnessed firsthand the power of collective violence. White authorities fretted eternally over the baleful influence these slaves had on Virginia's blacks, worrying, like Governor Monroe, that "the scenes which are acted in St. Domingo, must produce an effect on all the people of colour in this and the States south of us."[86]

Gabriel's insurrection suggested how revolutionary conceptions could lend slave rebellion a crucial sense of coherence and purpose. The conspirators viewed their actions not as a nihilistic race war but an insurgency of the oppressed that partook entirely of the radical tradition of the revolutionary Atlantic. Gabriel had sought to court the antislavery sympathies of likely whites, instructing his followers that as people "friendly to liberty," the "Quakers, Methodists, and French people" were to be spared in the onslaught. He envisioned the rebellion as a second American Revolution, which he hoped would enlist "the poor white people" and "the most redoubtable republicans" alongside the enslaved. Even more terrifying to authorities must have been the collusion of specific whites. Plying the taverns and public houses of Richmond, the literate and skilled Gabriel had apparently found sympathy among some working-class whites and free blacks, plebian Richmonders resentful of the deference required of them by the city's patrician class. Indeed, trial evidence suggests that the plot's leaders envisioned their uprising as embracing a host of discontented Virginians. Several free blacks were implicated but evaded punishment because the enslaved were not permitted to enter testimony against them. One conspirator testified that the rebels hoped to enlist "the nation of Indians called Catawbas," Native Americans with justified and long-standing grievances against Virginia. And some in Gabriel's ranks believed that a force of French radicals had landed nearby and would likely join them. Indeed, according to Gabriel, "two Frenchmen"—later identified as Charles Quersey and Alexander Beddenhurst—"had actually joined." The collusion of whites extended even to Gabriel's flight, which while betrayed by a slave, was abetted by Richardson Taylor, a ship captain who had recently converted to Methodism. Finally, the specter of St.

Domingue hung over all. Whites believed utterly that slave insurrectionaries in Virginia had been inspired by events in the French Caribbean. Delaware Senator Samuel White argued that only by ending "the horrid evil of slavery" could the nation "avoid the fate of St. Domingo,"[87] while one Federalist editor posed his warning in poetry:

> remember ere too late
> The tale of St. Domingo's fate,
> Though *Gabriel* dies, a host remain
> Oppress'd with slavery's galling chain,
> And soon or late the hour will come,
> Mark'd with Virginia's dreadful doom.[88]

Clearly, Gabriel's rebellion must be viewed within the context of revolutionary fervor sweeping the Atlantic. Of course, all New World slave societies had known the threat of rebellion from their very foundings. As far back as 1522, slaves on the Spanish island of Hispaniola had revolted against the rule of Christopher Columbus's son, while a 1663 conspiracy of slaves and white servants in Gloucester County, Virginia, marked the first instance of slave rebellion in British mainland North America. But Gabriel's rebellion marked a phenomenon new in the United States, one inaugurated in the Atlantic world by the Haitian Revolution. Revolutionary events and ideology lent old practices of collective resistance new potential. Slave rebellion in the age of democratic revolution laid full claim to that tradition's central assertion—that all people possessed natural liberty in the form of the absolute right to hold property, including their own bodies and its produce. For ever after, collective slave violence could invoke these central commitments of liberal metropolitan society. In the instance of Gabriel, this had occurred in the very land that had first and most powerfully theorized the rights of the subordinate to throw off their oppressors.

Yet the ideological content of slave rebellion often proved unintelligible to the custodians of the slave system. Whereas Gabriel may have predicated his actions on his understanding of the radical political currents of the Atlantic world, Virginia planters and Henrico County courts were unlikely to hear, let alone accede to, his reasoning. Even when authorities gleaned the connection between revolutionary principle and slave behavior, they were utterly disinclined to acknowledge its legitimacy. Invariably, slave powers responded to threats of rebellion with unbridled brutality. Conspiracies and insurrections served as jarring refutations of paternalistic claims that the enslaved benefitted from enlightened care, belying a reality of omnipresent, simmering resentment. After Gabriel's conspiracy, horror-struck white southerners acknowledged the fragility of their world. "Nothing but the interposition of Heaven," declared Delaware Senator Samuel White, "prevented the slaves . . . from destroying Richmond."[89]

Revolutionary era moves to ameliorate the condition of the slaves gave way to new efforts to restrict them. In 1782, the Virginia state legislature, inspired by antislavery activists and revolutionary principle, had provided for the private manumission of individual adults, a process that had enlarged the state's free black population from fewer than three thousand in 1782 to about twenty thousand by 1800.[90] In the wake of Gabriel's conspiracy, and still another in Virginia just two years later, the legislature moved swiftly to clamp down on the forces it believed had fostered rebellion. As one Virginian put it, "If we will keep a ferocious monster in our country, we must keep him in chains."[91] The legislature strengthened the policing of slaves in the city, and severely restricted the activities of African Americans along the waterways, which served as key channels of communication among the enslaved. It prohibited masters from hiring out their slaves, a practice that had given the skilled Gabriel opportunities to move freely in the city. And undoing most of the state's 1782 emancipation law, it required newly emancipated slaves to leave the state or confront reenslavement. These measures tightened the screws not just on the slave population, but on free blacks as well, who were deemed dangerous exemplars of the autonomy that "ruined" slaves and made them likely to revolt.[92]

A later plot, Denmark Vesey's Charleston, South Carolina, conspiracy of 1822, repeated the pattern evident in Gabriel's conspiracy. The man known originally as Telemaque had been born outside the United States, in Africa or the West Indies, and had spent his youth as a slave on commercial ships trafficking the Atlantic. His owner, Joseph Vesey, brought him as a youth to Charleston just after the American Revolution. In 1799, the year before Gabriel had planned his revolt, Telemaque (now known as Denmark) won a large sum in a public lottery, with which he purchased his freedom and opened a carpenter's shop. Like Gabriel, Denmark was an artisan, worked in the city, and intermingled with its mix of skilled slaves, free blacks, and plebian whites. A literate man, he would have encountered black refugees from St. Domingue, and heard of slave plots and rebellions in the region. According to one of his coconspirators, he read everything he could "that had any connexion with slavery," and especially all "that related to St. Domingo."[93] Conversant with the radical intellectual currents of the revolutionary Atlantic, his role in founding the local African Methodist Episcopal Church also indicated his fluency in the biblical language of deliverance prevalent in slave Christianity. Though the notion of rebellion had perhaps been brewing in him for some time, the city's suppression of his church congregation in the years preceding 1822 likely incited Vesey to organize in earnest.

For several years, he developed a leadership cadre and recruited enslaved and free blacks in both the city and countryside, planning an insurrection for July 14, to coincide with the anniversary of the day the Parisian mob stormed the Bastille and launched the French Revolution. Those in the know—numbering in the thousands, the evidence suggests—were to rise up and concentrate on Charleston. There, they would seize its armory and other strong points, burn the city, slay the whites, escape on a ship captured from the harbor, and flee to Haiti, whence some among the rebellion's leadership even promised military aid would arrive.

As in the case of Gabriel's conspiracy, the scheme was foiled by black informants, who revealed the plot in the weeks before the rebellion was to be launched. Authorities descended on the city's black population, arresting 131, executing 35, and exiling 37. Vesey himself was hung on July 2, alongside five of his leading coconspirators. Once again, insurrection had been crushed. But Vesey's conspiracy was, like Gabriel's, no sudden outburst of pent-up rage. Rather, it was a carefully organized plan, conceived in an ideological context of revolutionary antislavery and designed to strike a blow against the system of slavery itself. Also as in the case of Gabriel's rebellion, white authorities dimly understood the significance of Vesey's motives and intentions, gleaned as they were through a brutal trial process. Terrified, they responded as had Virginia legislators, clamping down ever more tightly on the lives of Charleston's African Americans. A municipal police force established to help guard the city began closely surveilling the black population, particularly the free community in which Vesey had operated. New laws struck at the fragile liberties of this class. One mandated that black sailors on ships docking in Charleston be imprisoned for the length of their stay. Ship captains refusing to cover the expense of the detention would forfeit their black sailors, who would be sold as "absolute slaves."

The Gabriel and Vesey rebellions did not exhaust the major plots and conspiracies that occurred in the United States between the end of the Haitian Revolution and 1831. If one abides the fears and suspicions of slaveholders themselves, dozens if not hundreds may be counted. Indeed, the largest slave revolt in American history occurred during the period, amid the sugar plantations of coastal Louisiana in 1811. Successful cane sugar cultivation had come late to the Gulf Coast, but expanded quickly—from one successful plantation in 1795 to some seventy-five plantations in 1802, which produced over three thousand tons of sugar per year.[94] Rapid development of an exploitation colony, though, created dangerous preconditions for slave revolt, especially in a largely Francophone territory in the immediate aftermath of the Haitian Revolution. The rapid introduction of slaves, many African, badly skewed the racial balance away from whites, while the harsh labor control required of sugar production bred discontent. In January 1811, three and a half months before Louisiana entered the Union as a state, several hundred slaves from sugar plantations along the German Coast of Louisiana rose up and marched on New Orleans. After burning several plantations and killing some whites, they encountered a militia force of planters who overcame them with mounted men and superior weaponry. The revolt left over fifty slaves dead, to which another hundred were added through postrevolt skirmishes or post-trial executions. Though the German Coast uprising of 1811 almost certainly involved greater numbers of slaves than any other in U.S. history, it long remained a neglected event, even among the most ardent historical excavators of slave rebellion. In some measure, this owed to the efforts of Louisiana's territorial governor, William C. C. Claiborne, to squelch knowledge of a catastrophe on his watch. Just as significantly, though, the fact that the rebellion occurred on the very frontiers of American society suggested the critical importance of metropolitan reaction to slave revolts. In Louisiana, Clairborne could imagine suppressing knowledge of the revolt. An insurrection in the capital of the nation's leading state attracted widespread attention; one in a frontier territory might not.

To the extent that slave rebels' motives can be gleaned from the scanty historical record, these uprisings in the Early Republic contribute to our understanding of a critical transformation in collective slave violence throughout the Atlantic. In the wake of the Haitian Revolution, a new brand of insurrection blossomed throughout the Atlantic Basin. Unrest in St. Domingue sparked immediate outbreaks in Jamaica and Martinique, and inflected many instances of rebellion thereafter. In the Atlantic world, a spirit of collective resistance had long prevailed wherever the enslaved concentrated. Large-scale insurrections had always been rare, and remained so in the early nineteenth century. When they did occur, though, rebellions after Haiti often reflected a general (but by no means absolute) transformation in means and ends.

For one, they increasingly involved creole slaves in their planning and organization. Creole awareness of the currents of metropolitan opinion and Atlantic events often proved the critical factor in deciding to rise up. The Easter Rebellion that struck Barbados in 1816 was instigated by elite slaves who believed their emancipation imminent. One of these leaders, Nanny Grigg, a domestic servant, preached to fellow slaves "that they were damned fools to work," for "the negroes were to be freed on Easter-Monday." If not, she suggested, slaves should "fight for it" and "set fire," for "that was the way they did on Santo Domingo." While no "free paper" or plan for mass emancipation actually existed, slave leaders were surely reacting to news that the Barbadian Assembly had recently rejected Parliament's plan to register slaves, part of an abolitionist campaign to ameliorate their condition.[95]

In addition to increasingly illustrating the acculturative process evident in creole leadership, revolts of the nineteenth century thus also reflected an ever-growing awareness of the power of emancipatory ideas among the enslaved, and their recognition of antislavery sentiment among the metropolitan publics that reacted to revolts. In the British sugar colony of Demerara, on the northern coast of South America, planters had, as in Barbados, balked at amelioration measures for the slaves. Elite slaves like Jack Gladstone and Quamina heard news of this, which in the slave community once again transformed into claims that the defiance of local planters impeded the Crown's purpose to free the slaves. English missionaries likely added fuel to the fire by establishing expectations that slaves could hold religious meetings, and pressing local authorities for the amelioration of harsh conditions.

The linkage of creoles and rebellion evident in these instances was by no means perfect. Creoles had been implicated in revolts before the revolutionary era, as when a handful of American-born slaves masterminded a broad conspiracy to revolt on Antigua in 1736.[96] And ethnic identity remained a vital force in slave rebellion during and after the age of revolution. One need only consider the Malê revolts by Muslim slaves from discrete African nations in northeastern Brazil from 1807 to 1835. In general, though, the locus of collective resistance shifted subtly over the age of revolutions, steadily favoring native-born leaders who would have refracted extant traditions of resistance through new ideas of revolution and Christian evangelicalism. In short, slave insurrectionaries' awareness of the shifting currents of metropolitan opinion clearly shaped their intentions and actions.

Yet, particularly in the United States, whites' reactions to slave conspiracies demonstrated a fundamental limitation of collective violence as a tool for slave liberation. Slave insurrectionaries may often have been exemplars of the radical principles of the Revolution, but those who policed the slave regime were more interested in benefitting from their exploitative labor system than adhering to their own liberal professions. Even the most enlightened of slavery's apologists might remain true to their core beliefs by harkening to the conservative impulse in liberal theory that protected the rights of property, even that held in persons. The status of humans as property remained a contested principle, after all, particularly in the United States, a nation half slave and half free. Slave rebellion was a risky, all-or-nothing gamble. Its chances of success were minuscule, and the inevitable response to failure was even greater repression. The Haitian instance had been exceptional; nowhere else did mass violence secure slaves their own independent state. It would take something more to leverage collective slave resistance into effective challenges to the slave regime. From within, slave behavior might shake the foundations of the institution, but alone it was insufficient to destroy them. Translating the meaning of slave revolt to potentially sympathetic democratic publics took other kinds of work, by other actors.

The Age of Immediatism

CHAPTER 5

Minds Long Set on Freedom

Rebellion, Metropolitan Abolition,
and Sectional Conflict

BLACK SPIRITS AND WHITE
Slave Rebellion and the Foundations of
Radical Abolitionism in the United States

Now imagine another Virginia slave, on another summer night, some hundred miles to the south of the Richmond where Gabriel had launched his uprising thirty-one years earlier. This night, August 21, 1831, witnessed a similar gathering of enslaved African Americans, this time in a remote wood in the southeastern part of the state, not far from the Great Dismal Swamp, an area long known to harbor runaway slave maroons. Half a dozen men gathered to eat, drink, and await their leader. In the wee hours of the night, Nat Turner arrived. The band moved to the home of Turner's owner, Joseph Travis, and killed his entire family as it slept. Into the morning their slaughter spread, with no whites spared among the rural households nearby. By the coming noon, the militia had been alerted, and a confrontation ensued with Turner's band. About fifty slave rebels, many armed with muskets and riding on horseback, fell back. By the time white reinforcements arrived, the rebels had been scattered, having tallied some five dozen lives.

For the whites, the worst was over, and the retaliation that followed was swift and brutal. A massive force, eventually numbering up to three thousand armed civilians and government troops, flooded the area, rounding up suspected insurrectionaries and summarily executing close to two hundred—a number well exceeding the size of Turner's force. The heavy hand of the law followed, with a series of trials intended to secure "justice." Official sentences of death numbered thirty, with many more slaves sold away from kith and kin to other states. Turner himself evaded capture for over two months, but was finally brought to bay on October 30. Imprisoned and quickly tried, he died at the end of a rope on November 11.

Nat Turner's rebellion constituted the last of the four great slave rebellions in U.S. history. Much of what historians think they know about Turner's outlook and motivations derives from the remarkable but problematic document prepared by Thomas R. Gray, a local slaveholder and attorney, in the wake of the uprising. Gray spoke with the insurrectionary for three days before his execution, then rushed to print a volume purporting to be "confessions" that Turner had "fully and voluntarily made." Filtered through Gray's own values, outlooks, and motives, Turner's words must be treated with great care. But the document reveals a remarkable man whose narrative the trial record often corroborates. In it, Turner appears not so much a figure of the revolutionary black Atlantic as a militant prophet of the Second Great Awakening, the wave of Protestant revivalism that swept the United States in the early nineteenth century. This religious and cultural phenomenon began around the turn of the nineteenth century, as itinerant preachers throughout the country spread a revitalized form of Protestant Christianity that stressed conversion to a life in Christ, strict reliance on biblical authority, and personal communication with the divine. Historians debate the extent to which Christianity permeated communities of the enslaved, but it is clear that Turner's perspective was heavily influenced by the tenets of Christian millennialism, or the belief in the imminent return of Christ and the establishment of God's kingdom on earth.

Messianic motifs permeated every aspect of Turner's confession. Marked early in life by black and white alike as highly intelligent and imbued with a special destiny, he lived a life of "austerity" that further distinguished him from others, and garnered him a reputation as a spiritual figure. He rejected folk belief—"conjuring and such like tricks"—as a means of obtaining influence over his comrades, and instead wrapped himself in "mystery," devoting his time to "fasting and prayer." He once even returned from a successful escape attempt because his Christian belief directed him to a higher spiritual purpose. A decade-long series of personal visions then revealed his divine mission. In one such revelation, he reported, "I saw white spirits and black spirits engaged in battle, and the sun was darkened—and thunder rolled in the Heavens, and blood flowed in streams." Three years before his fateful insurrection, another vision told Turner that he was to take up Christ's "yoke" and "fight against the Serpent, for the time was fast approaching when the first should be last and the last should be first." In short, Turner believed himself to be called to bring about "the great day of judgment"—a moment when God would return to earth, Christ would separate saints from sinners, and time would end. Turner bided his time, waiting for further "signs in the heavens" before he would "commence the great work," which was to "slay my enemies with their own weapons." In February 1831, he took a solar eclipse to be the predicted sign. "The seal was removed from my lips," he testified, and he entrusted his mission to four confidants. Turner's illness delayed a plan set for the Fourth of July, a date likely chosen both to catch whites unaware and to mock national promises of equality for all. Not until August 13 did another portent appear, and one week later Turner and his men moved.[1]

Contemporaries, as have many since, viewed Turner's revolt as insanity—a nihilistic expression of rage tinged with religious fanaticism. But the prophet's messianism helps illuminate the differences between his rebellion and the ones preceding his. Why did Turner resolve to conduct an impossible war of annihilation against an overwhelming enemy? Earlier slave rebels, as challenging as were their tasks, had enjoyed advantages Turner did not. Like Denmark Vesey, Turner was a preacher. Unlike Vesey, he had not won his freedom and thus could not exhort in a church—even an embattled black church like Vesey's Charleston AME. Turner's church must be considered an "invisible institution," in the words of historian Albert Raboteau—an informal spiritual community.[2] Neither did Turner, like Gabriel and Vesey before him, work in an urban environment that offered relative freedom of movement, potential allies, and in Vesey's case even an escape plan. Turner's status as a slave in a rural community confined possibilities for rebellion. Whereas in the case of the German Coast uprising of 1811 slaves constituted nearly 60 percent of the affected frontier parish, enslaved people constituted less than half of Turner's Southampton County, which was also well established and heavily policed.[3]

But Turner did have something. His most potent resource was the tradition of biblical prophecy that formed the core of his thinking. He could not have contemplated his revolt without recourse to passages such as Matthew 6:33, which he quoted in the *Confessions*: "Seek ye the kingdom of Heaven and all things shall be added unto you." Turner had imbibed and reinterpreted Virginia's tradition of evangelical Christianity just as surely as Gabriel had its legacy of revolutionary liberalism. Still, religious enthusiasm offered a weak substitute for weapons and free allies. It was no surprise that a strong note of fatalism attended Turner's apocalyptic race war. The same voices that revealed his role to him also enjoined him to accept his destiny: "Such is your luck, such you are called to see, and let it come rough or smooth, you must surely bare it," the Holy Spirit had told him. And when asked in jail if the insurrection's failure revealed his visions to be false, Turner responded simply, "Was Christ not crucified?"[4] Turner's apocalypticism thus not only reflected assimilation of the religious revivalism of his day, but fitted the desperation of his straits. Inspired by the word of God, how could he not act? And yet, how, without believing in the imminence of the divine, could he have even imagined success?

Despite its apparent futility, Turner's revolt rippled consequence through the state and nation. Among Virginia's elites, it instigated yet another cycle of repression, recrimination, and reconsideration. As in most other cases of rebellion, the slave power immediately responded by brutally cracking down on black life. In the Turner case, the Virginia General Assembly targeted two particular concerns—literacy and religious expression—believed to be responsible for the insurrection. It became forbidden to teach bondspersons to read and write. Slaves were expressly prohibited from preaching, or holding "any assembly or meeting" for any purpose whatsoever.[5] Notably, many of the new laws, such as the injunction against assembly, applied to free African Americans as well. Inspired by the fear that unenslaved blacks offered dangerous examples to the bound, legislators sought to close off any hope of liberty. Then they passed a "police bill" that rushed some three hundred free blacks in Southampton County off to Liberia under the auspices of the American Colonization Society. Those remaining lost their right to a trial by jury, and confronted new laws providing for their sale into slavery upon criminal offence.[6] Neighboring states like North Carolina and Maryland followed suit with similar provisions. As far away as New Orleans, legislators inspired by the Southampton insurrection tightened old controls on black life, and applied new ones.[7]

Horrendous as it was, the sweeping campaign of oppression that followed the rebellion was less surprising than the Virginia General Assembly's next move. As had happened in the wake of Gabriel's rebellion, some whites questioned retaining an institution so manifestly dangerous. This time, though, the legislature actually considered alternatives. In January 1832, the Virginia General Assembly began debating a measure to abolish slavery gradually in the state. Extraordinarily, a slave rebel had indirectly brought the abolition of slavery to the floor of the oldest and most powerful slaveholding state of the Union. With the rebellion "destroying for a time all feeling of security and confidence," reasoned Virginia law professor Thomas R. Dew at the time, it was not to be wondered that "many should have seriously inquired, if this supposed monstrous evil could not be removed from her bosom."[8] The Virginia proposal was hardly a gesture of racial equality. Lawmakers managed to forge an abolition bill which, in its efforts to enforce the boundaries of caste, far exceeded anything contemplated in the North. Starting July 4, 1840, all slaves would become property of the state upon reaching the age of maturity. Before that point—age twenty-one for men and eighteen for women—owners could sell their slaves to other states, and indeed would have every reason to try. Any freed African Americans remaining in the state after the bill went into effect would be forcibly removed. The point was obvious: slavery should be abolished because it imperiled the state, not because people of African descent possessed any innate right to liberty. As ran the tenor of race relations in the North, those who had been enslaved would be extirpated as thoroughly as slavery itself. For months lawmakers debated and amended the measure. But the powerful planters of the Tidewater region refused to embrace even this much-compromised plan for ending slavery. The bill went down in defeat.

Nonetheless, something critical had happened. Turner had not succeeded in his impossible aim of bringing about the final judgment. Nor had he come close to earlier insurrectionaries' goals of founding or joining a black state. But his actions had had a marked impact on the slave power, sufficient to cause one of the most prestigious slaveholding regimes on the planet to seriously consider self-abolition. The Turner rebellion marked a critical turning point in the story of slavery's demise in the United States. The preceding conspiracies had been more careful in their planning and more rational in their aims, yet less successful in their outcomes. The Gabriel and Vesey rebellions had been rooted in the logic of Atlantic social revolution and the example of Haiti. The Turner rebellion lacked these elements, yet nonetheless succeeded, at least inadvertently, in putting a serious gradual abolition measure on the floor of the Virginia legislature. What had happened?

The key difference lay in context. By 1831, several decades of sectional strife had seeped their way into national politics. Widespread emancipation in the North, awareness of Atlantic trends toward abolition in Latin America, and the amelioration of slavery in much of the Caribbean all helped identify slavery in the United States as a regional peculiarity. The work of Federalist critics of southern power, and of the gradual abolitionists who had melded into the colonization movement, was just beginning to give way to a new breed of antislavery agitator. Throughout Virginia's reaction to the Turner rebellion, slaveholders charged that northerners had filled the heads of blacks with aspirations of freedom. Virginia governor John Floyd believed that Turner's revolt "had its origin, and eminated from, the Yankee population"—"most especially the Yankee pedlers and traders." He complained that outsiders had brought two dangerous ideas to the slaves. Christianity fostered the notion that the spiritual equality of all people before God could easily translate into civic and political equality here on earth, and the Revolution taught the enslaved that just as "the white people rebelled against England to obtain freedom, so have the blacks a right to do." The education of slaves, which had been intended as a benevolent gesture to help them understand the scriptures, had only given them access to antislavery literature. Religious gatherings had provided cover for conspiracy. Worst of all were the "incendiary publications" that had found their way into the hands of Virginia slaves. Floyd was convinced that "Northern presses" were distributing plans for rebellion throughout the South, which black preachers and other "leading and intelligent men" among the slaves were acting upon.[9]

Floyd's fears reflected an important change from the days of 1800, or even of

1822. It was not that northerners were actively promoting slave rebellion; it was that a fresh generation of abolitionists was calling American slaveholding into question in bold new ways. Though the new breed of antislavery activists constituted the smallest fraction of northern society and opinion, their vocal efforts drew considerable attention, and in fact altered the national political agenda. No single figure more clearly stood for the new strain of antislavery than William Lloyd Garrison, the editor of the abolitionist newspaper the *Liberator*, which began publication in the same year that Turner launched his revolt. Born in 1805 to a poverty-stricken but pious Massachusetts family, Garrison apprenticed as a newspaper man in Newburyport. After heading several unsuccessful papers, he began editing a Boston serial, the *National Philanthropist*, which preached the gospels of temperance (abstaining from the consumption of alcohol) and moral reform. He caught the attention of Benjamin Lundy, a Quaker abolitionist then editing a Baltimore newspaper, the *Genius of Universal Emancipation*, which positioned itself on the antislavery wing of the colonization movement. Garrison began co-editing the journal. He took up the message, breaking completely with colonization and converting to immediate abolitionism. After a brief stint at the *Genius*, he moved back to Boston, and on January 1 released the first edition of the *Liberator*, the weekly he would edit until slavery ended in 1865.

More than any other single white figure, Garrison represented a new strain of uncompromising antislavery thought. He discredited colonization as a scheme "inadequate in its design, injurious in its operation, and contrary to sound principle."[10] In 1832, he published an extended refutation of the American Colonization Society's central claims, titled *Thoughts on African Colonization*, in which he compiled voluminous evidence to demonstrate that the society's concern for black welfare was specious, and that African Americans themselves overwhelmingly rejected it. As he wrote to a colleague shortly after the pamphlet's publication, "I look upon the overthrow of the Colonization Society as the overthrow of slavery itself—they both stand or fall together."[11] The cornerstone of Garrisonian abolitionism, though, was a call for the immediate and uncompensated end to slavery. Garrison rejected the very principle of gradualism implicit in colonization, and indeed in all plans for emancipation heretofore considered or implemented. Garrison and his followers well knew that their stridency alienated the moderate center of the American public, but they considered it a moral duty to stand against an execrable national crime. Garrison responded to criticism of his radicalism in the inaugural edition of the *Liberator*:

> On this subject, I do not wish to think, or speak, or write, with moderation. No! no! Tell a man whose house is on fire, to give a moderate alarm; tell him to moderately rescue his wife from the hand of the ravisher; tell the mother

to gradually extricate her babe from the fire into which it has fallen;—but urge me not to use moderation in a cause like the present. I am in earnest—I will not equivocate—I will not excuse—I will not retreat a single inch—AND I WILL BE HEARD.[12]

With this approach, Garrison steered antislavery into uncharted waters. Earlier reformers had called for the immediate end to bondage, but never before had a white activist bundled together so many radical messages: the uncompromising tone, the moral righteousness, the call for immediate change, the utter neglect of slaveholder interest and sentiments. He attracted enormous attention. A growing trickle of northern whites, eager to put their reform commitments to practical use, "converted" from the gradualism of colonization to immediate abolition. Notably, Garrison championed new places for women in reform, offering them a novel public realm for the expression of their gendered roles as moral nurturers. By 1840, American antislavery societies could boast a total membership of two hundred thousand.[13] But Garrison's dogmatic challenge to the status quo of antebellum America inspired more detractors than adherents. In northern cities between 1833 and 1838, some thirty-five riots targeted abolitionists or African Americans.[14] In October 1835, a Boston mob prevented Garrison from addressing a meeting of the Female Anti-Slavery Society. According to a contemporary account, Garrison was "seized and dragged through the streets with a rope around his body," and "threatened with tar and feathers." Only the intervention of the mayor, who placed Garrison in jail, saved the abolitionist from further harm.[15] But infamy worked nearly as well as praise for Garrison, for it, too, focused national concern on the crime of slavery and the plight of its victims.

It came as no surprise, then, when slaveholders singled out Garrison for instigating the Turner insurrection. Governor Floyd named the abolitionist specifically as one who produced "incendiary publications" with the "express intention of inciting the slaves and free negroes . . . to rebellion."[16] This statement should not be taken as the mere hyperbole of an embattled governor of a slave state. Floyd may have discounted Garrison's oft-avowed pacifism, and in his paranoia overstated possibilities for communication between abolitionists and the enslaved. But he had alighted upon the defining principle of the new antislavery. The slaves were no longer on their own. The paternalistic tones of gradual reformers were being replaced by the unforgiving demands of activists who had forsaken compromise. The new style of abolitionism posed such potent challenges to the slave power because radical abolitionists considered themselves unqualified champions of the oppressed; they were the representatives of those legally denied any other form of representation. Immediatists might be a "despised minority," but they were no more despised than the slaves they stood for. Radical abolitionists' own marginality stood for the marginality of those denied basic rights and liberties. Their numbers were small but grew, and every new apostle added one more white caste traitor to the cause of ending slavery. True, most white abolitionists carried their own, considerable racial baggage. Some wrestled with it, while others ignored it.[17] But their uncompromising campaign against chattel bondage posed the possibility of altering the "public mind" on the morality of the South's bedrock institution.

Their most critical function, in fact, lay in communicating the interests of the enslaved to a public composed of the free. Garrison himself used the charge that he instigated rebellion as one such opportunity. In answering his critics over the Southampton insurrection, he sought to educate the public on the meaning of slave rebellion more generally. "The slaves need no incentives at our hands," he wrote; "they will find them in their stripes." Such statements folded otherwise incomprehensible slave actions into a framework of meaning that people in the nonslaveholding North might understand and act on. In Garrison's hands, Nat Turner may indeed have been a violent religious fanatic. His actions were not an unfortunate aberration, though, but the logical outcome of a system that denied the slaves their fundamental humanity. Bloody rebellion was to be expected as the tragic yet inevitable consequence of bondage. Turner's revolt constituted "but the beginning of our sorrows," Garrison warned. "The same causes are at work which must inevitably produce the same effects." He also placed Turner's actions in a broad historical context of revolutionary activity. While little suggests that Turner himself called upon the American revolutionary tradition, Garrison offered such a Turner to the northern public. For him, the Southampton slaves merely fought for their liberty, as was every human's right. They thus deserved "no more censure" than any of the other peoples who were at the time seeking to throw off their oppressors, such as "the Greeks in destroying the Turks, or the Poles in exterminating the Russians, or our fathers in slaughtering the British." To think anything else of them, Garrison intoned, constituted the basest hypocrisy.[18] Here was the Revolution writ anew, with old cries of inconsistency now in the hands of an uncompromising rhetorical powerhouse.

It was a potent message, but Garrison had not been the first to make it. He had been inspired, in fact, by free African Americans themselves, who pioneered the craft of interpreting the meaning of slave rebellion in the public forum. When, for example, Garrison responded to the Turner rebellion by warning that only emancipation would relieve the threat of further violence, he was following David Walker, his fellow Bostonian, who had published a militant pamphlet in 1829. Garrison, calling "IMMEDIATE EMANCIPATION" the only hope for salvation, admonished: "Wo to this guilty land, unless she speedily repent of her evil doings!" His language directly echoed that of Walker, who just two years prior had exhorted white America, "unless you speedily alter your course, you and your Country are gone!" Indeed, Governor Floyd listed Walker first and Garrison second in his catalog of dangerous antislavery propagandists. And while there is no evidence that Nat Turner ever came close to a copy of the *Liberator*, it is known that African American sailors smuggled copies of David Walker's *Appeal* into Virginia ports such as Norfolk.[19] In addition, Garrison's rejection of colonization owed completely to his understanding that African Americans themselves overwhelmingly objected to it. His famous pamphlet, *Thoughts on African Colonization*, included a seventy-six-page chapter crammed with evidence to this effect, compiled from African Americans throughout the North and upper South. "African colonization is directly and irreconcilably opposed to the wishes of our colored population as a body," Garrison wrote, and then promptly produced the minutes of meeting after meeting testifying to this effect. Once again, he trod a path already blazed by Walker, who spent an entire chapter of his *Appeal* denouncing colonization as a nefarious scheme to buttress slavery by removing slaves' most powerful potential allies from their midst. "If the free are allowed to stay among the slaves," Walker wrote sardonically, "they will intercourse together, and, of course, the free will learn the slaves *bad habits*, by teaching them that they are MEN, as well as other people, and certainly *ought* and *must* be FREE."[20]

In fact, the entire phenomenon of radical immediatism may never have happened in the United States had it not been for the critical connection white reformers made with the prominent African Americans who led the institutions northern blacks had created in freedom. It is unlikely that, absent this connection, Garrison would have undergone such a rapid and complete conversion to the immediatist cause. Surely, Garrison's personality, rooted as it was in alienation and recrimination, factored crucially. But he, like other radical abolitionists, directed his reforming energies at one among many possible concerns: the plight of enslaved African Americans. He could do so only because African Americans themselves had constructed a platform on which he could stand. Only their self-publicized struggles with freedom in the North, and their connections to slavery in the South, induced reformers such as Garrison to expend their talents on behalf of the slaves rather than on comparable reforms such as temperance. In publicizing blacks' protest messages, Garrison and the immediatists, as maligned as they were, possessed at least one critical resource their inspirers' lacked. Their white racial identity guaranteed them a degree of attention blacks could never have attained on their own.

MUST NOT WORK AGAIN
Slave Rebellion and Metropolitan Abolition in the Caribbean

In the United States, black activists and white immediatists worked together to form a new generation of antislavery workers, which revolutionized
the practice of abolition. Ending bondage required a bloc with the potential to
become a powerful force in the public discourse of a nation. This was particularly
so in the United States, because the slave power was so deeply entrenched. Slave
owners there were not as secure as in Brazil, where no concerted opposition to
slavery existed in free society, nor perhaps the Spanish Caribbean, where Cuba
and Puerto Rico were quickly becoming the world's most important producers
of cane sugar. But in mainland Spanish Latin America, slavery either had fallen
or was falling. And in the remainder of the Caribbean, slavery was truly under
siege by 1831. In the period between Nat Turner's rebellion in 1831 and the end
of the Mexican-American War in 1848, slavery in the non-Spanish Caribbean
largely collapsed, leaving the United States the world's premier slaveholding
state. It was the most industrialized nation in the world to maintain slavery, as
well as the wealthiest to countenance slavery within its national borders.[21]

The process of "metropolitan abolition," through which European powers
ended their practice of colonial slavery, was inextricably intertwined with a new
wave of insurrection that blossomed in the wake of the Haitian Revolution. Unrest in St. Domingue sparked immediate outbreaks in Jamaica and Martinique,
and inflected many instances of rebellion thereafter. In the Atlantic world, a
spirit of collective resistance had long prevailed wherever the enslaved concentrated. Large-scale insurrections, though, had always been rare, and remained so
in the early nineteenth century. When they did occur, though, rebellions after
Haiti often reflected a transformation in means and ends. Notably, their planning and execution fell more and more to creole slaves, who evinced a remarkable awareness of the currents of metropolitan policy and opinion. Earlier revolts
had often been led by Africans, and indeed had often centered on one particular
ethnic group. For example, Wolof slaves of Hispaniola staged the first large-scale
revolt in the Americas. Similarly, Kongolese slaves rose up in South Carolina's
Stono Rebellion of 1739, and Koramantse slaves led Tacky's Rebellion in Jamaica
in 1760. Rivalries among African ethnic groups could even impair rebellions, as
happened in 1724 among Angolan and Yoruban slaves, who rose up separately
in Minas Gerais, Brazil.[22] With the age of revolution, though, American-born
slaves increasingly played key roles in Atlantic slave rebellions. During the summer of 1776, creole slaves in Hanover parish, Jamaica, aware of events in the
mainland thirteen colonies, joined a large plot to revolt. A white resident found

the conspiracy all "the more alarming" in that island-born slaves had joined "the Salt-water negroes"—an event, he said, "which never happened before."[23]

The trend toward creole leadership of slave rebellions suggests the degree to which general patterns of acculturation impacted the shape of collective resistance in the postrevolutionary era. As was happening to even greater degrees in the heavily creole United States, distinct slave cultures were melding. While saltwater Africans flowed into burgeoning plantation regimes such as Cuba and Puerto Rico, the slave populations of long-established societies became increasingly American-born in the early nineteenth century. Knowing firsthand no culture but the Afro-Caribbean world into which they had been born, creole slaves assumed important roles in nineteenth-century slave societies. Even when outnumbered by imported Africans, the creoles offered newcomers a dynamic and malleable cultural hearth, anchoring notions of identity and collective consciousness all enslaved people could contribute to and share. And, as had been the case with the skilled Gabriel, creole slaves often possessed skills and knowledge that both enhanced their status and made them effective leaders. Often entrusted with authority by whites, they were more likely than Africans to be literate, and to understand the political and military developments that might signal propitious times for collective action.

The creolization of the slave population was particularly clear in the British West Indies. In 1807, all had understood that choking off slave supplies to the British Caribbean doomed slavery to eventual demise. This speculation bore fruit in ensuing decades. While nearly fifty thousand Africans entered the British Caribbean between the legal end of the trade and abolition in 1833,[24] smuggled imports could never compensate for the natural population decline endemic to the brutal work and disease regimes of the West Indies. Between 1807 and 1833 the slave population of the British Caribbean fell from 776,000 to 668,000.[25] This general decline concentrated the native born in the remaining population.[26] Long-standing colonies were already mostly creole; Africans predominated only in newly acquired territories such as Trinidad and Berbice.[27] Not even half of the slave populations of Demerara and Jamaica were American-born in the 1820s, while that of Barbados was over 90 percent in 1816.[28] (In the United States, creoles formed an even larger majority of the slave population, but their very predominance there denoted that the slave population itself was rising—from 1.13 million in 1810, to just under 2 million in 1830.[29] Slavery was not dying a natural death in the United States; it was growing on its own.)

Policymakers' awareness of demographic trends in the Caribbean may even have enhanced the creolization process. Some planters, anticipating that abolition of the slave trade would foster labor shortages and soaring costs, sought to ameliorate the conditions of slaves in hope of enhancing natural population growth. British abolitionists shared their aim, though they deplored planters' selfish motives. Their efforts resulted in laws such as the 1819 Slave Registration Act, which created a central storehouse of information on slaves and their conditions, and the amelioration policy of 1823, which encouraged planters to provide religious instruction, reduce corporal punishment, and separate Sabbath and market days.[30] By mildly improving conditions where they were implemented, such moves further augmented the creole portions of colonial slave populations, unintentionally heightening slaves' sense of collective identity and group cohesion.

Creoles' awareness of Atlantic events and the currents of metropolitan opinion often proved critical in decisions to rebel. Rumors of impending amelioration or emancipation frequently led slaves to conclude that the current of policy moved in their favor, but was being bucked by local authorities.[31] The Easter Rebellion that struck Barbados in 1816 (also named Bussa's Rebellion after one of its leaders) was instigated by elite slaves who believed their emancipation imminent. One of these leaders, Nanny Grigg, a domestic servant, told fellow slaves "that they were damned fools to work," for "the negroes were to be freed on Easter-Monday." If not, she suggested, slaves should "fight for it" and "set fire," for "that was the way they did in Santo Domingo." While no "free paper" or plan for mass emancipation actually existed, slave leaders surely were reacting to news that the Barbadian Assembly had recently rejected Parliament's slave registration plan.[32] One Barbadian planter blamed "mischievous persons" and "indiscreet conversation" for permitting such news to reach the slaves, but island whites had publicly announced their opposition.[33]

The Demerara Rebellion of 1823 similarly illustrated that slave insurrectionaries' awareness of the shifting currents of metropolitan opinion clearly shaped rebels' intentions and actions. In this British sugar colony on the northern coast of South America, planters had, as in Barbados, balked at amelioration measures. Elite slaves like Jack Gladstone and Quamina heard news of this, which in the slave community once again transposed into claims that local planters were defying the mother country's intention to free them. English missionaries, illustrating the new power of evangelical Protestantism throughout the Atlantic, likely added fuel to the fire by establishing expectations for slave religious meetings, and pressing local authorities to better deplorable conditions.[34]

The objectives of these West Indian revolts offer yet another sign of the centrality of transatlantic awareness among the enslaved. Neither the Easter Rebellion of 1816 nor the Demerara Rebellion of 1823 envisioned the indiscriminate slaughter of whites. In both instances, leaders planned to launch a general cessation of work to protest worsening conditions and the denial of rumored help from governors in the mother country. Indeed, one British commentator declared that the Demerara uprising looked more like "a combination of European workmen to strike for wages, for time, or other indulgence, than a rebellion of African slaves."[35] True, violence was integral to the effort, as it was in the instance of free labor radicalism. Against an intransigent and nearly omnipotent planter class, armed resistance offered the only means possible for establishing a basis of negotiation. Militance sought to achieve the limited though still formidable aim of improving work conditions: an extra day to tend and market garden produce, or limitations on the use of the whip. In both instances, leaders enjoined their followers to keep white casualties to a minimum. They also hoped that the king's troops, and particularly those of African descent, would refuse to kill those they might see as countrymen.

This limited objective of seeking further amelioration within the system prevailed in other revolts as well. In 1830, Bahamian slaves on Exuma Island resisted sale to other plantations. They fled to the bush for several weeks, then sailed a pilfered boat to the capital of Nassau, where they put their case to the governor of the colony.[36] Such tactics were a far cry from the resistance typical of the prerevolutionary age. They signaled a new era, in which bondspersons sought to engage the slave power as rough political equals working within a common system. While earlier maroons had often treated with local regimes, their goals had generally been to secure their autonomy from colonial governance, not reform it. Oftentimes, maroons actually served the plantation system by returning fugitives to the plantation or even taking up arms against rebels in instances of insurrection, as happened during Tacky's War in Jamaica in 1760.[37]

The largest rebellion of the post-Haitian age further illustrates the trend toward strike actions and away from maroonage. In 1831, the creole Baptist deacon Samuel Sharpe spearheaded a widespread work shutdown in Jamaica that sparked the rebellion of tens of thousands of slaves.[38] Discouraged by the colony's failure to implement the 1823 amelioration measures, Sharpe induced his followers to "sit down" and cease work on Christmas day, which was commonly set aside for the enslaved to gather with families. Adherents swore that they "must not work again unless we got half pay," but also that they "must not trouble anybody or raise any rebellion."[39] Hopes for a nonviolent confrontation once again proved chimerical, however, as the conflation of angry slaves and obdurate whites was likely to produce only one outcome. In the resulting Baptist War, which also became known as the Christmas Rebellion, ten days of armed conflict with militia and regular troops wreaked a swath of destruction across the western portion of the island. But, again, the initial aim had been to seek a more equitable position within existing power structures rather than flee the system and seek to live as proto-peasant maroons on the margins of Atlantic society. And, also again, sensitivity to metropolitan opinion dictated that white casualties be kept minimal—a difficult goal indeed once passions were loosed and the conflict escalated into an all-or-nothing contest of arms.

The Baptist War constituted West Indian slaves' most promising effort to speed a general emancipation, representing the height of post-Haitian rebellion in the British West Indies. In different ways, historians such as Eugene Genovese and Michael Craton have posed this transition in the goals of slave rebellions as a consequence of the revolutionary era. Whether considering Gabriel's desire to "drink and dine with the merchants of the city" in Richmond in 1800, or Demerara rebels' intention to send a freedom plan to the governor, many of the post-Haitian rebellions were conceived in decidedly modern terms.[40] The revolutionary period marks the point at which slaves' appropriation and refashioning of metropolitan political and religious idioms transformed their collective resistance, moving it from "restorationist" efforts to re-create the premodern social relations of Africa, to efforts to seek power within the Atlantic political and economic order, even to the point of ending slavery itself by ameliorating it out of existence.[41]

In the short term, the new revolts produced disastrous results. Local authorities more than repaid the temerity of slave rebels. Local militias, ill disciplined and bloodthirsty, responded first to insurrections, typically slaughtering dozens of slaves indiscriminately before the facade of regular justice could legitimate the murder of suspected rebels. Regular troops claimed their own numbers, and the inevitable wave of show trials and public executions claimed still more. Michael Craton estimates that in the Barbados uprising, fighting took 50 slaves' lives, while militias indiscriminately killed another 70 and executions took 144 more. In Demerara, a total of 250 slaves lost their lives. In Jamaica, rebels killed only 14 whites but lost about 200 themselves, with authorities executing an additional 344 in the aftermath.[42] Most revolts also set back the abolitionist movement, at least temporarily. Ever vulnerable to the claim that they sowed "servile insurrection," antislavery reformers reacted cautiously to such events. White evangelical missionaries active among the slaves came under special fire. Planters charged, not without some justice, that the preachers' sermons inspired revolt while their religious services provided cover for organizing. After the Barbados insurrection, even the noble Wilberforce advised abolitionists to "lie upon our oars" instead of pressing to enforce the slave registration laws that had already been passed.[43]

In the longer term, though, the rebellions played decisive roles by impacting metropolitan opinion, a key motive force behind metropolitan abolition. The planter regime's widespread and indiscriminate butchery of slave rebels served as poor advertisements for the institution's humanity. White vengeance in the periphery backfired by offering clear evidence of the brutal extremes required to maintain plantation discipline. Henry Taylor, an antislavery sympathizer who worked in the Colonial Office, which oversaw affairs in the Caribbean, later recalled the tactics employed. Government agents in the colonies would submit biannual reports, "in which every outrage and enormity perpetrated on the slaves was duly detailed." Taylor and his colleagues then "laid the reports and despatches before Parliament as fast as they were received and written." The antislavery press also received copies, "by which they were circulated far and wide through the country." By this means, "unquestionable facts" that had been "officially authenticated" were made to complement "the howling of the saints," as British abolitionists were known.[44] In the case of Demerara, English abolitionists parlayed tales of slaveholder inhumanity into powerful rhetorical tools for swaying public opinion, as when Thomas Buxton told Parliament the story of the slave Billy, who became a rebel only after his family was separated by sale.[45]

The British public recoiled at the vehemence with which plantation regimes sought retribution for insurrection, but more significant than the many slave lives taken was the lone Englishman lost to postrebellion trials. The death of John Smith, a London Missionary Society minister who had been preaching to the slaves in Demerara since 1817, galvanized public opinion, punctuating a transition to the final abolitionist campaigns. Men such as Smith inspired some comfort, but more dread, among slaveholders. On the one hand, Christian preaching could stress the Bible's injunction against disobedience to worldly authority. On the other, it could inspire liberation movements such as the one that freed the Israelites from Egyptian rule. Such preaching often fell to clergymen of antislavery bent aligned with the "nonconformist" or "dissenting" Protestant sects in England, so named for standing apart from the state-sanctioned Anglican church. Initially, many observers considered the Gospel an overall boon to plantation discipline. One plantation manager in Demerara reportedly confessed to being "astonished at the wonderful change that has taken place" among the slaves since their commencement of religious instruction. "They formerly were of a very rebellious disposition, and not at all backward to insurrections," he related, "but now their leisure time is spent in prayer."[46]

Yet as the enslaved availed themselves of the opportunity to avoid labor and gather at services, planters' suspicions bloomed. When they found Smith's own congregants at the center of the Demerara revolt, they court-martialed him. He was convicted of complicity with the rebels, and of failing to notify officials of the impending insurrection. For two months, Smith languished in prison, sentenced to die. Shortly before a royal reprieve could effect his deportation, consumption took him. Smith's martyrdom animated public outrage in Britain far more than did the killings of 250 slave rebels. Whereas the Barbados debacle had placed abolitionists on the defensive, Smith's death permitted abolitionists to condemn slaveholder barbarism without risk of endorsing the slaves' violence.

"The blood of the martyred Missionary . . . will not be silent," intoned one British antislavery journal. "Already its sound has gone forth throughout the land; and from every corner of it the most energetic expressions of public feeling have begun to proceed."[47]

If the British public's reaction to Smith's death in 1824 helped turn the tide of opinion against the slave power, public response to the Baptist War of 1831 proved decisive in the final ending of slavery in the British Empire. Reports of the indiscriminate butchery of Jamaican insurrectionaries intensified abolitionists' long-standing propaganda efforts. Returning to England, ministers such as Thomas Burchell focused public attention on the treatment of respectable white preachers at the hands of Jamaica's "savage hordes" of slaveholders: "Have his blood," "shoot him," and "hang him" they had cried as Burchell fled Montego Bay after the rebellion.[48] Once again, missionaries from the island "stole the martyr's crown," as historian Michael Craton puts it.[49] Petitions calling for immediate emancipation began flooding Parliament. Abolitionists called upon candidates for elective office to pledge their support for abolitionist measures. Antislavery lecturers blanketed the country, spreading the word to hundreds of thousands, and establishing over a thousand local branches. Nonconformist evangelicals played critical roles in linking the antislavery cause with the will of God and the interests of humanity. The earlier emphasis on gradual measures gave way to calls for immediate emancipation. In short, the period following the Jamaican uprising witnessed an as yet unparalleled example of the mobilization of public opinion in the service of a major legislative action.[50] As French observer Alexis de Tocqueville described the impulse for abolition, "the popular torrent prevailed and swept it along."[51]

Events in the metropole promoted the reform spirit that led to abolition. In 1829, Parliament sought to quiet long years of Irish unrest by repealing long-standing restrictions on Catholics' political and civil rights. In July 1830, Parisian mobs overthrew the French King Charles X and installed a constitutional monarchy under Louis Philippe. Though it fell far short of the violence and radicalism of the French Revolution, the transition in power triggered separatist crises in the Netherlands (Belgium) and Russia (Poland), and warned Britain's ruling class of the limits of its own oligarchic tendencies. For decades parliamentary representation had fallen ever further away from actual sources of wealth and population in Britain. "Rotten" boroughs conferred political power on magnates who controlled these seats, despite that over time they had come to represent very few Britons at all. One of these notorious boroughs, Old Sarum, had for several centuries elected two members to the House of Commons despite that no resident voters actually lived there. Likewise, Dunwich in Suffolk elected two MPs, despite that most of it had fallen into the sea centuries before. With three houses and a population of fifteen, its seats in Parliament had become marketable commodities. Meanwhile, the thriving industrial city of Manchester, with a population of 142,000 in 1831, was considered a part of Lancashire County, and lacked its own representatives. In 1832, long calls for the reform of the political system culminated in the social unrest of the "Days of May." A broad coalition of middle- and working-class citizens took to the streets to object to the House of Lords' veto of a reform measure, threatening Britain with the possibility of revolution. Finally, in June 1832, public pressure caused even entrenched conservatives in the Lords to relent, and a bill passed. The Great Reform Bill of 1832 expanded the electorate, cleaned up many rotten boroughs, and created new seats to reflect changes in population. By retaining a considerable property qualification on voting, the bill frustrated the aims of working-class radicals, but by offering real concessions to public opinion Parliament had averted a constitutional crisis and preempted more sweeping change.

The same spirit of concession attended Parliament's next great act of reform, the abolition of slavery. The Reform Act Crisis had forestalled consideration of an abolition measure, but with news of the Christmas Rebellion in Jamaica fully entering the public consciousness in the spring of 1832, abolition and political reform became linked. The Reform Bill materially helped abolitionist efforts by creating new seats in Parliament likely to go to abolition's supporters, and removed some belonging to West Indian proprietors.[52] The campaign mounted, featuring two new arguments that had a powerful effect on political discussions surrounding slavery. First, British abolitionists embraced the slaves' own conception of their struggle, steadily fitting rebellions into a framework of thought that understood collective violence as an outgrowth of liberal sentiment. According to some in Parliament, executed Jamaican slave rebels "died glorying in their death."[53] In the midst of the political upheaval of 1830, British abolitionists connected the slaves' desires with Britons' own. "At a moment when Britons were struggling for what they conceived to be their inalienable rights," asked one, "would not one and all say they were averse to slavery, and ardent for the liberty of 800,000 of their fellow-subjects?"[54]

Abolitionists thus began posing insurrection as an expression not just of generic resistance, but of the slaves' yearning for freedom on the Western model. "The feeling of liberty appears to have gone abroad among the negroes," reported one Jamaican missionary to Parliament. This was a phenomenon impelled by abolitionism itself. "The negroes are very sensible . . . of all that is taking place in their favour," he continued; "their minds have been long set on freedom, and they never will be satisfied without it."[55] Slave rebels consciously shaped their actions around their understanding of public opinion and popular values back in the metropole, as when leaders called for minimizing the killing of whites during insurrections. Though antislavery missionaries claimed credit for preaching the new, pacific approach of slave uprisings, religious instruction alone could never have accomplished the feat. Instead, we may credit slaves' own gleaning of revolutionary principles and their refabrication of Christian liberation. Abolitionists, marking the self-imposed limits of slave insurrections, posed mass emancipation as the safe alternative to more violent possibilities. "There would be more danger from withholding emancipation than from bestowing emancipation," they claimed.[56] In the wake of the Baptist War, this perspective became dominant. The enslavement of those who yearned for liberty risked anarchy and destruction for all. "Emancipation alone will effectively avert the danger," argued Prime Minister Charles Grey.[57] Such arguments heralded emancipation in the West Indies, and became important examples for American abolitionists.

Events moved. In May 1832, Parliament formed a select committee "to consider and report upon the Measures which it may be expedient to adopt for the purpose of effecting the Extinction of Slavery throughout the British Dominions." In August 1833, Parliament passed An Act for the Abolition of Slavery throughout the British Colonies, which decreed the end of slavery in most of the British Empire on August 1, 1834. Two important components of the bill mitigated its impact, rendering it more palatable to the West Indian slave power and considerably diminishing its significance as a manifesto of universal liberty. First, the government was to reimburse slave owners the unimaginable sum of twenty million pounds for the property they were losing. This provision conceded not simply considerable wealth to planters, but also the principle that, at least in the colonies, property could be held in man. Second, the final bill immediately freed only those slaves under six years of age. The remainder were subjected to a period of "apprenticeship," which, as in the postrevolutionary U.S. North, was euphemistically imagined as a time during which former slaves could be prepared for the responsibilities of freedom. With these patronizing connotations, apprenticeship thus indemnified slave owners for their lost labor by providing a period during which a master could treat a laborer "as a Slave [as] if this Act had not been made."[58] Apprentices involved in agricultural labor would be freed after a period of six years, and those in domestic or other service after four. Given that planters estimated the value of their human property at forty-five million pounds, these two measures went far toward soothing the sting of abolition.[59] Abolitionists grieved, but the concessions worked. According to historian Robin Blackburn, only two of the MPs who owned West Indian plantations voted against the measure, one because he had converted to abolitionist sympathies and could not morally abide compensation![60] In any case, abolitionists had cause for joy in 1838, when peaceful protests in the colonies led Parliament to abolish the apprenticeship system, and grant full and immediate freedom to all.

The metropolitan abolitions that followed were but epigones of the British original. No other European power developed a mass movement to rival that of the most powerful industrial and trading nation in the world. In Britain, circumstances favored the rapid progress of a mass abolition movement, at least relative to the continent. For one, the mass campaigns founded to end the slave trade bequeathed a legacy of antislavery institutions and leaders, establishing momentum for successive waves of mass action. Historian Seymour Drescher calculates that while sixty to seventy-five thousand signed about one hundred antislavery petitions in 1788, nearly half a million signed over five thousand petitions in 1833.[61] Perhaps because England's example was so epochal, abolition in peer nations did not require comparable movements. England's "mighty experiment" loosened slavery's stranglehold on other nations, for whatever abolition cost them in wealth or national interest would at least already have been offset by Britain. It was perhaps also the case that West Indian emancipation generated antislavery momentum among other nations' elites such that less was required to effect the destruction of slavery. In the "continental" pattern of metropolitan abolition, social and political notables sought not to create a mass movement, but pressed those in power to pursue incremental measures, operating much as the colonizationists had in the young United States. To the extent that mass movements did emerge elsewhere, they did so much on the British model.

France trailed Britain. Gallic abolitionists, their nation having abolished slavery during the Revolution only to have it reimposed by Napoléon, could hardly declare the institution's end inevitable. In addition, the Anglophobia generated by long years of war with Britain inhibited the adoption of English styles and methods of abolitionism. Finally, despite British antislavers' sanguine predictions that free labor would prove more productive than enslaved, production declined after mass emancipation in the British West Indies, setting an uninspiring example for others. Nonetheless, a French abolition movement did exist. It had helped France agree to abolish its slave trade at the Congress of Vienna in 1818, and had played a role in the strengthening of anti-slave-trade measures in 1830. Its membership was small and privileged, drawn primarily from Paris's social and intellectual elite. Heir to the revolutionary era's Société des Amis des Noirs (Society of the Friends of the Blacks), the Société française pour l'abolition de l'esclavage (French Abolition Society) moved cautiously in the wake of the July Revolution of 1830. Only in 1845 were ameliorative measures passed, and these were reluctantly implemented. In the following two years, something akin to a mass movement appeared, built largely from British examples and even British funds. While French petition drives never yielded anything close to the number of signatures appearing on English counterparts, abolitionists there nonetheless could claim thirty thousand names in early 1848.[62]

This rapid but late rise of a mass movement for immediate abolition was forestalled by yet another revolution, that of 1848, which created unintentional but fortuitous opportunities for a dedicated core of high-ranking French notables to influence slave policy. As Paris workers prepared to man the barricades in protest of conservative rule and declining economic opportunity, a provisional government appointed Victor Schoelcher, perhaps the country's leading abolitionist, to the position of undersecretary for the colonies. Schoelcher promptly called for a commission to craft a measure abolishing slavery, which the government approved a mere eight weeks later. In April, France abolished slavery in Martinique, Guadeloupe, French Guiana, and Réunion. A year later, it approved the raising of 120 million francs (24 million U.S. dollars) to compensate slave owners for the 248,560 bondspersons set free. France had legally eradicated slavery a second time.

Slave violence in the periphery did not instigate the abolition of 1848, but it had played a role. Learning of the imminent announcement of emancipation, bondsmen in Martinique struck work, leaving the countryside to await further news in the town. In May, the tense situation erupted into violence, with thirty-five slave lives lost. These events hastened emancipation, if only by eleven days, as local governors sought to avert further calamities by prematurely declaring slavery dead.

Collective action also pressured the Danish government, which ended slavery in its small Caribbean colonies at virtually the same time. The country had been the first European power to abolish its slave trade (1792), and its Virgin Island possessions were of minimal and declining significance. In 1847, King Christian VIII acted with the popular will in decreeing a post-nati emancipation measure that also freed existing slaves after a period of twelve years. The following February, unrest broke out on St. Croix when nearly half the island's seventeen thousand slaves struck work to demand immediate emancipation. A crisis ensued, in which eight slave "rebels" were executed. Nonetheless, colonial governor Peter von Scholten acceded, and in July 1848 all slaves in the Danish Virgin Islands were liberated.

In the Dutch Caribbean, too, word of emancipation measures on nearby islands fostered collective slave action to hasten emancipation. On the island of St. Martin, which the Dutch and French split, news of the impending freedom on the French side of the island led to insurrection on the Dutch side. Slaves refused to work, and local authorities proved powerless to make them. In this fashion, the several hundred Dutch slaves on St. Maarten effected their de facto liberation.[63] Full freedom would take fifteen more years. Only in the South American colony of Suriname, with a slave population hovering between thirty-five and forty thousand,[64] was plantation slavery still a viable enterprise in the Dutch New World. But just as the examples of British and French abolition impelled the Netherlands to follow, so too postemancipation declines in both empires cautioned the Dutch. When the Hague finally did pass an emancipation measure in 1863, it included a decade-long period of apprenticeship, the longest any European nation successfully enacted.

UNDISGUISED TRUTHS
National Showdowns over Slavery in the United States

Amid the broad patterns of Atlantic abolition, the United States occupied a unique position. The northern states had abolished slavery, as had most newly independent states of mainland Spanish Latin America. As we have seen, mass emancipation had resulted from colonial wars for independence that played out amid a field of new ideological possibilities. Roughly coincident with these "revolutionary" emancipations, "metropolitan" movements for abolition emerged first in Britain, and then France, Denmark, and the Netherlands. The northern United States, having established the pattern of revolutionary emancipation above the Mason-Dixon line, then became home to a metropolitan-style movement to end slavery in the South. While abolitionists in Britain sought to emancipate all in the West Indian colonies, those in the North sought the same in a geo-contiguous portion of their own nation. The North had joined the ranks of Atlantic societies becoming free, yet the South had remained slave country, along with the Spanish Caribbean and Brazil. The North's situation around 1831 thus roughly mirrored that of Britain after 1772, when Lord Mansfield's ruling in Somerset's Case had divided British dominions between a periphery where slavery was permissible and a metropole where it was forbidden.

The U.S. North became as European states to their colonies, but with a critical difference. In the planters of the South, the forces of abolition faced a slave power far heartier than most of its contemporaries. The federal nature of the American compact, and particularly the three-fifths clause of the Constitution, had conferred on the South influence in the federal government well beyond what its own free population would have merited. Because of this, there was no likelihood of the southern plantation regime crumbling in the face of mere British precedent, elite abolitionism, or even its own slave revolts. A more potent constellation of forces, composed of all of these and more, would be necessary. The task was formidable but not wholly impossible, for the slave power of the South was not, like Brazil, its own sovereign entity, unassailable except from without. Neither was it, as in the case of Cuba, the colonial appendage of a decaying European national empire, hardly likely to destroy a key source of its failing national wealth. Instead, the presence of a slave-oriented agricultural periphery within the same national boundaries as a growing industrial metropole created ongoing conflict, along with enormous possibility.

Only in the United States, where incessant friction between free states and slave generated an accelerating sense of crisis, did activists replicate an antislavery crusade to rival the scale and significance of Great Britain's. The North launched its own metropolitan-style movement to abolish slavery in the South. This exogenous pressure proved a necessary component of any successful attempt to destroy slavery across American soil, for once the industrial revolution spurred a worldwide demand for cotton, there was little prospect of slavery's "natural" decay. Four impressive slave revolts and the full panoply of individual and collective slave resistance had proven insufficient on their own to destroy slavery. In the United Kingdom a mass abolition movement had been necessary to overcome historical inertia and generate the political momentum required to initiate a wave of metropolitan emancipations. In the United States, where a hyper-empowered periphery made the job so much more difficult, another metropolitan-style mass abolition movement proved a necessary component of abolition.

All the factors spurring the British movement pertained in the U.S. North. Both featured expanding urban metropoles with their own centers of finance, new forms of production, and thriving public fora. But as a source of antislavery, the North had much ground to make up on Britain. It began the game late, for while English abolitionists could hearken to popular anti-slave-trade organizing stretching back to the 1780s, the mass movement that took off in the 1830s in the United States had to be pieced together from English models and whole cloth. The American abolition of the slave trade had not exercised the energies of the public on anywhere near the scale it had in Britain; instead, ending the trade had been a concern of national legislators. And while mass party politics in the Early Republic had formed in part around the North-South divide, the gradual and moderate impulses of colonization had subsumed most antislavery thought in America between 1816 and 1831. The fight against slavery began to concentrate the energies of large numbers of Americans only in the early 1830s.

The organization of power in national government particularly challenged American abolitionists. The slave power in the United States, compared to its rivals in the European empires, benefitted from a national system of governance in which it was fully, and in fact disproportionately, empowered. At the local level in the European colonies, colonial assemblies commanded by planter interests controlled most affairs, just as southern planters tended to dominate local politics throughout much of the South. The difference lay in American planters' influence in national politics. In European national tribunals, slave powers had enjoyed no direct representation; their political subordination in fact defined them as colonies. In England, they had relied instead on the representation granted by elected members of Parliament who might also happen to be West Indian proprietors, and by a network of lobbying groups paid well to influence legislative matters in their favor. Figures such as William Beckford, whose fortune depended on his Jamaican plantations, occupied powerful positions both in Parliament and as Lord Mayor of London. Organizations such as the West India Planters Association and the West India Planters and Merchants defended the empire's sugar interests in London.[65] Throughout most of the eighteenth century, these mechanisms had served planter interests well. Toward the end of West Indian slavery, though, they faltered, fatally. Though proslavery apologists proffered their own stream of propaganda, planters' lobbies could not compete with the swell of national antislavery opinion. The structure of government offered relatively little defense short of a conservative House of Lords, which ultimately failed to block the emancipation bill. In the continental model of abolitionism, planters had had even fewer avenues of recourse once the leadership classes resolved to end slavery. In the United States, however, southern planters served as political leaders in a national system already weighted in their favor. True, there was opposition, but whereas in the early 1830s none of Garrison's radical bent had a hope of gaining a seat in Congress, considerably many of equal proslavery commitment had achieved just that, and more.

From the late 1820s through the 1840s, a series of national political struggles illustrated new conflicts over the place of slave country in the expanding nation, with ever-worsening implications for national unity. For example, the displacement of Native American populations from the southern interior cleared new ground for slavery. Five "civilized" tribes—the Cherokees, Chickasaw, Choctaw, Creeks, and Seminoles—occupied lands recognized as theirs by long-standing treaties with the federal government. Notwithstanding, proponents of slavery's expansion coveted their holdings. Georgians in particular sought control of Cherokee territory, on which gold had recently been discovered. In 1830, Congress passed the Indian Removal Act, which permitted President Andrew Jackson to trade with native groups: their valuable property on the frontier in exchange for poor new lands west of the Mississippi. In practice, the exchange often entailed treaty violations, manipulation of native subgroups, outright fraud, and, in the cases of the Creeks and Seminoles, open warfare. Ultimately, over fifty thousand Native Americans endured migration to the barren lands of present-day Oklahoma. Many who did not perish on this arduous "trail of tears" succumbed to disease and impoverishment. All this had come to pass through a bill that passed the House of Representatives with a slim five-vote majority, suggesting the importance of the twenty-three "slave seats" the southern states enjoyed in Congress by virtue of the three-fifths compromise.[66]

Contemporaneously, sectional acrimony brewed over South Carolina's nullification of federal tariff laws. In 1824, Congress had imposed a new protective tariff on goods entering the country. By collecting a 35 percent tax on imports,

proponents of the tariff hoped to nurture American industries against rival manufacturers in Great Britain and Europe. Originally conceived as a gesture of economic nationalism, these exorbitant tariff measures wound up sowing sectional
discord. Many northern politicians favored protection of the nascent industries
of their states, while those in the Northwest hoped to benefit from the roads, ca-
nals, and other internal improvements the new revenue would help fund. Southerners, though, had little in the way of domestic manufactures to protect, and
benefitted less from internal improvements. They feared that the tariff would
raise costs on the manufactured goods they did not produce and hence needed
to import, and would invite retaliatory tariffs that would diminish profits from
the export of their precious cotton.

South Carolina in particular, which was home to some of the wealthiest
planters of the South, objected. John C. Calhoun, the South Carolinian then sitting as Andrew Jackson's vice president, helped engineer a new tariff in 1828. In
this political maneuver, an extremely high tariff was meant to embarrass northern politicians, who would be forced to vote it down out of sheer self-interest. The scheme failed, however, for this new "Tariff of Abominations" actually
passed, imposing enormous hardship on the agricultural states. South Carolinians claimed that a 40 percent tariff on cotton amounted to northerners con-
fiscating four of every ten bales of southern cotton. Calhoun anonymously authored the state's rebuttal to the tariff. His *South Carolina Exposition and Protest*
argued that since sovereignty ultimately lay with the states enacting the federal
compact, each state had the constitutional power to "nullify" measures it deemed
contrary to its fundamental interests. As a model of federalism, this principle of
"interposition" was difficult to distinguish from states' right to unilaterally veto
any federal law. But Calhoun posed it as a more moderate alternative to the
secession that his hot-headed compatriots advocated. In 1832, the South Carolina state legislature declared the tariff void in the state, sparking a showdown
with President Andrew Jackson, the strongest executive of the age. As Jackson
declared nullification a doctrine "incompatible with the existence of the Union,"
and one "contradicted expressly by the letter of the Constitution," South Carolina began preparing for a clash of arms.[67] In early 1833, Congress passed Jackson's Force Bill, which authorized the use of federal troops and state militias
to collect tariff revenue. As tensions mounted, Kentucky Senator Henry Clay,
architect of the Missouri Compromise of 1820, stepped in. He negotiated a compromise tariff measure, which gradually lowered rates and resolved the crisis.

The nullification controversy had highlighted slaveholders' fears of their
growing marginality. Northern and southern economies were growing further
and further apart, and their respective interests and social values with them. An
energized abolition movement, though small and reviled, had raised the rhe-

torical stakes on discussions of slavery. Calhoun sensed the threat in a private letter, writing that the tariff was but a symptom of a deeper malady. "The truth can no longer be disguised," he wrote. "The peculiar domestick institution of the Southern States . . . has placed them in regard to taxation and appropriations in opposite relation to the majority of the Union." Because the sectional balance was swinging toward the North, inaction invited disaster. "If there be no protective power in the reserved rights of the states they must in the end be forced to rebel, or, submit to have their paramount interests sacrificed, their domestic institutions subordinated by Colonization and other schemes, and themselves and children reduced to wretchedness."[68] By invoking the threat of disunion that had hovered over the national project since its founding, the radical wing of the slave power demonstrated its willingness to risk sundering the Union to meet the challenge of the growing North.

The nullification controversy also marked a critical point at which political leaders in the South pivoted on their stance toward federal power. Faced with the possibility of declining relative significance in the national government, the slave states of the South would increasingly invoke the doctrines of federalism and states' rights. Such claims often served immediate rhetorical exigencies, inviting charges of hypocrisy. Under the benign reign of the Virginia dynasty, fears of encroaching federal power had been few. But as the northern states' critique of southern power evolved, southern politicians increasingly expressed anxiety over the potential of a national government that included slavery's detractors. In 1824, Virginia Congressman John Randolph objected to federal support for "internal improvements," fearing that if Congress had the power to fund the growth of transportation networks, "they may emancipate every slave in the United States."[69] Southern leaders subordinated ideals of the federal-state relationship to their ultimate priority of protecting slavery. For the next several decades, southern slaveholders would inconsistently promote or criticize an active federal government, depending on whether its power was likely to uphold or undermine slavery.

In the mid-1830s southern legislators spared few efforts to use their power in national government to counter abolitionist tactics. A new crisis arose as northern abolitionists began emulating the British movement and flooded Congress with antislavery petitions. From its founding in 1833, the American Anti-Slavery Society had been the premier immediatist organization in the country, publishing innumerable free pamphlets decrying the inhumanity of slavery, which it distributed liberally both North and South. The society also organized petitions to Congress, requesting that it abolish slavery in the District of Columbia, over which Congress had direct legislative control. More than 130,000 of these deluged the Capitol in 1837 and 1838 alone. It was novel that women made up the bulk of the signatories. The names of hundreds of thousands would eventually fill the pages of antislavery petitions, indicating the critical new role female activists played in the movement.[70] On the floor of the House of Representatives, these requests had usually been presented and then consigned to legislative perdition. At the start of the 1835 session of Congress, though, a Maine representative presented the House with yet another memorial, this one signed by 172 women from Fairfield, Maine, repeating the desire that Congress abolish slavery where it could. Rather than following standard practice by tabling the petition, southern congressmen demanded a more emphatic rejection, deeming it the product of "ignorant fanatics" who infringed on the "rights of the southern people."[71] Widely backed by southern members and Democrats from all regions, the 1836 gag rule sought to restore "tranquility to the public mind" by mandating that for the present session, Congress would take no action on any memorial relating to slavery.[72] Over the course of eleven years, members of the House fought repeatedly over whether such petitions would be heard.

John Quincy Adams, the former president who had returned to serve Massachusetts in the House, led the charge against the gags, challenging them in each subsequent session of Congress. Echoing abolitionist views, Adams deemed the right to petition one fundamental to American liberty. During the crisis that had led to the American Revolution, colonists had protested that their "humble" petitions to the king had been met only with further repression. As the Declaration of Independence asserted, this denial of the right of the ruled to petition their rulers constituted one of the acts "which may define a Tyrant . . . unfit to be the ruler of a free people." Such concerns had led directly to the incorporation of an explicit right to petition in the First Amendment to the Constitution. Now Congress's denial of the right spurred many northerners to charge gag proponents with antirepublicanism. The controversy inflamed sectional passions. The number of antislavery societies grew, as did their total membership. Abolitionists stepped up the petition campaign, barraging their legislators with new memorials every year. In the House, Adams employed a range of clever procedural maneuvers to try to rescind the gag. At one point, when he offered a petition written by slaves themselves, exasperated southern representatives roundly censured him for once again fomenting slave revolt. "By extending to slaves a privilege only belonging to freemen," an Alabama congressman tiredly reiterated, Adams "directly incites the slave population to insurrection." Adams them calmly explained that the slave petition in question actually argued *against* abolition.[73] After years of this kind of wrangling, Adams's work finally 'ᵉ fruit, in 1844, when the House voted down the gag rule. It would never be reimplemented.

Much damage had been done, and of an unintended sort. Adams had spoken for many in challenging the gag rule on the grounds that it undermined democratic process. Throughout the North, newspapers complained that it restricted the constitutional liberties of free white citizens, reducing them to political slaves just as Great Britain had done in the previous century. "If we give up the right of petitioning, or cease to exercise it in this cause then we are indeed slaves," declared one northern abolitionist. Wrote another, "The actual slavery of one portion of a people must eventually lead to the virtual slavery of the other."[74] Even those indifferent to abolitionism worried about the consequences of the new House rules. The *Boston Advocate* objected to this "renewed attempt to infringe the liberty of the press," while the *Massachusetts Spy* asserted that those willingly submitting to the gag law would earn themselves the title, "the *white slaves of the north*."[75]

Popular antipathy to the gag eventually infiltrated formal politics, threatening the fragile foundations of the two-party political system taking shape in the 1830s. Andrew Jackson's Democratic Party had swept into power in 1828, just as sectional concerns over the tariff issue brewed. The strong-willed Tennessean led a party that, like its Jeffersonian forebears, claimed a national identity but enjoyed its strongest support in the South. A new counter to the Democrats, the Whigs, began forming in the wake of Jackson's election, as opponents of his policies—ranging from northeastern advocates of a national bank to the large slaveholders whom Jackson had overmastered in the Nullification Crisis—coalesced into a viable opposition. Despite some real and many rhetorical differences between the two, neither party's leadership had much interest in championing sectionally divisive issues, lest they split their own geographically diverse ranks and concede vital ground to their opponent. These parties, and particularly those Democrats adhering to the principles established by Jackson's vice president, Martin Van Buren, pioneered the elements of modern party process: the primacy of party unity, the subordination of individual ambition to party well-being, and the use of mechanisms such as the caucus to avoid public splits among the party faithful. Neither of the two dominant parties welcomed debates in Congress over slavery, for these threatened to elevate sectional over national party loyalties. Submerging such issues became a key goal of party stalwarts. In fact, as Jackson's successor, President Van Buren had favored the gag rule precisely because he hoped it would quell debate in Congress and hence minimize sectional divisions that might split the northern wing of his party off from its powerful southern base.

It did not. Originally intended to maintain party integrity against the divisive force of abolitionism by simply forbidding discussion of slavery, the gag rule wound up threatening party unity. The intransigence of southern representatives of slavery in Congress undermined Van Buren's plan. Votes in the House of Representatives demonstrate that over time, as southern firebrands sought ever greater insulation against the threat of antislavery petitions, party loyalties gave way to sectional identity. In the slave power's desire for impossible levels of security from the threat posed by the petitions, it sought increasingly strict gag measures, such as declaring antislavery petitions unconstitutional, or demanding perpetual rather than session-limited gags. Such moves backfired. Extreme positions inflamed public opinion in the North, making it ever more difficult for moderate members of the House to support the gag. From 1836 to 1844, House votes over various exclusionary rules demonstrate a clear erosion of support from northern Democrats. As political scientists Jeffery Jenkins and Charles Stewart have demonstrated, new classes of freshman congressmen broke ranks with the Democratic leadership, dropping their support and dealing a death blow to efforts to restrict the acceptance of antislavery petitions.[76]

The episode exemplified an ever-intensifying pattern, in which antislavery agitation provoked southern overreaction, which in turn raised fears in the North about the sanctity of civil liberties. Southern congressmen sought to secure their institution from the new threat of immediatism, marginal though the movement was, through measures to resecure the slave power in Congress. These necessarily sacrificed freedoms, though not of enslaved people, for whom the vast majority of the northern public had little regard. Rather, they eroded the liberties of northern whites themselves, who may have cared little for "fanatical" abolitionists, but cared much for the fundamental civil liberties guaranteed by their cherished Constitution. As historian William W. Freehling writes, "The gag-rule debacle illustrates the way these irrational southern explosions helped break through the North's massive indifference to the antislavery campaign."[77]

The same could be said of slaveholders' call to censor the southern mails. When abolitionists sought to flood the South with antislavery tracts in the middle of the 1830s, President Andrew Jackson's postmaster general, Amos Kendall, upheld southern state laws prohibiting the delivery of "incendiary papers" designed to produce "domestic violence" among the "servile population."[78] When southern politicians called for a federal law to prevent distribution of seditious literature, abolitionists justly pointed to the threat to civil liberties. "Every freeman would be roused to a sense of his danger," one wrote of the prospect of such a law. "The people would simultaneously spring to their feet in self-defence, to rescue from the hand of tyranny all which is comprehended in the sacred words—OUR LIBERTIES."[79] The national debates over slavery engendered by efforts to protect the institution had little need to consider the slaves themselves. Instead, the threat posed to whites' civil liberties polarized sectional rhetoric, creating an ever-widening gulf that made compromise increasingly difficult. At any given point in the emergence of this dialectic, immediate winners and losers may have been debatable: abolitionists lost the right of petition, only to gain it back; the slave power secured itself from antislavery memorials to Congress, only to undo itself on the issue by pressing too hard. Either way, discussions over slavery polarized debate, infusing the issue with apocalyptic significance. "Liberty and slavery cannot exist together," warned abolitionists; "either liberty will abolish slavery, or slavery will extirpate liberty."[80] Laden with such significance, slavery-related issues steadily appeared as unavoidable items on the national political agenda. Despite the party leaders' earnest efforts to the contrary, concerns around slavery came to dominate national politics, and even threaten the cohesion of the party system itself. Northern Democrats in particular found it increasingly difficult to maintain solidarity with their southern brethren; their own constituents increasingly demanded representatives willing to check the overweening power of the South.

New crises over national expansion continued to weaken the party system by dividing it along sectional lines. The admittance of Missouri into the Union had initiated a political crisis in 1820, but one largely confined to the halls of government. By the 1840s, when events in Mexico introduced new questions of expansion, politics had become a truly mass affair. In the 1824 elections, only 27 percent of the electorate actually turned out to vote. By 1836, that number climbed to 58 percent. In the 1840 election, it would reach 80 percent.[81] So when in 1845 the leaders of the newly independent Republic of Texas sought admittance into the Union, the matter became contested not simply in the halls of Congress, but in the streets, lecture halls, and cheap daily newspapers of the nation's cities. Once again, questions over the relative power of slave versus free states in government incited conflict.

The Texas story was one of two revolutions. Mexico, having broken free of Spain in 1821 after over a decade of revolutionary struggle, had abolished slavery in 1829, yet permitted American migrants from the United States in its sparsely populated northern region to keep their slaves. American settlers such as Stephen Austin vigorously promoted the opportunities Texas offered for Americans seeking new land for the expansion of the cotton economy. Southerners flooded into the rich coastal counties, such that by 1830 they constituted three-quarters of the population.[82] The number of slaves in Texas rose markedly. Around the turn of the nineteenth century, the slave population had numbered in the dozens; by the 1830s, it had climbed to well above a thousand.[83] The growth of an American-style slave economy led directly to the independence movement. Tensions between an antislavery government and slaveholding settlers flared incessantly. The former sought to enact a commitment to liberty inspired by its own revolutionary independence movement, while the latter resisted all efforts to be deprived of their human property. Austin feared the "pernicious and dangerous influence" of "a population of fanatical abolitionists" in the region were Mexican plans for abolition to be fully enacted. As he wrote in private correspondence,

"Texas must be a slave country. It is no longer a matter of doubt."[84] In 1835, American settlers in Texas launched their own "revolution," and declared the state's independence.

With victory won the following year, the Lone Star Republic enshrined slavery in its new constitution, and began calling for annexation by the United States. Northern politicians balked, fearing the entrance of a new slave state into the Union. Newspapers railed against the consequences of admitting vast new lands into the Union as slave country. For the *Daily National Intelligencer*, which asserted no love for "contemptible abolitionists," Texas was a "glittering prize" for the "ambition and avarice" of the South, which sought above all "the extension of slavery and Southern influence." Incorporating the new slave state into the Union would "scatter among us the elements of disunion, weaken the national feeling, and, finally, work out a dissolution of all the ties which make us kindred, and constitute us as one People."[85]

Southerners' own statements lent credibility to such claims. As the new secretary of state, John C. Calhoun, the former vice president from South Carolina who had spearheaded the southern position during the Nullification Crisis, wrote a letter to British minister Richard Pakenham, who supported the possibility that some of Texas might be annexed to the United States as free territory. Calhoun lambasted Britain's aim "to procure the general abolition of slavery throughout the world," and not least in Texas, where he suspected a British plot to gain influence over Mexico and undermine American interests. Calhoun went on to defend slavery in Texas and throughout the South, arguing that when freed as in the North, "the condition of the African, instead of being improved, has become worse." In contrast, he insisted, where slavery persisted, conditions for blacks "have improved greatly in every respect."[86]

The debate in Congress reflected this controversy. Some 180,000 petitions objecting to the annexation of Texas took pride of number among the innumerable slavery-related memorials the gag order had been designed to ignore.[87] So vociferous was objection in Congress that in 1844 expansionists failed to secure the two-thirds of the Senate necessary to ratify a treaty of annexation. Instead, Congress took the unprecedented step of annexing Texas with a joint resolution, which required only a majority of both houses of Congress. The measure passed, but the defection of 35 percent of House Democrats from the North revealed an important sectional rift in the dominant party's ranks.[88] Martin Van Buren's own faction, which had been instrumental in instituting an age of strict partisan voting, broke with the party leadership. Nonetheless, the resolution passed, and Texas became a part of the Union, with a provision to break it up into as many as five separate states, each with its own two senators and slave-buoyed representatives in the House.

Annexation only inflamed tensions over the expansion of slavery. Mexico had never conceded Texas's independence, and consequently considered annexation a provocation to war. In 1845, the new president, Tennessee Democrat and expansionist James K. Polk, pressed the issue. He ordered American troops across the historic border of the Nueces River farther south, to the Rio Grande. Ostensibly an effort to protect American interests, the move induced the response Polk intended. In April 1846, a Mexican force attacked. In May, not even half a year after the annexation of Texas, Mexico and the United States declared war on each other. The course of events on the battlefield portended a rapid and complete American victory. A small but professional force of American troops overmastered an opponent reliant on outdated weaponry and beset with internal divisions. The affair lasted until February 1848. Before the conflict was over, the U.S. army had invaded Mexico City to dictate terms, having lost not even two thousand men to death on the battlefield.

Long before this, though, American lawmakers had begun debating the fate of any new lands that would be gained in the conflict. Some northern politicians on both sides of the aisle objected to the war, asserting that the conflict was being fought largely in the interests of the South. Northern Democrats in particular confronted a difficult time in maintaining party unity behind a policy they knew would endanger their standing with a public increasingly mistrustful of the slave power. New York Senator John M. Niles wondered at southern politicians unwilling to understand that northern Democrats had their constituents to consider. "Do you think the N. York members have no sagacity, no instinct to discover the public sentiment in their districts?" he asked. A "strong infusion of the spirit of abolitionism" was making it harder and harder for men such as Niles to hold their seats.[89] In addition, Van Buren's "Bucktail" faction had expected consideration for supporting annexation over the concerns of those they claimed to represent. Instead, Polk had reneged on his promise to seek all of the Oregon Territory also claimed by Britain, proceeded with annexation plans that evaded all promises of leaving some Texas lands free, and denied the Bucktail faction patronage positions in the new government. Meanwhile, northern Whigs and antislavery dissidents made hay of their counterparts' apparent support for the slave power, threatening Democrats' fragile hold on critical states such as New York.

Once bitten by Texas, these northern Democrats were twice shy to concede to southern interests in the Mexican conflict. Some of the northern Democrats who had acceded to Texas's annexation now withdrew their unbridled support for their president's war effort. Others sought to forestall another step toward political suicide by seeking a measure that would guarantee, before the war with Mexico had barely begun, that at least some of whatever territory was gained would remain void of slavery. When President Polk requested from the House two million dollars to cover the costs of the war, David Wilmot, then a little-known Democratic congressman from Pennsylvania, introduced an amendment to the bill, requiring that "neither slavery nor involuntary servitude shall ever exist in any part" of territory taken from Mexico.[90] As amended the bill passed the House, with the vote on the proviso itself split severely along sectional rather than party lines. Southerners howled. John C. Calhoun vowed that his section would never "acknowledge inferiority" to the North on the matter.[91] Georgia Senator John M. Berrien warned that Wilmot's amendment would "give the control of the Government entirely" to northerners; "the African, and his owner, will both be slaves."[92] Happily for such men, the Senate remained under the control of southern Democrats and their "dough face" allies from the North, and it passed the bill without the proviso. Stuck, Congress tried to pass a similar funding measure the following year, and succeeded only in granting the funds minus Wilmot's amendment. The slave power had prevailed, but the failed proviso resolved nothing, serving only as a rallying cry for antislavery politicians for the next several years.

Slavery's expansion into the West marked a crucial tipping point in American politics. By continually raising questions about the balance of sectional influence, the territorial aggrandizement of the nation exacerbated long-standing tensions over the slave power's disproportionate strength in government. From the days of the Early Republic, New England Federalists had complained of the South's overweening control of government, yet had themselves lacked the strength to contest them nationally. The formation of the second American party system in the late 1820s and 1830s had entrenched southern power, as the dictates of party unity acceded to the demands of the powerful South. The rise of Whig opposition did little to counter southern power, for as another national party, the Whigs, too, sought to submerge sectional interests under a broad national platform. But the contemporaneous emergence of radical abolitionism had slowly begun to alter public opinion. It was not that the bulk of northern popular thought ever swung around to the abolitionists' view of slavery as an unmitigated national sin, for this remained a minority position even into the Civil War. It was that more moderate elements of the abolitionist message—particularly the fear that southern leaders' commitment to slavery outweighed their dedication to constitutional liberties—were becoming ever more widespread in the North. These were fears white northerners could share regardless of their attitudes toward people of African descent. By threatening to further unbalance the fragile sectional compromise, expansion heightened these concerns above the Mason-Dixon line. The same held true in the South. Each section accused the other of seeking to upend the wavering ship of state.

The emergence of a strong national dialectic over slavery severely stressed the two-party political system. The South increasingly turned toward a politics of sectional identity that threatened to trump party loyalties. For example, the challenge posed by the Wilmot Proviso caused even many southern Whigs to abandon their aversion to expansion and close ranks with southern Democrats. In 1847, a North Carolina newspaper declared that it was "time for party distinctions to sleep, and for the South to present a united front."[93] In the North, the situation was even more dire. In strongholds of antislavery opinion, elements of both parties had to give way or risk national failure. To be sure, at the time of the Mexican war most northern Whigs, like most northern Democrats, remained committed to a more centrist politics that would not alienate the vast majority of the American electorate, which either cared little for slavery, actively sought to protect it, or dared not risk national disunion over the issue. Yet northern "Conscience" Whigs representing antislavery strongholds began increasingly to challenge their party's neglect of the issue. As inheritors of the Federalist tradition, New York and New England Whigs had a long-standing interest in contesting southern power. Some felt strongly enough to jettison party loyalty for the cause of the slave.

This double threat from both sections would eventually help destroy the Whigs in the early 1850s. The process began as early as 1839, when northern dissidents from both parties met to form the Liberty Party, which was dedicated to fostering antislavery views in the political process. In the 1840 presidential election, the party ran former slave owner and abolitionist James G. Birney for president, garnering only some 7,000 votes nationwide. Four years later, though, Birney ran again, on a platform resolving that southern slavery violated "the principles of American Liberty," and constituted "a deep stain upon the character of the country."[94] This time, Birney captured over 62,000 votes. In New York, his popular vote exceeded the margin of difference between the successful Democratic nominee, James K. Polk, and the unsuccessful Whig candidate, Henry Clay. Had but a third of the 15,800 voters who cast ballots for Birney voted instead for Clay, the Whigs would have carried New York state, won its thirty-six electoral votes, and captured the White House.

Despite this impact, the challenge of developing an antislavery third party must not be understated. Any single-issue party had to contend not simply with a two-party system effective at submerging sectionally divisive issues, but also with the antislavery movement's own faithful, who argued eternally over principles, strategy, and tactics. A radical core of abolitionists viewed any engagement in the political system as hopelessly compromising their vision of a perfected moral order. Those such as William Lloyd Garrison, for whom the Constitution itself constituted a "covenant with death" and "an agreement with Hell," were unlikely to view formal politics as a solution.[95] "Political action is not moral action," Garrison wrote. By "absorbing the moral energies and pecuniary means

of its members," he accused, the Liberty Party would "retard the moral revolution that is needed for the overthrow of slavery."[96] To some extent, Garrison was
right. Political abolitionists frequently scaled back their private commitments to
abolition and equal rights, publicly championing more conservative positions in
the hopes of broadening the party's appeal. Thus while some in the party viewed
civil rights for northern free blacks as central to the party's mission, others cautioned the party to avoid such radical positions.

Strategic moderation did indeed temper the party's views, in a process that
would only hasten over time. In 1848, for example, most members of the Liberty Party folded into the Free Soil Party, a yet more moderate incarnation of
antislavery politics. That the party ran Martin Van Buren for president bespoke
the degree to which some northern Democrats had forsaken alliance with their
southern counterparts, as well as how badly the slavery issue had shaken traditional party structures. How remarkable for a former president and the architect
of the modern two-party political system to become the most prominent representative of an antislavery third party to date. Such antislavery parties became
increasingly popular in the North, but broadened their constituencies only by
watering down their message. Nonetheless, the political antislavery of the 1840s
represented the first serious attempt in the nation's history to build a national
movement for abolition. And while political antislavers often ran afoul of the
more strident moralists in the movement, they also proved to be the most practically minded activists on behalf of the antislavery cause. Eventually, they reformulated the party political process in ways that led directly to secession and the
Civil War.

By the end of the Mexican-American War in 1848, the stage had been set.
The U.S. South was the largest of the few remaining slave societies in the world.
With a slave population of 3,950,000 in 1861,[97] it dwarfed Cuba, which held
367,400 slaves in the same year,[98] and outpaced Brazil, with 1,715,000 in 1864.[99]
With the exceptions of those societies, it had known unparalleled power in its
nation. But its predominance had been threatened by a movement whose influence was beginning to shake the foundations of national politics. Historian
Leonard Richards writes eloquently of what was at stake: "In the sixty-two years
between Washington's election and the Compromise of 1850, for example, slaveholders controlled the presidency for fifty years, the Speaker's chair for forty-one
years, and the chairmanship of House Ways and Means for forty-two years. The
only men to be reelected president—Washington, Jefferson, Madison, Monroe,
and Jackson—were all slaveholders. The men who sat in the Speaker's chair the
longest—Henry Clay, Andrew Stevenson, and Nathaniel Macon—were slaveholders."[100] The next twelve years would witness a series of dramatic showdowns
between the largest mass movement for metropolitan abolition and the most
potent slave power on earth.

That abolitionist movement had begun in the North's own push for revolutionary emancipations, and been energized in the 1830s by the emergence of a new strain of radicalism that called for the immediate and uncompensated end to slavery. The slave power against which it struggled had been protected since the Constitution by a federal system designed to grant it an influence in national politics greater than its numbers of free people would indicate. Despite that the United States had devised a party political system intended to obviate the divisive influence of sectional issues, these two powerful forces clashed. Each sought to intrude its interests into the halls of power. In the wake of the Mexican-American War, that system would be rent asunder by sectional divisions that the existing party system could not contain. Ultimately, the breakdown meant that formal politics could no longer perform the very function for which they existed—to balance competing interests without recourse to violence.

CHAPTER 6

Ere the Storm Come Forth
*Antislavery Militance and the
Collapse of Party Politics*

YOURS FOR THE SLAVE
Militant Antislavery Activism before 1850

The transformations that struck American politics in the decades before
the Civil War might appear at first glance to have been unrelated to the actions
of the enslaved themselves. Questions of slavery's expansion, or the sectional
balance of power in Congress, seemed to have little to do with those who toiled
on southern plantations. And no major insurrection had imperiled American
slaveholders since Nat Turner's rebellion struck during the first years of the radical abolition movement. And yet the reformulation of American politics soon
led to a national crisis that created secession—the event that led to the war that
led to emancipation.

Contrast African Americans' apparent insignificance in this process with
pre-emancipation sites elsewhere in the New World, where slave resistance had
played a complex but decisive role in bringing about the end of slavery. Individual acts of resistance had always registered a constant flow of evidence that the
enslaved did not find slavery the uplifting and civilizing influence its advocates
depicted. Collective violence had made the point all the more clear. Once ideological developments made it possible for metropolitan publics and governors
to conceive that slavery could end, the enslaved's appropriation of revolutionary
idioms often made them their own best arguments for freedom. Still, it was easy
for free whites in the metropole to consider slave violence evidence of the innately brutish nature of Africans. The work of imparting the meaning of slave
resistance to the public fell to antislavery activists. They acted as proxies for the
enslaved, amplifying their will and translating their behavior into terms intelligible to the publics and elites who drove politics, and ultimately abolished slavery.

The importance of this combination of forces throughout the Atlantic cannot be understated. Revolt in the periphery melded with antislavery sentiment in the metropole to create a complex dialectic that led—haltingly, to be sure—to mass emancipation. Just as slave insurrections in the early nineteenth-century Caribbean had incorporated understandings of metropolitan events, so too metropolitan publics had played vital roles by giving meaning to collective slave resistance. Slave revolt alone was unlikely ever to produce a policy of abolition; in the short term, insurrections usually inspired fierce campaigns of repression. Conversely, abolitionism could hardly exist without evidence that the enslaved themselves preferred liberty. Instead, the two worked together. Resistance and rebellion provided abolitionists critical evidence in arguing that slavery should be abolished. Slave action, when filtered through the values and rhetoric of sympathetic allies in the metropole, could take on emancipatory potential. In abolitionist hands, slave behavior became an argument for the humanity of the enslaved and their inviolable right to self-ownership—liberty. With this aid, it became possible for those in the metropole to understand slave resistance not as evidence of Africans' innately savage natures, but as the slaves' own demand for the very freedom so highly prized by whites across the modern Atlantic. By translating slaves' acts of resistance into the idioms of Atlantic liberalism, or by amplifying slaves' own appropriation of those idioms, metropolitan abolitionists in Britain had swayed public opinion. That public then called upon its political representatives to abolish slavery. And British abolition set off a chain of metropolitan abolitions that left most of the Caribbean free. In varying ways throughout the Atlantic world, slave resistance in the periphery thus melded with antislavery ideology in the metropole to help end slavery.

But the unique circumstance of the United States weakened the prospects of a similar confluence of slave resistance and metropolitan abolitionism. In the United States, where the slaveholders of the South commanded so much control of the nation relative to their counterparts in most other places in the Atlantic, the threshold for government enactment of abolition was far higher than it had been in the British, French, Dutch, and Danish cases. In the United States, abolition would have to fight a hyper-empowered slave interest with enormous influence in government, and do so through a party political system that fought tooth and nail to submerge the divisive issue. In that desperate struggle, the behavior of the enslaved themselves played a critical, underappreciated role. As in Britain, public opinion would once again serve as the terrain of contest. In the United States, a true mass abolition movement—the only one comparable to the British original—would prove necessary to defeat a slave power that enjoyed political advantages woven into the very parameters of the national government's organization. In such a contest, every asset counted. If slave resistance proved critical to impelling abolition elsewhere, it was all the more significant where the task was so much more difficult.

The leaders of the free African American communities established in the Early Republic took the lead in forging links between slave action and abolitionist rhetoric. The valediction that pervaded their epistolaries—"yours for the slave"—suggested their roles as representatives for those who could not otherwise be heard. They undertook the earliest efforts to harness slave resistance to the abolitionist cause. From the 1830s on, black activists used the press, the lecture hall, and the pulpit to interpret the meaning of slave resistance throughout the Atlantic world. In the battle for public opinion, the understandings of slave rebellion they generated helped make an important case: a policy of emancipation lay in whites' very self-interest. The paucity of major slave uprisings in the United States after 1831 did not prohibit black ideologues from invoking the specter of collective violence, for actions taken by enslaved Africans throughout the history of the Atlantic slave system left traces in the historical record that could constantly be invoked and given meaning. Before the Civil War, for example, no fewer than three prominent African Americans wrote extended treatments of the Haitian Revolution.[1] The foundations of the black historiographical tradition lay in understanding the role of slave rebellion throughout the Atlantic.

But recalling instances of slave violence such as Haiti posed challenges. Antislavery reformers, already labeled "incendiaries" for their public agitation, risked even further ostracization through association with slave violence. Slavery's defenders frequently alleged that abolitionists inspired insurrection through their dangerous calls for freedom. The "busy intermeddling of visionary fanatics" had "set the revolt of the blacks in St. Domingo in motion," according to one Virginia politician.[2] White abolitionists in particular took special pains to distance themselves from charges of inciting insurrection, calling such allegations "a wanton perversion of the truth, and . . . a downright libel on the character, conduct and motives of the friends of the abolition cause."[3] With slave violence so heavily laden with treasonous implications, black activists and white abolitionists sought to redeem slave violence by associating it with the rebelliousness that had birthed the United States. The African American writer William Wells Brown, for example, compared Haitian revolutionary Toussaint Louverture to George Washington, noting that "each was the leader of an oppressed and outraged people, each had a powerful enemy to contend with, and each succeeded in founding a government in the New World." But they differed, argued Brown, in that "Toussaint liberated his countrymen" while "Washington enslaved a portion of his."[4] Even James G. Birney, the white abolitionist who ran for president on the Liberty Party ticket in 1840, remarked that "the Haitians achieved their Independence as our forefathers did ours—by rebellion."[5] Associating slave resistance with the liberty-seeking violence of colonial patriots, black activists found a way to invoke militancy while remaining true to American ideals. The struggle to attain freedom—through arms, if necessary—was no effort to destroy the Union. Rather, they posed it as entirely consonant with the mission of the nation. Black activists viewed their goal as not to rend the country, but to purify it—to cleanse the "foul stain" that slavery cast upon the nation's "otherwise pure drapery."[6]

The critical point was that liberty would prevail, one way or another. History pointed to an end in which freedom would triumph. *Freedom's Journal* quoted Scottish divine Alexander Stewart on this widely held Atlantic principle. Liberty was a "desire which glows more intensely than every other in the human breast"—one even "dearer than life itself."The past was but a record of"the struggles, the conflicts, and the triumphs by which the yoke of oppression has been broken, & the liberty of nations has been vindicated and established."[7] Time and again black activists framed the struggle against slavery within this Whiggish, even millennial framework of conflict between liberty and tyranny. In 1841, one black newspaper believed that a rumored slave conspiracy demonstrated "the natural desire for freedom implanted in every man's breast."The implication for those in chains was clear. If left without peaceful means to find freedom, slaves would seek alternatives. This, for black activists and white abolitionists alike, was the great lesson of the Haitian Revolution and other Caribbean insurrections. William Wells Brown thus wondered if some Toussaint, Christophe, or Rigaud—heroes of Haiti—might appear in the American South. "That they are there, no one will doubt," he cautioned. "That their souls are thirsting for liberty, all will admit. The spirit that caused the blacks to take up arms, and to shed their blood in the American revolutionary war, is still amongst the slaves of the south; and, if we are not mistaken, the day is not far distant when the revolution of St. Domingo will be reenacted in South Carolina and Louisiana."[8]

Black activists and white abolitionists contrasted the frightening prospects of slave revolt with emancipation's relative ease, frequently citing evidence that Great Britain's 1833 abolition of slavery in the West Indies demonstrated that emancipation could proceed peacefully. As did many abolitionist newspapers, the *Colored American* cited Joseph H. Kimball's influential *Emancipation in the West Indies: A Six Months' Tour in Antigua, Barbados and Jamaica, in the Year 1837* (1838) to demonstrate the bucolic course of emancipation. Kimball described a world desolated by slavery but finding a new life in freedom, with the former slaves enterprising, peaceful, and hopeful: "The spirit of a new life is enlightening and invigorating the mind, unshackling and kindling the heart, purifying the morals, and giving to enterprise new objects and impulses. Peace, and industry, and knowledge, and religion—all the results of freedom are spreading among all classes."[9] In annual "August First" commemorations of mass emancipation in the West Indies, white and black abolitionists in the United States propounded on the harmonious character of the postemancipation Caribbean. Jeremiah Shadd, a black activist from Wilmington, Delaware, recalled that "instead of the high expectation of the fires of rebellion being lit by a feeling of lawless revenge on the part of the freed bondmen," liberty had instead been characterized by "contentment and good will."[10]

Indeed, many argued that the very forces proslavery apologists found so reprehensible had served to maintain their fragile regime far beyond its years. Why had there been no major uprisings since 1831? In truth, many factors may be cited, such as the largely creole nature of the American slave population and the overwhelming power of the white majority throughout most of the plantation region. But black activists and white abolitionists pointed to the antislavery movement itself. In 1859, black editor Thomas Hamilton declared that the northern movement to abolish slavery was far from "inimical to the institution of slavery." Rather, it served "as its greatest safety valve; the escape pipe through which the dangerous element incident to slavery found vent."[11] The *Colored American* concurred with this rhetorical gesture, claiming that only the South's close ties with the North had prevented it from exposure to "HEAVEN'S CURSE," and the "REVENGE OF BLOOD GUILTINESS." Leave the South to itself, it continued, "and her *patriotic slave system* would soon work out its own redemption through *rivers of blood*."[12] White abolitionists picked up the theme, stressing that history demonstrated that amelioration and emancipation were the paths of safety, for the innate desire of man for liberty would, if left no hope, devolve into bloody demand. Thus the abolitionist poet John Greenleaf Whittier could write,

> Oh rouse ye, ere the storm comes forth—
> The gathered wrath of God and man—
> Like that which wasted Egypt's earth,
> When hail and fire above it ran.
> Hear ye no warnings in the air?
> Feel ye no earthquake underneath?
> Up—up—why will ye slumber where
> The sleeper only wakes in death?[13]

By 1860, when Lydia Maria Child published a book whose title made the same case—*The Right Way the Safe Way, Proved by Emancipation in the British West Indies, and Elsewhere*—the argument had become a familiar component of abolitionists' rhetorical arsenal. Freedom was coming—peacefully and safely, if planters heeded the wisdom of voluntary emancipation, but violently if not. As black activist and fugitive slave H. Ford Douglas warned at an August First speech, "You must either free the slaves, or the slaves will free themselves. All history confirms the fact."[14] The innate love of liberty that beat in the breast of every man would demand release. If channeled safely, a calm and prosperous transition to freedom could be imagined. If not, abolitionists could not be held responsible for the consequences.

Black and white abolitionists' invocations of a history of slave resistance formed one of the movement's central arguments. More than their imprecations against the breakup of slave families and the horrors of plantation punishments, more than their paeans to the efficiency of free labor and their derogation of the slave power, their marshaling of actual slave behavior linked the slaves to their free allies. These two forms of antislavery resistance existed side by side. The enslaved, lacking rights and access to the public forum, had no alternative but direct action; abolitionists, on the other hand, could claim a voice in public, but feared that militant action might create a backlash that would endanger the entire movement.

Over the course of the antebellum decades, the distance between the slaves' and abolitionists' streams of antislavery dwindled. In the twenty years between the emergence of immediatism around 1830 and the Compromise of 1850, as abolitionists disputed the role action and militance should play in the movement in light of ongoing events, the two streams moved ever closer together. Immediatism in the United States, with its roots in Quaker pacifism and elite benevolent reform, had begun as a movement purely of words. In the early 1830s, the movement frequently attested to its faith in pacifistic means, even as its rhetoric became more and more uncompromising. The first issue of the *Liberator* rhapsodized to the slaves, "Not by the Sword shall your deliverance be; Not by shedding of your master's blood."[15] Recalling the patronizing tones of the early century's elite reformers, the Massachusetts Anti-Slavery Society resolved that "by the patient endurance in their wrongs . . . the slaves will hasten the day of their peaceful deliverance from the yoke of bondage; . . . whereas by violent and bloody measures they will prolong their servitude, and expose themselves to destruction."[16] In the wake of the antiabolition riots of the mid-1830s, though, many in the movement began to question the efficacy of "moral suasion" alone. In 1838, when a mob in Alton, Illinois, sought to destroy the press of antislavery newspaper editor Elijah Lovejoy, the abolitionist returned bullets with bullets, claiming the life of a mob member. In return, the crowd fired into Lovejoy's sanctuary, riddled him with gunfire, and destroyed his press. Questions over the propriety of Lovejoy's violent response to the mob exacerbated nascent divides within the movement. Garrisonians grew ever more committed to pacifism, founding institutions such as the New England Non-Resistance Society in 1838. Others, though, grew increasingly frustrated with the movement's idealism, and began to broaden the range of acceptable approaches.

In 1840, American abolitionists split, divided by such questions. Garrison's American Anti-Slavery Society remained steadfastly committed to nonresistance, support for women's rights, and nonparticipation in politics based on the principle that the Constitution endorsed slavery. In forming the American and Foreign Anti-Slavery Society, Lewis and Arthur Tappan, James G. Birney, and others opposed this view. They saw the Constitution as more antislavery than proslavery, and hence considered formal politics a viable arena for antislavery activity. Garrison aptly accused these Liberty Party founders of a willingness to compromise principle for party success, but their willingness to part with nonresistance permitted some to grow into the most practically militant antislavery activists of the era.[17]

African Americans, though they played notable roles in both camps, pioneered the use of action. From the earliest days of their community organizing, free blacks had been more likely to confront directly the forces arrayed against them. Black parades at public celebrations, for instance, engendered hostility among urban whites partly because they presented the image of African Americans in martial regalia, claiming the streets of northern cities as equals.[18] Those bearing the scars of recent bondage, or with family and friends still enslaved, could ill afford the luxury of nonresistance. The enslaved themselves pressed the issue by crossing the geographic divides that separated lands of slavery and lands of freedom. Free black communities in the North became havens for those who fled from slavery, and free black activists were the first to take active roles in aiding fugitives. As early as 1797, Philadelphia leaders petitioned Congress to rescind the Fugitive Slave Act of 1793, which caused free blacks and enslaved alike to be "hunted by armed Men" and "brought back in chains to those who have no just claim upon them."[19] In ensuing years, black Philadelphians intervened repeatedly in the recovery of suspected fugitives, as when in 1824 a group of 150 African Americans, "armed with bludgeons," intercepted white officials transporting a runaway.[20] Similar cases arose in the 1830s throughout the North, with informal collections of working-class African Americans spearheading efforts to rescue or hide fugitives. The Underground Railroad, though cloaked in a historical mythology that tends to laud white abolitionists, actually began in black-led organizations known as "vigilance committees." Founded by African Americans in northern cities, these groups hid fugitives from the South, started them on lives in freedom, and forged crucial networks with white abolitionists. In New York City in the 1830s, the radical black activist David Ruggles led the charge; it was he who first housed the fugitive Frederick Douglass. In Boston,

Lewis Hayden carried the load; in Detroit, it was George DeBaptiste; and in Philadelphia, William Still. Others, such as the astoundingly courageous Harriet Tubman, physically traversed the boundary between North and South to aid border state slaves on their flight to freedom. Over time, the networks grew along with the legends, until it became possible for fugitives to find aid in every northern state.

To be sure, free black northerners did not speak with one voice on the role of militance in the movement. Well-to-do leaders tended to evince more deferential approaches, while working-class activists tended to favor direct action. Garrison's preeminence kept some notable African American activists in the nonresistant fold, but others maintained a rigorous commitment to what they termed "practical abolitionism." Over time, though, the tightening reigns of white supremacy pushed many toward ever more radical stances. One such instance occurred in the lives of black leaders Henry Highland Garnet and Alexander Crummell, who as youths in the early 1830s both attended the integrated Noyes Academy in Canaan, New Hampshire. When hostile whites attacked the school, the young Garnet returned fire with a shotgun. His actions did not prevent the mob from burning the building and dragging its foundation into a nearby swamp, but Crummell credited Garnet with saving their lives.[21] His militance became renowned. In 1843, he urged a national convention of African Americans to endorse his "Address to the Slaves of the United States." Setting black rebels such as Denmark Vesey amid other heroes in "the great cause of universal freedom," Garnet instructed the slaves to demand liberty from their masters. "Inform them that all you desire is FREEDOM, and that nothing else will suffice," he urged. Should the masters refuse, Garnet offered a stirring motto: "rather die freemen than live to be slaves."[22] The convention reacted with uproar, hotly debating but ultimately rejecting the address. Frederick Douglass objected that "there was too much physical force" in it; he was "for trying the moral means a little longer."[23] But by 1848, when Garnet finally published the address (in a pamphlet that also included David Walker's *Appeal*), many black leaders were tending in his direction.

Hesitantly, white abolitionists endorsed, then began adopting, the tactics of direct intervention that black communities had pioneered. A notable minority of white abolitionists—men such as Calvin Fairbank, Charles T. Torrey, and William L. Chaplin—began participating in fugitive slave rescues.[24] Two notable cases of shipboard rebellion also went far to inspire white abolitionists' conversion to more direct efforts to free slaves. In 1839, a group of bondsmen on the Cuban slave-trading ship *La Amistad* took over, slew most of the crew, and compelled two remaining crewmen to return them to Africa. Instead, the sailors steered toward the eastern coast of North America, where the starving ship finally landed to seek provisions. The Africans wound up in Connecticut, where the antebellum version of the Coast Guard encountered them. A lengthy court battle, landing eventually in the Supreme Court, decided their fate. Abolitionists organized around the case, financing the rebels' defense. Following an impassioned plea by John Quincy Adams, the Court decided that the Africans had been illegally enslaved, and hence were free. In a similar case in 1841, American slaves being transported from Virginia to Louisiana on the brig *Creole* seized the ship and took it to the British Bahamas. Because the Somerset principle, by which those setting foot on free soil instantly became free, now applied to the emancipated British West Indies, the *Creole* slaves gained their liberty. Once again, slave actions had steered the course of events, with abolitionists following. The *Creole* case led antislavery Congressman Joshua Giddings to break the gag rule in Congress by resolving that the insurrectionaries "violated no law of the United States, incurred no legal penalty, and are justly liable to no penalty."[25] Through acts of resistance and flight, the enslaved intruded themselves into realms where the law did not automatically presume they were rightless slaves, but instead presumed their liberty, and gave them access to the courts and resources due citizens. Most white abolitionists still called for peace—"be patient, long-suffering and submissive," Garrison continued to caution the slaves[26]—but the set of acceptable responses to slavery was growing. Steadily, the two streams of antislavery—slaves' behavior and abolitionists' words—were drawing together.

DANGEROUS DALLIANCES
Sectional Conflicts and the Party System, 1848–60

Between 1848 and 1860, the national political system in the United States broke down. It failed to serve as the mechanism for adjudicating fierce disputes between groups of states. The Mexican-American War served as the starting point, for it was here that the weakness of the existing two-party system became clearly evident. The failure of the Wilmot Proviso to prohibit slavery from the Mexican cession portended continuing sectional strife between a growing contingent of antislavery northern politicians and an increasingly vociferous brand of southern "fire-eaters." The successful conclusion of the Mexican-American War bequeathed the United States a host of unresolved sectional issues. In the Treaty of Guadalupe Hidalgo of 1848, Mexico ceded the United States some 525,000 square miles, a swath of territory so enormous that all or some of seven states would be carved from it. Conflict over the fate of slavery in these lands boiled over, marking a new era of particularly anxious sectional politics. Southern hotheads had reacted to the Wilmot Proviso with anger, posing its ban on slavery in any newly acquired territories as yet another incursion into the "liberties" of those who enslaved others, and an affront to southern "honor."

Northerners proved equally steadfast in defense of their principles. Wilmot himself declared that "to compromise on this question is to surrender the right and establish the wrong."[27] In the 1848 campaign cycle, like-minded antislavery Democrats stormed out of New York's party convention. They joined with "conscience" Whigs frustrated with their party's neutrality on slavery, and melded into the Liberty Party. Liberty's new incarnation softened its stand on black civil rights and militant antislavery, instead focusing on a kind of bread-and-butter antislavery that might appeal to the rank and file of northern whites. The platform of the new Free Soil Party declared its first commitment not to ending slavery, but to upholding "the rights of free labor against the aggressions of the Slave Power." It acknowledged the legality of slavery in the southern states, and vowed explicitly to avoid "interference by Congress with Slavery within the limits of any State." Instead, preventing the expansion of slavery into the territories through an act of Congress constituted its primary platform plank.[28] By softening the message, the party garnered over 290,000 votes for its presidential candidate, former Democrat and White House occupant Martin Van Buren. Its solid 10 percent of the popular vote in the 1848 election established it as a viable national political force.

With the fate of slavery in the Mexican cession unresolved, the next session of Congress began in tension. In the House of Representatives, the Free Soilers gained nine seats, one more than the Whigs lost. The South recoiled, and talk of secession ran freely. When sectional divisions prevented the House of Representatives from even resolving an election for Speaker, Georgia representative Robert Toombs charged antislavery politicians with "attempting to fix a national degradation upon half the States of the Confederacy." If such were the case, he declared, "*I am for disunion.*"[29] Compromise seemed equally impossible in the more temperate Senate, at least initially. There, John C. Calhoun declared that his region had "no compromise to offer," and called for a constitutional amendment to "restore to the South . . . the power she possessed of protecting itself, before the equilibrium between the sections was destroyed."[30] William H. Seward, antislavery senator from New York, argued that slavery was already protected in the national government. Regardless, he declared, there was "a higher law than the Constitution," a divinely sanctioned history of progress that thrived on "the security of natural rights, the diffusion of knowledge, and the freedom of industry." Slavery contravened these impulses toward liberty. "Just in proportion to the extent that it prevails and controls in any republican state, just to that extent it subverts the principle of democracy, and converts the state into an aristocracy or a despotism."[31] Seward's words repackaged an antislavery message as old as Jefferson's: slavery fundamentally contradicted freedom, and thus blighted any society premised on universal liberty.

Finally, the aging Henry Clay stepped up to offer a series of resolutions designed to quiet sectional discord, at least for a time. California would enter the Union with Congress silent on its status; as the territory's constitutional convention had already chosen to prohibit slavery, the matter would be closed. Texas would lose its considerable claims to lands farther west, but Congress would compensate it by assuming its debts. Congress would also remain silent on the remaining territories taken from Mexico; their status would be left to the popular will of their residents. Despite that much of this land lay below the thirty-six degrees, thirty minutes line established by the Missouri Compromise of 1820 as slavery's southern border, many believed the infertile territory unsuited for slavery—a tenuous conclusion given developing practices of irrigation. In addition, the slave trade in the federally controlled District of Columbia would be abolished, but slavery itself would remain, and Congress would affirm the legitimacy of the domestic slave trade in the states. Finally, Congress would pass a comprehensive new fugitive slave bill, which would help assure slaveholders that their property would remain safely theirs even if it ran away to free states. After heated discussion and considerable legislative wrangling, the measures passed.

In the short term, the Compromise of 1850 relieved pressure on the political system. New Hampshire statesman Daniel Webster commented, "We have gone through the most important crisis which has occurred since the foundation of the government, and whatever party may prevail thereafter, the Union stands firm."[32] National political leadership had resolved a seemingly intractable problem, and returned the nation to a path of peace. But the system had been shaken; mutual distrust between the sections had grown. The Whig Party, polarized into a southern "cotton" faction and a northern "conscience" group, split badly over the compromise measures. Two years later, Whigs put together a party platform acquiescing to the hated Fugitive Slave Law, and deprecating "all further agitation of the question thus settled, as dangerous to our peace."[33] Conscience Whigs reacted with disgust. "We defy it, we execrate it, spit upon it," scathed New York *Tribune* editor Horace Greeley of the platform.[34] In the presidential election of 1852, the split cost the Whigs badly. Their candidate, Mexican War hero Winfield Scott, lost to a "doughface" Democrat from New Hampshire, Franklin Pierce. The margin of 215,000 popular votes more than covered the 155,000 garnered by the antislavery Free Soil Party, but divisions in the northern electorate surely hurt its chances.[35] Shortly after, the Whigs fragmented into insignificance.

The dissolution of the Whigs played havoc with political alignments. In both sections, splinter parties sought to occupy the vacuum. One of these captured votes by appealing to widespread fears of foreign immigration. Between the turn of the nineteenth century and the start of the Civil War, some 5.4 million free foreigners landed on American shores, with the decade of the 1840s alone witnessing the immigration of over 1.5 million.[36] Nativists railed against the damage so many immigrants allegedly would cause. Known colloquially as "Know Nothings" for the response required of them when asked about their secret organizations, they feared that Irish Catholics in particular threatened American liberty, charging that new immigrants' first loyalty would lay with pope and church rather than adopted nation. The platform of the movement's leading political arm, the American Party, demanded that *"Americans must rule America,"* and called for lengthening the period of naturalization from five to twenty-one years.[37] More radical nativist platforms advocated "war to the hilt, on political Romanism," and "Death to all foreign influences, whether in high places or low."[38] In recording his impressions of immigrants becoming naturalized citizens, New York City attorney George Templeton Strong expressed nativist views typical of his privileged caste: "It was enough to turn a man's stomach to see the way they were naturalizing this morning. Wretched, filthy, bestial-looking Italians and Irish, the very scum and dregs of human nature filled the office so completely that I was almost afraid of being poisoned by going in."[39] In the 1856 presidential election, the American Party's presidential candidate, Millard Fillmore, garnered 22 percent of the popular vote, a remarkable total for a new party in a crowded field. That Fillmore won the electoral votes only for Maryland, not nearly the hotbed of nativism that northern states such as New York and Massachusetts were, suggests that the American Party benefitted as much from the Whig implosion as from widespread nativist sentiment. American Party support in the 1856 presidential race mapped neatly onto old sources of Whig support in the upper South and among the most wealthy slave counties in the country. The lessons were clear. Opposition to the dominant Democrats would fare best if it coalesced into a strong national party. Those most capable of fashioning an appeal broad enough to attract a mass audience would inherit the rump of the Whigs, and stand a good chance of contesting national political power. What had changed since 1848 was that one issue above all others, even the nativists' xenophobia, could no longer be shunted aside.

That issue, of course, was slavery, which had long agitated party politics. Nativists, as contenders for the Whig legacy, could not draw on the organizing history and prowess of the political abolitionists, who since the late 1830s had been constructing the institutional mechanisms of a legitimate third party. They had established geographic strongholds, a slate of nationally known leaders, and strong mechanisms for communicating to the public. The Liberty Party had run presidential candidates in the elections of 1840 and 1844, the Free Soil Party in 1848 and 1852. Four presidential election cycles had grown their brand, while national events had only made the issues they addressed more pressing. The election cycle of 1856 witnessed yet a new incarnation of political antislavery, the Republican Party. The party fully inherited Free Soil's leadership and constituency. It further incorporated old Whig leaders and planks, advocating federal support for internal improvements and a homestead act to grant free western lands to a rising middle-class yeomanry. In addition, as the party sought to move beyond its roots in a single issue and become a true coalition, a broad range of moral reformers and temperance advocates made a home among its ranks; even some nativists found succor among the Republicans.

More than anything, though, the Republicans opposed the expansion of slavery into the western territories. The party began among the "anti-Kansas-Nebraska" organizations that rose up following passage of the Kansas-Nebraska Act of 1854, which organized the territory west of Missouri. The bill had been championed by Stephen Douglas, Democratic senator from Illinois, who had moved heaven and earth to overcome stiff resistance among northern legislators even in his own party. The planter interests that dominated the Democratic Party refused to support the bill unless it permitted the possibility of slavery north of the thirty-six degrees, thirty minutes parallel, which in 1820 the Missouri Compromise had established as slavery's northern border. Douglas thus championed the admission of Kansas into the Union under the principle of "popular sovereignty," by which residents of a territory could vote slavery up or down when they formed a state. The Compromise of 1850 incorporated this solution to resolving slavery's status in some of the territories ceded by Mexico, thus permitting the possibility of slavery's establishment north of Missouri's southern border. But while in 1850 many believed the mountain territories of the far west unsuited to slavery, the same could not be said of the more populous Kansas and Nebraska Territory in 1854, which both sections coveted for their fertile prairies, proximity to existing states, and influence in swaying the sectional balance in Congress.

Having successfully engineered the bill's passage, Douglas faced a storm of reaction throughout the North. Illinois Republican Abraham Lincoln declared the idea of popular sovereignty, by which a democratic majority could uphold the enslavement of others, "a dangerous dalliance for a free people."[40] Many northerners considered the Missouri Compromise a "sacred compact," and excoriated those who nullified it. Wrote the New York *Tribune*, "These deliberate violators of solemn compacts, these vagabond repudiators of obligations the most sacred, deserve to be roasted by the hottest fires of public indignation."[41] Douglas's ill-conceived plan had bestowed an enormous gift on the slave power, but at the cost of reigniting fierce sectional antagonisms. Opponents of slavery in the North needed no more evidence that southern slaveholders sought to expand their dominion into new lands, nor that northern doughface politicians would aid them in doing so. Nonetheless, more evidence was available—in the

South's efforts to purchase or take Cuba from Spain, for example, or its support for the clandestine intervention of American "filibusters" in the political affairs of Mexico and Central America. In the mid-1850s, the audaciousness of the slave power seemed to know no bounds. John A. Quitman, a slaveholding congressman from Mississippi, declared before Congress in 1856, "We claim the right of expansion as essential to our future security and prosperity." Slaveholders required "elbow-room" to prevent a plantation system "confined to narrow limits."[42]

The new Republican Party constituted the last and most successful attempt to organize politically against the expanding slave power. While the party's platform addressed an array of issues oriented toward Whig and reform-minded constituents, its foundation lay in opposing the spread of slavery into the territories. "The normal condition of all the territory of the United States is that of freedom," declared the party's platform. "We deny the authority of Congress, of a Territorial Legislature, or of any individuals, to give legal existence to slavery in any territory of the United States."[43] Selling this argument to a broad electorate was not easy, though, particularly given white northerners' manifest hostility to people of African descent. How could the party pose a fundamentally antislavery message to a public with little sympathy for the enslaved? The answer lay in two central arguments that political antislavers had been developing for some time: opposition to the slave power, and support for "free labor."

The free labor component of the Republican message derived from the Free Soil Party's concern with keeping western lands open for development by white men. Implicitly, free soilism critiqued slavery for depriving free people of opportunity. Where slave labor thrived, free labor languished. Bound labor associated physical work with social debasement, driving down the value of free labor. Slaves had no incentive but the lash to work, and were kept in the worst possible conditions; free labor elevated workers by offering healthy incentives to achieve ever better standards of living. "Slavery withers and blights all it touches," declared an Iowa Republican. It "is a foul political curse upon the institutions of our country; it is a curse upon the soil of the country, and worse than that, it is a curse upon the poor, free laboring white man."[44] In Republicans' idealized description of the free states, all had a chance in the race of life; all could rise, if given a fair opportunity to develop their intellects and cultivate their virtues. "By popular education and continual change of condition the dividing lines between the ranks and classes are almost obliterated," Carl Schurz eulogized. "Look upon our system of public instruction, which places even the lowliest child of the people upon the high road of progressive civilization."[45] Slavery undid all this. Were the western territories open to slavery, the argument went, free white men would compete against a system that would always prove cheaper. As David Wilmot stated, "where the negro slave labors, the free white man cannot labor by his side without sharing in his degradation and disgrace."[46]

Free soilism constituted a considerable declension from the first principles of the radical abolitionists. Many Free Soilers, such as the former Illinois Congressman Abraham Lincoln, had grown into antislavery politicians from roots in colonization rather than immediate abolitionism. The very purpose of the Free Soil message, after all, was to attract the broadest possible array of white voters, whose concern for people of African descent was negligible at best. After years of effort, the slave power's opponents had developed a form of antislavery that forsook the moral concerns of the despised abolitionists in favor of the social mobility of rank-and-file white northerners. "There are Republicans who are Abolitionists; there are others who anxiously desire and labor for the good of the slave," acknowledged the New York *Tribune*. "But there are many more whose main impulse is a desire to secure the new Territories for Free White Labor, with little or no regard for the interests of negroes, free or slave."[47]

This primary interest in the middling whites who made up the party's best hope for a broad electoral base left considerable room for the white supremacy that suffused the nation in the nineteenth century. Miraculously, the Republicans had found a way to argue against slavery without challenging white Americans' widespread racial hostility. "We, the Republican party, are the white man's party," declared Illinois Senator Lyman Trumbull. "We are for free, white men, and for making white labor respectable and honorable, which it never can be when negro slave labor is brought into competition with it."[48] David Wilmot himself voiced the white supremacist underpinnings of the free soil appeal. "I have no squeamish sensitiveness upon the subject of slavery, nor morbid sympathy for the slave," he declared. "I plead the cause of the rights of white freemen. I would preserve for free white labor a fair country, a rich inheritance, where the sons of toil, of my own race and own color, can live without the disgrace which association with negro slavery brings upon free labor."[49]

Black activists and white abolitionists castigated the system that produced such unprincipled antislavery. "The Democrats have declared themselves our enemies, and the Republicans have not declared themselves our friends," Frederick Douglass editorialized. The Republicans' exclusionary free-soil stance on Kansas served as a case in point. While Democrats "would admit the black man into Kansas as a slave," Douglass challenged, Republicans "would seem to wish to exclude him as a freeman. . . . One party would enslave him, and the other party would drive him from the face of all the earth over which they have power."[50] Still, the Republican road was hard. Party leaders constantly rebutted charges of seeking "social equality" for blacks, or associating with abolitionist radicals. One Ohio newspaper worried that in Minnesota territory, which was seeking entrance into the Union, "black Republicans" like Lyman Trumbull were working for a "nigger constitution" that would grant equality to African Americans.[51] By painting Republicans as fanatics, Democrats hoped to push them out of the mainstream, and capture the broad center of the northern electorate.

As a contender for leadership in the new Republican Party, Abraham Lincoln himself felt it necessary to pander to the racist spirit of the age. Though his personal writings reflect a thoughtful approach to questions of racial equality, his public statements sought to reassure northern voters that he had no inclination to upset the racial order. Lincoln was, after all, a politician, and understood well the attitudes held by the vast majority of his countrymen. Among many voters, Republicans' antislavery, as lukewarm as it was, constituted an enormous liability, which Democrats proved all too ready to exploit. During Lincoln's famous debates with Stephen Douglas in 1858 for an Illinois Senate seat, the Democratic contender had relished the opportunity to paint his rival as an apostle of racial equality. "I do not question Mr. Lincoln's conscientious belief that the negro was made *his* equal, and hence is *his* brother," said Douglas to widespread laughter in the audience, "but for my own part, I do not regard the negro as my equal, and positively deny that he is my brother or any kin to me whatever." Lincoln's response revealed the depths to which any personal belief in racial equality he may have held gave way to the dictates of popular politics in a country absolutely suffused with racism. "I am not, nor ever have been, in favor of bringing about in any way the social and political equality of the white and black races," he responded.

> I am not, nor ever have been, in favor of making voters or jurors of negroes, nor of qualifying them to hold office, nor to intermarry with white people; and I will say in addition to this that there is a physical difference between the white and black races which I believe will forever forbid the two races living together on terms of social and political equality. And inasmuch as they cannot so live, while they do remain together there must be the position of superior and inferior, and I as much as any other man am in favor of having the superior position assigned to the white race.

Lincoln offered but a small coda to the more liberal attitudes he expressed in private. "I do not perceive that because the white man is to have the superior position the negro should be denied everything," he added.[52] Such utterances reveal the tortured path any antislavery politics trod on the road to national victory. A party built around opposition to slavery could not also risk appearing to advocate a racial equality anathema to the great majority. As Lincoln's fate in 1858 demonstrated, the path was narrow and delicate. His race with Douglas brought him to national prominence, but failed to win him the Senate seat he coveted.

After the free labor appeal, the Republicans' second great argument revivified old concerns that slaveholders constituted a discrete interest in the nation, one dedicated to securing slave property against the will of the majority, even to the point of dispensing with the fundamentals of democratic life. Since the earliest days of the Federalist Party, northern politicians had expressed concern with the constitutional compromise over slavery. Republicans revitalized these fears, fitting them into an understanding of events over the last several decades. In a speech before Congress in January 1860, Henry Wilson, senator from Massachusetts, recounted a history in which the Founding Fathers had deemed slavery a "local and temporary evil," only to have the nation witness the rise of a "slave power" that had achieved "complete domination" over the federal government. "That power has established in the slave States a relentless despotism over the freedom of speech and of the press, and of correspondence through the mails," Wilson charged. "That power will not permit American citizens to entertain, utter, print, or circulate, sentiments and opinions concerning slavery, which were avowed by Jefferson, Henry, Mason, and the great men of Virginia of the Revolutionary era." Wilson quoted—copiously but selectively—antislavery Founders on the threat bondage posed to the fragile Republic. "Slavery is inconsistent with the genius of republicanism, and has a tendency to destroy those principles on which it is supported," Luther Martin had addressed the constitutional convention of 1787. His fellow Marylander, William Pinkney, had agreed. "The effect of *slavery* is to destroy that REVERENCE FOR LIBERTY, WHICH IS THE VITAL PRINCIPLE OF A REPUBLIC. . . . If slavery continues fifty years longer, its effects will be seen in the decay of the spirit of liberty in the free States."[53] Wilson thus powerfully marshaled the antislavery impulses of the nation's founding to portray southern slaveholders as power-hungry opponents of American liberties.

Scholars once viewed such fears of a slave power "conspiracy" to destroy American liberties as evidence of a "paranoid style" in American politics, more expressive of social tensions in the North than illustrative of the realities of southern policy.[54] It is difficult, though, to view the span of national agitation over slavery from the Revolution to 1860 without appreciating the earnestness with which slaveholders and their political proxies sought to protect the institution. The very power of Republicanism owed to the plausibility of these charges in the public mind. The slave power's dominance of the Democratic Party, its effort to benefit from the Mexican cession, its concern with expanding the national boundaries of slavery, and its apparent willingness to abridge the civil liberties of free citizens in defense of the institution—all helped otherwise disinterested northerners fear that little was beyond the reach of the plantation regime. Increasingly, the very institutions designed to mediate the slavery dispute seemed incapable of performing their functions. The rules of apportionment in the House and Electoral College had undermined faith in electoral politics as an effective arbiter of sectional disputes. The party system had been rent asunder and was reforming along sectional lines. Then, in the late 1850s, even the Supreme Court lost its credibility as a neutral adjudicator of sectional disputes.

Nothing inflamed trepidations of a slave power conspiracy more than the Supreme Court's 1857 decision in the case of *Dred Scott v. Sandford*. Dred Scott, an enslaved African American born in Virginia, had lived along the western frontier with various owners. One of these, Dr. John Emerson, had taken Scott to Fort Snelling in Wisconsin Territory, which by virtue of the Missouri Compromise was free land. In 1846, Scott's case came to the attention of abolitionists, who helped him sue for his freedom. A winding path through the judicial system finally brought the case to the Supreme Court in 1855, which heard oral arguments in 1856. The timing of the case was delicate, for its appearance on the docket coincided with the first presidential election since the Whig implosion. In 1856, the Democrats secured the White House against the upstart Republican and American Parties, and sectional tensions were running high. To make matters worse, it became known that the president-elect, doughface Democrat James Buchanan, had corresponded with members of the Court, seeking a clear decision that would end the legal controversy over slavery in the territories. Having been secretly informed by Chief Justice Roger Taney that the decision would fall against Dred Scott's freedom, Buchanan publicly promised to stand by whatever opinion the Court rendered.

When, two days after Buchanan's inauguration in March, the Court spoke, it hardly quelled the controversy. Taney's rambling ruling proclaimed that Scott had no standing to sue in court. Because he was of African descent, Scott could not be a citizen of the United States. He had no right of access to the law, hence the case should never have been heard in federal court. Taney then went on to declare that, even had Scott the right to sue, his plea would have been denied, for the Missouri Compromise, in prohibiting "a citizen from holding and owning property of this kind in the territory . . . is not warranted by the Constitution." In fact, the Court, exercising its power of judicial review for only the second time in its history, declared the Missouri Compromise unconstitutional. The federal government had no right to outlaw slavery in any federal territory. "Neither Dred Scott himself, nor any of his family, were made free by being carried into this territory."[55] Taney had, in effect, turned the logic of Somerset's Case on its head. In that 1772 instance, an English court had ruled that people might be made property, but property of a special kind, the enjoyment of which required "positive law"—explicit statutes asserting the legality of slavery. Such law might exist in the colonies, Lord Mansfield had ruled, but not England, where the assumed status of all people was free. In contrast, Taney seemed to argue that the law presumed the opposite—that slaveholders' right to property overrode the default assumption of liberty. Even Congress's explicit denial of the right to slave property could not withstand what Taney viewed as the Constitution's guarantee.

Taney based his decision on a decidedly flawed interpretation of history. Rather than acknowledge the Founders' manifest ambivalence over bondage, he declared that at the time of the Founding blacks had been regarded "as being of an inferior order, and altogether unfit to associate with the white race, either in social or political relations." In fact, blacks were "so far inferior, that they had no rights which the white man was bound to respect; and that the negro might justly and lawfully be reduced to slavery."[56] This was clearly not the case. To the argument that some African Americans had, and still, possessed rights of citizenship in several of the northern states, Taney responded that state citizenship differed from national citizenship. A free state might grant blacks full and equal rights, but the rights of national citizenship, including the right to bring suit in federal court, were distinct and unrelated. This novel notion of "dual citizenship" seemed to defy both common sense and the Constitution's promise in article IV, section 2—that "the Citizens of each State shall be entitled to all Privileges and Immunities of Citizens in the several States." Nonetheless, the decision stood. A bright line had indeed been drawn.

Republicans and abolitionists denounced the ruling as poorly argued and politically motivated. The slave power seemed once again to have unfairly manipulated the levers of power to protect itself. Frederick Douglass saw the decision as yet one more nail in the coffin of liberty. "Step by step we have seen the slave power advancing; poisoning, corrupting, and perverting the institutions of the country; growing more and more haughty, imperious, and exacting. The white man's liberty has been marked out for the same grave with the black man's."[57] The Court had ruled that slavery could not be prohibited from the territories, a cataclysmic rebuttal to the principle of sectional balance which for four decades had maintained a fragile peace. Republicans now worried that the Court had opened the door to an even more egregious dissolution of the boundaries between slavery and freedom. Reformer Henry B. Stanton argued that the Supreme Court had effectively ruled "that Slavery is not a local system . . . but is a national institution," now "inviolable everywhere."[58] Following the decision, a meeting of outraged New Yorkers called on the northern public to "wrest the General Government from the hands of the Slave Power" so that "they may prevent Slavery from . . . stealthily planting its foot upon the soil of every Free State in the Union."[59]

None other than Abraham Lincoln gave clearest voice to such fears. Though remembered for its signature line, his famous "House Divided" speech, which he gave during his senatorial race with Stephen Douglas in 1858, consisted mostly of an explication of the slave power and its operation. Tracing events from the Kansas-Nebraska Act through the Dred Scott decision, Lincoln described nothing less than a concerted plan to expand slavery. He charged that recent events showed that slavery's "advocates will push it forward till it shall become alike lawful in all the States, old as well as new."[60] The Taney Court had ruled that Congress could not prohibit slavery in the territories; Lincoln pointed out that it had conspicuously neglected to declare whether or not states were similarly bound. Indeed, in his assent, one of the Supreme Court judges concurring with Taney had anticipated just this issue, ominously declaring that "when that question arises, we shall be prepared to decide it."[61] Lincoln was not far-fetched, then, in fearing the nationalization of slavery. "What Dred Scott's master might lawfully do with Dred in the free State of Illinois," Lincoln said, "every other master may lawfully do with any other one or one thousand slaves in Illinois, or in any other free state."[62]

This was not paranoid rhetoric, but a credible appraisal of future possibilities. An even more portentous case was wending its way toward the Supreme Court—that of the Lemmon slaves. In 1852, when Juliet Lemmon carried her chattels through New York City on a steamship journey from Virginia to Texas, black activists had successfully petitioned the state court to have them freed. Lemmon appealed, claiming that the privileges and immunities clause of the Constitution (art. IV, sec. 2, cl. 1) guaranteed her right to slave property throughout the nation. The case gained widespread notoriety, and wound up in the Supreme Court in 1857, mere months after the Court had rendered its verdict in the Dred Scott case. Thus the Court was soon to hear a case, the facts of which compelled it to decide the very issue the Dred Scott case had left unsettled. If Congress lacked the constitutional authority to prohibit slavery in the territories, by what right could states prohibit it? "What will the decision be?" asked Ohio Senator Salmon Chase about the Lemmon case. He feared that the Court would decide that slaveholders "can take their slaves into New York over the railroads of New Jersey, through Pennsylvania and through Ohio, Indiana, Illinois to any state of the North, and that they can hold them there during all the time that it is convenient for them to be passing through."[63] Such a decision would, in effect, nationalize slavery, making the practice legal in every state in the Union.

The Dred Scott decision constituted just the most recent bit of evidence that a conspiracy existed to expand the institution of slavery across the nation. Events over the course of the decade convinced many northerners that the slave power plotted to undermine the liberties of white men everywhere. The fugitive slave law would "enslave you and me as well as the black man," wrote one concerned abolitionist. "IT WILL MAKE SLAVES OF US ALL." Another believed that "the question of African Slavery sinks into insignificance compared with the enslavement of the people of Kansas, and the subjugation of all the free states to the principles of Dred Scott vs. Sanford."[64] These metaphors of white enslavement, so redolent of the rhetoric of the Revolution, did little justice to the experience of those African Americans who actually labored under the lash. But the comparison was made, if only indirectly, on their behalf, and against the mechanisms that kept bondspersons in chains. Their purpose, and ultimate effect, was to mobilize against slavery a public unlikely to be moved solely by the cause of the slave.

The slave power conspiracy, along with the party's concern that the West be preserved as a realm of opportunity and social mobility for the virtuous free laborer, constituted the Republican Party's strongest antislavery appeal. Buoyed by these, the party gained traction in the second half of the 1850s. In 1856, with the Whig Party gone, the party's presidential candidate, John C. Frémont, the frontier explorer and former military governor and senator from California, polled 33 percent of the popular vote. His 38 percent of the electoral vote won him eleven of sixteen free states, placing him quite respectably behind Democrat James Buchanan, and solidly ahead of the nativist American Party. Aided by the Whig collapse, the new party had performed remarkably well in its first presidential outing. Political antislavers could be pleased at the stronghold the party was building in many northern districts. "They have not yet got a President," declared a Philadelphia abolitionist, "but they have what is better, a North."[65] The party picked up forty-four seats in the House of Representatives, raising its proportion of House seats to 38 percent. Between the nativist American Party and the nominally antislavery Republicans, the latter seemed best positioned to inherit the northern Whig voter base. With popular reaction to the Dred Scott debacle polarizing northern opinion, the next election cycle promised a dramatic showdown—between the Democrats, now purged of their most antislavery northern members, and the Republicans, a sectional interest quickly building a marginally antislavery party on Whig foundations.

CHAINED TOGETHER
Militant Antislavery and the Fugitive Slave Law

In the Atlantic world, the United States stood alone in the degree to which the end of slavery owed to the conjoining of slave resistance and abolitionism. We have seen that the planter interest of the U.S. South was particularly empowered in its national system of governance. While not, perhaps, as unassailable as its counterparts in Brazil or the Spanish Caribbean, which were largely uncontested from within, it was well connected to the most dynamic sectors of the industrializing Atlantic economy. This unique American circumstance, in which the nation contained an expanding industrial metropole within the same borders as an expansive slave regime in the agricultural periphery, did more than simply empower that periphery, though. It also permitted the possibility of a uniquely potent *opposition* to slavery. Popular British abolitionism required a remarkable exercise of imagination, in which everyday Britons came to empathize with the plight of largely unseen Africans, thousands of miles away. In the United States, evidence of liberty's denial could be found much closer to hand; it pressed upon the legal and political system in undeniable ways. The free states, politically linked to the slave periphery through federalism, could not help but become implicated in slaves' struggles to free themselves.

Those struggles had always depended on the confluence between the enslaved and their free allies. In mainland Spanish Latin America, bondspersons had gained their freedom by participating in violent revolutionary wars of independence led by creole whites; in the Caribbean, they exploited changes in public opinion in the metropole to hasten the coming of freedom through mass resistance. In the United States, though, revolutionary conditions had long since passed, and the barriers to overcoming the planter interest in government were much higher than they had been in Britain and its imperial peers. Perhaps because of this, southern slaves launched no major slave rebellions after Nat Turner's futile insurrection in 1831. Instead, they ran away. Most who fled the plantation did so to protest local or temporary conditions, and most returned to the plantation after a period of "hiding out." But some, particularly in the border states, and numbering up to perhaps a thousand a year, relied on the proximity of the free states, and fled to the North. This steady stream of fugitives ignited abolitionist action, posing courts insoluble problems, and implicating white liberties.[66] It created contentious national conflicts, which helped rend the party system itself.

This circumstance was singular. In the colonies of the Caribbean, fugitive slaves had few options. Geographically isolated, the islands permitted flight only to maroon communities in the interior. At best, fugitives there would live lives of tenuous subsistence; at worst, the maroons might adhere to treaty obligations with slave regimes and return them. Some scholars have posed the North to which the fugitives ran as a form of maroon society, but in actuality it was much more.[67] In the northern United States, escaped slaves might find white allies tirelessly dedicated to their freedom. They might even benefit from a legal system that presumed their innocence and offered them due process. Truly, life for fugitives was tenuous in the North, for runaways might be reenslaved and sequestered without due process of law. Even free African Americans were vulnerable. In one instance, Solomon Northup, a New York musician, was kidnapped into slavery while touring the nation's capital and sold to a plantation in Louisiana, where he toiled for more than a decade on cotton and sugar plantations.[68] But in no maroon society did anything exist close to the body of contested law and abolitionist resources that could be marshaled on behalf of the accused runaway. After all, Northup was ultimately rescued by abolitionists, who then helped him write and publish his story.

Neither did there exist communities of other African Americans, whether free for generations or runaways themselves, whose own experiences of oppression made them generally impoverished but ardently dedicated advocates for universal liberty. The limited freedoms that unenslaved African Americans enjoyed in the free states permitted them to act as surrogates for those lacking rights and a voice in public debates. Their liminal status—as neither enslaved nor wholly free, as occupying a world between the agricultural periphery and the cosmopolitan metropole—permitted them a special capacity for doing this. And the fact that social distinctions among African-descended people in the United States were far more muted than elsewhere in the New World meant that free blacks were inclined to help. Recall that all people of African descent did not automatically see themselves as united by a common history and destiny; distinctions in class and color rent black identity in most places in the Atlantic, and operated to lesser degrees in the United States. Black northerners had to construct a unified racial identity through hard ideological work, but construct it they did.[69] The black national convention of 1848 put the matter beautifully. Though free blacks in the North remained "slaves to the community," they were "far enough removed from the actual condition of the slaves" to permit them to help. Many, in fact, had known the dreaded institution firsthand: "Our backs are yet scarred by the lash, and our souls are yet dark under the pall of slavery," the convention declared. It could therefore affirm the unity of all blacks in the country, slave or free. "We are as a people, chained together. We are one people—one in general complexion, one in a common degradation, one in popular estimation.—As one rises, all must rise, and as one falls all must fall."[70]

Northern black communities thus played a role far more potent than that of any other free black community in any other Atlantic slave society. Nowhere else did free and enslaved blacks join forces so spectacularly. The very conditions that made slavery so robust in the United States—an artificially empowered and geocontiguous slave periphery within the borders of the nation—also promoted the course of abolition by fostering contact between the enslaved and free black allies. The latter acted as the living embodiment of the antislavery argument's most important premise, that above all black people desired freedom. Through free black activists, the collective resistance of the enslaved in the periphery melded with the ideology of antislavery as set forth in metropolitan centers of opinion and governance. By publishing newspapers and pamphlets, and gathering in conventions and public meetings, African American ideologues broadcast their own unrelenting stream of criticism of the slave power, and thus acted as the critical membrane between the worlds of slave resistance and public sphere discourse. They helped interpret slave action and translate it into an ideological vocabulary intelligible to potential converts. And they inspired white abolitionists, challenging the movement to think beyond antislavery to deeper questions of racial equality.

As the phenomenon of slave flight demonstrated, the porous boundary between southern periphery and northern metropole that permitted such activist communities also engendered enormous problems for policing the slaves. Bondspeople, by "stealing themselves" and crossing the geographic divide between slave and free states, placed these questions on the national agenda. In the form of the Fugitive Slave Act of 1850, southern response to those problems undermined whites' civil liberties, strained the constitutional arrangements that bound the states, and helped erode the functionality of the party system.

As part of the 1850 compromise that temporarily resolved the crisis created by the question of slavery in the new territories, Congress passed a new fugitive slave law, the first since the Republic's initial decade. Following the Constitution's "extradition" clause, which had provided that those "who shall flee from Justice" across state lines would be "delivered up" to their home states, the 1793 act had empowered slaveholders and their agents to "seize or arrest" a "fugitive from labor" who crossed state borders. Upon presentation of satisfactory evidence of ownership, local courts were compelled to deliver runaway slaves to their home states.

From the early 1830s, though, abolitionists had sought to use northern courts and laws to protect the rights of African Americans in the North who were suspected of being fugitives. In one notable instance, a woman named Margaret Morgan, who was technically enslaved but had long lived as a free woman in Maryland, moved to Pennsylvania. When representatives of her "owners" abducted her, Pennsylvania prosecuted them under a state law prohibiting the fraudulent enslavement of free African Americans. In 1842, the case made it all the way to the Supreme Court, which decided against Morgan on the basis that federal law superseded state law. But the decision left open the possibility that states could pass laws specifically prohibiting state authorities from intervening in fugitive slave renditions. If northern states passed such laws, which many soon did, only federal agents would retain the authority to recapture runaway slaves in the North. In 1847, Virginia statesman C. J. Faulkner captured succinctly the southern response to the "personal liberty" laws that had begun appearing in the North. Their existence was "not only a flagrant violation of the spirit of the Federal Constitution," but a "deliberate *insult* to the whole Southern people," amounting to "a *just cause of war*." Insofar as they constituted "an invitation to our slaves to abscond from their masters," such laws undermined all of southern slavery, he complained.[71]

The Fugitive Slave Act of 1850 addressed the problem with a series of new provisions. It created a class of federal commissioners to oversee cases of suspected fugitives, who would receive a fee of ten dollars for every successful recapture, but only five dollars for every failed recapture. Suspected fugitives were forbidden from invoking the constitutional right of habeas corpus and testifying in their own defense, while their accusers required only an unadjudicated claim to invoke the law. Free-state citizens could be compelled to serve by posse comitatus to assist in the capture of fugitives, while those impeding recapture of fugitives were subject to thousand dollar fines. As a gesture of conciliation, the law helped southern lawmakers swallow the bitter pills contained in the Compromise of 1850: California's admittance into the Union as a free state, and Texas's loss of sizable land claims. But the law infuriated northerners.

Once again, the dominant concern was less for the African Americans it directly impacted and more for the broader civil liberties it undermined. Four hundred Wisconsin citizens declared the law "an outrage upon the rights of the people" and "offensive to our sense of justice and propriety."[72] According to a broadside from Worcester, Massachusetts, the law disregarded "all the ordinary securities of personal liberty," and "tramples on the Constitution, by its denial of the sacred rights of trial by jury, habeas corpus, and appeal." It also suppressed rights of conscience, declaring that "the cardinal virtues of Christianity shall be considered, in the eye of the law, as crimes, punishable with the severest penalties,—fines and imprisonment."[73] These concerns easily melded into growing concerns about the slave power. In Trumbull County, Ohio, antislavery men declared the law "only another, but greatly aggravated aggression of the slave power on our rights as citizens of a free State, and we will not, under any circumstances, render obedience thereunto."[74]

Abolitionists' umbrage knew few bounds. Antislavery activists gathered throughout the North to protest Congress's passage of an "unconstitutional and nefarious Law," and called for its immediate repeal.[75] Ministers preached against an act that "makes crime [that] which to our religion is a Christian duty, prohibiting us from doing what Christianity requires us to do under pain of fine and imprisonment."[76] Reaction could have far-reaching effects. In Brunswick, Maine, a sermon excoriating the law gave a professor's wife an epiphany—the vision of a saintly slave being whipped to death at the hand of a cruel master. The woman, Harriet Beecher Stowe, rushed home and began writing the most famous novel of nineteenth-century America, *Uncle Tom's Cabin; or, Life Among the Lowly* (1852). More than any other single piece of writing, this enormously influential book evangelized abolitionism, offering a moderate antislavery that appealed to the bourgeois domestic ideals of an expanding middle class. An episodic and sentimental story told through the plight of black and white characters equally ensnared by an inhumane institution, *Uncle Tom's Cabin* spawned a host of literary imitators and theatrical spinoffs. Frederick Douglass extolled the novel for having "baptized with holy fire myriads who before cared nothing for the bleeding slave."[77]

Most immediately impacted, of course, were African Americans themselves. The passage of the Fugitive Slave Act sent shockwaves through northern black communities, inducing hundreds if not thousands to emigrate to Canada.[78] Free black activists excoriated the law throughout the North. African Americans in Philadelphia's AME Church captured the mood, resolving,

> While we have heretofore yielded obedience to the laws of our country, however hard some of them have borne upon us, we deem this law so wicked, so atrocious, so utterly at variance with the principles of the Constitution; so subversive of the objects of all law, the protection of the lives, liberty, and property of the governed; so repugnant to the highest attributes of God, justice and mercy; and so horribly cruel in its clearly expressed mode of operation, that we deem it our sacred duty, a duty that we owe to ourselves, our wives, our children, and to our common nature, as well as to the panting fugitive from oppression, to resist this law at any cost and at all hazards; and we hereby pledge our lives, our fortunes, and our sacred honor so to do.[79]

Frederick Douglass, who had favored moral suasion in the 1840s, took a decisive step toward militance. "The only way to make the Fugitive Slave Law a dead letter is to make half a dozen or more dead kidnappers," he told a Free Soil convention.[80]

Black activists and white abolitionists did not restrict their response to words, no matter how powerful. Rather than settle questions and quell dissent, the Fugitive Slave Law engendered a campaign of civil disobedience rivaling any in the nation's history up to the civil rights movement of the 1960s. Antislavery activists redoubled their efforts to aid fugitives, openly challenging the law through increasingly militant actions. In Boston in 1850, a vigilance committee sheltered William and Ellen Craft, who had fled Georgia in a daring midday escape; Lewis Hayden threatened to detonate two kegs of gunpowder in his entryway should slave catchers invade their hiding place in his home. The next year in Boston, slave catchers arrested Virginia fugitive Shadrack Minkins. When the local judge refused him a writ of habeas corpus, a band of black and white abolitionists entered the courthouse and spirited him away. Minkins hid in Boston until he could escape to a new life in Canada. The same year, federal marshals arrested suspected runaway William Henry, known as "Jerry," in Syracuse, New York. A crowed gathered outside the office where Jerry was being held, battered down the door, and carried the fugitive to freedom. The most violent confrontation also occurred in 1851, when four slaves of Maryland slaveholder Edward Gorsuch found a haven in Christiana, Pennsylvania, where longtime fugitive William Parker had helped establish an informal vigilance network among local African Americans. When Gorsuch brought a small posse and a federal marshal to reclaim his property, he found his slaves fortified in a stone house with Parker and others. A firefight ensued, leaving several on both sides wounded, Gorsuch dead, and the African Americans free.[81]

Many successful cases of fugitive slave rendition offset these notable successes, testifying to the legal conflicts the law created. In Baltimore, on September 18, not even two weeks after passage of the act, marshals prosecuted fugitive James Hamlet under the law.[82] Others quickly followed, with free blacks swept into the maw as well. Over the course of the decade, 80 percent of all cases prosecuted under the law returned slaves to the South. Nonetheless, antislavery agitation made enforcement no easy task. In 1854, Boston activists gathered to free Anthony Burns, a fugitive from Richmond. The biracial crowed failed in its effort to storm the courthouse, and in the process a federal marshal lost his life. When Burns's ensuing show trial remanded him to slavery, some fifty thousand Bostonians lined streets decked in black crepe to watch him be carried away, shouting, "Kidnapper! Slave Catcher! Shame! Shame!"[83] The administration of Democratic President Franklin Pierce had to impose martial law, placing federal troops on the streets of the city. Ultimately, the cost of Burns's capture, trial, and return topped forty thousand dollars. The problem, of course, was that no law so abhorrent to the conscience of the public it affected could be easily enforced. As the Fugitive Slave Act's very author, South Carolina Senator Andrew P. Butler, admitted, the spirit of laws "must live and be preserved in the willing minds and good faith of those who incurred the obligation to maintain them."[84]

As had the South's earlier efforts to protect slavery through the gag order, the Fugitive Slave Act created a backlash of public opinion more dangerous to slavery than the evil it was intended to remedy. The doughface administrations of Fillmore and Pierce dedicated themselves to prosecuting the law to the full extent, charging violators with the capital offense of treason. The resulting trials tested the law, bringing as much attention to the issue as did the cases themselves. White attorneys—men such as Richard Henry Dana, James Birney, Salmon Chase, Joshua Giddings, and Samuel Sewall—made names for themselves by representing alleged runaways or fighting the law's constitutionality. Those involved in keeping the Gorsuch slaves free enjoyed defense by no less than Thaddeus Stevens, the prominent Pennsylvania member of the House of

Representatives, who secured the exoneration of all of the forty-one charged.[85] Also notable were the African Americans who helped break the legal profession's color barrier—men such as Robert Morris and John Mercer Langston—who made their careers fighting on behalf of fugitives.

These efforts to marshal the power of law in a free society dovetailed with slave resistance in the form of escape to produce calamitous effects for the legal system. As historian James Oakes has argued, the resistance entailed in individuals' choices to flee across the boundaries between slave and free states had far-reaching implications. Through flight, slaves' actions could, regardless of their motive or intent, pose crippling conundrums for a legal culture built on the assumption and protection of liberty. To what extent could protecting the right to hold humans as property intrude on free people's right to act according to their consciences? What was the proper role of the federal government in adjudicating conflicts between slave and free states on these issues? And how fragile had the system become when such small expressions of slave agency could send such disturbing ripples through the entire structure? In 1831, it had taken Nat Turner's notorious rebellion to shake the foundations of slavery in Virginia. By the 1850s, even single instances of nonviolent flight were raising the most fundamental questions about the nature of the federal compact.[86] What was more, such questions were quickly animating an otherwise indifferent public. Massachusetts manufacturer Amos Adams Lawrence experienced events such as the Anthony Burns rendition as catalyzing moments which converted otherwise complacent northerners to antislavery positions. "We went to bed one night old fashioned, conservative, Compromise Union Whigs & waked up stark mad Abolitionists," he reflected.[87]

This "conflict of the laws" arose not simply because fugitives ran to the North, but because allies there worked tirelessly to convince their local and state governments to guarantee minimum standards of liberty for all who occupied free soil. Several northern legislatures responded to the Fugitive Slave Law with a new round of personal liberty laws, finely tailored to circumvent the new mandate. Vermont, New Hampshire, Maine, Massachusetts, Connecticut, Rhode Island, Ohio, Michigan, and Wisconsin all established measures guaranteeing the right of habeas corpus to suspected fugitives, providing them with jury trials, and protecting northern authorities who acted discordantly with the federal law. Many of these personal liberty statutes latently invoked the doctrine of "interposition" that John C. Calhoun had formulated during the Nullification Crisis of 1832, affirming states' right to pass laws nullifying the effect of federal statute. As before, a showdown with federal power ensued. This time, though, when in 1859 the Supreme Court overturned a Wisconsin personal liberty law in the case of *Abelman v. Booth*, the slave power could cheer the triumph of federal authority over states' rights. Indeed, in the 1850s the voices of disunion hailed from both sections. In the North, men such as Charles Sumner likened resistance to the Fugitive Slave Law as analogous to American patriots' denial of the British Stamp Act.[88] In the South, Senator Robert Barnwell Rhett of South Carolina predicted that northern agitation over the act would rend "the whole fabric" of the Union, which would fall into "a vast pile of ruin and desolation."[89] He and his fellow South Carolinians had even met in convention in 1852 to consider seceding from the Union altogether. The delegates affirmed states' right to secede based on what they viewed as "the frequent violations of the Constitution of the United States by the Federal Government," including northern states' refusal "to enforce and carry out the existing constitutional provisions on the subject of rendition of fugitive slaves."[90] Runaway slaves had thus inadvertently triggered new threats of southern secession.

MINGLED BLOOD
Showdowns in Kansas and Virginia

At the same time that Anthony Burns was being forced back into slavery, new strains of militance emerged in the territories. Under the popular sovereignty provision of the Kansas-Nebraska Act, which negated the Missouri Compromise of 1820, the people of the Kansas Territory would themselves decide whether or not slavery would exist in the new state. The irony of this ostensibly democratic solution to the problem of slavery was not lost on the northern press. Last on a list of "inalienable rights of Americans" *not* enumerated in the Declaration of Independence, the Philadelphia *Daily Register* sarcastically placed the right "to hold slaves, and prate of freedom. To make Franklin Pierce Autocrat of Kansas and Nebraska, and clamor about 'popular sovereignty.'"[91] By making the matter of slavery one of numbers, the Kansas scheme created incentives for each side in the struggle to pack the territory with as many partisans as possible. "We will engage in competition for the virgin soil of Kansas," William Henry Seward challenged the slave states, "and God give the victory to the side which is stronger in numbers, as it is in right."[92]

Seward spoke no mere rhetoric. While the Kansas-Nebraska Act's instigators assumed that the more northerly territory would balance the new slave state of Kansas, free soilers were not about to let the abrogation of the "sacred compact" of 1820 pass without a fight. Slaveholders from adjacent Missouri arrived first, but antislavery northerners soon organized the New England Emigrant Aid Company to send men and material to Kansas. The latter included clandestine shipments to the antislavery settlers of Sharps rifles, known popularly as "Beecher's Bibles." The name honored New England minister Henry Ward

Beecher, who reportedly stated that "there was more moral power in one of those instruments, so far as the slaveholders of Kansas were concerned, than in a hundred Bibles."[93] Over twelve hundred settlers dedicated to the antislavery cause migrated to Kansas, including six members of the family of John Brown, an aging abolitionist who, following Elijah Lovejoy's martyrdom in 1837, had consecrated his life "to the destruction of slavery."[94]

Early on, proslavery forces seemed to secure the upper hand. In November 1854, the territory's lone congressional delegate went to proslavery forces in an election rife with fraud and ballot stuffing. In March of the next year, the same faction packed Kansas's first territorial legislature. When the new lawmakers began passing a series of measures legalizing slavery in Kansas, antislavery men organized a "Free State" shadow government in Topeka that banned slavery. President Franklin Pierce denounced the state constitution drafted by the free-staters. Declaring it "of a revolutionary character," he ordered federal troops to disperse the convention that crafted it.[95] Kansas descended into a welter of small-scale but vicious guerrilla battles. Missouri Senator David Rice Atchison declared his desire "to kill every God-damned abolitionist in the district."[96] In November 1855, proslavery settlers shot free-stater Charles Dow, and in the next month the antislavery Thomas Barber died at the hands of proslavery "border ruffians" from Missouri. These shortly laid siege to Lawrence, which free-staters used as a defense point in the growing Wakarusa War in eastern Kansas. On May 21, 1856, some eight hundred proslavery men sacked the town, destroyed its newspaper presses, looted its residences, and left a burning ruin of the hotel used as a command post.

The violence in "bleeding Kansas" spread even to the halls of Congress, when Massachusetts Senator Charles Sumner rose to deplore the Kansas-Nebraska Act. Sumner charged that the "slave power" had inflicted a "crime against Kansas," calling it "the rape of a virgin Territory," and singling out South Carolina Senator Andrew Butler for approbation for championing the act. Preston Brooks, Butler's nephew and a congressman from South Carolina, took exception to the slight on his uncle's honor, for Sumner had accused Butler of having taken "the harlot, slavery" as his "mistress."[97] The very day following the sack of Lawrence, Brooks confronted Sumner in the Senate chamber, beating him so severely that Sumner ripped his desk from its floor bolts. Sumner suffered the effects of the thrashing for years later, but the act had more significant implications on the country as a whole. While a few southern politicians expressed private disapproval, many in the South lauded the measure as a justified response to Sumner's affront. Butler received canes to replace the one he broke on Sumner in the attack. Abolitionists had been "suffered to run too long without collars," approved a Richmond paper. "They must be lashed into submission."[98]

When news of the sack of Lawrence arrived at virtually the same time word of the Butler outrage spread, the North erupted in indignation. Edward Everett, the moderate Whig senator from Massachusetts, reported "an excitement in the public mind deeper and more dangerous than I have ever witnessed," and worried "that events are even now in train, with an impulse too mighty to be resisted, which will cause our beloved country to shed tears of blood through all her borders for generations to come."[99] In rallies and speeches throughout the North, speakers linked the defense of slavery to the erosion of liberty. To many, the twin outrages of "Bleeding Kansas" and "Bleeding Sumner" reinforced the growing belief that the institution of slavery bred a disregard for the freedoms of all people, not just those of African descent. Transcendentalist intellectual Ralph Waldo Emerson used the incidents to conclude that the nation's two systems were fundamentally incompatible. "I do not see how a barbarous community and a civilized community can constitute one state," he stated. "I think we must get rid of slavery, or we must get rid of freedom."[100] The New York *Evening Post* made the connection explicit. "The friends of slavery at Washington are attempting to silence the members of Congress from the free states by the same modes of discipline which make the slaves units on their plantations," declared editor William Cullen Bryant. "Are we too, slaves, slaves for life, a target for their brutal blows, when we do not comport ourselves to please them?"[101] The polarizing effect of the incidents was palpable. The British *Economist* calculated that the new Republican Party "will find itself much strengthened by the feelings engendered by the outrage on Sumner and by the violent attacks of the slavery party on Kansas."[102]

In Kansas itself, antislavery men were not content to let the political process work its inertial course. The sack of Lawrence and the caning of Sumner plunged the territory into a wave of paramilitary violence. John Brown, having arrived to aid his family, led a raid to avenge the destroyed town and the beaten senator. Brown's band, including four of his sons, attacked a proslavery settlement at Pottawatomie Creek, butchering five men innocent of the attack on the free-state stronghold. Proslavery retaliation ensued, and throughout the summer of 1856, eastern Kansas turned into a war zone in miniature. The imposition of thirteen hundred federal troops and an amnesty for the warring parties helped quell the violence, but skirmishing in Kansas ultimately claimed the lives of perhaps as many as two hundred before the outbreak of the Civil War.

Nearly as fierce was the struggle to create a viable constitution for Kansas statehood—the ostensible reason for packing the state in the first place. Emboldened by the White House's denunciation of free-staters' Topeka Constitution, proslavery men met at Lecompton in September 1857 to draft their own. Once again, voting fraud and opposition boycotts impaired the results, but the new Democratic president, James Buchanan, endorsed the document, and enough of the Senate succumbed to Stephen Douglas's influence to pass it. Only the House's rejection kept Kansas from becoming the country's sixteenth slave state.

Having found his calling as a guerrilla, John Brown left Kansas in the fall of 1856, to gather men and resources for an entirely new crusade against slavery. Now renowned for his actions and with a price on his head, he stole out of the territory and made his way east, where he began a campaign to enlist moneyed abolitionists in an elaborate plan. On the Kansas frontier, Brown had learned his efficacy in matching the violence of the slave power with the violence of righteous antislavery. Now, Brown would "carry the war into Africa," taking the fight to the slaveholding states.[103] In the parlors of abolitionists such as Thomas Wentworth Higginson, Samuel Gridley Howe, the Reverend Theodore Parker, and Gerrit Smith, Brown elaborated a plan, growing in his mind since the 1840s, to attack slavery through a "Subterranean Passway" in the Appalachians. This would funnel a huge stream of fugitives north and eventually to Canada, enlarging the Underground Railroad and bringing it above ground.

The scheme evolved into something more akin to establishing a maroon community in the heart of the Appalachian Mountains. Brown would gather committed white and black antislavery activists, arm them, and establish a base in the remote, defensible regions of western Virginia. Patterned on the larger maroon groups of Jamaica or Suriname, this would offer a haven for fugitive slaves, and a center from which further attacks on slavery could be made. Its avowed purpose would be, unlike that of maroon societies, not mere subsistence or survival, but the destruction of the slave system itself, preferably through a mass uprising that would impel a nationwide struggle against the slave power. Brown had read broadly on guerrilla actions throughout history, making a special study of "the wars in Hayti and the islands round about," and imagined his actions sparking "insurrectionary warfare." One of Brown's men testified that the captain believed "all the free negroes in the Northern States would immediately flock to his standard," along with "all the slaves in the Southern States," and "many of the free negroes in Canada."[104] Brown would exploit the long border between slavery and freedom, seeking forcibly to provoke the conditions of revolutionary chaos that had so effectively undermined slavery during the American, Haitian, and Latin American wars for independence.

Throughout 1857 and 1858, Brown coaxed financial and logistical support from skeptical auditors thrilled by his charisma and experiences. He recruited men—whites, free blacks, and fugitive slaves—to join him. Approaching African Americans in the fugitive sanctuary of Chatham, Ontario, he won the faith of notable black nationalist Martin Delany. At a convention there, Brown revealed his purpose and proposed his "Provisional Constitution and Ordinances for the People of the United States," a plan of governance for the territory to be conquered that constituted both a wartime emergency constitution as well as a utopian vision for a property-free society. The document also articulated Brown's underlying commitment to America; the plan did not "encourage the overthrow of any State Government of the United States" or seek "dissolution of the Union," but desired simply "Amendment and Repeal" of the existing system to omit slavery.[105] The closer the scheme came to fruition, though, the more Brown seemed inclined to spark a moment of apocalyptic violence. At Harpers Ferry, which lay at the northern mouth of the Shenandoah Valley in western Virginia, he would take the federal armory, confiscate its weapons, and arm slaves throughout the countryside. The inevitable response would be met with thousands of slaves raised from the surrounding area. When he confided this plan to Frederick Douglass, the abolitionist demurred, reporting later that he objected to the proposal "with all the arguments at my command." Douglass told Brown that "he was going into a perfect steel-trap, and that once in he would never get out alive."[106]

But Brown persisted. In the summer of 1859, he rented a farm in western Maryland, just five miles from Harpers Ferry. On October 16, he led a force of twenty-one men, including five African Americans, across the Potomac River Bridge. After quickly capturing the armory, arsenal, and gun works, things went awry. When a night watchman—who happened to be African American—ventured onto the bridge, Brown's band fired on him. A train passing through managed to pass news of the invasion along the line, and by early afternoon of the next day, militiamen had surrounded Brown's band in an engine house where they had taken some thirty hostages from the town. Later that evening, U.S. Marines arrived under the command of Colonel Robert E. Lee, aided by Lieutenant J. E. B. Stuart. The next morning, Brown rejected a surrender offer, and the Marines stormed the building. The captain and just four of his remaining men were captured alive, having themselves claimed the lives of four Virginians. The trial proceeded quickly, with Virginia passing a sentence of death for treason. But before Brown faced justice he spent nearly six weeks engaging in a remarkable campaign of writing and speaking from his jail cell. This time, during which the condemned insurrectionary justified himself lengthily, did more than anything to help northerners understand Brown's actions as a fight for liberty.

Most abolitionists repudiated Brown's violent approach, but sympathized with his yearning for black liberty. "We disclaim sympathy with Brown's scheme of emancipation," ran a typical editorial, "but we regret that so brave a man should fall a victim to the generous impulses of his patriotic heart." Others lamented the disjuncture between national and "higher" law that the raid exposed.

Representatives from Wisconsin churches resolved: "We mourn over the degeneration and guilt of our country, in having brought any of her citizens to the *necessity of disobedience* to human law, in order to render *loyalty to the laws of heaven!*" Those of a more radical bent quickly placed Brown among the most exalted of antislavery saints. Many posed him as an antislavery John the Baptist, preparing the way for universal emancipation. Ralph Waldo Emerson declared that Brown's imminent death "will make the gallows as glorious as the cross."[107] Brown's martyrdom drove even the most ardent nonresisters to countenance violence in the cause. William Lloyd Garrison himself endorsed this most extreme form of practical abolitionism: "Rather than see men wearing their chains in a cowardly and servile spirit, I would, as an advocate of peace, much rather see them breaking the head of the tyrant with their chains."[108]

Unsurprisingly, white southerners reacted with fear and contempt. For decades, slaveholders had incubated fears that abolitionists conspired to foment slave insurrection—charges abolitionists had long taken pains to deny. Now southern suspicions had been confirmed. *DeBow's Review*, a bastion of conservatism, declared the raid "the first act in the grand tragedy of emancipation, and the subjugation of the South in bloody treason."[109] Ran the Richmond *Whig*, "A wild, mad anti-slavery fanaticism has seized upon a portion of the citizens of the North, which nothing but the mournful practical realities of civil war and general bloodshed can ever appease." The attack was "calculated to add fuel to the flames of sectional excitement, and awaken a feeling of insecurity and vindictiveness all through the Southern States fatal to the peace and preservation of the Union."[110]

Brown's choice to target Harpers Ferry had doomed the scheme, but its conception uniquely combined myriad impulses in antislavery resistance. Brown was at once an abolitionist, an insurrectionary guerrilla, and a prophet—roles not easily harmonized. Perhaps Brown's military self-discipline gave way to his messianism. For even had the raid come off without its hitches—the early death of an innocent free black man on the bridge, Brown's choice to let a Baltimore and Ohio Railroad conductor proceed through town, the failure to hastily retreat from Harpers Ferry after successfully seizing its arms—its key premise was always faulty. Lacking ongoing revolutionary ferment or exceptionally grievous labor conditions, the surrounding Jefferson County, with not even four thousand scattered slaves in a total population of nearly fifteen thousand, would never rise up en masse to support an insurrection begun by fewer than two dozen men.[111] Brown seemed not to mind. Certainly, a Nat Turner–like air of fatalism hung over him. Like the prophet of Southampton, Brown had "long entertained" a plan "to make war on slavery."[112] Never much of a success in his business dealings, he seemed to view his martyrdom as the most he could offer the cause he held so dear. "God sees it," he had told one of his sons back in Kansas. "I have only a short time to live—only one death to die, and I will die fighting this cause."[113] Facing the gallows after the raid's failure, Brown reiterated this belief in stirring words: "If it is deemed necessary that I should forfeit my life for the furtherance of the ends of justice, and mingle my blood further with the blood of my children and with the blood of millions in this slave country whose rights are disregarded by wicked, cruel, and unjust enactments—I submit; so let it be done!"[114]

Brown mingled his blood with that of oppressed blacks not just in death. He evinced a rare willingness to commune with African Americans, a signal of perhaps his greatest significance. In 1838, he mortified his church by inviting a black family into his pew. When the wealthy Gerrit Smith offered grants of land in upstate New York to impoverished African Americans, Brown took a parcel as well. He committed "to live with those poor despised Africans" and promised to "be a kind of father to them."[115] More than other white abolitionists, Brown demonstrated a willingness to violate the boundaries of caste and identify with the plight of a despised race. "Though a white gentleman," Frederick Douglass reported after meeting the abolitionist back in 1848, Brown was "in sympathy a black man, and is as deeply interested in our cause, as though his own soul had been pierced with the iron of slavery."[116] To take up arms and fight for blacks' liberty was but a logical extension of Brown's cross-racial identification. On the day of Brown's death, J. Sella Martin, an escaped slave who became a Baptist minister in Boston, made the point in perhaps the most eloquent eulogy offered for the martyr. Noting abolitionists' fear to plainly endorse Brown's course, Martin approved of Brown's violent instruments. "I remember that our Fourth-of-July orators sanction the same thing," Martin intoned, noting battle after battle fought by American revolutionaries. "All go to approve the means that John has used; the only difference being, that in our battles, in America, means have been used for white men and that John Brown used his means for black men."[117] For many African Americans, Brown's crime consisted solely in doing for slaves what white men had done for themselves.

John Brown's raid represented the culmination of antislavery militance, a melding of the twin streams of slave resistance and metropolitan antislavery activism. For many, war was already under way—if not in Kansas, then in the militance with which African Americans and their abolitionist allies responded to the slave power's vigorous prosecution of the Fugitive Slave Law. Brown thought of it even more sweepingly. "Slavery was a state of war," he told Douglass, in a formulation recalling John Locke's portrayal of the institution as a more humane alternative to annihilation.[118] Black activists and the most radical abolitionists understood this, folding Brown's actions smoothly into yet further calls for slave resistance. To J. Sella Martin, Brown had been the meteor that strikes "the volcano of American sympathies," and causes it to "burst forth in one general conflagration of revolution that shall bring about universal freedom." Tellingly, Martin noted that the slaves were not to be left out of the equation. Brown's "adamantine courage" would "serve as the grit in the grindstone upon which the slave shall sharpen his weapon."[119]

Brown's melding of abolitionism and slave resistance illustrated the unparalleled tensions that the "house divided" had engendered in the United States. In no other slave society of the New World could be found a comparable case of a white antislaver actively engineering an armed revolt for the sole purpose of destroying slavery. Planters had accused English missionaries of fomenting rebellion in the British West Indies, but no British churchman had ever raised a sword to lead his flock in a campaign of armed resistance. In effect, Brown had tried to re-create the conditions of revolutionary chaos that had led to widespread emancipations earlier in the century throughout the Atlantic. Such, though, was the steadily rising tide of militance around the slavery issue in the United States that by 1859 Brown's raid could be contemplated, and even supported, by important antislavery leaders both white and black.

The raid reacted to the failure of change through formal politics, another circumstance unique in the Atlantic. Elsewhere, metropolitan movements for abolition had employed forceful but peaceful means to move the levers of governments and effect mass emancipation. With cautious optimism, African Americans and abolitionists viewed a broad sweep of Atlantic history that seemed to be moving steadily toward a future of liberty. But the slave power of the South impeded this trend by successfully exploiting a political system that had been rigged for slavery's defense. Then, when even this was insufficient to counter the growing tide of demographics and antislavery opinion, the slave power had proved all too willing to jettison the liberties of free whites to further secure its hold on a fundamentally antidemocratic institution. Whereas measured slave violence helped precipitate the end of slavery in the Caribbean, even abolitionists' moves toward militance in the United States appeared to be having no effect at producing gradual change. In the 1840s, Gerrit Smith and the non-resistant Garrison had gotten to the point of calling for slave strikes similar to those that had characterized the end of slavery in the Caribbean.[120]

Nothing, however, had availed, not even Brown's desperate attempt to lead a slave rebellion himself. Instead of yielding southern acquiescence on gradual emancipation laws as had happened elsewhere, decades of antislavery agitation in the United States had only emboldened the slave power, which used its political sway to buttress slavery through measures such as the Fugitive Slave Law or the Supreme Court's ruling in the Dred Scott case. In the Caribbean slavery had ended more or less peacefully. But to American blacks and abolitionists, democratic and peaceful means were not only failing, they were being denied by a government in the hands of the enemy. The range of alternatives to ending slavery steadily diminished into ever more extreme possibilities. John Brown's final message, written after even his exceptional effort went unfulfilled, must be understood in this context: "I, John Brown, am now quite certain that the crimes of this guilty land can never be purged away but with blood."[121]

The failure of less radical forms of change drew the twin streams of public protest and slave resistance ever closer together. For years, abolitionists and free black activists had been acting as surrogates and public proxies for those in bonds, rhetorically channeling slave action into arguments that might move indifferent free whites to act. As spokespersons, abolition's advocates undoubtedly were imperfect: white abolitionists with their own racial baggage often condescended to those they saw as objects of their benevolence, while even free black leaders conceded the "unelevated" nature of their enslaved brethren. Yet free allies had helped make slave action intelligible to a broader national community by situating the slaves' desire for freedom amid a long and cherished tradition of liberty-seeking revolution. As the struggle continued, though, and as peaceful means of change failed, abolitionists and black activists moved steadily toward more militant means of securing liberty. If fugitive slave rescues constituted individual manifestations of this melding, Brown's attempt to spark mass insurrection sought to conflate collective expressions of abolitionist and slave resistance. His effort failed, a victim of his need to die a martyr to the cause rather than launch the militant maroon haven he had originally envisioned. Had he maintained his strategic discipline, 1860 may have looked quite different.

As it was, Harpers Ferry served as a warning of what was likely to come. Since 1831, no major slave rebellion had beset the Old South. Now Brown's raid had fused the millennialism of Turner's insurrection with the political purpose and revolutionary ideology of Vesey's conspiracy of 1822 and Gabriel's rebellion of 1800. Then it placed them in the hands of a dedicated metropolitan abolitionist who had forsaken the movement's cant of nonresistance. Brown's failure had fateful consequences. As had been the case in instances of slave insurrection, the raid on Harpers Ferry acted first to galvanize the slave power. Its long-term significance was less clear. Certainly, the widespread public horror over Brown's actions threatened antislavery politicians, who faced a formidable task in dissociating themselves from Brown's tactics. "The republican party of the North is stained with the blood of insurrection," editorialized one Democratic newspaper from New Hampshire. "Let it be painted upon their banners—they are responsible before God for the victims at Harper's Ferry!"[122] Secessionists, emboldened by this backlash, positively delighted in the attack. "We can well afford the blow," crowed William Lowndes Yancey of Alabama. "The pain is sweet, for it will accomplish more in aid of disunion than all the platforms, resolves and agitations of a lifetime."[123] The raid thus weakened Republicans' claim to the moderate center. But by strengthening the secessionists' hand, it also fostered divisions within the Democratic Party that would prove decisive in 1860.

On a still larger scale, the raid had once again exposed the unique features of the struggle against slavery in the United States. With a lengthy border between geo-contiguous lands of slavery and freedom, the nation proved endlessly vulnerable to the inconsistencies posed by bondage in a land nominally dedicated to liberty. Proslavery intellectuals eloquently explained how the institution uplifted its charges and actually enhanced white liberty, but the actions of the slaves themselves stubbornly refused to vindicate such arguments. Instead, militant resistance that crossed the borders between free and slave states posed thorny questions about the boundaries between the law of slavery and the law of liberty. These intruded into the political system, steadily polarizing it until it ceased to function as a means of nonviolent dispute resolution. This was possible only because there existed in the North committed groups of antislavery agitators, willing and able to give meaning to slaves' actions. Their acts of translation—of interpreting the content of slave lives for the voters and politicians of the free states—moved legal levers and altered public opinion. The persistent drumbeat of slave defiance could even attract the most ardent of these antislavery activists to meld their abolitionism with the resistance of the enslaved, in a relentless effort to assail the national scourge.

In indirect but crucial ways, then, African Americans deeply shaped the breakdown of the party system and its reformulation around the slavery issue. Abolitionist arguments relying on the meaning of slave resistance informed national debates over such matters as slavery's expansion, or the relative political power of the sections. Beyond arguments, acts of civil disobedience taken by white abolitionists and free black activists lent these questions a concrete and practical reality that could not be avoided. In the end, the controversies they generated broke the two-party political system, and precipitated the secession that caused war.

SECTION 4

The Civil War and Reconstruction

CHAPTER 7

This Terrible War

Secession, Civil War, and Emancipation

A PREEMPTIVE CONSERVATIVE COUNTERREVOLUTION
The Meaning of Secession

On November 6, 1860, Americans elected a president for the eighteenth time. When the Kansas-Nebraska Act passed in 1854, the political party he represented had not existed. In the election of 1860, the name Abraham Lincoln did not even appear on the ballot in many southern states. When he nonetheless won, it took but a month for South Carolina, the leading slaveholding state of the Deep South, to secede from the Union and declare its independence—despite that the new president had often averred that slavery was legal in the states where it existed and had promised that under his presidency he would continue to protect it. "I have no purpose, directly or indirectly, to interfere with the institution of slavery in the States where it exists," he had stated. "I believe I have no lawful right to do so, and I have no inclination to do so."[1] Ten slaveholding states of the South nonetheless withdrew from the national compact. Their secession led, indirectly though inexorably, to the destruction of the very institution it sought to preserve. Chattel slavery as a legal entity in the United States ended as a consequence of the Civil War. And the war itself began because President Abraham Lincoln refused to accept the dissolution of the Union. The elevation to the presidency of a politician who stood against the expansion of slavery into the western territories thus triggered the formation of the Confederacy. And the war that was necessary to reunite the country destroyed slavery.

From the very founding, tension between the free and slave states had arisen not over the degraded position most Americans were all too willing to assign people of African descent, but over the disproportionate representation slave states received in the national government by virtue of the three-fifths clause of the Constitution. The formation of the party system subsumed and obscured the political struggle between slave and free states, while the growth of an industrial and urban market economy in the North exacerbated distinctions in the interests of the two regions. The country's success in the Mexican-American War placed it on a clear path to internal conflict by posing thorny new problems over slavery in the territories, and about the slave power's chokehold on the liberties of white northerners. The political system broke down around these issues, reformulating along sectional lines.

These factors were singular in Atlantic experience, for of all the instances of slavery's long death, the American Civil War ranks with the Haitian Revolution for its utter lack of precedence. Up to 1860, most Atlantic slaves had became free from processes of largely nonviolent metropolitan abolition. The revolutionary abolitions accompanying independence movements in mainland Spanish Latin America freed a fraction as many, though with more bloodshed. In none but the Haitian and American instances, though, did slavery itself serve as the root cause of warfare. And while the Haitian Revolution is best understood as a consequence of the enslaved's exploitation of the political chaos caused by the revolution in France, the American Civil War actually began over questions directly related to slavery. The United States stands alone as the only society in which controversies over slavery initiated the complete breakdown of national politics, and thus an incredibly bloody civil war that wound up destroying slavery.

The factor that made the story of slavery's ending in the United States so unparalleled was, of course, the strength of the southern slave power in national tribunals. The hyper-empowerment of the slaveholding regime had upheld American slavery far beyond the point at which analogous institutions in other highly developed Atlantic societies had abandoned it. Yet it was not that the American slave power was so strong that only a recourse to extralegal violence could defeat American slavery. It was that a slow and arduous process of marginalizing and containing southern slavery was actually on the verge of working. Southerners' stepped-up efforts to defend slavery from the onslaught of abolitionism and slave resistance generated reactions in the free states that spread antislavery feeling into the political mainstream. The prospect of peaceful change, effected through legitimate political institutions despite the slave states' lopsided control of government, precipitated sufficient numbers of the institution's defenders to make the critical choice to secede. War came because the slaveholders of the American South reacted to a shifting balance of power in the federal government that became evident in the decade after the Mexican-American War ended. Even with its artificially enhanced representation, the slave power of the United States confronted a future of doubt and declining relative strength, which it sought to forestall by staking all on a risky gamble for independence. Only the choice to sunder the Union created the necessity for an extralegal resolution to the problems slavery posed. In losing that gamble, the slave South plunged the nation into catastrophic violence, and lost the very thing it sought most to guard.

But the Union did not in fact begin the war with the goal of ending slavery. It began the war to end secession. The Confederacy initiated the conflict in order to protect slavery, but the Union did not accept war in order to abolish it. Indeed, the great majority of northern whites continued to maintain that abolitionists themselves were an incendiary band of "crack-brained fanatics." They retained their commitments to white supremacy and thought little for the humanity of the enslaved. But because of events in the 1850s, more and more in the North had come to view slavery itself as an institution antithetical to their ideal of American society. For these Americans, the social values and political order bred by slavery threatened whites' civil liberties and their opportunities for social mobility. This message worked its way into national politics, until it became the article of faith that drove many in the North to support a Republican candidate for office, and then a war against disunion.

Uniquely in the Atlantic world, popular politics became the terrain on which the battle was fought. The party system had cloaked the sectional conflict, overlaying a template of party politics on national debates over the peculiar institution. The Democratic Party assumed the role of chief defender of slavery and its expansion, but the workings of the two-party process muffled the sectional character of the parties. Eventually, though, public opinion in both sections polarized to the point that the parties could not avoid the issue. The two-party system of the 1840s imploded, to be replaced by a fractured new sectional one, overtly organized around slavery-related issues. Secession represented the withdrawal of most slaveholding states from this system. This breakdown was the critical precondition for war, the very function of politics being to resolve disputes without recourse to violence. So beholden to party struggle was ending slavery in the United States that some among earlier generations of historians, and many Americans into this day, have suggested that chattel bondage actually had little to do with secession at all. While the sectional crisis was indeed about the fate of slavery, outside of the declarations of radical abolitionists and southern fire-eaters, little in the 1850s would have suggested that the institution itself was in peril. Instead, national conversations concerned only the extension of slavery, or the question of states' relation to the federal government, or concerns over whites' civil liberties, or the relative power of the regions in the institutions of national governance, or even continual squabbles over the tariff. No other society in the Atlantic world contested slavery so long and bitterly, and yet so indirectly.

Nowhere else was such a long and politically tortured route to abolition necessary. Even in the instance of St. Domingue, where the Haitian Revolution came closest to matching the Civil War in bloodshed and loss of life,[2] war emerged quickly when free colored and slave rebels exploited a sudden political crisis among the island's free population. War had also spurred abolition amid the revolutionary independence movements of Latin America, but never with a domestic politics as arduously contested, and ultimately as violently fought, as in the United States. Great Britain witnessed the only popular abolitionist movement equal to America's, but by that time, West Indian planters could not mount a credible political defense, let alone imagine a military one. Lacking the commercial clout, political self-confidence, and sense of collective identity that characterized the slaveholders of the U.S. South, they never launched a viable bid for independence. With the exception of Spain, the nations of continental Europe abolished slavery in their New World dominions with little pretense that democratic mass movements had caused its end. Whether abolition was accomplished through the actions of constitutional monarchs such as Denmark's King Christian VIII or through the interim government of revolutionary France, democratic politics simply did not assume the key roles they did in the Atlantic's first metropolitan abolition (Great Britain) and its largest (the United States). And only in America did slavery itself cause a breakdown of the formal political process that descended into a clash of arms between rival white factions.

Democratic processes uniquely characterized American abolition, rendering it arduous and ultimately violent. At the time of the founding, the principles of political equality had in fact justified granting a slaveholding periphery equal (indeed, overweening) weight in the system of national governance. The operations of mass politics then helped the South maintain its hyper-empowered position in the two-party system. Finally, though, only mass politics could sway even the risk-averse two-party system into heeding the dictates of rank-and-file northerners who, despite their overwhelming disregard for the slaves themselves, came to view slave*holders* as a fundamental threat to liberty and opportunity. In the United States, the constitutional settlement had offered protections to slavery that, short of war, could be changed only through the political work of resolving the purposeful ambiguity of the nation's founding charter. Ending slavery in the United States required not simply passing a series of laws, but clarifying contradictions written into the very nature of the national government—conflicts that represented the growing strength of, and growing divides between, each section's distinct interests.

This formidable challenge was made no easier by the nature of American politics. In the United States, the political work of altering the federal compact had to be accomplished through a mass two-party system that the Founders had never envisioned, and which amplified the artificial strength the Constitution had conferred on southerners. For reasons we have seen, two-party politics submerged rather than foregrounded divisive issues such as slavery; the moderating influence of the party system had punished extreme positions and rewarded moderation. Only a long and concerted campaign of political agitation—one of the greatest social movements in the history of the Atlantic world—had compelled the system to react democratically, and incorporate onto party agendas what otherwise would have been politically suicidal. Because of this, when the system did grudgingly begin to acknowledge what so many Americans compelled it to, slavery as a concern in national tribunals emerged through proxy issues such as the tariff, or states' rights.

It is impossible, though, to imagine secession and the war that followed as disconnected to slavery. Lincoln put the matter concisely to Confederate Vice President Alexander Stephens in late 1860: "You think slavery is right and ought to be extended; while we think it is wrong and ought to be restricted. That I suppose is the rub. It certainly is the only substantial difference between us."[3] Discussions related to slavery broke the party political process to the point that only armed conflict remained a viable means of resolving the dispute. When overmatched even in a political system that artificially strengthened them, slaveholding leaders of the South chose to withdraw from the national compact rather than confront a future of unending decline. While cynical and destructive, their calculation was not without foundation. Slave systems were being steadily marginalized throughout the Atlantic by the maturation of new forms of industrial capitalism back in the metropole. It was not that the periphery's productivity or profits declined, for generally they did the opposite. It was that industrial capital's increase in wealth and power outpaced that of the periphery. Both grew, but the metropole's accelerating expansion from the last quarter of the eighteenth century on caused a *relative* decline in the economic, and hence political, might of the periphery in the Atlantic as a whole. This situation invited the periphery's political subjugation to the interests of the metropole. The ideological component of this took the form of broad and wide-ranging attacks on the periphery's unique labor system, which seemed to violate the evolving norms of the new bourgeois social order.

The Atlantic pattern was clearly evident in the United States. Demographically, the sections were unbalancing, with the North's advantage in capital accumulation quickly accelerating. Not even the three-fifths compromise could offset the consequences for representation of the disproportionate growth of the northern free population. After the first federal census, the northern states commanded 53 percent of the population as counted for purposes of apportioning the House of Representatives and seats in the Electoral College. By 1850, that figure had climbed to almost 62 percent, and in 1860 it reached 64 percent—on the verge of controlling two-thirds of the seats in the House.[4] History seemed to be moving against the South. What had begun as a marginal single-issue splinter party had grown into a national political force. A small and widely despised handful of radicals—the abolitionists—had managed over the course of decades to infiltrate both national discourse and the formal political system, even if the hard core disavowed the Republicans' cynical declension from original ideals. The agitation they generated transformed national politics, and eventually left a party committed to limiting slavery in control of the White House.

The story of the Civil War, then, is the story of how the slave power of the U.S. South lost a preemptive conservative counterrevolution designed to protect the institution at the core of its society.[5] Secession represented a counterrevolution in the sense that it reacted to a revolution already under way. The movement to abolish slavery in the South was of a piece with much broader impulses throughout the Atlantic world to abolish slavery everywhere. As we have seen, in world-historical terms this was a new impulse—generated by evolving notions of property, given shape by the tradition of liberal thinking inherent in the Atlantic revolutions, and energized by new strains of evangelical Protestantism. Southerners sought to counter these new concerns about slavery by removing themselves from a national state wherein they believed their interests had become hopelessly compromised. The *Charleston Mercury* spoke in such terms in 1860, asserting that "the distemper of our times has been gathering virulence through twenty years of progress and agitation." The South could no longer count on aid from northern quarters. "Our safety rests in ourselves," editors opined.[6]

In this respect, secessionists were also conservative, seeking to preserve an institution that, while it shifted dynamically to a range of times and places, had a long history in Atlantic life and thought. "We are not revolutionists—we are resisting revolution," the editor of the southern *DeBow's Review* declared; "we are conservative." The Confederacy viewed itself as but "upholding the great principles which our fathers bequeathed us," and "struggling for constitutional freedom"—a defensible position, given the Founders' failure to resolve the slavery issue. Finally, secession was preemptive, in that it reacted not to a crisis already extant, but to one the slave power thought was looming. By all constitutional and legal standards, slaveholding in the southern states was secure in the America of 1860—as safe as "in the days of Washington," Lincoln assured the South.[7] It was the possible direction of future events that drove slaveholders to advocate secession. With a political party in office that was predicated on the containment of slavery, slaveholders' long-standing but fragile grip on national power had collapsed, their delicate latticework of influence unlikely to be reconstituted. In his second inaugural address of February 1862, Confederate President Jefferson Davis noted this imminence in recalling the origins of secession: "To save ourselves from a revolution which, in its silent but rapid progress, *was about to* place us under the despotism of numbers, . . . we determined to make a new association, composed of States homogenous in interest, in policy, and in feeling."[8] Faced with a future in which even the three-fifths clause and dominance of the Democratic Party were insufficient to offer slavery the security its adherents demanded, leaders in southern politics moved to dissolve the national compact and form their own nation. Formal politics had ceased to offer a means of adjudicating the sectional conflict.

BAPTIZED IN BLOOD
The Election of 1860 and the Sundering of the Union

The election of 1860 broke the system. That year posed the upstart Republicans in their second presidential outing against a Democratic Party that had been strongly proslavery for decades. The Democrats, though, confronted tectonic divisions. Years of pressure on the party's weak northern wing combined with the ever-growing stridency of its southern members to widen the gulf between the two regional factions. When in April 1860 the party convened in Charleston, South Carolina, to name a presidential nominee, the convention split. Deep South planters and southern "fire-eaters" demanded support for a federal slave code to permit slavery in all the territories, regardless of location. Instead, they had to swallow leading candidate Stephen Douglas, whose Freeport Doctrine sought to mollify northern opinion by suggesting that regardless of the Supreme Court's ruling in the Dred Scott case, the people of the territories could pass positive law banning slavery. The southerners walked out, held their own convention, and eventually nominated Kentucky's John C. Breckenridge, the Kentucky senator who had served as James Buchanan's vice president. Yet another party, the Constitutional Union Party, acted as heirs to the southern Whigs, nominating John Bell of Tennessee to run on a platform conspicuously silent on slavery.

The Republicans had the best of it. Though the smaller party, they enjoyed all the unity the Democrats lacked. As heirs to the Whigs, Republicans had a long lead on their rivals in reformulating a splintered party around the slavery issue. The Whig collapse had cost opponents of the Democrats several election cycles, during which the latter wreaked havoc on sectional comity through measures such as the Ostend Manifesto and the Kansas-Nebraska Act. A situation of one-party dominance would never stand long, and northern outrage over Democratic policies ensured it. By 1860, the Republican Party had become a strong contender for national power. Though clearly sectional, the section it sought to represent composed the bulk of the country's free population, 69 percent in total.[9] The party had honed its appeal, relying on all the experience gleaned in two decades of political antislavery. Meanwhile, the Democrats had weathered the storms of the 1850s intact, only to confront a sectional reckoning that badly split the party as the 1860 presidential election loomed.

The Republicans, running against a divided Democratic opposition, faced a situation far more favorable than any sectional startup party had a right to. The novel quality of the 1860 election—it consisted of two distinct two-party races, one in the South and one in the North—made it unlikely that the victor would need a majority of the popular vote. The rules of the game dictated that the winning party would need only a majority of votes in the Electoral College to capture the White House. In 1860, that magic number was 152, just over half of the total of 303 electoral votes available. The math wound up being inexorable. The free states simply controlled a majority of these votes—183 in total. In a sectional contest of North versus South, the party representing a united North could not lose. The southern states, which had long exercised disproportionate control over the federal government, had always relied on their domination of a national party—the Democrats—to buttress their minority position. The sectional divide within the party obviated this, leaving the region on its own. Even had a single candidate, such as Breckenridge, taken all slaveholding states, he would still have lacked the necessary majority in the Electoral College to win the presidency. Even if such a candidate had taken the new western states of California and Oregon, he would not have had enough. Given a united and popular Republican Party, the Democratic split doomed the slave power. For the first time since the days of John Quincy Adams, it would not be able to count on a friend in the White House.

Though dividing the Democratic Party amounted to self-immolation, the southern "fire-eaters" who favored disunion had hoped for just such a result. Certainly, the election to the presidency of a candidate whose name had not even appeared on the ballot in many southern states inflamed talk of secession. "How can the South be saved from injury if the Republican party succeeds in the coming Presidential election?" asked South Carolina Congressman Lawrence Keitt. "*I answer only by dissolving the Government immediately.* If this party succeeds, *loyalty to the Union will be treason to the South.*"[10] Newspaper editors throughout the South railed of impending doom. "Black Republicans" in power would now be free to encourage racial amalgamation in the South, and foment slave insurrection through the mails.[11] Though moderate voices in both sections cautioned against courting the perils of civil war, many in both sections were becoming consigned to a final showdown. "No one can dread war more than I do," wrote Frances Seward, the wife of the antislavery senator from New York. "Yet I could not to day assent to the perpetuation or extension of slavery to prevent war."[12] In October 1860, *DeBow's Review*, the voice of southern conservatism, declared that "war is not the only, nor is it the greatest evil to which a people can be subjected"; it was preferable to "dishonor" and "a perpetual sense of insecurity." History demonstrated "that liberty can only be won and maintained at the costly sacrifice of human life," for "no great political principle has ever been achieved except by the baptism of blood."[13]

For many in the South, Lincoln's success at the ballot box merely confirmed the need to secede. Having won a plurality of the popular vote with the lowest successful total in American history (39.6 percent), he had been rejected by the national majority. His northern rival Stephen Douglas had polled well in the southern counties of Illinois and Indiana, but the only state he captured outright was Missouri, which duly conferred its nine electoral votes on the Little Giant. New Jersey, which split its electoral vote, gave him three to Lincoln's four. Lincoln won a clear majority in the Electoral College, garnering 28 more votes than the 152 necessary for a majority, for a total of 180. The Democratic split sealed Douglas's fate. Lacking the 18 percent of the popular vote that went to southern Democrat John Breckenridge, Douglas's 30 percent landed him in last place in the four-way electoral race.

Fire-eaters in the South moved quickly. On December 20, 1860, a special convention met in South Carolina to unanimously approve secession from the Union. In January, Mississippi, Florida, Alabama, Georgia, and Louisiana followed. Texas seceded on February 1, and shortly after representatives from these seven states met in Montgomery, Alabama, to adopt a constitution for the new Confederate States of America. Southern congressmen and senators resigned their seats, many to take up positions in a new Confederate government. Bypassing a popular election, delegates from the seceding states quickly chose Jefferson Davis, the experienced former senator from Mississippi, as president, and named Alexander Stephens, a former representative from Georgia, vice president.

Any doubts that southern leaders fled the Union to protect their interests in slavery were roundly belied by the declarations the secessionists themselves crafted to justify their departure. Mississippi disunionists declared forthrightly, "our position is thoroughly identified with the institution of slavery."[14] Others rehearsed the growth of antislavery agitation, culminating in the election to the presidency of Lincoln—a candidate whose avowed purpose, Georgia declared, "is to subvert our society and subject us not only to the loss of our property but the destruction of ourselves, our wives, and our children, and the desolation of our homes, our altars, and our firesides."[15] South Carolina seceded because a party had come to power which, it charged, had declared "that a war must be waged against slavery until it shall cease throughout the United States."[16] Many baldly expressed the white supremacist underpinnings of the social orders they sought to safeguard. Texas, for example, seceded to protect the "beneficent and patriarchal system of African slavery" against those "proclaiming the debasing doctrine of equality of all men, irrespective of race or color—a doctrine at war with nature, in opposition to the experience of mankind, and in violation of the plainest revelations of Divine Law."[17]

The Confederate Constitution itself, which was adopted in March 1861, differed from the U.S. Constitution largely in its overt protections of slavery. Whereas the Framers of the U.S. Constitution had assiduously eschewed direct references to chattel bondage, the new document used the term repeatedly and boldly: "No bill of attainder, ex post facto law, or law denying or impairing the right of property in negro slaves shall be passed," it declared. The Confederate Constitution overtly protected the right to slave property in the territories, and permitted the importation of bondspersons from slave states still in the United States. Tellingly, it retained the three-fifths clause, thus ensuring slaveholders' dominance over nonslaveholders even within the Confederacy.[18] Confederate Vice President Alexander Stephens removed any questions about the racial bases of the new nation in a speech given in March 1861. Recalling a history that stretched back to the Founders, Stephens highlighted the ambivalence of the Framers, who had worried that "the enslavement of the African was in violation of the laws of nature." As a consequence, the Founders had bequeathed future generations an ambivalent legacy that had created "agitating questions" that eventually had ruptured the Union. The U.S. Constitution had incorporated slavery into the nation as a necessary evil. "Our new Government is founded upon exactly the opposite ideas," Stephens explained. "Its foundations are laid, its cornerstone rests, upon the great truth that the negro is not equal to the white man; that slavery, subordination to the superior race, is his natural and normal condition."[19]

The establishment of a new Confederate nation, even on such execrable principles, did not in itself trigger war. Some in the North favored the departure of the slave states. Winfield Scott, the highest ranking general in the U.S. army, suggested telling the seceded states, "*Wayward Sisters, depart in peace!*"[20] Antislavery editor Horace Greeley picked up this formulation, repeating it in the leaves of his *Tribune* in November 1860. Notable antislavery activists, such as Wendell Phillips, adopted this position as well. Garrison, long a disunionist, wondered "whether the Union, under any such circumstances as we have been compelled to behold it, is after all, so valuable a boon and worthy of so great sacrifice."[21]

Throughout the secession winter of 1860 to 1861, though, moderate politicians North and South urgently sought compromise measures that would avert both secession and war. Kentucky Senator John C. Crittenden sponsored the

most credible of these, a proposal for six constitutional amendments and a series of congressional resolutions designed to placate the South by assuring that
slavery would be protected in the states and territories. The line of the Missouri
Compromise prohibiting slavery north of the thirty-six degrees, thirty minutes
parallel would be extended to all western territories. The federal government
could not prohibit slavery in its jurisdiction, including the District of Columbia,
and Congress could not interfere with the domestic slave trade. Strict new fugitive slave provisions would punish those who helped bondspersons escape. Finally, in a novel gesture, none of these provisions, enacted as amendments to the
Constitution, could themselves be amended, thus ensuring the legality of slavery
in perpetuity. Throughout December 1860 Congress debated these compromises,
but in the end both houses rejected them. With little to offer the free states
except a temporary halt to disunion, the bargain was no Compromise of 1850.
Similar proposals for constitutional amendments that would prohibit Congress
from amending the Constitution to "abolish or interfere" with slavery also failed
to gain momentum. So, too, stalled a peace effort launched in February 1861,
during which a special committee of Congress struggled toward compromise.
The Senate rejected its frantically composed results, which, like the Crittenden
measures, sought primarily to extend the Missouri Compromise line westward.

Lincoln, not yet president, discounted such efforts. As he wrote to a colleague
in the midst of the secession crisis, "We have just carried an election on principles fairly stated to the people. Now we are told in advance the government
shall be broken up unless we surrender to those we have beaten, before we take
the offices." He accused secessionists of "extorting a compromise" with threats of
disunion. "If we surrender," he wrote, "it is the end of us and of the government.
They will repeat the experiment upon us *ad libidium*. A year will not pass till we
shall have to take Cuba as a condition upon which they will stay in the Union."[22]
Lincoln would opt for war with the secessionists over extorted conciliation. "Entertain no compromise in regard to the extension of slavery," he instructed a Republican negotiator during the secession crisis. "The tug has to come," Lincoln
wrote; "better now than later."[23]

The tug did indeed come, over the issue of federal property—post offices,
arsenals, military outposts—steadily falling into the hands of the southern states
surrounding them. Only a few opportunities to defend federal territory in the
South presented themselves—notably Fort Pickens in Pensacola, Florida, and
Fort Sumter in the harbor of Charleston, South Carolina—and these bedeviled
the president-elect. Should Union forces fire the first shots of the war, even in
defense of federal property, a critical psychological and moral advantage would
be lost. Yet to concede defensible military posts to the secessionists would signal
the weakness of the new government at its most critical moment. It might even

inspire the eight slave states as yet still in the Union to join the Confederacy. The problem remained as Lincoln addressed the nation at his inauguration on March 4, 1861. As president, he would, if possible, place the onus for initiating hostilities on the Confederacy. "In your hands, my dissatisfied fellow-countrymen, and not in mine, is the momentous issue of civil war," he told the seceded states. "You can have no conflict without being yourselves the aggressors."[24] But with the forts blockaded and supplies failing, Lincoln had few options. He cleverly chose to resupply Sumter by sea without the use of arms, a move that sparked Confederate aggression. On April 12, Confederate guns began bombarding the fort, firing the first shots of the war. The next day, Sumter surrendered without a fatality. Georgia Senator Robert Toombs considered the attack on Sumter very poorly advised: "It is unnecessary; it puts us in the wrong; it is fatal."[25] Despite this, four more slaveholding states—Virginia, Arkansas, North Carolina, and Tennessee— quickly joined the Confederacy, citing Lincoln's "inhuman design" to "coerce any State that had seceded from the old Union" to return.[26]

But the Confederate firing on Fort Sumter ratified the Union's commitment to war. Lincoln quickly called for seventy-five thousand volunteers, to put down "combinations too powerful to be suppressed by the ordinary course of judicial proceedings"—a phrase he hoped would avoid the implication that the Union contended with a legitimate enemy state.[27] Under Lincoln's leadership, Union political leaders, and ultimately the Union public, did not permit the seceding states to leave. Many Republicans argued that the Union was inviolable, but the case was not entirely clear. Even Lincoln acknowledged the "most sacred right" of revolution, which American Founding Fathers had invoked to justify the War for Independence. But while this could be a "moral right," Lincoln declared that it was "never a legal right."[28] Rather, as he argued in his first inaugural address, "the central idea of secession is the essence of anarchy." This was the new president's own version of the "baptism by blood" argument: the states might secede, but only through illegal or treasonous action, the ultimate legitimacy of which could be confirmed only by a successful contest of arms. That so many among the northern public acceded to this view is testimony to the depths to which anti-slavery-related notions had permeated American nationalism. For those raised on two generations of the slave power argument, secession seemed to be the South's final attempt to preserve a social order built on tyranny.

Secession repudiated the democratic tradition as many northerners understood it. For Republican leaders and the sizable portion of the northern electorate that followed them, it represented the triumph of tyranny over a civil religion built on liberty, and reversing it constituted a national mission. A meeting of Chicago Unionists declared that the United States had been assigned by Providence "the high and important mission of working out the great idea of national self-government." It should not shirk from demonstrating "that the people in their collective majority are sufficient without the aid of titled monarchs or standing armies to maintain their own government against every treasonable conspiracy for its destruction." The Philadelphia *Public Ledger* announced that a "great fundamental principle of republican Government" hung in the balance— "the right of the majority to rule." The looming war would "prove to the world, that the free Democratic spirit which established the government, is equal to its protection and its maintenance."[29] Young men themselves testified to this underlying conception of the war's purpose as they rushed to join the Union army. One Indiana youth enlisted "to aid my country in her desperate struggle against oppression and slavery, against Rebels and Traitors." Even when slavery itself was not the target of volunteers' ire, the undermining of liberty that slave society represented was. "This contest is not the North against the South," wrote another Union recruit, "it is government against anarchy, law against disorder."[30] For many northerners, nothing less than the fate of democracy was at stake. Lincoln codified the notion in a message to Congress delivered that July. The Union war was "a struggle for maintaining in the world that form and substance of government whose leading object is to elevate the condition of men." Its purpose was to teach "men that what they cannot take by an election, neither can they take it by war."[31] The president refined this message nearly three years later in the Gettysburg Address, terming the war a test of whether "government of the people, by the people, for the people, shall not perish from the earth." For now, to defend such principles, the Union would fight.

POLITICS BY OTHER MEANS
Grand Strategy in the Civil War

War, the Prussian military theorist Carl von Clausewitz famously declared, is but the pursuit of politics through other means.[32] During the Napoleonic Wars that Clausewitz witnessed in the early nineteenth century, European nation-states pursued war as one of many instruments of statecraft. Just as diplomacy and trade policy were subordinated to the interests of state, so too could be military action or its threat. Warfare, then, served as one of many tools of "policy," albeit one with its own distinct internal logic and self-generating imperatives. This formulation is particularly useful in thinking about the American Civil War, which clearly began as a consequence of the breakdown of the formal political system that had kept the Union intact since 1787. Political leaders of the seceding states resolved that continued participation in the political union with nonslaveholding states no longer served their interests, and sundered the Union; political leaders of the remaining states and the national government refused to accept this. Lincoln recalled it this way in his second inaugural address in 1865: "Both parties deprecated war, but one of them would *make* war rather than let the nation survive, and the other would *accept* war rather than let it perish, and the war came."[33]

Clausewitz's dictum does not mean that once war began, "politics," or non-violent forms of contest, stopped. As Mao Tse-tung famously reformulated the great Prussian's dictum, "politics is war without bloodshed while war is politics with bloodshed."[34] Warfare and formal politics continued to operate within a broader realm of activities that influenced relations between states and within them.[35] These included warfare, of course, but also nonviolent interactions such as diplomacy, which might continue even through the course of a war. Like-wise, each combatant state continued its own course of domestic politics, as established by constitution and law. Even less formal manifestations of political contest persisted, such as the processes of public debate that deeply inform the operations of government (scholars speak of discussions in the "public sphere," for example), or even the latent attitudes that informed popular understandings of good and bad governance (often termed "political culture"). Once war starts, then, politics in its myriad forms does not stop. A war more or less successfully waged on the battlefield might be stymied by domestic politics, as happened to the United States during the Vietnam War. Conversely, an unsuccessfully fought war might lead to domestic upheaval, as happened to Russia at the end of World War I. The Civil War was no exception to this general rule that war is never solely a matter of events on the battlefield. Warfare and other forms of politics—both the internal politics of each combatant state as well as the nonmilitary political struggle between those two states—remained active and dynamically linked.

Military operations in the Civil War remained subordinated to these broader questions of the political goals of the Union, the Confederacy, and their member states. Appreciating the shifting context of strategic imperatives helps us understand the remarkable relationship that unfolded between war and emancipation. Each side in the contest had distinct, asymmetrical goals, which each hoped war might abet. Because the Confederacy entertained war as a means of protecting its independence, it enjoyed all the benefits of the defender. Its soldiers would be fighting on and for native soil, and its forces would profit from shorter distances in bringing resources to bear in its defense. Most important, the Confederacy did not have to take the strategic initiative, for if neither side did a thing, Confederate independence would become a reality. Time would reify the autonomy of the new state. Leading world powers would recognize the Confederacy as a sovereign entity, and secession would triumph. In contrast, the Union had the formidable goal of crossing onto Confederate soil and using force of arms to compel the seceded states back into the Union. This would require attacking across a border some twelve hundred miles wide, filled with a white population largely determined to resist invasion of its homeland. Furthermore, the end point in the Union struggle would be difficult to define: the destruction of the Confederate capacity to make war might end formal hostilities, but the imposition of Union rule over a recalcitrant population would test the Union's claims to being a democratic republic ruled by the consent of the governed. The contest between Union and Confederacy was thus no chess match, with both sides striving for an identical victory condition. A Confederate victory required far less than a Union one.

Offsetting the Confederacy's lower threshold for victory, though, was the Union's vast advantage in material. In this sense, too, the Civil War was no chess match, with each side possessing identical forces. As a nascent industrial society, the Union far exceeded the largely agricultural Confederacy in its capacity to finance, build, and equip a modern army. The Union was simply wealthier, possessing a greater than fourfold advantage in bank deposits, twelvefold advantage in bank capital, ninefold advantage in capital investment, elevenfold advantage in the value of manufactured goods, and sixfold advantage in manufacturing establishments. It benefitted from 12 times more industrial workers as the Confederacy, 2.4 times more miles of railroad track, 16 times more shipping tonnage, 26 times more pig iron, and 21 times more coal. The value of the firearms it produced exceeded the Confederacy's 31 times over. These numbers demonstrated the might of new forms of industrial capital over older forms of plantation-based wealth.

Only in agricultural production could the Confederacy compete, but it still produced less than half the Union's corn, wheat, and draft animals. Only in the cash crops of the slave economy did it enjoy clear advantages. In 1860, the Confederacy's 5.3 million bales of cotton dwarfed the Union's paltry 43,000.[36] Many agreed with South Carolina Senator James Henry Hammond, who in 1858 had argued that cotton's critical role in the textile manufacturing process offered the South an enormous strategic asset in the event of a clash with the North. Countries dependent on southern cotton, such as England, "dare not make war on cotton. No power on earth dares to make war upon it. Cotton is king."[37] In any military clash between North and South, English "Lords of the Loom" would support the southern "Lords of the Lash" on whom they depended. Britain and its powerful navy would enter the war on behalf of the Confederacy, just as France had supported the independence of the colonies during the Revolution. This faith proved to be misplaced. Union blockades of the Confederacy did in fact imperil the flow of cotton to Britain, but cotton plantations were not like factories, which required extensive long-term investment to create. During the war, Britain's Egyptian and Indian colonies increased cotton production to make up for much of the loss. No agricultural product, not even one as central to industrialization as cotton, could replace factories themselves as a strategic asset.

Of all the material advantages the Union enjoyed, however, raw manpower would prove the most decisive. Here, too, the Union possessed a notable lead, with a 2.5 to 1 advantage in total population and a 4.2 to 1 lead in free white men in the prime years of military service. In any long war of attrition, the Union's enormous superiority in raw numbers would tell. The manpower question had yet another dimension, though. As Clausewitz had noted, the loyalty of the people themselves constituted a critical strategic resource for war—and one that deeply shaped the course of events during the Civil War. The citizenry, after all, supplied the labor that produced arms and supported armies, and it constituted the pool from which soldiers could be drawn. Most important, people provided the political assent necessary for a state to continue making war. This was so even in authoritarian societies, where a population disaffected by the sacrifices necessary of long and destructive wars could pressure a state to end its war making, or even cause the state to collapse. In a highly democratic society such as the United States, where formal processes of electoral politics remained in force throughout the entire war in both the Union and the Confederacy, popular support for war making mattered enormously. The Civil War, then, became a contest not simply of arms, but of the popular wills of each combatant nation—"a People's contest," as Lincoln put it.[38] The state most capable of mobilizing popular support would possess a valuable advantage.

On this score, both combatants began with high but hardly unanimous degrees of popular enthusiasm for the war effort. The true test would come only in the event of a protracted struggle requiring great sacrifice. Would the bulk of the southern white population continue to support a war fought largely on behalf of a minority of slaveholders? Would the northern public continue to support a costly battle against an opponent merely seeking liberty and independence, or one that had become a struggle to liberate a despised race? In each section, political leaders confronted the challenge of divining the unknowable threshold of sacrifice that would determine the point at which the state could no longer rally its public to support the war effort. Domestic politics would be as important as battlefield clashes between enemy states.

Lincoln began the war deftly intuiting these considerations. The Republicans had won a fair political contest, and Lincoln was not about to relinquish that victory by conceding to secessionist blackmail. He would entertain the prospect of war with the slave power instead. But he also understood that the popular will that had elevated his party to power was deeply ambivalent on the issue of slavery itself. It was one thing to struggle politically against the expansion of the slave power into the territories or the incursions of southern "justice" into the freedoms of northerners; it was quite another to wage an actual armed struggle to destroy slavery where it had long existed. Lincoln's electoral victory had hardly constituted a mandate for war. He confronted an electorate enthused to chasten traitors and secessionists, but ambivalent on the question of slavery itself. Northern public opinion, so deeply rooted in white supremacy, simply did not support emancipation as a war aim.

This did not, though, prevent black activists and white abolitionists from excoriating Lincoln for what they viewed as a lost opportunity to stand boldly for freedom. The war began as a war for union, William Lloyd Garrison conceded in May 1861, but little had been said of slavery. "Why overlook *the cause of all this?*" he asked. "If this war shall put an end to that execrable system, it will be more glorious in history than that of the Revolution. If it shall leave it unscathed, . . . there will be nothing to look for but heavier judgments and an irrevocable doom!"[39] Union leaders' decision to exclude African Americans from joining the fight as soldiers drew the particular ire of African American activists. "We are fully aware that there is no more soul in the present administration on the great moral issues involved in the slavery question and the present war, than has characterized previous administrations," conceded Philadelphia black activist Alfred M. Green. But that only taught "the necessity of making ourselves felt as a people at this extremity of our national government worthy of consideration and of being recognized as a part of its own strength."[40]

Lincoln, though, envisioned matters quite differently in 1861. His grandest hope was that Confederate political leaders had beguiled whites in the southern states into supporting secession; if he prosecuted the war firmly but lightly, he might capitalize on latent unionism throughout the South. The southern public would see the folly of secession, and return to the Union fold on generous terms. Slaveholders might keep their slaves, along with their country. Of greatest concern to Lincoln was the fate of the four slaveholding states of the upper South that yet remained in the Union. Those four—Delaware, Kentucky, Maryland, and Missouri—contained one-third of the free population of the South, and the bulk of its industry.[41] Moreover, the presence of slaveholding states in the Union shored up Union claims that disunion, rather than abolition, impelled the conflict. The retention of border-state loyalty thus dominated Lincoln's calculations. When approached early in the war by clergymen suggesting that a policy of emancipation would yield divine favor for the Union cause, the president demurred, fearing that such a move would cost him the loyalty of the slave states still in the Union. "I hope to have God on my side," he reportedly said, "but I must have Kentucky."[42] Retaining the loyalty of these states comprised Lincoln's most formidable task. Precipitous or overly aggressive prosecution of the war might cause these wavering states to join the Confederacy, but too soft a touch would cause Lincoln to appear weak, threaten his standing among the "radical" antislavery Republicans in his own party, and undermine his role of reuniting the Union.

WARFARE BY OTHER MEANS
The Evolution of an Emancipation Policy

While black activists and white abolitionists approached the war with cautious hopes that the conflict between the states might become a war for liberty, most in government began it of Lincoln's mind. Union commanders in the field received instructions to tread lightly on slaveholders wherever they were encountered. In June 1861, mere days after the Union's ignominious defeat in the first significant battle of the war at Bull Run in Virginia, both houses of Congress resolved that the Union would not wage war "in any spirit of oppression, nor for any purpose of conquest or subjugation, nor purpose of overthrowing or interfering with the rights or established institutions" of the seceded states, but only "to defend and maintain the supremacy of the Constitution, and to preserve the Union."[43] As late as July 1862, a full year into the conflict, George B. McClellan, commander of the Union Army of the Potomac, sought to sway Lincoln against those seeking to prosecute the war more vigorously. "It should not be a War looking to the subjugation of the people of any state," he lectured his commander in chief, but one waged only "against armed forces and political organizations." Most important, McClellan wrote, chattel bondage should not be disturbed. "Neither confiscation of property, political executions of persons, territorial organization of states or forcible abolition of slavery should be contemplated for a moment."[44] For many important Union officials, then, slavery's destruction figured lowly if at all on the wartime agenda. That very August, Lincoln himself publicly responded to abolitionist criticisms that he moved too slowly against the institution. The antislavery editor Horace Greeley, in a public letter printed in his widely read New York *Tribune*, had complained that Lincoln had taken to heart "timid counsels." The president's deference to slaveholders' property rights had led him to underappreciate how much a blow against bondage would strike at the rebellion, the editor charged. Lincoln's famous reply clarified his priorities: "I would save the Union," he stated plainly, "in the shortest way under the Constitution." This would offer the best chance to restore "the Union as it was." Would slavery then persist? He continued,

> My paramount object in this struggle is to save the Union, and is not either
> to save or to destroy slavery. If I could save the Union without freeing any

slave I would do it, and if I could save it by freeing all slaves I would do it; and if I could save it by freeing some and leaving others alone I would also do that. What I do about slavery, and the colored race, I do because I believe it helps to save the Union; and what I forbear, I forbear because I don't believe it would help to save the Union.[45]

At the time he crafted this reply, however, Lincoln had already decided on a momentous move that would transform both the war and slavery. The measure he had resolved to implement—a sweeping proclamation that would free slaves in rebel-held territories—had been unthinkable at the war's start. That it had become possible owed largely to two factors. The first of these was the failure of the battlefield to yield a series of decisive Union victories that could reverse secession. Early in the war, poor Union commanders in the critical eastern theater of the war failed to leverage their advantages in men and materiel into decisive victories.

More broadly, though, responsibility lay with technological innovations caused by the industrial revolution. The soldiers who fought in the Civil War were armed with weapons unknown at the time of the Mexican-American War. Technological developments in the 1850s had outpaced battle tactics developed for Napoleonic era armaments. A new infantry weapon appeared: the rifled musket, employing a closed ignition system relying on a percussion cap and firing a conical lead bullet known as a Minié ball. These innovations increased the range and accuracy of firearms by several times and reduced misfire rates by two orders of magnitude.[46] The new rifled musket lent an enormous advantage to the defense, with devastating implications. A half century earlier, aggressive commanders could soften an enemy position with artillery and then charge it with massed cavalry or infantry columns. Napoléon had used such tactics to bring almost every continental power to its knees through decisive battle. By the 1860s, though, it had become much, much more difficult to cross open ground and deliver the shock attack that routed enemies and delivered clear victory. Firearms accounted for up to 90 percent of all Civil War deaths—far more than the artillery fire or saber cuts that had taken so many in Napoléon's time.

Death rates climbed. Casualty rates in major Civil War battles often topped 20 or even 25 percent, with little difference distinguishing winner from loser. The Civil War remains the most lethal conflict American armies have ever endured. For every thousand Union troops, 21.3 were killed in action; in comparison, 12 per thousand were killed in action during World War I, the most destructive industrial war for frontline soldiers in history.[47] In fact, the Civil War developed battlefields that looked much more like the Somme than Leipzig. With troops in constant contact, soldiers built trenches to protect themselves, which only enhanced the defense all the more.[48] Recently, demographic historian J. David Hacker has upwardly revised the Civil War's horrendous death toll of 618,000—already more numerous than American losses in any other war—to between 752,000 and 851,000.[49]

Despite enormously high casualty rates, decisive victories that broke the strategic deadlock were virtually impossible to achieve. In July 1861, Confederate victory at the First Battle of Bull Run demonstrated that the seceded states would not quickly yield to the pressure of northern numbers and industry. Bloody Union defeats at battles such as Second Bull Run and costly Union victories like those at Shiloh and Antietam demonstrated that technological advances in weaponry had rendered the battlefield a source of stalemate. War, the very purpose of which was to resolve contests unresolvable by nonviolent political means, could not perform its function. The high human price of victory loosened restraints on many Union commanders' prosecution of the war. Before his costly victory at Shiloh in April 1862, Union General Ulysses S. Grant had vowed "to protect the property of the citizens whose territory was invaded"; after, he determined "to consume everything that could be used to support or supply armies."[50] Long-standing constraints on military behavior, informed by respect for Fifth Amendment protections of property and driven by the Union's grand strategy of courting the loyalty of border states Unionists in the Confederacy, gave way to the need to escalate the means used to fight the war. Both sides would steadily do this, despite the high political costs of instituting unpopular measures such as conscription. The transformation of the conflict from a Napoleonic-style war of maneuver into an industrial war of attrition created incentives for finding new mechanisms for prosecuting the war.

The enslaved themselves helped offer a solution to breaking the stalemate. Through patterns of mass flight, the behavior of bondspersons relentlessly intruded into Union policy, helping to force mass emancipation on the agenda. From the very earliest days of the war, African Americans in the South demonstrated that they were not property, lacking agency and will. In March 1861, with federal forces struggling to hold a few last strongholds in the South, twelve slave fugitives fled to Fort Pickens, seeking refuge. According to an astonished Union officer at the scene, they arrived "entertaining the idea that we were placed here to protect them and grant them their freedom."[51] In much the same way that West Indian slaves had interpreted metropolitan moves toward amelioration, or rebellious slaves in Richmond and Charleston had believed contemporary radicalism offered exploitable opportunities for their own struggle for liberty, so too the enslaved in the Civil War South stayed closely attuned to the opportunities afforded by the political circumstances surrounding them. By using escape to register their desire for liberty, enslaved blacks challenged the Union government to formulate policies that effectively degraded slavery.

The first critical moment occurred in May 1861, when General Benjamin Butler, the commander of the Union-held Fortress Monroe on Virginia's Atlantic coast, received into his lines a number of slaves who had fled from nearby Confederate forces, where they had been put to work building earthworks and fortifications. Despite the administration's direction to treat slave property with care, Butler "determined to employ . . . the able-bodied persons in the party" for his own purposes. "As a military measure," Butler suggested to his superiors, "it would seem to be a measure of necessity to deprive their masters of their services."[52] By thus declaring slaves used in aid of the rebellion "contraband of war" akin to interdicted arms or animals—the slaves themselves quickly became known simply as "contrabands"[53]—Butler had found a way for Union forces to capitalize on slaves' initiative. He did so at the cost of treating humans as property, and the Lincoln administration was slow to adopt a general policy, but Butler's actions signaled a pattern that would bedevil efforts to keep slavery out of the war. Union officers in the field clearly saw the trend. As Charles Harvey Brewster of the Tenth Massachusetts wrote in November 1861, "This war is playing the Dickens with slavery and if it lasts much longer will clear our Country's name of the vile stain and enable us to live in peace hereafter."[54]

The growing difficulties of fighting a stalemated war placed a premium on capitalizing on the slaves' willingness to work and fight against the Confederacy. From initially seeking to exclude runaway slaves from Union lines—in Kentucky, General William T. Sherman considered welcoming fugitives a policy "by which Union men are estranged from our Cause"[55]—the Union army gradually began to accept runaways as a practical necessity. Initially determined to uphold the Fugitive Slave Act, Union commanders in the field steadily began to figure slaves' military value into the calculus of war. Some overtook the slow evolution of the administration's resolve. On August 30, 1861, General John C. Frémont, the former Republican presidential nominee now in command of the Western Department of the Union army, declared martial law in Missouri in response to widespread guerrilla warfare. Frémont's order confiscated the property of those in arms against the government, and declared their slaves "free men."[56] Lincoln rescinded the order, fearful that such a drastic measure would cost him support in the critical border states. Kentucky, which had declared a fragile neutrality, particularly concerned him. "I think to lose Kentucky is nearly the same as to lose the whole game," the president fretted.[57]

Yet eventually, as Union armies began conquering Confederate territories in the plantation zone, slaves found themselves behind Union lines without ever having moved. Such was the case in May 1862, when General David Hunter, who oversaw Union efforts in the southeastern states, declared slavery "incompatible" with martial law, and ordered that slaves in Georgia, Florida, and South Carolina would be "forever free."[58] An avowed antislavery man, Hunter began enlisting freed slaves into a special regiment. Again, Lincoln immediately rescinded the move as too sweeping. Declaring publicly that only he, as president, had the power to emancipate slaves, Lincoln promised to do so only should it "become a necessity indispensable to the maintenance of the Government."[59]

Yet if the administration appeared to dawdle, Congress also had the power to affect slavery. While Lincoln's administration wrestled with conflicting strategic imperatives, Congress, now purged by secession of its proslavery members, moved more decisively. As soon as Fort Sumter had been fired on, Massachusetts Senator Charles Sumner, still recovering from the caning incident of 1856, advised Lincoln that "under the war power the right had come to him to emancipate the slaves."[60] It did not take long for antislavery congressmen to register the problem of slave refugees in the field. In July 1861, the House resolved that "it is no part of the duty of the soldiers of the United States to capture and return fugitive slaves."[61] The same month, Congress passed the First Confiscation Act, which authorized the army to seize slave property used in support of the rebellion.[62] A year later, with Union forces reeling from McClellan's failed campaign to take the Confederate capital of Richmond, Virginia, from the southeast, Congress passed two more pieces of legislation designed to capitalize on slaves' initiative: the Second Confiscation and the Militia Acts. Whereas the First Confiscation Act had affected only those slaves employed in the Confederate war effort, and perversely made the Union army their new owners, the Second targeted slaves of all openly disloyal masters now behind Union lines, declaring them "captives of war" who "shall be forever free of their servitude." It also authorized the president to use "persons of African descent" in any way necessary to suppress the rebellion.[63] Along with the Militia Act, which authorized the army's use of African Americans as laborers and soldiers, formally freeing them and their families, this measure accelerated the transformation of U.S. policy. In the spring, Congress had already passed bills forbidding Union officers from returning fugitive slaves to their masters, ending slavery in the District of Columbia with compensation to their owners, and prohibiting slavery in the territories.[64] These measures offered logical responses to the problem of battlefield stalemate. If war could not effectively pursue politics through other means, perhaps politics—particularly the politics of slavery—could be made to more effectively prosecute war.

Slowly, Lincoln came around, impelled by growing frustration with the border states' hesitation to adopt emancipation measures of their own. Sensing the pressure wartime demands were placing on slavery, he time and again offered graceful exits to the slaveholding four. In the fall of 1861, he sought to make Delaware a precedent, offering a generous plan for compensated, gradual emancipation of the state's mere eighteen hundred slaves. "If I can get this plan started in Delaware I have no fear but that all the other border states will accept it," he told representative George Fisher.[65] Delaware, though, did not bite. In March 1862, Lincoln sought to broaden the plan, successfully requesting Congress to compensate slave owners in border states that adopted their own plans for emancipation. Again, he found no takers. In May, he repeated his appeal, beseeching the Union border states to embrace the offer of compensated manumission.[66] And in July, he once more advised the border states to take the offer, warning them that if they did not avail themselves of the opportunity, the mere "friction and abrasion" of war might deprive them of their slaves before a compensation plan could be formulated.[67]

State-initiated emancipation offered two advantages to Lincoln. First, it would place the onus of liberation on the states themselves, where the right to abolish slavery resided, and thus avoid burdening the office of the Executive with the troublesome question of the limits of its war powers. Lincoln well understood that, exigencies of war or not, the maintenance of democratic assent for the conflict demanded that he operate, whenever possible, within the bounds of the Constitution. He had already suspended the writ of habeas corpus in order to more effectively prosecute spies and traitors in the North, a move that had widely earned him criticism from the opposition press. "Abraham Lincoln," charged the Democratic *Daily Age*, "aspires to greater power than was claimed by [British King] George, the Tyrant, and has already violated, with even more ruthless hand, the very dearest of those rights for which our ancestors fought."[68] In 1864, Lincoln worried that overweening exercise of his war powers on the slavery question would place him on the "boundless field of absolutism." He asked his treasury secretary, "Would not many of our own friends shrink away appalled? Would it not lose us the elections, and with them, the very cause we seek to advance?"[69] In addition to protecting him against charges of aggrandizing the power of the Executive, state-initiated abolition would also achieve Lincoln's most fervent wish, by securing forever the border states for the Union cause. Had the states adopted emancipation plans, he admonished them in July, "the war would now be substantially ended," for the prospect of their unification with the Confederate states would have been obviated. "But you cannot divest them of their hope to ultimately have you join them so long as you show a determination to perpetuate the institution within your own states." He hoped the Union slave states would "break that lever before their faces," and end Confederates' hopes of the border states' defection.[70]

By the middle of the month, he had had enough of the reticence. McClellan's costly failure in the Peninsula Campaign in Virginia demonstrated the desperate need to find alternatives to the battlefield. Lincoln's insistence that Confederate states would return to the fold if treated gently, which had exhausted the patience of antislavery members of Congress, had to give way to a more forceful approach. "This government cannot much longer play a game in which it stakes all, and its enemies stake nothing," the president scolded a New York Democrat who requested leniency for Confederate slaveholders. "Those enemies must understand that they cannot experiment for ten years trying to destroy the government, and if they fail still come back into the Union unhurt."[71] In a July 13 carriage ride with two members of his cabinet, Lincoln revealed his intention to emancipate the slaves if "the Rebels did not cease to persist in their war on the Government and the Union." Lincoln had concluded that such a move was "a military necessity absolutely essential for the salvation of the Union." As he explained, "we must free the slaves or be ourselves subdued."[72] Meeting with his cabinet shortly thereafter, Lincoln announced that he had "determined to take some definitive steps in respect to military action and slavery."[73] The proclamation he proposed again offered financial assistance to any Union slave states embarking on a program of gradual emancipation. Then it veered into new terrain, announcing that on January 1, 1863, any slaves in territories still in rebellion "shall be then, thenceforward, and forever free." In the intervening hundred-day period, any Confederate state could avoid this fate simply by returning to the Union. Whereas Congress's Confiscation Acts had liberated slaves behind Union lines who had been used in support of the rebellion, Lincoln's measure would apply to those still in lands largely held by rebels.[74] Congress had determined to make slaves of rebels free; Lincoln made all slaveholders in Confederate territory rebels.

On January 1, 1863, Lincoln signed the final draft of the proclamation, as he had promised. Slaves in most Confederate territory became free, their liberty to be defended by military authorities. Instantly, the document liberated tens of thousands of enslaved African Americans in designated rebel territories under Union control.[75] For those as yet unaffected, the proclamation transformed Union forces, whose success would now make them armies of liberation, freeing slaves as they conquered new Confederate territory. More and more African Americans would gain their practical liberty. Gone was the presumption of slaveholders' rights in property; now the slaves' manpower could be marshaled by the United States, predicated on a promise of liberation for millions of enslaved people. This was a momentous change, constituting an instant, comprehensive, and elegant reformulation of Union war aims. With a stroke of his pen, Lincoln had transformed a war for union into a war against slavery.

The Emancipation Proclamation offered a stunning illustration of how the slaves themselves had altered the political calculus of war. The measure would have been unthinkable as a military gesture had not bound African Americans demonstrated their awareness of events around them, and exploited the opportunities these created for attaining liberty. As had been the case in other instances of Atlantic emancipation, the enslaved had intruded themselves into the political world of the free by enacting their desire for freedom through acts of flight and resistance. The unpredictable nature of war had amplified their actions, creating exigencies that pressured policymakers to imagine what shortly before had been unimaginable. The war served as the great catalyzer of emancipation—the novel component that gave new meaning to decades of steady agitation by slaves and abolitionists. The military situation, and in particular the Union's failure to parlay its enormous advantages in manpower and resources into rapid victory, created demands that only an audacious policy of abolition could meet. Lincoln told New York Judge Edwards Pierrepont that emancipation was his "last card" in the fight against the Confederacy; "I will play it and may win the trick."[76] The military trajectory of the Civil War thus dealt a grievous blow to slavery in the South, the most potent defender of chattel bondage in the world. The war itself had come because politics could not resolve disputes between the slaveholding and nonslaveholding states. But neither, the war proved, could the force of arms alone—at least, not in a time amenable to the political survival of the ruling Republican Party and perhaps the Union state. Other means were needed to prosecute the war, and emancipation became the most potent of these. If the war itself constituted the pursuit of policy by other means, emancipation constituted the pursuit of war by other means.

The conflict had not started as a war to end slavery, but it ended as such. Before the war, most white northerners expressed far more concern about the slave powers' depredations than about the equal rights of the enslaved, and the North's white supremacy remained robust throughout the conflict. Abolitionists championed the slaves' humanity, but in 1860, only the most sanguine of them dared prophesize that the cursed institution would end soon. Lincoln himself, who during the war did more than any other single person to advance the destruction of chattel bondage, could not imagine a quick end. When in 1858 he had spoken of putting slavery on a path of "ultimate extinction," he had meant that it might die not "in a day, nor in a year, nor in two years," but in "less than a hundred years."[77] But much changed in a few short but cataclysmic years, and in 1864 Lincoln conceded that events had moved beyond the capacity of anyone to predict or control. "The nation's condition is not what either party, or any man, devised or expected" before the war's start, he wrote.[78]

By the last year of the conflict, it was hard for anyone to imagine how slavery might survive. Lincoln meant to nail the coffin shut. The Union's real, if unsteady and costly, military successes propelled the Republican Party's victory in the 1864 elections, guaranteeing that abolition as a war policy would be sustained. Lincoln, concerned that the Supreme Court might ultimately declare the Emancipation Proclamation an unconstitutional exercise of his war powers, continued to press the Union border states to abolish slavery themselves. Even now they proved recalcitrant. In 1863, the entrance into the Union of the state of West Virginia, formed from Union-held territory in Virginia, toppled the first domino. Missouri and Maryland surrendered the institution next, but Kentucky and Delaware proved tardier even than the reconstructed states of Louisiana, Arkansas, and Tennessee, which abolished slavery as they returned to the Union fold. Lincoln, buoyed by electoral success in late 1864, vigorously lobbied Congress to toll the knell of slavery's final death in the Union by passing a constitutional amendment abolishing the institution entirely. On January 31, 1865, the House seconded the Senate's endorsement of the previous spring, and the measure went to the states. By May, the Confederacy had been defeated, and no longer existed as an independent state. The reconstructed governments of the former Confederate states considered the measure as they reentered the Union. When, in December, Georgia became the twenty-seventh state to ratify it, the Thirteenth Amendment became a part of the U.S. Constitution, declaring that "neither slavery nor involuntary servitude, except as a punishment for crime whereof the party shall have been duly convicted, shall exist within the United States, or any place subject to their jurisdiction." By then, the Confederate States had been defeated, and no longer existed as an independent entity. Slavery in the United States was dead.

To be sure, the process had not been easy. At the start of the war, public opinion would never have supported a policy of abolition. Only the lengthening of the conflict and its drastic escalation—Lincoln called it "this terrible war" in his second inaugural—made mass emancipation a viable political possibility. Of course, antislavery forces celebrated that it did, and pressed for more. "Such rejoicing I never before witnessed, cannons firing, people hugging and shaking hands, white people I mean, flags flying." Thus Frederick Douglass's son Charles excitedly reported to his father the mood in Washington following Congress's passage of the Thirteenth Amendment. "If only they will give us the elective franchise," he added.[79] Lincoln may have been too optimistic when he suggested that the northern public had been "educated into abolition" by the war, but the dramatic transformations wrought by the fighting had caused an important fraction to indeed come around, if slowly and incompletely.[80]

Yet the political wisdom of emancipation had long been in doubt. Union dissenters excoriated antislavery radical Republicans and the administration, convinced that a policy of abolition would derail efforts to keep the border states in the Union, embolden the rebels, and even cause widespread slave insurrection. "Your anti-slavery crusade adds to the rebel army day after day thousands of soldiers," Ohio Congressman Samuel Cox had lambasted the Radicals in Congress in June 1862. It would convert the war "into a St. Domingo-insurrection" by placing "the saber, the musket, and the torch in the hands of the enfranchised African."[81] The persistence of such voices suggested that whatever effect the war had wrought on northern opinion, fierce critics remained. Peace Democrats openly charged "King Lincoln" with "crushing out liberty and erecting a despotism."[82] When Union General Ambrose Burnside issued a general order forbidding Union dissenters' "habit of declaring sympathies for the enemy," authorities foolishly arrested one of the most vociferous of these "Copperheads," Clement Vallandigham of Ohio, who became a martyr to civil liberties, and fueled still more domestic dissent to the Republican administration. Days after the Emancipation Proclamation took effect, New York Governor Horatio Seymour labeled it bloody, barbarous, revolutionary, and unconstitutional.[83] For several days in July 1863, the streets of his state's largest city become the site of a civil war within a civil war, as working-class whites rose up to protest emancipation and forced conscription into the Union army. For four days rioting consumed New York City, during which time Irish immigrants and poor whites pointed their wrath over economic inequality at symbols of the African American community. Before Union troops could return from Gettysburg to quell the violence, the rioters had claimed the lives of at least a hundred black New Yorkers, destroyed shops and homes, and torched the Colored Orphan Asylum, displacing over two hundred black children.

The costs of emancipation, then, had been high, and remained so. In the summer of 1864, with Union forces stalled outside of Petersburg and Atlanta, Republicans reformulated their ticket for the upcoming elections in November. They faced a Democratic opposition led by ousted Union general George B. McClellan, whose popularity owed to widespread war weariness and opposition to emancipation. So certain was Lincoln in his impending defeat that he had asked his cabinet members to sign an oath supporting McClellan should he win, vowing to help "save the Union" for the remainder of their time in office.[84] To avoid association with their radical wing, the Republicans renamed themselves the National Union Party. They jettisoned the antislavery vice president Hannibal Hamlin, and replaced him with the former senator and military governor of Tennessee, Andrew Johnson—a fateful choice, as it turned out. Sherman's capture of Atlanta in early September buoyed Union morale and helped secure Lincoln's reelection, which in turn helped guarantee emancipation. The administration's November triumph demonstrated just how much the terrain of political discourse had changed. In the face of a war that demanded ever-increasing commitments, the vital center of public opinion—so long the coveted target of party struggle—fell away. Secession had shorn popular politics of its southern moderates, while the need to escalate the stalled Union war effort demanded policy solutions such as confiscation, conscription, and emancipation. The uncompromising positions demanded by the deepening war increasingly polarized northern public opinion, rendering middle paths ever less tenable. Such were the exigencies wrought by war.

Nothing more readily illustrated this than the wartime fate of colonization, long Lincoln's remedy for the nation's racial ills. Lincoln had assiduously courted the conservative antislavery center for his entire political career, building his public identity on a delicate tightrope walk over the roiling political rapids of the 1850s. Raised politically on the example and philosophy of the great Kentucky Whig Henry Clay, Lincoln had posed African colonization as the viable middle ground on which a mass politics of antislavery could be erected. In 1854 he had told Peorians that he could not blame southerners "for not doing what I should not know how to do myself" about slavery. His "first impulse" was "to free all the slaves, and send them to Liberia," though he admitted the impracticality of such a plan.[85] In an 1857 speech, he conceded that "the separation of the races is the only perfect preventative of amalgamation" and that "such separation, if ever effected at all, must be effected by colonization."[86] Lincoln used colonization to oppose the slave power while simultaneously pandering to the widespread white supremacy of his day. Deep into the war Lincoln continued to pin his hopes on this position. His preliminary draft of the Emancipation Proclamation had promised to continue "the effort to colonize persons of African descent, with their consent, upon this continent, or elsewhere," and Congress had twice appropriated funds to aid wartime colonization schemes in Central America and elsewhere. A month before issuing the preliminary draft, Lincoln had even addressed a cohort of black leaders in the White House on the matter. "But for your race among us there could not be war, although many men engaged on either side do not care for you one way or the other," he told them, bizarrely intimating that blacks as victims of slavery were somehow responsible for the war. Even then, in August 1862, with plans for a preliminary emancipation proclamation under way, he advanced the self-colonization option, despite understanding that most African Americans had no desire whatsoever to leave the land of their birth. He even dared call their reticence "an extremely selfish view of the case."[87]

Eventually, though, the radical impulse of events outran Lincoln's moderation. He lacklusterly followed through with an ill-fated colonization experiment at Île-à-Vache, Haiti, but following the Emancipation Proclamation he loosened his grip on the option of racial separation.[88] In the final version, he replaced the prospect of removal with a momentous alternative—an invitation for formerly enslaved African American men to join the Union military machine. Instead of exiling former slaves, he would use them to fight.

SOLDIERS IN WAR, CITIZENS IN PEACE
African Americans in Arms and the Coming of Freedom

The marshaling of the military labor of liberated slaves during the Civil War constituted the most revolutionary aspect of mass emancipation in the United States. It proved decisive in defeating the slave power of the American South and placing Atlantic slavery on its last legs. Emancipation destroyed three billion dollars' worth of property in human beings. Militarily, incorporating enslaved African Americans from the seceded states into Union armies deprived the Confederacy of critical manpower, transferred the benefit of that manpower to the Union cause, and undermined the stability of southern society. As Secretary of the Navy Gideon Welles explained on the eve of mass emancipation, "The slaves were now an element of strength to the Rebels," whom they served as "laborers, producers, and army attendants."[89] The Emancipation Proclamation would transfer this strength to the Union, where it made a critical difference. Before the war's end 179,000 African Americans served, constituting altogether some 10 percent of its enlisted men. Another 7,000 served in the navy. Nearly 99,000 of these 186,000 were recruited from the overrun Confederate states.[90] They served in segregated units officered by white men, some of whom—Thomas Wentworth Higginson, Robert Gould Shaw—boasted impeccable abolitionist credentials. Some units were raised in the slave South, such as the First South Carolina Volunteers, and some in the free North, such as the Fifty-Fourth Massachusetts Colored Infantry. Both kinds of troops fought valiantly in major engagements, such as those at Port Hudson, Louisiana; Fort Wagner, South Carolina; and Milliken's Bend, Louisiana. By the end of the war, some 140 black regiments had participated in 449 engagements, including 39 major battles.[91]

Time and again Union officials affirmed the benefits of arming freed slaves. In August 1863, Joseph Holt, the Union's judge advocate general, informed Secretary of War Edwin Stanton that "the tenacious and brilliant valor" displayed by black troops "has sufficiently demonstrated to the President and to the country the character of service of which they are capable."[92] The same month, Grant wrote to Lincoln from the field to say that emancipation and recruitment were proving to be "the heaviest blow yet given the Confederacy."[93] In June 1864, Lincoln visited Grant at the front and reflected on the value of black troops. "I was opposed on nearly every side when I first favored the raising of colored regiments," Lincoln recalled, "but they have proved their efficiency, and I am glad they have kept pace with the white troops in the recent assaults."[94] In September of that year, Lincoln explained once again the import of the African Americans who served the Union cause. "We can not spare the hundred and forty or fifty thousand now serving us as soldiers, seamen, and laborers. This is not a question of sentiment or taste, but one of physical force which may be measured and estimated as horse-power and Steam-power are measured and estimated. Keep it and you can save the Union. Throw it away, and the Union goes with it."[95]

Persistent prejudice justified this defense of the emancipation and recruitment policy. While some Union officials believed that such biases were "rapidly giving way" in the face of black troops' illustrations of their capacity to fight alongside whites,[96] emancipation clearly emboldened Lincoln's critics, who derided the abolitionist turn. Shortly after Lincoln signed the Emancipation Proclamation, Clement Vallandigham declared, "war for the Union was abandoned; war for the negro openly begun."[97] One white Union soldier wrote that his fellows "do not wish to think that they are fighting for Negroes, but to put down the Rebellion. We must first conquer & then its time enough to talk about the *damn'd niggers*."[98] To this Lincoln steadfastly asserted the necessity and utility of emancipation. Rather than "carrying on this war for the sole purpose of abolition," Lincoln prosecuted it "for the sole purpose of restoring the Union." Emancipation formed a necessary component of that struggle. "No human power can subdue this rebellion without using the Emancipation lever as I have done," he said.[99] Though it inflamed the latent prejudices of northern society, emancipation lifted many burdens of war. "I thought that in your struggle for the Union, to whatever extent the negroes should cease helping the enemy, to that extent it weakened the enemy in his resistance to you," Lincoln addressed critics in the army. "I thought that whatever negroes can be got to do as soldiers, leaves just so much less for white soldiers to do, in saving the Union."[100]

Ultimately, the strategy worked, both politically and militarily. The Republicans won reelection in 1864, a sign that a year's trial of emancipation had yielded no loss "anyhow or anywhere" in "our home popular sentiment."[101] In the field, the emancipation policy worked to exploit the Confederacy's greatest weakness, and indeed its very reason for being: an enormous servile population requiring constant vigilance. In addition to putting nearly a hundred thousand slaves in Union blue, the Emancipation Proclamation went far to undermine the discipline of the plantation workforce. The slaves slowed down their work, denying masters their labor and obedience. Grant communicated these effects of the proclamation to Lincoln: Confederates had been "united in their action" before the proclamation, for "with the negro under subjection [they] could spare their entire white population for the field." But passage of the proclamation undermined productivity and security of the plantation home front, requiring more whites to oversee the fields. "Now they complain that nothing can be got out of their negroes," he reported.[102] The Emancipation Proclamation heralded an enormous manifestation of the same kind of resistance that had characterized West Indian slaves in their final revolts. The slaves withheld their labor. W. E. B. Du Bois, the great historian of African Americans during the Civil War period, put it in precisely this way: "As soon . . . as it became clear that the Union armies would not or could not return fugitive slaves, and that the masters with all their fume and fury were uncertain of victory, the slave entered upon a general strike against slavery by the same methods that he had used during the period of the fugitive slave. He ran away to the first place of safety and offered his services to the Federal Army."[103] In this sense, southern slaves manifested the same remarkable engagement with the shifting currents of metropolitan policy as did slave rebels in the British West Indies, who led collective actions designed to leverage growing calls for amelioration into expanded liberty, and even abolition.

Confederate leaders' efforts to cope with the practical consequences of emancipation suggested the depth of their bind. In October 1862, they anticipated the effects of the pending Emancipation Proclamation, the preliminary draft of which Lincoln had announced the previous month. Amending their first conscription law of April 1862, they raised the age of draftable men from thirty-five to forty-five. They also exempted those who owned twenty slaves or more, on the theory that such men served best by maintaining security and productivity on the plantation. The apparently unequal effects of conscription fostered complaints that the war represented a "rich man's war, poor man's fight," a view justified by the distribution of slaveholding in the Confederate population. In 1860, 394,000 people in the states that would form the Confederacy owned one or more slaves; the remaining 8.8 million, or 94.3 percent, did not. Assuming an average of one slaveholder per family, this meant that almost 70 percent of all free white families in the Confederacy owned no human property at all.[104] Confederate recruitment and conscription, however, fell heavily on the nonslaveholding class. Governor Joseph E. Brown of Georgia worried that the new conscription measure tended to "crush out the spirit of freedom and resistance to tyranny which was bequeathed to us by our ancestors of the Revolution of 1776."[105] The enslaved, by resisting plantation discipline, demanded a considerable diversion of resources from the front lines to the home front, thus exacerbating class tensions in a highly unequal society that was already demanding much sacrifice from the nonslaveholding. Confederate soldier Sam Watkins, who served in a Tennessee regiment, recalled the effect of the "twenty negro law" on his fellows: "It gave us the blues; we wanted twenty negroes." According to Watkins, the iniquitous conscription policy wreaked havoc on soldiers' morale. "The war might as well have ended then and there. The boys were 'hacked,' nay, whipped."[106] Together with the inexorable march of Union troops, which was made all the easier by the transfer of black labor from Confederate to Union forces, the social disruptions caused by a policy of emancipation contributed to the breakdown of Confederate political will, and helped destroy the Confederacy's capacity to compete militarily with the Union. None of this would have been possible had not African Americans registered their willingness to serve the cause of liberty.

Confederate officials viewed the Union emancipation policy as a clear incitement to insurrection. A war measure "leveled against the citizens of the Confederate States," the Emancipation Proclamation invited "an atrocious servile war"; it constituted a "gross violation of the usages of civilized warfare," and "an outrage on the rights of private property."[107] Historian Steven Hahn has suggested that Confederate outrage surpassed mere rhetoric; instead, he raises the possibility that in the Union's recruitment and employment of the enslaved, scholars "have missed what may have been the greatest slave rebellion in modern history."[108] And true, from the start of the conflict, the prospect that the enslaved might take advantage of the war to rise up terrorized southern whites. In public, the planters might pose their slaves as loyal wards who appreciated the civilizing influences of bondage, but in private, they well understood the potential of slaves' awareness of events around them. In the midst of the Confederate firing on Fort Sumter, Mary Chesnut, the privileged wife of prominent South Carolina planter James Chesnut, confided her anxieties to her diary. "Not by one word or look can we detect any change in the demeanor of these negro servants," she wrote. "They carry it too far. You could not tell that they even hear the awful row that is going on in the bay, though it is dinning in their ears day and night. And people talk before them as if they were chairs and tables. And they make no sign. Are they stolidly stupid or wiser than we, silent and strong, biding their time?" Later in the year, she reflected again on her slaves' capacity to dissemble: "Their faces are as unreadable as the sphinx."[109] Many white southerners feared that Yankees might actively incite slaves to rebel. Just days after the firing on Fort Sumter, a Louisiana planter wrote to Confederate President Jefferson Davis about such a possibility: "Should . . . a John Brown Raid occur, what with the sparse population—and a deep seated anxiety in regard to *negroes*, Such a panic would ensue as would be ruinous to our cause."[110]

Initially, Union leaders hesitated to undertake any action that might be interpreted as an echo of John Brown's. Even those who did not prioritize the persistence of the southern social order could still fear the political backlash of appearing to support slave insurrection through a policy of emancipation. Treasury Secretary Salmon Chase feared that Lincoln's momentous move would open the floodgates to slave resistance, leading to "depredation and massacre on the one hand, and support to the insurrection on the other."[111] When the preliminary draft of the Emancipation Proclamation declared that the federal government would undertake no action to "repress" those declared free "in any efforts they may make for their actual freedom"—a phrase applying to slave runaways, but one widely interpreted as support for slave insurrection—the administration found itself back-pedaling furiously.[112] The final draft of the proclamation clearly entreated the slaves "to abstain from all violence" and when permitted "labor faithfully for reasonable wages."

African Americans themselves generally proved eager to participate in any struggle for liberty. They fought as well as or better than white troops and exhibited exceptional motivation despite enduring a mortality rate (18.5 percent) much higher than that of white troops (13.5 percent).[113] Their natural affinity to the Union cause made them excellent spies, as heralded figures such as Harriet Tubman illustrate. Military service could transform former slaves into avenging angels. Consider the exemplary instance of Private Spotswood Rice, who fled slavery to join the Union army, leaving his wife and daughter behind in Glasgow, Missouri. When his mistress, a woman named Kitty Diggs, refused to sell the child to him, Rice fired off an angry missive. "I want you to understand that mary is my Child and she is a God given rite of my own," he wrote to Diggs. "The longor you keep my Child from me the longor you will have to burn in hell and the qwicer youll get their." Rice promised a retribution only possible because of his position within the Union army: "We are now makeing up a bout one thoughsand blacke troops to Come up . . . through Glasgow and when we come wo be to Copperhood rabbels and to the Slaveholding rebbels for we dont expect to leave them there root neor branch. . . . [W]hen I get ready to come after mary I will have bout a powrer and autherity to bring hear away and to exacute vengencens on them that holds my Child."[114]

The broader political implications of such apparently individual and domestic motivations must not be underestimated. The enslaved possessed the strongest reasons to take up arms. During the secession crisis, Frederick Douglass had predicted that "the slave population of South Carolina may at last prove the most serious check upon disunion." Understanding the point of resistance, the slaves "might burst forth and spread havoc and death among slaveholders to an extent never surpassed even in the annals of St. Domingo."[115] As he continued his tireless efforts to promote the use of black troops in the army early in the war, Douglass again noted the value to the Union of the slaves' commitments. At a time when "every resource of the nation . . . could be well employed to avert the impending ruin," the government refused "to receive the very class of men which have a deeper interest in the defeat and humiliation of the rebels, than all others." Douglass contended that "one black regiment in such a war as this is, without being any more brave and orderly, would be worth to the Government more than two of any other."[116]

Younger activists from the free North helped enact Douglass's vision. Decades of organization in northern black communities had already produced a strong martial tradition, resulting in at least two dozen black military companies formed between 1850 and the start of the Civil War.[117] When the conflict began, many free African Americans jumped at the opportunity to strike a blow for liberty. Denied the opportunity to serve until 1863, these men became the core of the thirty-eight thousand black free-staters who mustered into the U.S. Colored Troops (USCT).[118] Regiments such as the Fifty-Fourth Massachusetts Volunteer Infantry boasted the names of highly politicized members of the families of racial activists, including two of Frederick Douglass's sons. Two other members of the regiment, James Henry Gooding and George Stephens, became regular correspondents to northern newspapers. Martin R. Delany, one of the most militant of antebellum black nationalists, recruited for the USCT and served as an officer. Free African Americans from the North thus entered the ranks with a highly developed sense of racial politics, which they then enlarged through their experiences, and shared with recently enslaved compatriots in newly forming units.[119] Such soldiers acted as living conduits between the public antislavery of northern activists and the collective resistance of the enslaved.

Consider the significance of this. John Brown's raid had represented a desire to bring together the twin streams of slave resistance and abolitionist ideology. As Lincoln noted with some accuracy, "it was an attempt by white men to get up a revolt among slaves, in which the slaves refused to participate."[120] The emancipation policy, though, effectively melded slave action and antislavery ideology. Lincoln even made the link explicit in a White House discussion with Frederick Douglass in the spring of 1864. Concerned that too few slaves were making it to Union lines, the president proposed that Douglass undertake the formation of "a band of scouts, composed of coloured men, whose business should be somewhat after the original plan of John Brown." They would "go into the rebel States, beyond the lines of our armies, and carry the news of emancipation, and urge the slaves to come within our boundaries."[121] The Civil War thus powerfully merged free black activism and slave militance, fulfilling at last the militant vision of 1859. Both African Americans and the Union administration benefitted from this melding. The government enjoyed the bayonets of nearly two hundred thousand men, many of whom otherwise would have been put to work for the Confederacy. African Americans benefitted from the opportunity to put their commitments to black liberty in action without risking certain failure in an unpropitious peacetime uprising.

Shackling the cause of the slaves to the Union army did, though, come with costs. For one, black soldiers faced an enemy unwilling to consider them legitimate combatants. As Confederate armies began encountering African Americans with Union forces in late 1862, rebel field officers ordered their men "to shoot, wherever & whenever captured, all negroes found armed & acting in concert with the abolition troops either as guides or brothers in arms." Rebel authorities scrambled to formulate an official policy. On November 30, 1862, Confederate Secretary of War James Seddon declared that "slaves in flagrant rebellion are subject to death by the laws of every slave holding State." African Americans in uniform "cannot be recognized in anyway as soldiers subject to the rules of war." Seddon deemed it "essential that slaves in armed insurrection should meet condign punishment" in the form of "summary execution."[122] In the field, Confederate troops frequently gave no quarter to black soldiers, and in the invasions of Maryland (1862) and Pennsylvania (1863), Confederate forces rounded up African Americans, the free along with the fugitive, and sent them south into slavery.[123] In 1864, Confederates ruthlessly massacred black troops during the Battle of Fort Pillow in Tennessee and at Saltville in Virginia.

The merging of African American resistance into the Union war effort also tempered black resisters' autonomy, limiting their range of action and subordinating it to the interests of institutions that prioritized them below the cause of union. At the war's start, free black activists had hesitated to offer their support, fearing just such an eventuality. In an incisive letter to the *Anglo-African*, black New Yorker Robert H. Vandyne understood the desire to fight, but foresaw the problem: "Once under army discipline, subject to the control of government officers or military leaders, could we dictate when and where the blow should be struck?" With considerable prescience, Vandyne worried that without a greater Union commitment to true racial equality, African American veterans of such a war would have to settle for "a casual mention of our heroic deeds upon the field of battle" by ancestors "doomed" to a "heart-crushing prejudice" that had never been stamped out.[124] While the course of events suggested a limited transformation in the racial sentiments of some white northerners, even the enormity of the war that unfolded could not revolutionize them.

The Union army's practical treatment of African American soldiers and their families reinforced the point. Kept in segregated units and paid less than their white counterparts, black soldiers had to contend with racist Union officials, inferior treatment, and higher rates of disease. While the families they left behind often suffered cruel fates at the hands of vengeful masters, those who accompanied them to Union lines often endured hardships equally severe, ranging from malnutrition to forced labor to sexual abuse. By December 1863, Lincoln could boast to Congress that "no servile insurrection or tendency to violence or cruelty has marked the measures of emancipation and arming the blacks."[125] What African Americans could boast was less clear. Vandyne had been right: white authorities overwhelmingly directed the course of black resistance during the war, limiting in unimaginable ways the political will of the African Americans who fought in blue. This domestication of slave resistance must severely temper any claim that African American recruitment constituted "the greatest slave rebellion" in history.

The promise of citizenship implicit in black military service offset these limitations. The struggle against inferior treatment in the Union ranks constituted one of African Americans' crowning achievements in the course of the war, as it directly fostered the recognition of blacks' civic equality. It took time, though, to forge the link between military service and equal rights. From the start, Lincoln had to explain to his critics why the government should reward the slaves with even freedom, let alone equality. "Negroes, like other people, act upon motives," he told an Illinois audience. "Why should they do any thing for us, if we will do nothing for them? If they stake their lives for us, they must be prompted by the strongest motive—even the promise of freedom."[126] Questions about the status of African Americans once in arms then prompted Union officials to clarify the meaning of that freedom.

Confederate resolve to treat black soldiers as slave insurrectionaries enjoined Union leaders to defend the liberty of African Americans in arms. In July 1863, Lincoln declared Confederate policy on captured black troops "a relapse into barbarism, and a crime against the civilization of the age"; in retaliation, he announced that "for every one enslaved by the enemy or sold into slavery, a rebel soldier shall be placed at hard labor on the public works and continued at such labor until the other shall be released and receive the treatment due to a prisoner of war."[127] In fact, the only conviction of a Confederate official for a war crime—Major Henry Wirz, who oversaw Union prisoners at Camp Sumter near Andersonville, Georgia—resulted from the Union government's demand for equal treatment of black soldiers. The Confederate government's failure to treat black Union soldiers as legitimate combatants prompted the Union army Commander in Chief Ulysses Grant to deny the equal exchange of prisoners of war. As a direct consequence, Andersonville prison overflowed, with almost thirteen thousand Union prisoners losing their lives to illness, malnutrition, and abuse.

But the growing Union defense of black soldiers' rights ultimately had the effect those such as Frederick Douglass had predicted. "Once let the black man get upon his person the brass letters, U.S., let him get an eagle on his button, and a musket on his shoulder and bullets in his pocket, there is no power on earth that can deny that he has earned the right to citizenship."[128] The army's little-heralded declaration in August 1863 that under the Militia Act "free persons of African descent are treated as 'citizens of the United States' in the sense of the law," grudgingly fulfilled the promise African American leaders had seen in the recruitment policy, and acknowledged that all those who fought for the Union deserved to be treated as equals.[129]

Union service paved the road to equality in other ways as well, such as through the struggle for education. Long denied basic literacy by law, many enslaved African Americans who joined the Union cause encountered their first tastes of literacy in camp schools. Reported one chaplain of a black regiment in Louisiana, "A majority of the men seem to regard their book as an indispensable portion of their equipments, and the cartridge box and spelling book are attached to the same belt."[130] The acquisition of literacy enhanced the autonomy and self-confidence of blacks in uniform, and helped placed them on a plane of equality with whites. As one African American soldier wrote to the *Christian Recorder*, "Freedom and education are the essential properties to make a great and powerful nation. . . . We need not fear for the future of our race, if based upon those principles."[131]

The fight for equal pay constituted another case in which the struggle for equal treatment helped translate into a broader equality. The Union initially paid black troops only ten dollars per month, deducting three dollars for clothing; white troops received thirteen dollars per month with no deduction. In November 1863, Sergeant William Walker of the Third South Carolina Volunteers convinced a group of compatriots to lay down their arms and resign from the army, a protest against pay inequity that earned him a court-martial and execution on a charge of mutiny. More effective was the approach of James Henry Gooding of the Fifty-Fourth Massachusetts, who wrote to President Lincoln in September 1863. "We have done a Soldiers Duty," he stated; "why cant we have a Soldiers pay?" He argued that if the Union government "insists on having all her Soldiers, of whatever, creed or, Color, to be treated, according to the usages of War"—a reference to Confederate treatment of captured black soldiers—it should follow its own policy and pay them equally.[132] Such appeals ultimately succeeded when in June 1864, Congress granted equal pay to black soldiers, retroactive to the beginning of the year.

In both instances, African Americans worked to ensure that the Union kept promises of liberty implicit in military service. Fighting next to white troops offered African Americans the rough parity accruing to those who can equally die for a state. But rendering meaningful this morbid equality required special efforts to enforce the long-standing principle in Atlantic societies that military service and citizenship rights went hand in hand. Paradoxically, by subjecting themselves to the constrained freedom of military discipline, black soldiers demonstrated to a prejudiced public their fitness to wield the supreme symbol of political liberty: the vote. Louisiana, which fell early to Union control, first considered the great experiment. In March 1864, Lincoln met with representatives of New Orleans's antebellum free people of color, who from the days of French settlement had reflected the privileged caste status that often accrued to the Caribbean's free people of mixed racial origins. The day after, Lincoln wrote to loyalist Governor Michael Hahn, suggesting the possibility of granting the right to vote to African Americans. "I barely suggest for your private consideration, whether some of the colored people might not be let in—as, for instance, the very intelligent and especially those who have fought gallantly in our ranks."[133] Lincoln's very last public address, in fact, reiterated his support for black voting rights in Louisiana, which had gained considerable support in the intervening year. Standing outside the White House on April 11, 1865, the president stated publicly that he hoped the right to vote "were now conferred on the very intelligent, and on those who serve our cause as soldiers."[134]

African Americans themselves had long anticipated such a move, and now stood ready to cement in the public mind the connection between military service and the right to vote. In January 1865, for example, Nashville blacks asked, "If we are called on to do military duty against the rebel armies in the field, why should we be denied the privilege of voting against rebel citizens at the ballotbox? The latter is as necessary to save the Government as the former."[135] The motto on the regimental flag of the Twenty-Fourth USCT put the matter concisely, "Let soldiers in war, be citizens in peace."[136] As the war closed, support for extending the suffrage to African Americans grew. If "freedom" consisted solely of "the privilege of not being chained," Ohio Congressman James Garfield told an Ohio Independence Day gathering in 1865, "then freedom is a bitter mockery, a cruel delusion."[137] Union General Sherman concurred: "When the fight is over, the hand that drops the musket cannot be denied the ballot."[138]

Despite the growth of such sentiments among many Union politicians, mass emancipation did not translate into voting rights for African Americans. John Wilkes Booth's assassination of Abraham Lincoln on April 15, 1865, deprived blacks of a reluctant but crucial supporter. Lincoln's successor, Andrew Johnson, was no such champion. The conservative and bullheaded Tennessean bypassed the will of Congress, instituting a plan for reconstruction that offered former rebels widespread amnesty. Johnson himself expressed concern that black suffrage would result in bloodshed and "a war of the races," and promised to leave the matter to the states.[139] Unsurprisingly, the former Confederate states that returned to the Union under Johnson's lenient terms restricted the elective franchise to white people. A longer struggle would be required to achieve the elimination of racial restrictions on voting.

Given the myriad direct and indirect ways that military service could promote racial equality, it was no wonder that the Confederacy contemplated the possibility of slave recruitment only as a last, desperate measure. Early in the war a very few Confederate voices had suggested the possibility of enlisting slaves in exchange for liberty, but the great majority, particularly among the Confederate leadership, refused even to contemplate such a move. A very few African-descended people in arms served the Confederate cause, such as the First Louisiana Native Guard, a militia regiment composed of free people of color largely from New Orleans, which Confederate leaders never risked testing in battle. Overwhelmingly, though, the Confederates used African Americans, mostly enslaved, as laborers and servants. Only late in the war, with the manpower shortage clearly telling, did Confederate leaders begin seriously considering a policy of slave recruitment. In January 1864, General Patrick Cleburne wrote a remarkable letter to his commanders, conceding that "slavery, from being one of our chief sources of strength at the commencement of the war, has now become, in a military point of view, one of our chief sources of weakness." A Confederate policy of liberation and recruitment would "strike dead all John Brown fanaticism" in the North, permit the raising of troops necessary for "carrying on a protracted struggle," and remove all "fear of insurrection in the rear."[140] Confederate officials rejected the plan only to have the desperate Lee promote it again the next January. In the Confederate Congress, Speaker Howell Cobb of Georgia rebuked him. "The day you make soldiers of them is the beginning of the end of the revolution. If slaves will make good soldiers our whole theory of slavery is wrong."[141] By March 1865, when Congress finally permitted masters to voluntarily relinquish slaves who would then be emancipated into Confederate armies, the end of the war was too near for the policy to make a difference in the course of the war.[142]

The Confederacy's desperate gamble to enlist freed slaves fit within historical patterns of Atlantic slave societies, differing only in southern slaveholders' extreme reluctance to consider measures that every other slave power at war enacted at some point. As such, it symbolized the extreme degree to which the identity of the Confederacy depended on an ideological defense of slavery. This, in turn, signaled the deeply embattled nature of a slave power so firmly committed to the vision of slave society as an ideal in itself. No other Atlantic slave power—not even the Brazilian planters who stood largely unopposed within their nation until the 1870s—so fiercely constructed ideological defenses of slavery as a legitimate, and indeed beneficial, modern social institution. Southern planters had chosen to seek to preserve slavery through a contest of arms rather than through a formal political system in which they believed themselves to be overmatched. The use of their own slaves against them demonstrated that they were militarily overmatched as well.

The Civil War's use of the enslaved as combatants already had a long history in the Atlantic world, stretching back to the foundations of New World plantation societies. Sparsely populated settlements had often turned to their bondsmen in times of military crisis. But slaves could not be expected to fight for nothing. As Thomas Jefferson had put it, "If a slave can have a country in this world, it must be any other in preference to that in which he is born to live and labour for another."[143] The price of loyalty was the liberty so coveted by those in chains. During the conflicts between the Dutch and Portuguese over control of northeastern Brazil in the first half of the seventeenth century, sugar planters had promised freedom and to pay for "every black, Arda, Mina, Anglola, creole, mulatto, métis, free or slave, who does his duty in defense of divine liberty."[144] The British General Lord Dunmore had famously offered to exchange freedom for service during the American Revolution, a move northern colonies also embraced in the later years of the war. Slaves became the backbone of the French Revolutionary Army in St. Domingue, and forces fighting on all sides in the Latin American wars of independence turned to slave liberation and recruitment in their struggles.

The broad phenomenon of emancipation in the United States fits several of these patterns, but defies simple placement among any of the historical models that preceded it. In the United States, a series of revolutionary emancipations had liberated slaves in the northern part of the nation, though it left them victims of a vicious racial prejudice. The remaining slave states grew into the strongest and most powerful slave regime on the planet, but one opposed by a potent movement of metropolitan abolitionism that sought slavery's end from outside. In the Civil War, the Union government sought first for its slaveholding states to embark on a program of gradual, compensated emancipation, which would isolate the slave states that had seceded. Even before the failure of this initiative, the Union Congress had begun legally dismantling an institution that war and the slaves themselves had already been subverting. "You would not have become free," a black leader reminded South Carolina blacks toward the end of the war, "had we not armed ourselves and fought out our independence."[145] The Emancipation Proclamation constituted the signal recognition of this reality, but as elsewhere, only the war created the imperatives necessary to make emancipation a political possibility, palatable to the public of a highly democratic society. White abolitionists and black activists understandably criticized the administration for its slow adoption of an emancipation policy. But in Atlantic terms

Congress's and the president's moves in 1862 far outstripped in size and impact any similar measure taken anywhere else in the New World, with the possible exception of Haiti. No precedent existed for the liberation by fiat of over three million slaves, all to appropriate their labor for the express purpose of destroying the very slave power that oppressed them.

CHAPTER 8

One Hundred Years

Reconstruction

REHEARSAL FOR RECONSTRUCTION
Wartime Experiments in Free Labor

In early November 1861, a scant half year after the start of the Civil War, a Union naval flotilla, launched from Hampton Roads, Virginia, swept down the coast and attacked two forts protecting the harbor of Port Royal, South Carolina. On November 7, Confederate forces abandoned Forts Walker and Beauregard, leaving these guardians of the harbor to enemy marines. Union forces soon occupied the nearby towns of Port Royal and Beaufort, securing a base from which gunboats could help enforce a massive naval blockade of the Confederacy. Captain Samuel Francis DuPont, the commander of the squadron, effused over this success. "You can form no idea of the terror we have spread in the whole Southern country," he reported. "Beaufort is deserted. . . . The enemy flew in panic leaving public and private property, letters, portfolios, all their regimental archives, clothes, arms, etc."[1]

A triumph of military planning, the Battle of Port Royal revealed an equivalent lack of preparation for the aftermath. Even at this early stage of the war, the advance of Union armies raised unanticipated questions about the fate of the slaves. As early as May 1861 Union General Benjamin Butler had begun receiving runaway slaves into Union lines at Fortress Monroe, Virginia, which the Union had held from the start of the war. Now, though, Union forces were taking over territory actually held by Confederates. In the case of the Battle of Port Royal, Union troops came to control some of the most densely populated slave country in the South. Beaufort and Colleton Counties, which straddled the site of the Union invasion, were home to some sixty-five thousand enslaved African Americans, roughly 16 percent of the state's entire bound population. Slaves constituted over 75 percent of the people in these counties, the second and third highest rates of enslavement in the state. The counties' coastal lowlands were especially rich in slaves. The long-staple cotton plantations of islands such as Port Royal, St. Helena, Ladies', and Hilton Head were among the most valuable slaveholdings in the country. Of South Carolina's 449 plantations with over one hundred slaves in 1860, nearly a third lay along the coastal region of Beaufort and Colleton.[2]

Union commanders should not, then, have been surprised to encounter slaves. When Sea Island planters hastily fled the invading army, their human property sought to remain behind. Former slave Sam Mitchell recalled the scene from his childhood: the master demanding his father abandon his rail-splitting work to row the boat that would carry the whites to Charleston; his mother sternly countermanding the order. "You ain't gonna row no boat to Charleston, you go out dat back door and keep a-going," she told Sam's father.[3] The Union army found itself in control not simply of Confederates' plantations and personal property, but thousands of their enslaved laborers as well. Officials quickly noted the first concern of these slaves, who by virtue of the policy pioneered at Fortress Monroe were being termed "contraband of war." As DuPont reported immediately after the invasion, "the contrabands are wild and sacking Beaufort, in return for being shot down because they would not leave with their masters." The enslaved more typically exhibited simple relief from bondage, expressed in spirituals recorded by white observers. Ran one,

> No more driver's lash for me,
>   no more, no more,—
> No more driver's lash for me,
>   Many thousands go.[4]

In the weeks and months following the invasion, the army found itself pressed ever harder to cope with the implications of military success for the institution of slavery. Charged with control of lands abandoned by rebel planters, the Treasury Department took responsibility for the situation on the Sea Islands. Administrators prioritized the reestablishment of cotton production, which would help cover the costs of war, confirm Union control of Confederate lands, and occupy the contrabands in paying for their own care. Treasury Secretary Salmon Chase sent Edward L. Pierce, a Massachusetts attorney who had first supervised contraband laborers at Fortress Monroe, to assess the situation at Port Royal. Pierce reported favorably on the prospects for employing the slaves as a productive labor force, affirming many northerners' faith that slavery might be replaced by something better. He declared the contrabands themselves capable of becoming a thrifty workforce. Some were indeed "of very low intellectual development," but only a few were "too low to be reached by civilizing influences." The key was to establish a free labor system that taught the contrabands independence, self-sufficiency, and the value of hard work. "When properly organized, and with proper motives set before them," Pierce attested, "they will, as freemen, be as industrious as any race of men are likely to be in this climate."[5] Under free labor, Port Royal might become a model for what military victory might proffer elsewhere throughout the South.

The government adopted Pierce's proposal. Treasury agents and military officials soon flocked to the region with the intention of implementing a system of free labor to replace slavery. Thus began the Union's first large-scale attempt to prepare for the aftermath of slavery, a widely publicized effort followed closely by the press and in the halls of government. Both champions and detractors understood the significance of this "Port Royal experiment." On its success or failure hung something even greater than the fate of up to ten thousand slaves who suddenly found themselves behind Union lines in South Carolina. The disposition of slavery, and the prospects for freedom throughout the South, stood in the balance. Could a large population of formerly enslaved laborers—now poised in legal limbo between bondage and freedom—become productive workers?

Many Union officials thought not. In Congress, Representative William Henry Wadsworth of Kentucky complained that while the government's missionaries were "endeavoring to instill some ideas of freedom, &c., into the negro mind," the contraband's "idea of freedom is that of a state in which he will be exempt from labor."[6] It did not help that Union officers in the field often expressed open contempt for the contrabands. Hazard Stevens, who served as an aide-de-camp to a Union commander stationed in Beaufort, described apocalyptic scenes of Sea Islands slaves' reactions to the flight of the planters. "Native Africans" plunged in "the densest ignorance" held "high carnival in the deserted mansions, smashing doors, mirrors, and furniture, and appropriating all that took their fancy." After, they "reveled in unwonted idleness and luxury, feasting upon the corn, cattle, and turkeys of their fugitive masters."[7] For those already fearful of the consequence of emancipation, this was hardly a promising vision of freedom.

Understandably, advocates of emancipation disagreed. One black newspaper argued that success would serve as an "irresistible" argument "against slavery, and in favor of free labor."[8] William Lloyd Garrison declared Port Royal "the next stage in the great abolition movement." The Sea Islands were to be "the scene of an experiment which will test the great question of free labor, negro capacity, and the productiveness of Southern soil under the application of science." Many abolitionists leaped at the opportunity to transplant northern ideals to southern soil. "Northern men with noble hearts and full heads are about to take the place of slave-drivers in the seat of despotic ease," Garrison contended, going on to envision the Yankee Utopia in store for postemancipation South Carolina: "Northern capital and enterprise will find here a sure investment; and the world will behold here another gateway to the South, through which Northern art, science and institutions will hereafter flow. Enlivened and sustained by freedom, this great commercial centre shall yet be the pride of the North to pervade with its free spirit the industrial and social interests of that charming section of our united and happy country."[9]

Only one variable remained unknown. The success of the experiment teetered on the capacity of the enslaved to live up to standards set for them by metropolitan opinion. Detractors believed the blacks of the Sea Islands innately incapable of self-motivation and self-governance; supporters conceded their present degradation but viewed them as upliftable. Consequently, no facet of the experiment drew more attention than the effort to educate the contrabands. Of course, simply remedying the slaves' enforced ignorance constituted a high priority. The contrabands themselves proved eager to gain the basic literacy and numeracy that might put them on a par with whites. Reported one Yankee educator in the Sea Islands, "All expressed a desire to have their children learn something, if they themselves knew nothing."[10]

Even more, though, education promised to train the contrabands for new lives in a free marketplace and a democratic society. The earliest plans for coping with the Sea Islands contrabands acknowledged the critical role of this training for freedom. "Their teaching will by no means be confined to intellectual instruction," resolved a commission on education for Sea Island contrabands. "It will include all the more important and fundamental lessons of civilization,— voluntary industry, self-reliance, frugality, forethought, honesty and truthfulness, cleanliness and order. With these will be combined intellectual, moral and religious instruction."[11] Military officials concurred. In January 1862, General T. W. Sherman requested "suitable instructors" to teach the contrabands "all the necessary rudiments of civilization." He concluded, "They must be trained and instructed into a knowledge of personal and moral responsibility."[12] In response, a bevy of well-meaning missionaries and teachers—known colloquially as "Gideon's Band," after the Old Testament prophet who had assembled a core of faithful warriors to fight off Israel's enemies—arrived at Port Royal, with others to follow. Funded by wealthy abolitionists and supplemented by fundraising efforts throughout the North, educators such as Elizabeth Hyde Botume and Laura Towne opened schools in the area of Yankee occupation. Charlotte Forten, daughter of Philadelphia's first family of free black activists, went with them, reporting back that she "never saw children so eager to learn."[13]

Ideally, in the minds of reformers, the charity represented by the educational mission would make itself obsolete as freedpeople learned how to behave in the competitive social order of freedom. Frederick Law Olmsted, the prominent landscape architect and polymath who had written a searing indictment of slavery's economic inefficiency in the 1850s, captured the logic succinctly in a letter to Abraham Lincoln in March 1862. The "duty and function of government with regard to the negroes," he argued, was quite limited. Government had a minimal obligation to "save the lives of the negroes" from the "rampages of war." Beyond this, it had only a charge to "*train or educate*" the contrabands "in a few simple, essential and fundamental social duties of free men in civilized life." These included the ability to provide for themselves "independently of charity," and the substitution of "subordination to the will of their former owners" with "submission to Laws or rules of social comity." The contrabands were to be free, perhaps, but only to adopt the ethos of the competitive market order into which they had been liberated—with no capital. Olmsted even accepted the deaths of idle slaves as "a natural punishment of neglect of duty," the first of which was the obligation to work. For defenders of the Port Royal experiment, the aid offered to the contrabands was to be of a very temporary sort, intended not to rectify several centuries' worth of expropriated labor, but only to launch them quickly into self-sufficiency. As Edward Pierce put it, the government's policy toward the freedpeople should be viewed as "a paternal discipline for the time being, intended for present use only." As soon as they demonstrated themselves "fitted for all the privileges of citizens, the contrabands were to be dismissed from the system and allowed to follow any employment they please, and where they please."[14]

Port Royal showed that abolitionism embodied far more than just a rejection of slavery. Affirming the wisdom of emancipation—a cause over which as many as a million would die as a result of the war—meant ratifying the theory behind it. This stated that slavery was not simply a moral evil, but a violation of the basic principles underlying progressive, democratic, and "civilized" society. Antislavery positively asserted the moral economy of nineteenth-century liberalism: the benign workings of the neutral marketplace, the consanguinity of labor and capital, the minimal role of the state in market affairs, and the centrality of individual character in predicting success in the race of life. Counterposed with bondage, these values had buttressed the ideological fight against slavery. Now it was time to implement them in the South. More than anywhere else, the effort would take place in the fields, with the transition to a free labor system of agricultural production. The key component, land, came from the planters themselves. Under the First and Second Confiscation Acts, and then the Direct Tax Act of June 1862, the Union government claimed rebel landholdings, which it then sought to sell to recoup lost taxes and restart the cotton economy.

A hazy policy provided for a system of "preemption," modeled on practices on the western frontier, which would permit freedpeople who had cultivated and improved abandoned lands an early chance to purchase their plots at rates below full market value. General Rufus Saxton, the military governor of the region, viewed such measures as "the dictate of simple justice" for a people who had "paid for it many times over" through "wages withheld and accumulated for generations."[15] But in the eyes of other Gideonites, preemption violated the strict rules of the market. "A system of selling to any people any property whatever for less than its market value" would fail to teach the freedpeople the value of work and "would beget idleness and unthrifty habits," complained Edward Philbrick, a Gideonite who speculated vigorously in abandoned Sea Island plantations. "Negro labor has got to be employed, if at all, because it is *profitable*, and it has got to come into the market like everything else, subject to . . . supply and demand."[16] Thus crystallized two visions of postemancipation labor that would bedevil the efforts of even the most well-meaning of the freedpeople's champions. In arguing against the sale of abandoned lands on the open market, Edward Pierce had foreseen the conflict. "No man, not even the best of men," he said, "should be put in a position where there would be such a conflict between his humanity and his self-interest."[17] But questions remained. Were the freedpeople to become independent smallholders on the model of the yeoman farmers of the North or wage workers, also on the northern model, strictly subordinated to a fluid labor market?

To the freedpeople's dismay, the Philbricks had the better of it. Freed slaves wound up with some land set aside by the government for their use, but could not compete with northern money. Philbrick represented a cabal of investors who purchased eleven plantations, covering seven thousand acres and employing some 950 African American tenants. By the spring of 1864, the question had been largely settled. Freedpeople had purchased a fraction of the available acreage on favorable terms, but whites had purchased the rest. Lacking land, most former slaves on the Sea Islands remained landless laborers, tenants, and field hands on the plantations of others. Even before the end of the war, the Port Royal experiment had yielded its grim results.

For all its novelty and notoriety, the experience of wartime reconstruction in the Sea Islands was not singular. Throughout the South, as Union forces captured land claimed by the Confederacy, similar questions arose, only to be resolved with different permutations of the same solutions. Notable examples appeared in the western theater of war, where Union forces traveled up the Mississippi from New Orleans and down from western Tennessee. In the state of Mississippi, a freed slave converted the model antebellum plantation of Davis Bend into a new experiment in free labor and communal living. Yet even more than the Port Royal experiment, the plantation's significance lay more in its suggestion of the possible than its representation of the likely.

In contrast, the Union army in Louisiana took nearly complete control over the wartime regulation of plantation labor. As many as fifty thousand black laborers fell under the control of Union officials, who compelled them to accept wage contracts to work on plantations at preset rates. General Nathaniel Banks, Union commander in the region, insisted that this system best met the needs of wartime reconstruction and the slaves' transition to freedom. He offered no promises of land ownership, instead envisioning the freedpeople as an elastic, inexpensive, and docile force of wage laborers. Champions of the plan argued that this temporary abrogation of the rules of the market was necessary for the freedpeople. "To have allowed them that kind of liberty, which in reality is license and not liberty, would have resulted in making the change in their condition one of injury and not of benefit."[18] This of course melded well with the desires of the planters, who complained bitterly about their loss of control, demanding "such power & authority as will enable us to preserve order & compell the negroes to work so as to make the crops necessary for the support of our families & of the negroes themselves."[19] The freedpeople, though, chafed under strictures that felt more like slavery than freedom; the government's labor regulations forbade hands to move from the plantation without a pass, or even to "roam at will" around their home plantations after sundown.[20] In taking issue with the Banks plan, Frederick Douglass appealed to the popular gospels of limited government and self-help, arguing that American principles dictated that the freedpeople be left free to work out their destiny without repressive measures designed to "prepare" them for freedom. "What shall we do with the Negro?" he asked, repeating the stock question of the day. "Do nothing with us!" he replied. "If the Negro cannot stand on his own legs, let him fall. . . . The fault will not be yours."[21]

Wartime reconstruction in Louisiana established a pattern that became typical throughout the postemancipation South. Strict market solutions, such as Philbrick's, were harsh enough. But the exceptional exigencies of war combined with fierce demands to resurrect the plantation economy to guarantee that the principles of laissez-faire would be circumvented in favor of forced contract—in liberal theory, a clear contradiction. What resulted was neither slavery nor clearly freedom.

DISCOURSES ON THE NEGRO QUESTION
The Problem of Labor in the Postemancipation Plantation Zone

While the details of these wartime experiments in reconstructing a black labor force varied, similar questions underlay them—questions that appeared wherever Atlantic slave societies confronted mass emancipation. In the plantation zones, the key conflicts posed the interests of freedpeople against the interests of the slave power's legatees, as well as of the metropolitan regimes that had deprived them of their property in man. What would happen to the plantation economy? How would former slaves work? What rights would freedom imply for them? Both planters and the metropole demanded the rapid reformulation of a profitable plantation economy. Generally, former slave owners sought a labor system as close to slavery as possible, while metropolitan concerns concentrated on the reconstitution of the plantation regime on principles of free, but none-theless fruitful, labor. The slave power had lost the struggle to retain its human property, but the state itself possessed a strong incentive to uphold the plantation economy. After all, metropolitan capital had financed the plantation, while met-ropolitan consumers had created the demand that made the sale of plantation products so profitable. How, then, to maintain production? Many abolitionists had argued that free labor offered a more moral and efficient alternative to servi-tude, but planters remained convinced that only an exploitable labor force could make the plantation profitable. In freedom, they argued, blacks would respond to the incentives of the marketplace, asserting that "the negro has the same self-ish element in him which induces other men to labor."[22] But, as the conflict at Port Royal demonstrated, the exact form that free labor might take fell instantly into question. The "free" in free labor could as easily mean "freely replaceable" as "free from slavery."

The emancipated had different ideas altogether. Unsurprisingly, rather than spend sunup to sundown toiling in the fields, they preferred to preserve the lei-sure time that made life in freedom worth living. Similarly, they evinced little en-thusiasm for working cash crops, preferring the independence that might come from growing food for consumption and barter. Virtually everywhere, these de-sires collided with the interests of both the planters and the state, resulting in a general reduction in the labor available to the plantation economy. "Exactitude of labour is lacking," complained French abolitionist Auguste François Perrinon, observing the freedpeople's reluctance to work in Martinique. "Subordination to an overseer is [as] repugnant to them as is submitting to roll-call. They see in these formalities reminders of slavery."[23] In nearly every plantation society that ended slavery before the American Civil War, production declined. In the five years following freedom in the Caribbean colonies, Martinique lost 30 percent of its sugar production, St. Croix 25 percent, and Dutch Surinam 38 percent. In the United States itself, cotton production in the five years following the Civil War sank from its pre-emancipation level by 23 percent, tobacco by 35 percent, rice by 61 percent, and sugar by 59 percent.[24] Haiti's earlier, war-torn path to emancipation had particularly crippled its capacity to produce. From 1791 to 1818, sugar production fell over 98 percent.[25] In 1800, Toussaint Louverture had im-posed a system of forced labor to compel freed slaves to produce the crops so necessary for the fragile state's survival, but to no avail.

In freedom, the emancipated slaves of the Atlantic generally sought to become peasant proprietors—autonomous, self-sufficient, and traditional. In the Caribbean and Sea Islands of the U.S. South, work patterns under slavery had prepared them for this with a system of task labor that permitted slaves the time to work their own provision grounds. The slaves had transformed this duty into a right, securing fixed days to tend garden plots and trading their surplus in local markets to supply themselves with critical supplements to their diet. Now, in freedom, they claimed their garden plots as theirs by right, and their key to autonomous, collective living. Officials noted with dismay the freedpeople's troubling tendency to treat the provision grounds they had worked under slavery as their own private property in freedom.

Wherever mass emancipation occurred, struggle ensued. White authorities proved loath to concede the freedpeople the autonomy they sought. Planters retained control of the primary source of capital in the form of land, and the state retained a strong desire to reconstitute a plantation labor force. But the former slaves now possessed the enormous asset of their own bodies. Much as slaves had withheld their labor to impel the movement to mass emancipation, freedpeople withheld their sole source of power to leverage a meaningful freedom out of emancipation. When possible, they moved to towns and cities, where wage work might offer relief from the toil of the fields. Or they might claim interior lands or ground less favorable to the production of cash crops like sugar. The governor of Demerara related "the painful truth that the emancipated peasantry are withdrawing themselves more and more from productive industry, and settling themselves in greater numbers up the rivers and creeks of this vast place."[26] This option proved most viable in places such as British Guiana and Trinidad, which were late, expansive entrants into the sugar game. On the other extreme were colonies such as Barbados, small islands with denser populations and long histories of development, where the scarcity of land made gaining independence more difficult. Jamaica, an established colony with a large population, stood in the middle; its sizable mountain interior had long supported communities of maroons who lived fragile lives of subsistence. The general pattern, then, favored the freedpeople where they had the most options—where labor was scarce and alternatives to plantation work, particularly in the form of unoccupied land, plentiful.

Everywhere in the Caribbean, though, control of local governance remained largely in the hands of the planters. They worked fiercely, often in conjunction with metropolitan officials, to prevent flight from the plantations and to restrict the freedpeople's options. In the British West Indies, the very design of emancipation limited freedpeople's choices by transitioning them to freedom through a period of "apprenticeship." The policy, enacted upon the declaration of mass emancipation in August 1834, compelled slaves aged six and older to serve their owners for a number of years—four years for those designated house slaves, six for field workers. On top of the astronomical compensation of twenty million pounds to the planters, apprenticeship cushioned the plantation economy from the collapse many had feared by guaranteeing a supply of labor lasting several years. Ultimately, though, apprenticeship pleased neither party. The apprentices bridled against their semifreedom, at times engaging in the kinds of work stoppages that had impelled slavery's abolition. "Me free, no bind, no work," declared one striking St. Kitts apprentice.[27] In turn, the planters resented the authority of the colonial magistrates who had been charged with preventing their abuse of the freedpeople. Complained one such official of the planters, "Those gentlemen cling to habits contracted by slavery, which the jealousy of their lost authority fosters up."[28] Popular pressure on the islands ended the apprenticeship system two years prematurely, in 1838.

Even without the support of apprenticeship, planters possessed considerable power to regulate the lives of the freedpeople and compel them into plantation labor. Resurrected from medieval origins, vagrancy laws designed to punish idleness and force the freedpeople into plantation work appeared throughout the postemancipation Atlantic. The Jamaican Vagrancy Act of 1840 exemplified the ways planters could use their control of colonial government to regulate black labor even after apprenticeship. The law declared that "every person who is able to labour" but who was instead "found wandering abroad" or begging could be defined as an "idle and disorderly person." Those found in this condition could be sentenced to hard labor on the testimony of a single "credible witness" brought before a justice of the peace, who was likely a planter himself. An exhaustive list of activities that might keep blacks out of productive plantation work helped define the "rogue and vagabond": dealing in the folk religions of "obeah or myalism," telling fortunes and reading palms, squatting in unoccupied buildings or plantation grounds, gambling, making any "indecent exhibition" of themselves or of prints and pictures, using physical deformities to beg for alms, possessing weapons or implements of thievery, "not having any visible means of subsistence," or simply "not giving any good account of himself or herself."[29] More stringent than similar vagrancy measures in Britain, laws passed by colonial assemblies such as this one clearly operated to reduce freedpeople's options for labor off the plantation. Those who chose not to work would be compelled to.

Onerous new tax codes also impeded the freedpeople's search for autonomy. In the Caribbean, the transformation to a wage system placed heavy burdens on cash-strapped colonies. When withdrawal of freedpeople from the fields collapsed the sugar economy of the West Indies, the real estate market followed. This, along with taxes on slaves themselves, had generated the revenue that funded colonial governments. Emancipation placed yet additional burdens on local governance by making matters long kept private into matters of public policy. Under slavery, masters themselves took responsibility for disciplining and punishing the enslaved, but freedom demanded the expense of new, public systems to manage criminality, such as courts, jails, and workhouses. Reconstructing the plantation economy along free labor lines thus required new sources of solvency for the colonies. In the 1840s, British colonial policy began shifting the primary burden of taxation from cash-strapped planters onto the freedpeople themselves. Import taxes on staple foodstuffs, for example, helped impoverish the freedpeople by elevating the costs of necessary supplies. For the state, the strategy offered the double benefit of reducing the financial strain on the shaky planter class while also creating new incentives for the freedpeople to undertake plantation labor. Under officials such as colonial secretary Earl Grey, taxes on luxury imports fell, only to be offset by taxes directly levied on the freedpeople. Not only did planters find themselves relieved of some financial burden, freedpeople found themselves compelled to engage in wage labor to pay their tax obligations.[30]

Such measures hardly proved foolproof in recapturing lost plantation labor, but the power of the state did aid the recovery of the economy. Small islands with established populations such as St. Kitts, Antigua, and Barbados witnessed fairly rapid reconstitutions of their sugar industries. Within eight years of slavery's final end they had increased production over pre-emancipation levels by 3.8, 5.5, and 8.7 percent, respectively. In contrast, islands with large interiors, less concentrated populations, or shorter histories of development tended to suffer. Eight years after emancipation, Jamaica's sugar production remained at less than half its pre-emancipation levels. British Guiana suffered almost as badly.[31] The pattern was clear: unless compelled by circumstance and law, freed laborers could not be counted on to do the work of slaves. Like whites themselves, they preferred to control their own land, time, and labor. Antislavery free labor theorists had been wrong on crucial points. The freed slave sought to become not a thrifty rural proletarian so much as an autonomous rural peasant. The labor demands of the plantation economy could not easily be met with free workers; the whips of slavery proved more effective than the carrots of only nominally free labor. Production could not be restored except through coercion and control, even if laboring bodies themselves could no longer be owned as property.

Some British abolitionists did object to overt efforts to diminish the value of freedpeople's liberty by regulating their labor. But more typically, those who had fought to free the slaves neglected them in liberty. With the sin of slavery removed, and the freedpeople steadily refuting the basic assumptions of antislavery labor theory, concern for the plight of the former slaves slowly gave way to indifference, or even outright hostility. In 1849, Thomas Carlyle, the Scottish historian, philosopher, and essayist, captured the age's disenchantment in a coarse satire titled "Occasional Discourse on the Negro Question." Carlyle's fictional speaker envisions "Quashee," the generic lazy ex-slave of the West Indies, "sunk to the ears in pumpkin," an easily grown subsistence crop of little value for overseas trade. The problem, as Carlyle saw it, was that the freedpeople could too easily choose an easy subsistence over productive toil; only compulsion could make them produce crops for export. "If Quashee will not honestly aid in bringing out those sugars, cinnamons, and nobler products of the West India islands, for the benefit all mankind, then, I say, neither will the powers permit Quashee to continue growing pumpkins there for his own lazy benefit." In this view, the freedpeople could purchase the privilege of subsistence only with toil dictated by the empire. "Not a square inch of soil in those fruitful Isles, purchased by British blood, shall any Black man hold to grow pumpkins for him, except on terms that are fair towards Britain," Carlyle decreed.[32]

His callous insensitivity to the plight of the freedpeople owed as much to common presumptions regarding the primacy of the market as to the blatant racism that suffused his essay. So long as the profitability of the plantation took precedence over the equality of the freed, emancipation would prove troublesome. Abolitionists had posed slavery as the antithesis of progress and efficiency, offering free labor as an alternative ideal relation between labor and capital. Whereas slavery was compelled, contract was volitional. Free labor thus appeared to be the humane alternative, for no worker would willingly opt to be oppressed. But the freedpeople's choice to avoid labor on exploitative terms threatened the plantation production on which a thriving free market economy also depended. Free labor, scarce and necessary, was expensive labor—particularly relative to the bargain that had been slavery. Which would take precedence: the right of the freedpeople to withdraw from production or the imperative to reconstruct the plantation economy?

A deeper commitment to free labor and free markets might have yielded a meaningful liberty for the freedpeople, but such was the imperative of restoring plantation profits that the blame for failure often fell on former slaves themselves. In metropolitan eyes, the problem was not that the laws of labor supply and demand made the plantation unprofitable with free labor but that blacks refused to submit to the level of exploitation required to keep the plantation economically competitive. Everywhere emancipation happened, this "negro question" arose. The failure, those such as Carlyle reasoned, must lie in blacks themselves. Race thus helped perform the work of labor control, in the process denigrating the sanctity of free labor in favor of the demand for profit. The freed slaves had not, as many had hoped, become a thrifty rural proletariat, eager to embrace the discipline of wage labor in order to better their lot in life through consumption. Rather than engage with the market economy on degrading terms, the freedpeople too often sought to encounter it on their own, or not at all. Their flight from the plantation illustrated that if they could not win, they would try not to play. This undoubtedly reasonable and indeed predictable response to freedom frustrated everyone who sought the reconstitution of the plantation complex. Yet rather than question the free market economic values that had in fact impelled abolitionism, postemancipation theorists concluded that a plantation labor force required compulsion. It could not be enslaved, but neither could it be entirely free.

Spurred by what they viewed as the failure of free labor, Caribbean planters and metropolitan authorities pioneered a momentous new policy whereby contract workers would be imported from South and East Asia and from Africa. Much like the white indentured servants who had helped settle the New World, these workers received passage across the Atlantic in exchange for a commitment to work for a term. Unlike the earlier servants, the contract laborers of the nineteenth century would receive wages, if very low, instead of a promise of land to settle once their contract expired. The new system proved as open to abuse as the old had been. Labor contracts often regulated nearly every facet of daily life, and planters frequently refused to honor their obligations on the basis of workers' perceived violations. The laborers themselves had little recourse in such instances, since the machinery of justice lay in the hands of the governing class.

Metropolitan writers appreciated the irony of superseding slavery with a system that exploited masses of imported nonwhite workers to produce tropical crops in the colonies. British abolitionists worried that England, "once more [able] to allow its subjects to buy Africans, even for the avowed purpose of making them free," created an enormous "stimulus" to the slave trade of other nations, "with all its horrible accompaniments." Just as bad, those who had worked so hard to free black slaves worried about the moral character of non-Christian migrants, complaining about the "horrible contamination" of the "native peasantry" that would "inevitably result from the importation of these sensual and idolatrous Hindoos."[33] Other writers, demonstrating even less sympathy than the abolitionists, equivocated more readily. Of course, argued a commentator in the English Catholic journal the *Tablet*, no one could think of reimposing slavery. "We might be compelled to tolerate a great national crime, so long as it was a political fact, but once removed, it would be a greater crime than ever to restore it," the journal proclaimed. But contract labor was different. It remained "free," with "immigrants bound over by indentures of five and seven years to secure their steady industry." Still, the plan posed problems for the *Tablet*'s editors. Echoing the growing racism of the postemancipation era, they asked, "Would the savages be at all likely to make nice distinctions between driving a herd of captives to the slave-dealer's stores or to the immigrant offices? Would even the officials of the latter be very scrupulous, in the face of the necessity which exists for labourers to be found somehow or other?"[34]

Necessity settled the matter. It seemed to make little sense to abolish slavery only to encourage a "worse slavery" elsewhere by purchasing cheap sugar from slave societies such as Brazil and Cuba, and in the process drive Britain's own planter class to ruin. Importing poorly paid, semifree "coolie" labor kept costs down and the British sugar trade competitive. With Britain lowering its protective tariffs and dismantling its colonial monopolies in the name of free trade, only such measures kept the plantation profitable. In the 1830s, the decade of abolition, England imported over 8,000 indentured workers into the British Caribbean. The following decade, that number rose to over 72,000. Competitors such as France, which would soon trace Britain's path to mass emancipation, confronted the same challenges, and followed suit. In the years from 1851 to 1860, almost 27,000 indentured workers entered the French Caribbean. Cuba, still enslaved but quickly developing a hybrid system of slave and indentured labor on its thriving sugar plantations, imported almost 50,000 from 1851 to 1860, and almost 60,000 the following decade. In the end, the Caribbean became the workplace of 59,000 contract laborers from Africa, 162,000 from China, and an incredible 552,000 from India.[35]

The indentured labor solution helped fulfill the plantation's insatiable thirst for cheap, controllable workers. It succeeded only at the cost of vastly diminishing metropolitan commitments to liberty and exposing the limits of the liberal imagination. Ultimately, the "negro question" centered on the meaning of freedom. It was one thing for the developed nations of the Western world to decide that humans could no longer be held as property. It was quite another to define the rights of the freed. As historian Eric Foner reminds us, the colonial world of European empires was not, after all, very democratic. As a constitutional monarchy, Britain did not extend full rights of citizenship, such as the right to vote for members of the House of Commons, even to all propertied white men living there. France had its own strong yet contentious history of democracy, with the Second Republic that had inaugurated abolition in 1848 lasting only three short years before Louis-Napoléon Bonaparte staged a coup and initiated the Second Empire. With the rights of whites at home so deeply contested, the metropole felt little inclination to consider the rights of colonial subjects. The entire point of empire, after all, was to aggrandize the mother country at the expense of the colony.[36] In this context, defining and enhancing the rights of the freed were subordinated to securing the profitability of the plantation.

The situation differed markedly in the United States. As the largest mass emancipation in the history of Atlantic slavery, the American instance amplified patterns evident elsewhere. But distinct factors rendered the aftermath of slavery exceptional in the United States. The fact that emancipation came about as a consequence of a massive civil war in a highly democratic society, and a war begun over slavery, conditioned every aspect of emancipation in the United States. All mass emancipations created pressures to rapidly reconstitute the plantation economy. The disruptions wrought by the Civil War and the imperative to quickly reunite the national polity increased these pressures enormously. Where the slave power had felt strong enough to launch a military challenge to the national government, adjustment to a postslave labor system was likely to be particularly fraught. The planters would be vital to any reconstruction. Slave owners had lost somewhere between three and three and a half billion dollars' worth of human property, a source of capital even more valuable than the land they had claimed in 1860.[37] They were not likely to let even military failure utterly destroy them. War, after all, does not always conclude the political struggles that start it; when wars end, their causes may not. The Union's point in engaging in armed conflict had been to contest ten southern states' rupture of the national state. In negating secession and reunifying the nation, war had proved decisive: results on the battlefield had demonstrated that the Confederacy could not sustain itself as an independent country. But Union military victory could not utterly negate the ideological, social, and economic commitments that had inspired the slave power's secession in the first place. War might have decided the question of Confederate independence, but it could not decide the question of southern loyalty. In the wake of defeat, on what terms would the southern populace return to the Union fold?

The fate of slavery, the other great issue of the war, had been decided as well, though not by initial design. The Civil War had represented much more than a great slave uprising; it had melded traditions of collective slave resistance with the force of metropolitan abolitionism. The enslaved themselves, along with their free black and white abolitionist allies in the North, exploited the imperatives of war to compel an enormous, critical shift in Union war aims: emancipation. This confluence of forces would prove critical in defining freedom during Reconstruction. But the obstacles were many. Abolitionists and the enslaved had pressed for emancipation, but as Lincoln's subordination of emancipation to the higher priority of reunification suggested, the rights and interests of blacks had hardly been paramount. Only military desperation had driven the Union to abolish slavery. This hasty, ad hoc solution, improvised rather than planned, left enormous questions about the labor system that would replace chattel bondage. These two issues—southern loyalty and the fate of postemancipation labor— would dominate the process of national reunification, or reconstruction.

The same political system whose rupture had caused the war itself would resolve these questions. We have seen how the war came about as a consequence of contesting slavery in a highly democratic society, in which the slave periphery was no colonial appendage, but a fully—indeed excessively—empowered interest, enjoying a potent position in a federal system of governance that granted full equality to all its component states. The highly democratic nature of the American political system had meant that only the mobilization of mass opinion could topple the world's largest and most powerful slave regime. Reconstruction would likewise depend on the operations of a highly democratic political system with a federal form of governance. Once again, democratic politics could cut two ways. The same principles abolitionists could use to argue for blacks' full freedom could be used by the remnants of the slave power to argue that they should not be disenfranchised, even for treason. And the same federalism that secessionists could use to quickly rejoin the Union on equal terms could be employed by abolitionists to guarantee equal treatment of freed slaves in those states.

In the United States, then, a contested two-party political system uniquely mediated postemancipation conflicts, ensuring that popular electoral politics, and not simply the policies of a powerful imperial state, would determine the eventual outcome. With the country nominally reunited, formal politics reemerged as the central arena of contest. The state would once again become the terrain of conflict—this time among the planter interest, the various representatives of Union victory, and the freedpeople and their allies. Another group—one largely absent in Caribbean contestations—would also play a vital role: the sizable population of whites in the plantation zone who had never held slaves but possessed a deep investment in white supremacy. The parties would vie for the loyalty of these various constituencies. The Republicans, radicalized by the electoral successes of 1864, could boast both responsibility for Union victory and a commitment to a meaningful brand of liberty for African Americans. The Democratic Party, the traditional home of the slave power, represented an opposition whose wartime criticisms had sometimes meandered into outright disloyalty. But in the postwar world, it still served as the home of anyone opposing the Republicans. Each party viewed the former Confederate states as bountiful sources of support, which had to be cozened lest their votes be conceded to the other. And because it had been defeated militarily but not ideologically, the planter interest still possessed the will to contest state power through popular politics. It remained to be seen if formal politics could contain this struggle.

A CONTEST NOT CLOSED
Presidential Reconstruction

The contest began, literally, with a bang. The gunshot that ended Abraham Lincoln's life on April 14, 1865, elevated to the presidency Andrew Johnson, an eastern Tennessee Unionist whose political commitments lay in a Jacksonian repugnance of the large slaveholders who had dominated southern politics before the war. Lincoln had never much championed equal rights, but his political skills and sensitivity to the changes wrought by war had kept in abeyance a growing rift on reconstruction policy between the White House and radical Republicans in Congress. Outlined first in his "Proclamation of Amnesty and Reconstruction" of December 1863, Lincoln's wartime plan for Reconstruction had required Confederate states seeking readmission into the Union to abolish slavery. Beyond this, though, he had pledged not to object to any state's "temporary arrangement" to regulate the freedpeople in a manner consistent with "their present condition as a laboring, landless, and homeless class."[38] Thereafter, Lincoln had urged a reconstructed Louisiana state government to confer the vote on black soldiers and those freedpeople found to be "very intelligent"—a request he repeated in his last public statement.[39] Johnson posed his plan for Reconstruction as the continuation of Lincoln's, neglecting that Lincoln had formulated his as a war measure designed to undermine the Confederate will to fight by permitting readmission to the Union on lenient terms.

With the war over and Congress out of session, Johnson continued his predecessor's wartime forbearance, with disastrous effect. "Treason must be made odious, and traitors must be impoverished," he had stated toward the end of the war.[40] Yet during the spring and summer of 1865, he implemented a generous policy of amnesty, whereby most Confederates who had taken up arms could restore their citizenship by taking an oath of loyalty to the Union. Under Johnson's own proclamation of May 1865, high Confederate officials and officers above the rank of colonel could apply for clemency, which Johnson promised would be "liberally extended."[41] True to his word, he pardoned innumerable ex-Confederates, including Alexander Stephens, vice president of the Confederacy, and Dr. Samuel Mudd, alleged to have conspired to assassinate Abraham Lincoln. A second amnesty of 1867 left only about three hundred former Confederates bereft of their rights, and a final act of 1868 extended Johnson's pardon "unconditionally and without reservation, to all and to every person who, directly or indirectly, participated in the late insurrection or rebellion."[42]

Naturally, former Confederates swept back into office in the southern states. Johnson, free to act with Congress out of session, argued that since secession had never been legal, the states of the former Confederacy had never actually left the federal compact. "These States have not gone out of the Union," he argued, "therefore reconstruction is unnecessary."[43] Since the war had been a function of rebellious individuals, the fundamental relation between the states and the Union had never changed. Reuniting the country required only the resumption of normal federal-state relations. During the summer of 1865, the governors Johnson appointed oversaw the election of state constitutional conventions. These conventions, and the new state governments they would form, would be open to and elected by the voting populace as it stood in 1860, excepting those yet denied amnesty. Members of the old ruling class soon occupied governors' mansions, local judiciaries, and state legislatures. Once a state repealed its ordinance of secession, repudiated its war debts, and ratified the Thirteenth Amendment abolishing slavery, it could return to the Union. Of course, this meant delivering a full complement of senators and representatives to the national legislature as well. The former Confederate states sent to the second session of the Thirty-Ninth Congress men who had served as Confederate state officials, representatives to the Confederate Congress, colonels and generals in the Confederate army (four of each), and the former Confederate vice president (the recently pardoned Stephens).[44] When Congress reconvened in December 1865, it refused to seat those elected from the former Confederate states, asserting its constitutional right to judge the qualifications of its own members.[45]

As for the freedpeople, Johnson adopted a laissez-faire approach to emancipation, amending it with his own deep strains of racial prejudice. Privately, he felt from the start that "white men alone must manage the South."[46] Publicly, he was just as straightforward, declaring that "in the progress of nations Negroes have shown less capacity for government than any other race of people."[47] Such views echoed patterns from the Caribbean, where no one expected emancipated slaves to wield even the limited political rights due colonial subjects. Also as happened in the Caribbean, Johnson envisioned little special provision for the freed. "The career of free industry must be fairly opened to them, and then their future prosperity and condition must, after all, rest mainly on themselves," he stated. Ultimately, the freedpeople were on their own. "If they fail, and so perish away," he continued, "let us be careful that the failure shall not be attributable to any denial of justice."[48]

But the leaders of the states that had once been the Confederacy had no intention of letting the free market dictate their success or failure in the post-emancipation world. Throughout the postwar South, reports of abuse filtered back to Union officials. One officer in Mississippi captured the mood effectively:

> Wherever I go . . . I hear the people talk in such a way as to indicate that they are yet unable to conceive of the Negro as possessing any rights at all. Men who are honorable in their dealings with their white neighbors will cheat a Negro without feeling a single twinge of their honor. To kill a Negro they do not deem murder; to debauch a Negro woman they do not think fornication; to take the property away from a Negro they do not consider robbery. The people boast that when they get freedmen affairs in their own hands, to use their own classic expression, "the niggers will catch hell."[49]

The new state legislatures of the South enshrined such attitudes in law. They crafted a series of measures, built on those passed in the British West Indies, to control black labor. These "black codes," which varied from state to state, defined the former slaves' fragile freedom, acknowledging their legal right to marry, sign contracts, hold property, and bring suit in court. They also strictly controlled the work lives of the freedpeople, as even a small portion of South Carolina's provision reveals: "On farms or in out-door service, the hours of labor, except on Sunday, shall be from sun-rise to sun-set, with a reasonable interval for breakfast and dinner. Servants shall rise at dawn in the morning, feed, water and care for the animals on the farm, do the usual and needful work about the premises, prepare their meals for the day, . . . and begin the farm work or other work by sun-rise."[50] Other black codes provided for legal segregation in public accommodations, and all excluded African Americans from juries and prohibited racial intermarriage. Some required African Americans to obtain expensive licenses if they wished to engage in any other than agricultural labor—a benefit to white mechanics and tradesmen who feared black competition. Others contained vagrancy provisions that imposed strict penalties on those deemed unemployed, idle, or merely spendthrift. Many defined crimes so vaguely that virtually any black behavior out of keeping with planters' desires could fall under them. Mississippi's was typical in this regard, defining the imprisonable "rogue and vagabond" as "idle and dissipated persons, beggars, jugglers, or persons practicing unlawful games or plays, runaways, common drunkards, common night-walkers, pilferers, lewd, wanton, or lascivious persons, in speech or behavior, common railers and brawlers, persons who neglect their calling or employment, misspend what they earn, or do not provide for the support of themselves or their families, or dependents, and all other idle and disorderly persons, including all who neglect all lawful business, habitually misspend their time by frequenting houses of ill-fame, gaming-houses, or tippling shops."[51] The codes thus intruded into every aspect of black life. Many states' codes included apprenticeship provisions, which made a mockery of freedom by giving planters control of the underage children of freedpeople. Other new laws criminalized a wide variety of behaviors—from displaying impudence to white employers to preaching the Gospel without a license.[52]

As in the Caribbean, the black codes sought to reestablish planters' control over the labor of African Americans by replacing the dominance of the slave master with the oppressive oversight of the state. But the South was not the Caribbean. The states that had seceded formed part of a national union that had triumphed in a test of arms against the slave power. The Union public that had sacrificed so much for victory had little tolerance for regulations that looked so much like slavery. Newspapers throughout the North declared that "there can be no 'Black Codes'" in the South—that "all laws applicable to one race shall apply to the other."[53] As before the war, the threat to liberty posed by a resurrected slave power also proved a potent rouser of northern objections. One newspaper spread the story that in some places in the South "any man who questions the justice of local enactments or Black Codes is to be imprisoned."[54] Complaints against the codes filtered their way up to members of Congress, such as Senator Henry Wilson of Massachusetts, who told the southern states, "You must repeal your humiliating and degrading black codes, and give suffrage to the loyal men of the country without distinction of color."[55]

The black codes invited backlash by raising legitimate questions over whether the war was actually over. True, Union armies had caused battlefield hostilities to cease, but the passage of the codes suggested that the interests that had led eleven southern states to secede had not died. "Neither the Rebellion nor Slavery is yet ended," William Lloyd Garrison declared in the fall of 1865. "Slavery has been abolished in name; but that is all."[56] One might have expected such a stance from America's foremost abolitionist, but even the opposition press concurred. "The contest was not closed when Lee surrendered," argued the editor of the *St. Louis Democrat*. "The rebel puts aside the bayonet, and takes up the ballot." The freedmen could not be left "at the mercy of those who so long held them in slavery."[57] Complained Virginia freedpeople, "We are 'sheep in the midst of wolves.'" Former Confederates' new statements of loyalty were but a "cover" to achieve their goal of "getting restored to their former relations with the Federal Government," at which point they would "render the freedom you have given us more intolerable than the slavery they intended for us."[58]

That mercy was not forthcoming was made brutally evident in two riots that struck the South the year after formal hostilities ended: Memphis in May, New Orleans in July. The Memphis violence, occasioned by street clashes between mustered-out black veterans and white police, illustrated the social tensions fostered by the immigration to the city of thousands of refugee freedpeople, seeking sustenance and work. The three days of violence claimed the lives of at least forty-six African Americans and two whites. The destruction included dozens of burned black homes, three black churches, and eight black schoolhouses, totaling one hundred twenty thousand dollars in property damage. The working-class white policemen who sparked the riot freely robbed individual veterans of the pay they had just received from mustering out of the army—amounts ranging from five to five hundred dollars.[59] A Union official condescendingly ascribed the "remote cause" of the riot to "a bitterness of feeling which has always existed between the low whites & blacks, both of whom have long advanced rival claims for superiority, both being as degraded as human beings can possibly be." But the northern press's even-handed assessments—*Harper's* reported that the "lower class of white citizens were as responsible as were the soldiers"[60]—belied the experience of Memphis blacks themselves. One African American witness testified that white policemen began the fray when a group of freedmen "stepped off the sidewalk to allow the policemen to pass." When one of the officers tripped, the others "drew their revolvers"; one "struck one of the Negroes on the head with his pistol, breaking it."[61] Another black witness saw a band of policemen march down an otherwise quiet street firing indiscriminately at blacks. "The Negroes ran away without offering any resistance, the police following & shooting," he continued.[62] Nothing that happened on the street could have justified the violation of black homes that accompanied the riot. In one typical instance, a freedwoman testified that whites broke into her house and "abused me very badly"—a euphemism for rape—and set fire to her home. When the woman's husband ran outside to douse the fire, the rioters shot and robbed him.[63]

If the Memphis riot spoke to long-standing racial tensions between black and white working classes, the violence in New Orleans illustrated the fragility of formal politics in the immediate aftermath of war. The trouble began when radical Republicans sought to reconvene the state's constitutional convention to eliminate discriminatory black codes and voting exclusions. Some hundred African Americans, many of them former soldiers seeking their rights, marched in support to the convention hall. An armed white mob, composed largely of former Confederate soldiers, greeted them. Pistol shots punctuated heated discussion, and several hours of open warfare erupted in the streets. Less prepared for violence, many blacks retreated to the convention hall, where, short of ammunition, they succumbed to an enemy that gave them no quarter. Contemporary accounts described "negroes mutilated and literally beaten to death as they sought to escape."[64] The violence left 38 dead, all but 4 of whom were black, and 146 injured, again mostly black. While a conservative Richmond newspaper blamed the riot on a "radical conspiracy" to disfranchise "nine-tenths of the white inhabitants of Louisiana" and "bring about a war of the races at the South," *New York Tribune* editor Horace Greeley pointed to the White House: "The policy of Andrew Johnson engendered the demon fury which has shed blood in the streets of the Crescent City."[65] The Republican *Chicago Tribune* similarly linked the New Orleans bloodshed to larger trends: "The rebels of New Orleans have proved worthy of their cousinship to the rebels in Memphis. They have fleshed their maiden swords in the blood of the negro."[66] No African American could have missed the point. The war for union may have been over, but the one for equality had just begun.

Between the black codes and the riots, consensus grew that the government had some role, even if highly limited, in guaranteeing the rights of the freed. The concept was not entirely new. Since the war itself, Union leaders had understood the need for federal action to help secure the rights of the freedpeople. In 1863, Secretary of War Edwin Stanton charged a three-man committee of prominent northern reformers with investigating the state of African Americans throughout the South. Their report surveyed the slaves' prospects for liberty, arguing that the federal government had an important, if transient, role to play in the transition to freedom. For the report's authors, the nation confronted the question of whether or not the free slave "will be able peacefully to maintain his new rights" and "protect himself against undue ascendency and imposition from the white man." More than the freedpeople's long habits of dependence, whites' own habits of prejudice posed the great challenge to postemancipation peace. Would the freed slave bear white hostility "as patiently in his capacity of freedman as he has borne it under subjection as a slave?" wondered the commission.[67] Congress adopted its recommendation for a new federal agency, which would launch the process of educating the former slaves and "guard them against the virtual restoration of slavery in any form."[68] In March 1863, Congress established the Bureau of Refugees, Freedmen, and Abandoned Lands, commonly known as the Freedmen's Bureau. This agency would have "control of all subjects relating to refugees and freedmen from rebel states," including relief and shelter, and the provision of forty-acre plots of abandoned Confederate land for former slaves (a plan that failed to materialize).[69] Over time, the bureau would come to oversee the negotiation of labor contracts between freedpeople and planters, and establish a network of schools throughout the South.

As an experiment in governance, the bureau represented a novel if not revolutionary intervention, far exceeding anything ever contemplated in the Caribbean. As an instrument of transition to freedom, though, it fell far short of the need. The same laissez-faire principles that undergirded the Port Royal experiment dictated that the bureau could never be a permanent institution. The Freedmen's Inquiry Commission had stressed that such an agency would be a "temporary necessity" only, for the sooner the freedpeople could "stand alone and make their own unaided way, the better both for our race and for theirs."[70] The bureau's head, Union General Oliver Otis Howard, kept faith with this principle, issuing orders to his state assistant commissioners to ensure that the freedpeople would not become dependent on government largesse. "Every effort will be made to render the people self-supporting," he wrote. "Government supplies will only be temporarily issued to enable destitute persons speedily to support themselves."[71] Assistant commissioners dutifully relayed the message to the freedpeople, urging them to be "industrious and frugal," and warning them that the lazy "will not be allowed to live in idleness when there is work to be had." At the same time that bureau agents promised freedpeople government help "if others fail to recognize your right to equal freedom with white persons," they also stressed the temporary nature of the effort, cautioning that "the special care that the Government now exercises over you as a people, will soon be withdrawn, and you will be left to work and provide for yourselves."[72] The bureau thus faced the same challenge that confronted Port Royal: what role, if any, could government play in the transition to a free labor economy of minimal state inference?

The bureau became a conservative bête noire throughout the nation. Southern white politicians such as Wade Hampton of South Carolina objected to its "pernicious and mischievous interference," declaring "the strong but paternal hand" of the former masters of "the nergo" to be "the only hope of rendering him either useful, industrious or harmless."[73] Others, such as J. D. B. DeBow, told Congress that the Freedmen's Bureau was "only productive of mischief" and that "the whole regulation" of the freedpeople should be "left to the people of the communities in which they live."[74] The image of the bureau as little more than a government almshouse found traction even in the North. In Pennsylvania's gubernatorial election of 1866, Democrat Heister Clymer attacked his Republican opponent, Union General John W. Geary, for supporting "an agency to keep the negro in idleness at the expense of the white man." A campaign poster making this case depicted a Sambo-like African American lounging in ease while whites labored around him. A depiction of the U.S. Capitol building stood in the background, its pillars labeled "indolence," "white women," "idleness," and "apathy" (figure 8.1).[75]

FIGURE 8.1. *The Freedman's Bureau! An Agency to Keep the Negro in Idleness at the Expense of the White Man* (1866).
Library of Congress, Rare Book and Special Collections Division, Washington, D.C.

True to his roots as a Jacksonian Democrat, President Johnson sided with the conservatives. In February 1866, he vetoed a bill renewing and expanding the work of the Freedmen's Bureau, basing his decision on a very narrow reading of the executive's constitutional power. "The bill before me contains provisions which, in my opinion, are not warranted by the Constitution," he declared. In particular, Johnson objected to the bill's new system of bureau courts, which permitted the freedpeople an alternative to prejudiced local courts where they could find no justice. As the bureau courts would reside under the Department of War, the bill entailed a vast expansion of "military jurisdiction," with no "legal supervision." To the objection that the spirit of the Confederacy lived on in measures repressing the freedpeople, Johnson announced that the nation was no longer at war, and any assertion to the contrary would "unnecessarily disturb the commerce and credit and industry of the country."[76] Congress twice overrode Johnson's veto, demonstrating the Republicans' domination of the national legislature, but clearly Johnson did not stand alone.

Conflict over the Freedmen's Bureau dovetailed with the return of former Confederates to state and local office, the black codes, and the riots to trigger a showdown between White House and Congress over Reconstruction policy. At issue was nothing less than the meaning of the Civil War, and even of freedom. Would the United States, as Johnson and the planter interest intended, follow the path of the Caribbean and seek to force the freedpeople into becoming a rural proletariat with tightly circumscribed legal rights? Or would it seek, as blacks and their anti-slavery-minded allies desired, the full citizenship and equality promised by the nation's founding charters? The question involved not simply the interests of the freedpeople, but the destiny of the nation. To many in the North, the course of events suggested that if left unimpeded the southern states would quickly return the freedpeople to servility—a virtual negation of Union sacrifice and victory. Editors of the *Chicago Tribune* objected to Mississippi's black code on such grounds, vowing that "the men of the North will convert the State of Mississippi into a frog pond before they will allow any such laws to disgrace one foot of soil in which the bones of our soldiers sleep and over which the flag of freedom waves."[77] Thus many who otherwise might have cared little for the freedpeople came to advocate measures to protect blacks' civil rights.

Of course, defenders of the planter interest fought back vociferously, repeating, as did the renowned southern conservative George Fitzhugh, the cant that southern white men best knew about "managing the negroes." In the absence of slavery, Fitzhugh argued, "a great deal of severe legislation will be required to compel negroes to labor as much as they should do." The innate inferiority of people whom law, custom, nature, and God had placed under whites required this. "Never did the black man come into contact with the white man," Fitzhugh argued, "that he did not become his subordinate, if not his slave."[78] The ongoing contest over the place of the freedpeople in Reconstruction thus forced the nation to clarify the ambiguous nature of freedom, and even of blacks themselves.

A GOVERNMENT THUS OUTRAGED
Congressional Reconstruction

In the face of conservative intransigence, Republicans in Congress began pressing for a federal statute to protect the freedpeople's rights from the interference of hostile southern state governments. The result, which became the momentous Civil Rights Act of 1866, defined the rights that attended freedom. The bill stipulated that the freedpeople had rights "to make and enforce contracts, to sue, be parties, and give evidence, to inherit, purchase, lease, sell, hold, and convey real and personal property, and to full and equal benefit of all laws and proceedings for the security of person and property, as is enjoyed by white citizens, and shall be subject to like punishment, pains, and penalties." This stunning statement sought to end forever the possibility that American freedpeople would fall into the status of the rights-limited colonial subjects of the Caribbean. It fundamentally altered the character of citizenship in the federal Republic, declaring that if the states would not protect the rights of their citizens, the national government would.

Johnson vetoed it. His March 1866 statement on the matter repeated his earlier concerns with the bill to renew the Freedmen's Bureau—that it constituted yet "another step, or rather stride, toward centralization and the concentration of all legislative powers in the National Government." For Johnson, a measure ensuring the equality of a special group targeted for oppression constituted an extraordinary exercise of government on their behalf—what was commonly termed "class legislation." In protecting the rights of the freedpeople, Johnson argued, the bill established "safeguards which go infinitely beyond any that the General Government has ever provided for the white race. In fact, the distinction of race and color is by the bill made to operate in favor of the colored and against the white race."[79] The bill did no such thing, of course; it merely guaranteed certain minimal rights all Americans were legally qualified to enjoy on the basis of their citizenship. The *Liberator* quickly noted the hypocrisy of a president who decried any form of class legislation benefitting the freedpeople, but countenanced black codes that marked freedpeople "as a class for separate and specially stringent legislation."[80] Though Congress overrode Johnson's veto, many shared his sentiments. Democratic newspapers denounced the bill as a "scheme of the abolition traitors of Congress to override and destroy the States" by allowing them to be "swallowed up in a centralized despotism."[81] The Harrisburg *Patriot* feared that the bill, in effectively enfranchising blacks, would permit the radical Republican "revolutionists" to wield the "blindly ignorant power" of the black vote and thus complete their plans to turn the nation into a "consolidated central despotism" that would be "as despotic in its sway as the Old World monarchies."[82] One Kentucky state legislator charged that the nation was "drifting into a centralized despotism," while another, with no apparent sense of irony, vowed that he "would rather die a freeman than live a slave to a despotic power."[83]

This extraordinary concern with maintaining a limited role for government demonstrated that the great political battles of Reconstruction were fought not only on the terrain of race, but also on the ground of constitutional law. Those who would defend the rights of the freedpeople contended not simply with the hostility of the slave power and an overwhelmingly prejudiced public. They also confronted their own long-standing commitments to limited government. Since the American system was founded in fears of consolidated power, the federal government had been granted only the minimal authority necessary to keep the Union together. John Adams had written words on the eve of the Revolution that innumerable midcentury Americans cherished: "Nip the shoots of arbitrary power in the bud, is the only maxim which can ever preserve the liberties of any people."[84] Federal authority had been tested over the decades since, to be sure. Andrew Jackson, the very president who warned Congress "against all encroachments upon the legitimate sphere of state sovereignty," had also stared down South Carolina nullifiers in 1832 with the threat of federal troops.[85] But Jackson's own presumption, and the philosophy of the party he created, had always favored the rights of states, where liberty was deemed most safely guarded. Democratic Presidents James K. Polk and Franklin Pierce both vetoed bills funding transportation improvements, based on a very narrow view of the acceptable reach of federal power. In 1846, Polk had argued that such an exercise of national authority "tends imperceptibly to a consolidation of power in the Government intended by its framers to be thus limited in its authority." Pierce vetoed a similar funding measure in 1854 because it constituted a "dangerous augmentation of the political functions" of the national government.[86] In vetoing the Civil Rights Act of 1866, Andrew Johnson merely followed this well-worn lead.

But Reconstruction posed a problem for limited government more intractable than the one presented by the war itself. On the one hand, who could deny the Union's right to ensure the fruits of its hard-won victory by protecting the rights of those it had freed? Many Republicans thought the Union owed the rebel states little. Recalling that secession had sparked a war "of the greatest magnitude," Congress's Joint Committee on Reconstruction argued that "a government thus outraged had a most perfect right" to prevent "recurrence of such outrages in the future."[87] Republican Richard Henry Dana, Jr. put the matter even more baldly. "When one nation has conquered another, . . . the victorious nation does not retreat from the country and give up possession of it, because the fighting has ceased," he declared in a Boston speech. "The conquering party may hold the other in the grasp of war until it has secured whatever it has a right to require."[88] Fellow Massachusetts Senator Henry Wilson concurred, suggesting that representatives of the slave power had gambled all on secession, and lost: "They went into civil war to get the right to carry slaves into the territories, and they came out of it without the right to hold slaves in the States."[89] For men like Wilson, the black codes, race riots, and other efforts to limit black rights and options in freedom suggested that the peace had not yet been won, and that extraordinary measures were required to vindicate the war effort.

Against this stood long traditions—bound in both jurisprudence and popular political culture—stressing the overwhelming importance of limited government. The Civil War had posed a crisis that required the vast expansion of federal power: the selective suspension of the normal court system, the implementation of national conscription, the imposition of a federal income tax, and of course emancipation. But these had been temporary wartime necessities, not fundamental changes in the nature of the government. Once the war ended, enormous pressures existed to scale back the reach of the national state, even among radical Republicans. A Republican newspaper from Philadelphia explained that the war had "so effectually disposed of" the "State sovereignty heresy" that Americans now saw "a tendency toward the other extreme"—"a perilous aggregation of power at Washington." War had "rendered unavoidable the use by the government of all the powers possible within the limits of the Constitution." Now, though, the time had come to scale back the national authority.[90] One need consider only the rapid demobilization of the Union army for evidence of this commitment. From a force numbering over a million men in May 1865, the army mustered out over eight hundred thousand troops in a matter of months; a year after the war's end, it numbered only eleven thousand.[91]

What would this dedication to minimal government mean to those for whom the war had been fought? In a speech in 1866, Republican leader Carl Schurz explained that the "principal difficulty" of Reconstruction was that the political system of the United States "rests upon the right of the people to control their local concerns" through self-governance. He honored this ideal, but should the nation simply return to its previous system, it would reinstate "the very people who had been in rebellion against the Government." They would be allowed to "control the very results which had been won." Such a result "would have been a surrender of the consequences of our victory to the discretion of the defeated."[92] How then to secure the fruits of victory while remaining true to the principles of limited and local government the Union had fought to preserve? No measure to aid the freedpeople in securing their rights was likely to succeed should it overstep the acceptable role of federal authority. Even "grasp of war" theorist Richard Henry Dana tempered his rhetoric with a clear statement of faith in limited central government. The United States had never been willing to embrace a "consolidated democratic republic," and Dana did not intend to urge one now; in a balance of state and federal power "is our safety," he wrote.[93]

The Civil Rights Act of 1866, as the other great laws and constitutional amendments of Reconstruction that followed it, must be understood in this context. The act did indeed represent a remarkable reformulation of the relationship between the states and the federal government, and it did expand the power of the national government by making it the guarantor of citizens' rights when states failed to do so. But it did all this only as an alternative to the much more disagreeable option of direct intervention into state affairs. Granting civil rights to the freedpeople, rather than violating the principle of limited government, actually helped keep the government out of local matters.

Republicans hoped that black enfranchisement would give the freedpeople the means to protect themselves, thus obviating the need for more invasive federal intrusions. "The arm of the Federal government is long, but it is far too short to protect the rights of individuals in the interior of distant States," Frederick Douglass argued. "They must have the power to protect themselves, or they will go unprotected, spite of all the laws the Federal Government can put upon the national statute-book."[94] From the start of Reconstruction, Carl Schurz, the antislavery Republican, had used such reasoning in urging Andrew Johnson to press for blacks' civil rights. The right to vote offered the freedpeople "the best protection" against the hostility of both state government and individual whites. Best of all, giving the freedpeople representation in their own governance would render unnecessary "the interference of the national authority" into the "home concerns of the southern States."[95] Champions of the civil rights bill constantly stressed the limited nature of the power expansion it contemplated. Lyman Trumbull, the Illinois senator who authored the bill, acknowledged that it could be criticized for "drawing to the Federal Government powers that properly belong to 'States.'" But he stressed that the bill "will have no operations in any State where the laws are equal, where all persons have the same civil rights without regard to color or race."[96] Even Jacob Cox, the conservative governor of Ohio, endorsed this reasoning. If the "State laws and State authorities" provide equal protection for civil rights, "there will be no need of federal legislation on the subject, and the power will remain in abeyance."[97]

Congress overrode Johnson's veto and passed the Civil Rights Act of 1866, then went on to do much, much more. First, it began moving the Fourteenth

Amendment to the Constitution. If nothing else, Johnson's vetoes had suggested the fragility of any purely legislative solution to the problem of equal rights. A constitutional amendment promised to protect the act's provisions from a hostile president, future Congresses, or a recalcitrant judiciary. Like the Civil Rights Act, the amendment asserted the rights of citizenship due all native-born Americans. In explicitly defending the Fifth Amendment's protections of life, liberty, and property from state incursion, it rescinded the principle of dual citizenship that Chief Justice Roger Taney had introduced in *Dred Scott v. Sandford*. The amendment also disenfranchised Confederate leaders who had renounced their position in the government of the United States, thereby reversing Johnson's lenient amnesty policy. And it repudiated all Confederate losses or debts, thus ensuring that slaveholders could never call on the federal government to repay foreign loans made to the Confederacy, or seek indemnification for the losses of their slaves. When the states ratified the amendment in 1868, they dealt a final death blow to the Confederacy.

But the amendment went one step short of protecting black voting rights outright. Instead, its second section acted as a kind of reverse three-fifths clause. Rather than rewarding states with representation for people denied rights, it penalized them for denying the elective franchise on the basis of race.[98] For the purposes of calculating representation in the House and Electoral College, a state's population would be reduced by the proportion of adult men the state prohibited from voting. In the 1870 census, African American men twenty-one years or older constituted roughly a third of the entire adult male population of the former slave states. Had all of those states prohibited these million men from voting, 4.5 million people would have been struck from the entire South's basis of representation. The loss would have meant an enormous swing in sectional political power. Under the most punitive scenario, the northern states would have gained 25 seats in the House (of a total of 292), while the South would have lost 25. The situation in the Electoral College would have reflected these same proportions, with the southern states losing 16 percent of their influence.[99]

As it was, most southern states had little inclination to impose any racial liabilities on the franchise, for the next Congress passed a series of sweeping measures designed to restructure state governments along Congress's vision. The Reconstruction Acts passed by Congress from March 1867 to March 1868 removed from the Union and placed under temporary military rule ten of the eleven states that had made up the Confederacy. (Tennessee, having ratified the Thirteenth Amendment, avoided military reconstruction.) In order to seek readmission, the states had to hold new constitutional conventions, which were to be open to delegates regardless of race, who would be voted on by citizens regardless of race. The conventions had to create new state governments that abolished slavery, ratified the Fourteenth Amendment, and eliminated racial barriers to enfranchisement. What ensued was nothing short of a political revolution in the South. The new governments constituted the Atlantic's first meaningful experiment in biracial democracy. African American men not only voted in enormous numbers, up to two thousand of them served in varying federal, state, and local offices. Once portrayed as unlettered and politically inept, these often obscure figures have been revealed by more recent research to have been remarkably skilled and generally well educated.[100] Under Republican rule, many former Confederate states even sent black men to Washington. Blanche K. Bruce and Hiram Revels served as U.S. senators from their home state of Mississippi, while South Carolina sent a complement of African American representatives to the House, including Robert Smalls, J. H. Rainey, and Robert Brown Elliot. P. B. S. Pinchback of Louisiana became the first black governor of a state, while a host of lesser positions, from lieutenant governor to coroner, went to African Americans. To consolidate these gains, in February 1869 Congress passed the Fifteenth Amendment prohibiting the denial of suffrage on the basis of race; the following spring, the states ratified it.

Collectively, the actions of the Thirty-Ninth and Fortieth Congresses constituted a wholesale overturning of Presidential Reconstruction. President Johnson wielded the veto pen vigorously but futilely. Congress overrode his objections, and eventually impeached him for his opposition. In the history of the Atlantic, no other metropole so assertively sought to fetter a slave power after emancipation. That it happened in the United States owed to Union politicians' commitments to ensuring that the costly war that had ended slavery affirmed the basic promises of freedom in a democratic society. The slave power had brought on itself this novel reaction by challenging the result of the Civil War and seeking to reconstitute slavery in all but name. The Republican regimes that swept into state office throughout the South in the wake of the Reconstruction Acts overturned the power of the planters. Rooted in the newly enfranchised black vote but buoyed by masses of southern whites who had long had cause to resent the slave power, the Reconstruction state governments embarked on a campaign to redefine southern life. Throughout much of the region, Republican-controlled state legislatures initiated systems of taxpayer-supported public education, funded internal improvements in transportation infrastructure, offered debt relief and lien protection for smallholders, and sponsored the creation of asylums and other institutions designed to aid the destitute. Most of all, political participation offered the freedpeople an opportunity to police their own states, by electing representatives and local officials who could protect their interests or by joining state militias that could counter the omnipresent threat of racial violence.

Such measures constituted a virtual revolution in the domestic governance of the South. On the surface, the states that had held slaves retained their power in national tribunals. In 1860, they had contained 32 percent of the nation's free population but, with the benefits of the three-fifths clause, 35 percent of the seats in the House and nearly 40 percent of the votes in the Electoral College. Much changed in a single decade. With slavery gone, the free population of the South rose dramatically—from 6.4 million, or 28 percent of the country's entire population in 1860, to 13.4 million, or 35 percent of the national population in 1870.[101] Millions of new free black citizens more than offset the number of slaves who had been counted for representation by the three-fifths clause. The southern states remained a potent force in national politics. As a black politician from South Carolina would later say of the slave states in 1860, "the existence of the institution of slavery cemented their personal interests and compelled them to act in concert in political matters."[102] But with the slaves freed and enfranchised, the South no longer stood united in protecting white supremacy. Now an entire class of people, who had had no voice but had nonetheless boosted the South's representation, could participate in the process. Within each state, the freedpeople and their allies could fight for their equality, while within the nation the South could no longer function as a united bloc dedicated to serving the planter interest. Southern elites who had once contended primarily with northern states to protect their interests now found themselves confronted with a political uprising of their subordinate classes.

THE TRAGIC ERA
The Undoing of Reconstruction

In 1867, at the start of Congressional Reconstruction, the freedpeople's position appeared to be more enviable than that of any other group that had achieved freedom in an Atlantic slave society. As in the Caribbean, the planter interest in the U.S. South had attempted to replace servitude with a stringent set of laws designed to keep nominally "free" black labor docile, immobile, and inexpensive. But because slavery in the United States ended as the result of a war fought over the institution, the victors proved unwilling to let the planters retain their power. Determined to wrest meaning from the sacrifices of the Civil War, the Union government sought to ensure that freed slaves enjoyed at least a minimal level of freedom. Republican-led Congresses wrote these guarantees into the Constitution, in the process asserting the federal government's ultimate role in securing liberty. A casual observer would have pronounced the slave power dead.

In a mere decade, though, the promise of Reconstruction dissolved. One by one, Republicans lost control of every southern state government to Democratic rivals. The political representatives of the freedpeople fell, and with them the protection of government. Even worse, the national government itself became indifferent, and then hostile, to their concerns. In 1876, a disputed election for president ended the last federal efforts to police racial discord in the South. In the following year, Democrats toppled the last of the Republican state governments, leaving the freedpeople largely unaided at any level. At the same time, the federal court system began systematically rolling back the constitutional protections provided by the Reconstruction amendments, stripping them of their intent and power. Black people in the South would be left on their own. The Civil War and Reconstruction did destroy the slave power, but in its place arose a system of sharecropping that reduced the freedpeople to debt peonage. Just as bad, unlike in the Caribbean, most freedpeople in the United States lived amid a large, militarized white settler population that clung tenaciously to its racial privileges.

The damage had been long in coming. From its very start, Congressional Reconstruction had faced determined opposition. "The white people of our State will never quietly submit to negro rule," South Carolina whites told Congress.[103] In every southern state, representatives of the old order sought political power under the banner of the Democratic Party. In some states, black majorities helped maintain Republican control. In others, though, conservative forces gained early toeholds, and swept the Republicans out. In Virginia, radical Republicans overplayed their hand, split their party, and lost the statehouse to conservative opponents in 1870. In Georgia, Democrats and breakaway Republicans colluded to deny blacks the right to hold office in the new state governments. A September 1868 massacre of black Republicans at a political rally in Camilla emphasized the point. Calls to return Georgia to military rule failed, and the state legislature fell into Democratic hands in 1870. North Carolina, too, suffered an early return to conservative rule, propelled by charges of Republican corruption and mismanagement. Other Republican state governments survived longer. South Carolina, Mississippi, Florida, and Louisiana, for example, remained in Republican hands until the completion of the 1875–76 election cycle.

Everywhere, though, conservative rule eventually returned. The narrative varied from state to state, but the general pattern of Republican failure followed a distressingly common trajectory. Factionalism defined the first component, as many of the Reconstruction state governments foundered on internal divisions. Northern politicians active in Republican politics in the South often sought to take leading roles in a party that necessarily relied on the support of white southerners. The latter, who often hailed from the ranks of wartime Unionists and prewar nonslaveholders (and who were referred to in Reconstruction lore as "scalawags"), resented the focus of "carpetbaggers" (northerners allegedly seeking to exploit the defeated South) on issues of racial equality and economic development. They also made strange bedfellows with the party's other great bloc, the freedpeople. Overwhelmingly, freed slaves cared less about the debt relief that concerned their white colleagues and more about civil rights, less for punishing the planters and more for buttressing their own fragile security. Keeping the two groups united under the Republican banner proved a difficult but crucial task, for no group was more critical to the success of Republican Reconstruction than southern whites. With carpetbaggers far too few to influence electoral outcomes, and African Americans a large minority safely in the camp of the Republicans, southern whites constituted the crucial swing votes that delivered elections. With them, Republicans could hope to win; without them, Republicans could not help but lose.

The Republicans' failure to maintain the faith of southern whites owed in part to fundamental incoherence in the Republican message. Emancipation from the long domination of the planter class most attracted southern whites to the party. Measures such as the Southern Homestead Act of 1866 sought to secure a base of support for Republican policies by offering accessible land to a class long denied it. Other Republican platform planks offered relief from the omnipresent threat of debt in a cash-poor economy. It was no surprise that Republicans found their strongest white support outside the plantation zone, and particularly in the upcountry counties lining the Appalachians—in northern Alabama, the western Carolinas, and eastern Tennessee.

But to these, as well as to many African Americans, the Republicans offered something neither group particularly desired—a distinctly northern vision of a highly capitalistic postemancipation world, wherein the planter class would be supplanted by a new agricultural system modeled on the ideal of the thrifty yeoman farmer of the North. Freed of planter control, all would have the chance to rise through energetic participation in a thriving market economy. As emblem of this commitment, Republican leaders in the reconstructed states championed the vigorous construction of internal improvements. State-backed bonds would spur investment in railroads, which would tie the South together in a web of commerce similar to that which had made the North so powerful. Ultimately, this platform failed to maintain the loyalty of many southern whites, who had long expressed ambivalence toward the emerging market economy anyway. Perhaps, as carpetbagger Albion Tourgée suggested, Republicans moved too fast. "That was our mistake," he put it in his 1883 novel, *A Fool's Errand.* "We tried to superimpose the civilization, the idea of the North upon the South at a moment's warning."[104]

More practically, the sheer expense of freedom exacerbated the situation immensely. The social costs of the Old South had been borne primarily by the wealthy, paternalistic elites of southern society. In freedom, the basic public services necessary to care for large new numbers of freedpeople, all entitled to the benefits of citizenship, rose considerably. Furthermore, the Republican state governments of Reconstruction distributed their increased costs more evenly than before. Tax burdens increased on nonelite southern whites, who spent more and more of their scanty dollars supporting a black population for whom they felt little sympathy. A storm of Democratic propaganda declaring the Reconstruction governments corrupt took root, and the southern whites who had initially supported the Reconstruction governments began to turn against them.[105]

Latent tensions in the vision of liberal capitalism itself fueled this fire. Did the Republican Party stand for individual economic opportunity and uplift through hard work and moral virtue? Or did it stand for the concentration of capital through aggressive profit seeking and economic consolidation? As the Port Royal experiment had demonstrated, free market success could just as easily mean the exploitation of working people as it might their "elevation." Ultimately, charges of corruption proved no more well founded in the Reconstruction South than anywhere else in American society at the time. But they succeeded in helping to peel off southern whites because they resonated with root anxieties over the state's connection to the trajectory of industrial capitalism.

The most critical component of failure lay in the racial animus so deeply woven into southern society. In all the states of the former Confederacy, the forces of conservatism reasserted their power through campaigns of violence with no analogue in other postemancipation slave societies. The efforts began among groups such as the Ku Klux Klan and Knights of the White Camelia, Confederate veteran organizations formed shortly after the Civil War. When Congressional Reconstruction opened the franchise to African Americans, and Republican majorities consequently took over statehouses, these groups grew into the paramilitary wing of the conservative opposition in the South.

Assuming disguises that preserved individuals' anonymity, their members pursued tactics of political and social terror. "Night rides" to the homes of politically active freedpeople and their families ended with whippings, beatings, rape, arson, and murder. Klansmen menaced black and Republican voters at polling places, intimidated Republican officeholders, conducted daylight political assassinations of their political opponents, instigated race riots, and even conducted small-scale warfare against Republican state regimes. They played the most critical role in counties where blacks constituted an important but not overwhelming portion of the population, and they swung many elections toward the Democrats. Local Klan leaders often hailed from the ranks of Confederate officers and southern social elites; the organization could boast the names of former Confederate generals such as Nathan Bedford Forrest and John B. Gordon among its

FIGURE 8.2. Thomas Nast, *This Is a White Man's Government*,
"We Regard the Reconstruction Acts (So Called) of Congress as
Usurpations, and Unconstitutional, Revolutionary, and Void"—
Democratic Platform, *Harper's Weekly* 12 (September 5, 1868): 568.
Library of Congress, Prints and Photographs Division, Washington, D.C.

founders. Its rank and file drew from "common whites," who may have had little concern with black labor, but had an enormous interest in protecting the privileges of their racial caste status from the competition of newly free, and now enfranchised, African Americans. The nonslaveholders who before the war had composed the groups who patrolled the countryside for errant bondsmen now acted to police the caste boundaries that freedom threatened to undermine. The title of Thomas Nast's famous 1868 *Harper's Weekly* cartoon of Democrats standing atop the body of a murdered freedman captured their concerns well: "this is a white man's government" (figure 8.2).[106]

The lawlessness of such groups provoked national debate. Northern newspapers began running regular columns documenting "Ku-Klux Outrages" throughout the South.[107] Editors insisted that "loyal citizens should be protected at all hazards, and every hour wasted in other legislation . . . is a wanton disregard of a high and sacred duty."[108] Democrats denied charges of abuse, or insisted that blacks deserved whatever violence they had suffered for stepping out of their proper, subordinate place in southern society. Southern accounts claimed that the freedmen "carried things with a high hand"—that in their "arrogance" they sought "to reduce the whites of the South to political vassalage."[109] Democratic papers throughout the country ignored or justified the violence. An 1872 cartoon by Matt Morgan, Thomas Nast's Democratic rival, offers a solid example. In "Too Thin, Massa Grant," President Ulysses Grant props up stick-figure Klansmen fabricated to inspire fearful blacks to vote Republican; the freedman at whom they are directed, though, sees through the chicanery (figure 8.3).[110]

But the violence was real, and Republicans in the national government could not permit conditions to persist. Not only did Klan intimidation directly threaten the electoral processes that kept Republicans in power, it undermined the very legitimacy of Republican governments by making them appear powerless to guarantee democratic governance. "The poor negro begins to feel that he must protect himself, for the government seems to be deaf to all appeals for protection," complained one sympathetic editorial.[111] Congress and the president did respond, passing three new measures designed to punish Klan lawlessness. The Enforcement Act of 1870 provided penalties for inhibiting the right to vote on the basis of race, and authorized the national executive to use the army and federal marshals to enforce the law. It even permitted suspension of the writ of habeas corpus, the great symbol of lawful civil governance. A second act of 1871 clarified the measures of the first, and a third, which became known as the Ku Klux Klan Act of 1871, expanded them. It made federal crimes of many typical Klan tactics and permitted the president to call out the militia and impose martial law on regions in disorder.[112]

FIGURE 8.3.
Matt Morgan, "Too
Thin, Massa Grant,"
*Frank Leslie's Illustrated
Newspaper* 35 (September 14,
1872): 1.

Though they did dampen some of the worst outrages, state and federal government measures failed to stem political violence in the long run. At the local
level, Klan sympathizers or members might control local offices and courts. Republican governors sometimes declared martial law, but such assertive executive responses were as likely to generate sympathy for the Klan as they were to
degrade it. And few governors risked the inevitable backlash invited by relying on small state militias composed largely of African Americans. Republicans
did defend themselves, as at Colfax, Louisiana, on Easter Sunday 1873. But the
massacre that ensued that day taught sobering lessons. As one black legislator
recounted to Congress, "When the sun went down that night, it went down on
the corpses of two hundred and eighty negroes."[113]

Even the federal effort failed. Congress held innumerable hearings to document outrages, and Grant's attorney general, Amos Akerman, moved to prosecute Klan leaders. But moving the machinery of government took time, and
the most prominent Klan figures evaded capture, living on to lead the era's final

battles. Federal authorities arrested thousands of suspected Klansmen throughout the South, but overwhelmed courts acquitted or plea-bargained most of the cases. Many of those convicted received light sentences or fines, with only sixty-five winding up serving time in federal prison. Frustrated, Akerman concluded that the instances of political terrorism he prosecuted "really . . . amount to war" and "cannot be effectively crushed on any other theory."[114] Union General Philip Sheridan agreed, arguing that "banditti" in the South should be left to the army, which would arrest and try them before military tribunals.[115]

There was much to such views. Organized paramilitary violence effectively drove Republicans from office, suppressed the Republican vote, and chastened those who stood up to such bullying. The failure of Republican officials at all levels to police it heartened southern conservatives and built confidence in political terror as an effective tool. Even en masse, groups such as the Klan could never have succeeded in an all-out military challenge to Union authority. Instead, they mounted a classic insurgency—an asymmetrical war of (relatively) low-level violence against civilian targets. The mechanisms of government simply could not contend with the scale of lawlessness. Buttressing them through the vigorous exercise of military authority violated widely held sanctions against the concentration of authority. In a republic dedicated to minimal national government and ever-fearful of the growth of central power, military intervention could not be maintained indefinitely in a society that thought itself at peace. The Reconstruction measures had provided blacks legal mechanisms that they themselves could trigger to protect their rights. But protection required an executive willing and able to enforce the law by prosecuting violations of freedpeople's civil rights, or maintaining order at elections. Klan violence demonstrated that the states alone, even when safely in Republican hands, lacked the legal and material force necessary to do this. Since state militias could not overwhelm the paramilitaries, federal force proved necessary.

Ultimately, Klan tactics succeeded by raising the political costs of Reconstruction on the Republicans implementing it. Regardless of how justified they were, impositions of military force carried heavy political penalties. To the northern public, the "Southern question" descended into an endless series of charges and countercharges: Republicans highlighted Klan depredations while southern conservatives pointed to Republican corruption and "negro insolence." The growing weariness of the northern public made fertile ground for men such as George Fitzhugh, the old defender of slavery and critic of free labor. "Let not our Northern friends . . . fear to turn the freedmen over to us," he wrote, promising "special protection by legal regulations to the inferior races."[116] Democrats from the North softened the offer. "You need but to cease hostilities and the general tranquility will be restored," tempted former attorney general Jeremiah

Black.[117] As disingenuous as such statements may have sounded, they appealed to a public weary of "bayonet rule" in the South. "The people of the Northern States are very tired of . . . the continual calls for federal interference which it involves," conceded a Republican newspaper. "They would very much like to see those States manage their own local affairs."[118] In effect, southern militants sought to parlay the widespread desire for peace into acquiescence to home rule and white supremacy. A public hungry to return to the operations of "normal" politics proved itself unwilling to tackle a domestic insurgency.

The will to continue to exert federal authority to protect the freedpeople's rights began to dissolve. There came a point when even die-hard Republicans resolved that nothing more could be done to shelter the freedpeople—not without damaging the very principles of republican governance for which they fought. In the 1872 election cycle, national Democrats reformed their message, accepting the basic fact of Reconstruction while turning a blind eye to ongoing problems of disorder. They succeeded in capturing several important "liberal" Republicans, including Charles Sumner and Horace Greeley. No figure exemplified the shift better than Carl Schurz, the man who had so ardently advocated black civil rights during the Johnson administration. Schurz could no longer accept the lengths to which federal authority had been exercised in defense of freedpeople's liberty. He charged that laws such as the Enforcement and Ku Klux Acts "break down the bulwarks of the citizen against arbitrary authority, and by transgressing all Constitutional limitations of power, endanger the rights of all." Echoing the growing Democratic chorus, he blamed "unprincipled and rapacious leaders at the head of the colored population" for most of the trouble. And while he conceded that surrendering the South meant giving it to those who "stood against us during the civil war," he asserted that "it cannot be avoided, unless you adopt a system of interference which will subvert the most essential principles of our government."[119] Other prominent radical Republicans expressed similar sentiments on the critical matter of constitutional limits. Salmon Chase, once Lincoln's secretary of the treasury and now chief justice of the Supreme Court, reflected that "there should have been as little military government as possible; no military commissions; no classes excluded from suffrage; and no oath except one of faithful obedience and support to the Constitution and laws."[120]

Grant won reelection in 1872 against a coalition of liberal Republicans and New Departure Democrats, but the damage had been done. Southern conservatives began learning the limits of acceptable federal intervention, honing their approach to future elections. Formally, the Klan dispersed, but the attitudes and practices it had pioneered lived on. In the 1876 cycle, paramilitary groups—the White Leagues in Louisiana, White Liners and Rifle Clubs in Mississippi, Red Shirts in South Carolina—acted as the Klan redux, minus the hoods and robes, delivering these states to Democratic politicians through outright fraud, intimidation, and violence. Lawlessness pervaded all the remaining reconstructed states, but Mississippi set the tone. There, African Americans beseeched Governor Adelbert Ames to intervene on their behalf, proclaiming, "We will not vote at all, unless there are troops to protect us."[121] President Grant, though, chastened Ames. "The whole public are tired out with these annual autumnal outbreaks in the South, and the great majority are ready now to condemn any interference on the part of the Government," he snapped.[122] Ames lost his governorship, and black Mississippians their legislature. The "Mississippi Plan" of organized intimidation, fraud, and violence became a template for the remaining states in the South, and by 1877 Louisiana, South Carolina, and Florida had been similarly "redeemed" by white conservatives operating under the banner of the Democratic Party. The president withdrew what federal troops remained, and the experiment in Reconstruction was over.

Blacks' few remaining defenders howled in protest at southern conservatives' success. "They want the negro as a slave," one northern editor protested; "if they cannot have him in this way, they will deprive him of civil and political rights, if they can, and bring him down as nearly as possible to the condition of slavery."[123] Garrison railed that slave owners' awareness that "their former chattels are now constitutionally enfranchised American citizens" caused them to "writhe in agony, gnaw their tongues for pain," and resolve that the freedpeople "be reduced as near as possible to a state of serfdom."[124] The southern press largely acceded to the notion that conservatives engaged in an insurgency to return to the old racial order. For one Mississippi editor, the 1875 election amounted to "something more earnest and holy" than a mere political contest; it was a "rebellion," a "revolution"—"a struggle to regain a mastery that has been ruthlessly torn from them by selfish white schemers and adventurers, through the instrumentality of an ignorant horde of another race which has been as putty in their hands."[125] The outcome of these elections signaled that the North had given up the struggle. "The negro will disappear from the field of national politics," prophesied a prominent national journal. "Henceforth, the nation, as a nation, will have nothing more to do with him."[126]

The final nail in the coffin followed soon thereafter. If the outcome of the 1875 and 1876 elections gave the former Confederate states to conservative Democrats, the resolution of the disputed presidential election of 1876 established this principle of "home rule" on a national scale. New York Democrat Samuel J. Tilden won the popular vote against Ohio Republican Rutherford B. Hayes, but the electoral vote fell into contention due to the widespread fraud prevalent in Florida, Louisiana, and South Carolina. Through a series of novel and complex machinations, southern electors permitted an electoral victory for Hayes, but only at the cost of removing federal troops from southern soil, effectively leaving the South uncontested terrain for the Democrats.

The rollback of Reconstruction happened in the courts, too. The Supreme Court, guided by the same constitutional conservatism that had limited the federal government's ability to protect blacks' equal rights, began eviscerating the Fourteenth Amendment five short years after its passage. In the *Slaughter-House Cases* of 1873, the Court ruled that the Fourteenth Amendment did not make national and state citizenship equal, but only distinguished the two, thus resurrecting the dual citizenship loophole created by the Dred Scott decision in 1857. In *Minor v. Happersett* (1875), the Court ruled that the Fourteenth Amendment did not cover political rights, such as the right to vote, only civil rights. And in *United States v. Cruikshank* (1876), the Court ruled that the Fourteenth Amendment applied only to discriminatory actions taken by the state, not individuals. In 1885, the Court struck down the Civil Rights Act of 1875 as unconstitutional on the grounds that it applied to private rather than state instances of discrimination. In that case, the Court ruled, with Andrew Johnson–like logic, that blacks had been "the special favorite of the laws." Dissenting justices could not help but conclude "that the substance and spirit of the recent amendments of the Constitution have been sacrificed by a subtle and ingenious verbal criticism."[127]

Finally, in 1896, the Supreme Court famously found, in *Plessy v. Ferguson*, separate treatment of blacks and whites on public conveyances to be consistent with the Reconstruction amendments. The issue had arisen as the white South coped with the same "problem" of freedom the antebellum North had confronted on a smaller scale decades before—of how to maintain in freedom the caste distinctions that slavery had once imposed. Enshrining the principle of "separate but equal," the Court ruled that the law could do no more to enforce the nominal political equality blacks had achieved. "If one race be inferior to the other socially, the constitution of the United States cannot put them upon the same plane," it reasoned. In any case, it continued, any inferiority implied by separate facilities existed only in the minds of blacks themselves. If "enforced separation of the two races stamps the colored race with a badge of inferiority," it was "solely because the colored race chooses to put that construction upon it." The majority's remarkable blindness to the very point of segregation, which separated the races in order to create caste distinctions, signaled that prejudice had become the law of the land.[128]

What Peace among the Whites Brought

Reconstruction failed to secure equal rights and meaningful equality for African Americans in the long run. For a brief moment—no more than a decade—black people had exercised the political and civil rights promised by the nation's founding commitments to universal equality. The incorporation of African Americans into the political systems of the southern states represented a remarkable revolution, one unthinkable before the war, or in any other large slave society. Since the time of the Revolution, free African Americans had organized quasi-political bodies on their own, starting with local churches and mutual aid societies and building up to a national convention movement. Their forced isolation from the formal politics of the Early Republic had nurtured a self-reliance that blossomed into a potent tradition of activism. In the three decades before the Civil War, white abolitionists had fused with the black freedom movement, lending it resources, spokespersons, and attention that had helped black activism infiltrate national political agendas. Some African American activists had accepted this patronage, while others had long stressed the need for independent action. Even in the midst of the Civil War, such African Americans had organized independently, as when in 1864 blacks meeting at a national convention in Syracuse, New York, formed the National Equal Rights League to press for the freedpeople's citizenship. The spirit of reliance held true immediately after the war as well, as freedmen throughout the South convened to protest the black codes' diminution of their rights in freedom.[1]

While Reconstruction under President Andrew Johnson threatened to return blacks to subordinate status, Congressional Reconstruction promised the remarkable prospect of full political participation. African Americans embraced the opportunity to join with the Republicans who had secured the great objects of liberty and citizenship, but their alliance came with a cost. Racial restrictions on the franchise had fallen, but racist sentiment remained strong throughout the country. Republicans relied on southern blacks to anchor their state governments, but how far would they be willing to go to protect the interests of a group deemed safely in their corner? In even the earliest days of Congressional Reconstruction, African Americans expressed hardheaded skepticism about what might be expected. "We do not wish to try the depth of the Republican love for us," wrote black activist Abraham Shadd in 1867. "While we acknowledge our dependence upon the Republican Party, we hold that dependence is mutual, and that they are as fully dependent upon us."[2] Alliance with Republicans offered African Americans their only realistic opportunity to benefit from freedom. Yet it may also be said that in the same way that enlistment in the Union army channeled black resistance during the Civil War, so too participation in formal politics limited possibilities for black political expression in Reconstruction. Largely confined to a Republican Party that offered little in return for their assumed loyalty, African American leaders chafed under white patronage and unresponsive platforms.

The problem grew worse as national enthusiasm for Reconstruction waned. In 1875, Frederick Douglass worried of "a disposition to get rid of us" within the Republican Party. "A disposition is seen to shake off the negro and accept the old master's class," he warned.[3] Frustrated with the party's neglect of their concerns and its patronizing assumption that they had no other options, some African Americans eventually bolted. The *Christian Recorder* took to task the "dozen hypocritical negroes" who argued against passage of the Civil Rights Act of 1875, only to shortly after lament blacks' paucity of power in the party. "Unless the negro is prepared to vote to his own hurt and to his country's distraction," editors sighed, "there is nothing left for him to do but vote the Republican ticket."[4] The most prominent of black bolters, Martin Delany, the great prewar nationalist and now frustrated South Carolina politician, threw his support to Wade Hampton and his paramilitary Red Shirts in the election of 1876. Nothing could have more clearly signaled the retreat from Reconstruction.

While the failure of the experiment in biracial democracy was tragic, in comparative terms it was exceptional that allies in the metropole had championed full black equality at all. Compared to the fate of freedpeople elsewhere in the Atlantic to 1865, the experience of the United States stood out. The slave periphery existed within the boundaries of a nation configured on principles of liberty, even if that liberty had often been nominal or highly contested. Reconstruction failed because the federalism so key to that liberty had permitted those defeated in the Civil War to reassert their domination of southern blacks, all in the name of exercising their rights as free Americans.

Despite its many failings, Reconstruction did break up the basis of the plantation regime. From 1860 to 1870, the number of huge, five-hundred-acre plantations in the South declined from thirteen thousand to six thousand, while farms of less than fifty acres increased by over 250 percent. The same period also saw the amount of arable land on small farms grow almost three times, while arable land on large plantations declined even more precipitously. By 1880, plantations of over two hundred acres constituted less than 1 percent of all farms in the South.[5] This massive transformation in southern agriculture owed directly to the freedpeople's efforts to exert control over their own work. The Port Royal experiment had demonstrated that freed slaves disliked systems of labor control that overly regulated their lives. Many northerners had envisioned the freedpeople becoming a kind of rural proletariat, but cash was scarce, and African Americans bridled against forms of labor oversight that resembled slavery. When possible, they rejected gang systems that asked them to split profits from a small share of the crop they brought in. Often, if they did not like the terms of labor, they simply left, seeking a better deal. Recalling the early days of freedom, former slave Robert Falls captured well the freedpeople's search for acceptable terms on which to work:

> I remember so well how the roads was full of folks walking and walking along when the niggers were freed. Didn't know where they was going. Just going to see about something else somewhere else. Meet a body in the road and they ask, "Where you going?" "Don't know." "What you going to do?" "Don't know." And then sometimes we would meet a white man and he would say, "How you like to come work on my farm?" And we say, "I don't know." And then maybe he say, "If you come work for me on my farm, when the crops is in I give you five bushels of corn, five gallons of molasses, some ham-meat, and all your clothes and vittals while you works for me." Alright! That's what I do.[6]

As a consequence of freedpeople's resistance to exploitation, white farmers grew desperate for black workers. Shortly after the war one southern planter complained that "more than fifty per cent, of black labor has disappeared from the fields." He implored his northern creditors, "Give us cash capital and labor; certainty of labor, and its control."[7] The freedpeople had been released into a competitive capitalist economy with no capital, positioned against former masters who controlled the land and a federal government desperate for them to work. They had little leverage, but they did have their feet.

Steadily, new norms for black farmwork emerged from innumerable small negotiations conducted throughout the South. Sharecropping, an old agricultural labor arrangement that had been employed in parts of the postemancipation Caribbean, became the primary arrangement. In sharecropping, the landowner rented a small parcel of land to a freed family—not for cash, but for a share (typically half) of the profits of the harvest crop (usually cotton). The arrangement benefitted both sides. The freedpeople worked in families with far greater autonomy than was possible in the gang systems initially attempted after emancipation and stood to benefit from their own hard work when the crop came in. Landowners lacking cash were able to secure workers who were invested in the success of the farm.

In many ways sharecropping rewarded the freedpeople for driving a hard bargain. They generally worked less than under slavery. Freedom removed the compulsion that drove ten- to twelve-hour workdays before the war, leaving black sharecroppers with more free time to enjoy family and community. In addition, freedwomen generally removed themselves from the fields, so that they could care for their families and adopt norms of family life other Americans sought. Southern planters worried endlessly about the loss of this vital source of labor. Shortly after the war, one Georgia planter complained to the Freedmen's Bureau that freedwomen with husbands "are nearly as idle as it is possible for them to be, pretending to spin—knit or something that really amounts to nothing." He wondered if vagrancy laws could be used to end this "great evil" by compelling freedwomen back into the fields.[8] There was little, though, that planters could do without risking their labor supply. By 1890, a quarter of all farms in the former Confederate states were operating on the sharecropping principle. In Georgia and Texas, more than a third were.[9]

Despite freedpeople's success in putting their agency to work, they faced economic and legal systems arrayed against them. The contracts that bound freedpeople in sharecropping arrangements often controlled every aspect of their lives. Provisions such as "no cropper to work off the plantation when there is any work to be done on the land he has rented, or when his work is needed by me or other croppers" undermined the autonomy of nominally free laborers.[10] Freedpeople, often lacking literacy and confronting local justice systems firmly in the grasp of hostile whites, could do little to resist. Sharecropping devolved into a nightmare of economic dependency and legal vulnerability.

Credit was the culprit. Freed with nothing, former slaves depended on white landowners or local merchants to "furnish" them the food, clothing, and supplies necessary to survive the growing season and profit from the harvest. A system of local creditors lent these needed goods, but at exorbitant rates of interest that could exceed 100 percent.[11] With cotton often baled at these same merchants' gins, and the terms of contracts vague and exploitative, it was not surprising when creditors declared that sharecroppers had failed to meet their obligations. At this point, a creditor could further ensnare his prey by offering even more extortive terms for the following season, or he could simply take everything the sharecropper had worked to accumulate. Alabama sharecropper Ned Cobb remembered how a local landowner defrauded his neighbor Lark in the early 1900s: "Lark made about fifteen bales of cotton that year on that man's place, and fall come he took everything he had. He charged Lark enough in the deal for what he was furnishin him—took all the cotton, mules back, wagon back, and everything. Just took all that to clear him. He didn't leave Lark with nothing."[12] The cycle of debt this crop-lien system plunged black farmers into could be impossible to escape. Eventually, the problem became so bad that the U.S. Justice Department opened investigations into black debt peonage in the South.[13]

Compared to the freedpeople of the Caribbean, most southern blacks came to occupy something in between the poles of autonomous peasantry and agricultural proletariat. The U.S. South of course occupied far more physical space than did any West Indian island, or even the mainland South American colonies of the Guianas. But with virtually all the land in the control of a large white settler population, American freedpeople still possessed few alternatives to plantation labor. Their limited agency helped them achieve the compromise result of sharecropping, but the collusion of whites undermined any claims to free market autonomy the system's advocates may have made. Throughout the South, whites conspired to deny freedpeople access to the unfettered market, just as they deprived blacks of the land that might have offered independence, status, and economic mobility. "The feeling against any ownership of the soil by Negroes is so strong that the man who should sell small tracts of them would be in actual personal danger," wrote a northern correspondent shortly after the war.[14] Time did little to change this. Historians Roger L. Ransom and Richard Sutch calculate that in 1880 African Americans owned just 7.3 percent of farms in the cotton South.[15] By 1910, the census reported that blacks owned not quite 7 percent of all southern farms, despite constituting nearly 30 percent of the southern population.[16] Such statistics belied the progress alleged by boosters of a "New South" who proclaimed the region "a perfect democracy," in which "the relations of the southern people with the negro are close and cordial."[17]

That such words could have been uttered amid the maelstrom of disfranchisement, segregation, and racial violence in the late nineteenth-century South offers compelling testimony to the resurgent power of white supremacy throughout post-Reconstruction America. Toward the end of Reconstruction, Frederick Douglass asked, "If war among the whites brought peace and liberty to the blacks, what will peace among the whites bring?"[18] Here was his answer. In 1877, a Georgia writer offered British imperialists in South Africa some advice on coping with their labor problem. "The only way to treat the negroes in South Africa is to enslave them," he wrote. "Nothing but slavery will ever raise the savage negro to a condition approximating to civilization, and nothing but slavery, as our own unhappy experience since the war had demonstrated, will ever make him industrious."[19] The writer's confidence in suggesting that the British reimpose slavery on their colonies was nothing short of astounding, coming as it did a mere twelve years after southern slaveholders had lost their secession wager in a war that utterly destroyed their institution and at a cost of three-quarters of a million souls. Such, though, was the hubris bred by Redemption.

The failure of Reconstruction even impacted the memory of the long process through which the nation threw off chattel bondage. In the history of slavery's demise in the Atlantic world, the thoroughness with which the Civil War's causes were expunged from the historical record is remarkable. With Redemption, the Confederate view of history became the standard interpretation for much of the next century. Abolitionism became a small movement of fanatics, secession the product of legitimate squabbles over states' rights. The war itself became a noble tragedy, and Reconstruction the triumph of civilization over the forces of barbarism and tyranny. It is sometimes said that the winners write history. Perhaps, but it is difficult to think of another modern instance in which the losers came to exercise such enormous control over a national story. Textbooks incorporating elements of this warped past prevailed well past the Second World War, and sizable aspects of it persist to this day in public discussions and national political debates.

Rewriting the history of slavery's long death in the United States is still under way. Placing that process amid a broader Atlantic story may help us appreciate the depths to which slavery and white supremacy have informed our national narrative. Those in the United States were certainly not alone in depending on chattel bondage for their settlement and growth. But the slavery that developed in the colonies and United States possessed a distinct set of qualities. It often was not as physically harsh as slavery in most of the Caribbean because it occupied relatively benign environments, which by fostering natural population growth helped the American system grow into the largest slave society the Atlantic world would ever know. The large settler population of these climes meant that the American slave periphery would be peopled by whites who could not be denied an equal share of national influence. The massive war required to end the bedrock institution of such an impressive slave power took decades to make, and came about through the political process so circuitously that slavery itself almost got written out of its story.

But just as we cannot plausibly imagine a Civil War without slavery, neither can we portray abolitionism as an unqualified triumph. As a product of the liberal imagination of the late eighteenth and nineteenth centuries, antislavery throughout the Atlantic stalled badly at the moment of emancipation. It could imagine slavery as a violation of the norms of market society and the expanding world of industrial capitalism, but it could not sufficiently critique those norms to prevent the virtual reenslavement of black labor after emancipation. Everywhere, most freedpeople in plantation societies confronted subjugation to wage labor or the legacy of underdevelopment that accompanied peasant proprietorship. Nowhere did they gain the rights attending free subjects back in the colonial metropoles, just as nowhere did the economy of freedom permit them the social elevation it had so optimistically prognosticated. Only in the United States, where traditions of federalism and democratic participation demanded something else, did the freedpeople enjoy full political and civic equality, and this lasted for a mere moment before passing away. Reconstruction's collapse drove the children of slaves into a world of disfranchisement, segregation, discrimination, lynching, and pogrom. The popular will could find its way to accepting the war that ended bondage, but it had never been sufficiently dedicated to antislavery's humanitarian impulse to prevent "freedom" for blacks from becoming a byword. It is cliché but true: slavery died, racism persisted.

The pattern was not new. Just as the post-Revolution northern states had replaced slavery with a host of restrictions on free black life, so too did the postwar South. In 1821, a delegate to the New York state constitutional convention could reject black suffrage on no grounds other than that whites simply would not accept blacks as social equals: "If the time should ever arrive, when . . . the colours shall intermarry—when negroes shall be invited to your tables—to sit in your pew, or ride in your coach, it may then be proper to . . . remodel the constitution so as to conform to that state of society."[20] Seventy-five years and a massive civil war that ended slavery later offered no improvement. In the *Plessy* case of 1896, the highest court of the land insisted that "if the two races are to meet on terms of social equality, it must be the result of natural affinities, a mutual appreciation of each other's merits and a voluntary consent of individuals."[21] In the eyes of postemancipation Americans, law could make men free, but it could not make them equal.

The remarkable persistence of racial thinking baffled contemporary reformers. Largely convinced that prejudice grew from slavery, black activists and white abolitionists looked for a sea change in racial attitudes after emancipation. Before the war, black activists in the North had spoken of prejudice as "the spirit of slavery"—the "deadly poison" that the institution "disseminated from the torrid regions of the South to the frigid North."[22] After it, they declared that prejudice "stands upon the ruins" of its foundation in slavery, and would gradually pass away.[23] Of course, nothing like this happened. As products of the same liberal worldview that had constructed slavery as a violation of the right to self-ownership, even the most ardent racial activists failed to appreciate how easily the principles of liberalism could incorporate racist assumptions. It took little for a conservative such as Andrew Johnson to blame blacks themselves should they "fail, and so perish away" in freedom, for Johnson had never been sincere in promising that "the failure shall not be attributable to any denial of justice."[24] It is more difficult to understand Frederick Douglass's faith that such an experiment was ever possible. "If the Negro cannot stand on his own legs, let him fall," he had told whites; "the fault will not be yours."[25]

The attempt failed largely because the heirs of the slave power did their utmost to make it fail, and thus retain blacks as an exploitable labor force. In doing so, they followed long-standing interests and proclivities. Less explicable were the readiness with which champions of liberal values accepted the outcome and their willingness to lay responsibility for it at the feet of its objects. The destruction of slavery constituted the central reform of all nineteenth-century liberalism. For decades antislavery prophets had posed free labor as the progressive, Christian alternative to a barbaric system. Union victory and mass emancipation constituted a stunning vindication of their assertion that property could not be held in man, and antislavery reformers everywhere looked to the speedy affirmation of their theory in the rapid "elevation" of the freedpeople. It mattered little that the expectations were unsound, or that the experiment was never fairly tried. When the freedpeople did not rise as predicted, the fault became their own.

This, too, partook of a liberal ideology largely blind to its own iniquitous and exploitative tendencies. Reflecting at the end of the Civil War, British biologist Thomas Henry Huxley declared that just as the end of slavery had freed the slaves, it had also emancipated whites from responsibility for their fate: "Whatever the position of stable equilibrium into which the laws of social gravitation may bring the negro, all responsibility for the result will henceforward lie between nature and him. The white man may wash his hands of it, and the Caucasian conscience be void of reproach for evermore. And this, if we look to the bottom of the matter, is the real justification for the abolition policy."[26] Slavery, the great symbol of racial injustice, had been destroyed. Was not that sufficient? Confronted with ongoing racial inequities whose blame could be laid only at the feet of liberal capitalism or of blacks themselves, the latter were held to account. Only such leaps of logic could have justified national acquiescence to the grave injustices of the Jim Crow era.

If the perspective of a century and a half suggests sources of failure quite different from those assigned by the Redeemers themselves, it also poses quite different protagonists. The role that black people played in their own liberation has long been underappreciated. In 1928, a popular biography of General Grant denied that blacks had had any role in abolishing slavery whatsoever. "The American negroes are the only people in the history of the world . . . that ever became free without any effort of their own," W. E. Woodward wrote. While civil war raged about them, he continued, "they twanged banjos around the railroad stations, sang melodious spirituals, and believed that some Yankee would soon come along and give each of them forty acres of land and a mule."[27] The racism of a white biographer writing in the late 1920s is dismaying but not surprising. More shocking is to find a national black leader offering such similar words in a speech in 1875: "The fact is . . . our progress and present position are due to causes almost wholly outside of our own will and our exertions."[28] Frederick Douglass, of all people, should have known better.

Largely denied access to the public forum, the enslaved throughout the Atlantic lacked the capacity to argue on their own behalf. Often, they acted rather than spoke, and while white authorities usually met their actions with contempt and repression, slave behavior did make a difference. Slaves in the United States confronted an even more difficult struggle to become free, since they lived in the largest, wealthiest, and most politically empowered periphery in the Atlantic. But they also enjoyed the benefits of living in a nation that contained one of the largest and most dynamic industrial societies in the Atlantic. There, communities of blacks in the nominally free states—the fruits of the revolutionary antislavery struggle—could ally with white activists and give voice to the enslaved. These men and women founded a great tradition of public protest that implored the nation to adhere to its best vision of itself, urging white "advocates of freedom" to cease sullying "what they profess to adore."[29] As these pages detail, the long and complex history of total emancipation in the United States involved innumerable social and political actors. Perhaps more than any other single group, though, these neglected Americans may deserve credit for bringing slavery to its knees.

NOTES

ABBREVIATIONS

HSUS   Susan B. Carter, Scott Sigmund Gartner, Michael R. Haines, Alan L. Olmstead, Richard Sutch, and Gavin Wright, eds., *Historical Statistics of the United States, Earliest Times to the Present: Millennial Edition* (New York: Cambridge University Press, 2006)

ICPSR3   "Inter-University Consortium for Political and Social Research. Historical, Demographic, Economic, and Social Data: The United States, 1790–1970 (ICPSR3)" [Computer file] (Ann Arbor, Mich.: Inter-University Consortium for Political and Social Research)

PROLOGUE: A HOUSE DIVIDED

1. *The Collected Works of Abraham Lincoln*, ed. Roy P. Basler (New Brunswick, N.J.: Rutgers University Press, 1953), 2:461. The "house divided" phrase echoed the moment in the Gospels when the Pharisees charged that Jesus, in casting out demons, was serving Satan. Matthew 12:25: "And Jesus knew their thoughts, and said unto them, Every kingdom divided against itself is brought to desolation; and every city or house divided against itself shall not stand." Mark 3:25: "And if a house be divided against itself, that house cannot stand."

2. *Dred Scott v. Sandford*, 60 U.S. 393 (1857); *Lemmon v. New York*, 20 N.Y. 562 (1860).

3. Abraham Lincoln to Hon. J. T. Hale, January 11, 1861, in *Abraham Lincoln: Complete Works, Comprising His Speeches, Letters, State Papers, and Miscellaneous Writings*, ed. John G. Nicolay and John Hay (New York: Century, 1907), 1:664.

4. William H. Seward, *The Irrepressible Conflict: A Speech by William H. Seward* (New York: New York Tribune, 1858).

5. Abraham Lincoln to William Kellogg, December 11, 1860, in *Abraham Lincoln: Speeches and Writing 1859–1865*, ed. Don E. Fehrenbacher (New York: Literary Classics of the United States, 1989), 190.

6. J. David Hacker, "A Census-Based Count of the Civil War Dead," *Civil War History* 57, no. 4 (December 2011): 307–48.

INTRODUCTION: THE SLAVE POWER

1. Alice Dana Adams, *The Neglected Period of Anti-slavery in America, 1808–1831* (Boston: Ginn and Co., 1908). The complex process of abolition in the North is the subject of chapters 1 and 2. For now, suffice it to say that slavery fell through a series of gradual and

incremental measures passed by the northern states. Some of these worked by declaring enslaved African Americans free after some certain point in the future—in some cases a specific date, in others when slaves reached a certain age. By 1827, when the last slaves in New York were declared free, all northern states but New Jersey (which followed in 1846) had provided for the immediate or eventual emancipation of all slaves within their borders. By 1830, the U.S. census listed 3,538 slaves living in the so-called free states; 2,254 (64 percent) of these lived in New Jersey. It is thus difficult to provide a final date for the antebellum abolition of slavery in the North, but 1827 serves well to divide the period when northerners considered slavery on their own soil from the period when northerners turned their eyes southward to consider slavery. Figures calculated from federal census (ICPSR3) and apportionment data found in John P. McIver, "Apportionment of the House of Representatives: 1787–2000," table Eb1–56 in HSUS.

2. I am indebted to Eric Foner for this insight, which I merely propose to flesh out here. See *Nothing but Freedom: Emancipation and Its Legacy* (Baton Rouge: Louisiana State University Press, 1983).

3. Estimates of the slave trade are highly contentious and necessarily imprecise. The most authoritative source of numbers—the Trans-Atlantic Slave Trade Database—estimates that between 1501 and 1866, 12.5 million Africans embarked on slave ships leaving Africa, and 10.7 million disembarked on American shores. Voyages: The Trans-Atlantic Slave Trade Database, http://slavevoyages.org/tast/assessment/estimates.faces?yearFrom =1501&yearTo=1866.

4. Igor Kopytoff and Suzanne Miers, "African 'Slavery' as an Institution of Marginality," in *Slavery in Africa: Historical and Anthropological Perspectives* (Madison: University of Wisconsin Press, 1977), 3–81.

5. Ivana Elbl, "The Volume of the Early Atlantic Slave Trade, 1450–1521," *Journal of African History* 38, no. 1 (1997): 32, 73.

6. David Eltis, "The Volume and Structure of the Transatlantic Slave Trade: A Reassessment," *William and Mary Quarterly*, 3rd ser. 58, no. 1 (January 2001): 45.

7. Stuart B. Schwartz, *Sugar Plantations in the Formation of Brazilian Society* (Cambridge: Cambridge University Press, 1985), 168.

8. Sidney W. Mintz, *Sweetness and Power: The Place of Sugar in Modern History* (New York: Viking, 1985), 73.

9. Johannnes Postma, "The Dimension of the Dutch Slave Trade from Western Africa," *Journal of African History* 13, no. 2 (1972): 246.

10. For the interesting role of Sephardic Jewish traders in the transmission of sugar technology from Brazil to the Caribbean, see Richard Sheridan, *Sugar and Slavery: An Economic History of the British West Indies* (Baltimore: Johns Hopkins University Press, 1974), 367; Stephen Alexander Fortune, *Merchants and Jews: The Struggle for British West Indian Commerce, 1650–1750* (Gainesville: University Press of Florida, 1984); Jonathan Irvine Israel, *European Jewry in the Age of Mercantilism, 1550–1750* (New York: Oxford University Press, 1985). For the transmission of the technology more generally, see J. H. Galloway, "Tradition and Innovation in the American Sugar Industry, c. 1500–1800: An Explanation," *Annals of the Association of American Geographers* 75, no. 3 (September 1985): 334–51.

11. Eltis, "Volume and Structure of the Transatlantic Slave Trade," 43.

12. James I (1566–1625), *A Counterblaste to Tobacco* (London: R. Barker, 1604).

13. Robert C. Nash, "The English and Scottish Tobacco Trades in the Seventeenth and Eighteenth Centuries: Legal and Illegal Trade," *Economic History Review*, new ser. 35, no. 3 (August 1982): 354–72, 356.

14. Philip D. Curtin, *The Rise and Fall of the Plantation Complex: Essays in Atlantic History* (Cambridge: Cambridge University Press, 1990), 14–16.

15. Timothy R. Walton, *The Spanish Treasure Fleets* (Sarasota, Fla.: Pineapple Press, 2002), 85.

16. Stanley L. Engerman, "A Population History of the Caribbean," in *A Population History of North America*, ed. Michael R. Haines and Richard H. Steckel (Cambridge: Cambridge University Press, 2000), 494.

17. Alfred W. Crosby, *Ecological Imperialism: The Biological Expansion of Europe, 900–1900* (Cambridge: Cambridge University Press, 1986).

18. John Winthrop, "A Modell of Christian Charity" (1630), in *The Puritans: A Sourcebook of Their Writings*, ed. Perry Miller and Thomas H. Johnson (Mineola, N.Y.: Dover, 2001), 198–99.

19. Ira Berlin, *Many Thousands Gone: The First Two Centuries of Slavery in North America* (Cambridge, Mass.: Belknap, 1998).

20. For mainland North American figures, see table Eg21–59 in HSUS; for Caribbean figures, see John J. McCusker, "The Economy of the British West India, 1763–1790: Growth, Stagnation, or Decline?," in *Essays in the Economic History of the Atlantic World* (New York: Routledge, 1997), 206.

21. The concepts of *metropole*, *core*, and *periphery* come from world-systems analysis. For starting places and examples, see Immanuel Maurice Wallerstein, *The Modern World-System* (New York: Academic Press, 1974); Terence K. Hopkins, *World-Systems Analysis: Theory and Methodology* (Beverly Hills, Calif.: Sage, 1982); Christopher Chase-Dunn and Thomas D. Hall, eds., *Core/Periphery Relations in Precapitalist Worlds* (Boulder, Colo.: Westview, 1991); P. Nick Kardulias, ed., *World-Systems Theory in Practice: Leadership, Production, and Exchange* (Lanham, Md.: Rowman & Littlefield, 1999); Thomas D. Hall, ed., *A World-Systems Reader: New Perspectives on Gender, Urbanism, Cultures, Indigenous Peoples, and Ecology* (Lanham, Md.: Rowman & Littlefield, 2000); Immanuel Wallerstein, *World-Systems Analysis: An Introduction* (Durham, N.C.: Duke University Press, 2004).

22. This is Eric Williams's famous thesis. See Eric Williams, *Capitalism and Slavery* (Chapel Hill: University of North Carolina Press, 1944); Barbara L. Solow and Stanley L. Engerman, eds., *British Capitalism and Caribbean Slavery: The Legacy of Eric Williams* (Cambridge: Cambridge University Press, 1987); Heather Cateau and S. H. H. Carrington, eds., *Capitalism and Slavery Fifty Years Later: Eric Eustace Williams—A Reassessment of the Man and His Work* (New York: Peter Lang, 2000); Colin A. Palmer, *Eric Williams and the Making of the Modern Caribbean* (Chapel Hill: University of North Carolina Press, 2006).

23. R. R. Palmer, *The Age of the Democratic Revolution: A Political History of Europe and America, 1760–1800* (Princeton, N.J.: Princeton University Press, 1959–64).

24. Kenneth Morgan, *Slavery and the British Empire: From Africa to America* (Oxford: Oxford University Press, 2007), 202.

25. Quoted in Michael Craton, "Proto-Peasant Revolts? The Late Slave Rebellions in the British West Indies, 1816–1832," *Past and Present* 85 (November 1979): 104.

26. Thomas Smith, *The History and Origin of the Missionary Societies, Containing Faithful Accounts of the Voyages, Travels, Labours, and Successes of the Various Missionaries* (London: Thomas Kelly and Richard Evans, 1825), 342.

27. Rebecca Scott, *Slave Emancipation in Cuba: The Transition to Free Labor, 1860–1899* (Princeton, N.J.: Princeton University Press, 1985), 22; Manuel Moreno Fraginals, "Plantation Economies and Societies in the Spanish Caribbean, 1860–1930," in *Cambridge History of Latin America*, ed. Leslie Bethell (Cambridge: Cambridge University Press, 1986), 4:205.

28. Seymour Drescher, "Brazilian Abolition in Comparative Perspective," *Hispanic American Historical Review* 68, no. 3 (August 1988): 429.

29. Ibid., 443.

30. Robert Edgar Conrad, *The Destruction of Brazilian Slavery, 1850–1888* (Berkeley: University of California Press, 1972), 285.

CHAPTER 1: IMPIOUS PRAYERS

1. [Samuel Johnson], *Taxation No Tyranny: An Answer to the Resolution and Address of the American Congress*, 4th ed. (London: T. Cadell, 1775), 89.

2. Ibid., 50–51.

3. Ibid., 41, 38.

4. Ibid., 89, 77.

5. Pierre L. Van den Berghe, *Race and Racism: A Comparative Perspective* (New York: Wiley, 1967); George M. Fredrickson, *White Supremacy: A Comparative Study in American and South African History* (New York: Oxford University Press, 1981).

6. Edmund S. Morgan, *American Slavery, American Freedom: The Ordeal of Colonial Virginia* (1975; repr., New York: Norton, 1995), 380, 376.

7. "Speech on Conciliation (1775)," in *Edmund Burke: Selected Writings and Speeches*, ed. Peter J. Stanlis (1963; repr., New Brunswick, N.J.: Transaction, 2009), 192.

8. See also Jack P. Greene, "'Slavery or Independence': Some Reflections on the Relationship among Liberty, Black Bondage, and Equality in Revolutionary South Carolina," *South Carolina Historical Magazine* 80 (1979): 203–4.

9. John Shy, *A People Numerous and Armed: Reflections on the Military Struggle for American Independence*, rev. ed. (Ann Arbor: University of Michigan Press, 1990), 249–50. See also Howard H. Peckham, ed., *The Toll of Independence: Engagements and Battle Casualties of the American Revolution* (Chicago: University of Chicago Press, 1974).

10. William Blackstone, *Commentaries on the Laws of England* (Oxford: Clarendon, 1765–69), 1:125, 135.

11. New York Petition to the House of Commons, October 18, 1764, in *Prologue to Revolution: Sources and Documents on the Stamp Act Crisis, 1764–1766*, ed. Edmund S. Morgan (Chapel Hill: University of North Carolina Press, 1959), 9.

12. Stamp Act Congress, "Declaration of Rights and Grievances," October 19, 1765, in

Journal of the First Congress of the American Colonies, in Opposition to the Tyrannical Acts of the British Parliament (New York: E. Winchester, 1845), 12.

13. First Continental Congress, "Declaration and Resolves of the First Continental Congress," October 14, 1774, in *Journals of the Continental Congress, 1774–1789*, ed. Worthington C. Ford (Washington, D.C.: GPO, 1904–37), 72.

14. Igor Kopytoff and Suzanne Miers, "African 'Slavery' as an Institution of Marginality," in *Slavery in Africa: Historical and Anthropological Perspectives* (Madison: University of Wisconsin Press, 1977), 101–5. See also Paul Lane, "Introduction: Slavery, Social Revolutions, and Enduring Memories," in *Comparative Dimensions of Slavery in Africa: Archaeology and Memory*, ed. Paul Lane and Kevin C. MacDonald (New York: Oxford University Press, 2012).

15. Blackstone, *Commentaries on the Laws of England*, 1:412.

16. Orlando Patterson, *Slavery and Social Death: A Comparative Study* (Cambridge, Mass.: Harvard University Press, 1982).

17. John Locke, *Two Treatises of Government* (London: Whitemore and Fenn, 1821), 207.

18. *A Complete Collection of State Trials and Proceedings for High Treason and Other Crimes and Misdemeanors*, comp. T. B. Howell (London: T. C. Hansard, 1814), 20:51.

19. Calculated from Voyages: The Trans-Atlantic Slave Trade Database, www.slavevoyages.org.

20. Mark S. Weiner, "New Biographical Evidence on Somerset's Case," *Slavery and Abolition* 23, no. 1 (April 2002): 121–36; Steven M. Wise, *Though the Heavens May Fall: The Landmark Trial That Led to the End of Human Slavery* (Cambridge, Mass.: Da Capo Press, 2005); George van Cleve, "'Somerset's Case' and Its Antecedents in Imperial Perspective," *Law and History Review* 24, no. 3 (Fall 2006): 601–45.

21. *London Chronicle*, June 20, 1772.

22. William Cowper, *The Task, Book II, A Time-Piece* (1784).

23. *Virginia Gazette* (Purdie and Dixon), September 30, 1773.

24. Blackstone, *Commentaries on the Laws of England*, 1:119 (emphasis in original).

25. Quoted in Emmauel Chukwudi Eze, "Hume, Race, and Human Nature," *Journal of the History of Ideas* 81, no. 4 (October 2000): 691.

26. Thomas Jefferson, *Notes on the State of Virginia*, ed. Merrill D. Peterson (1781–82; repr., New York: Library of America, 1984), 264, 270.

27. Quoted in Charles Elliott, *Sinfulness of American Slavery* (Cincinnati: L. Swormstedt, 1850), 238.

28. Jefferson, *Notes on the State of Virginia*, 288, 264, 270.

29. Thomas Jefferson to John Holmes, April 22, 1820, in *The Writings of Thomas Jefferson*, ed. Paul Leicester Ford (New York: Putnam, 1899), 10:157–58. Ford erroneously transcribed "ear" as "ears."

30. Thomas Jefferson to Edward Everett, February 24, 1823, in *The Writings of Thomas Jefferson: Being His Autobiography, Correspondence, Reports, Messages, Addresses, and Other Writings, Official and Private*, ed. H. A. Washington (Washington, D.C.: Taylor and Maury, 1854), 7:273.

31. See Richard L. Greaves, "Concepts of Political Obedience in Late Tudor England: Conflicting Perspectives," *Journal of British Studies* 22, no. 1 (Autumn 1982): 23–34.

32. See Peter A. Dorsey, *Common Bondage: Slavery as Metaphor in Revolutionary America* (Knoxville: University of Tennessee Press, 2009); F. Nwabueze Okoye, "Chattel Slavery as the Nightmare of the American Revolutionaries," *William and Mary Quarterly*, 3rd ser. 37, no. 1 (January 1980): 3–28.

33. John Jay, "Address to the People of Great Britain" (1774), in *The Correspondence and Public Papers of John Jay*, ed. Henry P. Johnston (New York: Putnam, 1890–93), 1:18, 27, 30.

34. [Silas Downer], "A Son of Liberty," *A Discourse Delivered at the Dedication of the Tree of Liberty* (1768), in *The American Republic: Primary Sources*, ed. Bruce Frohnen (Indianapolis: Liberty Fund, 2002), 143.

35. "Hancock's Oration [March 5, 1774]," *Niles' Weekly Register* 2, no. 28 (March 14, 1812): 40.

36. Quoted in Kenneth S. Greenberg, "Revolutionary Ideology and the Proslavery Argument: The Abolition of Slavery in Antebellum South Carolina," *Journal of Southern History* 42, no. 3 (August 1976): 366.

37. George Washington to Bryan Fairfax, August 24, 1774, in *The Papers of George Washington, Colonial Series* (Charlottesville: University of Virginia Press, 1983–93), 10:156.

38. Samuel Adams, "The Rights of the Colonists," in *The Writings of Samuel Adams*, ed. Harry Alonzo (New York: Putnam, 1904–8), 2:355.

39. James Otis, "The Rights of the British Colonies Asserted and Proved," in *Tracts of the American Revolution, 1763–1776*, ed. Merrill Jensen (1966; repr., Indianapolis: Hackett, 2003), 28.

40. Simeon Howard, *A Sermon Preached to the Ancient and Honorable Artillery-company, in Boston, New-England, June 7th, 1773* (Boston: John Boyle, 1773), 7, 24.

41. James Prior, *Life of the Right Honourable Edmund Burke* (London: H. G. Bohn, 1854), 143.

42. Ibid.; Edmund Burke, *The Works of the Right Honourable Edmund Burke* (London, 1887), 2:180.

43. "Declaration and Resolves on Colonial Rights of the First Continental Congress," October 14, 1774, in *Journals of the Continental Congress, 1774–1789*, ed. Worthington C. Ford (Washington, D.C.: GPO, 1904–37), 1:71.

44. *A Declaration by the Representatives of the United Colonies of North-America, Now Met in Congress at Philadelphia, Setting Forth the Causes and Necessity of Their Taking Up Arms* (Philadelphia: n.p., 1775), 2.

45. See also Bernard Bailyn, *The Ideological Origins of the American Revolution* (Cambridge, Mass.: Harvard University Press, 1967), 119–22, 232–46.

46. James Otis, *The Rights of the British Colonies Asserted and Proved* (Boston: Edes and Gill, 1764), 29.

47. Arthur Lee, "Address on Slavery" (March 19, 1767), in *Am I Not a Man and a Brother: The Antislavery Crusade of Revolutionary America, 1688–1788*, ed. Roger Bruns (New York: Chelsea House, 1977), 112.

48. Quoted in Arthur Zilversmit, *The First Emancipation: The Abolition of Slavery in the North* (Chicago: University of Chicago Press, 1967), 95.

49. [John Allen], *An Oration upon the Beauties of Liberty, or the Essential Rights of the Americans* (Boston: E. Russell, 1773), 75.

50. Abigail Adams to John Adams, September 24, 1774, in *Familiar Letters of John*

Adams and His Wife Abigail Adams, ed. Charles Francis Adams (New York: Hurd and Houghton, 1876), 41–42.

51. Nathaniel Appleton, *Considerations on Slavery* (1767), in Bruns, *Am I Not a Man and a Brother*, 136.

52. Thomas Day, *The Fragment of an Original Letter on the Slavery of the Negroes*, Early American Imprints, ser. 1, no. 18437 (Philadelphia, 1784), broadside.

53. Thomas Hutchinson, *Strictures upon the Declaration of the Congress at Philadelphia*, ed. Malcolm Freiberg (London, 1776; repr., Boston: Old South Association, 1958), 11.

54. Jacob Green, *A Sermon Delivered at Hanover, (in New Jersey), April 22nd, 1778* (Chatham, N.J.: Shepard Kollock, 1779), 13.

55. John Jay to Robert Livingston and Gouverneur Morris, April 29, 1777, in *Correspondence and Public Papers of John Jay*, 1:136.

56. John Jay to Egbert Benson, September 17, 1780, in *Correspondence and Public Papers of John Jay*, 1:407.

57. William Jay, *The Life of John Jay: With Selections from His Correspondence and Miscellaneous Papers* (New York: J. and J. Harper, 1833), 1:231.

58. Richard Price, *Observations on the Importance of the American Revolution, and the Means of Making It a Benefit to the World* (Boston: Powars and Willis, 1784), 68.

59. *New Jersey Gazette*, September 20, 1780, quoted in Zilversmit, *First Emancipation*, 142.

60. "The Germantown Protest, 1688," in *Slavery in America: A Reader and Guide*, ed. Kenneth Morgan (Athens: University of Georgia Press, 2005), 370–71.

61. Anthony Benezet to Granville Sharp, April 14, 1772, in *Memoirs of Granville Sharp, Esq.*, ed. Prince Hoare (London: Henry Colburn, 1820), 99.

62. See, for example, Elizabeth B. Clark, "'The Sacred Rights of the Weak': Pain, Sympathy, and the Culture of Individual Rights in Antebellum America," *Journal of American History* 82, no. 2 (September 1995): 463–93.

63. David Brion Davis, *The Problem of Slavery in the Age of Revolution, 1770–1823* (Ithaca, N.Y.: Cornell University Press, 1975).

64. Peter Bestes et al., unnamed broadside, Library of Congress, Printed Ephemera Collection, portfolio 37, folder 16 (digital ID hdl.loc.gov/loc.rbc/rbpe.03701600).

65. *Collections of the Massachusetts Historical Society*, 5th ser., vol. 3 (Boston, 1877), 436–37.

66. "Petition of 1779 by Slaves of Fairfield County for the Abolition of Slavery in Connecticut," in Vincent J. Rosivach, "Three Petitions by Connecticut Negros for the Abolition of Slavery in Connecticut," *Connecticut Review* 17, no. 2 (Fall 1995): 79–92.

67. "Petition of a Number of the Negroes Now Detained in Slavery at Portsmouth, &C.," *New-Hampshire Gazette* 24, no. 1233 (July 15, 1780).

68. Samuel Hopkins, *A Dialogue Concerning the Slavery of the Africans; Showing It to Be the Duty and Interest of the American Colonies to Emancipate All Their African Slaves* (Norwich, Conn.: Judah P. Spooner, 1776).

69. See, for example, Joanna Brooks, "The Early American Public Sphere and the Emergence of a Black Print Counterpublic," *William and Mary Quarterly*, 3rd ser. 62, no. 1 (January 2005): 67–92.

70. Philip D. Morgan and Andrew Jackson O'Shaughnessy, "The Arming Slaves in the American Revolution," in *Arming Slaves: From Classical Times to the Modern Age*, ed.

Christopher Leslie Brown and Philip D. Morgan (New Haven: Yale University Press, 2006), 198.

71. William Livingston to Samuel Allinson, July 25, 1778, in *New Jersey in the American Revolution, 1763–1783: A Documentary History*, ed. Larry R. Gerlach (Trenton, N.J.: New Jersey Historical Commission, 1975), 384.

72. Edward Needles, comp., *An Historical Memoir of the Pennsylvania Society, for Promoting the Abolition of Slavery* (Philadelphia: Merrihew and Thompson, 1848), 24.

73. The Earl of Dunmore to the Earl of Hillsborough, May 1, 1772, quoted in George Bancroft, *History of the United States of America, from the Discovery of the Continent* (Boston: Little, Brown, 1879), 4:231. See also Peter Wood, "'Impatient of Oppression': Black Freedom Struggles on the Eve of White Independence," *Southern Exposure* 12, no. 6 (November–December 1984): 12.

74. William Draper, *The Thoughts of a Traveller upon Our American Disputes* (London: J. Ridley, 1774), 21.

75. Jefferson, *Notes on the State of Virginia*, 226.

76. George Milligen-Johnston, *A Short Description of the Province of South-Carolina: With an Account of the Air, Weather, and Diseases, at Charles-Town* (London: John Hinton, 1770), 26. See also Robert A. Olwell, "'Domestick Enemies': Slavery and Political Independence in South Carolina, May 1775—March 1776," *Journal of Southern History* 55, no. 1 (February 1989): 21–48.

77. James Madison to William Bradford, November 26, 1774, in *The Papers of James Madison*, ed. William T. Hutchinson et al. (Chicago: University of Chicago Press, 1962), 1:129–30.

78. Philip D. Morgan, "Black Society in the Low Country, 1760–1810," in *Slavery and Freedom in the Age of the American Revolution*, ed. Ira Berlin and Ronald Hoffman (Charlottesville: University of Virginia Press, 1983), 92, 129.

79. South Carolina, General Committee, *South-Carolina. The Actual Commencement of Hostilities Against This Continent*, Early American Imprints, Series 1, no. 42942 (1775), broadside.

80. *Diary and Autobiography of John Adams*, ed. L. H. Butterfield et al. (Cambridge, Mass.: Belknap, 1961), 2:182–83.

81. "Municipal Common Hall to Governor Dunmore: An Humble Address," *Virginia Gazette* (Pinkney), April 20, 1775, 2.

82. "Deposition of Dr. William Pasteur," in "Virginia Legislative Papers (Continued)," *Virginia Magazine of History and Biography* 13, no. 1 (July 1905): 49.

83. Quoted in Michael Lee Lanning, *African Americans in the Revolutionary War* (New York: Citadel, 2000), 51.

84. Quoted in Hugh F. Rankin, *The North Carolina Continentals* (1971; repr., Chapel Hill: University of North Carolina Press, 2005), 24.

85. *Virginia Gazette* (Dixon and Hunter), November 5, 1775.

86. George Washington to Joseph Reed, December 15, 1775, in *The Writings of George Washington from the Original Manuscript Sources*, ed. John C. Fitzpatrick (Washington, D.C.: GPO, 1931), 4:167.

87. "A Declaration," December 13, 1775, in *The Proceedings of the Convention of Delegates*

for the Counties and Corporation in the Colony of Virginia (Richmond: Ritchie, Trueheart, and Du-Val, 1816), 64.

88. Jefferson, *Writings of Thomas Jefferson: Being His Autobiography*, 2:23.

89. As perverse as this logic was, it was widely endorsed at the time, especially after the Somerset ruling. Other commentators understood slavery to have become a distinctly New World practice, which civilized Europe had progressed beyond. For example, a preliminary preamble to Pennsylvania's gradual abolition law of 1780 would call America "the scene of this new invasion of the rights of mankind, after the spirit of Christianity had abolished it from the greater part of Europe." Reprinted in *The Friend, A Religious and Literary Journal* (Philadelphia) 36, no. 38 (May 23, 1862).

90. Thomas Jefferson, "Autobiography," in *The Writings of Thomas Jefferson*, ed. Andrew Lipscomb (Washington, D.C.: Thomas Jefferson Memorial Association, 1904), 1:28.

91. "Proposed Constitution for Virginia" (June 29, 1776), in *The Works of Thomas Jefferson*, ed. Paul L. Ford (New York: Putnam, 1905), 2:163.

92. "Speech on Conciliation" (1775), in Stanlis, *Edmund Burke: Selected Writings and Speeches*, 200.

93. Thomas Jefferson to Dr. William Gordin, July 16, 1788, in *Writings of Thomas Jefferson*, 5:40.

94. Gary Nash, *Race and Revolution* (Madison, Wis.: Madison House, 1990), 60.

95. Philip Morgan and Andrew Jackson O'Shaughnessy, "The Arming of Slaves in the American Revolution," in *The Arming of Slaves from Classical Times to the Modern Age*, ed. Christopher Leslie Brown and Philip Morgan (New Haven: Yale University Press, 2006), 190.

96. *Memoirs of the Life of Boston King, a Black Preacher, Written by Himself* (London, 1798), in *"Face Zion Forward": First Writers of the Black Atlantic, 1785–1798*, ed. Joanna Brooks and John Saillant (Boston: Northeastern University Press, 2002).

97. Morgan and O'Shaughnessy, "Arming of Slaves," 198–99.

98. Thomas Paine, "African Slavery in America" (Boston, 1775), in *The Writings of Thomas Paine*, ed. Moncure Conway (New York: Putnam, 1894), 1:8.

99. Alexander Hamilton to John Jay, March 14, 1779, in Carol Sue Humphrey, ed., *Voices of Revolutionary America: Contemporary Accounts of Daily Life* (Santa Barbara, Calif.: Greenwood, 2011), 210.

100. Quoted in Robin D. G. Kelley and Earl Lewis, eds., *To Make Our World Anew: Volume I: A History of African Americans to 1880* (Oxford: Oxford University Press, 2000), 116.

101. John Laurens to George Washington, May 19, 1782, in *Proceedings of the Massachusetts Historical Society* (Boston, August 1862), 222.

102. Quoted in Henry Wiencek, *An Imperfect God: George Washington, His Slaves, and the Creation of America* (New York: Farrar, Straus and Giroux, 2003), 215.

103. *London Chronicle*, September 14, 1775; Benjamin Quarles and V. P. Franklin, *The Negro in the Making of America* (New York: Collier Books, 1987), 58.

104. John Shy, "The American Revolution: The Military Conflict Considered as a Revolutionary War," in *Essays on the American Revolution*, ed. Stephen G. Kurtz and James H. Hutson (Chapel Hill: University of North Carolina Press, 1973), 121–56.

105. *Letters from America, 1776–1779: Being Letters of Brunswick, Hessian and Waldeck; Officers with the British Armies during the Revolution*, ed. Ray W. Pettengill (Cambridge, Mass.: Riverside Press, 1924), 119.

106. Lanning, *African Americans in the Revolutionary War*, 177.

107. See, for example, William C. Nell, *The Colored Patriots of the American Revolution, with Sketches of Several Distinguished Colored Persons* (Boston: Robert F. Wallcut, 1855).

108. Felix Gilbert, "Machiavelli: The Renaissance of the Art of War," in *Makers of Modern Strategy from Machiavelli to the Nuclear Age*, ed. Peter Paret (Princeton, N.J.: Princeton University Press, 1986), 11–31.

109. Morgan and O'Shaughnessy, "Arming of Slaves," 184.

110. Ibid., 184–85.

111. Ibid., 186.

112. "Petition of Several Poor Negroes and Mulattoes, Who Are Inhabitants of the Town of Dartmouth," in George Washington Williams, *History of the Negro Race in America, from 1619 to 1880* (New York: Putnam, 1883), 2:126.

113. Entry for November 28, 1776, in Johann Ewald, *Diary of the American War: A Hessian Journal*, trans. Joseph P. Tustin (New Haven: Yale University Press, 1979), 340–41.

CHAPTER 2: HALF SLAVE AND HALF FREE

1. David Cooper, *A Serious Address to the Rulers of America on the Inconsistency of Their Conduct Respecting Slavery* (Trenton, N.J.: Isaac Collins, 1783), 4.

2. See Arthur Zilversmit, *The First Emancipation: The Abolition of Slavery in the North* (Chicago: University of Chicago Press, 1967), 111, 120, 123.

3. "September Meeting," *Proceedings of the Massachusetts Historical Society* 10 (1868): 332.

4. In 1761, the reformist prime minister Marquis de Pombal abolished slavery in Portugal, though not in the colonies. It is sometimes pointed out that the Republic of Vermont was an independent sovereign state between 1777, when it declared its independence, and 1791, when it was admitted into the Union.

5. "In Re Vermont Constitution of 1777, as Regards Its Adoption, and Its Declaration Forbidding Slavery; and the Subsequent Existence of Slavery within the Territory of the Sovereign State," *Proceedings of the Vermont Historical Society* (1919–20): 247.

6. Miss Sedgewick, "Slavery in New England," *Bentley's Miscellany* 34 (1853): 421.

7. "Brief of Levi Lincoln in the Slave Case Tried 1781," *Collections of the Massachusetts Historical Society*, 5th ser. 3 (1877): 440.

8. Quoted in John D. Cushing, "The Cushing Court and the Abolition of Slavery in Massachusetts: More Notes on the 'Quock Walker Case,'" *American Journal of Legal History* 5, no. 3 (April 1961): 133.

9. "The Commonwealth v. Nathaniel Jennison," *Proceedings of the Massachusetts Historical Society* 13 (1873–75): 294.

10. ICPSR3.

11. Patrick Rael, "The Long Death of Slavery in New York," in *Slavery in New York*, ed. Ira Berlin and Leslie Harris (New York: New Press, 2005), 122–25.

12. "Methodist Petition Against Slavery, November 8, 1785," in *A Necessary Evil? Slavery and the Debate over the Constitution*, ed. John P. Kaminski (Madison, Wis.: Madison House, 1995), 34.

13. Thomas Jefferson Randolph, ed., *Memoir, Correspondence, and Miscellanies, from the Papers of Thomas Jefferson*, 2nd ed. (Boston: Gray and Bowen, 1830), 1:1, 40.

14. "Methodist Petition Against Slavery, November 8, 1785," in Kaminski, *A Necessary Evil?*, 34.

15. Ira Berlin, *Slaves without Masters: The Free Negro in the Antebellum South* (New York: Pantheon Books, 1974), 30.

16. William Wirt Henry, ed., *Patrick Henry: Life, Correspondence and Speeches* (New York: Scribner, 1891), 1:152.

17. George Washington to Robert Morris, April 12, 1786, in *The Writings of George Washington*, ed. Jared Sparks (Boston: Ferdinand Andrews, 1835), 9:159.

18. Berlin, *Slaves without Masters*, 46.

19. Ira Berlin, "The Revolution in Black Life," in *The American Revolution: Explorations in the History of American Radicalism*, ed. Alfred F. Young (DeKalb: Northern Illinois University Press, 1976), 349–82.

20. David Brion Davis, *The Problem of Slavery in the Age of Revolution, 1770–1823* (Ithaca, N.Y.: Cornell University Press, 1975), 100n23.

21. Figures derived from ICPSR3.

22. See, for example, "Brutus III (Melancton Smith), *New York Journal*, November 15, 1787," in Kaminski, *A Necessary Evil?*, 127–28.

23. Counterfactual estimates rely on the apportionment basis used for the census year. Figures calculated from federal census (ICPSR3) and apportionment data found in John P. McIver, "Apportionment of the House of Representatives: 1787–2000," table Eb1–56 in HSUS.

24. "Ordinance of 1787, July 13, 1787," in *Documents Illustrative of the Formation of the Union of the American States*, ed. Charles C. Tansill (Washington, D.C.: GPO, 1927), 54.

25. "We will neither import nor purchase, any slave imported after the first day of December next; after which time, we will wholly discontinue the slave trade, and will neither be concerned in it ourselves, nor will we hire our vessels, nor sell our commodities or manufactures to those who are concerned in it." Articles of Association, October 20, 1774, in *Journals of the Continental Congress, 1774–1789*, ed. Worthington C. Ford (Washington, D.C.: GPO, 1904–37), 1:77.

26. August 25, August 22, "Journal of the Constitutional Convention of 1787," in *The Writings of James Madison*, ed. Gaillard Hunt (New York: Putnam, 1903), 2:303, 2:271.

27. Jonathan Elliot, ed., *The Debates in the Several State Conventions on the Adoption of the Federal Constitution* (Washington, D.C.: Taylor and Maury, 1836), 3:599, 4:286.

28. August 8, August 21, July 11, in "Journal of the Constitutional Convention of 1787," 2:135, 2:264, 1:397.

29. June 11, August 8, July 9, in "Journal of the Constitutional Convention of 1787," 1:143, 2:136, 1:384.

30. July 11, July 12, in "Journal of the Constitutional Convention of 1787," 1:398, 1:412.

31. A similar debate occurred in Congress during the Revolution, over the issue of taxing slaves especially. Thomas Lynch of South Carolina argued that since slaves were property, "why should they be taxed more than the land, sheep, cattle, horses, &c.?" The inimitable Benjamin Franklin quickly rebuked him: "There is some difference between them and sheep," he noted. "Sheep will never make any insurrections." Albert Bushnell

Hart, ed., *American History Told by Contemporaries: Building of the Republic, 1689–1783* (New York: Macmillan, 1927–29), 2:540.

32. "John Adams' Notes of Debate," July 30, 1776, in *Letters of Delegates to Congress*, ed. Paul H. Smith (Washington, D.C.: Library of Congress, 1976–2000), 4:568.

33. August 21, August 21, in "Journal of the Constitutional Convention of 1787," 2:264, 2:265.

34. August 22, July 12, July 12, August 25, in "Journal of the Constitutional Convention of 1787," 2:265, 1:411, 1:412, 2:304.

35. According to the federal census of 1790, the free population of North Carolina, South Carolina, and Georgia totaled 487,231. At 239,395, the slave population constituted 33 percent of the total population of these states. ICPSR3.

36. Merrill Jensen, ed., *The Documentary History of the Ratification of the Constitution* (Madison: State Historical Society of Wisconsin, 1978), 3:263.

37. August 22, August 22, in "Journal of the Constitutional Convention of 1787," 2:265–66, 2:269.

38. Henry Knox to George Washington, July 7, 1789, in *American State Papers: Indian Affairs, Volume Four, Part One* (Washington, D.C.: Gales and Seaton, 1834), 53.

39. David C. Hendrickson, *Peace Pact: The Lost World of the American Founding* (Lawrence: University Press of Kansas, 2006).

40. James Madison to Daniel Webster, May 27, 1830, in *Letters and Other Writings of James Madison* (Philadelphia: J. B. Lippincott, 1865), 4:85.

41. John Adams to John Jay, May 8, 1787, in *The Works of John Adams*, ed. Charles Francis Adams (Boston: Little, Brown, 1853), 439.

42. August 29, in "Journal of the Constitutional Convention of 1787," 2:329.

43. August 22, in "Journal of the Constitutional Convention of 1787," 2:268–69.

44. *Federalist 39*, "The Conformity of the Plan to Republican Principles: An Objection in Respect to the Powers of the Convention, Examined," in *Federalist, on the New Constitution* (Philadelphia: Benjamin Warner, 1817), 208–9.

45. John Dickinson, "Document IV: Notes for a Speech, July 9–14(?), 1787," in James H. Hutson, "John Dickinson at the Federal Constitutional Convention," *William and Mary Quarterly*, 3rd ser. 40, no. 2 (April 1983): 280.

46. August 22, August 25, in "Journal of the Constitutional Convention of 1787," 2:269, 2:305–6.

47. See, for example, the resolution adopted at the annual meeting of the Massachusetts Anti-Slavery Society in 1843: "The compact which exists between the North and the South is a 'covenant with death, and an agreement with hell ,'—involving both parties in atrocious criminality,—and should be immediately annulled." *Liberator* (Boston), March 17, 1843.

48. "February 27, 1860—Address at Cooper Institute, New York," in *Abraham Lincoln: Complete Works, Comprising His Speeches, Letters, State Papers, and Miscellaneous Writings*, ed. John G. Nicolay and John Hay (New York: Century, 1894), 1:605.

49. In the Caribbean: Jamaica, Antigua, Barbados, Dominica, Grenada, Montserrat, Nevis, St. Kitts, St. Vincent, Tortola, and Tobago. In Canada: Newfoundland and Nova Scotia. Britain possessed many other lands as territories or protectorates. Andrew

J. O'Shaughnessy, *An Empire Divided: The American Revolution and the British Caribbean* (Philadelphia: University of Pennsylvania Press, 2000).

50. Stanley L. Engerman, "France, Britain and the Economic Growth of Colonial North America," in *The Early Modern Atlantic Economy*, ed. John J. McCusker and Kenneth Morgan (Cambridge: Cambridge University Press, 2000), 247. See also Helen Dewar, "Canada or Guadeloupe? French and British Perceptions of Empire, 1760–1763," *Canadian Historical Review* 91, no. 4 (December 2010): 637–60.

51. Seymour Drescher, *Econocide: British Slavery in the Era of Abolition*, 2nd ed. (Chapel Hill: University of North Carolina Press, 2010), 22.

52. O'Shaughnessy, *Empire Divided*, chaps. 8–9.

53. Alfred W. Crosby, *Ecological Imperialism: The Biological Expansion of Europe, 900–1900* (Cambridge: Cambridge University Press, 1986).

54. The term "creole" has many academic and colloquial meanings. Here, the term is used consistently to distinguish people of European or African descent born in the Americas (creoles) from those born in Europe or Africa.

55. Selwyn H. H. Carrington, "The American Revolution and the Sugar Colonies, 1775–1783," in *A Companion to the American Revolution*, ed. Jack P. Greene and J. R. Pole (Malden, Mass.: Blackwell, 2004), 521.

56. Quoted in O'Shaughnessy, *Empire Divided*, 87.

57. Computed from Stanley L. Engerman and B. W. Higman, "The Demographic Structure of the Caribbean Slave Societies in the Eighteenth and Nineteenth Centuries," in *General History of the Caribbean, Volume III: The Slave Societies of the Caribbean*, ed. Franklin W. Knight (London: UNESCO Publishing, 1997), 49.

58. Edward Long, *The History of Jamaica* (London: T. Lownes, 1774), 4:309–10.

59. Quoted in O'Shaughnessy, *Empire Divided*, 50–51.

60. Ibid., 56.

61. Richard B. Sheridan, "The Jamaican Slave Insurrection Scare of 1776 and the American Revolution," *Journal of Negro History* 61, no. 3 (July 1976): 300, 301.

62. Edmund Randolph, *History of Virginia* (Charlottesville: University of Virginia Press, 1970), 253. Some reassured Nicholas that slaves "could never pretend to any benefit from such a maxim," while others asserted that "with arms in our hands, asserting the general rights of man, we ought not to be too nice and too much restricted in the delineation of them."

63. Phocion [Henry William De Saussure], *Letters on the Questions of the Justice and Expediency of Going into Alterations of the Representation in the Legislature of South-Carolina, as Fixed by the Constitution*, Early American Imprints, ser. 1, no. 28562 (Charleston: Markland and Miver, 1795).

64. ICPSR3.

65. Selwyn H. H. Carrington, "The American Revolution and the British West Indies' Economy," in *British Capitalism and Caribbean Slavery: The Legacy of Eric Williams*, ed. Barbara L. Solow and Stanley L. Engerman (Cambridge: Cambridge University Press, 1987), 135.

66. Quoted in ibid., 145.

67. Ibid., 148.

68. Calculated from Voyages: The Trans-Atlantic Slave Trade Database, http://www.slavevoyages.org.

69. Maurice Jackson, *Let This Voice Be Heard: Anthony Benezet, Father of Atlantic Abolitionism* (Philadelphia: University of Pennsylvania Press, 2009); Christopher Leslie Brown, *Moral Capital: Foundations of British Abolitionism* (Chapel Hill: University of North Carolina Press, 2006); Seymour Drescher, *Capitalism and Antislavery: British Mobilization in Comparative Perspective* (Oxford: Oxford University Press, 1987).

70. *The Papers of George Washington, Presidential Series*, ed. W. W. Abbot (Charlottesville: University of Virginia Press, 1987), 2:163.

CHAPTER 3: A HOUSE DIVIDING

1. "Governor Violeménil to the Minister of the Marine and the Colonies, September 14, 1789," in *Slave Revolution in the Caribbean, 1789–1804*, ed. Laurent Dubois and John B. Garrigus (Boston: Bedford/St. Martin's, 2006), 64.

2. Copy of a Letter from the Slaves of Martinique, August 29, 1789, in Dubois and Garrigus, *Slave Revolution*, 65–66.

3. Antoine Dalmas, "History of the Revolution of Saint-Domingue" (1814), in Dubois and Garrigus, *Slave Revolution*, 93.

4. Pierre Mossut, "Letter to the Marquis de Gaillifet" (September 19, 1791), in Dubois and Garrigus, *Slave Revolution*, 94.

5. Quoted in Jeremy D. Popkin, *You Are All Free: The Haitian Revolution and the Abolition of Slavery* (Cambridge: Cambridge University Press, 2010), 131.

6. "Rights of Black Men," *Argus* (Boston), November 22, 1791.

7. George Washington to Colonel John Laurens, July 10, 1782, in *The Writings of George Washington from the Original Manuscript Sources, 1745–1799*, ed. John C. Fitzpatrick (Washington, D.C.: GPO, 1938), 24:421.

8. George Washington to M. De Ternant, Minister from France, September 24, 1791, in *The Writings of George Washington*, ed. Jared Sparks (Boston: Ferdinand Andrews, 1836), 10:194.

9. Thomas Jefferson to James Madison, February 12, 1799, in *The Works of Thomas Jefferson*, ed. Paul L. Ford (New York: Putnam, 1905), 9:39, quoted in Douglas R. Egerton, *Gabriel's Rebellion: The Virginia Slave Conspiracies of 1800 and 1802* (Chapel Hill: University of North Carolina Press, 1993), 47.

10. Quoted in Gary Wills, *Negro President: Jefferson and the Slave Power* (Boston: Houghton Mifflin, 2003), 44.

11. Quoted in Laurent DuBois, *Avengers of the New World: The Story of the Haitian Revolution* (Cambridge, Mass.: Belknap, 2004), 111.

12. Thomas Jefferson to John Drayton, December 23, 1793, in *The Writings of Thomas Jefferson*, ed. Andrew Lipscomb (Washington, D.C.: Thomas Jefferson Memorial Association, 1903), 9:275.

13. Quoted in Herbert Aptheker, *American Negro Slave Revolts* (1943; repr., New York: International Publishers, 1987), 96–97.

14. Deposition of John Randolph, July 21, 1793, in *Calendar of Virginia State Papers and Other Manuscripts* (Richmond, Va.: A. R. Micou, 1886), 6:453.

15. George Reid Andrews, *Afro-Latin America, 1800–2000* (New York: Oxford University Press, 2004), 38.

16. Seymour Drescher and Pieter C. Emmer, eds., *Who Abolished Slavery? Slave Revolts and Abolitionism: A Debate with João Pedro Marques* (New York: Berghahn Books, 2010), 48.

17. Quoted in John Lynch, *Simón Bolívar: A Life* (New Haven: Yale University Press, 2007), 151.

18. See Andrews, *Afro-Latin America*, 57; Drescher and Emmer, *Who Abolished Slavery?*, 48–51.

19. Reprinted in Brycchan Carey, *From Peace to Freedom: Quaker Rhetoric and the Birth of American Antislavery, 1658–1761* (New Haven: Yale University Press, 2012), 74–76.

20. J. R. Oldfield, *Popular Politics and British Anti-Slavery: The Mobilisation of Public Opinion Against the Slave Trade, 1787–1807* (Manchester: St. Martin's, 1995), 1.

21. The phrase "national sin" was Sharp's. Srividhya Swaminathan, *Debating the Slave Trade: Rhetoric of British National Identity, 1759–1815* (Farnham: Ashgate, 2009), 74.

22. Calculated from Voyages: The Trans-Atlantic Slave Trade Database, www.slavevoyages.org.

23. Toyin Falola and Amanda Warnock, eds., *Encyclopedia of the Middle Passage* (Westport, Conn.: Greenwood, 2007), s.v. "British slave trade" (82).

24. Calculated from Voyages: The Trans-Atlantic Slave Trade Database, www.slavevoyages.org.

25. "Sixth Annual Message," December 2, 1806, in Ford, *Works of Thomas Jefferson*, 7:482.

26. *Annals of Congress*, 9th Cong., 2nd Sess., 202.

27. Ibid., 221.

28. Ibid., 266.

29. Ibid., 477.

30. Ibid., 626.

31. *Remarks of Henry B. Stanton: In the Representatives' Hall* (Boston: Isaac Knapp, 1837), 75.

32. See Matthew E. Mason, "Slavery Overshadowed: Congress Debates Prohibiting the Atlantic Slave Trade to the United States, 1806–1807," *Journal of the Early Republic* 20, no. 1 (Spring 2000): 59–81.

33. Steven Deyle, "An 'Abominable' New Trade: The Closing of the African Slave Trade and the Changing Patterns of U.S. Political Power, 1808–60," *William and Mary Quarterly*, 3rd ser. 66, no. 4 (October 2009): 833–50.

34. George Washington to John Francis Mercer, September 9, 1786, in *Writings of George Washington*, 29:5.

35. Thomas Jefferson to George Rogers Clark, December 25, 1780, in *The Papers of Thomas Jefferson*, ed. Julian P. Boyd et al. (Princeton, N.J.: Princeton University Press, 1950–), 4:237–38.

36. "Cotton, cottonseed, shorn wool, and tobacco—acreage, production, price, and cotton stocks: 1790–1999 [Annual]," table Da755–765 in HSUS.

37. Roger L. Ransom, "The Economics of the Civil War" (February 1, 2010), eh.net/encyclopedia/article/ransom.civil.war.us.

38. ICPSR3.

39. U.S. Department of Commerce, Bureau of the Census, *Historical Statistics of the United States, 1789–1945* (Washington, D.C.: GPO, 1949), 313, 220, 219, 200.

40. Between 1820 and 1840 the immigrant population increased by a factor of ten, from 8,300 to 84,000. Ibid., 29, 34.

41. Robert A. Davison, "Comment on New York Foreign Trade," in *The Growth of the Seaport Cities, 1790–1825*, ed. David T. Gilchrist (Charlottesville: University of Virginia Press, 1967), 70.

42. George Rogers Taylor, "Comment on Population," in Gilchrist, *Growth of the Seaport Cities*, 44.

43. Charles Grier Sellers, *The Market Revolution: Jacksonian America, 1815–1846* (New York: Oxford University Press, 1991); Scott C. Martin, ed., *Cultural Change and the Market Revolution in America, 1789–1860* (Lanham, Md.: Rowman & Littlefield, 2005).

44. Angus Maddison, *The World Economy: Historical Statistics* (Paris: Development Centre of the Organisation for Economic Co-operation and Development, 2003), 46–47, 85, 87, 132, 136, 146. GDP figures given in standardized international (Geary-Khamis) dollars.

45. "Foreign Commerce of the Country," March 25, 1825, in *Parliamentary Debates, New Series* (London: T. C. Hansard, 1825), 12:1200.

46. "Trade between Great Britain and the United States," *Niles's Weekly Register* 32, no. 826 (July 14, 1827): 330–31.

47. Memorial of the Pennsylvania Society for Promoting the Abolition of Slavery to the Senate and Representatives of the United States, February 3, 1790, in Julius Rubens Ames, *"Liberty." The Image and Superscription on Every Coin Issued by the United States of America* (1837), 20. Also available at the Historical Society of Pennsylvania (Philadelphia), Pennsylvania Abolition Society Papers (collection 490), box 5B.

48. "Abolition of Slavery" (House), February 12, 1790, in *Abridgement of the Debates of Congress, from 1789 to 1856* (New York: Appleton, 1861), 1st Cong., 2nd Sess., 1:208.

49. Quoted in Jay Winik, *The Great Upheaval: America and the Birth of the Modern World, 1788–1800* (New York: HarperCollins, 2007), 186.

50. *William Plumer's Memorandum of Proceedings in the United States Senate, 1803–1807* (New York: Macmillan, 1923), 111, quoted in Everett S. Brown, "The Senate Debate on the Breckinridge Bill for the Government of Louisiana, 1804," *American Historical Review* 22, no. 2 (January 1917): 345.

51. George Cabot to Thomas Pickering, December 10, 1803, in Henry Cabot Lodge, ed., *Life and Letters of George Cabot* (Boston: Little, Brown, 1877), 334.

52. Quoted in Matthew Mason, *Slavery and Politics in the Early American Republic* (Chapel Hill: University of North Carolina Press, 2006), 53–54.

53. Samuel Eliot Morison, *The Life and Letters of Harrison Gray Otis, Federalist, 1765–1848* (Boston: Houghton Mifflin, 1913), 263.

54. Quoted in William Chauncey Fowler, *The Sectional Controversy, or, Passages in the Political History of the United States* (New York: Scribner, 1864), 62. See also Albert F. Simpson, "The Political Significance of Slave Representation, 1787–1821," *Journal of Southern History* 7, no. 3 (August 1941): 315–42; Matthew Mason, "'Nothing Is Better Cal-

culated to Excite Divisions': Federalist Agitation Against Slave Representation during the War of 1812," *New England Quarterly* 75, no. 4 (December 2002): 531–61.

55. For examples, see Stephen Nissenbaum, "New England as Region and Nation," in *All over the Map: Rethinking American Regions*, ed. Edward L. Ayers and Patricia Nelson Limerick (Baltimore: Johns Hopkins University Press, 1996), 38–61; Joseph Conforti, *Imagining New England: Explorations of Regional Identity from the Pilgrims to the Mid-twentieth Century* (Chapel Hill: University of North Carolina Press, 2001).

56. Quoted in Mason, *Slavery and Politics*, 53; Manumission Society of Tennessee, *An Address Delivered by a Member of the Manumission Society, on the 17th of August, 1816, and Again on the 1st of January, 1817*, Early American Imprints, ser. 2, no. 39927 (Knoxville, Tenn.: Heiskell and Brown, 1817), 14.

57. Revised figures are based on the original apportionment basis. Author's analysis of John P. McIver, "Apportionment of the House of Representatives: 1787–2000," table Eb1–56 in HSUS.

58. Brian D. Humes, Elaine K. Swift, Richard Valelly, Kenneth Finegold, and Evelyn C. Fink, "The Representation of the Antebellum South in the House of Representatives: Measuring the Impact of the Three-Fifths Clause," in *Party, Process, and Political Change in Congress, Volume 1: New Perspectives on the History of Congress*, ed. David Brady and Mathew McCubbins (Palo Alto, Calif.: Stanford University Press, 2002), 666.

59. Morison, *Life and Letters of Harrison Gray Otis*, 263. See also Humes et al, "Representation of the Antebellum South in the House of Representatives," 670.

60. Leonard L. Richards, *The Slave Power: The Free North and Southern Domination, 1780–1860* (Baton Rouge: Louisiana State University Press, 2000), 68–69; Wills, *Negro President*, 7.

61. Jonathan Elliot, ed., *The Debates in the Several State Conventions on the Adoption of the Federal Constitution*, 2nd ed. (Philadelphia: J. B. Lippincott, 1836), 4:300; James Madison to Edmund Randolph, April 8, 1787, in ibid., 4:108 (emphasis in original). See also Wills, *Negro President*, 57–58.

62. "Missouri State Government—Restriction on the State" (House), February 15, 1819, in *Abridgment of the Debates*, 15th Cong., 1st Sess., 6:346.

63. Josiah Quincy, *Memoir of the Life of John Quincy Adams* (Boston: Crosby, Nichols, Lee, 1860), 108–9.

64. Richards, *Slave Power*, 80.

65. Henry Wilson, *History of the Rise and Fall of the Slave Power in America*, 4th ed. (Boston: James R. Osgood, 1875), 1:138.

66. Thomas Jefferson to John Holmes, April 22, 1820, in Ford, *Works of Thomas Jefferson*, 12:158.

67. "Maine and Missouri" (Senate), January 19, 1820, in *Abridgment of the Debates*, 15th Cong., 1 Sess., 6:400.

68. Quincy, *Memoir of the Life of John Quincy Adams*, 109.

69. See, for example, Dale W. Tomich, *Through the Prism of Slavery: Labor, Capital, and World Economy* (Lanham, Md.: Rowman & Littlefield, 2004), chap. 3; Anthony E. Kaye, "The Second Slavery: Modernity in the Nineteenth-Century South and the Atlantic World," *Journal of Southern History* 75, no. 3 (August 2009): 627–50.

70. Richard Graham, "Slavery and Economic Development: Brazil and the United States South in the Nineteenth Century," *Comparative Studies in Society and History* 23, no. 4 (October 1981): 620–55.

71. Ransom, "Economics of the Civil War."

CHAPTER 4: TO BECOME A GREAT NATION

1. ICPSR3.

2. William Jay, *The Life of John Jay: With Selections from His Correspondence and Miscellaneous Papers* (New York: J. and J. Harper, 1833), 1:231.

3. Quoted in Arthur Zilversmit, *The First Emancipation: The Abolition of Slavery in the North* (Chicago: University of Chicago Press, 1967), 146, 176, 177, 179.

4. *Journals of the Provincial Congress, Provincial Convention, Committee of Safety and Council of Safety of the State of New York* (Albany, 1842), 1:887.

5. Quoted in Zilversmit, *First Emancipation*, 179.

6. Daniel R. Ernst, "Legal Positivism, Abolitionist Litigation, and the New Jersey Slave Case of 1845," *Law and History Review* 4, no. 2 (Autumn 1986): 337–65.

7. Quoted in Zilversmit, *First Emancipation*, 187.

8. *New Jersey Journal*, quoted in ibid., 143–44.

9. Quoted in ibid., 150.

10. William Frederick Poole, *Anti-Slavery Opinions before the Year 1800* (Cincinnati: Robert Clarke, 1873), 11.

11. Quoted in David Brion Davis, *The Problem of Slavery in the Age of Revolution, 1770–1823* (1975; repr., Oxford: Oxford University Press, 1999), 331.

12. *Minutes of the Proceedings of the Ninth American Convention for Promoting the Abolition of Slavery and Improving the Condition of the African Race*, Early American Imprints, ser. 2, no. 5699 (Philadelphia: Solomon W. Conrad, 1804), 32–33.

13. "To the Free Africans and other free People of color in the United States," in *Minutes of the Proceedings of the Third Convention of Delegates from the Abolition Societies Established in Different Parts of the United States*, Early American Imprints, ser. 1, no. 29947 (Philadelphia: Zachariah Poulson, 1796).

14. Poole, *Anti-Slavery Opinions*, 46n18.

15. See also "Advice Given Negroes a Century Ago," *Journal of Negro History* 6, no. 1 (January 1921): 103–12.

16. Lois Horton, "From Class to Race in Early America: Northern Post-emancipation Racial Reconstruction," in *Race and the Early Republic: Racial Consciousness and Nation-building in the Early Republic*, ed. Michael A. Morrison and James Brewer Stewart (Lanham, Md.: Rowman & Littlefield, 2002), 65.

17. Thomas Jefferson, *Notes on the State of Virginia*, ed. Merrill D. Peterson (1781–82; repr., New York: Library of America, 1984), 270.

18. Benjamin Rush, "Observations Intended to Favor a Supposition That the Black Color (As It Is Called) of the Negroes Is Derived from the Leprosy," in *Transactions of the American Philosophical Society* (Philadelphia: Thomas Dobson, 1799), 6:289, 295, 296. See also Winthrop Jordan, *White over Black: American Attitudes toward the Negro, 1550–1812* (Baltimore: Penguin, 1968), 518–19; Ronald Takaki, *Iron Cages: Race and Culture in 19th-Century America* (1979; repr., New York: Oxford University Press, 2000), 33.

19. Colin Kidd, *The Forging of Races: Race and Scripture in the Protestant Atlantic World, 1600–2000* (Cambridge: Cambridge University Press, 2006), 136.

20. James Thackera, *A New Mode of Perfuming & Preserveing Clothes from Moths* (etching with color; Philadelphia, 1819; Historical Society of Pennsylvania, Philadelphia). See also Phillip Lapsansky, "Graphic Discord: Abolitionist and Antiabolitionist Images," in *The Abolitionist Sisterhood: Women's Political Culture in Antebellum America*, ed. Jean Fagan Yellin and John C. Van Horne (Ithaca, N.Y.: Cornell University Press, 1994), 217–18, 220.

21. Edward Clay, *Life in Philadelphia*, plate 4 (lithograph; Philadelphia: S. Hart, 1829; Library Company of Philadelphia, Philadelphia).

22. *Zip Coon, a Favorite Comic Song, Sung by Mr. G. W. Dixon* (sheet music cover; New York: J. L. Hewitt, 1834).

23. Jeremy Engels, *Enemyship: Democracy and Counter-Revolution in the Early Republic* (East Lansing: Michigan State University Press, 2010), 316. See also Ronald P. Formisano, *For the People: American Populist Movements from the Revolution to the 1850s* (Chapel Hill: University of North Carolina Press, 2007).

24. David N. Gellman and David Quigley, eds., *Jim Crow New York: A Documentary History of Race and Citizenship, 1777–1877* (New York: New York University Press, 2003), 125.

25. Ibid., 116, 123.

26. Ibid., 129.

27. Ibid., 121, 128, 117, 122.

28. Rhoda Golden Freeman, *The Free Negro in New York City in the Era before the Civil War* (New York: Garland, 1994), 92–93.

29. Pierre L. Van den Berghe, *Race and Racism: A Comparative Perspective* (New York: Wiley, 1967).

30. "An Act, to Regulate Black and Mulatto Persons," January 5, 1804, in *Acts of the State of Ohio, Second Session of the General Assembly* (Chillicothe, Ohio: N. Willis, 1804; repr., Norwalk, Ohio: Laning, 1901), 2:63–66.

31. Fred Lockley, "Some Documentary Records of Slavery in Oregon," *Oregon Historical Quarterly* 17, no. 1 (March 1916): 110.

32. "An Act, to Prevent Negroes and Mulattoes from Coming to, or Residing in Oregon," September 26, 1849, in *Statutes of a General Nature Passed by the Legislative Assembly of the Territory of Oregon* (Oregon City: Asahel Bush, 1851), 181–82.

33. See Alexander Keyssar, *The Right to Vote: The Contested History of Democracy in the United States* (New York: Basic Books, 2000), 54–60, tables A.2–A.4.

34. Mary Beth Norton, "The Fate of Some Black Loyalists of the American Revolution," *Journal of Negro History* 58, no. 4 (October 1973): 402–26.

35. Paul Cuffee, *Memoir of Captain Paul Cuffee, a Man of Colour* (Philadelphia: Kimber and Sharpless, 1816).

36. Tom W. Shick, "A Quantitative Analysis of Liberian Colonization from 1820 to 1843 with Special Reference to Mortality," *Journal of African History* 12, no. 1 (1971): 45–59.

37. "American Colonization Society," *African Repository and Colonial Journal* 1, no. 1 (March 1825): 2.

38. Isaac V. Brown, *Biography of the Rev. Robert Finley, D.D.*, 2nd ed. (Philadelphia: John W. Moore, 1857), 123.

39. Quoted in William Lloyd Garrison, *Thoughts on African Colonization*, ed. William Loren Katz (1832; repr., New York: Arno Press, 1969), ix.

40. See, for example, Folarin Shyllon, *Black People in Britain, 1555–1833* (London: Oxford University Press, 1977), 128; Norton, "Fate of Some Black Loyalists."

41. Garrison, *Thoughts on African Colonization*, 1:125, 128, 127, 135, 136.

42. "Colonization," *African Repository* 27, no. 11 (November 1851): 349; "The Liberian Colony," *African Repository* 10, no. 7 (September 1834): 207; "Dr. S.H. Cox and Colonization," *African Repository* 10, no. 4 (June 1834): 113.

43. David R. Roediger, *The Wages of Whiteness: Race and the Making of the American Working Class* (London: Verso, 1991).

44. Graham Russell Hodges, *Black Itinerants of the Gospel: The Narratives of John Jea and George White* (Madison, Wis.: Madison House, 1993); Susan Houchins, ed., *Spiritual Narratives* (New York: Oxford University Press, 1988); Rebecca Jackson, *Gifts of Power: The Writings of Rebecca Jackson, Black Visionary, Shaker Eldress*, ed. Jean McMahon Humez (Amherst: University of Massachusetts Press, 1981); William L. Andrews, ed., *Sisters of the Spirit: Three Black Women's Autobiographies of the Nineteenth Century* (Bloomington: Indiana University Press, 1986).

45. "A Narrative of the Proceedings of the Black People During the Late Awful Calamity in Philadelphia" (1794), in Richard Newman, Patrick Rael, and Phillip Lapsansky, eds., *Pamphlets of Protest: An Anthology of Early African American Protest Literature, 1790–1860* (New York: Routledge, 2001), 38.

46. Henry Sipkins, "An Oration on the Abolition of the Slave Trade" (1809), in *Early Negro Writing, 1760–1837*, ed. Dorothy Porter (1971; Baltimore: Black Classic Press, 1995), 371.

47. Jupiter Hammon, "Address to the Negroes in the State of New York" (1787), in Porter, *Early Negro Writing*, 322.

48. Peter Williams, "An Oration on the Abolition of the Slave Trade" (1808), in Porter, *Early Negro Writing*, 348, 352–53.

49. John W. Lewis, "Essay on the Character and Condition of the African Race," in *The Life, Labors, and Travels of Elder Charles Bowles, of the Free Will Baptist Denomination* (Watertown, N.Y.: Ingalls and Stowell's Steam Press, 1852), 228.

50. Frankie Hutton, *The Early Black Press in America, 1827 to 1860* (Westport, Conn.: Greenwood, 1993), 165–66.

51. Quoted in John M. Werner, *Reaping the Bloody Harvest: Race Riots in the United States during the Age of Jackson, 1824–1849* (New York: Garland, 1986), 58, 56.

52. Howard Holman Bell, *Minutes of the Proceedings of the National Negro Conventions, 1830–1864* (New York: Arno Press, 1969).

53. Patrick Rael, *Black Identity and Black Protest in the Antebellum North* (Chapel Hill: University of North Carolina Press, 2002), 27–44.

54. Prince Hall, "A Charge" (1797), in Newman, Rael, and Lapsansky, *Pamphlets of Protest*, 47; James Forten, "Series of Letters by a Man of Colour" (1813), in Newman, Rael, and Lapsansky, *Pamphlets of Protest*, 71.

55. Rael, *Black Identity and Black Protest*, chap. 2.

56. Winthrop D. Jordan, "American Chiaroscuro: The Status and Definition of Mulattoes in the British Colonies," *William and Mary Quarterly*, 3rd ser. 19, no. 2 (April 1962): 183–200.

57. Hammon, "Address to the Negroes," 5–6.

58. Quoted in Joanna Brooks, "John Marrant's Journal: Providence And Prophecy in the Eighteenth-Century Black Atlantic," *North Star* 3, no. 1 (Fall 1999), http://www.princeton.edu/~jweisenf/northstar/volume3/brooks.html. See also Joanna Brooks and John Saillant, eds., *"Face Zion Forward": First Writers of the Black Atlantic, 1785–1798* (Boston: Northeastern University Press, 2002).

59. Absalom Jones, "A Thanksgiving Sermon . . . on Account of the Abolition of the Slave Trade" (1808), in Porter, *Early Negro Writing*, 337–40. The Joseph motif is apparent as well in A Member of the African Society in Boston, "The Sons of Africans: An Essay on Freedom" (1808), in Porter, *Early Negro Writing*, 17–18.

60. Paul Cuffee to William Allen, April 22, 1811, in Sheldon H. Harris, "An American's Impressions of Sierra Leone in 1811," *Journal of Negro History* 47, no. 1 (January 1962): 39.

61. Hall, "A Charge," 47.

62. See Prince Sanders, *Haytian Papers: A Collection of the Very Interesting Proclamations and Other Official Documents . . . of the Kingdom of Hayti* (London: W. Reed, 1816).

63. Quoted in James Oliver and Lois E. Horton, *In Hope of Liberty: Culture, Community, and Protest among Northern Free Blacks, 1700–1860* (New York: Oxford University Press, 1997), 201.

64. See Rael, *Black Identity and Black Protest*, chap. 3.

65. Garrison, *Thoughts on African Colonization*, 2:63; "Meeting of the People of Color of Philadelphia, January 1817," in ibid., 1:9; Prince Saunders, "An Address, Delivered at Bethel Church, Philadelphia" (1818), in Herbert Aptheker, ed., *A Documentary History of the Negro People in the United States* (New York: Citadel Press, 1966–67), 1:73.

66. See New York statutes from 1806, 1808, and 1817; the Illinois statute from 1819; and federal statutes from 1807, 1808, and 1820. "An Act Relative to Slaves and Servants," in *Laws Relative to Slaves and Servants, Passed by the Legislature of New-York, March 31st, 1817. Together with Extracts from the Laws of the United States Respecting Slaves* (New York: Samuel Wood and Sons, 1817), 3, in Paul Finkelman, ed., *Slavery, Race, and the American Legal System, 1700–1872, Series VII: Statutes on Slavery* (Clark, N.J.: Lawbook Exchange, 2007), 1:85–124; *Laws Relative to Slaves and the Slave-Trade* (New York: Samuel Stansbury, 1806), reprinted in Finkelman, *Slavery, Race*, 1:55–84; *Selections from the Revised Statutes of the State of New York: Containing All the Laws of the State Relative to Slaves, and the Law Relative to the Offence of Kidnapping* (New York: Vanderpool and Cole, 1830, reprinted in Finkelman, *Slavery, Race*, 2:1–46; *Slave Code of the State of Illinois, Being an Abstract of Those Laws Now in Force in This State, Which Affect the Rights of Colored People, as Such, Both Bond and Free* (n.p.: Will Co. Anti-Slavery Society, 1840), in Finkelman, *Slavery, Race*, 2:81–92; *Illinois Slavery. The Laws Now in Force, Which Oppress and Hold in Bondage the Colored People* (n.p., n.d.), in Finkelman, *Slavery, Race*, 2:97–100.

67. *Selections from the Revised Statutes of the State of New York: Containing All the Laws of the State Relative to Slaves, and the Law Relative to the Offence of Kidnapping* (New York: Vanderpool and Cole, 1830), in Finkelman, *Slavery, Race*, 2:5, 7.

68. Garrison, *Thoughts on African Colonization*, 2:46.

69. *Colored American* (New York), August 19, 1837.

70. William Hamilton, *An Address to the New York African Society, for Mutual Relief* (New York, 1809), in Porter, *Early Negro Writing*, 37.

71. David Walker, *David Walker's Appeal to the Coloured Citizens of the World*, ed. Peter P. Hinks (1829; repr., University Park: Pennsylvania State University Press, 2000).

72. Hammon, " Address to the Negroes," 322.

73. "To the People of Colour," in A[bsalom], J[ones], and R[ichard] A[llen], *A Narrative of the Proceedings of the Black People, during the Late Awful Calamity in Philadelphia, in the Year 1793* (Philadelphia: William W. Woodwaard, 1794), 27.

74. Williams, "Oration on the Abolition," 350; Henry Sipkins, *An Oration on the Abolition of the Slave Trade* (New York, 1809), in Porter, *Early Negro Writing*, 371.

75. Thomas Hodgkin, *An Inquiry into the Merits of the American Colonization Society* (London, 1833), 7.

76. *Freedom's Journal* (New York), October 5, 1827.

77. "Address to the Citizens of New York," in *Resolutions of the People of Colour at a Meeting Held on the 25th of January, 1831* (New York, 1831), in Porter, *Early Negro Writing*, 285.

78. Jermain Wesley Loguen, *The Rev., J.W. Loguen, as a Slave and as a Freeman* (Syracuse, N.Y., 1859), viii.

79. *Colored American* (New York), September 30, 1837.

80. Joseph Sidney, "An Oration, Commemorative of the Abolition of the Slave Trade in the United States" (1809), in Porter, *Early Negro Writing*, 358.

81. Nathaniel Paul, *An Address, Delivered on the Celebration of the Abolition of Slavery, in the State of New-York* (Albany: J. B. Van Steenbergh, 1827), 19–20.

82. "The Trial of Gabriel," in *Calendar of Virginia State Papers and Other Manuscripts*, ed. H. W. Flournoy (Richmond: James E. Goode, 1890), 9:165.

83. I rely heavily on Douglas R. Egerton's excellent analysis in *Gabriel's Rebellion: The Virginia Slave Conspiracies of 1800 and 1802* (Chapel Hill: University of North Carolina Press, 1993), chap. 5.

84. "Speech of a Slave at His Trial," in *Anti-Slavery Record* 1, no. 12 (December 1835): 143.

85. "Substance of the Testimony Given in the Trial of Jack Bowler," *Calendar of Virginia State Papers*, 9:160.

86. Douglas R. Egerton, "The Scenes Which Are Acted in St. Domingo: The Legacy of Revolutionary Violence in Early National Virginia," in *Antislavery Violence: Sectional, Racial, and Cultural Conflict in Antebellum America*, ed. John R. McKivigan and Stanley Harrold (Knoxville: University of Tennessee Press, 1999), 41–64.

87. Everett S. Brown, "The Senate Debate on the Breckinridge Bill for the Government of Louisiana, 1804," *American Historical Review* 22, no. 2 (January 1917): 347.

88. [Theodore Dwight], "Triumph of Democracy," *Connecticut Courant*, January 1, 1801, in Richard Alsop and Theodore Dwight, *The Echo, with Other Poems* (New York: Porcupine Press, 1807), 274.

89. Brown, "Senate Debate on the Breckinridge Bill," 347.

90. The 1800 figure is based on the author's analysis of IPUMS3. The 1782 figure is from Luther P. Jackson, "Manumission in Certain Virginia Cities," *Journal of Negro History* 15, no. 3 (July 1930): 282.

91. "A Gentleman: 'Extract of a Letter,'" *Virginia Herald* (Fredericksburg), September 23, 1800, in Patricia L. Dooley, *The Early Republic: Primary Documents on Events from 1799 to 1820* (Westport, Conn.: Greenwood, 2004), 83.

92. Egerton, *Gabriel's Rebellion*, chap. 11.

93. "The Confession of Jack Purcell," in James Hamilton, Jr., *Negro Plot. An Account of the Late Intended Insurrection among a Portion of the Blacks of the City of Charleston, South Carolina*, 2nd ed. (Boston: Joseph W. Ingraham, 1822), 46.

94. Daniel Rasmussen, *American Uprising: The Untold Story of America's Largest Slave Revolt* (New York: Harper, 2011), 47.

95. Quoted in Michael Craton, "Proto-Peasant Revolts? The Late Slave Rebellions in the British West Indies, 1816–1832," *Past and Present* 85 (November 1979): 117.

96. David Barry Gaspar, "The Antigua Slave Conspiracy of 1736: A Case Study of the Origins of Collective Resistance," *William and Mary Quarterly*, 3rd ser. 35, no. 2 (April 1978): 308–23.

CHAPTER 5: MINDS LONG SET ON FREEDOM

1. Thomas Gray, ed., *The Confessions of Nat Turner, the Leader of the Late Insurrection in Southampton, Va.* (Baltimore: Lucas and Deaver, 1831), 3, 9–11.

2. Albert J. Raboteau, *Slave Religion: The "Invisible Institution" in the Antebellum South* (New York: Oxford University Press, 1978).

3. ICPSR3.

4. *Confessions of Nat Turner*, 9, 10, 11.

5. Quoted in Nicholas May, "Holy Rebellion: Religious Assembly Laws in Antebellum South Carolina and Virginia," *American Journal of Legal History* 49, no. 3 (July 2007): 252.

6. Louis P. Masur, "Nat Turner and Sectional Crisis," in *Nat Turner: A Slave Rebellion in History and Memory*, ed. Kenneth S. Greenberg (Oxford: Oxford University Press, 2003), 161.

7. Judith Kelleher Schafer, "The Immediate Impact of Nat Turner's Insurrection on New Orleans," *Louisiana History: The Journal of the Louisiana Historical Association* 21, no. 4 (Autumn 1980): 361–76.

8. *The Pro-Slavery Argument, as Maintained by Our Most Distinguished Writers of the Southern States* (Philadelphia: Lippincott, 1853), 289–90.

9. Virginia Governor John Floyd to South Carolina Governor James Hamilton Jr., November 19, 1831, in *The Confessions of Nat Turner and Related Documents*, ed. Kenneth S. Greenberg (Boston: Bedford/St. Martin's, 1996), 110.

10. William Lloyd Garrison, *Thoughts on African Colonization: Or, An Impartial Exhibition of the Doctrines, Principles, and Purposes of the American Colonization Society* (Boston: Garrison and Knapp, 1832), 2.

11. William Lloyd Garrison to Henry E. Benson, July 21, 1832, in *The Letters of William Lloyd Garrison*, ed. Walter M. Merrill and Louis Ruchames (Cambridge, Mass.: Belknap, 1971–81), 2:158.

12. *Liberator* (Boston), January 1, 1831.

13. William E. Cain, ed., *William Lloyd Garrison and the Fight against Slavery: Selections from the Liberator* (Boston: Bedford/St. Martin's, 1995), 14.

14. Leonard L. Richards, *Gentlemen of Property and Standing: Anti-Abolition Mobs in Jacksonian America* (New York: Oxford University Press, 1970), 14–15.

15. Horace Greeley, *The American Conflict: A History of the Great Rebellion in the United States of America, 1860–'65* (Hartford, Conn.: O. D. Caes, 1865), 2:127.

16. Virginia Governor John Floyd to South Carolina Governor James Hamilton Jr., November 19, 1831, in Greenberg, *Confessions of Nat Turner*, 110, 107.

17. See, for example, Leon Litwack, "The Emancipation of the Negro Abolitionist," in *African-American Activism before the Civil War: The Freedom Struggle in the Antebellum North*, ed. Patrick Rael (New York: Routledge, 2008), 39–49.

18. "The Insurrection," *Liberator* (Boston), September 3, 1831.

19. Peter P. Hinks, *To Awaken My Afflicted Brethren: David Walker and the Problem of Antebellum Slave Resistance* (University Park: Pennsylvania State University Press, 1997); David Walker, *David Walker's Appeal to the Coloured Citizens of the World*, ed. Peter P. Hinks (1829; repr., University Park: Pennsylvania State University Press, 2000).

20. Ibid., 49.

21. Scholars estimate the GDP of Brazil in 1820 to have been 2.9 billion in constant dollars, and the entire Caribbean 5.3 billion. The GDP of the United States in 1820 stood at 12.5 billion. Angus Maddison, *The World Economy: Historical Statistics* (Paris: Development Centre of the Organisation for Economic Co-operation and Development, 2003), 114, 84.

22. Eugene Genovese, *From Rebellion to Revolution: Afro-American Slave Revolts in the Making of the Modern World* (Baton Rouge: Louisiana State University Press, 1978), 99; Walter Rodney, "Africa in Europe and the Americas," in *The Cambridge History of Africa*, ed. J. D. Fage and Roland Anthony Oliver (Cambridge: Cambridge University Press, 2003), 4:616.

23. Richard B. Sheridan, "The Jamaican Slave Insurrection Scare of 1776 and the American Revolution," *Journal of Negro History* 61, no. 3 (July 1976): 290–308.

24. Calculated from Voyages: The Trans-Atlantic Slave Trade Database, www.slave-voyages.org.

25. B. W. Higman, *Slave Populations of the British Caribbean, 1807–1834* (Baltimore: Johns Hopkins University Press, 1984), 417–18, table s1.2.

26. "Colonial Summary. March, 1817," *Colonial Journal* (London) 3, no. 5 (March 1817): 141.

27. Higman, *Slave Populations of the British Caribbean*, 458, table s3.6.

28. Kenneth Morgan, *Slavery and the British Empire: From Africa to America* (Oxford: Oxford University Press, 2007), 144.

29. ICPSR3.

30. William A. Green, *British Slave Emancipation: The Sugar Colonies and the Great Experiment, 1830–1865* (Oxford: Clarendon, 1976), 103.

31. See also Hilary Beckles, "The Wilberforce Song: How Enslaved Caribbean Blacks Heard British Abolitionists," *Parliamentary History* 26 (Supplement 2007): 113–26.

32. Michael Craton, *Testing the Chains: Resistance to Slavery in the British West Indies* (Ithaca, N.Y.: Cornell University Press, 1982), 259–62.

33. Quoted in Michael Craton, "What and Who to Whom and What: The Significance of Slave Resistance," in *British Capitalism and Caribbean Slavery: The Legacy of Eric Williams*, ed. Barbara L. Solow and Stanley L. Engerman (Cambridge: Cambridge University Press, 1987), 266.

34. Craton, *Testing the Chains*, chap. 21; Emília Viotti da Costa, *Crowns of Glory, Tears of Blood: The Demerara Slave Rebellion of 1823* (Oxford: Oxford University Press, 1994);

Joshua Bryant, *Account of an Insurrection of the Negro Slaves in the Colony of Demerara, Which Broke Out on the 18th of August, 1823* (Demerara: A. Stevenson, 1824).

35. "Art. X," *Edinburgh Review, or Critical Journal* 41, no. 81 (October 1824–January 1825): 209.

36. Michael Craton, "We Shall Not Be Moved: Pompey's Slave Revolt in Exuma Island, Bahamas, 1830," *New West Indian Guide/Nieuwe West-Indische Gids* 57, no. 1 (1983): 26.

37. Genovese, *Rebellion to Revolution*, chap. 2.

38. Michael Craton, "Proto-Peasant Revolts? The Late Slave Rebellions in the British West Indies, 1816–1832," *Past and Present* 85 (November 1979): 123; Morgan, *Slavery and the British Empire*, chap. 6.

39. Craton, *Testing the Chains*, 300.

40. Quoted in Douglas R. Egerton, *Gabriel's Rebellion: The Virginia Slave Conspiracies of 1800 and 1802* (Chapel Hill: University of North Carolina Press, 1993), 51, 109; quoted in Craton, *Testing the Chains*, 285.

41. Genovese, *Rebellion to Revolution*, intro.

42. Craton, *Testing the Chains*, 24, 288, 314.

43. Quoted in Reginald Coupland, *Wilberforce: A Narrative* (Oxford: Clarendon, 1923), 458.

44. Henry Taylor, *Autobiography of Henry Taylor, 1800–1875* (London: Longmans, Green, 1885), 1:122–23.

45. Gelien Matthews, *Caribbean Slave Revolts and the British Abolitionist Movement* (Baton Rouge: Louisiana State University Press, 2006), 82.

46. Quoted in Craton, *Testing the Chains*, 274.

47. [John Smith], "No. VIII. Insurrections in the West Indies: St. Lucia–Trinidad–Dominica–Jamaica–Demerara," in *Negro Slavery* (London: Ellerton and Henderson, 1824), available online at John Rylands University Library Image Collections, http://enriqueta.man.ac.uk/luna/servlet.

48. Francis Augustus Cox, *History of the English Baptist Missionary Society: From A.D. 1792 to A.D. 1842* (Boston: Isaac Tompkins, 1844), 215.

49. Craton, *Testing the Chains*, 319.

50. Seymour Drescher, "Public Opinion and the Destruction of British Colonial Slavery," in *Slavery and British Society, 1776–1846*, ed. James Walvin (London: Macmillan, 1982), 216–21.

51. Quoted in Seymour Drescher, "History's Engines: British Mobilization in the Age of Revolution," *William and Mary Quarterly*, 3rd ser. 66, no. 4 (October 2009): 756.

52. Izhak Gross, "The Abolition of Negro Slavery and British Parliamentary Politics 1832–3," *Historical Journal* 23, no. 1 (March 1980): 84.

53. "Analysis of the Report of a Committee of the House of Commons on the Extinction of Slavery—Evidence of W. Taylor, Esq.," *Anti-Slavery Reporter* 5 (January 1832–February 1, 1833), 352.

54. "Proceedings of a General Meeting of the Anti-slavery Society and Its Friends, Held at Exeter-Hall, on Saturday, the 12th of May, 1832," *Anti-Slavery Reporter* 5, no. 5 (May 1832): 138.

55. *Report from the Select Committee on the Extinction of Slavery throughout the British Dominions* (London: J. Haddon, 1833), 97.

56. Ibid.

57. Quoted in Wolfgang Zach, Ulrich Pallua, Adrian Knapp, and Cynthia Rauth, "Slavery and Literature: The Abolition Period in Britain, Main Results of a Research Project," *Racism, Slavery, and Literature*, ed. in Wolfgang Zach and Ulrich Pallua (Frankfurt: Peter Lang, 2010), 113.

58. "An Act for the Abolition of Slavery throughout the British Colonies; for promoting the Industry of the manumitted Slaves; and for compensating the Persons hitherto entitled to the Services of such Slaves" (August 28, 1833), in *The Statutes of the United Kingdom of Great Britain and Ireland, 3 & 4 William IV*, vol. 73 (London, 1833), 666–91.

59. "Supplement, No. 1: Draft of Report Proposed by the Chairman," *Parliamentary Papers, House of Commons and Command* 23, no. 4 (1847–48): 44.

60. Robin Blackburn, *The Overthrow of Colonial Slavery, 1776–1848* (London: Verso, 1988), 457.

61. Seymour Drescher, *Capitalism and Antislavery: British Mobilization in Comparative Perspective* (Oxford: Oxford University Press, 1987), 93–94.

62. "British Way, French Way: Opinion Building and Revolution in the Second French Slave Emancipation (1991)," in Seymour Drescher, *From Slavery to Freedom: Comparative Studies in the Rise and Fall of Atlantic Slavery* (New York: New York University Press, 1999), 178.

63. Seymour Drescher and Pieter C. Emmer, eds., *Who Abolished Slavery? Slave Revolts and Abolitionism: A Debate with João Pedro Marques* (New York: Berghahn Books, 2010), 54–58; Blackburn, *Overthrow of Colonial Slavery*, chap. 12.

64. Humphrey E. Lamur, "Demographic Performance of Two Slave Populations of the Dutch Speaking Caribbean," *Boletín de Estudios Latinoamericanos y del Caribe* 30 (June 1981): 95.

65. B. W. Higman, "The West India 'Interest' in Parliament, 1807–1833," *Historical Studies* 13, no. 49 (1967): 1–19; Andrew Jackson O'Shaughnessy, "The Formation of a Commercial Lobby: The West India Interest, British Colonial Policy and the American Revolution," *Historical Journal* 40, no. 1 (1997): 71–95; David Lambert, "The Counter-Revolutionary Atlantic: White West Indian Petitions and Proslavery Networks," *Social and Cultural Geography* 6, no. 3 (2005): 405–20.

66. Leonard L. Richards, *The Slave Power: The Free North and Southern Domination, 1780–1860* (Baton Rouge: Louisiana State University Press, 2000), 81.

67. Joseph Story, *Commentaries on the Constitution of the United States*, 3rd ed. (Boston: Little, Brown, 1858), 729.

68. Gaillard Hunt, *John C. Calhoun* (Philadelphia: George W. Jacobs, 1907), 73.

69. Quoted in Albert J. Beveridge, *The Life of John Marshall* (1916; New York: Cosimo, 2005), 4:420.

70. Richards, *Slave Power*, 136; Susan Zeaske, *Signatures of Citizenship: Petitioning, Antislavery, and Women's Political Identity* (Chapel Hill: University of North Carolina Press, 2003), 8.

71. "Slavery in the District of Columbia" (House), December 18, 1835, *Congressional Debates*, 24th Cong., 1st Sess., 12:1967.

72. Ibid., pt. 3, 12:3750.

73. *House Journal*, 24th Cong., 2nd Sess. (February 6, 1836), 352.

74. Both quoted in Elizabeth R. Varon, *Disunion! The Coming of the American Civil War, 1789–1859* (Chapel Hill: University of North Carolina Press, 2008), 113–14.

75. "Gag Law," *Gloucester Democrat* (Massachusetts), January 27, 1835; "The Palladium," *Massachusetts Spy* (Worcester), August 12, 1835.

76. Jeffery A. Jenkins and Charles Stewart III, "The Gag Rule, Congressional Politics, and the Growth of Anti-Slavery Popular Politics" (unpublished paper, April 16, 2005), http://web.mit.edu/cstewart/www/gag_rule_v12.pdf.

77. William W. Freehling, *Prelude to Civil War: The Nullification Controversy in South Carolina, 1816–1836* (New York: Oxford University Press, 1965; repr., Oxford: Oxford University Press, 1992), 358.

78. "Report of the Postmaster General," December 1, 1835, *Congressional Debates*, 24th Cong., 1st Sess., 12:24.

79. Cincinnatus [William Plumer], *Freedom's Defence; or, A Candid Examination of Mr. Calhoun's Report on the Freedom of the Press* (Worcester, Mass.: Dorr, Howland, 1836), 3.

80. "Slavery," *Genius of Universal Emancipation* 3, no. 10 (August 1833): 149.

81. John P. McIver, "Voter Turnout in Presidential Elections, by State: 1824–2000," table Eb62–113 in HSUS.

82. John H. Schroeder, "Annexation or Independence: The Texas Issue in American Politics, 1836–1845," *Southwestern Historical Quarterly* 89, no. 2 (October 1985): 140.

83. Randolph B. Campbell, *An Empire for Slavery: The Peculiar Institution in Texas, 1821–1865* (Baton Rouge: Louisiana State University Press), 11; Donald E. Chipman and Harriett Denise Joseph, *Spanish Texas, 1519–1821* (Austin: University of Texas Press, 1992), 220; Sean Kelley, "'Mexico in His Head': Slavery and the Texas-Mexico Border, 1810–1860," *Journal of Social History* 37, no. 3 (Spring 2004): 709–23.

84. Stephen F. Austin to Mary Austin Holley, August 2, 1835, in Eugene C. Barker, "Stephen F. Austin and the Independence of Texas," *Quarterly of the Texas Historical Association* 13, no. 4 (April 1910): 271.

85. "Independence of Texas and Its Annexation to the United States," *Daily National Intelligencer* (Washington, D.C.), April 11, 1837.

86. *Proceedings of the Senate and Documents Relative to Texas, from Which the Injunction of Secrecy Has Been Removed*, 28th Cong., 1st Sess., 1844 (serial 435), 50–53.

87. *Fifth Annual Report of the Executive Committee of the American Anti-Slavery Society* (New York: William S. Dorr, 1838), 48.

88. Analysis based on *U.S. House Journal* (28th Cong., 2nd Sess., January 3, 1845), 165–66. Information on party and sectional affiliations of the Representatives derived from *The Biographical Directory of the American Congress: 1774–1996* (Alexandria, Va.: CQ Staff Directories, 1997).

89. Quoted in Eric Foner, "The Wilmot Proviso Revisited," *Journal of American History* 56, no. 2 (September 1969): 270.

90. *Senate Journal*, 29th Cong., 1st Sess. (August 10, 1846), 37:527.

91. Debate over "Three Million Bill," February 18, 1847, *Abridgement of the Debates of Congress, from 1789 to 1856* (New York: Appleton, 1861), 29th Cong., 2nd Sess., 16:85.

92. Quoted in Michael F. Holt, *The Rise and Fall of the American Whig Party: Jacksonian Politics and the Onset of the Civil War* (New York: Oxford University Press, 1999), 465.

93. *Raleigh Register* (North Carolina), February 28, 1847, as quoted in Joseph Grégoire

de Roulhac Hamilton, "Party Politics in North Carolina, 1835–1860," *James Sprunt Historical Publications* 15, nos. 1–2 (1916): 122.

94. *A Political Text-book for 1860: Comprising a Brief View of Presidential Nomination and Election, Including All the National Platforms Every Yet Adopted,* comp. Horace Greeley and John F. Cleveland (New York: Tribune Association, 1860), 14.

95. Wendell Phillips Garrison and Francis Jackson Garrison, *William Lloyd Garrison, 1805–1879: The Story of His Life Told by His Children* (Boston: Houghton Mifflin, 1889), 3:412.

96. *Liberator* (Boston), March 10, 1846.

97. ICPSR3.

98. Philip D. Curtin, *The Atlantic Slave Trade: A Census* (Madison: University of Wisconsin Press, 1969), 34.

99. Robert Edgar Conrad, *The Destruction of Brazilian Slavery, 1850–1888* (Berkeley: University of California Press, 1972), 283.

100. Richards, *Slave Power*, 9.

CHAPTER 6: ERE THE STORM COME FORTH

1. John Brown Russwurm, "The Condition and Prospects of Haiti," commencement address given at Bowdoin College, September 6, 1826, published in the *Eastern Argus* (Portland, Maine), September 12, 1826, and in the *Boston Courier*, September 14, 1826; reprinted in Philip S. Foner, ed., *The Voice of Black America: Major Speeches by Negroes in the United States, 1797–1971* (New York: Simon & Schuster, 1972), 43; James McCune Smith, "Extracts from a Lecture Delivered at the Stuyvesant Institute, New York, for the Benefit of the Orphan Asylum, February 26, 1841," in Alice Moore Dunbar-Nelson, *Masterpieces of Negro Eloquence: The Best Speeches Delivered by the Negro from the Days of Slavery to the Present Time* (New York: Bookery, 1914), 19–32 (see also McCune Smith's two-part series "Haytien Revolutions," *Colored American* [New York], September 18 and 25, 1841; William Wells Brown, *St. Domingo: Its Revolutions and Its Patriots. A Lecture, Delivered before the Metropolitcal Athenæum, London, May 16, and at St. Thomas' Church, Philadelphia, December 20, 1854* (Boston: Bela March, 1855), reprinted in Richard Newman, Patrick Rael, and Phillip Lapsansky, eds., *Pamphlets of Protest: An Anthology of Early African American Protest Literature, 1790–1860* (New York: Routledge, 2001), 240–53.

2. "St. Domingo. The Misrepresentation," *National Era* (Washington, D.C.), April 13, 1848.

3. "Slavery. Spirit of the Lord's Freemen!," *Liberator* (Boston), November 7, 1835.

4. Brown, "The History of the Haitian Revolution," in Newman, Rael, and Lapsansky, *Pamphlets of Protest*, 253.

5. "Letter of James G. Birney, Esq.," *Colored American* (New York), June 27, 1840.

6. Austin Steward, *Twenty-Two Years a Slave, and Forty Years a Freeman: Embracing a Correspondence of Several Years, while President of Wilberforce Colony, London, Canada West* (Rochester, N.Y.: William Alling, 1857), 323.

7. "Liberty," *Freedom's Journal* (New York), February 21, 1829. For original, see Alexander Stewart, *Discourses on Some Important Points of Christian Doctrine and Duty* (Edinburgh: Oliver and Boyd, 1829), 52.

8. Brown, " History of the Haitian Revolution," 245.

9. "Ruin of the West Indies," *The Colored American* (New York), November 4, 1837. For

the book, see James A. Thome and Joseph Horace Kimball, *Emancipation in the West Indies: A Six Months' Tour in Antiqua, Barbados, and Jamaica, in the Year 1837* (New York: The American Anti-Slavery Society, 1839).

10. "First of August in Wilmington," *Colored American* (New York), August 24, 1839. For a paean by William Lloyd Garrison, see "ADDRESS Delivered at the Broadway Tabernacle, N.Y. on the FIRST OF AUGUST, 1838, By request of the People of Color of That City, in Commemoration of the Complete Emancipation of 600,000 Slaves on That Day in the British West Indies,—BY WILLIAM LLOYD GARRISON, OF BOSTON," *Colored American* (New York), August 25, 1838.

11. *Weekly Anglo-African*, November 5, 1859, in Martin E. Dann, ed., *The Black Press, 1827–1890: The Quest for National Identity* (New York: Putnam, 1971), 77. Elsewhere, Hamilton termed the Underground Railroad and Christianity "the two great safety-valves" that released or subdued "the restless and energetic among the slaves." *Anglo-African Magazine* 1, no. 1 (January 1859), in Herbert Aptheker, ed., *Documentary History of the Negro People* (New York: Carol, 1990), 1:415.

12. *Colored American*, September 2, 1837.

13. John Greenleaf Whittier, "Our Countrymen in Chains!" (1837).

14. "Speech of Hezekiah F. Douglas, at the Sixteenth Anniversary of West Indian Emancipation, at Cleveland, August 1, 1850," *Anti-Slavery Bugle* (Salem, Ohio), August 31, 1850, in *Black Abolitionist Papers, 1830–1865* (microform), ed. George E. Carter et al. (Sanford, N.C.: Microfilming Corp., 1981), reel 6, frame 560. David Walker launched the most strident attacks of all, warning white Americans "that unless you speedily alter your course, *you* and your *Country are gone!!!!!!* For God Almighty will tear up the very face of the earth!!! . . . Oh Americans! Americans!! I warn you in the name of the Lord, (whether you will hear, or forbear,) to repent and reform, or you are ruined!!!" David Walker, *Walker's Appeal, in Four Articles; Together with a Preamble, to the Coloured Citizens of the World, but in Particular, and Very Expressly, to Those of the United States of America* (Boston: David Walker, 1830), 45.

15. "Universal Emancipation," *Liberator* (Boston), January 1, 1831.

16. William Lloyd Garrison, *An Address Delivered in Marlboro Chapel, Boston, July 4, 1838* (Boston: Isaac Knapp, 1838), 23.

17. See, for example, the essays in John R. McKivigan and Stanley Harrold, eds., *Antislavery Violence: Sectional, Racial, and Cultural Conflict in Antebellum America* (Knoxville: University of Tennessee Press, 1999).

18. Patrick Rael, *Black Identity and Black Protest in the Antebellum North* (Chapel Hill: University of North Carolina Press, 2002), chap. 2; Shane White, "'It Was a Proud Day': African Americans, Festivals, and Parades in the North, 1741–1834," *Journal of American History* 81, no. 1 (June 1994): 13–50; Mitch Kachun, *Festivals of Freedom: Memory and Meaning in African American Emancipation Celebrations, 1809–1915* (Amherst: University of Massachusetts Press, 2006).

19. "A Petition of Absalom Jones and others, December 30, 1799," in *Landmark Documents on the U.S. Congress*, ed. Raymond Smock (Washington, D.C.: Congressional Quarterly, 1999), 92.

20. "Chronicle. 1824," *Niles Weekly Register* (Baltimore), September 11, 1832.

21. Milton C. Sernett, *Abolition's Axe: Beriah Green, Oneida Institute, and the Black Freedom Struggle* (Syracuse, N.Y.: Syracuse University Press, 1986), 54; James Oliver Horton

and Lois E. Horton, *In Hope of Liberty: Culture, Community and Protest among Northern Free Blacks, 1700–1860* (Oxford: Oxford University Press, 1997), 215.

22. Henry Highland Garnet, "Address to the Slaves of the United States" (1848), in Newman, Rael, and Lapsansky, *Pamphlets of Protest*, 160–64.

23. "Debate over Garnet's 'Address to the Slaves of the United States of America,'" in Newman, Rael, and Lapsansky, *Pamphlets of Protest*, 158.

24. Stanley Harrold, "John Brown's Forerunners: Slave Rescue Attempts and the Abolitionists, 1841–51," *Radical History Review* 55 (Winter 1993): 89–110; Stanley Harrold, *The Abolitionists and the South, 1831–1861* (Lexington: University Press of Kentucky, 1995), 67–83.

25. "Creole Case," in *The Political Text-book, or Encyclopedia: Containing Everything Necessary for the Reference of the Politicians and Statesmen of the United States*, ed. Michael W. Cluskey (Washington, D.C.: Cornelius Wendell, 1857), 121.

26. William Lloyd Garrison, "Address to the Slaves of the United States" (1843), in *The Rise of Aggressive Abolitionism: Addresses to the Slaves*, ed. Stanley Harrold (Lexington: University Press of Kentucky, 2004), 176.

27. "I Plead the Cause of White Freemen" (1847), in *The Civil War and Reconstruction: A Documentary Collection*, ed. William E. Gienapp (New York: Norton, 2001), 27.

28. *The Platform Text-book: Containing the Declaration of Independence, the Constitution of the United States, and All the Platforms of All Parties* (Omaha: Vincent, 1900), 46.

29. Ulrich Bonnell Phillips, *The Life of Robert Toombs* (New York: MacMillan, 1913), 68.

30. "Mr. Clay's Compromise Resolutions" (Senate), March 4, 1850, *Abridgement of the Debates of Congress, from 1789 to 1856* (New York: Appleton, 1861), 31st Cong., 1st Sess., 16:414.

31. George E. Baker, ed., *The Works of William H. Seward* (New York: Redfield, 1853), 1:74, 76.

32. Daniel Webster to Peter Harvey, October 2, 1850, in *The Writings and Speeches of Daniel Webster*, ed. Edward Everett (Boston: Little, Brown, 1903), 16:568.

33. Horace Greeley, ed., *The American Conflict: A History of the Great Rebellion in the United States of America, 1860–'64* (Hartford: O. D. Case, 1864), 1:223.

34. *Tribune* (New York), June 21, 1852.

35. John P. McIver, "Electoral and Popular Votes Cast for President, by Candidate: 1789–2000," table Eb149–153 in HSUS.

36. Richard Sutch, "Net Immigration—Various Estimates: 1774–1860," table Ad16–20 in HSUS.

37. "Platform of the American Party," in William G. Brownlow, *Americanism Contrasted with Foreignism, Romanism and Bogus Democracy, in the Light of Reason, History, and Scripture* (Nashville, 1856), 11.

38. "The Know Nothing Platform" (Duke University Special Collections Library), http://library.duke.edu/rubenstein/scriptorium/americavotes/know-nothing.html.

39. Allan Nevins and Milton Halsey Thomas, eds., *The Diary of George Templeton Strong* (New York: Macmillan, 1952), 1:94.

40. "Speech at Peoria, Illinois, October 16, 1854," in *The Collected Works of Abraham Lincoln*, ed. Roy P. Basler (New Brunswick, N.J.: Rutgers University Press, 1953), 2:274.

41. "The Rascals at Washington," *Tribune* (New York), January 26, 1854.

42. "Speech of Hon. J.A. Quitman, of Mississippi," December 18, 1856, *Congressional Globe*, 34th Cong., 3d Sess., appendix, pt. 2, 118. See also Matthew Pratt Guterl, *American Mediterranean: Southern Slaveholders in the Age of Emancipation* (Cambridge, Mass.: Harvard University Press, 2008).

43. Benson J. Lossing, *Harpers' Popular Cyclopædia of United States History: From the Aboriginal Period to 1876* (New York: Harper, 1882), 2:1139.

44. *The Debates of the Constitutional Convention of the State of Iowa* (Davenport: Luse, Lane, 1857), 2:682.

45. Frederic Bancroft, ed., *Speeches, Correspondence and Political Papers of Carl Schurz* (New York: Putnam, 1913), 1:131.

46. "Restriction of Slavery. Speech of Mr. D. Wilmot, of Pennsylvania, in the House of Representatives," February 8, 1847, *Congressional Globe*, 29th Cong., 2nd Sess., appendix, 317.

47. *New York Daily Tribune*, October 15, 1856.

48. *Facts for the People: A Valuable Campaign Document—Lincoln's Springfield Speech—Trumbull's Chicago Speech—Douglas at Chicago vs. Douglas at Freeport—What the Southern Papers Say—and the Political Record of Stephen A. Douglas* (Springfield, Ill.: Daily Journal, 1860), 12.

49. "Restriction of Slavery," *Congressional Globe*, 29th Cong., 2nd Sess., appendix, 1847, 317.

50. "The Kansas Constitutional Convention," *Douglass' Monthly* (Rochester, N.Y.), August 1859.

51. "The Aim of Black Republicanism in Minnesota," *Daily Ohio Statesman* (Columbus), June 8, 1857.

52. *Political Debates between Hon. Abraham Lincoln and Hon. Stephen A. Douglas, in the Celebrated Campaign of 1858, in Illinois* (Columbus: Follett, Foster, 1860), 71, 136.

53. Henry Wilson, *Territorial Slave Code: Speech of Hon. Henry Wilson, of Massachusetts* (Washington, D.C.: Buell and Blanchard, 1860), 2, 6, 5.

54. David Brion Davis, *The Slave Power Conspiracy and the Paranoid Style* (Baton Rouge: Louisiana State University Press, 1969).

55. *Dred Scott v. Sandford*, 60 U.S. 393 (1857).

56. Ibid.

57. Frederick Douglass, "The Dred Scott Decision, Speech Delivered Before American Anti-slavery Society, New York, May 14, 1857," in *Two Speeches by Frederick Douglass: West India Emancipation, and the Dred Scott Decision* (Rochester, N.Y.: C. P. Dewey, 1857), 33.

58. "The Dred Scott Case. Remarks of Hon. H. B. Stanton," *Cabinet* (Schenectady, N.Y.), April 21, 1857.

59. "The Dred Scott Meeting at the Capitol," *Albany Evening Journal*, April 13, 1847.

60. "Fragment of a Speech," *Collected Works of Abraham Lincoln*, 2:453.

61. Benjamin C. Howard, *Report of the Decision of the Supreme Court of the United States: And the Opinions of the Judges Thereof, in the Case of Dred Scott Versus John F. A. Sandford* (Washington, D.C.: Cornelius Wendell, 1857), 74.

62. "Fragment of a Speech," *Collected Works of Abraham Lincoln*, 2:453.

63. Quoted in Paul Finkelman, *An Imperfect Union: Slavery, Federalism, and Comity* (Union, N.J.: Lawbook Exchange, 2000), 315.

64. Quoted in Larry Gara, "Slavery and the Slave Power: A Crucial Distinction," *Civil War History* 15, no. 1 (March 1969): 15, 14.

65. W. H. Furness to Charles Sumner, November 9, 1856, quoted in ibid., 17.

66. James Oakes, "The Political Significance of Slave Resistance," *History Workshop* 22, no. 1 (Autumn 1986): 89–107.

67. See, for example, Steven Hahn, *The Political Worlds of Slavery and Freedom* (Cambridge, Mass.: Harvard University Press, 2009), chap. 1.

68. *Twelve Years a Slave: Narrative of Solomon Northup, a Citizen of New-York, Kidnapped in Washington City in 1841, and Rescued in 1853* (Auburn, N.Y.: Derby and Miller, 1853).

69. Patrick Rael, "Black Identity Formation in the Diaspora: The Strange Case of the Antebellum North," *Maryland Historian* 28, nos. 1–2 (Fall/Winter 2003): 47–68.

70. *Report of the Proceedings of the Colored National Convention, Held at Cleveland, Ohio, on Wednesday, September 6, 1848* (Rochester: John Dick, 1848), 18. See also Henry Highland Garnet's call for slave rebellion: "While you have been oppressed," he wrote his brethren in bonds, "we have been partakers with you; nor can we be free while you are enslaved. We, therefore, write to you as being bound with you." Newman, Rael, and Lapsansky, *Pamphlets of Protest*, 160. See also David Ruggles's formulation that free blacks were "slaves whose condition is but a short remove from that of two millions of our race who are pining in their bloody chains." Quoted in Graham Russell Gao Hodges, *David Ruggles: A Radical Black Abolitionist and the Underground Railroad in New York City* (Chapel Hill: University of North Carolina Press, 2010), 79.

71. C. J. Faulkner to John C. Calhoun, July 15, 1847, *The Papers of John C. Calhoun*, ed. Robert L. Meriwether (repr., Columbia: University of South Carolina, 1998), 24:444.

72. "By Telegraph. By Speed's Line. Reported for the Sentinel and Gazette. Kenosha, Oct. 19," *Milwaukee Sentinel*, October 21, 1850.

73. *Read and Ponder the Fugitive Slave Law!*, American Broadsides and Ephemera, ser. 1, no. 14388 (Worcester, Mass.: Spy Office, 1850), broadside.

74. Public Meetings at the North, *National Era* (Washington, D.C.), December 19, 1850.

75. "The Liberator. No Union with Slaveholders!," *Liberator* (Boston), March 28, 1851.

76. "The Fugitive Slave Law,—its Unrighteous Character," *Liberator* (Boston), December 12, 1850.

77. *Frederick Douglass' Paper* (Rochester, N.Y.), April 29, 1853.

78. James Oliver Horton and Lois E. Horton, "A Federal Assault: African Americans and the Impact of the Fugitive Slave Law of 1850," *Chicago-Kent Law Review* 68 (1993): 1187–89.

79. Quoted in Margaret Hope Bacon, *But One Race: The Life of Robert Purvis* (Albany: State University of New York, 2007), 118.

80. "The Fugitive Slave Law, Speech to the National Free Soil Convention at Pittsburgh," *Frederick Douglass' Paper* (Rochester, N.Y.), August 1852.

81. See William Parker, "The Freedman's Story: In Two Parts," *Atlantic Monthly* 17 (February 1866): 152–66, and (March 1866): 276–95.

82. "Slave Catching in New York—First Case under the Law," *Plain Dealer* (Cleveland), September 30, 1850.

83. Quoted in Albert J. Von Frank, *The Trials of Anthony Burns: Freedom and Slavery in Emerson's Boston* (Cambridge, Mass.: Harvard College, 1998), 210.

84. "Recovery of Fugitives from Labor. Speech of Mr. Butler, of South Carolina," January 24, 1850, *Congressional Globe*, 31st Cong., 2nd Sess., 79.

85. Back in 1841, Lincoln himself had successfully convinced the Supreme Court of Illinois to grant the freedom of an enslaved woman sold into free territory. *Baily v. Cromwell*, 4 Ill. 71 (1841).

86. Oakes, " Political Significance of Slave Resistance."

87. Amos A. Lawrence to Giles Richards, June 1, 1854, in AAL Letterbook, 2:338, as quoted in David R. Maginnes, "The Case of the Court House Rioters in the Rendition of the Fugitive Slave Anthony Burns," *Journal of Negro History* 56, no. 1 (January 1971): 34.

88. *The Works of Charles Sumner* (Boston: Lee and Shepard, 1875), 3:144.

89. Marion Mills Miller, ed., *Great Debates in American History: Slavery from 1790 to 1857* (New York: Current Literature, 1915), 4:252.

90. *Journal of the State Convention of South Carolina; Together with the Resolution and Ordinance* (Columbia, S.C.: Johnston and Cavis, 1852), 17–18, 24.

91. Reprinted in "Miscellaneous. Inalienable Rights of Americans," *Frederick Douglass' Paper* (Rochester, N.Y.), August 18, 1854.

92. "The Nebraska and Kansas Bill—Debate," March 3, 1854, *Congressional Globe*, 33rd Cong., 1st Sess., appendix, 769.

93. "Ward Beecher on the Observer. Sharp's Rifles as a Moral Agent," *New York Tribune*, February 8, 1856.

94. Quoted in "Lovejoy's Influence on John Brown," *Magazine of History* 23, nos. 3–4 (September–October 1916): 96.

95. Horace Greeley, *A History of the Struggle for Slavery Extension or Restriction in the United States, from the Declaration of Independence to the Present Day* (New York: Dix, Edwards, 1856), 92.

96. *Report of the Special Committee Appointed to Investigate the Troubles in Kansas: With the Views of the Minority of Said Committee*, House Report 200, 34th Cong., 1st Sess. (1856), 357.

97. *The Crime Against Kansas: The Apologies for the Crime. The True Remedy. Speech of Hon. Charles Sumner, in the Senate of the United States* (Boston: John P. Jewett, 1856), 5, 9.

98. *Inquirer* (Richmond, Va.), June 12, 1856, as quoted in William Day, *Slavery in America Shown to Be Peculiarly Abominable Both as a Political Anomaly, and an Outrage on Christianity*, 2nd ed. (London: Harrison, 1857), 37.

99. Quoted in William E. Gienapp, "The Crime Against Sumner: The Caning of Charles Sumner and the Rise of the Republican Party," *Civil War History* 25, no. 3 (September 1979): 223.

100. "The Assault upon Mr. Sumner: Speech at a Meeting of the Citizens in the Town Hall, in Concord, May 26, 1856," in *The Complete Works of Ralph Waldo Emerson* (Boston: Houghton, Mifflin, 1903–4), 11:247.

101. "The Outrage on Mr. Sumner, May 23, 1856," in *Power for Sanity: Selected Editorials of William Cullen Bryant, 1829–1861*, ed. William Cullen Bryant II (New York: Fordham University Press, 1994), 289–90.

102. "The Outrage on Mr. Sumner," *Living Age* 50, no. 637 (August 9, 1856): 376.

103. Oswald Garrison Villard, *John Brown, 1800–1859: A Biography Fifty Years After* (Boston: Houghton Mifflin, 1911), 248.

104. *Reports of the Select Committee of the Senate on the Harper's Ferry Invasion*, Senate Committee Report 278, 36th Cong., 1st Sess. (1860), 96, 97.

105. "Provisional Constitution and Ordinances for the People of the United States," in Richard J. Hinton, *John Brown and His Men: With Some Account of the Roads They Traveled to Reach Harper's Ferry*, rev. ed. (New York: Funk and Wagnalls, 1894), 619–33.

106. Frederick Douglass, *Life and Times of Frederick Douglass, Written by Himself*, new rev. ed. (Boston: DeWolfe and Fiske, 1892), 389.

107. S. D. Carpenter, ed., *Logic of History: Five Hundred Political Texts, Being Concentrated Extract of Abolitionism* (Madison, Wis.: S. D. Carpenter, 1864), 69, 70.

108. Wendell Phillips Garrison and Francis Jackson Garrison, *William Lloyd Garrison, 1805–1879: The Story of His Life Told by His Children* (Boston: Houghton Mifflin, 1889), 3:492.

109. S. D. Moore, "The Irrepressible Conflict and Impending Crisis," *DeBow's Review* 28, no. 5 (May 1860): 546.

110. "The Harper's Ferry Riot," *Richmond Whig*, October 21, 1859.

111. ICPSR3.

112. Villard, *John Brown*, 46.

113. Ibid., 248.

114. "John Brown's Last Speech," in *Memoirs of John Brown*, ed. F. B. Sanborn (Concord, Mass., 1878), 99.

115. Ibid., 67.

116. "Editorial Correspondence," *North Star* (Rochester, N.Y.), February 11, 1848.

117. "The Liberator. No Union with Slaveholders," *Liberator* (Boston), December 9, 1859.

118. Douglass, *Life and Times of Frederick Douglass*, 341.

119. "The Liberator. No Union with Slaveholders," *Liberator* (Boston), December 9, 1859.

120. Gerrit Smith, "Address of the Anti-Slavery Convention of the States of New-York to the Slaves in the U. States of America," in Harrold, *Rise of Aggressive Abolitionism*, 153–62.

121. Sanborn, *Memoirs of John Brown*, 94.

122. *New Hampshire Patriot* (Concord, N.H.), November 9, 1859.

123. Carpenter, *Logic of History*, 70.

CHAPTER 7: THIS TERRIBLE WAR

1. *Political Debates between Hon. Abraham Lincoln and Hon. Stephen A. Douglas, in the Celebrated Campaign of 1858, Illinois* (Columbus: Follett, Foster, 1860), 75.

2. The death toll of the Haitian Revolution has been notoriously difficult to determine, but likely ran to several hundred thousand. Historians long held that 618,222 died in the American Civil War, but recent work has elevated that number to between 752,000 and 851,000. "Haiti," in *Encyclopedia of African-American Politics*, ed. Robert C. Smith (New

York: Facts on File, 2003), 166; J. David Hacker, "A Census-Based Count of the Civil War Dead," *Civil War History* 57, no. 4 (December 2011): 307–48.

3. Abraham Lincoln to Hon. J. T. Hale, January 11, 1861, in *Letters and Addresses of Abraham Lincoln* (New York: Howard Wilford Bell, 1903), 181.

4. ICPSR3.

5. James McPherson first used the phrase "pre-emptive counterrevolution" with respect to the Civil War, drawing from the ideas of Arno Mayer. James M. McPherson, *Battle Cry of Freedom: The Civil War Era* (New York: Oxford University Press, 1988), 245.

6. "The Condition of the South," *Charleston Mercury*, June 13, 1860.

7. "Art. IV.—Our Danger and Our Duty," *DeBow's Review* 7, no. 1 (May–August 1862): 44. Abraham Lincoln to Hon. J. T. Hale, January 11, 1861, in *Letters and Addresses of Abraham Lincoln*, 180.

8. Quoted in Frank H. Alfriend, *The Life of Jefferson Davis* (Cincinnati: Caxton, 1868), 350 (my emphasis).

9. ICPSR3.

10. "The Conspiracy Against the Union," *Richmond Whig*, September 4, 1860.

11. Donald E. Reynolds, *Editors Make War: Southern Newspapers in the Secession Crisis* (Nashville: Vanderbilt University Press, 1970).

12. Quoted in Doris Kearns Goodwin, *Team of Rivals: The Political Genius of Abraham Lincoln* (New York: Simon & Schuster, 2005), 303.

13. A. Roane, "The South—In the Union or Out of It," *DeBow's Review* 29, no. 4 (October 1860): 457.

14. *An Address Setting Forth the Declaration of the Immediate Causes Which Induce and Justify the Secession of the State of Mississippi from the Federal Union* (Jackson: Mississippian, 1861), 3.

15. *Journal of the Public and Secret Proceedings of the Convention of the People of Georgia* (Milledgeville, Ga.: Doughton, Nisbet and Barnes, 1861), 113.

16. "An Ordinance to Dissolve the Union between the State of South Carolina and Other States United with Her under the Compact Entitled 'The Constitution of the United States of America,'" in *Ordinances of Secession and Other Documents, 1860–1861*, ed. Albert Bushnell Hart and Edward Channing (New York: A. Lovell, 1893), 9.

17. "A Declaration of the Causes Which Impel the State of Texas to Secede from the Federal Union," in John Henry Brown, *History of Texas: From 1685 to 1892* (St. Louis: L. E. Danielle, 1893), 2:394.

18. Constitution of the Confederate States of America, art. 1, sec. 9(4); art. 4, sec. 3; art. 1, sec. 2(3).

19. Henry Cleveland, *Alexander H. Stephens in Public and Private: With Letters and Speeches, Before, During, and Since the War* (Philadelphia: National, 1866), 721.

20. Winfield Scott to W. H. Seward, March 3, 1861, in *Letters and Literary Memorials of Samuel J. Tilden*, ed. John Bigelow (New York: Harper, 1908), 1:157.

21. "The Dissolution of the Union and the 'Southern Confederacy,'" *Liberator* (Boston), January 4, 1861.

22. Abraham Lincoln to Hon. J. T. Hale, January 11, 1861, in *Letters and Addresses of Abraham Lincoln*, 180.

23. Abraham Lincoln to William Kellogg, December 11, 1860, in *Abraham Lincoln: Speeches and Writing 1859–1865*, ed. Don E. Fehrenbacher (New York: Literary Classics of the United States, 1989), 190.

24. "March 4, 1861.—First Inaugural Address," in *Abraham Lincoln: Complete Works, Comprising His Speeches, Letters, State Papers, and Miscellaneous Writings*, ed. John G. Nicolay and John Hay (New York: Century, 1894), 2:7.

25. "Jefferson Davis and Robert Toombs," *Confederate Veteran* 20, no. 4 (April 1912): 171.

26. "An Ordinance to Dissolve the Union Now Existing between the State of Arkansas and the Other States United with Her under the Compact Entitled 'The Constitution of the United States of America,'" in *The War of the Rebellion: A Compilation of the Official Records of the Union and Confederate Armies* (Washington, D.C.: GPO, 1900), ser. 4, 1:287.

27. Charles McClure, ed., *A Digest of Opinions of the Judge-Advocates General of the Army*, rev. ed. (Washington, D.C.: GPO, 1901), 770n1; April 15, 1861, in *The Tribune Almanac for the Years 1838 to 1868, Inclusive*, ed. Horace Greeley (New York: New York Tribune, 1868), 39.

28. "Message to Congress in Special Session," July 4, 1861, in *The Collected Works of Abraham Lincoln*, ed. Roy P. Basler (New Brunswick, N.J.: Rutgers University Press, 1953), 4:434.

29. "Self-Government on Trial," *Tribune* (Chicago), January 7, 1861, and "In Defense of the Ballot Box," *Public Ledger* (Philadelphia), June 7, 1861, in *The Causes of the Civil War*, 3rd rev. ed., ed. Kenneth Stampp (New York: Simon & Schuster, 1991), 191, 192–93.

30. Quoted in James M. McPherson, *For Cause and Comrades: Why Men Fought in the Civil War* (New York: Oxford University Press, 1977), 18. McPherson found 68 percent of his sample group of Union soldiers reporting patriotic motives for fighting (101).

31. "Doc. 66: Message of President Lincoln, July 4, 1861," in *The Rebellion Record: A Diary of American Events, with Documents, Narratives, Illustrative Incidents, Poetry, Etc.*, ed. Frank Moore (New York: Putnam, 1862), 2:228.

32. Carl von Clausewitz, *On War*, trans. J. J. Graham (London: Kegan Paul, Trench, Trübner, 1908), 3:121. Peter Paret offers a useful introduction in "Clausewitz," in *Makers of Modern Strategy from Machiavelli to the Nuclear Age*, ed. Peter Paret (Princeton, N.J.: Princeton University Press, 1986), 186–215.

33. "Second Inaugural Address," March 4, 1865, in *Collected Works of Abraham Lincoln*, 8:332–33.

34. Mao Tse-tung, "On Protracted War" (May 1938), in *Selected Works of Mao Tse-tung* (Peking: Foreign Languages Press, 1967), 152–53.

35. Politics is, after all, essentially the word we use to describe social contests over "who gets what, when, and how," according to political scientist Harold Lasswell. Harold Lasswell, *Politics: Who Gets What, When, How* (New York: McGraw-Hill, 1936).

36. "The Resources of the Union and the Confederacy (1861)," in *The Civil War and Reconstruction: A Documentary Collection*, ed. William Gienapp (New York: Norton, 2001), 76–77.

37. "Speech on the Admission of Kansas, under the Lecompton Constitution, Delivered in the Senate of the United States, March 4, 1858," in *Selections from the Letters and*

Speeches of the Hon. James H. Hammond, of South Carolina (New York: John F. Trow, 1866), 317.

38. "Message to Congress in Special Session," July 4, 1861, in *Collected Works of Abraham Lincoln*, 4:438.

39. "The War—Its Cause and Cure," *Liberator* (Boston), May 3, 1861.

40. Quoted in James M. McPherson, ed., *The Negro's Civil War: How American Blacks Felt and Acted during the War for the Union* (New York: Pantheon, 1965), 32.

41. ICPSR3.

42. The origins of this widely quoted witticism are obscure. One source—reporter Albert Richardson's 1865 account of the war—cites the abolitionist and Unitarian minister Moncure Conway, who lampooned Lincoln's reticence on emancipation, suggesting that Lincoln's nightly prayer went: "O Lord, I desire to have Thee on my side, but I must have Kentucky!" Albert Deane Richardson, *The Secret Service, the Field, the Dungeon, and the Escape* (Hartford, Conn.: American, 1865), 136.

43. *House Journal*, 37th Cong., 1st Sess. (July 26, 1861), 123.

44. *War of the Rebellion*, ser. 1, vol. 2, pt. 2:73–74.

45. Greeley's letter appears in L. U. Reavis, *A Representative Life of Horace Greeley* (New York: G. W. Carleton, 1872), 253–58. Lincoln's reply follows on 258–59. Lincoln's reply is also in *Collected Works of Abraham Lincoln*, 5:388–89.

46. Trevor Nevitt Dupuy, *The Evolution of Weapons and Warfare* (New York: Da Capo Press, 1984), chap. 21.

47. Richard M. Garfield and Alfred I. Neugut, "The Human Consequences of War," in *War and Public Health*, ed. Barry S. Levy and Victor W. Sidel (Oxford: Oxford University Press, 1997), 31.

48. Earl J. Hess, "Tactics, Trenches, and Men in the Civil War," in *On the Road to Total War: The American Civil War and the German Wars of Unification, 1861–1871*, ed. Stig Förster and Jörg Nagler (Washington, D.C.: German Historical Institute, 1997), 481–96.

49. Hacker, "Census-Based Count of the Civil War Dead."

50. Ulysses Simpson Grant, *Personal Memoirs of U. S. Grant* (New York: Charles L. Webster, 1892), 1:368–69.

51. *War of the Rebellion*, ser. 1, 1:362.

52. Benj. F. Butler to Lieutenant Genl. Scott, May 27, 1861, in *Freedom: A Documentary History of Emancipation, 1861–1867, Series I, Volume 1, The Destruction of Slavery*, ed. Ira Berlin, Barbara J. Fields, Thavolia Glymph, Joseph P. Reidy, and Leslie Rowland (Cambridge: Cambridge University Press, 1985), 71.

53. Kate Masur, "'A Rare Phenomenon of Philological Vegetation': The Word 'Contraband' and the Meanings of Emancipation in the United States," *Journal of American History* 93, no. 4 (March 2007): 1050–84.

54. David Blight, ed., *When This Cruel War Is Over: The Civil War Letters of Charles Harvey Brewster* (Amherst: University of Massachusetts Press, 1992), 57.

55. "Commander at Camp Nevin, Kentucky, to the Commander of the Department of the Cumberland; and the Latter's Reply," November 5, 1861, in Berlin et al., *Destruction of Slavery*, 519–20.

56. "Gen. Fremont's Proclamation," in Moore, *Rebellion Record*, 3:10.

57. Abraham Lincoln to Hon. O. H. Browning, September 22, 1861, in John George Nicolay and John Hay, *Abraham Lincoln: A History* (New York: Century, 1890), 4:422.

58. Robert Tomes and Benjamin George Smith, *The War with the South: A History of the Late Rebellion* (New York: Virtue and Yorston, 1864), 2:278.

59. James D. Richardson, ed., *A Compilation of the Messages and Papers of the Presidents* (New York: Bureau of National Literature, 1914), 4:3292.

60. Ellis Yarnall, *Wordsworth and the Coleridges: With Other Memories, Literary and Political* (New York: Macmillan, 1899), 8.

61. "Military Treatment of Captured and Fugitive Slaves," *War of the Rebellion*, ser. 2, 1:749.

62. "An Act to Confiscate Property Used for Insurrectionary Purposes," *U.S. Statutes at Large*, 37th Cong., 1 Sess. (1861), 319.

63. "An Act to Suppress Insurrection, to Punish Treason and Rebellion, to Seize and Confiscate the Property of Rebels, and for Other Purposes," *U.S. Statutes at Large*, 37th Cong., 2d Sess. (1862), 589–92.

64. *U.S. Statutes at Large*, 37th Cong., 2d. Sess. (1862), 354, 376, 432.

65. Quoted in William Richard Cutter, ed., *American Biography: A New Cyclopedia* (New York: American Historical Society, 1919), 6:266.

66. Proclamation of May 19, 1862, Richardon, *Compilation of the Messages and Papers*, 4:3293.

67. "Appeal to Favor Compensated Emancipation, Read by the President to Border-State Representatives, July 12, 1862," in *Complete Works of Abraham Lincoln*, 7:271–72.

68. "A Parallel. The Tyrant, George III., and Abraham Lincoln," *Daily Age* (Philadelphia), November 19, 1863.

69. "Draft of Letter to Secretary Chase," September 2, 1862, in *Abraham Lincoln: Complete Works*, 2:403.

70. Henry J. Raymond, ed., *The Life and Public Services of Abraham Lincoln* (New York: Derby and Miller, 1865), 235.

71. "Letter to August Belmont," July 31, 1862, in *Abraham Lincoln: Complete Works*, 2:217.

72. Edgar T. Welles, ed., *Diary of Gideon Welles: Secretary of the Navy under Lincoln and Johnson* (Boston: Houghton Mifflin, 1911), 1:70.

73. July 21, 1862, in *The Salmon P. Chase Papers*, ed. John Niven (Kent, Ohio: Kent State University Press), 1:348.

74. "Preliminary Emancipation Proclamation," September 22, 1862, in *Collected Works of Abraham Lincoln*, 5:434.

75. Keith Poulter, "Slaves Immediately Freed by the Emancipation Proclamation," *North and South* 5 no. 1 (December 2001): 48.

76. July 31, 1863, in *A Memoir of Robert C. Winthrop*, 2nd ed., ed. Robert C. Winthrop, Jr. (Boston: Little, Brown, 1897), 229.

77. *Political Debates between Hon. Abraham Lincoln and Hon. Stephen A. Douglas*, 157.

78. "Letter to A. G. Hodges," April 4, 1864, in *Abraham Lincoln: Complete Works*, 2:509.

79. Quoted in David W. Blight, *Frederick Douglass' Civil War: Keeping Faith in Jubilee* (Baton Rouge: Louisiana State University Press, 1989), 186.

80. Don E. Fehrenbacher and Virginia Fehrenbacher, eds., *Recollected Words of Abraham Lincoln* (Stanford: Stanford University Press, 1996), 174.

81. Samuel E. Cox, *Eight Years in Congress, from 1857 to 1865* (New York: Appleton, 1865), 238.

82. Whitelaw Reid, *Ohio in the War: Her Statesmen, Her Generals, and Soldiers, Volume I: History of the State during the War, and the Lives of Her Generals* (New York: Moore, Wilstach, and Baldwin, 1868), 104.

83. Horatio Seymour, "Inaugural Message as Governor, Jan. 7, 1863," in *Public Record: Including Speeches, Messages, Proclamations, Official Correspondence, and Other Public Utterances of Horatio Seymour; from the Campaign of 1856 to the Present Time*, ed. Thomas M. Cook and Thomas W. Knox (New York: I. W. England, 1868), 104.

84. "Memorandum Concerning His Probable Failure of Re-election," in *Collected Works of Abraham Lincoln*, 7:514.

85. "Speech at Peoria, Illinois," October 16, 1854, in *Collected Works of Abraham Lincoln*, 2:255.

86. "Speech in Springfield, Illinois," June 26, 1857, in *Abraham Lincoln: Complete Works*, 1:235.

87. "Address on Colonization to a Deputation of Negroes," August 14, 1862, in *Collected Works of Abraham Lincoln*, 5:372.

88. Michael Vorenberg, "Abraham Lincoln and the Politics of Black Colonization," *Journal of the Abraham Lincoln Association* 14, no. 2 (Summer 1993): 119–22.

89. *Diary of Gideon Welles*, 1:159.

90. Ira Berlin, Barbara J. Fields, Steven F. Miller, Joseph P. Reidy, and Leslie S. Rowland, eds., *Slaves No More: Three Essays on Emancipation and the Civil War* (New York: Cambridge University Press, 1992), 203; Joseph Reidy, "Armed Slaves and the Struggles for Republican Liberty in the U.S. Civil War," in *Arming Slaves: from Classical Times to the Modern Age*, ed. Christopher Leslie Brown and Philip D. Morgan (New Haven: Yale University Press, 2006), 285.

91. L. D. Reddick, "The Negro Policy of the United States Army, 1775–1945," *Journal of Negro History* 34, no. 1 (January 1949): 27.

92. J. Holt to Hon. E. M. Stanton, August 20, 1863, in *War of the Rebellion*, ser. 3, 3:696.

93. U. S. Grant to Abraham Lincoln, August 23, 1863, in *Grant: Memoirs and Selected Letters* (New York: Literary Classics, 1990), 1031.

94. Horace Porter, *Campaigning with Grant* (New York: Century, 1907), 219.

95. "Unfinished Draft of Letter to I. M. Schermerhorn," September 12, 1864, in *Abraham Lincoln: Complete Works*, 2:576.

96. J. Holt to Hon. E. M. Stanton, August 20, 1863, in *War of the Rebellion*, ser. 3, 3:696.

97. *Speeches, Arguments, Addresses, and Letters of Clement L. Vallandigham* (New York: J. Walter, 1864), 430.

98. Quoted in Bell Irvin Wiley, *The Life of Billy Yank: The Common Soldier of the Union* (1952; repr., Baton Rouge: Louisiana State University Press, 2008), 42.

99. "Interview with Alexander W. Randall and Joseph T. Mills," August 19, 1864, *Collected Works of Abraham Lincoln*, 7:507.

100. August 26, 1863, in *Collected Works of Abraham Lincoln*, 6:409.

101. "Letter to A. G. Hodges," April 4, 1864, in *Abraham Lincoln: Complete Works*, 2:509.

102. Ulysses S. Grant to Abraham Lincoln, August 23, 1863, in *Grant: Memoirs and Selected Letters*, 1031.

103. W. E. B. Du Bois, *Black Reconstruction in America 1860–1880* (1935; repr., New York: Free Press, 1998), 57.

104. ICPSR3.

105. *Special Message of His Excellency Joseph E. Brown, to the Legislature, upon the Subjects of Conscription, Martial Law, Habeas Corpus and the Impressment of Private Property by Confederate Officers, November 6th, 1862* (Milledgeville, Ga.: Boughton, Nisbet, and Barnes, 1862), 14.

106. Samuel R. Watkins, *1861 vs. 1862: "Co. Aytch," Maury Grays, First Tennessee Regiment; or, A Side Show of the Big Show* (Nashville: Cumberland Presbyterian, 1882), 39.

107. Orville James Victor, *The History, Civil, Political and Military, of the Southern Rebellion, from Its Incipient Stages to Its Close* (New York: James D. Torrey, 1861), 3:359.

108. Steven Hahn, *The Political Worlds of Slavery and Freedom* (Cambridge, Mass.: Harvard University Press, 2009), 97.

109. Mary Boykin Miller Chesnut, *Mary Chesnut's Civil War*, ed. C. Vann Woodward (New Haven: Yale University Press, 1981), 48, 233.

110. Charles J. Mitchell to Jefferson Davis, April 27, 1861, in *The Papers of Jefferson Davis*, ed. Lynda Lasswell Crist and Mary Seaton Dix (Baton Rouge: Louisiana State University Press, 1992), 7:143.

111. Tuesday, July 22nd, 1862, Niven, *Salmon P. Chase Papers*, 1:351.

112. "Preliminary Emancipation Proclamation," in *Collected Works of Abraham Lincoln*, 5:434.

113. Margaret Humphreys, *Intensely Human: The Health of the Black Soldier in the American Civil War* (Baltimore: Johns Hopkins University Press, 2007), 11.

114. "Doc299B: Missouri Black Soldier to His Daughter's Owner," September 3, 1864, in *Freedom: A Documentary History of Emancipation, 1861–1867, Series II, The Black Military Experience*, ed. Ira Berlin, Joseph P. Reidy, and Leslie S. Rowland (Cambridge: Cambridge University Press, 1982), 690.

115. "Dissolution of the American Union," *Douglass' Monthly* (Rochester, N.Y.), January 1861.

116. "Fighting Rebels with Only One Hand," *Douglass' Monthly* (Rochester, N.Y.), September 1861.

117. Jeffrey Kerr-Ritchie, "Rehearsal for War: Black Militias in the Atlantic World," *Slavery and Abolition* 26, no. 1 (April 2005): 1–34.

118. Berlin et al., *Slaves No More*, 203.

119. Thomas Holt, *Black over White: Negro Political Leadership in South Carolina during Reconstruction* (Urbana: University of Illinois Press, 1979), 66, 77.

120. "Address at Cooper Institute, New York," February 27, 1860, in *Abraham Lincoln: Complete Works*, 1:609.

121. Frederick Douglass, *The Life and Times of Frederick Douglass: From 1817–1882*, ed. John Lobb (London: Christian Age, 1882), 313.

122. "Doc. 224: Commander of an Alabama Confederate Regiment to the Headquarters of the Confederate District of the Gulf," November 8, 1862, in Berlin et al., *Black Military Experience*, 570–71; "Doc 225: Confederate Secretary of War to the Commander of the Confederate Department of South Carolina, Georgia, and Florida," November 30, 1862, in Berlin et al., *Black Military Experience*, 572.

123. Ted Alexander, "'A Regular Slave Hunt': The Army of Northern Virginia and Black Civilians in the Gettysburg Campaign," *North and South* 4, no. 7 (September 2001): 82–89.

124. Alfred M. Green, *Letters and Discussion on the Formation of Colored Regiments and the Duty of the Colored People in Regard to the Great Slaveholders' Rebellion in the United States of America* (Philadelphia: Ringwalt and Brown, 1862), 16.

125. "Annual Message to Congress," December 8, 1863, in *Abraham Lincoln: Complete Works*, 2:454.

126. "Unfinished Draft of Letter to C. D. Robinson," August 17, 1864, in *Abraham Lincoln: Complete Works*, 2:564.

127. "Order of Retaliation," July 30, 1863, in *Collected Works of Abraham Lincoln*, 6:357.

128. "Enlistment of Colored Men," *Douglass' Monthly* (Rochester, N.Y.), August 1863.

129. J. Holt to E. M. Stanton, August 20, 1863, in *War of the Rebellion*, ser. 3, 3:696.

130. "Doc. 252: Chaplain of a Louisiana Black Regiment to the Commander of a Black Division," April 8, 1864, in Berlin et al., *Black Military Experience*, 618.

131. "Florida Correspondence," *Christian Recorder* (Philadelphia), August 6, 1864.

132. "Doc. 157A: Massachusetts Black Corporal to the President," September 28, 1863, in Berlin et al., *Black Military Experience*, 385–86.

133. "To Michael Hahn," March 13, 1864, in *Collected Works of Abraham Lincoln*, 7:243.

134. "Last Public Address," April 11, 1865, in *Collected Works of Abraham Lincoln*, 8:403.

135. "Doc. 362: Nashville Blacks to the Union Convention of Tennessee," January 9, 1865, in Berlin et al., *Black Military Experience*, 812.

136. "Presentation of Colors to the 24th Regt. U.S.C.T.," *Christian Recorder* (Philadelphia), April 22, 1865. The image may be found online at http://www.loc.gov/pictures/item/2010647924/.

137. "Suffrage and Safety. Oration Delivered at Ravenna, Ohio. July 4, 1865," in *The Works of James Abram Garfield*, ed. Burke A. Hinsdale (Boston: J. R. Osgood, 1882), 1:86.

138. John Jay, *The Political Situation in the United States: A Letter to the Union League Club of New York* (London: Rivingtons, 1866), 51.

139. "Interview with George L. Stearns," October 3, 1865, in Edward McPherson, *A Handbook of Politics for 1868* (Washington, D.C.: Philp and Solomons, 1868), 49.

140. Patrick R. Cleburne, et al., to Joseph E. Johnston, et al., January 2, 1864, in *War of the Rebellion*, ser. 1, vol. 60, pt. 2:589.

141. Howell Cobb to James A. Seddon, January 8, 1865, in *War of the Rebellion*, ser. 4, 3:1009.

142. "An Act to Increase the Military Force of the Confederate States," March 23, 1865, in *War of the Rebellion*, ser. 4, 3:1161.

143. Thomas Jefferson, *Notes on the State of Virginia* (Boston: David Carlisle, 1801), 241.

144. Quoted in Henrik Kraay, "Arming Slaves in Brazil," in Brown and Morgan, *Arming Slaves*, 155.

145. Ira Berlin, Steven Hahn, Steven F. Miller, Joseph P. Reidy, and Leslie S. Rowland, "The Terrain of Freedom: The Struggle over the Meaning of Free Labor in the U.S. South," *History Workshop*, no. 22 (Autumn 1986): 123–24.

CHAPTER 8: ONE HUNDRED YEARS

1. Samuel Francis DuPont to Louis Malesherbes Goldsborough, November 9, 1861, in *Samuel Francis Du Pont: A Selection from His Civil War Letters*, ed. John D. Hayes (Ithaca, N.Y.: Cornell University Press, 196), 1:229.

2. ICPSR3.

3. George Rawick, ed., *The American Slave: A Composite Autobiography, Volume 3, South Carolina Narratives, Parts 3 and 4* (Westport, Conn.: Greenwood, 1972), 203.

4. Thomas Wentworth Higginson, *Army Life in a Black Regiment* (Boston: Lee and Shepard, 1882), 218.

5. Edward L. Pierce, *The Negroes at Port Royal: Report of E. L. Pierce, Government Agent, to the Hon. Salmon P. Chase* (Boston: R. F. Wallcut, 1862), 10, 17.

6. "Fortification of Appropriation Bill," January 15, 1862, *Congressional Globe*, 37th Cong. 2nd Sess., 357.

7. Hazard Stevens, *The Life of Isaac Ingalls Stevens* (Boston: Houghton Mifflin, 1901), 2:364–65.

8. "The Freed Blacks at Port Royal," *Christian Recorder* (Philadelphia), July 12, 1862.

9. "Then and Now," *Liberator* (Boston), March 21, 1862.

10. Elizabeth Hyde Botume, *First Days amongst the Contrabands* (Boston: Lee and Shepard, 1893), 86.

11. "Appeal of the Educational Commission," in Pierce, *Negroes at Port Royal*, 36.

12. General Thomas W. Sherman to Adjutant-General U.S. Army," January 15, 1862, in *The War of the Rebellion: A Compilation of the Official Records of the Union and Confederate Armies* (Washington, D.C.: GPO, 1886–1901), ser. 2, 1:802–3.

13. [Charlotte Forten], "Life on the Sea Islands," *Atlantic Monthly* 13, no. 74 (May 1864): 591.

14. Pierce, *Negroes at Port Royal*, 28.

15. *War of the Rebellion*, ser. 3, vol. 4, 1:1025.

16. Elizabeth Ware Pearson, ed., *Letters from Port Royal, Written at the Time of the Civil War* (Boston: W. B. Clarke Co., 1906), 276, 221.

17. Pierce, *Negroes at Port Royal*, 24–25.

18. "Report of the Bureau of Free Labor to Major Gen. Banks," *Liberator* (Boston), October 21, 1864.

19. "Louisiana Planters to the Commander of the Department of the Gulf," January 14, 1862, in *Freedom: A Documentary History of Emancipation, 1861–1867, Series I, Volume 3: The Wartime Genesis of Free Labor: The Lower South*, ed. Ira Berlin et al. (Cambridge: Cambridge University Press, 1990), 408–10.

20. "Regulations by the Superintendent of Plantations in the Treasury Department 5th Special Agency," New Orleans, February 1864, in Berlin et al., *Wartime Genesis of Free Labor*, 527–28.

21. Frederick Douglass, "What the Black Man Wants" (1865), in *Great Speeches by Frederick Douglass*, ed. James Daley (Mineola, N.Y.: Dover, 2013), 57–58.

22. J. M. Forbes to Edward Atkinson, May 23, 1862, in *Letters and Recollections of John Murray Forbes*, ed. Sarah Forbes Hughes (Boston: Houghton Mifflin, 1899), 1:313.

23. Quoted in Dale W. Tomich, *Through the Prism of Slavery: Labor, Capital, and World Economy* (Lanham, Md.: Rowman & Littlefield, 2004), 181.

24. Herbert S. Klein and Stanley L. Engerman, "The Transition from Slave to Free Labor: Notes on a Comparative Economic Model," in *Between Slavery and Free Labor: The Spanish-Speaking Caribbean in the Nineteenth Century*, ed. Manuel Moreno Fraginals, Frank Moya Pons, and Stanley L. Engerman (Baltimore: Johns Hopkins University Press, 1985), 262.

25. Ibid.

26. "Copy of a Despatch from Governor Barkly to Earl Grey," April 17, 1850, in *Accounts and Papers of the House of Commons* (February 4–August 8, 1851), 9:76–77.

27. Quoted in Mary Turner, ed., *From Chattel Slaves to Wage Slaves: The Dynamics of Labour Bargaining in the Americas* (Kingston: Ian Randle, 1995), 13.

28. John Bowen Colthurst, *The Colthurst Journal: Journal of a Special Magistrate in the Islands of Barbados and St. Vincent, July 1835—September 1838*, ed. Woodville K. Marshall (Millwood, N.Y.: KTO Press, 1977), 71.

29. "An Act for the Punishment of Idle and Disorderly Persons, Rogues and Vagabonds, and Incorrigible Rogues," December 5, 1839 (Vict. c. 18, no. 3315), in "Minutes of Evidence Taken before the Select Committee on Sugar and Coffee Planting," March 29, 1848, *Sessional Papers Printed by Order of the House of Lords* (1847–48), 36:136.

30. William A. Green, *British Slave Emancipation: The Sugar Colonies and the Great Experiment, 1830–1865* (Oxford: Clarendon, 1976), 186.

31. Stanley L. Engerman and Kenneth L. Sokoloff, "Institutional and Non-Institutional Explanation of Economic Differences," in *Handbook of New Institutional Economics*, ed. Claude Ménard and Mary M. Shirley (Heidelberg: Springer-Verlag, 2008), 655, table 4.

32. [Thomas Carlyle], "Occasional Discourse on the Negro Question," *Fraser's Magazine* 40 (December 1849): 672, 675, 676. In 1853, Carlyle published an updated version of the essay with the even more denigrating title *Occasional Discourse on the Nigger Question* (London: Thomas Bosworth, 1853).

33. *British and Foreign Anti-Slavery Reporter* (London) 7 (December 1, 1846): 199, 200.

34. "The West India Colonies—'Suggestions For Saving Them,'" *Tablet* (London), February 3, 1849.

35. Derived from figures 2.1 and 2.2 in David Northup, *Indentured Labor in the Age of Imperialism, 1834–1922* (Cambridge: Cambridge University Press, 1995), 156–60.

36. Eric Foner, *Nothing but Freedom: Emancipation and Its Legacy* (Baton Rouge: Louisiana State University Press, 1983), 46. Foner quotes Douglas Lorimer in *Colour, Class and the Victorians: English Attitudes to the Negro in the Mid-Nineteenth Century* (Leicester: Leicester University Press, 1978): "The question, 'does a black man equal a white man?' had little meaning in an age when few thought all white men deserved equality" (15).

37. Roger L. Ransom, *The Confederate States of America: What Might Have Been* (New York: Norton, 2005), 27; David Brion Davis, "The Impact of British Abolitionism on American Sectionalism," in *In the Shadow of Freedom: The Politics of Slavery in the National Capital*, ed. Paul Finkelman and Donald R. Kennon (Athens: Ohio University Press, 2011), 21.

38. "December 8, 1863—Proclamation of Amnesty and Reconstruction," in *Abraham Lincoln: Complete Works, Comprising His Speeches, Letters, State Papers, and Miscellaneous Writings*, ed. John G. Nicolay and John Hay (New York: Century, 1894), 2:444.

39. "To Michael Hahn," March 13, 1864, 7:243, and "Last Public Address," April 11, 1865, 8:403, both in *The Collected Works of Abraham Lincoln*, ed. Roy P. Basler (New Brunswick, N.J.: Rutgers University Press, 1953).

40. *Modification of the Oath of Office*, House Report 51, 39th Cong., 1st Sess. (serial 1272), 4.

41. John Savage, *The Life and Public Services of Andrew Johnson* (New York: Derby and Miller, 1865), 371–73.

42. Eric L. McKitrick, *Andrew Johnson and Reconstruction* (1960; repr., New York: Oxford University Press, 1988), 143–44; *The American Annual Cyclopædia and Register of Important Events of the Year 1868* (New York: Appleton, 1869), 8:753.

43. Quoted in Dan Monroe and Bruce Tap, *Shapers of the Great Debate on the Civil War: A Biographical Dictionary* (Westport, Conn.: Greenwood, 2005), 146.

44. Margaret E. Wagner, Gary W. Gallagher, and Paul Finkelman, eds., *The Library of Congress Civil War Desk Reference* (New York: Simon & Schuster, 2002), 766.

45. Article I, section 5.

46. Quoted in Eric Foner, *Reconstruction: America's Unfinished Revolution, 1863–1877* (New York: Harper & Row, 1988), 180.

47. Andrew Johnson, "Third Annual Message," December 3, 1867, in *A Compilation of the Messages and Papers of the Presidents, 1789–1897*, ed. James D. Richardson (Washington, D.C.: GPO, 1897), 6:565.

48. *House Journal*, 39th Cong., 1st Sess. (December 5, 1865), 24.

49. Report of Samuel Thomas, in *Message of the President of the United States*, Senate Ex. Doc. 2, 39th Cong., 1st Sess. (1865), 81.

50. "Laws in Relation to Freedmen," in *Freedman's Affairs*, Senate Ex. Doc. 6, 39th Cong., 2nd Sess. (1865), 202–20.

51. "The 'Black Codes' of 1865–1866," in *Laws Relating to Freedmen, 1865–1866, West Virginia University Documents Relating to Reconstruction*, no. 8, ed. Walter L. Fleming (Morgantown, W.Va., 1904), 11.

52. A compilation of the black codes appears in *Letter of the Secretary of War, Communicating, in Compliance with a Resolution of the Senate of December 17, 1866, Reports of the Assistant Commissioners of Freedmen, and a Synopsis of Laws Respecting Persons of Color in the Late Slave States*, Senate Ex. Doc. 6, 39th Cong., 2nd Sess. (serial 1276), 170–230.

53. *New Orleans Tribune*, December 24, 1865.

54. *Columbian Register* (New Haven), November 25, 1865.

55. "Speech of Hon. Henry Wilson. At the Meeting of the Colored National Monument Association of Washington, July 4, 1865," *New-Hampshire Sentinel* (Keene), July 20, 1865.

56. *Liberator* (Boston), September 22, 1865.

57. W. M. Grosvenor, "The Rights of the Nation, and the Duty of Congress," *New Englander and Yale Review* 24, no. 93 (October 1865): 768.

58. "The Late Convention of Colored Men; Address to the Loyal Citizens of the United States and to Congress," *New York Times*, August 13, 1865.

59. "Report of an investigation of the cause, origin, and results of the late riots in the city of Memphis made by Col. Charles F. Johnson, Inspector General States of Ky. and Tennessee and Major T. W. Gilbreth, A. D. C. to Maj. Genl. Howard, Commissioner

Bureau R. F. & A. Lands," available online at the Freedmen's Bureau Online, http://freedmensbureau.com/tennessee/outrages/memphisriot.htm.

60. "The Memphis Riots," *Harper's Weekly* 10, no. 491 (May 26, 1866), 1.

61. Affidavit of Rachael A. Ditts, available online at the Freedmen's Bureau Online, http://freedmensbureau.com/tennessee/affidavits/ditts.htm.

62. Affidavit of Alex McQuatters, available online at the Freedmen's Bureau Online, http://freedmensbureau.com/tennessee/affidavits/mcquatters.htm.

63. Affidavit of Mandy Wilburn, available online at the Freedmen's Bureau Online, http://freedmensbureau.com/tennessee/affidavits/wilburn.htm.

64. *New Orleans Times,* July 31, 1866.

65. *Richmond Times*, August 2, 1866, in *The Reconstruction Era: Primary Documents on Events from 1865 to 1877*, ed. Donna L. Dickerson (Westport, Conn.: Greenwood, 2003), 141–42.

66. *Chicago Tribune*, August 1, 1866.

67. *Preliminary Report Touching the Condition and Management of Emancipated Refugees* (New York: John F. Trow, 1863), 22.

68. "Final Report of the American Freemen's Inquiry Commission to the Secretary of War," May 15, 1864, in *War of the Rebellion*, ser. 3, 4:381–82.

69. *An Act to Establish a Bureau for the Relief of Freedmen and Refugees* (March 3, 1865), *U.S. Statutes at Large*, 38th Cong., 2nd Sess., chap. 90, 507–9.

70. "Final Report of the American Freemen's Inquiry Commission to the Secretary of War," May 15, 1864, in *War of the Rebellion*, ser. 3, 4:381–82.

71. *Circular No. 5: Rules and Regulations for Assistant Commissioners*, House Ex. Doc. 11, 39th Cong., 1st Sess., serial 1256 (1866), 102.

72. Orestes Brown, Bureau of Refugees, Freedmen and Abandoned Lands, "To the Freedmen of Virginia," Richmond, Virginia, July 1, 1865, House Ex. Doc. 70, 39th Cong., 1st Sess., 125.

73. Wade Hampton to Andrew Johnson, 1866, in Walter L. Fleming, ed., *Documentary History of Reconstruction: Political, Military, Social, Religious, Educational, and Industrial, 1865 to the Present Time* (Cleveland: A. H. Clark, 1906–7), 1:368–69.

74. Testimony of James D. B. DeBow, March 28, 1866, in *Report of the Joint Committee on Reconstruction*, 39th Cong., 1st Sess. (1866), 4:134.

75. *The Freedman's Bureau! An Agency to Keep the Negro in Idleness at the Expense of the White Man* (woodcut, 1866), Library of Congress Broadside Collection, portfolio 159, no. 9a c—Rare Book Collection (digital ID http://hdl.loc.gov/loc.pnp/cph.3a41094).

76. Benjamin Perley Poore, ed., *Veto Messages of the Presidents of the United States*, (Washington, D.C.: GPO, 1886), 290–91.

77. Quoted in William Archibald Dunning, *Reconstruction Political and Economic: 1865–1877* (New York: Harper and Brothers, 1907), 57.

78. George Fitzhugh, "What's to Be Done with the Negroes?" *DeBow's Review* 1, no. 6 (June 1866): 577–81.

79. Poore, *Veto Messages of the Presidents*, 304.

80. *Liberator* (Boston), December 15, 1865.

81. "The Rights of the States President Johnson," *Evening Union* (Washington), April 16, 1866.

82. "Bill for a Consolidated Central Despotism," *Patriot* (Harrisburg, Pa.), June 2, 1866.

83. "Kentucky Legislature," *Cincinnati Daily Gazette*, February 14, 1866.

84. Charles Francis Adams, ed., *The Works of John Adams, Second President of the United States* (Boston: Little, Brown, 1851), 4:43.

85. Andrew Jackson, "First Annual Message," December 8, 1829, in *Addresses and Messages of the Presidents of the United States from Washington to Tyler*, 3rd ed. (New York: Edward Walker, 1842), 363.

86. Poore, *Veto Messages of the Presidents*, 187, 223. In Pierce's eyes, Congress possessed only the powers the Constitution had specifically adumbrated: "such as to establish post-offices and post-roads; to declare war; to provide and maintain a navy; to raise and support armies; to regulate commerce; and to dispose of the territory and other public property of the United States." He even vetoed a bill to grant western lands to impoverished handicapped people, arguing that the Constitution never enumerated any power "making the Federal Government the great almoner of public charity throughout the United States" (224, 213).

87. *Report of the Joint Committee on Reconstruction*, 39th Cong., 1st Sess. (1866), 1:xi.

88. "'Grasp of War' Speech," June 21, 1865, in *Richard Henry Dana, Jr.: Speeches in Stirring Times and Letters to a Son*, ed. Richard Henry Dana, III (Boston: Houghton Mifflin, 1910), 246.

89. "Speech of Hon. Henry Wilson. At the Meeting of the Colored National Monument Association of Washington, July 4, 1865," *New-Hampshire Sentinel* (Keene), July 20, 1865.

90. "Doctrines Well Put," *North American and United States Gazette* (Philadelphia), September 13, 1865.

91. Gary W. Gallagher, *The Union War* (Cambridge, Mass.: Harvard University Press, 2011), 125.

92. "The Logical Results of War," in *Speeches, Correspondence and Political Papers of Carl Schurz*, ed. Frederic Bancroft (New York: Putnam, 1913), 1:378–79.

93. "'Grasp of War' Speech," June 21, 1865, in *Richard Henry Dana, Jr.*, 259.

94. Frederick Douglass, "Reconstruction," *Atlantic Monthly* 18, no. 110 (December 1866): 762.

95. "Report of Carl Schurz on the States of South Carolina, Georgia, Alabama, Mississippi, and Louisiana," in *Message of the President of the United State*, Senate Ex. Doc. 2, 39th Cong., 1st Sess. (serial 1237), 42–43.

96. "Protection of Civil Rights," January 29, 1866, *Congressional Globe*, 39th Cong., 1 Sess., 476.

97. "Annual Message of the Governor of Ohio, to the Fifty-Seventh General Assembly," January 2, 1867, in *Message and Annual Reports for 1866, Made to the General Assembly of the State of Ohio* (Columbus: L. D. Myers and Bro., 1867), pt. 1, 282. See also Michael Les Benedict, "Preserving the Constitution: The Conservative Basis of Radical Reconstruction," *Journal of American History* 61, no. 1 (June 1974): 77n28.

98. This section used the word "male" for the first time in the Constitution, setting off a furor among advocates for women's rights, and effectively splitting the movement on the issue of race.

99. Author's analysis.

100. Eric Foner, *Freedom's Lawmakers: A Directory of Black Officeholders during Reconstruction* (New York: Oxford University Press, 1993), xviii, xxii, xxiv.

101. In 1860 in the slave states, each electoral vote had represented the will of 53,438 free citizens, while the comparable figure for the free states was 65,503—a ratio of 1:1.37. In 1872, the South had lost only a bit of this ground. In the states where slavery had been legal in 1860, each electoral vote represented the will of 102,609 free people, whereas the comparable figure for the states that had been free was 122,154—a ratio of 1:1.31.

102. "Speech of Hon. Robert Small, of South Carolina, in the House of Representatives, February 24, 1877," in *Black Congressmen during Reconstruction: A Documentary Sourcebook*, ed. Stephen Middleton (Westport, Conn.: Greenwood, 2002), 336.

103. "Objections to the New Constitution of South Carolina," in Fleming, *Documentary History of Reconstruction*, 1:456.

104. Albion Winegar Tourgée, *A Fool's Errand, by One of the Fools* (London: George Routledge, 1883), 300.

105. See, for example, Heather Cox Richardson, "A Marshall Plan for the South? The Failure of Republican and Democratic Ideology during Reconstruction," *Civil War History* 51, no. 4 (December 2005): 378–87; J. Mills Thornton III, "Fiscal Policy and the Failure of Radical Reconstruction in the Lower South," in *Region, Race, and Reconstruction: Essays in Honor of C. Vann Woodward*, ed. J. Morgan Kousser and James M. McPherson (New York: Oxford University Press, 1982), 349–94.

106. "This is a White Man's Government," *Harper's Weekly* 12 (September 5, 1868).

107. See, for example, "Ku-Klux Outrages," *Washington Reporter* (D.C.), November 11, 1868.

108. "The Ku Klux," *Providence Evening Press* (Rhode Island), March 10, 1871.

109. "The Ku Klux in Union County," *New York Herald*, November 15, 1871; "The Military and the Southern Secret Societies," *Georgia Weekly Telegraph* (Macon), April 24, 1868.

110. Matt Morgan, "Too Thin, Massa Grant," *Frank Leslie's Illustrated Newspaper* 35 (September 14, 1872).

111. "Ku-Klux Outrages," *Washington Reporter* (D.C.), November 11, 1868.

112. "An Act to enforce the Right of Citizens of the United States to vote in the several States of his Union, and for other Purposes" (May 31, 1870), *U.S. Statutes at Large*, 41st Cong., 2 Sess., chap. 114, 140–46; "An Act to amend an Act approved May Thirty-One, Eighteen Hundred and Seventy, Entitled 'An Act to enforce the Rights of Citizens of the United States to Vote in Several States of This Union, and for Other Purposes'" (February 28, 1871), *U.S. Statutes at Large*, 41st Cong., 3 Sess., chap. 99, 433–40; "An Act to Enforce the Provisions of the Fourteenth Amendment to the Constitution of the United States and for Other Purposes" (April 20, 1871), *U.S. Statutes at Large*, 42nd Cong., 1 Sess., chap. 22, 13–15.

113. "Testimony of John G. Lewis," March 30, 1880, in *Proceedings of the Select Committee of the United States Senate to Investigate the Causes of the Removal of the Negroes from the Southern States to the Northern States*, Senate Report 693, 46th Cong., 2nd Sess., part 2 (1880), 433.

114. Quoted in Richard Zuczek, *State of Rebellion: Reconstruction in South Carolina* (Columbia: University of South Carolina Press, 1996), 100.

115. Edward McPherson, ed., *A Hand-book of Politics for 1876: Being a Record of Important Political Action, National and State, from July 15, 1874, to July 15, 1876*, 7th ed. (Washington, D.C.: Solomons and Chapman, 1876), 29.

116. George Fitzhugh, "The Freedman and His Future: A Rejoinder," *Lippincott's Magazine* 5 (February 1870): 191–97.

117. "An Open Letter. Hon. Jeremiah S. Black to Gen. James A. Garfield," *Washington Review and Examiner* (Washington, Pa.), September 27, 1876.

118. "An Opportunity for Governor Tilden," *New York Herald*, July 18, 1876.

119. Carl Schurz, "Why Anti-Grant and Pro-Greeley," speech given July 22, 1872, in Bancroft, *Speeches, Correspondence and Political Papers*, 2:398, 437, 438.

120. J. W. Schuckers, *The Life and Public Services of Salmon Portland Chase* (New York: Appleton, 1874), 585.

121. Quoted in Foner, *Reconstruction*, 560.

122. Edwards Pierrepont to Adelbert Ames, September 14, 1875, in "Executive and Department Doings," *Republic* 5, no. 4 (October 1875): 269.

123. "About the Negro Question," *Massachusetts Spy* (Worcester), September 29, 1876.

124. "The Voice of the Old Leaders. Words of Warning from Wendell Phillips and William Lloyd Garrison," *Weekly Louisianian* (New Orleans), February 6, 1875).

125. *Examiner* (Aberdeen, Miss.), October 7, 1875, in Fleming, *Documentary History of Reconstruction*, 2:394.

126. "The Political South Hereafter," *Nation* 24, no. 614 (April 5, 1877), 202.

127. *Civil Rights Cases*, 109 U.S. 3, 27 L. Ed. 836, 3 Sup. Ct. Rep. 18 (1883).

128. *Homer A. Plessy v. John H. Ferguson*, 163 U.S. 537 (1896).

CONCLUSION: WHAT PEACE AMONG THE WHITES BROUGHT

1. See Philip S. Foner and George E. Walker, eds., *Proceedings of the Black National and State Conventions, 1865–1900* (Philadelphia: Temple University Press, 1986).

2. "Who Are Our Friends?," *Christian Recorder* (Philadelphia), August 10, 1867.

3. Frederick Douglass, "The Color Question," in *The Frederick Douglass Papers, Series One: Speeches, Debates, and Interviews*, ed. John W. Blassingame and John R. McKivigan (New Haven: Yale University Press, 1991), 4:417–18.

4. "A Colored Man's View of the Question—Certain Republicans," *Christian Recorder* (Philadelphia), August 6, 1874; "How?," *Christian Recorder* (Philadelphia), February 18, 1875.

5. Roger L. Ransom and Richard Sutch, *One Kind of Freedom: The Economic Consequences of Emancipation* (Cambridge: Cambridge University Press, 1977), 71, table 4.5, 69, table 4.3.

6. Norman R. Yetman, *Voices from Slavery* (New York: Holt, Rinehart and Winston, 1970), 118.

7. Francis William Loring and Charles Follen Atkinson, *Cotton Culture and the South Considered with Reference to Emigration* (Boston: A. Williams, 1869), 113.

8. Letter of M. C. Fulton, April 17, 1866, in "Afro-American Families in the Transition from Slavery to Freedom," ed. Ira Berlin, Steven F. Miller, and Leslie S. Rowland, *Radical History Review* 42, no. 3 (Fall 1988): 112–13.

9. ICPSR3.

10. Robert D. Marcus and David Burner, eds., *America Firsthand*, 4th ed. (New York: St. Martin's, 1997), 2:51.

11. Ransom and Sutch, *One Kind of Freedom*, 240, table D.2.

12. [Ned Cobb], *All God's Dangers: The Life of Nate Shaw*, ed. Theodore Rosengarten (New York: Knopf, 1974), 112.

13. See *The Peonage Files of the U.S. Department of Justice, 1901–1945* (Frederick, Md.: University Publications of America, 1989), microform.

14. Whitelaw Reid, *After the War: A Southern Tour: May 1, 1865, to May 1, 1866* (London: Sampson Low, Son, and Marston, 1866), 564.

15. Ransom and Sutch, *One Kind of Freedom*, 84, table 5.1.

16. ICPSR3.

17. Henry W. Grady, "The New South," *New England Magazine* 2, no. 1 (March 1890): 88.

18. Douglass, "Color Question," 4:420.

19. "Civil Rights in Africa," *Georgia Weekly Telegraph* (Macon), July 6, 1875.

20. Ibid., 116, 123.

21. *Plessy v. Ferguson*, 163 U.S. 537, 539 (1896).

22. Speech by Andrew Harris delivered at the Broadway tabernacle, New York City, May 7, 1839, *The Emancipator*, May 15, 1839, in *The Black Abolitionist Papers*, ed. C. Peter Ripley, Jeffrey S. Rossbach, et al. (Chapel Hill: University of North Carolina Press, 1985), 3:295.

23. "The Dawn of the Future," *Christian Recorder* (Philadelphia), May 19, 1866.

24. *House Journal*, 39th Cong., 1st Sess. (December 5, 1865), 24.

25. Frederick Douglass, "What the Black Man Wants" (1865), in *Great Speeches by Frederick Douglass*, ed. James Daley (Mineola, N.Y.: Dover, 2013), 57–58.

26. Thomas Henry Huxley, "Emancipation—Black and White (1865)," in *Thomas Henry Huxley, Science and Education Essays* (New York: Appleton, 1895), 67.

27. W. E. Woodward, *Meeting General Grant* (New York: Horace Liveright, 1928), 372.

28. Douglass, "Color Question," 4:416.

29. Prince Hall, "A Charge" (1797), 47, and James Forten, "Series of Letters by a Man of Colour" (1813), 71, both in *Pamphlets of Protest: An Anthology of Early African American Protest Literature, 1790–1860*, ed. Richard Newman, Patrick Rael, and Phillip Lapsansky (New York: Routledge, 2001).

RACE IN THE ATLANTIC WORLD, 1700–1900

Diplomacy in Black and White: John Adams, Toussaint Louverture, and Their Atlantic World Alliance
BY RONALD ANGELO JOHNSON

Enterprising Women: Gender, Race, and Power in the Revolutionary Atlantic
BY KIT CANDLIN AND CASSANDRA PYBUS

Eighty-Eight Years: The Long Death of Slavery in the United States, 1777–1865
BY PATRICK RAEL

CPSIA information can be obtained at www.ICGtesting.com
Printed in the USA
BVOW05*1505120615

404155BV00002B/3/P

9 780820 333953